Economic Analysis of Law in European Legal Scholarship

Volume 15

The purpose of the book series "Economic Analysis of Law in European Legal Scholarship" is to publish high quality volumes in the growing field of law and economics research in Europe, from a comprehensive theoretical and practical vantage point. In particular, the series will place great emphasis on foundational and theoretical aspects of economic analysis of law and on interdisciplinary approaches in European Legal Scholarship. Following Nobel laureate Ronald Coase's famous essay "The Problem of Social Cost" (1960) fifty years ago law and economics has become the lingua franca of American jurisprudence. In recent decades, law and economics has also gained widespread popularity in Europe and its influence on Legal Scholarship is growing significantly.

Therefore, the economic analysis of law in European Legal Scholarship academic book series illustrates how law and economics is developing in Europe and what opportunities and problems – both in general and in specific legal fields – are associated with this approach within the legal traditions of European countries. Rather than further exploring economic analysis as such, the main focus of this series lies on the implementation of economic methods in legislation and legal adjudication from a European perspective. It takes into account the particular challenges the European legal systems face. Volumes will address law and economics research in Europe from a critical and comparative viewpoint. The studies in this series are strong and bold narratives of the development of economic analysis of law in European Legal Scholarship. Some are suitable for a very broad readership.

Contributions in this series primarily come from scholars in Europe. The purpose is to provide the next generation of European lawyers with the models and skills needed to understand and improve the economic analysis of law in their own legal field. The series includes monographs focusing on specific topics as well as collections of essays covering specific themes.

Klaus Mathis · Avishalom Tor
Editors

Law and Economics of the Digital Transformation

Springer

Editors
Klaus Mathis
Faculty of Law
University of Lucerne
Lucerne, Switzerland

Avishalom Tor
School of Law
University of Notre Dame
Notre Dame, IN, USA

ISSN 2512-1294 ISSN 2512-1308 (electronic)
Economic Analysis of Law in European Legal Scholarship
ISBN 978-3-031-25058-3 ISBN 978-3-031-25059-0 (eBook)
https://doi.org/10.1007/978-3-031-25059-0

This Springer imprint is published by the registered company Springer Nature Switzerland AG
The registered company address is: Gewerbestrasse 11, 6330 Cham, Switzerland

Preface

This edited volume "Law and Economics of the Digital Transformation" is a collection of papers which were due to be presented at the annual Law and Economics Conference in Lucerne on the 8th and 9th April 2022, co-organised by the University of Lucerne, Institute for Economy and Regulation, and the Notre Dame Research Program on Law and Market Behaviour (ND LAMB). This volume consists of contributions to current issues concerning the economic analysis of the ongoing digital transformation.

The main focus of this volume lies in presenting European legal scholars' perspectives on the issues surrounding the digital transformation of the economy and society from a Law and Economics perspective. These are complemented by insights from distinguished scholars from the United States in order to foster the international dialogue among the different legal cultures. The thematic scope of this volume spans both the theoretical foundations and specific practical applications of Law and Economics within the digital transformation, its immediate impacts and developments and future possibilities.

We take this opportunity to thank all those who have contributed to the successful completion of this volume. In particular, we are grateful to Lyanne Elsener, MLaw, Philipp Gisler, BLaw and Lea Röthlin, BLaw for their diligent proofreading. Finally, we also thank Anja Trautmann and Sathya Subramaniam at Springer Publishers for overseeing the publishing process.

Lucerne, Switzerland
Notre Dame, IN, USA
October 2022

Klaus Mathis
Avishalom Tor

Contents

Contributors

Ido Baum Haim Striks Faculty of Law, College of Management-Academic Studies (COLMAN), Rishon LeTsiyon, Israel;
Louis Brandeis Institute for Society Economy and Democracy, COLMAN, Rishon LeTsiyon, Israel

Jarosław Bełdowski Department of International Comparative Studies, Warsaw School of Economics, Warszawa, Poland

Mira Burri University of Lucerne, Lucerne, Switzerland

Łukasz Dąbroś Warsaw School of Economics, Collegium of Economic Analysis, Warszawa, Poland

Danny Friedmann Associate Professor of Law, Peking University School of Transnational Law, University Town, Nanshan District, Shenzhen, China

Mariusz Jerzy Golecki Faculty of Law and Administration, University of Lodz, Łódź, Poland

Lisanne M. F. Hummel Utrecht University, Utrecht, Netherlands

Salil K. Mehra Charles B. Klein Professor in Law and Government, Temple University, Philadelphia, US

Katarzyna Południak-Gierz Jagiellonian University, Cracow, Poland

Lejla Ramić University of Sarajevo, Sarajevo, Bosnia and Herzegovina

Tilman Reinhardt Faculty of Life Sciences: Food Nutrition and Health, University of Bayreuth, Kulmbach, Germany

Rute Saraiva University of Lisbon Law School, Alameda da Universidade, Lisbon, Portugal

Evelyne A. Tauchnitz Institute of Social Ethics ISE, University of Lucerne, Lucerne, Switzerland

Alexandra Telychko Faculty of Law, University of Geneva, Geneva, Switzerland

Piotr Tereszkiewicz Jagiellonian University, Cracow, Poland;
University of Leuven, Leuven, Belgium

Avishalom Tor School of Law, University of Notre Dame, Notre Dame, IN, USA

Kalpana Tyagi Maastricht University, Maastricht, Netherlands

Massimiliano Vatiero University of Trento, Trento, Italy;
(Law Institute, IDUSI), Lugano, Switzerland

Rolf H. Weber University of Zurich, Zürich, Switzerland

Part I: Insights from Behavioural Economics

Digital Nudges: Contours and Challenges

Avishalom Tor

Abstract Digital nudges—that is, significantly behavioral interventions that use software and its user-interface design elements—are an increasingly pervasive feature of online environments that shapes behavior both online (e.g., changing online privacy settings) and offline (e.g., taking a flu vaccine due to a text message reminder). Although digital nudges share many characteristics of their offline counterparts, they merit particular attention and analysis for two important reasons: First, the growing ubiquity of digital nudges makes encountering them nearly unavoidable in daily life, thereby bringing into sharper relief the promise and perils of nudges more generally. Second, the potentially greater potency of digital—compared to offline—nudges, the greater opacity of their instruments and behavioral mechanisms, and the typically dominant role of private intermediaries or independent private actors in their implementation all raise unique or qualitatively different challenges from those presented by their better-studied offline predecessors.

Keywords Behavioral regulation · Behavioral insights · Nudge · Costs and benefits · Artificial intelligence · Machine learning · Intermediaries

1 Introduction

For some time now, governments and other organizations have been employing behavioral interventions—also known as nudges—to advance their policy goals, but the rapid advent of digital nudges is relatively recent.[1] Digital nudges are distinct from their offline counterparts in their deployment of software and its user-interface design elements and are an increasingly pervasive feature of online environments.[2]

[1] Mathis and Tor (2016), Oliver (2017), Tor (2022).
[2] Weinmann et al. (2016).

A. Tor (✉)
School of Law, University of Notre Dame, Notre Dame, IN, USA
e-mail: ator@nd.edu

K. Mathis and A. Tor (eds.), *Law and Economics of the Digital Transformation*, Economic Analysis of Law in European Legal Scholarship 15,
https://doi.org/10.1007/978-3-031-25059-0_1

These instruments increasingly shape behavior both online and offline. For instance, in the former domain they may encourage people to change their privacy settings or update a password while in the latter domain they may lead a person wearing a Fitbit tracker to adjust her physical activity or a driver to follow the route recommended by his GPS.

Although digital nudges share many features of their offline predecessors, they merit particular attention and analysis for two important reasons: First, the ubiquity of digital nudging across online platforms, social networks, other applications, and electronic devices makes it a nearly unavoidable feature of daily life, thereby bringing into sharper relief the promise and perils of nudges more generally. Second and more importantly, digital nudging raises unique—or at least qualitatively different—issues compared to offline nudging, because of its potentially greater potency (e.g., due to the possibility of dynamic, personalized interventions), the opacity of the technological and behavioral mechanisms through which it shapes behavior (as when using artificial intelligence and machine learning), and the central role of independent private actors—most notably, private intermediaries such as internet platforms—in its implementation.[3]

Part 2 of this chapter therefore opens with a review of offline nudging that clarifies relevant terms and sets the stage for the later analysis. Part 3 then explores the main contours of digital nudges and distinguishes between two types of such interventions—namely, behavioral interventions that are "digital" only in that they operate via a digital medium and nudges that can only be employed in digital environments. Part 4 examines the challenges entailed by the use of digital nudging as a means from promoting public and private welfare, and focuses on the special concerns raised by the tools of digital nudging and the digital environment within which they operate. Part 5 concludes.

2 Offline Nudging

Behavioral regulation has been on the rise for the last 15 years.[4] To achieve their policy goals, both governments and public and private organizations are increasingly turning to nudges in an attempt to shape individual behavior in most major policy domains including health, safety, education, finance, environmental protection, tax compliance, public service delivery and more.[5] Indeed, recent national responses to the coronavirus pandemic vividly illustrated this behavioral turn, with governments facing the high costs and limited efficacy of traditional regulatory tools employing

[3] This chapter considers the welfare effects of these instruments—namely, their private benefits and costs—though nudges generally and digital nudges in particular raise numerous other legal questions and normative concerns; Tor (2020).

[4] E.g., Mathis and Tor (2016), Oliver (2017), Tor (2023).

[5] Tor (2022).

nudges to encourage widespread vaccination as well as to complement quarantine, masking, or social distancing mandates.[6]

Nudging draws on behavioral science to inform policy design, drawing in particular on the evidence of systematic differences between real human behavior and the hypothetical rationality that standard economic models assume.[7] Thus, while traditional regulatory instruments affect behavior by imposing constraints (as mandates or bans do), using economic incentives (as in the case of taxes or subsidies), or disclosing unavailable or costly information, nudges rely on "softer" behavioral tools, like more effective or persuasive information presentation, the framing of the available choices, the selection of defaults, or the communication of social information.[8]

Thaler and Sunstein, who coined the term, offered an ostensibly narrow definition of nudging as a form of "libertarian paternalism" that "preserves freedom of choice but... encourages both private and public institutions to steer people in directions that will promote their own welfare."[9] On this account, what renders an intervention libertarian paternalistic—that is, a nudge—is the unique combination of its private welfare goal and choice-preserving tools.[10] Yet even Thaler and Sunstein themselves already describe as nudges certain interventions that exceed the boundaries of their own definition, including policies that are choice-preserving but not paternalistic but rather concerned with public welfare; instruments that are paternalistic but not truly choice-preserving and thus not libertarian; and even interventions that are neither libertarian nor paternalistic.[11]

At any rate, the expansive literature on behavioral regulation now encompasses a variety of nudge usages. Some scholars in this interdisciplinary field follow Thaler and Sunstein's narrower libertarian paternalistic definition,[12] others have proposed a variety of alternative definitions,[13] and some have gone so far as to designate as nudges even traditional price instruments like taxes and subsidies, merely because they do not literally compel a particular choice.[14] More commonly, however, the literature uses nudging simply as a loose shorthand for policies with some behavioral component or connection, irrespective of their goals or the specific mechanisms through which they generate their effects.[15]

For clarity, therefore, this chapter follows a broad yet well-delineated definition of nudges as significantly *behavioral instruments*—that is, as policies that seek to shape behavior, at least in significant part, through the activation of behavioral

---

[6] OECD (2020), The White House (2021), Teichman and Underhill (2021).

[7] Madrian (2014), Tor (2016).

[8] Sunstein (2016), Thaler and Sunstein (2008), Tor (2019, 2021).

[9] Sunstein and Thaler (2003, p. 120), Thaler and Sunstein (2008).

[10] Tor (2016).

[11] Hausman and Welch (2010), Tor (2022).

[12] De Haan and Linde (2018), Oliver (2015).

[13] E.g., Grune-Yanoff and Hertwig (2016).

[14] Le Grand and New (2015).

[15] Sibony and Alemanno (2015).

processes that strictly rational actors would have found irrelevant.[16] Notwithstanding its breadth, this definition avoids being overinclusive by excluding all traditional regulatory instruments that are not "significantly" behavioral, such as traditional instruments whose influence is due in part to behavioral factors (e.g., highly visible taxes) or traditional disclosure policies that do not rely on behavioral factors to provide information. At the same, it not only encompasses policies that involve some combination of behavioral and traditional elements (e.g., highly emotive information disclosures, like Graphic Warning Labels on cigarette packaging), but also includes common behavioral interventions that exceed the official confines of "libertarian paternalism".

The popularity of offline nudging owes, in large part, to the perception that it offers a more palatable form of regulation that is highly cost-effective, a perception driven by the typically low implementation costs of behavioral interventions.[17] Because they do not rely on resource-intensive enforcement efforts and do not burden the public purse as traditional incentive-based policies sometimes do, nudges impose less strain on limited regulatory budgets.[18] Policy makers may also believe that nudges often are politically more feasible than traditional regulation, since large segments of the public—often a majority—in many democratic nations appear to find many nudges acceptable.[19] In addition, regulators in democratic societies may find appealing the notion of non-coercive behavioral interventions that leave citizens with greater freedom of choice than some forms of traditional regulation.[20]

Notwithstanding these and other benefits of behavioral interventions, more recent scholarship highlights some of their limitations and costs. For one, empirical studies of nudge efficacy suggest that although nudges can be efficacious the magnitude of their effects is often modest. A quantitative review by Hummel and Maedche identified 100 higher-quality primary publications with 317 independent effect sizes spanning policy areas including health, finances, the environment, energy use, and more, which reported sufficient statistical information for quantitative comparisons.[21] Overall, the nudges in the sample had a median relative effect size of 21% and an average effect size of 30% (excluding outliers), with the effects in specific studies ranging widely. Effect size variability across nudge types also was dramatic: Defaults, the most common and most effective behavioral instrument in the literature, showed a large median effect size of 50%, while that of simplification—the next most common nudge category—was only 20%. Other common instruments of reminders and pre-commitments produced only small median relative effect sizes of 8% and 7% respectively. Hence, most behavioral interventions other than defaults exhibited limited effectiveness.[22]

---

[16] Tor (2022).

[17] Tor (2022).

[18] Benartzi et al. (2017), Tor and Klick (2023).

[19] E.g., Jung and Mellers (2016), Sunstein et al. (2019).

[20] Sunstein and Reisch (2019).

[21] Hummel and Maedche (2019).

[22] Hummel and Maedche (2019).

Recent meta-analyses further show that the effects of many real-world nudges are substantially smaller than those reported in the literature and limited in their absolute magnitude. DellaVigna and Linos compared the results of behavioral policies in research studies with those documented for large-scale interventions by two governmental "nudge units" in the United States. After narrowing down the dataset to render the included interventions more comparable to one another, the authors retained a final sample of 126 randomized controlled trials (RCTs) involving 243 nudges and over 23 million target participants, which they compared to a similar subsample from the set of academic studies that Hummel and Maedche reported on that consisted of 26 RCTs with 74 nudges and more than 500,000 participants.[23]

DellaVigna and Linos found that the nudges in their academic subsample produced an average relative effect size increase of 33.5% in the desired behavior over the 26.0% baseline of the control groups, or an 8.7% average absolute increase in the frequency of the nudged behavior. On the other hand, the nudge unit data showed a dramatically smaller average relative effect size increase of 8.1% from a 17.2% control baseline, or a 1.4% average absolute increase in the frequency of the nudged behavior—that is, only about one-sixth of the magnitude of the academic subsample effect size.[24]

These findings suggest that nudges can be effective when implemented at scale, but that the magnitude of their effects under these circumstances may often be small in absolute terms even if statistically significant. At the same time, the results of behavioral interventions in the academic sample indicate that some nudges—like default arrangements—can produce substantially larger effect sizes, with the efficacy of specific interventions depending on myriad factors, including the type of nudge involved, its specific features, the behaviors it targets, whether it complements a traditional intervention or substitutes for it, and more.[25]

Beyond concerns about efficacy, current research further reveals that behavioral interventions can be costlier than they initially appear. Specifically, nudges that entail only limited direct implementation costs can generate significant private costs, particularly when they are efficacious. These costs include direct cognitive, emotional, or monetary costs variously imposed on some of the individuals targeted by behavioral policies, as well as the costs borne by private third parties due to behavior changes brought about by successful nudging.[26]

However, the most significant costs of most behavioral regulation typically are the private opportunity costs to individuals whose behavior it successfully changes.[27] All successful interventions, including those that produce net social benefits, entail opportunity costs—namely, the now-forgone benefits that individuals obtained from their former course of action. Yet, successful nudges can also cause people to

---

23 DellaVigna and Linos (2021).

24 DellaVigna and Linos (2021).

25 Tor (2022).

26 Tor (forthcoming 2023).

27 Tor (2021).

make personally detrimental behavior changes.[28] For instance, regulators may seek to reduce harmful environmental externalities by nudging consumers to conserve energy (e.g., by mailing them Home Energy Reports ("HERs")—letters that compare their consumption to that of their neighbors and imply a social norm favoring energy conservation.[29] All successfully nudged households inevitably forgo the benefits of their previous, higher energy usage (e.g., greater indoor comfort). Moreover, at least some energy consumers—like those who reduce usage only to avoid violating a perceived social norm or comparing unfavorably to their more efficient neighbors—can be made worse off when reducing their energy consumption.[30]

As with traditional regulation, the behavior changes produced by nudging can impose economic costs on non-consumer third parties. To illustrate, HERs that lead consumers to reduce their energy consumption produce net revenue losses for energy retailers due to their diminished sales.[31] From the perspective of energy retailers, in fact, the losses from reduced use are the same irrespective of the mechanism employed to change consumer behavior.

Of course, the private costs that may accompany behavioral interventions do not necessarily render these policies undesirable. Nudges increase social welfare when their overall benefits exceed their overall costs, and they are particularly attractive when they produce net private benefits—that is, when they improve individual well-being on balance enough to also make up for any attendant costs to their targets as well as to third parties. Nonetheless, the prevalence and magnitude of private costs militate for requiring a demonstration that proposed behavioral interventions offer society net benefits, just as expected of traditional regulation.[32]

3 The Basic Contours of Digital Nudging

The relatively recent and ongoing development of digital nudges is at the intersection of behavioral science and technological innovation in digital environments. Digital behavioral instruments can be distinguished from their offline predecessors by the unique medium they use to deliver interventions. Specifically, digital nudges employ software and its user interface design elements[33]—those aspects of computer systems with which humans interact—to shape the behavior of the individuals they target.[34]

In the current technological environment, people spend much of their time interacting with sophisticated computer systems, from personal computers, through smartphones, to countless other digital devices that pervade daily life at home, work,

---

[28] Tor (2023).

[29] Allcott (2011).

[30] Allcott and Kessler (2019).

[31] Allcott and Kessler (2019), Tor and Klick (2023).

[32] Tor (2023), Tor and Klick (2023).

[33] Weinmann et al. (2016).

[34] Stone et al. (2005).

or other public and private settings. This reality increases both the opportunities for and the incidence of digital nudging. Local governments can nudge residents to pay taxes on time by highlighting social norms of tax payment or framing the penalties for overdue payments as psychologically painful losses; charitable organizations can nudge individuals to donate more by offering donation menus that lead them to select favored options or triggering emotional reactions; social media platforms can nudge individuals to follow news from media outlets those platforms deem reliable; and even private email providers may nudge their customers with a simple reminder to follow up on an email they sent five days ago that received no reply.

Of course, though digital nudging occurs online, its behavioral effects are not limited to digital environments. Online interactions may produce offline effects incidentally, because the online behaviors that people are nudged towards have offline parallels: The nudged tax payment may be done with a physical check or even in person; the emotionally-triggered donation may take place at a local charity; successfully-nudged social media consumers may subscribe to a physical edition of a favored newspaper; and even the automated email nudge may lead one to knock on a colleague's office door to follow up in person on an unanswered email.

In such cases, the offline effects of digital nudging are mere byproducts of online interventions whose primary goal is the shaping of online behavior. Yet digital nudges are frequently implemented specifically to change offline behavior. This is the case, for instance, with health apps or gadgets that nudge individuals to increase their physical activities; with text messages that nudge people to engage in targeted real-world health behaviors, like taking a flu vaccine; or with websites or mobile phone apps that closely resemble those physical Home Energy Reports and seek to lower consumers' home energy use.

Digital nudges also vary in the degree to which they are uniquely digital. Some nudges are digital primarily in the sense that they operate through some digital medium, as when citizens receive a "reminder" to pay taxes on time via email or text rather than by a physical letter in the mail. Other behavioral interventions are more uniquely digital in that they exploit features of the digital environment that are unavailable to their offline counterparts. For example, when originally conceived as an accompaniment to physical utility bills, Home Energy Reports only offered monthly feedback on a household's overall consumption over a previous month, while the digital version of the same reports or similar apps can provide ongoing, immediate, and far more granular, energy-use or social comparison information.

The advantages of digital nudges are not limited to their potentially rapid response times or their access to current information. For one, the flexible and technologically advanced nature of common digital interfaces offer those who employ them, to shape behavior, a wide array of visual and auditory effects to direct attention, emphasize or deemphasize information, or trigger affective or intuitive psychological reactions, in ways that usually are unavailable to offline nudges. Additionally, digital nudges can use artificial intelligence that benefits from machine learning, big data analytics, and more to track and evaluate individual behavior and develop more nuanced and personalized interventions, with ongoing content modification as new information is obtained. Studies show, for instance, how data on Facebook "likes" can predict different personal characteristics, such as demographics or even personality traits (e.g., extraversion or openness), with some accuracy.[35] Such predictions, in turn, can form the basis of more effective behavioral interventions that are adapted to the identified characteristics.[36]

Beyond the technological strengths of digital interfaces and the software underlying them, which may enable more effective behavioral interventions, digital environments also yield novel opportunities for nudging that simply do not exist offline. Online social networks (e.g., Facebook or Instagram) and other online social groups (such as gaming communities) are a familiar case on point. Such networks and communities are uniquely online fora, with no direct offline counterparts. They allow for data collection, analysis, and use in the service of behavioral policy interventions, just as they do for commercial interests (e.g., through advertising).[37] Moreover, with the increasing importance of such online fora in people's social lives and interactions, digital nudges that recruit social information—like social comparisons, social norms, or social recognition—are capable of exerting ever stronger influence on their targets' behavior.

To illustrate the potential for leveraging digital social interaction and technology to shape offline behavior, consider a recently proposed Japanese Covid-19 contact-tracing mobile phone app. The app included both a gaming element—in the form of a "fortune slip" that downloads automatically when a person with the app checked in at a new physical location where social interaction could take place—and, importantly, a socially displayed digital art that becomes increasingly elaborate with each additional app user who is physically present in a physical social setting. The latter element in particular aimed to encourage app use by generating social recognition effects that clearly single out app users—as well as those who do not use the app—in social settings. Besides its immediate powerful social recognition nudge, moreover, a sufficiently popular app of this sort might also facilitate the creation of novel social norms that favor or at least accept contact tracing.[38]

4 Challenges Posed by Digital Nudging

The factors that render digital nudges potentially more efficacious also bring with them attendant risks and costs.[39] Most importantly, behavioral interventions delivered by digital means can generate opportunity costs and other private costs that are similar in kind but, at times, substantially greater in magnitude than the comparable costs of offline nudges.

---

[35] Kosinski et al. (2013).

[36] Matz et al. (2017).

[37] Matz and Netzer (2017).

[38] Kanamitsu et al. (2021).

[39] Cf. Yeung (2017).

The greater magnitude of digital nudge costs is due to a number of reasons: First, more successful interventions—offline and digital alike—usually generate higher private costs because they entail more dramatic or widespread behavior changes on the part of their targets. A policy that succeeds in leading its targets to conserve more energy, for instance, inevitably causes them to sacrifice more of the energy-use benefits they previously enjoyed and entails a greater social cost, as reflected in the net revenue losses to energy retailers from diminished consumption.[40]

Hence, those unique characteristics of digital nudges that render them potentially more effective—such as their reliance on algorithms that can employ machine learning and improve their performance with big data, the associated rapid and dynamic personalization of user experience, or the use of engaging and multi-sensory interfaces—can also lead people to make personally costly behavior changes. Indeed, some digital nudges are capable of changing behavior irrespective of whether such changes turn out to be beneficial on balance.

The potentially greater private costs of digital nudges are nicely illustrated by the Japanese contact-tracing app described above, which used both a gaming element and social recognition effects to encourage people to download and use the app. This app could be particularly powerful because it provides individuals with a strong social recognition signal. Notably, this public signal not only demonstrates to others that one is using the contact-tracing app, but also identifies those who are avoiding the app by the lack of a change in the public digital art when they join others in a social setting. In some social circumstances, such a powerful nudge could pressure individuals who do not wish to surrender their privacy to nevertheless use the app and submit to contract tracing that they would have preferred to avoid.

More generally, as this illustration demonstrates, the same tools and data that increase the potential effectiveness of digital nudging can also increase its private costs and occasionally lead targeted individuals to make personally costly behavior changes. The social recognition aspect of the Japanese contact-tracing app could not work without constantly tracking its users' whereabouts, collecting and using personal information, benefiting from rapid feedback, employing a multi-sensory interface, and so on. Yet by building upon such data and technology, this digital nudge could lead people to accede to a contact-tracing method they would have otherwise refused.

Similar technologies and data can underpin digital nudges that seek to promote other public welfare goals (e.g., a reduction in household energy consumption) or individual well-being (e.g., a more healthful diet or an increased rate of saving for retirement). In the case of many such common interventions, therefore, digital nudges may impose substantial private opportunity costs and occasionally also entail private costs to third parties (e.g., the net revenue losses to energy providers or less-healthful food sellers due to diminished consumption).[41] As in the case of offline nudges, these private costs may not render digital behavioral interventions altogether unappealing,

---

[40] Allcott and Kessler (2019).

[41] Tor and Klick (2023).

but they must be weighed, together with all other policy costs, against whatever private or public benefits these nudges provide.

Second, beyond concerns about the private costs that result from their greater efficacy, digital nudges often rely on opaque algorithms that make it exceedingly difficult to determine their benefits and costs. Like other current applications of artificial intelligence ("AI") in the commercial sphere, behavioral interventions can employ machine learning ("ML") systems to identify the individuals they target and determine when and how to nudge them. These software systems are trained on, and learn from, a great deal of individual-level data (e.g., people's online behavior) that allow algorithms to predict which outcome would optimize a set of parameters.[42] AI/ML systems can act in ways that are not strictly pre-programmed and adapt their actions to changing environments; once trained, they rely on recursive feedback to organically continue learning from new information to improve their predictions and thus the interventions implemented.[43]

Importantly, the adaptive nature of AI/ML systems can make it particularly difficult to determine precisely why they nudged a given individual (or why they selected a specific nudge variant for implementation in a given case).[44] An AI/ML system designed to encourage household energy conservation, for instance, may seek individuals whose preferences it predicts to favor energy conservation, people it predicts to consume more energy irrespective of whether their preferences favor conservation, or simply consumers whom the system estimates to be the most susceptible to a particular nudge based on their known or estimated personal characteristics. Yet we may not be able to ascertain for which of these reasons an individual was selected for nudging, only that the AI/ML system predicted that nudging that person will best optimize its energy conservation parameters.

This uncertainty is exacerbated by the further challenge of identifying the specific behavioral processes an algorithm recruited to encourage individuals to conserve more energy. After all, even a single offline intervention may recruit multiple behavioral processes—as when the traditional Home Energy Reports included a combination of social comparison information (comparing the household to a group of "efficient neighbors"), purported injunctive social norms favoring energy conservation (with smiley faces for those who conserve more than average), and energy conservation tips.[45] Consequently, it may be unclear which specific behavioral process led to a behavior change in any given case. After all, the energy conservation nudge may have assisted some who already wished to conserve more energy than their peers to follow through (e.g., by providing a social comparison benchmark), in which case they were likely made better off. But it may have led others to reduce energy consumption for fear of violating a purported social norm (such as through smiling/unsmiling face icons) or even just because they were susceptible to the pressure of repeated

[42] Chagal-Feferkorn and Elkin-Koren (forthcoming).

[43] Chagal-Feferkorn and Elkin-Koren (forthcoming).

[44] E.g., Mahmoodi et al. (2017).

[45] Tor (2022).

reminders (say, of their daily energy consumption). In the latter cases, however, those who conserved more energy have been made worse off.[46]

Third, in addition to producing potentially higher private costs that can be difficult to identify, digital nudging often occurs outside official government websites or online interfaces, taking place on the platforms and websites of private intermediaries. Of course, governments can and already do use behavioral instruments on their own websites, to facilitate their online interactions with citizens, as when they remind visitors to pay taxes on time, default them into specific selection of government benefits, and so on.[47] The same happens routinely on the websites of private, non-commercial organizations that seek to advance specific policy goals—such as increasing donations or changing public beliefs or preferences with respect to the issues they champion—through web design that includes a variety of nudge elements, such as framing, order effects, visual displays that direct attention or generate affect, and more.[48]

In addition, a growing number of local governments are developing "smart cities"—urban centers that use advanced technologies, such as smart devices and the collection and analysis of big data, to advance the innovative character of their cities and improve their functioning.[49] Besides its potential for improving the lives of residents and visitors, smart cities also offer new digital means for local governments to shape behavior. As the Behavioral Insights Team—formerly the United Kingdom's "nudge unit" and now a global social purpose organization—notes in its "behavioural government" report, smart cities can employ technology to make government requests of its citizens more effective.[50] Early examples of such digital nudging already exist, from Boston's partnering with private companies to develop and encourage the adoption of an app that collects personal and urban data on traffic safety and provides safe driving feedback based on the driver's speed, acceleration, braking, cornering, and phone distraction to the North Carolina city of Durham's partnering with private industry and employers to nudge residents to choose public transportation over private vehicles, by emailing personalized route maps from individuals' homes to work, showing different private and public transportation options.[51]

Nonetheless, to nudge individuals outside the limited confines of official websites and communications or specialized and voluntarily-downloaded apps, governments

---

[46] Tor and Klick (2023).

[47] For example, the United Kingdom's Department of Transportation encourages vehicle owners to register for reminders to avoid failing to comply with mandatory annual road safety tests, https://www.gov.uk/mot-reminder#:~:text=Sign%20up%20to%20get%20free,large%20trailer%20MOT%20is%20due (last access 27 January 2023).

[48] See, for instance, the various strategies employed by Oxfam, which describes itself as "a global movement of people, working together to end the injustice of poverty." https://www.oxfam.org/en (last access 27 January 2023).

[49] Ranchordás (2020).

[50] Behavioural Insights Team (2018).

[51] Ranchordás (2020).

and other organizations currently must turn to a variety of private online intermediaries, including social networks like Facebook, Instagram, or Twitter; e-commerce websites like Amazon, eBay, or Etsy, and more.[52] The benefits of delivering digital nudges using such intermediaries are obvious: These private platforms provide nudgers with access to a vast audience, sophisticated advertising, and powerful analytics services based on privately-held big data, all of which stands to increase the efficacy of digital nudging without requiring public entities to build specialized technology, accumulate big data, or develop the advanced and specialized marketing capabilities of private industry.

This reality, in which government will depend on private online intermediaries to implement many of its digital nudges, is of some concern. After all, the legal scrutiny and limits of regulatory interventions (e.g., the formal requirement that they pass a cost–benefit analysis), are usually not applied even to offline nudges and are thus unlikely to constrain the use of digital behavioral instruments. Moreover, privately-delivered online nudges are also unlikely to be significantly limited by consumer law, particularly in the United States.[53] Consumer protection laws are geared towards regulating false or misleading advertising by businesses that seek to sell consumers products or services. These rules therefore have limited bearing on digital nudging that involves no false or misleading claims as these terms are traditionally understood and are outside the typical seller-consumer relationship.

If that were not enough, the advertising and other services provided by commercial intermediaries to government agencies are equally available to private organizations, be they nonprofits or business entities. Indeed, the tools of digital nudging are the same effective and well-developed tools that for-profit businesses use routinely and extensively to market their products and services. The very capabilities that enable Google to personalize its search results or Facebook to provide its users with a personalized feed, for instance, are increasingly used in digital interventions aiming to nudge users towards online and offline behaviors that these platforms or their various private customers view as socially desirable.

Recently publicized evidence on some of the information-related activities of Facebook during the COVID-19 pandemic offer a striking illustration of the central and potentially problematic role of platform intermediaries in the service of digital nudging, initiated by governments, other organizations, or the intermediaries themselves.[54] While some of the actions taken by Facebook to promote the uptake of Covid vaccines and quash opinions and information that contradicted the official

---

[52] See, e.g., the COVID-19 Public Education Campaign of the Department of Health and Human Services, which included an effort to encourage vaccination through the dissemination of graphics on social media at https://wecandothis.hhs.gov/resource/ccc-find-a-covid-19-vaccine (last access 27 January 2023) and the extensive COVID-19 vaccination campaigns on Facebook directed at minority and religious communities in the U.S. described by de Vere Hunt et al. (2022).

[53] Bar-Gill and Ben-Shahar (2021).

[54] The redacted evidence is linked in a Wall Street Journal commentary from January 8, 2023 at https://www.wsj.com/articles/white-house-covid-censorship-machine-social-media-facebook-meta-executive-rob-flaherty-free-speech-google-11673203704?mod=Searchresults_pos1&page=1 (last access 27 January 2023).

government position went well beyond mere nudges, the platform combined these more extreme interventions with digital behavioral instruments. These included, for instance, using "trusted messengers", targeted ads, personalized messaging, and developing a wide-ranging social information campaign showing users other individuals that they trust taking these vaccines.

Notably, the company further reported providing "more than $30 million in ad credits to help governments, NGOs and other organizations reach people with COVID-19 information and other important messages. These information campaigns resulted in an estimated 10 billion ad impressions globally."[55] In other words, a powerful platform intermediary not only facilitated governmental efforts, but also supported the activities of private organizations that all advanced the official narrative on vaccinations and other COVID-19 related behaviors, while striving to reduce access to contradictory opinions and evidence, even when offered by experts with contrary positions.

Such potentially powerful digital nudging and broader platform conduct that is subject to little scrutiny may appear palatable, even desirable, to those whose beliefs or policy goals align with the platform's efforts. Yet the same effective tools are available to online intermediaries and the organizations who use their services when they seek to advance more controversial policy goals (e.g., encouraging COVID-19 booster shots for young children or discouraging abortion) outside established legal and regulatory institutions and processes or public political debate. All told, therefore, these private intermediaries can implement digital behavioral interventions to shape citizen behavior without being subject to substantial legal scrutiny or even to the most basic constraints that apply to the standard regulatory activities of governments.

5 Conclusion

Digital nudges are increasingly ubiquitous and their prevalence is only bound to increase in the coming years. They can offer more effective means for shaping people's judgments and decisions than offline behavioral instruments and may be easier for governments and private organizations to implement at scale. However, the greater efficacy of digital nudging, the opacity of the means it employs to change behavior, and the centrality of online platforms and other private actors in delivering or commissioning digital interventions raise significant challenges that merit further scrutiny and assessment.

It is apparent that digital nudging that uses the same capabilities that successfully advance the commercial interests of private industry is here to stay, whatever its consequences. Even more than in the case of offline nudges, therefore, the

[55] Id. (emphasis added).

various costs and risks involved should be weighed against the benefits of potentially efficacious digital behavioral interventions.[56] Beyond such case-by-case assessment of benefits and costs, however, there is a pressing need for developing appropriate responses—legal and technological—to address at least the more problematic instances of digital nudging.[57]

Acknowledgements The research underlying this chapter has benefited from the generous support of Notre Dame Law School and the helpful comments of participants at the Lucerne conference on Law and Economics of the Digital Transformation, the Copenhagen Business School conference on Personalisation and Discrimination in a Fundamental Rights Perspective, and the Hebrew University of Jerusalem Law and Economics Workshop. Isabella Wilcox provided excellent research assistance.

References

Allcott H (2011) Social norms and energy conservation. J Public Econ 95:1082

Allcott H, Kessler JB (2019) The welfare effects of nudges: a case study of energy use social comparisons. Am Econ J Appl Econ 11:236

Bar-Gill O, Ben-Shahar O (2021) Rethinking nudge: an information-costs theory of default rules. U Chi L Rev 88:531

Behavioural Insights Team (BIT) (2018) Behavioural government. The Behavioural Insights Team, London. https://www.bi.team/publications/behavioural-government/. Last accessed 3 Feb 2023

Benartzi S et al (2017) Should governments invest more in nudging? Psych Sci 28:1041

Chagal-Feferkorn K, Elkin-Koren N, LEX AI: revisiting private order by design. Berkeley Tech L J, forthcoming

City of Boston, Department of New Urban Mechanics, Safest driver competition. https://www.boston.gov/departments/new-urban-mechanics/bostons-safest-driver-competition. Last accessed 27 Jan 2023

De Haan T, Linde J (2018) Good nudge lullaby: Choice architecture and default bias reinforcement. Econ J 128:1180

DellaVigna S, Linos E (2021) RCTs to scale: comprehensive evidence from two nudge units (SSRN working paper. https://www.nber.org/papers/w27594. Last accessed 27 Jan 2023

European Commission (2021) Proposal for a regulation of the European Parliament and of the council laying down harmonized rules on artificial intelligence (Artificial Intelligence Act) and amending certain union legislative acts 2021/0106 (COD)

European Union (2022) Regulation (EU) 2022/1925 of the European Parliament and of the Council of 14 September 2022 on contestable and fair markets in the digital sector and amending Directives (EU) 2019/1937 and (EU) 2020/1828 (Digital Markets Act)

Glowacki M (2016) Nudging cities: innovating with behavioral science: lessons at the 15th convening of the project on municipal innovation, data-smart city solutions, May 17, 2016. https://datasmart.ash.harvard.edu/news/article/nudging-cities-innovating-with-behavioral-science-833. Last accessed 3 Feb 2023

Grune-Yanoff T, Hertwig R (2016) Nudge versus boost: how coherent are policy and theory? Mind Mach 26:149

[56] Tor (2022); cf. Sunstein (2018).

[57] The challenges involved in developing such regulatory responses are clearly demonstrated by European Union's recent efforts with respect to digital markets, artificial intelligence, and more. See, e.g., the EU's Digital Markets Act (2022) and the EC's Artificial Intelligence Act proposal (2021).

Hausman D, Welch B (2010) Debate: To nudge or not to nudge. J Pol Phil 18:123
Hummel D, Maedche A (2019) How effective is nudging? A quantitative review on the effect sizes and limits of empirical nudging studies. J Behav Exp Econ 80:47
Hunt IV et al (2022) A social media-based public health campaign encouraging COVID-19 vaccination across the United States. Am J Public Health 112(9):1253
Jung J, Mellers B (2016) American attitudes toward nudges. Judgm Decis Mak 11:62
Kanamitsu Y et al (2021) Using interaction as nudge to increase installation rate of COVID-19 contact-confirming application. In: Adjunct proceedings of the 2021 ACM international joint conference on pervasive and ubiquitous computing and proceedings of the 2021 ACM international symposium on wearable computers
Kosinski M, Stillwell D, Graepel T (2013) Private traits and attributes are predictable from digital records of human behavior. Proceed Nat Acad Sci 110:5802
Le Grand J, New B (2015) Government paternalism: Nanny state or helpful friend? Princeton University Press, Princeton New Jersey
Madrian BC (2014) Applying insights from behavioral economics to policy design. Ann Rev Econ 6:663
Mahmoodi J et al (2017) Big data approaches in social and behavioral science: four key trade-offs and a call for integration. Current Op Behav Sci 18:57
Matz SC, Netzer O (2017) Using Big Data as a window into consumers' psychology. Curr Opin Behav Sci 2017(18):7
Matz SC et al (2017) Psychological targeting as an effective approach to digital mass persuasion. Proceed Nat Acad Sci 114:12714
Mathis K, Tor A (eds) (2016) Nudging—possibilities, limitations and applications in European law and economics. Springer, Switzerland
Oliver A (2015) Nudging, shoving, and budging: Behavioral-economic informed policy. Pub Admin 93
Oliver A (2017) The origins of behavioural public policy. Cambridge University Press, pp 110–111
Organisation for Economic Co-operation and Development (OECD) (2020) Regulatory policy and COVID-19: Behavioural insights for fast-paced decision making
Sibony A-L, Alemanno A (2015) The emergence of behavioural policy-making: A European perspective. In: Alemanno A, Sibony, A-L (eds) Nudge and the law: A European perspective. Hart Publishing, Oxford United Kingdom p 1–25
Sibony AL, Alemanno A (2016) The emergence of behavioural policy-making. In: Alemmano A, Sibony AL (eds) A European perspective. Hart, Oxford, pp 1–2
Stone D et al (2005) User interface design and evaluation, 1st edn. Elsevier, p 4
Sunstein CR, Thaler R (2003) Libertarian paternalism. 93 Am Econ Rev 93:175
Sunstein CR (2016) The council of psychological advisers. Ann Rev Psychol 67: 713
Sunstein CR (2018) The cost-benefit revolution. The MIT Press
Sunstein CR, Reisch LA (2019) Trusting nudges: toward a bill of rights for nudging, 1st edn. Routledge
Sunstein CR, Reisch LA, Kaiser M (2019) Trusting nudges? Lessons from an international survey. J Eur Pub Pol'y 26:1417
Ranchordas S (2020) Nudging citizens through technology in smart cities. Intl'l Rev L Computers & Tech 34:254
Teichman D, Underhill K (2021) Infected by bias: behavioral science and the legal response to COVID-19. Am J L Med 47:205
Thaler RH, Sunstein CR (2008) Nudge: improving decisions about health, wealth, and happiness. Penguin Books, New York
The White House (2021) Fact sheet: President Biden to announce new actions to get more Americans vaccinated and slow the spread of the delta variant. https://www.whitehouse.gov/briefing-room/statements-releases/2021/07/29/fact-sheet-president-biden-to-announce-new-actions-to-get-more-americans-vaccinated-and-slow-the-spread-of-the-delta-variant/ last accessed 3 Feb 2023

Tor A (2016) The critical and problematic role of bounded rationality. In: Mathis K, Tor A (eds) Nudging—possibilities, limitations and applications in European law and economics. Springer, Switzerland
Tor A (2019) All nudges are not the same: why rationality matters for welfare (manuscript)
Tor A (2020) Nudges that should fail. Behav Pub Pol'y 4:316, n 1
Tor A (2021) The target opportunity costs of successful nudges. In: Mathis K, Tor A (eds) Consumer law and economics. Springer, Switzerland, p 3
Tor A (2022) The law and economics of behavioral regulation. Rev L & Econ 18:1
Tor A (2023) The private costs of behavioral interventions. Duke L J 72, forthcoming
Tor A, Klick J (2023) When should governments invest more in nudging? Revisiting Benartzi et al. (2017) Rev L & Econ, forthcoming
Wall Street Journal (2023) The White House Covid Censorship Machine, January 8
Weinmann M, Schneider C, vom Brocke J (2016) Digital nudging. Bus Inf Syst Eng 58:433
Yeung K (2017) Hypernudge: big data as a mode of regulation by design. Inf Commun Soc 20(1):118

Part II: Contracts in Digital Markets

Do Smart Contracts Incur Higher Transaction Costs Than Traditional Contracts?

Massimiliano Vatiero

Abstract A smart contract is an agreement enforced by blockchain technology. It supposedly allows the parties involved to conduct transactions more efficiently than a traditional contract, which is based on legal (costly) enforcement. This chapter challenges this claim. Given the need for an efficiency-enhancing adaptation of institutional arrangements—a chief problem of Oliver Williamson's transaction cost economics—smart contracts may incur higher transaction costs than traditional contracts.

Keywords Smart contracts · Blockchain · Adaptation · Incomplete contracts · Transaction costs · Enforcement costs · Consensus mechanism · Governance · Mancur Olson's Logic

1 The Issue

The common colloquialism "set in stone" can be used to explain one of the prominent requisites for good contracts and, more generally, for rules in a community.[1] In this analogy, the blockchain represents the stone for smart contracts. A smart contract contains a series of promises made about a transaction, written in computer code and enforced by blockchain technology. In a smart contract, each transaction is translated into a computer code, placed into a digital block, and once a "consensus mechanism" is applied, the block is placed into a perpetually growing chain of

[1] Unsurprisingly, in the Judeo–Christian tradition, the Ten Commandments were written on stone tablets by God and handed down to Moses on Mount Sinai. Similarly unsurprising is that the Babylonian Code of Hammurabi, dated roughly 1772 BC and consisting of 282 laws, including the famous "eye for an eye" (*lex talionis*), was etched in stone.

M. Vatiero (✉)
University of Trento, DEM), Trento, Italy
e-mail: massimiliano.vatiero@unitn.it

(Law Institute, IDUSI), Lugano, Switzerland

K. Mathis and A. Tor (eds.), *Law and Economics of the Digital Transformation*, Economic Analysis of Law in European Legal Scholarship 15,
https://doi.org/10.1007/978-3-031-25059-0_2

blocks, hence the term *blockchain*. This chapter addresses agreements that exploit blockchain technology—namely, smart contracts—through the lens of transaction cost economics.[2]

A smart contract codifies parties' responsibilities and obligations *ex ante*, and the blockchain executes them with certainty *ex post*; in other terms, smart contracts afford no room for second thoughts unless the parties have incorporated a clause to halt the blockchain's execution *ex ante*. Unlike traditional contracts, in which the parties can decide whether to fulfil their obligations, considering the risk of being held liable for damages, smart contracts cannot be breached. The "inflexible" nature of the blockchain[3] poses particular implications for contractual agreements: For an investment in a contractual relationship to thrive, clauses agreed upon should be stable and resistant to unilateral renegotiations.

Given that blockchain technology prevents renegotiations as well as avoids the malfeasance of a third party or external intermediary due to its decentralized nature, the blockchain represents a "trust machine"[4] that creates a reliable environment for agreements—smart contracts—among people who have no particular confidence in each other. The range of possibilities that can be derived from the basic idea of smart contracts is ample.[5] For instance, smart contracts may be used to improve rental cars,[6] to enable employees to be paid on an hourly or daily basis,[7] or to provide musical artists with a means of receiving music usage fees and royalties.[8]

Although scholarly interest in the subject is growing rapidly, to date, an analysis of smart contracts from the perspective of transaction cost economics is severely lacking.[9] The main motivation of this chapter lies in the naïve view of smart contracts, according to which smart contracts are supposed to be cheaper than traditional contracts. This chapter shows that when the problem of *adaptation* is seriously taken into account, smart contracts may incur higher (and not lower) transaction costs than traditional contracts.

Using a simple example of a rental car, this chapter first defines the chief characteristics of smart contracts and the principal differences compared to traditional contracts. Second, this chapter shows that, because smart contracts are constructed to avoid or limit legal enforcement (typically by a court), they also avoid or limit a potentially *efficient legal adaptation*. Furthermore, this chapter investigates the forking process of adapting a smart contract (and blockchain in general) and shows

[2] On transaction costs economics, see among others, Pagano and Vatiero (2015) and Vatiero (2018a), (2021).

[3] See, among others, Sklaroff (2017).

[4] Cf. *The* Economist (2015) and Werbach (2018).

[5] Cf. Swanson (2014).

[6] Cf. http://darenta.io (last access 12 July 2022).

[7] Cf. www.bitwage.co (last access 12 July 2022).

[8] Cf. www.mediachain.io (last access 12 July 2022).

[9] Relevant exceptions are Yermack (2017), Vatiero (2018b), Holden and Malani (2018) and Catalini and Gans (2018).

Table 1 Smart contracts and transaction costs

Transaction costs	
Decreasing	Increasing
Blockchain avoids any deviation from smart contracts	Blockchain also prevents efficiency-enhancing adaptation Transaction costs due to a lack of *legal adaptation*
Due to the consensus mechanism, a blockchain's participants can adapt the blockchain and smart contracts to new needs	Consensus mechanism may lead to an uncertain, majority-driven adaptation Transaction costs for a *bad adaptation*

that such a process is threatened by Mancur Olson's *logic*,[10] namely the risk that a sub-group of a blockchain's participants may dominate and manipulate the evolution of a blockchain and then of agreements using that blockchain (i.e., smart contracts). There are, then, transaction costs that result from this risk of *bad adaptation.* Table 1 synthesizes the transaction costs of smart contracts.[11]

The remainder of this chapter unfolds as follows. The next section describes the main differences between a smart contract and a traditional contract. Section 3 illustrates the transaction costs in a smart contract due to a lack of legal adaptation. Transaction costs resulting from a bad adaptation are discussed in Sect. 4. Section 5 is dedicated to the concluding remarks.

2 What Is a Smart Contract?

In a traditional contract, the parties write a state-contingent contract and rely on an external third party or enforcer to settle their conflicts ex post. However, in the parlance of incomplete contract theory,[12] the parties' conduct and the exact nature of their transaction are not ex ante completely predictable by the terms of the contract since unforeseen events occur, or, at least, are only imperfectly (i.e., costly) verifiable by the enforcer. In short, in this literature on incomplete contracts, there are enforcement costs, namely transaction costs, in each traditional contract. On the other hand, a smart contract is an agreement[13] that exploits the blockchain as the enforcement medium, limiting or avoiding transaction costs related to the *costly* legal enforcement that applies to traditional contracts.

Let me describe the main differences between a traditional contract and a smart contract. Assume that the author of this chapter (hereinafter MV) is the owner of

[10] See Olson (1965, 1982).

[11] I do not discuss a few other types of transaction costs that might stem from smart contracts, such as the cost of energy (cf. Biais et al. 2018) or costs for hacking incidents (cf. Werbach 2018).

[12] E.g. Williamson (1985) and Vatiero (2018a), (2021).

[13] It is not clear whether smart contracts are legally valid. See, among others, Werbach and Cornell (2017). For this reason, instead of "contracts" I refer to "agreements" between parties.

Ferrari California[14] and that Cruella De Vil[15] wants to use this car for a weekend. Suppose that MV and Cruella De Vil agree that MV will lend his Ferrari to Cruella De Vil in accordance with the following price scheme: 10 CHF per kilometre if Cruella De Vil drives MV's Ferrari on the city roads, whereas if she drives on the highway during that weekend, the price rises to 1,000 CHF per kilometre—MV is worried by the fact that his Ferrari is on the highway and therefore he asks for a significantly higher price. There is also an extra rate of 50% in case Cruella De Vil exceeds the speeding limits.

Now, consider that MV and Cruella De Vil decide to state their agreement via a contract. Then, they "translate" this agreement into contractual clauses, specifying every condition—including the price if Cruella De Vil drives on a highway. From an economic perspective, a contract consists of a list of contingencies (e.g., Cruella De Vil drives on a highway), a list of "conduct" (Cruella De Vil pays 1,000 CHF per kilometre), and a correspondence between contingencies and conduct (*if* Cruella De Vil drives on a highway, *then* she pays 1,000 CHF per kilometre). Finally, assume that, after the rental, using a GPS tracking inserted in the Ferrari, MV notes that Cruella De Vil drove on a highway for 10 kms, exceeding speeding limits, and then MV asks for payment of 15,000 CHF (= 1,000 CHF * 10 km * 150%). However, Cruella De Vil claims that she entered a highway, exceeding limits, because MV had asked her to take him urgently to the hospital. For this reason, she does not want to pay the price of 1,000 CHF per kilometre and the extra rate for exceeding speeding limits. MV sues Cruella De Vil and the Judge, say, Guido Richard,[16] will observe Cruella De Vil's and MV's (proxies of) conduct and, eventually, will make a decision based on (proxies of) their conduct. Note that Judge Guido Richard, like any other judge, decides after the occurrence of an event (e.g., Cruella De Vil drives on the highway, but she does not want to pay the highway rate price).

Now, consider that MV and Cruella De Vil write a smart contract. First, they "translate" their agreement into a computer language and specify every condition—including the price rate if Cruella De Vil drives on a highway. As in the traditional contract, in a smart contract, the parties specify the correspondence between contingencies and conduct (*if* Cruella De Vil drives on a highway, *then* she pays 1,000 CHF per kilometre). Unlike traditional contracts, there are two important differences. First, enforcement is represented by blockchain technology; second, as discussed earlier, the parties must write in computer code.

A blockchain is (supposed to be) a dis-intermediated and de-centralized digital ledger based on P2P governance. In particular, the blockchain "validates" the agreement using a consensus mechanism: Every participant is invited to (compete to) validate that agreement. There are two main consensus mechanisms: proof-of-work

---

[14] This is just an assumption. For sake of sincerity, the author of this paper does not own a Ferrari.

[15] Cruella De Vil is one of Walt Disney's most famous characters. She is generally depicted in the popular mind as the epitome of evil (indeed, the name Cruella de Vil is a pun of the words "cruel" and "devil") and therefore she may represent a person to avoid making an agreement with, and, as the Disney animated feature films describe her, not very safe driving a car.

[16] This a fictious name. It may represent a mix between Judge Guido (Calabresi) and Judge Richard (Posner), to emphasize that we will follow a law and economics perspective.

and proof-of-stake. In the case of a proof-of-work mechanism, participants confirm the agreement using their computational power. The agreement will be inserted and enforced in a blockchain if the majority of the computational power in the blockchain accepts this agreement. According to Bitcoin's pseudonymous creator, Satoshi Nakamoto, with a proof-of-work mechanism, people "*vote with their CPU power*, expressing their acceptance of the valid blocks by working on extending them and rejecting invalid blocks by refusing to work on them".[17] The proof-of-stake mechanism is a different way to validate transactions. Unlike the proof-of-work mechanism, in which users pay in the form of computational power, in the proof-of-stake system, the validator of a new block depends on the wealth of his or her digital wallet, or what is called a *stake*. In the proof-of-stake mechanism, every participant *votes* with his/her stake in a blockchain.[18] In both cases, a blockchain's participants vote (either with their computational power or stake); from this vote/consensus, the blockchain is updated, including the smart contract between MV and Cruella De Vil.

The second main difference between a traditional contract and a smart contract is that, in the latter, every clause is translated into a computer code. According to the inventor of smart contracts, Nick Szabo,

> The basic idea of smart contracts is that many kinds of contractual clauses (such as liens, bonding, delineation of property rights, etc.) can be embedded in the hardware and software we deal with, in such a way as *to make breach of contract expensive (if desired, sometimes prohibitively so) for the breacher*. A canonical real-life example, which we might consider to be the primitive ancestor of smart contracts, is the humble *vending machine*. Within a limited amount of potential loss (the amount in the till should be less than the cost of breaching the mechanism), the machine takes in coins, and via a simple mechanism, which makes a beginner's level problem in design with finite automata, dispense change and product fairly.[19]

In short, a smart contract can be programmed as a vending machine; if someone inserts a coin, then he or she automatically receives a can of soda. This means that each smart contract contains a set of rules that trigger automatic, predefined responses corresponding to particular contingencies in deterministic computational logic. So, if Cruella De Vil drives on the highway, then there is a transfer of crypto-coins from Cruella De Vil's digital wallet to MV's wallet. Neither Cruella De Vil nor MV can unilaterally deviate from the smart contract. It can be stopped only with a new smart contract, which will require the consensus (i.e., validation) of a blockchain's participants and, further, the "consensus" of the other party with whom the new smart contract is written (if Cruella De Vil wants to stop the current smart contract, she needs the consensus of MV, and vice versa).

Given that every contingency is translated in a deterministic language, i.e. the computer code, there is no possibility that the parties will deviate from what they agreed upon *ex ante*. Thus, computer code and blockchain technology guarantee that

---

[17] Nakamoto (2008), p. 8, italics added.

[18] This is a validation method that resembles decisions in a shareholders' assembly, which follow the vote basing on shares of a public company.

[19] Szabo (1997), italics added.

each transaction is performed automatically in keeping with the promises that MV and Cruella De Vil agreed upon *ex ante*. According to enthusiasts of smart contracts, smart contracts avoid all deviations of the parties without the *costly* intervention of a third party (e.g. Judge Guido Richard). The naïve view of smart contracts is that smart contracts are cheaper in terms of transaction costs than traditional contracts, a claim that I challenge in this chapter.

I argue that because of the need for an efficiency-enhancing adaptation of institutional arrangements, smart contracts may incur higher transaction costs than traditional contracts. Indeed, to achieve efficiency, a contract needs to be adaptable to unexpected, new circumstances. To quote Oliver Williamson, "[I]nasmuch as a full set of contingent claim markets is infeasible (by reason of bounded rationality), *adaptive*, sequential decision-making procedures need be devised."[20] Williamson later elaborated, "Intertemporal efficiency... requires that *adaptations to changing market circumstances be made*".[21] A similar claim regards efficient breach theory. Given that a contract that seemed sweet when agreed upon may turn sour in the interval prior to its performance, its renegotiation (e.g. breach of contractual promises) may be excusable.[22] Accordingly, an efficient contractual arrangement must facilitate adaptation in the face of mutable and unpredictable occurrences.

Indeed, assume that MV needs to be rushed to a hospital, and that Cruella De Vil, who rented the car, is available to drive him to the hospital faster than any other transport can by entering the highway. However, for the threat of a price of 1,000 CHF per kilometre on the highway plus an extra rate for exceeding speeding limits, Cruella De Vil could reject taking MV to the hospital until the new smart contract, which revokes the previous one, is agreed, written, and executed, which would require several minutes at least. As an alternative, Cruella De Vil may decide to trust that MV will recompensate her for the transfer of cryptocurrencies related to the entry onto the highway. Although unexpected events and emergencies could require driving beyond the boundaries established in the smart contract, the smart contract could inhibit such conduct.

The inflexibility of a smart contract may prevent efficient adaptation in this case. In that respect, compared with traditional contracts, smart contracts pose the principal disadvantage of inflexibility to *ex post* adaptation. Once submitted to the blockchain, the execution of a smart contract is entirely independent of any single party, including a legal party (Judge Guido Richard), unless the parties (MV and Cruella De Vil) deploying the smart contract have introduced a mechanism for that purpose *ex ante*. There are, in other terms, transaction costs due to a lack of legal adaptation (cf. Sect. 3 below).

Moreover, for the consensus mechanisms, the validation of a blockchain rests on a vote of a blockchain's participants, which poses the risk that a coalition of users might

---

[20] Williamson (1973), p. 318, italics added.

[21] Williamson (1979), p. 241, italics added.

[22] See, among others, Shavell (2009).

distort the development of the blockchain and its smart contracts.[23] Such a risk has become increasingly threatening as blockchain networks shift from the community at large to fewer and fewer hands that currently dominate the most popular blockchains. By using the consensus mechanism, blockchains and smart contracts entail the risk that their development will cater to the preferences of the majority and potentially against the interests of minorities. Adopting a transaction-cost politics perspective,[24] consensus mechanisms could determine that rules for smart contracts are aligned with the majority's preferences but are inefficient, unreliable, and unpredictable. This would increase transaction costs. In the example of the smart contract for the car rental, this could possibly mean that, if MV belongs to a group (e.g. a group of car owners) with enough power to affect the blockchain, then he and his group could distort the execution of the smart contract with Cruella De Vil. In more detail, Sect. 4 describes these transaction costs for a bad adaptation.

3 Transaction Costs Due to a Lack of Legal Adaptation

Smart contracts are constructed to avoid or limit external interventions. However, rich literature shows that, because the legal intervention takes place after the realisation of unpredictable events, legal enforcement can create benefits for the parties.[25] There is, in other terms, an increase in transaction costs for the parties if there is *no* room for a legal adaptation, as (it is supposed) in the case of smart contracts.

In the case of a traditional contract, Judge Guido Richard can (try to) observe the behaviours of the parties and decides, for instance, on a force majeure criterion: MV needed to go to the hospital, and the fastest way is on the highway. The judge can observe the Ferrari's track and collect information, such as a medical report on MV that attests that MV was in the hospital that day and hour. Thus, Judge Guido Richard can excuse Cruella De Vil's behaviour. *Trusting in legal intervention*, Cruella De Vil can take MV to the hospital without the threat of paying penalties. Due to legal intervention, there is an efficiency-enhancing adaptation of the agreement between MV and Cruella De Vil (without which the parties must write another contract).

The law and economics literature, in general, refers to two types of legal adaptation (which could be summed): the adjudicative-gap filling doctrine[26] and the theory of

---

[23] In a similar vein, in July 2014, the European Banking Authority (2015, p. 5) published a report highlighting those same concerns with virtual currencies (VCs): "The risks include the fact that a VC scheme can be created, and then its function subsequently changed, by anyone, and in the case of decentralized schemes, such as Bitcoin's, by anyone with a sufficient share of computational power".

[24] See Dixit (1996), Olson (1982), and Vatiero (2018a), (2021).

[25] E.g. Posner (2004), (2007); Schwartz and Scott (2003, 2010); and Shavell (2006), (2007); It is worthy to stress that also Old-Institutionalism (e.g. John R. Commons and John Maurice Clark) had a similar idea of legal adaptation that may create benefits for parties; see Fiorito and Vatiero (2011).

[26] E.g. Posner (2004), (2007) and Shavell (2006), (2007).

contract interpretation.[27] For the adjudicative-gap-filling doctrine, because there are costs of writing contracts (transaction costs), the parties may prefer leaving gaps in a traditional contract, and it is efficient that a judge, e.g. Judge Guido Richard, fills those gaps *when and if* they emerge. In the case of smart contracts, instead, the parties have to specify every contingency *ex ante* (which implies high transaction costs) if they do not want an external intervention. Moreover, what they specify *ex ante* will be performed *ex post* without the possibility of benefits coming from a legal adaptation, which is not always smart! Transaction costs may be very high due to this lack of legal adaptation. For the theory of contract interpretation, the court (e.g. Judge Guido Richard) may determine the meaning of contractual terms and, to a certain degree, interpret them in a way that adapts a contract to unexpected contingencies. In the case of smart contracts, instead, the parties should clarify the meaning of each contractual term, perhaps defining untranslatable terms, such as force majeure, good faith, and urgency. Again, in a smart contract, the lack of legal adaptation, intended as an interpretation, produces transaction costs for the parties.

More generally, in traditional contracts, an external party can intervene *ex post* to adapt to the contract. With smart contracts, clauses are not written in standard legal prose but memorialized in computer code using a strict, formal programming language (e.g. Solidity). Given its binary nature and inflexibility, computer code can neither include nor translate several important legal concepts characterizing the execution of traditional contracts, including force majeure, material breach, trade customs, commercial standards, fiduciary duty, and good faith, which give traditional contracts the flexibility that can be desired when so many contingencies cannot be defined *ex ante*.

Further, traditional contracts can also favour self-adaptation. Indeed, their contracting parties, who cannot construct bespoke contracts, may prefer to avoid litigation and resolve contract disputes informally (e.g. by gentlemen's agreements[28]). They could opt to resolve such disputes only *ex post*, for example, when contingencies occur. With a traditional contract, parties are free to dynamically shape their relationships by way of informal modifications or by selectively enforcing breaches. On the contrary, because the execution of a smart contract cannot be halted after it has been triggered by the parties, the parties cannot adapt the smart contract. Consider again the smart contract for a car rental. The smart contract should specify all minute aspects of the lesser-lessee transaction (e.g. its cleanliness, functioning, and condition of the car), which implies transaction costs in defining, potentially bargaining, and writing all possible clauses. Altogether, whereas smart contracts require the *ex ante* definition and translation into code of all future states of the world and correlated consequences, traditional contracts enable parties to use generally defined contractual terms as well as to create and enforce agreements without requiring complete knowledge of what might happen in the future. Hence, traditional contracts allow parties to conduct transactions more efficiently than smart contracts.

---

[27] E.g. Schwartz and Scott (2003, 2010).

[28] With traditional contracts, the parties may strike gentlemen's agreements instead of terms that attempt to be exhaustingly comprehensive.

4 Transaction Costs of a Bad Adaptation

The consensus mechanism is at the heart of blockchain technology. Briefly, consensus on a blockchain requires that only one block of chains exist, which all participants observe and upon which all agree. How this consensus is achieved affects the security and economic parameters of the protocol. The most-used consensus mechanism is called proof of work. To validate transactions, a miner—that is, a user in the blockchain network tasked with validating transactions—has to dedicate computational power to verify transactions and rapidly search through potential solutions to solve the mathematical puzzle associated with each block to obtain the reward. In doing so, miners vote with their computational power. Such a system supposes that miners have an incentive to act purely out of self-interest and, in the process, fulfil a socially beneficial role.[29]

However, an increasing concern with blockchain networks using proof-of-work systems is the risk of centralization. Amid the growing popularity of blockchains, the difficulty of the validation process has spiked, thus decreasing the probability that an individual using an everyday computer will mine a block. Therefore, in large blockchains such as Bitcoin's, the probability that any individual could mine a block using non-specialized hardware is low. Due to that dynamic, miners seeking to validate transactions have organized themselves into so-called "mining pools" in which they combine their computational resources and deploy specialized hardware to mine new blocks and share rewards. In other words, because rewards are distributed at infrequent, random intervals, miners who can be conceived as risk-adverse agents behave strategically and form mining pools to decrease the variance of their income rate.[30] Empirical evidence shows that the centralization of blockchains occurs. For instance, as of August 2018, four mining pools controlled 55% of the Bitcoin network (BTC.com: 17%, SlushPool: 15%, AntPool: 13%, BTC.TOP: 11%[31]), and five mining pools controlled more than roughly 80% of the Ethereum blockchain (Ethermine: 28%, SparkPool: 17%, F2Pool: 14%, Nanopool: 11%, MiningPoolHub_1: 9%[32]). The chief threat is that a group with sufficient computational power may prohibit certain transactions.

This risk, investigated at length with regards to economic institutions, relates to Mancur Olson's logic that subgroups (e.g. mining pools) may exploit the larger group (e.g. the blockchain network) because they act in support of their interests.[33] At stake in this dynamic is the loss of social welfare. More generally, the risk that mining pools may behave opportunistically can distort the choices of the parties to smart contracts and, therefore, create transaction costs.

---

[29] Eyal and Sirer (2014), Bonneau et al. (2015) and Biais et al. (2018) have described several circumstances in which benign strategies are *not* Nash equilibria for miners.

[30] Cf. Eyal and Sirer (2014).

[31] Cf. https://www.blockchain.com/it/pool (last access 12 July 2022).

[32] Cf. https://etherscan.io/stat/miner?range=7&blocktype=blocks (last access 12 July 2022).

[33] Olson (1965), (1982).

The hard fork process is another source of transaction costs. With a hard fork, a blockchain is split into two blockchains that start functioning as separate entities with different sets of rules. For instance, Ethereum experienced a hard fork in the summer of 2016. Following the hack of *The DAO*, members of the Ethereum community suggested rolling back the blockchain to cancel the transactions that diverted the fund's money. Given that several members of the network refused to alter the blockchain and rejected the hard fork, Ethereum split into two incompatible "worlds": one in which *The DAO*, along with all of the consequences of the hack, still exists (i.e. Ethereum Classic) and another in which *The DAO* never happened (i.e. Ethereum) and in which blocks of *The DAO* hacking incident were removed. Both worlds continue to survive. As Yermack has lucidly commented, that fork

> accomplished two things that were supposed to be impossible on a public blockchain: rewriting the history of transactions, and introducing human intervention to negate the unanticipated consequences of a self-executing smart contract. Implicitly, the event raised the possibility of future interventions in Bitcoin and other blockchains, even open ones, if a majority of the constituents wished to nullify a set of adverse economic outcomes after the fact. A minority of 15% of the Ethereum miners saw this precedent as dangerous and opposed the hard fork, creating a schism in Ethereum when they continued to mine and process transactions on the legacy blockchain.[34]

Hard forks, in other words, produce transaction costs.[35] First, because they can change the rules of a blockchain and, in turn, the institutional setting of smart contracts, hard forks create uncertainty for the parties of a smart contract. The hard fork negates the conclusiveness or immutability presumed by smart contracts.[36] Second, because every blockchain is joined with a cryptocurrency used as a means of payment in the blockchain platform, a hard fork can and often does alter the value of the cryptocurrency upon which the smart contract is established.[37] For instance, the value of Ethereum dropped when it split from Ethereum Classic, which added confusion to the marketplace and was liable to adversely affect all users. Last, when a coalition of a blockchain's participants (e.g. of mining pools) dominates that blockchain, according to Mancur Olson's *logic*, a hard fork can define rules that favour the majority and, thus, that are potentially inefficient, unreliable, and unpredictable for the entire community of that blockchain. Uncertainty and distorted incentives for groups' logic, therefore, determine transaction costs that are absent with traditional contracts.[38]

---

[34] Yermack (2017), p. 28, italics added.

[35] Hard forks are not uncommon. Bitcoin also underwent two hard forks in the summer and fall of 2017. The first stemmed from the size of blocks that could be mined on the blockchain and involved the split of the original Bitcoin blockchain into two branches, with two different cryptocurrencies: Bitcoin and Bitcoin Cash. The second fork, Bitcoin Gold, which occurred in the fall of 2017, has relied on a different proof-of-work algorithm than Bitcoin does.

[36] Cf. also Arruñada and Garicano (2018).

[37] See Thompson (2017).

[38] Regarding the group's *logic* in blockchain, it is worth considering that even traditional contracts may face the same problem. For example, in a parliamentary democracy, a group of citizens could vote for political parties to revise contract law according to their own, particular preferences, and at

5 Concluding Remarks

A smart contract represents an agreement that exploits blockchain technology as an enforcing medium. Departing from a naïve view of smart contracts (according to which smart contracts are supposed to reduce transaction costs, especially transaction costs for deviations from what parties agreed on *ex ante*), this chapter shows that, taking into account the need for an efficiency-enhancing adaptation, the smart contract may increase and not reduce transaction costs. Indeed, smart contracts are constructed to avoid or limit legal adaptation that may create benefits for the parties. Moreover, for a consensus mechanism, there is a risk of bad adaptation in an Olsonian logic of groups.

Thus, given the importance of adaptation, smart contracts may incur more transaction costs than traditional contracts.

References

Arruñada B, Garicano L (2018) Blockchain: the birth of decentralized governance. Economic working paper series, n. 1608, Universitat Pompeu Fabra

Biais B et al (2018) The blockchain folk theorem. Tolouse school of economics working paper, n. 17–817

Bonneau J et al (2015) SoK: research perspectives and challenges for bitcoin and cryptocurrencies. In: 2015 IEEE symposium on security and privacy

Catalini C, Gans JS (2018) Some simple economics of the blockchain. NBER working paper, n. 22952

Dixit A (1996) The making of economic policy: a transaction-cost politics perspective. MIT Press, Cambridge

The Economist (2015) The trust machine. The promise of the blockchain. October 31, 2015

European Banking Authority (2014) EBA opinion on "virtual currencies". 4 July 2014, http://www.eba.europa.eu/documents/10180/657547/EBA-Op-2014-08+Opinion+on+Virtual+Currencies.pdf. Last access 12 July 2022

Eyal I, Sirer EG (2014) Majority is not enough: bitcoin mining is vulnerable. In: Böhme R et al (eds) International conference on financial cryptography and data security. Springer, Berlin, pp 436–454

Fiorito L, Vatiero M (2011) beyond legal relations: Wesley Newcomb Hohfeld's influence on American institutionalism. J Econ Issues 45(1):199–222

---

the expense of the minoritarian groups. However, that circumstance is more costly than in the case of smart contracts, because a reform of contract law as well as each legal reform is intermediated by a costly and long legislative process that involves political parties and several socioeconomic stakeholders, and is characterized by a parliamentary debate. There are also constitutional norms in democratic countries that set limits and rigid procedures to change the rules to safeguard minoritarian parties. These limits and rigidities may reduce the flexibility of a legal ordering but create "legal certainty" for private parties, including minoritarian groups. Moreover, these constitutional norms that provide limits and rigidities can be changed only with specific and qualified procedures—for instance, with qualified majorities (for instance, in Switzerland, each amendment of the Swiss Federal Constitution requires the double majority: the majority of people and the majority of Cantons).

Holden R, Malani A (2018) Can blockchain solve the holdup problem in contracts? University of Chicago Coase-Sandor Institute for Law & Economics research paper, n. 846
Nakamoto S (2008) Bitcoin: a peer-to-peer electronic cash system. Available at https://bitcoin.org/bitcoin.pdf. Last access 12 July 2022
Olson M (1965) The logic of collective action. Harvard University Press, Boston
Olson M (1982) The rise and decline of nations: economic growth, stagflation, and social rigidities. Yale University Press, New Haven
Pagano U, Vatiero M (2015) Costly institutions as substitutes: novelty and limits of the Coasian approach. J Inst Econ 11(2):265–281
Posner R (2004) The law and economics of contract interpretation. Texas Law Rev 83:1581–1614
Posner R (2007) Economic analysis of law, 7th edn. Wolters Kluwer, Chicago
Schwartz A, Scott RE (2003) Contract theory and the limits of contract law. Yale Law J 113(3):541–619
Schwartz A, Scott RE (2010) Contract interpretation redux. Yale Law J 119(5):926–964
Shavell S (2006) On the writing and the interpretation of contracts. J Law Econ Organ 22(2):289–314
Shavell S (2007) Contract holdup and legal intervention. J Legal Stud 36(2):325–354
Shavell S (2009) Why breach of contract may not be immoral given the incompleteness of contracts. Mich Law Rev 107:1569–1581
Sklaroff J (2017) Smart contracts and the cost of inflexibility. Univ Pa Law Rev 166:263–303
Swanson T (2014) Great chain of numbers: a guide to smart contracts, smart property and trustless asset management. Amazon digital service
Szabo N (1997) The idea of smart contracts. Available at http://www.fon.hum.uva.nl/rob/Courses/InformationInSpeech/CDROM/Literature/LOTwinterschool2006/szabo.best.vwh.net/idea.html. Last access 12 July 2022
Thompson P (2017) How bitcoin forks influence bitcoin price rise and fall. Cointelegraph, Oct 28, available at https://cointelegraph.com/news/how-bitcoin-forks-influence-bitcoin-price-rise-and-fall. Last access 12 July 2022
Vatiero M (2021) The theory of transaction in institutional economics. Routledge, London
Vatiero M (2018a) Transaction and transactors' choices: What we have learned and what we need to explore. In: Ménard C, Shirley MM (eds) A research agenda for new institutional economics. Edward Elgar Publishers, pp 97–108
Vatiero M (2018b) Smart contracts and transaction costs. Oxford Business Law Blog, https://www.law.ox.ac.uk/business-law-blog/blog/2018b/10/smart-contracts-and-transaction-costs. Last access 12 July 2022
Werbach K (2018) Trust, but verify: why the blockchain needs the law. Berkeley Technol Law J 33:487–550
Werbach K, Cornell N (2017) Contracts ex machina. Duke Law J 67:313–382
Williamson OE (1973) Markets and hierarchies: some elementary considerations. Am Econ Rev 63(2):316–325
Williamson OE (1979) Transaction-cost economics: the governance of contractual relations. J Law Econ 22(2):233–261
Williamson OE (1985) The economic institutions of capitalism. Free Press, New York
Yermack D (2017) Corporate governance and blockchains. Rev Finance 21(1):7–31

Massimiliano Vatiero is a Professor of Economic Policy at the University of Trento (Italy) and Professor of Law and Economics at the Università della Svizzera italiana (Switzerland). His fields of interest include Law and Economics, Transaction Cost Economics and Corporate Governance.

Digitalization's Big Promise and Peril: The Personalization of Insurance Contracts and Its Legal Consequences

Katarzyna Południak-Gierz and Piotr Tereszkiewicz

Abstract This chapter analyzes the application of digital tools used to personalize consumer insurance contracts. First, a proper meaning of "personalization" is proposed, and its function in the insurance context is discussed. Subsequently, the paper illustrates the most important scenarios of incorrect personalization from the perspective of consumer insurance buyers. This enables an analysis of what legal remedies under contract and consumer law may be applied to protect the interests of consumer insurance buyers. The chapter's conclusion identifies a preferred and feasible solution from the perspective of insurance consumers themselves.

Keywords Personalization · Mispersonalization · Consumer insurance · Price discrimination · Insurance cover · Misselling · Insurance law · Unfair commercial practices

1 Introduction: The Notion of "Personalization"

In the third decade of the twenty-first century, the personalization of content presented to online users is widely discussed, raising interest among legal scholars. Crucially, it is not only the phenomenon itself that poses a challenge. The terminology itself requires explanation. Usually, *personalization* is understood to mean the process of adjusting the online content presented to individuals depending on data available on their situation, traits, and preferences.[1] The definition of personalization may depend

[1] Mik (2016), p. 19.

K. Południak-Gierz (✉) · P. Tereszkiewicz
Jagiellonian University, Cracow, Poland
e-mail: katarzyna.poludniak@uj.edu.pl

P. Tereszkiewicz
e-mail: piotr.tereszkiewicz@uj.edu.pl

P. Tereszkiewicz
University of Leuven, Leuven, Belgium

K. Mathis and A. Tor (eds.), *Law and Economics of the Digital Transformation*, Economic Analysis of Law in European Legal Scholarship 15,
https://doi.org/10.1007/978-3-031-25059-0_3

on whose perspective is assumed: the one of the traders using the personalizing tool in relations with clients, or that of the client who becomes targeted by the trader. From the perspective of the client, different methods of matching the content with the user may qualify as personalization. These methods may all lead the user to believe that online content was tailored individually for them. If personalization is understood in this manner, then it only occasionally entails *actual individualization*: the content may be adjusted not to an individual user, but to the context in which the information is presented (e.g., context advertising) or to typical characteristics of a targeted group (segment) of the population. From this perspective, personalization is an umbrella term encompassing practices during which not only an individual but also a group of individuals can be the addressee (target), in particular, practices such as online contextual, segmented, and behavioural advertising.[2] Yet, when deciding whether a certain practice should be regarded as personalization, one can also assume a perspective which places technology at the centre. From this point of view, personalization can be understood as a practice that involves using data collected from an individual's activity (e.g., purchase history, email activity, website behaviour) in order to deliver targeted content to that individual. Under this second approach, the terms "individualization" and "personalization" can be used interchangeably to describe the process in which the content is individually shaped for every addressee separately, based on their individual profile.[3] If a narrow view of personalization is adopted, one could claim that analyzing its legal consequences, at least in some sectors e.g., insurance, still appears a little premature.[4]

In this chapter, we adopt the first, broader understanding of the notion of personalization. The reason for this choice is that users who agree to their data being processed for the purposes of profiling and personalization[5] rarely know what the tailoring process looks like—especially whether they are subject to group or individual targeting. Regardless of the actual design of personalization mechanisms, they are prone to expect content adequately tailored to their needs, situation, or

---

[2] Fourberg et al. (2021), pp. 30–31; Townley et al. (2017), pp. 689–690.

[3] This can already be observed in the legal literature, see e.g.: Thouvenin et al. (2019); Infantino (2022). Sceptically: Helberger et al. (2021), p. 102; Personalization mechanisms frequently rely on predictive analytics using Big data sets—information fuelling the personalization process is not only derived from the data on this individual person but also from other data sets on "similar consumers" and statistical data. Mik (2016), p. 20. In fact, the better the latter proxies are, the less information is needed about the actual preferences of an individual. Consequently, it can be argued that during the process of tailoring the information the point of reference is not a particular individual. The benchmark is the "alter ego" of that individual, their digital representation construed within the digital environment, mostly for commercial purposes. This creates a problem which can be referred to as de-personalization by personalization tools: Helberger et al. (2021), pp. 103–104; Infantino (2022).

[4] Infantino (2022).

[5] Under Art. 5 1(b) GDPR such a general manner of describing the aims of data processing may be considered insufficient, therefore, as a rule, more information in this regard is expected to be given. Zuiderveen Borgesius and Poort (2017), p. 359; Steppe (2017), p. 778. It is recommended that examples and descriptions of general terms such as "personalized advertising" are given when specifying the purposes of data processing. Pałka (2020), p. 632.

specific features.[6] It is their trust in technology and the other party that increases their vulnerability.

At present, the relevant legal scholarship discusses the use of personalizing mechanisms in different markets[7] and the possible application of this technology by the regulator within the law-making process (i.e., to increase the granularity of legal norms).[8] One of the aspects of personalization, which, despite its importance, seems to have attracted the scant attention of legal scholars, is what legal consequences the mispersonalization can trigger.[9] Provided the variety of contexts in which personalization techniques are used, the question should not be discussed in the abstract. The legal consequences and subsequent response to improper personalization can differ depending on numerous variables, including the object of personalization (e.g., the law, content of the offer, marketing technique), its aim, the environment in which it is performed (online, offline), the scale (if it is used once or repetitively), and the resources applied (Big Data, individual data retrieval).

We approach the question of personalization from the perspective of general consumer insurance.[10] First, it is one of the areas where personalization may drastically influence the situation of a person to whom it is being applied. Second, the use of personalizing Big Data technologies is becoming a common practice in this sector.[11] However, tools applied for this purpose, and the process of personalization itself (including the data-gathering stage) are not always flawless. What is more, the effect intended by the entity applying personalizing mechanisms does not always align itself with what is objectively appropriate and desirable.[12] This increases the need for spelling out the typical consequences of mispersonalization that can be observed on the consumer insurance market and for determining the framework applicable in such instances. Depending on the form and effects of mispersonalization in this sector, the legal response may vary, allowing for the comparison of different models of sanctioning mispersonalization. Observations made in this specific context may contribute to the debate as to the appropriate legal response to the mispersonalization of contracts in sectors other than merely insurance.

---

[6] Mik (2016), p. 20.

[7] Inter alias: Namysłowska and Jabłonowska (2020); Południak-Gierz (2019); Wagner and Eidenmüller (2019); Zuiderveen Borgesius and Poort (2017); Mik (2016); Infantino (2022).

[8] On personalizing different branches of law, see e.g.: Denno (2019) (criminal law); Busch (2019); Ben-Shahar and Porat (2019) (contract law); Burk (2019); Libson and Parchomovsky (2019) (copyright law); Mora, "Personalized Law: Using Information from Previous Proceedings" available at www.studocu.com/it/document/universita-degli-studi-di-milano/diritto-internazionale/saggio/fulltext-dirittoprivatoedanni/2666055/view; Kugler and Strahilevitz (2019) (procedural law).

[9] On the reasons behind mispersonalization in the context of consumer insurance: Tereszkiewicz, Południak-Gierz (2021).

[10] Loacker (2015).

[11] On the applications of Big Data, see: International Association Of Insurance Supervisors (IAIS) (2020), pp. 14–30. Borselli (2020) pp. 101, 107–108. On the opposing legal response towards the use of personalization mechanisms in insurance, see: Thouvenin et al. (2019), p. 210; Infantino (2022).

[12] Tereszkiewicz and Południak-Gierz (2021).

This contribution starts by indicating the most common scenarios where certain consequences of the mispersonalization of consumer insurance agreements can occur. These are: the over- or under-pricing of an adequately tailored insurance product; the lack of insurance cover for certain risks or incomplete (partial) cover; excessive (unnecessary) insurance cover, which the customer neither needs nor wants. By contrast, instances where the personalization of the insurance contract is limited to the manner of its conclusion, namely the time, form, and channel of contracting, in principle, do not influence the adequacy of the offer. As they are unlikely to cause the mispersonalization of the contract, they are not dealt with in this chapter. Our analysis identifies those solutions which the law has made available to deal with typical patterns of mispersonalization. For the sake of convenience, our main focus is on European Union contract and consumer law; we also draw on Polish law as an example of a national legal system, including private law remedies. Further, we refer to selected provisions of the Principles of European Insurance Contract Law (PEICL), an academic restatement of insurance contract law in Europe.[13]

2 Typical Instances of Mispersonalization of Consumer Insurance Contracts

The effects of incorrect personalization in consumer insurance contracts vary. Usually, the inadequacy may be observed with respect to the premium due in return for cover. In principle, the premium is calculated based on a risk assessment (factors taken into account usually include personal information about the client, type and scope of cover, and a forecast regarding the extent of payout in case claims under the policy are made).[14] Furthermore, non-risk price discrimination in the insurance sector also occurs,[15] as, for instance, inertia pricing has already been observed for years.[16] In the context of online transactions, the range of factors that could be grounds for this type of discrimination is fairly broad, as the scope of information gathered by the insurance distributor encompasses different kinds of data that are not necessarily related to the peril insured against, for instance, what device the client is using to visit the distributor's website.[17] Having enough data about the client and an appropriate toolset makes it possible for distributors to offer a certain class of clients only a more expensive product (e.g., an "omnium"-cover).[18] As data flows rise due

[13] Basedow et al. (2015).

[14] McFall et al. (2020), pp. 3–4.

[15] Krikler et al. (2004) p. 71.

[16] Prices for new customers are lower than renewal prices for risk-equivalent insured. Thomas (2012), p. 27. Inertia pricing, upgraded with the Big Data analysis application, is still common. McFall et al. (2020), p. 4.

[17] In consumer e-commerce a trend was spotted to set higher price for those prospective clients who were accessing the website using an Apple device. Diganan (2012).

[18] Zuiderveen Borgesius and Poort (2017) pp. 352–353.

to technological developments, the efficacy of calculating clients' willingness to pay grows.[19] This may provide an incentive for insurers to increase premiums, so that they correspond with what an individual client might be inclined to pay instead of the market value of the insurance product.[20]

Moreover, Big Data not only drives price personalization, which has always been typical of insurance products, but even more importantly, the personalization of insurance products. Virtually, it becomes possible to automatically match or adjust the insurance cover to the specific circumstances and needs of a prospective client. Two examples can be provided. AI and advanced analytics may be launched to design an insurance product that covers risks resulting from the activity of an individual SME business owner. A car-owner who concluded a self-adjusting personalized car insurance contract may obtain an automatic insurance upgrade while driving on rough roads.[21]

When the tool used for personalizing offers does not function properly, this may result in an insurance contract which does not correspond to the specific features and needs of the policyholder. There are two typical outcomes of such mispersonalization: relevant risks are not covered or are covered only partially; insurance cover purchased is too broad and thus superfluous.[22] In both cases, it should be examined whether insurance distributors have correctly fulfilled their duty to provide advice to the client.[23]

One could view the mispersonalization of insurance contracts as the process of personalization that relies upon data which are not relevant for risk assessment, distorting its final effect. However, the reasons behind the personalization are not limited merely to the incorrect choice of data sets.[24] From the perspective of the interests of the client, the process of personalization does not really matter as long as its outcome is correct. As a result, our analysis is concerned with the consequences of the personalization.

The question arises then as to what type of legal sanction a mispersonalization of the insurance contract should trigger. It could be argued that not all cases of faulty personalization of insurance contracts should be sanctioned in the same manner, as their consequences may differ from the perspective of the policyholder.

---

[19] Townley et al. (2017), pp. 683–684.

[20] See Bar-Gill (2019), pp. 246–249. On the risk profile and willingness to pay as the points of reference during the individualization of an insurance product offer, see: Thouvenin et al. (2019), p. 210.

[21] On personalized and on-demand insurance products, see: https://www.capgemini.com/2018/11/advanced-analytics-enable-insurers-to-predict-customer-needs-and-personalize-services/ (last access 13 October 2022).

[22] International Association of Insurance Supervisors, Insurance Core Principles (2019), pp. 222–225; OECD, Regulatory and Supervisory Framework for Insurance Intermediation (2020), p. 29.

[23] Tereszkiewicz (2019), pp. 131–132; Tereszkiewicz and Południak-Gierz (2021).

[24] Tereszkiewicz and Południak-Gierz (2021).

2.1 *Incorrect Pricing of Insurance Cover*

When insurance premium is not fairly calculated ("mispersonalization of a price"), an insurance product itself may not necessarily be inappropriate for the purpose of the consumer. The mechanism used for calculating the premium fails to set what would be considered a fair market price. What we call "mispersonalization of price" can be caused either by inaccurate data or errors during the personalization process. Further, the algorithm applied by the product distributor may be designed to establish the consumer's willingness to pay based on their misperceptions, e.g., the value of the product for that consumer as they perceive it.[25] It follows that the algorithm may adjust the price upward to match the perception of the consumer.

In such cases, the main interest of the consumer is satisfied, as the insurance contract covers those risks that the consumer wished to have covered. Undesired effects of the mispersonalization are financial losses incurred by one of the parties to the insurance contract: the policyholder when cover is overpriced or the insurer when cover is underpriced. The loss would usually amount to the difference between a correctly calculated premium and the one determined by the algorithm.

Following this analysis, the direct consequence of improper pricing is overpriced insurance cover. This means that the contract confers a disproportionate benefit on one of the parties at the expense of the other. It is necessary to consider the legal implications of such contracts.

To begin with, the disproportion of benefits as such tends to be tolerated by private law systems, unless it is either gross or results from an unacceptable behaviour of the person who benefits from it.[26] For instance, insurance premiums may be increased to correspond with the growth in any perceived likelihood of an earthquake. The insurance distributor may target persons with more expensive offers when their misperception as to the actual risk of an earthquake is at its highest, e.g., shortly after they have learnt that their friend or family member lost their home during such a natural disaster. In situations where the said asymmetry is observed, the national provisions on unconscionability (unfair exploitation) may apply, providing for different sanctions across the European Union Member States.[27]

What needs to be taken into account is the fact that, in the case of personalization, the relationship between the consumer and the business may be classified as one based on trust and confidence.[28] In most legal systems, characterizing a legal relationship as

---

[25] Tereszkiewicz and Południak-Gierz (2021).

[26] See Gordley (1981); Thouvenin et al. (2019), p. 215.

[27] For instance, under Polish law the exploited party may demand a reduction of its performance or an increase of the performance due to this, and if both are excessively difficult it may demand that the contract be declared null and void. See: Tereszkiewicz and Południak-Gierz (2023) and Południak-Gierz (2023). On difficulties in establishing whether misrepresentation, mistake, duress, undue influence apply, see e.g. Mik (2016), pp. 25–31.

[28] Mik (2016), p. 20 (on the false sense of familiarity triggered by personalization); Południak-Gierz (2020), pp. 1015–1017.

one of "trust" implies a specific legal regime, usually a higher standard of conduct.[29] Another matter which needs to be considered is that if it is the inaccuracy of the data processed by the system, or the flaws of the personalization process itself, then the rules on unfair exploitation may apply only if the said defectiveness was intentionally induced by the insurance distributor.

Rules on unfair exploitation (unconscionability), however, work only in favour of the weaker party, being the consumer in the majority of scenarios. By contrast, under the regulation of mistake, provided that the premises on national rules on this vice of consent are fulfilled,[30] the contract can be challenged by either of the parties. However, this would rarely be the case due to the fact that the client to whom the personalization is applied has only little knowledge on how the personalization shall influence the insurance distributor's premium in a particular situation. Thus, in most instances the consumer will be unable to notice the error.

The process of premium (mis)personalization can constitute an unfair commercial practice, especially where the mechanism is designed to unlawfully stimulate an increase in client willingness to pay in order to abuse it.[31] One should bear in mind that consumers only navigate in the online environment, whereas traders are in control of that environment by operating the technological infrastructure or outsourcing its application to their benefit.[32] In such cases, remedies such as termination or price reduction based on Art. 11a of the Unfair Commercial Practices Directive[33] could be available to insurance consumers.

Finally, the insurance applicant's breach of the duty to disclose risk-relevant factors may give rise to specific insurance law sanctions.[34] However, once the automated data collection process is launched, there is little scope for the applicant to pro-actively inform the insurer about risk-relevant circumstances. With technological development, the traditional applicant's duty to disclose is evolving towards the insurer's obligation to collect relevant information from the applicant.[35] It is

---

[29] For instance in the context of Polish law, see: Tereszkiewicz (2015), pp. 443–444; Judgment of the Court of Appeal (Sąd Apelacyjny) in Warsaw of 14 March 2014, case number VI ACa 1183/13, LEX No. 1515319.

[30] For instance, under Polish law it would be required to demonstrate that the error concerned the contents of an act in law and if the declarant had not acted under the influence of the error and had judged the case reasonably they would not have made such a declaration of intent. However, if the declaration of intent was made to another person, the evasion of its legal effects is admissible only if that error was caused by that person, or if they were aware of the error or could have easily noticed it. Art. 84 Polish Civil Code. Tereszkiewicz and Południak-Gierz (2023).

[31] On when a personalization of price can be viewed as an unfair commercial practice, see e.g., OECD, Personalised Pricing in the Digital Era, Background Note by the Secretariat, 28 November 2018, pp. 34–35, available at https://one.oecd.org/document/DAF/COMP(2018)13/en/pdf (last access 13 October 2022).

[32] Mik (2016), p. 9.

[33] Introduced by Art. 3 point 5 Directive 2019/2161.

[34] Cousy (2012), pp. 125–126. Under Art. 2:102 (1) of the PEICL the insurer shall be entitled to propose a reasonable variation of the contract or to terminate the contract.

[35] Cousy (2012), pp. 123–131; Tereszkiewicz (2013b), pp. 473–506; Merkin and Gurses (2015), pp. 1004–1027.

submitted that where a potential client has agreed to their data being gathered for the purposes of personalization, in doing so, they have fulfilled their duty to disclose risk-relevant factors to the insurer.[36] As a result, it should be the insurer who bears the negative consequences related to mispersonalization caused by the failure to obtain all the necessary information on the risk-relevant circumstances.

In sum, it is submitted that there is a strong case in favour of challenging personalized insurance contracts where personalized premiums correspond with the consumer's willingness to pay based on this consumer's misperceptions: a consumer wants to cover the risks they overestimate and are willing to agree to higher premiums to have them covered. Insurance distributors prey on such misperceptions.

The party whose financial interests are infringed can seek protection within the individual protection mechanisms provided by national private law regulation (mistake or exploitation). Though the premises of these tend to be strict, such protection seems sufficient. The lack of strict equivalence of benefits exchanged under a contract is generally acceptable under private law and triggers regulatory response so long as it is caused by defects in the decision-making process. However, such mispersonalization infringes the financial interests without frustrating the purpose of the contract and, therefore, sanctions which bring about the annulment of the contract could be viewed as disproportionate. Yet, legal provisions which allow voiding contracts for mistakes or unfair exploitation usually apply in narrow circumstances—when voiding a contract is justified not solely by the unequal consideration, but when one of the parties has been tricked into the contract. As a result, the remedy of price reduction provided under the EU Unfair Commercial Practices Directive seems, from the perspective of the client, more adjusted to combat this type of irregularities.

2.2 *Inadequate Insurance Cover*

The improper functioning of the personalization mechanism may lead to the insurance product being inadequate for the needs of a particular consumer. The reasons for the malfunction may be different and could include situations where there is a mistake in the code applied, when the digital tool is not sufficiently sensitive, or when a prohibited goal of personalization is set and the like. The lack of or incomplete cover may result in the consumer being in a situation as if the insurance contract was not concluded at all. The mispersonalization prevents the insurance contract from fulfilling its main function, that is providing cover against the consequences of certain risks materializing. By contrast, the excessive cover may mean that the stronger party abuses contractual asymmetries to trick the consumer into a contract that they neither want nor need to conclude. Hence, such mispersonalization infringes on the consumer's decision-making autonomy.

[36] Borselli (2020), pp. 115, 131; Alkistis and Chatzara (2020), pp. 49–82, 60.

Such mispersonalization of a consumer insurance contract can trigger different legal responses, leading to various consequences, including invalidity or voidability of the contract, claim for damages, or contract adjustment. This part of the analysis focuses on examining the adequacy and effectiveness of possible sanctions instead of describing the current legal framework (this will be indicated briefly, to embed the inference in a regulatory context). In this manner, the chapter seeks to contribute to the debate on the design of any legal response to the mispersonalization of contracts.

2.2.1 Insurance Contract Being Null and Void

To begin with, the first solution would be to consider the mispersonalized contract null and void from the beginning. This sanction could stem from national general rules on contracts, such as Article 58 Sections 1 and 2 of the Polish Civil Code,[37] which state that a legal act contrary to the law or principles of community life is invalid. It is submitted that the insurance distributor's duty to provide advice to a prospective client gives rise to the obligation to adequately personalize the content of the contract. Thus, so runs the argument, one can claim that personalizing the contract against the best interests of the client could be contrary to the law.

The sanction of nullity is the most radical measure, which, in principle, should apply when other possible sanctions are not appropriate given the seriousness of the infringement of the parties' rights.[38] In most cases of mispersonalization of consumer insurance contracts, this sanction is neither proportionate nor adequate from the policyholder's perspective.[39]

This sanction is suboptimal from the point of view of the interests of a client who did not intend to assume a specific risk. First and foremost, the main purpose of the contract cannot be achieved in such a scenario – namely, the risk is not covered by the insurance contract as the latter ceases to exist. The fact that the consumer can demand reimbursement for the insurance payments he has already incurred does not compensate for that anyhow.

Further, one should bear in mind the broadly recognized principle that the consequences of nullity should not be more harmful to those they protect than the breach of the legal doctrine, which is sanctioned with the nullity itself.[40] If all instances of mispersonalization are sanctioned with insurance contracts being null and void, then the consumer would be deprived of even the partial or overpriced protection the mispersonalized insurance contract is granting, thus worsening their legal situation even further. As a result, the nullity might only be in the interests of the protected in these scenarios where the risks, which the consumer wanted to obtain cover for, are

---

[37] The Civil Code of 23 April 1964, [1964] Official Journal No. 16, Pos. 93 with subsequent amendments.

[38] Gutowski (2017) Chap. II, Sect. 2.

[39] On the nullity of contract as a sanction for breach of an applicant's duty to inform, see: Cousy (2012), p. 126.

[40] Skorupa (2019) Chap. VIII, Sect. 2.

not covered or where the risks which have been covered cannot materialize in their case.

Finally, when searching for an adequate sanctioning model for the mispersonalization of contracts in the insurance sector, the specific character of insurance products should also be taken into consideration. In most scenarios, clients discover that the contract was inappropriate for them only once the risk they wanted to be insured against has already materialized.[41] At that point, they can no longer meet their insurance needs by concluding a new insurance contract. Therefore, instead of arguing for the absolute invalidity of a mispersonalized contract (under Polish law pursuant to Article 58 of the Civil Code), it seems preferable to seek a sanctioning model which would allow one to keep the contract valid and binding for the parties.

2.2.2 Insurance Contract Being Voidable

Under a different legal solution, a policyholder could be entitled to rescind the insurance contract. The right to rescind a contract may be grounded on the general private law doctrines of error or fraud (i.e., Articles 84–86 of the Polish Civil Code). Specifically, policyholders could claim they were misled about the adequacy of the offer for their circumstances and needs, which resulted from the application of personalizing tools.[42]

Once we assume the approach of consumer law, the mispersonalization of an insurance product can be considered a misleading and thus an unfair commercial practice: a prospective client is being convinced that the offered product corresponds to their individual needs and situation (is fit for an individual purpose), which causes them to take a transactional decision that they would not have taken otherwise (Art. 6 section 1 letter b UCPD). Hence, a claim to have the insurance contract voided could also be grounded on provisions implementing Art. 11a of the UCPD, which obliges Member States to undertake measures granting consumers harmed by unfair commercial practices access to proportionate and effective remedies, including—where relevant—contract termination.[43]

The sanction of voiding the insurance contract might have the advantage of allowing insurance consumers to decide whether they want to invoke it against the provider or yet remain bound by the contract. At the same time, voiding the contract deprives insurance consumers of cover, and the insurance contract does not fulfil any socially valuable purpose.

---

[41] Tereszkiewicz (2013a), p. 236.

[42] On the personalized advertisement of insurance product from the perspective of insurance law, see: Południak-Gierz and Olechowski (2022).

[43] Under Art. 11a added to Directive 2005/29 by Art. 3 point 5 Directive 2019/2161 consumers harmed by unfair commercial practices, shall have access to proportionate and effective remedies, including where relevant, the termination of the contract.

2.2.3 Damages

Another option is that the agreement continues to bind the parties in its original form, but claims for damages arise. They may be founded upon different grounds, however.[44]

Provided that the mispersonalization of the insurance product was considered a misleading commercial practice, compensation claims could be based on national provisions implementing Art. 11a UCPD.[45] Claims for indemnification for lack of insurance cover may also stem from the specific provisions of national insurance law provisions,[46] tort law, or general provisions on precontractual liability.[47] Naturally, the scope of damages based on these grounds may vary. It could extend to expectation interest, which means covering all the damage incurred (from the financial perspective, the consumer would be in a similar situation as if the insurance contract was properly personalized), or be restricted to reliance interest only (the consumer would be in a situation as if the insurance contract has not been concluded).

Irrespective of the legal ground of the claim and the possible effectiveness of such protection, the main challenge here is that it would be extremely difficult for the consumer to prove the mispersonalization due to the information asymmetry and faulty technological infrastructure.

2.2.4 Contract Adjustment

Finally, in order to remedy the mispersonalization of the consumer insurance contract, its content could be adjusted. In principle, for the consumer to be entitled to demand that the contract be modified under Polish law, the requirements of undue exploitation must be fulfilled.[48] Alternatively, the adjustment could result from the correct interpretation of an insurance contract, reflecting the legitimate expectations of the consumer. For instance, if a standardized insurance product is distributed under a specific name on a given market, the consumer may reasonably believe that these products have all standard features (e.g., broad cover of typical risks in that product

---

[44] Project Group Restatement of European Insurance Contract Law, Principles of European Insurance Contract Law (PEICL) (2009), p. 100.

[45] Art. 7 s. 1 Directive (EU) 2019/2161 of the European Parliament and of the Council of 27 November 2019 amending Council Directive 93/13/EEC and Directives 98/6/EC, 2005/29/EC and 2011/83/EU of the European Parliament and of the Council as regards the better enforcement and modernisation of Union consumer protection rules (OJ L 328, pp. 7–28).

[46] For instance, in German law Sect. 6 (5) Insurance Contract Act; Tereszkiewicz (2013a), pp. 247–248.

[47] Loacker (2015).

[48] Under Polish law the doctrine of unfair exploitation (Article 388 Civil Code) would apply: a contract may be adjusted, where one of the parties, exploiting a forced situation or the inefficiency or inexperience of the other party, in exchange for its own performance accepts or stipulates for itself or for a third party a performance, the value of which at the time the contract is executed grossly exceeds the value of its own performance.

segment). Consequently, the contract will be interpreted as if the parties had agreed on all these typical features.[49]

When establishing the model of adjustment of the insurance contract, the main task is establishing a point of reference which is feasible and acceptable from the perspective of the parties as well as reflects legally protected interests. This point of reference would be crucial for determining whether the insurance contract was indeed mispersonalized, and—if that was the case—for providing a benchmark for its adjustment. There are different approaches that can be adopted.

First, when assessing whether a personalized insurance contract is appropriate for the needs and situation of the consumer, it could be examined what insurance product would be recommended in a face-to-face environment on the basis of the same information. An empirically sound assessment requires taking into consideration that human advisors make mistakes and their conduct may be inefficient.[50]

Second, it is possible to determine what insurance product would have been recommended to a client by an in-person advisor. The main disadvantage of this solution is that it does not allow one to take into consideration the functioning of the technology. Thus, on the one hand, it might be too demanding in certain scenarios, in particular when the technology is insensitive to certain factors which are intuitively and automatically taken into consideration by the human actor.[51] On the other hand, it may disregard the advances (benefits) offered by the use of the new technology.[52]

As a result, it is reasonable to set aside both the empirical standard and the human-based one, while determining what the optimal manner for the functioning of personalizing mechanism should be.[53] This should, on the one hand, allow one to avoid the above-mentioned weaknesses resulting from the application of the previous model. On the other, it would lead to the most favourable effect for the consumer who would have the contractual relationship shaped so that it corresponds with what the content of the contract should be, provided that the personalizing mechanism functioned correctly. Thus, the cover of the insurance contract would be re-tailored, so that the contract continues to bind the parties and their main interests remain protected. Similarly, the price could be re-calculated and the equivalence of the performance restored.

---

[49] In the context of German insurance law, see: Tereszkiewicz (2013a), p. 248; in the context of consumer law: Schulze and Zoll (2021), pp. 42–44, 151.

[50] Jungermann and Belting (2004).

[51] A good illustration of the difference between what is easy and manageable from the perspective of a human and highly challenging from the perspective of AI-based mechanisms is the case where a self-driving shuttle was hit by a lorry driving at slow speed (when the lorry started to approach the shuttle, the latter stopped instead of reversing). Lee (8 November 2017).

[52] In particular, processing vast amounts of data enables, first, discovering features of the person who is profiled even if that person is not aware of them, and second, making highly accurate assessments as to the future events, which in contrast, is not possible for a natural person giving the insurance applicant advice as to the choice of products.

[53] Południak-Gierz (2021), pp. 267, 270.

Proper consideration should be devoted to the legal significance of the personalization tool applied by the insurance distributor. What function should the personalization tool assume in our model? One possibility would be to regard it as a unilateral tool for protecting consumers (clients). A different possibility would be to see it as a mechanism for correcting the content of the contract. These questions can be illustrated with the following example: the errors of personalization lead to underpricing of the product, which, as a result, causes losses for the insurance provider. If the mechanism of contract adjustment was a tool of consumer protection, then it should not be triggered in such a case—the consumer's obligation stemming from the contract should not be increased, they could only benefit from the application of the tool. The risk of malfunction of the mechanism would be borne solely by the business party, which, in principle, is justified by the fact that it is the professional that ventures to harness new technologies to more effectively perform their business activities. Provided that the benchmark was the effect of a non-defective personalization process, this should not be seen as an instrument of a sanctioning character, nor should it increase the scope of liability of the business beyond the level that should have been expected when the process of personalization was initiated.

Alternatively, one could argue that adjusting a contract achieves an outcome that is desirable under the legal framework. It could work both ways. If the personalization mechanism used previously proved to be defective, an incorrect price could not only be diminished, but equally increased. Similarly, insurance cover could be modified regardless of how it affects the consumer's interest in having adequate cover. On this account, both the insurance client and the insurer bear the risk of deploying the new technology. Nevertheless, such an outcome appears questionable in the light of the goals of consumer law: it may result in the consumer losing the cover they would reasonably believe to have obtained under the insurance contract.[54]

3 Results and Conclusions

Our study allows for the following modest conclusions to be drawn.

Theoretically, the adjustment of the content of the insurance consumer contract seems to be the most effective solution, as it allows for an automatic (*ex lege*) modification of the agreement in line with reasonable expectations of the consumer to whom the personalization tool was applied. This could equally work with respect to improper price personalization and in a situation where the process of the personalization of an insurance product has failed. However, there are practical difficulties relating to the application of this model—first and foremost, the issue of setting an appropriate assessment benchmark—that diminish its usefulness.

---

[54] One should consider the following scenario: after the risk has occurred, the insurer wants to avoid making a payout and challenges the adequacy of personalization claiming that it was defective and the risk at hand should not have been covered by the insurance product. Had this been the case, the insurer would be exempt from liability.

During the comparison of alternative remedies for the mispersonalization of insurance contracts, the distinction made at the beginning of the chapter should be recalled: the negative consequences associated with the mispersonalization of price and product differ significantly. The former does not preclude the aim of the contract from being achieved. What is more, the disproportion of benefits should rarely allow for challenging the existence of the contract as the price tends to be one of the fundamental factors during the consumers' decision-making process.[55] Consequently, in such scenarios, remedies which allow only for the termination of the contract are, on the one hand, inadequate and, on the other, rarely applicable. Hence, the price reduction provided under the Unfair Commercial Practices Directive seems to be the main mechanism which could be invoked to combat this type of irregularities.

By contrast, the mispersonalization of an insurance product may easily lead to simple mis-selling. This may pass unnoticed by the consumer until it is too late (the risk they wanted to be insured against has meanwhile materialized), which renders the termination of the contract useless from their perspective. As a result, the only manner of protecting the interest the consumer has in mind when entering into the insurance contract is to allow for its automatic modification. This again steers us towards the application of interpretation tools that open the possibility of adjusting the contractual relationship to the legitimate expectations of the weaker party regardless of the provisions of the contract itself.

Acknowledgements This chapter has been written within the framework of the research project of the Narodowe Centrum Nauki, (NCN) [The National Science Centre] in Poland, Grant Number 2018/29/B/HS5/01281.

References

Alkistis C, Chatzara V (2020) The internet of things and insurance. In: Marano P, Kyriaki N (eds) InsurTech: a legal and regulatory view. Springer, Berlin/Heidelberg, pp 49–81

Bar-Gill K (2019) Algorithmic price discrimination when demand is a function of both references and (Mis)perceptions. Univ Chic Law Rev 86(2):217–254

Basedow J et al (eds) (2015) Principles of European insurance contract law. Sellier, Munich

Ben-Shahar O, Porat A (2019) Personalizing mandatory rules in contract law. Univ Chic Law Rev 86(2):255–282

Borselli A (2020) Smart Contracts in insurance: a law and futurology perspective. In: Marano P, Kyriaki N (eds) InsurTech: a legal and regulatory view. Springer, Berlin/Heidelberg, pp 101–125

Burk DL (2019) Algorithmic fair use. Univ Chic Law Rev 86(2):283–307

Busch C (2019) Implementing personalized law: personalized disclosures in consumer law and data privacy law. Univ Chic Law Rev 86(2):309–331

Cousy H (2012) About sanctions and the hybrid nature of modern insurance contract law. Erasmus Law Rev 5(2):123–131

Denno DW (2019) Neuroscience and the personalization of criminal law. Univ Chic Law Rev 86(2):359–401

[55] Grochowski (2017), pp. 89–93.

Diganan L (2012) Mac users pay more than PC users, says Orbitz, CNET https://www.cnet.com/news/mac-users-pay-more-than-pc-users-says-orbitz/. Accessed 23 Oct 2022

Fourberg N et al (2021) Online advertising: the impact of targeted advertising on advertisers, market access and consumer choice, Luxembourg 2021. http://www.europarl.europa.eu/RegData/etudes/STUD/2021/662913/IPOL_STU(2021)662913_EN.pdf. Accessed 24 Mar 2023

Gordley J (1981) Equality in exchange. Calif Law Rev 69(6):1587–1656

Grochowski M (2017) Postanowienia określające główne świadczenia stron (art. 385(1), § 1 k.c.): kryteria kwalifikacji w orzecznictwie Sądu Najwyższego. Palestra 9:81–85

Gutowski M (2017) Nieważność czynności prawnej. Chapter II, Sect. 2

Helberger N et al (2021) EU consumer protection 2.0, structural asymmetries in digital consumer markets. https://www.beuc.eu/sites/default/files/publications/beuc-x-2021-018_eu_consumer_protection_2.0.pdf. Accessed 24 Oct 2022

Infantino M (2022) Big data analytics, insurtech and consumer contracts: a European appraisal. Eur Rev Priv Law 30(4):613–634

International Association of Insurance Supervisors (IAIS), Insurance Core Principles (2019). https://www.iaisweb.org/uploads/2022/01/191115-IAIS-ICPs-and-ComFrame-adopted-in-November-2019.pdf. Accessed 24 Oct 2022

International Association of Insurance Supervisors (IAIS), Insurance Core Principles (2020) Issues paper on the use of big data analytics in insurance, basel, IAIS. https://www.iaisweb.org/uploads/2022/01/200319-Issues-Paper-on-Use-of-Big-Data-Analytics-in-Insurance-FINAL.pdf. Accessed 23 Oct 2022

Jungermann H, Belting J (2004) Wir verstehen uns doch—nicht wahr! Psychologische Aspekte der Altersvorsorge und Anlageberatung. Kritische Vierteljahresschrift für Gesetzgebung und Rechtswissenschaft 87(3):325–344. https://doi.org/10.5771/2193-7869-2004-3-325. Accessed 23 Oct 2022

Krikler S, Dolberger D, Eckel J (2004) Method and tools for insurance price and revenue optimisation. J Financ Serv Mark 9:68–79. https://doi.org/10.1057/palgrave.fsm.4770142. Accessed 23 Oct 2022

Kugler MB, Strahilevitz LJ (2019) Assessing the empirical upside of personalized criminal procedure. Univ Chic Law Rev 86(2):489–529

Lee D (2017) Self-driving shuttle bus in crash on first day. BBC News. https://www.bbc.com/news/technology-41923814. Accessed 23 Oct 2022

Libson A, Parchomovsky G (2019) Toward the personalization of copyright law. Univ Chic Law Rev 86(2):527–550

Loacker L (2015) Informed insurance choice?: The insurer's pre-contractual information duties in general consumer insurance. Edward Elgar Publishing, Cheltenham

McFall L, Meyers G, van Hoyweghen I (2020) Editorial: the personalisation of insurance: data, behaviour and innovation. Big Data & Soc 1. https://journals.sagepub.com/doi/full/10.1177/2053951720973707. Accessed 23 Oct 2022

Merkin R, Gurses O (2015) Insurance act 2015: rebalancing the interests of insurer and assured. Modern Law Rev 78:1004–1027

Mik E (2016) The erosion of autonomy in online consumer transactions. Law Innov Technol 8:1–38

Mora G (2017/2018) Personalized law: using information from previous proceeding. www.studocu.com/it/document/universita-degli-studi-di-milano/diritto-internazionale/saggio/fulltext-dirittoprivatoedanni/2666055/view. Accessed 23 Oct 2022

Namysłowska M, Jabłonowska A (2020) Personalizacja oparta na sztucznej inteligencji—nowe wyzwanie dla prawa konsumenckiego. In: Lai L, Świerczyński M (eds) Prawo sztucznej inteligencji. C.H. Beck, Warszawa, pp 95–112

OECD (2020) Regulatory and supervisory framework for insurance intermediation. https://www.oecd.org/daf/fin/insurance/Regulatory-and-Supervisory-Framework-for-Insurance-Intermediation.pdf. Accessed 23 Oct 2022

Pałka P (2020) Data management law for the 2020s: the lost origins and the new needs. Buffalo Law Rev 68:559–640

Południak-Gierz K (2019) Consequences of the use of personalization algorithms in shaping an offer—a private law perspective. Masaryk Univ J Law Technol 13(2):161–188

Południak-Gierz K (2020) Personalized agreement—a new contractual model. Vestnik of Saint Petersburg University. Law 4:1009–1021. https://doi.org/10.21638/spbu14.2020.411. Accessed 24 Mar 2023

Południak-Gierz K (2021) Personalization of consumer contracts—should we personalize interpretation rules? In: Green MD, Mercedes Lopez Rodriguez A, Kubica M (eds) Legal challenges in the new digital age. Brill

Południak-Gierz K (2023) Eco-reasonableness. Possibility of incorporating green principles into general private law clauses. In: Andenas M, Heidemann M (eds) Quo vadis commercial contract? Reflections on sustainability, ethics and technology in the emerging law and practice of global commerce. Springer Nature

Południak-Gierz K, Olechowski P (2022) Personalizacja reklam produktów ubezpieczeniowych—między teorią a praktyką. In: Namysłowska M (ed) Reklama. Aspekty prawne. Nowe wyzwania, Wolters Kluwer Polska

Project Group Restatement of European Insurance Contract Law (2009) Principles of European insurance contract law (PEICL), Sellier

Schulze R, Zoll F (2021) European contract law. C.H. Beck, Hart, Nomos

Skorupa P (2019) Nieważność czynności prawnej w prawie polskim na tle porównawczym. C.H. Beck, Warszawa

Steppe R (2017) Online price discrimination and personal data: a general data protection regulation perspective. Comput Law Secur Rev 33:768–785

Stuyck J (2000) European consumer law after the treaty of Amsterdam: consumer policy in or beyond the internal market? Common Market Law Rev 37:367–400

Tereszkiewicz P (2013a) The Europeanisation of the insurance contract law: the insurer's duty to advise and its regulation in german and european law. In: Devenney J, Kenny M (eds) The transformation of European Private Law: Harmonisation, Consolidation, Codification Or Chaos? Cambridge University Press

Tereszkiewicz P (2013b) Obowiązek informacyjny ubezpieczającego i skutki jego naruszenia z perspektywy prawno-porównawczej: Zmierzch uberrima fidei w epoce ochrony konsumenta? In: Pecyna M, Pisuliński J, Podrecka M (eds) Rozprawy cywilistyczne. Księga pamiątkowa dedykowana Profesorowi Edwardowi Drozdowi, Lexis Nexis, Warszawa

Tereszkiewicz P (2015) Obowiązki informacyjne w umowach o usługi finansowe. Wolters Kluwer Polska, Warszawa

Tereszkiewicz P (2019) Digitalisation of insurance contract law: preliminary thoughts with special regard to insurer's duty to advise. In: Marano P, Kyriaki N (eds) InsurTech: a legal and regulatory view. Springer, Berlin/Heidelberg

Tereszkiewicz P, Południak-Gierz K (2021) Liability for incorrect client personalization in the distribution of consumer insurance. Risks 9(5):83

Tereszkiewicz P, Południak-Gierz K (2023) Consumer protection in polish insurance law. In: Tereszkiewicz P, Golecki MT (eds) Protecting financial consumers in Europe. Comparative perspectives and policy choices. Brill

Thomas G (2012) Non-risk price discrimination in insurance: market outcomes and public policy. In: The Geneva papers on risk and insurance—issues and practice, vol 37, pp 27–46. https://link.springer.com/article/10.1057/gpp.2011.32#citeas. Accessed 23 Oct 2022

Thouvenin F et al (2019) Big data in the insurance industry. Leeway and limits for individualising insurance contracts. JIPITEC 10(2)

Townley C, Morrison E, Yeung K (2017) Big data and personalised price discrimination in EU competition law. Yearb Eur Law 36

von Bar C, Clive E, Schulte-Nölke H et al (eds) Principles, definitions and model rules of European private law draft common frame of reference (DCFR). Study group on a European civil code and the research group on EC private law (acquis group). https://www.law.kuleuven.be/personal/mstorme/european-private-law_en.pdf. Accessed 23 Oct 2022

Wagner G, Eidenmüller H (2019) Down by algorithms? Siphoning rents, exploiting biases, and shaping preferences: regulating the dark side of personalized transactions. Univ Chic Law Rev 86(2):581–609

Zuiderveen Borgesius F, Poort J (2017) Online price discrimination and EU data privacy law. J Consum Policy 40:347–366

Katarzyna Południak-Gierz is a Senior Lecturer at the Jagiellonian University of Cracow. Her fields of interest include Private Law and Technology, Consumer Law, Contract Law and Sustainability.

Piotr Tereszkiewicz is a Professor of Private Law at the Jagiellonian University of Cracow and Senior Research Affiliate, University of Leuven (KULeuven). His fields of interest include Private and Commercial Law (Law of Obligations, Insurance Law, Consumer Law, Financial Services), Comparative Law and Economic Analysis of Law.

Law Without Markets?

Salil K. Mehra

Abstract In a series of legal fields, from constitutional law to contracts to competition law, the market mechanism has provided a claimed neutral baseline against which to measure rights and remedies. While that neutrality was always somewhat fictional, its rhetorical strength bolstered classical liberals, Chicago School adherents, and others who favored the translation of market ordering into the positive legal framework. But increasingly, "the market" as an open, almost nature-given provider of neutral, homogenous prices may not be true. Increasingly, digital platforms match and target consumers with individualized offers and pricing. Law has relied on the concept of open, uniform markets—if this perception wanes, what will this mean for legal doctrines based on market neutrality as a keystone?

Keywords Markets · Algorithms · Law · Price discrimination · Targeting · Platforms · Technology

1 Introduction

Markets as a mechanism for allocating goods, services, and resources have long appeared inevitable. But even during the heyday of industrialism, it was recognized that the economy involved widespread tradeoffs between top-down control and decentralized market mechanisms.[1] While "market forces", such as the pursuit of profit, may be endemic, many systems of organization, such as governments, firms, and nonprofit organizations, depart from the market mechanism to allocate scarce benefits and resources.

Law and the legal system in industrialized countries developed in tandem with the traditional market mechanism. In a variety of areas, such as contract law, commercial

[1] Coase (1937); Robinson (1933).

S. K. Mehra (✉)
Charles B. Klein Professor in Law and Government, Temple University, Philadelphia, US
e-mail: salil.mehra@temple.edu

K. Mathis and A. Tor (eds.), *Law and Economics of the Digital Transformation*, Economic Analysis of Law in European Legal Scholarship 15,
https://doi.org/10.1007/978-3-031-25059-0_4

law, and competition law, there is an implicit assumption of a baseline reference transaction that would have taken place but for, say, respectively, a breach, a default, or punishable conduct. Both liability and judgments are shaped by this deeply embedded baseline.

However, society is increasingly characterized by a move away from traditional markets in which quantity and price are readily observable, and price is a uniform, monetary value. Two major trends are taking place that will undercut the existing legal doctrine's baseline and potentially erode citizens' trust in the legal system. First, an increasing number of transactions take place without a direct financial payment by the consumer. As explained below, these are not "free" in any honest sense of the word, but the absence of financial payment will complicate the application of the existing legal doctrine. Second, algorithmic matching increasingly substitutes for traditional market mechanisms in allocating goods, services, and resources. By doing so, algorithmic matching will make it harder to identify a counterfactual baseline against which to construct a legal judgment. While these trends towards zero-financial payment and algorithmic matching are firstly and most notably impacting competition law most notably first, the undercutting of a normative traditional market baseline will also impact law more generally in other areas.

2 The Problem of "Free"

Multisided platforms have long argued that they produce "free" services, and are therefore an unchallengeable boon to society.[2] A generation ago, Microsoft made such arguments about its provision of Internet Explorer.[3] More recently, Facebook argues that it provides "free" services to consumers.[4] But this kind of "free", is in fact, quite unfree.

The "rule of threes" recognizes that a person can survive three weeks without food, three days without water, but only three minutes without air.[5] At the end of Evelyn Waugh's *Brideshead Revisited,* a nobleman who has lived a dissolute life fairly free from the constraints of money or social norms gets his comedown in the shape of respiratory reliance on costly machinery.[6] COVID-19 has forced us to consider the freedom, in several senses, of our very breath.

---

[2] Section 2 draws on material originally published in Mehra (2021), and is used here with permission, for which the author is thankful.

[3] Blumenthal and Wu (2018), describing Microsoft attempt to defend itself by stating that is was giving away Internet Explorer for "free".

[4] See *FTC v Facebook/Meta*, slip op. at 29–30.

[5] Towell (2011), p. 154.

[6] "Free as air; that's what they say – 'free as air.' Now they bring me my air in an iron barrel." Waugh (1945).

It has long been said that "there ain't no such thing as a free lunch."[7] While the word "free" has several related meanings, they have in common the notion of being unconstrained, whether by a financial cost, physical bond, or legal or other restraint. Though popularized by the science fiction writer Robert Heinlein, the "free lunch" is believed to refer originally to the practice in nineteenth century American saloons of providing their customers with a "free lunch" consisting of a buffet of well-salted food likely to provoke further drinking. Free drinks were sometimes provided as well for youth, since, as the U.S. Brewers' Association proclaimed, "[a] few cents on free drinks for boys was a good investment; the money would be amply recovered as these youths became habitual drinkers!" However, the free lunch was often monitored by the tavern's bouncer to discourage too much eating[8]—an early example by which a high-consumption user might, literally, find himself "throttled".[9]

No payment now, but we *will* get you later is not anyone's definition of "free." Nor do many think "free" a good or service provided at no charge if you buy another product—you cannot successfully respond to a "buy one, get one free" offer by saying, "I'll take only the free one, thanks!" In a similar vein, "free" should not limit the legal system to the extent that free lunches are not a thing. "Free" goods and services often involve several kinds of "payment". First, and perhaps most familiarly, individuals trade personal data that benefits the seller for these "free" products—so they are not at all free, just "non-monetary-payment" required. Second, individuals receive "non-monetary-payment" products but thereby "lock in" other individuals, who "pay" instead. Finally, "free" products that trigger dopamine or other behavioral responses may alter individuals' brains to their detriment, as nineteenth century saloon owners knew. Just as we might take the air we freely breathe for granted until it suddenly turns potentially COVID-19 infective, we might consider that so-called "free" services may only be such at that instant, with possibly expensive consequences.

2.1 *Non-monetary-Payment Does not Necessarily Mean "Free"*

The law, especially that of contracts, has long recognized that not having to pay money for something is not the same thing as it being "free". If you provide a pharmaceutical company data on your body's reactions in a drug trial, its promise to give you a supply of its products in exchange is not a gift.[10] This is unsurprising; you

---

[7] Lender and Martin (1982), p. 104.

[8] Ibid.

[9] "Throttling" has been used metaphorically to refer to ISPs' constraining the use of those customers who, in the ISPs' view, excessively use "unlimited" data. See, e.g., Brodkin (2018), reporting allegations in lawsuit against Verizon.

[10] *Dahl v HEM Pharmaceuticals*, 7 F.3d 1399 (9th Cirl 1993). pointing out precedents for this view going back to *Hamer* v. *Sidway* (N.Y. 1891).

have provided the company with a benefit at its request.[11] Despite that, it is not rare to read someone arguing that, for example, competition law action against services that platforms provide to consumers without payment must be misguided—a trope that goes back to the turn-of-the-century *Microsoft* litigation.[12] Indeed, the economist Hal Varian has recently argued, in connection with the Department of Justice's ongoing action against Google, that the latter is no monopolist, despite an 80 percent market share in search, on the grounds that it offers a high-quality service to consumers "for free".[13]

To some extent, a serious discussion has long treated the "for free" argument as hollow. This idea was rebuffed by the district court in *U.S.* v. *Microsoft* more than 20 years ago,[14] based on the intuition that a firm cannot make money giving things away for free, so there must be some "catch"—"in other words, there ain't no such thing as a free lunch." More recently, social media and other Internet-based platforms have promoted a deeper understanding of no-payment services. Most prominently, Professor John Newman has provided an in-depth examination of what he calls not free but "zero-price" markets and introduced a taxonomy of consumer-facing costs to watch out for. In particular, he emphasizes a focus on costs to consumers that provide market signals as a keystone for antitrust enforcement.[15]

Fortunately, it appears that the version of "free" in which users "pay" producers benefits in non-monetary ways has been rejected as grounds for an "antitrust-free zone". First, the European Commission's Directorate-General for Competition and now the U.S. competition law authorities have focused their attention on Facebook and Google, both of which offer consumers a myriad of services without monetary payment. This energized scrutiny extends to the critical area of merger review—witness the UK's Competition and Markets Authority's blocking of Facebook's proposed acquisition of Giphy.[16] While the endgame of this revitalized enforcement awaits us, it seems as though the non-monetary-cost version of "free" may be through as a serious argument.[17]

---

[11] See Restatement (Second) of Contracts (American Law Institute, 1981), Sect. 71.

[12] See, e.g., Kennedy (2017), arguing against antitrust action because "many data-rich companies offer free or low-cost services that are extremely valuable to billions of people, most of whom have a pretty good idea of what data they are providing companies and how it might be used"; Sidak (2015), answering the title negatively.

[13] "Google Case is a Chance to Reframe Antitrust Debate" (2020), describing Varian's argument.

[14] 87 F. Supp. 2d. 30, 50 (D.D.C. 2000), concluding that "the fact that Microsoft ostensibly priced Internet Explorer at zero does not detract from the conclusion that consumers were forced to pay, one way or another, for the browser along with Windows".

[15] Newman (2015).

[16] McLaughlin (2021).

[17] See *FTC v Facebook/Meta* (D.D.C. Jan. 11, 2022), slip op. at 29–30, concluding that the FTC may prove anticompetitive effect due to "lower levels of service quality on privacy and data protection than [Facebook/Meta] would have to provide in a competitive market," even though the services at issue are provided to consumers at zero monetary cost.

2.2 *Making Someone Else Pay Does not Mean "Free"*

Another model of "free" is to offer goods and services to a consumer without payment in a way that extracts costs from someone else. The classic textbook—if quite gender-normative—example in economics is a local bar ladies' night when "discounted or even 'free' (in the sense of no monetary payment) drinks are offered to female customers."[18] Putting aside the ways in which the female customers may have to "pay" for cheap or free drinks by fending off unwanted attention,[19] the reality is that, as the textbooks suggest, the bar profits by the increased volume of sales to male customers seeking to socialize with the female customers drawn in by the discount.

But cross-subsidization with non-monetary charge products exists beyond nightlife. For example, while the COVID-19 vaccines may have been provided in the U.S. without monetary charge, vaccination is rapidly becoming a requirement to attend or teach at colleges and to hold one's job in many workplaces. Because many students, professors and workers who have been vaccinated do not wish to share the air they breathe with unvaccinated people, as the proportion who are vaccinated grows, it makes it easier for administrators and managers to impose vaccine requirements. As a result, the "free" vaccine has the effect of locking in or imposing costs—such as unemployment—on others.

Contract law has long recognized that the fact that a third party pays for something does not make it gratuitous. Indeed, the concept of exchange is not limited to two parties making an offer and an acceptance, including the enforcement of a promise based on consideration provided by someone other than the promisee.[20] Similarly, antitrust law should engage more deeply with "non-monetary-payment" services. The US Federal Trade Commission's complaint against Facebook in particular, is a step in the right direction, recognizing the lock-in effects that so-called "free" services can generate, so others effectively pay. Certainly, the Internet has encouraged the proliferation and increased economic importance of such business models, and there is nothing to suggest that they will disappear anytime soon.

---

[18] Parker et al. (2016), Chapter 2; Gwartney et al. (2016), pp. 200–203.

[19] This seems to have become a recurring source of pained comedy in pop music. See Allen (2006); Trainor (2015).

[20] See Restatement (Second) of Contracts, Sect. 71(4) (American Law Institute, 1981), stating that "[t]he performance or return promise [given as consideration making a promise enforceable]... may be given by the promisee or by some other person.".

2.3 *Altering Brains Does not Mean "Free"*

An additional example of "free" is to offer goods and services without monetary payment in order to get consumers "hooked"—a model well-known not just to nineteenth century saloon keepers but also to other sellers of addictive substances.[21] That said, the concept of a good, usually typified by heroin or cocaine, whose consumption increases the consumer's demand for more of that good, despite the law of diminishing marginal utility, has been taught in microeconomics for years.[22] While the boundaries of such goods have traditionally been set by legislatures rather than antitrust enforcers, technological advances may require more attention from the latter.

In particular, the ability of technology firms to trigger consumers' dopamine responses in an addictive way via apps may require competition law attention. In fact, antitrust scholars have long considered whether the consumer welfare standard should deem increased output of tobacco a positive thing for consumers, considering the product's addictive qualities and negative effects on user health.[23] That said, antitrust enforcers do continue to regulate conduct and mergers that may reduce the output of addictive products, notwithstanding their adverse health effects.[24]

The Internet, as well as smartphone and video gaming technology, have opened the door to non-monetary-charge services that the user can enjoy with little effort, but whose consumption may have literal mind-altering effects. This discussion has already commenced and is likely to continue.[25] In a similar manner to antitrust and tobacco, Professors Niels Rosenquist, Fiona Scott Morton, and Samuel Weinstein have pointed out that "robust medical evidence" is starting to show that digital platforms can be addictive and "harmful to users' mental health". As a result, where more use actually injures the consumer, the increased output of some addictive digital platforms may not be a reliable proxy for positive effects on consumer welfare. Such services are certainly not "free" just because no money is paid by the user; contract law has long understood that non-monetary detriment can ground an exchange. Antitrust commentators have an unfortunate tendency to wave away such problems as best dealt with by other areas of law or by Congress. While that may be true for some issues,

---

[21] *See infra* n. 3 and accompanying text; Fisman and Luca (2019), suggesting that free pens, meats and Christmas trees as gifts to physicians from Perdue Pharma representatives hawking OxyContin elicited a psychological response of gratitude in those physicians, who were then more likely to prescribe an addictive medication to their patients.

[22] Knopf (2014), p. 80, defining "diminishing marginal utility" as a "'law' in the marginal utility of consumption [that] states that as an individual consumes more and more of a good in a given time period, the satisfaction derived from each additional unit will be less than the satisfaction from the preceding unit", but stating that "[a] major exception to the law is an addictive drug such as heroin, cocaine or 'crack.'".

[23] See Crane (2005); Orbach (2010), questioning whether increased output of tobacco, with its harmful effects, does in fact benefit consumers, and if it does not, how the consumer welfare standard should be altered.

[24] See, e.g., Complaint, *U.S. v Anheuser-Busch InBev SA/NV and Grupo Modelo S.A.B. de C.V.* (Jan 31, 2013), challenging merger in beer industry.

[25] Rosenquist et al. (2021).

the Federal Trade Commission's long history with consumer protection and deception may make it particularly suited to considering how antitrust law should handle mergers and conduct involving firms that sell mind-altering, no-money-payment products and, if necessary, leading efforts to reshape antitrust accordingly.

2.4 Implications

Contract law has understood for centuries that a lack of a monetary payment does not make something free; antitrust law recognized this as far back as the *Microsoft* browser case. When a customer provides the seller benefits in non-monetary ways, or their action forces someone else to pay, or they suffer psychological change, a transaction cannot reasonably be called "free". The Internet and the changes it has spawned have raised the importance of non-monetary-payment services that are, in these ways, not "free". Just as the air we breathe can have costs we did not anticipate before COVID-19 first appeared in Wuhan, underestimating the implications of no-charge services is undermining consumers' faith in our law and our markets. The goal to breathe freely again requires an appropriate response. This may be quite difficult, however, because the disappearance of monetary prices is being accompanied by another transition, from traditional market mechanisms to algorithmic matching.

3 Algorithmic Matching

In the previously mentioned *Microsoft* case, legal doctrine raised, at least obliquely, the possibility of an emerging reality in which firms in network industries competed "for the market", in a Schumpeterian sense, to gain temporary dominance.[26] Under this account, promoting desirable creative destruction would require allowing a firm that gains a monopoly in a market to collect its monopoly rents—and even engage in exclusion—or society would suffer negative consequences.[27] Law built on a visible, traditional market model had, with effort, been able to handle this concept.[28]

But now, competition may be *literally* "for the market", in the sense that it is replacing the visible, traditional markets, which antitrust has handled, with algorithmic black box processes. In the past, market competition was the only efficient

[26] Farrell and Katz (1998), observing that "when firms recognize the possibility of tipping [due to network effects], they may compete vigorously to become the dominant supplier: so-called 'competition for the market'"; *United States v Microsoft,* 253 F3d 34, 49 (DC Cir 2001), describing tendency for competition in network-effects laden industries to be "'for the field' rather than 'within the field'", quoting Demsetz (1968).

[27] *Verizon v Trinko,* 540 US 398, 407–08, arguing that "[t]he opportunity to charge monopoly prices – at least for a short period – is what attracts 'business acumen'... [and] induces risk taking that produces innovation and economic growth.".

[28] United States v Alcoa (1945).

way to gather and process information and match producers and buyers in a modern economy—a key Hayekian insight that powered Chicago School thought.[29] However, technology has made alternatives once previously thought to be at the fringes of imagination, now, increasingly possible.[30]

Increasingly, multisided platforms employ matchmaking algorithms to take advantage of mass data collection, near-ubiquitous connectivity and fast computer processing to power increasingly opaque proprietary markets. Consider Uber, whose then-CEO stated of its "surge pricing" practice that raises prices for rides at particular times:

> Dynamic pricing algorithmically increases prices to encourage more drivers to come onto the platform and increase supply. . . [W]e are not setting the price, the market is setting the price . . . [W]e have algorithms to determine what that market is.[31]

From this perspective, the market is both an independent force that determines the price but also a result constructed at least in part by a proprietary algorithm. Of course, to the extent that consumers can switch between alternative black boxes—that is, multihome—competition may still be said to exist between multisided platforms that vie with each other to "make the market," as in the ongoing battle between ridesharing platforms such as Uber and Lyft, or meal delivery platforms such as Deliveroo and Grubhub. In doing so, such algorithmic matching systems may produce results that are unique to individuals, as opposed to supplying a uniform price, and they may do so in a way that is not a clear, unique equilibrium in the manner that law has assumed with traditional markets.[32]

3.1 Traditional Market Mechanics Versus Algorithmic Matching—Price, Markets, and Information

> If a universal mind existed . . . a mind that could register simultaneously all the processes of nature and society, that could measure the dynamics of their motion, that could forecast the results of their inter-reactions—such a mind, of course, could a priori draw up a faultless and exhaustive economic plan, beginning with the number of acres of wheat down to the last button for a vest. The bureaucracy often imagines that just such a mind is at its disposal; that is why it so easily frees itself from the control of the market and of Soviet democracy.

---

[29] Hayek (1948a), declaring the then unimaginability of "the mere assembly of data" and calculation of equilibria as "beyond human capacity" that led famed price-system proponent Friedrich Hayek to declare it the only option for economic ordering.

[30] Lange (1967), writing that "My answer to Hayek... would be: so what's the trouble? Let us put the simultaneous equations on an electronic computer and we shall obtain the solution in less than a second. The market process with its cumbersome tatonnements appears old-fashioned. Indeed, it may be considered a computing device of the pre-electronic age.".

[31] Matt Stoller (2014), quoting Uber's then-CEO Travis Kalanick.

[32] This is not to say that legal doctrine is correct in believing that traditional market mechanisms generate a single, uniform equilibrium, just that legal rules have been frequently designed with that assumption as a guiding norm.

> But, in reality, the bureaucracy errs frightfully in its estimate of its spiritual resources...The innumerable living participants in the economy, state and private, collective and individual, must serve notice of their needs and of their relative strength not only through the statistical determinations of plan commissions but by the direct pressure of supply and demand.—Leon Trotsky, The Soviet Economy in Danger (1932)

At first glance, a twentieth century debate about the practicality of Socialism might seem unconnected to our twenty-first century concerns about algorithmic processing and big data. But in fact, the "Socialist Calculation Debate", as it became known, brought about questions that are directly linked to these technologies, which are having such an impact on our current era. In light of these changes, the victory Friedrich Hayek and his followers claimed for markets over calculation to be re-examined; doing so raises questions about the deference to the Chicago School notion of tailoring governance to serve the assumed superiority of market ordering.

As the twentieth century turned into a confrontation between nations adopting Socialism versus those engaged in market-based Capitalism, economists too became drawn into a pitched battle of their own. In the era after World War I, with a newly socialist-run Soviet Union, the economist Otto Neurath suggested that the wartime experience had demonstrated that economies could be run under centralized control. In response, economists such as Hayek and Ludwig von Mises argued that comprehensive rational socialist economic planning could not work.

While von Mises pointed out the difficulty of measuring value without money, Hayek made several related arguments about information and the price system that had a long-term influence. In particular, Hayek's ideas led to a reconception of the market away from simply a mechanism for the physical allocation of goods between traders to a system of information transfer between agents.[33] First, Hayek pointed to the difficulties in gathering data concerning different agents' supply and demand, writing that "the mere assembly of these data" that Socialist calculation entailed was "a task beyond human capacity".[34] Additionally, even if such data could be assembled, trying to plan the appropriate quantities of various goods to produce would be complicated by the fact that the supply of each would be interdependent. In Hayek's view in 1935, "every one of these decisions would have to be based on a solution of an equal number of simultaneous differential equations, a task which, with any of the means known at the present, could not be carried out in a lifetime."[35] Thus, Hayek's view fundamentally was an instrumental defense of traditional markets based on the then-impossible tasks of gathering data and processing it that alternatives would require.

In making this argument, Hayek reconceived the market as a system for processing decentralized information. In one of his most famous statements about this idea, he asked:

> What is the problem which we try to solve when we try to construct a rational economic order? On certain familiar assumptions the answer is simple enough. If we possess all the

[33] See Mirkowski (2002), p. 235.

[34] Hayek (1948a), p. 187.

[35] Hayek (1935).

> relevant information, if we can start out from a given system of preferences, and if we command complete knowledge of available means, the problem which remains is purely one of logic . . . This, however, is emphatically *not* the economic problem which society faces . . . The peculiar character of the problem of a rational economic order is determined by the fact that the knowledge of the circumstances of which we must make use never exists in concentrated or integrated form but solely as dispersed bits of incomplete and frequently contradictory knowledge which all the separate individuals possess. The economic problem of society is thus not merely a problem of how to allocate "given" resources . . . it is a problem of the utilization of knowledge which is not given to anyone in its totality.[36]

From this perspective, in the absence of any other means of gathering, digesting, and coordinating dispersed bits of data, the traditional market could be the only practical economic operating system.

The Socialist Calculation Debate might appear to be a technical matter between dueling economists—after all, the debate itself did not result in the Soviet Union adopting market pricing, nor would we have expected an opposite result in the debate to have converted the capitalist West to socialist central planning. However, Hayek's instrumentalist argument for the traditional market-based price mechanism formed a keystone for the Chicago School edifice. There is both historical and theoretical evidence for this impact, and both proponents and opponents of the Chicago School and associated neoliberalist ideas agree on Hayek's influence.[37] Moreover, those making theoretical accounts of twentieth century American neoliberalism place Hayek's argument in favor of the traditional-market price mechanism at the forefront.[38]

Technological change has now made the bedrock Hayek view of traditional-market price mechanisms as superior contestable. As that view was based on pragmatic grounds, economists recognized decades ago that the actual problem of calculation would, in theory or in reality, be solved at some point.[39] As Oskar Lange noted about the potential development of computers:

> My answer to Hayek . . . would be: so what's the trouble? Let us put the simultaneous equations on an electronic computer and we shall obtain the solution in less than a second. The market process with its cumbersome tatonnements appears old-fashioned. Indeed, it may be considered a computing device of the pre-electronic age.—Oskar Lange, The Computer and the Market (1967)

Midway through the twentieth century, economists such as Lange and Leontief conjectured that computers would catch up with Hayek's critique.

---

[36] Hayek (1948b), pp. 77–78.

[37] See, e.g., Todd Henderson (2005) (empirical supporter); van Horn and Mirkowski (2009), historical account of influence by opponents.

[38] See, e.g., Chen and Hanson (2004), describing how Hayek's ideas influenced those of Friedman and thereby the programmes of Thatcher and Reagan; But see Posner (2005), identifying possible distinction between Hayek/Austrian economists and neoclassicists "about the degree to which government regulation is doomed to failure because of ability to obtain the information necessary for ascertaining value".

[39] Cockshott and Cottrell (1993), recognizing that the Leontief matrix calculations were then newly feasible, though a problem still remained as to the "task of gathering the vast amount of data required".

Technological progress took conjecture into reality a while ago, at least as far as computing power was concerned. In the 1990s, commentators observed that the simultaneous equations thought unsolvable in the 1930s would take late twentieth century computers mere minutes to solve—now that we carry smartphones with an order of magnitude more processing power than the IBM Deep Blue supercomputer that defeated Garry Kasparov in a six-game chess match in 1997.[40]

Even as Moore's Law eroded the "calculation" part of the Socialist Calculation Problem, the stumbling block that remained beyond processing power, however, was how to gather decentralized data—that part of Hayek's argument still had some bite to it.[41] After all, both Mises and Hayek had pointed to the price system's ability to collect and synthesize disaggregated data in the form of individual actors' supply and demand decisions. In the 1980s, economists advocating for reconsideration of socialist calculation's practicality suggested, perhaps hopefully, that what would suffice might be "an economy-wide network of cheap personal computers, running spreadsheets representing the conditions of production in each enterprise, in conjunction with a national Teletext system and a system of universal product codes."[42]

Such an interlinked data collection scheme sounds like an archaic vision of the future, like a socialist economic version of mid-century modernism—the 1964 World's Fair's dream of an Internet.[43] However, we can already have a glimpse into this world in which refrigerators can order refills when the milk runs out,[44] electric self-driving cars can pilot themselves to charging stations, and Internet retailers can suggest products you might want to buy with shocking accuracy.[45] Increasingly, decentralized supply and demand data is available, digestible, and actionable.

High-powered algorithmic processing is already well-established. The combination of a network-connected device ("IoT") with mass data collection ("Big Data") could yield the trove of decentralized data that would match or even exceed what Hayek thought only the price mechanism could. The next section turns to the impact that IoT and Big Data should have—post-Hayek and post-Chicago—on rethinking the relationship between the Internet, governance, and law.

---

40 TN (2014).

41 Cockshott and Cottrell (1993), p. 23.

42 Cockshott and Cottrell (1989).

43 Spicer (2014), describing the IBM Pavillion at the fair as the "second most popular stop," which was "[f]or a great number" of people "their first direct interaction with a computer of any kind," and which included exhibits of Russian-to-English "machine translation" and "the Information Machine" which could "give you a lot of information in a very short time".

44 Reilly (2016).

45 Simpson (2014), describing Amazon's "plan that would ship products to you before you even purchase them because Amazon knows what you want better than you do".

3.2 The Rise of Algorithmic Matching

Traditional markets have long been powerful mechanisms for expressing value and allocating resources. But there have long been alternative matchmaking mechanisms, where important non-economic values were at stake or where market allocation was considered repugnant. Think, for example, of the role of nonmarket alternatives in terms of allocating medical training, babies for adoption, or organs for transplant.[46] In the past, the additional cost of using a nonmarket alternative could only be justified in such relatively high-stakes scenarios.

But increased data collection and processing power has reduced nonmarket alternatives' cost disadvantage and allowed them to expand into other relatively lower-stakes areas, particularly where there are non-price, non-quantity considerations—consider Airbnb (host/guest reputation) and Uber (driver/passenger reputation) versus respective traditional alternatives such as hotels and taxis that did not assess such qualitative concerns to the same degree.[47]

Competition law continues to deal with an analogous problem. At the turn of this century, in the context of the *Microsoft* case, the antitrust field brought forth the argument that it would have to adapt to a new reality in which firms in network industries competed "for the market," in a Schumpeterian sense, to gain temporary dominance.[48] Under this account, promoting desirable creative destruction would require allowing a firm that gains a monopoly in a market to collect its monopoly rents—and even engage in exclusion—or society would suffer negative consequences.[49] Competition law, built on a visible, traditional market model, had long been able to handle this concept.[50]

But now, competition may be *literally* "for the market", in the sense that it is replacing the visible, traditional markets, which the law handled, with algorithmic black box processes. In the past, market competition was the only efficient way to gather and process information and match producers and buyers in a modern economy—a key Hayekian insight that powered Chicago School thought.[51] However,

---

46 See generally Roth (2016).

47 For an argument that there may be a downside to this type of growth, see Calo (2016).

48 Farrell and Katz (1998), observing that "when firms recognize the possibility of tipping [due to network effects], they may compete vigorously to become the dominant supplier: so-called 'competition for the market'"; *United States v Microsoft,* 253 F3d 34, 49 (DC Cir 2001), describing tendency for competition in network-effects laden industries to be "'for the field' rather than 'within the field'" (quoting Demsetz (1968).

49 *Verizon v Trinko,* 540 US 398, 407–408, arguing that "[t]he opportunity to charge monopoly prices – at least for a short period – is what attracts 'business acumen'... [and] induces risk taking that produces innovation and economic growth.".

50 United States v Alcoa (1945).

51 Hayek (1948a), declaring the then unimaginability of "the mere assembly of data" and calculation of equilibria as "beyond human capacity" that led famed price-system proponent Friedrich Hayek to declare it the only option for economic ordering.

technology has made alternatives once previously thought to be at the fringes of imagination, now, increasingly possible.[52]

Increasingly, multisided platforms employ matchmaking algorithms to take advantage of mass data collection, near-ubiquitous connectivity, and fast computer processing to power increasingly opaque proprietary markets. Consider Uber, whose then-CEO stated of its "surge pricing" practice that raises prices for rides at particular times:

> Dynamic pricing *algorithmically* increases prices to encourage more drivers to come onto the platform and increase supply. . . [W]e are not setting the price, the market is setting the price . . . [W]e have algorithms to determine what that market is.[53]

From this perspective, the market is both an independent force that determines the price but also a result constructed at least in part by a proprietary algorithm. Of course, to the extent that consumers can switch between alternative black boxes—that is, multihome—competition may still be said to exist between multisided platforms that vie with each other to "make the market", as in the ongoing battle between Uber and Lyft.

The possibility of switching or multihoming is a common retort to concerns about harm to competition stemming from algorithms, big data, and multi-sided platforms. As the cliché goes, "competition is only a click away." But that saying dates from the world of the open Internet and competition between HTML online shopfronts and web-based search engines running on desktop computers.[54] Much of what was then labeled the "World Wide Web" was transparently available to those launching online retail, search engines, or other Web 1.0-based ventures. G, however, the data collected nowadays, is increasingly proprietary and non-transparent. Increasingly, whether gathered by digital assistants like Amazon's Alexa, self-driving cars like Waymo's, or a myriad of smartphone apps, the "big data" that firms now gather resides in corporate silos that are not transparently available in the manner of the Internet a generation ago.

As a result, to say competition between different matchmaking platforms exists does not mean that antitrust law as it currently exists can easily address harms in this new kind of competition. Critically, algorithmic connectivity has made these platforms less transparent to regulators. Without intensive surveillance or analysis of massive historical data, can regulators determine whether the algorithms that Uber uses "to determine what that market is" are, in fact, leading to price-quantity-quality outcomes that are not harmful to consumers? It is easy enough to see consumer benefit in the case of Uber, which in many cases has undermined government-licensed taxi monopolies that served producers rather than users. But future applications of

---

[52] Lange (1967), writing that "My answer to Hayek... would be: so what's the trouble? Let us put the simultaneous equations on an electronic computer and we shall obtain the solution in less than a second. The market process with its cumbersome tatonnements appears old-fashioned. Indeed, it may be considered a computing device of the pre-electronic age.".

[53] Stoller (2014), quoting Uber's then-CEO Travis Kalanick.

[54] See, e.g., Willis (1998), arguing, a generation ago, that "[e]ven if Amazon does become profitable, its margins are likely to be paper-thin" because "competition is only a click away.".

algorithmic connectivity may combine opacity to regulators with goals less favorable to consumers.

The rising prominence of proprietary markets driven by algorithmic connectivity will be a challenge for competition regulators. Potentially, big data, mass interconnectivity and algorithmic processing can be leveraged to produce manipulated results in walled markets that shift welfare away from consumers towards walled market proprietors in ways that current antitrust doctrine and enforcement cannot handle well. Such results may require more direct intervention than antitrust is currently comfortable with. For example, when securities regulators in the United States became concerned that proprietary trading could balkanize public securities markets, they mandated a kind of forced interconnection between what otherwise would have become "walled markets" that might have sacrificed efficient capital allocation to focus on profits from captive investors. While there would be considerable resistance currently to an analogous antitrust policy that focused on, for example, Amazon, the replacement of markets transparent to regulators does require that we consider how to start redesigning antitrust to better secure competition in the future. Pursuing these goals in a fast-changing, technologically dynamic context makes this project more of an initial vault than a clean landing. But policymakers need a framework of questions to reconsider antitrust as markets as we have known them to vanish.

3.3 Algorithmic Matching Platforms Undercut the Assumption of a Unique, Stable Baseline Economic Equilibrium

3.3.1 Platforms and Law's Equilibrium Assumption

Antitrust, contract law and other areas have been constructed against a baseline model exemplified by the classic Economics 101 supply-and-demand diagram. While economists have long understood the assumptions and limitations of this model, it has nonetheless entrenched itself in law's conception of the proper baseline against which to measure wrongs and remedies. In competition law, the intersection of supply and demand has been a touchstone against which to weigh static and dynamic efficiency tradeoffs for decades.[55] In contract law, the remedy for the breach has been constructed against the conception of a single, market-clearing price.[56]

[55] Bork (1978), pp. 107–108, famously using an Econ 101 style diagram stating that "[t]his diagram can be used to illustrate all antitrust problems, since it shows the relationship of the only two factors involved, allocative inefficiency and productive efficiency.".

[56] Convention for the International Sale of Goods, Article 74, Advisory Council Opinion No. 6, Comment 3, stating that "[t]he aggrieved party is entitled to non-performance damages, which [are] typically measured by the market value of the benefit of which the aggrieved party has been deprived through the breach.".

Economists have recognized for a half-century that some markets may not tend towards a single, stable equilibrium in the manner that the typical Econ 101 diagram suggests.[57] Instead, given a push in one direction or another, they may "tip" towards different stable equilibriums. This has been particularly noted in the case of products with strong network externalities—for example, where the product's utility for consumers depends on its uptake by other consumers.[58]

Noteworthy cases involving platforms exhibit willful neglect, possibly to avoid the implications of tipping and multiple equilibria. For example, in the *Microsoft* case,[59] the D.C. Circuit court quickly brushed past the argument that competition in operating systems was "for the market", not "in the market". Small wonder, perhaps that the court sidestepped this question—had the court accepted that idea, it would have faced two possibilities: that Microsoft Windows would achieve a dominant position, or that Netscape Navigator would do so. To calculate a damages remedy would require assessing the probabilities of each end-state, an exercise conceptually at odds with the notion that markets provide courts with a single equilibrium as a neutral baseline. More recently, the *Ohio* v. *American Express* decision by the U.S. Supreme Court has been criticized for equating complained-of conduct to the validity of a business model as a whole rather than focusing on the direct marginal effects of such conduct.[60] Without defending the logic of that opinion, it is worth observing that the decision thereby managed to dodge questions of whether specific platform design decisions and exclusionary acts were necessary and well-tailored. These are the sorts of questions that may be unavoidable as platforms increasingly engage in algorithmic matching.

3.3.2 Algorithmic Matching Platforms

While market forces may stay similar, market mechanisms are quite different now than in the pre-Internet era. Many of the firms that are drawing antitrust attention now, from giants like Facebook, Google and Amazon to relatively smaller firms, but still with huge valuations and significant impact on labor markets, like Uber, employ algorithmic matching to bring buyers and sellers, or publishers and readers, or other pairs of external transactors.[61] The information held by the platform and the mechanics by which matching is done are relatively opaque to the external parties.

Algorithmic matching differs from the Econ 101 supply and demand diagram in that there may not be a single stable equilibrium where supply meets demand—an

[57] The economist Thomas Schelling introduced a general theory of tipping, in which the interaction of individual preferences in a market could lead to self-sustaining momentums that could result in multiple possible equilibria, tipping away from a starting point in one direction or another. Schelling (1969); Schelling (1971).

[58] Katz and Shapiro (1999), p. 39.

[59] See *US v Microsoft*, supra n. 49.

[60] Hovenkamp (2019), making this argument.

[61] *See* Complaint, *U.S.* v. *Google*; First Amended Complaint, *FTC* v. *Facebook*; See also Complaint, *D.C.* v. *Amazon*; *Meyer v Kalanick*.

image that is foundational to the twentieth century legal development.[62] However, one of the seminal works of algorithm design implies that multiple possible, stable matchings may be possible.[63] In particular, the Gale-Shapley algorithm—also known as the deferred acceptance algorithm—succeeds in producing stable matchings. But it can produce several such outcomes, and the desirability of each will vary with one's point of view—some will favor one group over another, depending on how the algorithm is designed.

One of the key breakthroughs in the algorithmic matching literature, in part for which Lloyd Shapley was recognized (along with Alvin Roth) with the economics Nobel in 2012, the Gale-Shapley, or "deferred acceptance", algorithm proceeds with the members of two groups of counterparties, such as applicants (or sellers) and employers (or buyers) privately submitting rank order list preferences for each member's preferred counterparties among the other group. Then, each employer makes an offer to its top-choice candidates. Each applicant looks at all her offers and then tentatively accepts the one she prefers, rejecting other offers. Then each employer that had an offer rejected in the prior step makes an offer to its next choice employee, if any remain. Then, each applicant considers the offer she has been holding together with any new offers, and tentatively accepts her preferred option, rejecting the others. This process repeats until no offer is rejected.

The logic of the Gale-Shapley algorithm forms a significant part of how matching platforms operate—versions of it have been used by a variety of platforms, from online dating sites to automated auctions for sponsored advertising on Internet search engines.[64] With the rise of data collection, algorithmic processing and automated decision making, such processes can be faster and cheaper than traditional markets, may better take into account non-price and quantity dimensions, and, for some transactions, may be less repugnant than, for example, a highest-price wins the auction. However, algorithmic matching may prioritize buyers over sellers, sellers over buyers, or platform operators over both buyers and sellers. As a result, it diverges from a market mechanism tending towards a single equilibrium where supply meets demand.

Specifically, Alvin Roth has described matching markets as critically differing from traditional markets for goods. According to him, in the latter, such as markets for groceries, commodities, or stocks, the "price decides who gets what", but in what he calls "matching markets", "prices don't work that way."[65] Because of the need to optimize several non-monetary variables, not just the price, matching markets for things such as college admissions slots, baby adoptions, and transplant organs require

---

[62] Bork (1978), p. 96, figure.

[63] See Kleinberg and Tardos (2005), pp. 4–7, explaining Gale-Shapley algorithm and its implications.

[64] See, e.g., Networks II info (2016), explaining how Airbnb, Lyft and Tinder can be "modeled by the Gale-Shapley algorithm; Wells (2018), explaining how Hinge online dating app is based on the Gale-Shapley algorithm; Harrenstein et al. (2013), describing use of Gale-Shapley algorithm in "auction mechanisms for sponsored search in Internet search engines ".

[65] Roth (2016), pp. 5–6.

a matching process.[66] This matching process is often the product of conscious design, which could produce different results based on that design.[67] Moreover, as technology progresses, it is becoming increasingly possible that the design choices will operate not just at the level of buyers vs. sellers, but may advance to include increasingly personalized offers and matches. While the overall impact of increasingly individualized market making is beyond this Article's scope, it is already drawing significant attention, and will likely exacerbate the problem of the law of relying on a single-supply–demand equilibrium yielding a single price.[68]

The reality of matching processes and the need for design choices means that the operator of an algorithmic matching process may have to choose one side of the platform's utility over another's. It could be argued that a platform that chooses to favor one group's preferences opens itself up to competition from another platform that makes a different choice. While that is possible, there are several reasons why an incumbent matching platform might deter competitive entry. Network effects may create formidable entry barriers, a phenomenon recognized by antitrust enforcers since at least the Microsoft litigation.[69] Switching and information costs may make it difficult for platform users to exit the incumbent platform or multihome (that is if they use two or more platforms); both switching and information costs were recognized by the Supreme Court over a generation ago as factors that can create entry barriers.[70] Exclusionary vertical contracts could exacerbate these issues, and designed-in exclusion in hardware and software could similarly frustrate entry.[71] Relatedly, while it could be argued that those harmed by the matching platforms could be made whole by side payments, in the real world, platform prohibitions on side dealing by matched parties are common.[72]

Several of the factors described above are at issue in the Google and Facebook antitrust cases now pending.[73] Whether they characterize other platforms will be a fact-intensive inquiry. But if they do, together with the potential for platforms to favor one group or another, it undercuts the assumption that market mechanisms will drive towards a single efficient result and correct false negatives the way it is alleged they did in the past.

---

[66] Ibid.

[67] Ibid.

[68] See, e.g., Symposium on Personalized Law (2019).

[69] *US v Microsoft* (D.C. Cir. 2001).

[70] *Kodak v Image Tech. Servs.* (1992).

[71] See, e.g., Fowler (2021), describing designed exclusion in home automation devices.

[72] *Ohio v American Express* (2018); *Epic v Apple* (N.D. Cal. 2021).

[73] See Meta (Facebook) and Google cases referenced in nn. 4 and 13.

4 Implications and Conclusions

Will traditional market mechanisms completely disappear? Quite possibly not. The argument here is not that all economic exchanges will migrate to zero-monetary payment and/or algorithmic matching formats. However, these alternative forms of goods, services, and resource allocation are becoming increasingly feasible and prominent. And law and the legal system are currently not well-situated to handle them.

Much of this paper has focused on competition law, where zero-monetary payment and algorithmic matching are at the heart of ongoing multi-continental cases against Facebook and Google. But the ability of states, firms, and other organizations to use these forms of exchange means that they may choose to do so when it suits them. And that includes those situations in which they seek to avoid legal rules or complicate their application. For example, the Convention on the International Sale of Goods measures damage by a seller's breach versus a baseline set by the market price of the goods in question.[74] Similar principles apply to the failure to perform promised services under both common and civil law. But how can courts measure such damages in situations where there is no monetary price, or where a black box algorithmic matching process has set up the exchange? Similar difficulties stemming from the displacement of the traditional market mechanism may crop up in commercial and tort law.

What can be done about this problem? We are at the relative incipience of zero-price and algorithmic matching forms of exchange. Any advocated steps must be tentative at this time. But at the very least, policymakers need to consider at least two possibilities. First, those involved in the law and regulation of markets must consider becoming comfortable with operating and advocating for models that simulate the baseline reference transactions that the law has heretofore relied on. Judges will also need to increase their sophistication in digesting the results. Second, and perhaps more controversially, policymakers may need to consider the degree to which they should incentivize the operation of traditional market mechanisms. Such steps will necessarily draw criticism that they would distort the choices of private firms and organizations. However, there may be public good aspects to the preservation of traditional market mechanisms that would justify such steps.

The steps advocated here are necessarily spare. This paper calls primarily for engagement with the problem; fuller, more defined prescriptions will have to wait for more experience and analysis. That said, the diminishment of the traditional market mechanism that law has relied on as a baseline will require that such engagement begin soon and amply.

[74] CISG Article 45.

References

Allen L (2006) Knock 'em out, alright still. Regal Recordings

American Law Institute (1981) Restatement (second) of contracts

Blumenthal R, Wu T (2018) What the microsoft case taught us. The New York Times. https://www.nytimes.com/2018/05/18/opinion/microsoft-antitrust-case.html. Accessed 19 Aug 2022

Bork R (1978) The antitrust paradox. Basic Books

Brodkin J (2018) Verizon throttled fire department's "unlimited" data during Calif. Wildfire. ARS Technica. https://arstechnica.com/tech-policy/2018/08/verizon-throttled-fire-departments-unlimited-data-during-calif-wildfire/. Accessed 19 Aug 2022

Calo R (2016) Privacy and markets: a love story. Notre Dame Law Rev 91:649–690

Chen R, Hanson J (2004) The illusion of law: the legitimating schemas of modern policy and corporate law. Mich Law Rev 103:1–149

CISG Advisory Council Opinion No. 6, Calculation of Damages under CISG Article 74. https://www.cisgac.com/cisgac-opinion-no6/. Accessed 19 Aug 2022

Coase R (1937) The Theory of the Firm. Economica 4:386–405

Cockshott PW, Cottrell AF (1993), Socialist planning after the collapse of the soviet union. Revue Européene des Sciences Sociales 31:167–185

Cockshott PW, Cottrell AF (1989) Labour value and socialist economic calculation. Econ Soc 18:71–99

Complaint (2013) United States v Anheuser-Busch InBev SA/NV and Grupo Modelo S.A.B. de C.V. (D.D.C.). https://www.justice.gov/atr/case-document/file/486606/download. Accessed 19 Aug 2022

Complaint (2020) United States v Google (D.D.C.). https://www.justice.gov/opa/press-release/file/1328941/download. Accessed 19 Aug 2022

Complaint (2021) Federal trade commission v facebook (D.D.C.). https://www.ftc.gov/system/files/documents/cases/ecf_75-1_ftc_v_facebook_public_redacted_fac.pdf. Accessed 19 Aug 2022

Complaint (2021) District of Columbia v Amazon (D.C. Super. Ct). https://oag.dc.gov/sites/default/files/2021-05/Amazon-Complaint-pdf. Accessed 19 Aug 2022

Crane D (2005) Harmful output in the antitrust domain: lesson from the tobacco industry. Georg Law Rev 39:321–410

Dahl v. HEM Pharmaceuticals, 7 F.3d 1399 (9th Cir 1993)

Demsetz H (1968) Why regulate utilities? J Law Econ 11:55–65

Editorial Board (2020) Google case is a chance to reframe antitrust debate. Financial Times. https://www.ft.com/content/3327579e-6ac9-49f8-b403-831f2bc32702. Accessed 19 Aug 2022

Epic v Apple, 559 F. Supp 3d 898 (ND Cal 2021)

Farrell J, Katz ML (1998) The effects of antitrust and intellectual property law on compatibility and innovation. Antitrust Bull 43:609–649

Fisman R, Luca M (2019) Did free pens cause the opioid crisis? The Atlantic. https://www.theatlantic.com/magazine/archive/2019/01/did-free-pens-cause-the-opioid-crisis/576394/. Accessed 19 Aug 2022

Fowler G (2021) How big tech monopoly made smart speakers dumber. Washington Post. https://www.washingtonpost.com/technology/2021/09/29/smart-home-monopoly/. Accessed 19 Aug 2022

Gwartney JD et al (2016) Microeconomics: private and public choice, 16th edn. Cengage

Harrenstein P, Manlove D, Wooldridge M (2013) The joy of matching. AI Game Theory. http://www.cs.ox.ac.uk/people/michael.wooldridge/pubs/ieeeis2013a.pdf. Accessed 19 Aug 2022

Hayek F (1948b) The use of knowledge in society. Am Econ Rev 35:519–530

Hayek F (1948a) Individualism and economic order. University of Chicago Press

Henderson TM (2005) The influence of F.A. Hayek on law: an empirical analysis. NYU J Law Lib 1:149–290

van Horn R, Mirowski P (2009) The rise of the Chicago school of economics and the birth of neoliberalism. In: The Road from Mont Pelerin, Harvard, pp. 139–178

Hovenkamp HJ (2019) Platforms and the rule of reason: the American express case. Columbia Bus Law Rev 2019:35–92

Katz ML, Shapiro C (1999) Antitrust in software markets. In: Eisenach JA, Lenard TM (eds) Competition, innovation and the microsoft monopoly: antitrust in the digital marketplace. Springer, pp 29–82

Kennedy J (2017) The myth of data monopoly: why antitrust concerns about data are overblown. Information Technology and Innovation Foundation. http://www2.itif.org/2017-data-competition.pdf. Accessed 19 Aug 2022

Kleinberg J, Tardos E (2005) Algorithm design. Pearson

Knopf KA (2014) A lexicon of economics. Academic

Kodak v Image Technical Services (1992), 504 U.S. 451

Lange O (1967) The computer and the market. In: Feinstein CH (ed) Socialism, capitalism and economic growth: Essays presented to Maurice Dobb. Cambridge University Press

Lender ME, Martin JK (1982) Drinking in America: a history. Free Press

McLaughlin D (2021) Facebook's stealth M&A puts focus on deals under antitrust radar, bloomberg. https://www.bloomberg.com/news/articles/2021-08-23/facebook-s-stealth-m-a-puts-focus-on-deals-under-antitrust-radar. Accessed 19 Aug 2022

Mehra SK (2021) Free as air? Competition policy international. https://www.competitionpolicyinternational.com/wp-content/uploads/2021/09/5-Free-as-Air-By-Salil-K.-Mehra.pdf. Accessed 19 Aug 2022

Meyer v Kalanick (2020) 477 F. Supp. 3d 52 (S.D.N.Y.)

Mirowski P (2002) Machine dreams: economics becomes a cyborg science. Cambridge University Press

Networks II (2016), Airbnb and the gale shapley algorithm. Cornell university course blog for INFO 4220. https://blogs.cornell.edu/info4220/2016/03/17/airbnb-and-the-gale-shapley-algorithm/. Accessed 19 Aug 2022

Newman JM (2015) Antitrust in zero-price markets: foundations. Univ Pa Law Rev 164:149–206

Ohio v. American Express (2018) 585 U.S.

Orbach BY (2010) The antitrust consumer welfare paradox. J Comp Law Econ 7:133–164

Parker GG, van Alstyne MW, Choudary SP (2016) Platform revolution: how networked markets are transforming the economy and how to make them work for you. Norton

Posner RA (2005) Hayek, law, and cognition. New York Univ J Law Lib 1:147–166

Reilly C (2016) Samsung's new fridge orders your groceries. CNET. https://www.cnet.com/au/news/samsung-family-hub-refrigerator-lets-you-order-groceries-from-woolworths/. Accessed 19 Aug 2022

Robinson J (1933) The economics of imperfect competition. Econ J 43:657–661

Rosenquist JN, Morton FMS, Weinstein SN (2021) Addictive technology and its implications for antitrust enforcement. North Carolina Law Rev 100:431–485

Roth A (2016) Who gets what and why. Eamon Dolan/Mariner Books

Schelling TC (1969) Models of segregation. Am Econ Rev 59:488–493

Schelling TC (1971) Dynamic models of segregation. J Math Sociol 1:143–186

Sidak JG (2015) Do free mobile apps harm consumers? San Diego Law Rev 52:619–694

Simpson C (2014) Amazon will sell you things before you know you want to buy them. The Atlantic. https://www.theatlantic.com/technology/archive/2014/01/amazon-thinks-it-can-predict-your-future/357188/. Accessed 19 Aug 2022

Slip Opinion (2022) Federal trade commission v meta platforms, inc. Mark Zuckerberg, and within unlimited, inc. (D.D.C.). https://www.documentcloud.org/documents/21177063-memorandum-opinion. Accessed 19 Aug 2022

Spicer D (2014) IBM and the 1964 world's fair, computer history museum. http://www.computerhistory.org/atchm/ibm-and-1964-worlds-fair/. Accessed 19 Aug 2022

Stoller M (2014) How uber creates an algorithmic monopoly to extract rents, naked capitalism. http://www.nakedcapitalism.com/2014/04/matt-stoller-how-uber-creates-an-algorithmic-monopoly.html. Accessed 19 Aug 2022

United States v Microsoft (2000) 87 F. Supp. 2d. 30 (D.D.C.)
Symposium (2019) Personalized law. Univ Chicago Law Rev 86(2)
TN (2014) A modern smartphone or a vintage supercomputer: which is more powerful?, phoneArena.com. http://www.phonearena.com/news/A-modern-smartphone-or-a-vintage-supercomputer-which-is-more-powerful_id57149. Accessed 19 Aug 2022
Towell C (2011) Essential survival skills, DK
Trainor M (2015) No, thank you, Epic
United Nations convention for the international sale of goods. Article 45
United States v Alcoa (1945) 148 F.2d 416 (2d Cir.)
United States v Microsoft (2001) 253 F3d 34 (D.C. Cir.)
Verizon v Trinko (2004) 540 US 398
Waugh E (1945) Brideshead revisited. Chapman/Hall
Wells S (2018) Hinge employs new algorithm to find your most compatible match, Techcrunch. https://techcrunch.com/2018/07/11/hinge-employs-new-algorithm-to-find-your-most-compatible-match-for-you/. Accessed 19 Aug 2022
Willis C (1998) Does Amazon.com really matter?, Forbes ASAP. https://www.forbes.com/asap/1998/0406/055_print.html. Accessed 19 Aug 2022

Salil K. Mehra is a Professor of Law and Government at Temple University, Beasley School of Law. His fields of interest include Competition Law, Law and Technology, Economic Analysis of Law.

Part III: Digitalisation and the COVID-19 Pandemic

Online Commercial Courts and Judicial Efficiency: Evidence from the COVID-19 Pandemic in Poland

Ido Baum, Jarosław Bełdowski, and Łukasz Dąbroś

Abstract This study aims to examine the impact of the transition of Polish commercial courts to remote working via online proceedings. To achieve this goal, we will exploit the natural experiment in 2020—the COVID-19 pandemic—which forced many areas of human activity (including the justice system) to move to the internet. Using data envelopment analysis and stochastic frontier analysis, we will show that the switch had no significant impact on the efficiency of Polish commercial courts. However, these results are to be treated with some caution. The efficiency benefits of the new technology may have been reduced by the steep learning curve and the fact that the decision to change was made suddenly and under the pressure of the disease. The topic requires, therefore, further scientific attention.

Keywords Judicial efficiency · Online courts · Data envelopment analysis · Stochastic frontier analysis

---

I. Baum
Haim Striks Faculty of Law, College of Management-Academic Studies (COLMAN), Rishon LeTsiyon, Israel
e-mail: baumi@colman.ac.il

Louis Brandeis Institute for Society Economy and Democracy, COLMAN, Rishon LeTsiyon, Israel

J. Bełdowski
Department of International Comparative Studies, Warsaw School of Economics, Al. Niepodległości 162, 02-554 Warszawa, Poland
e-mail: jaroslaw.beldowski@sgh.waw.pl

Ł. Dąbroś (✉)
Warsaw School of Economics, Collegium of Economic Analysis, Warszawa, Poland
e-mail: ld50376@doktorant.sgh.waw.pl; lukaszdabros@gmail.com

K. Mathis and A. Tor (eds.), *Law and Economics of the Digital Transformation*,
Economic Analysis of Law in European Legal Scholarship 15,
https://doi.org/10.1007/978-3-031-25059-0_5

1 Introduction

It is self-evident that the COVID-19 pandemic is one of the most transformational events of recent decades. The coronavirus outbreak in early 2020 caused a massive change in human behaviour worldwide. In particular, many areas of human activity, e.g., services, education, governance, and public administration, were forced to move to the virtual domain of the internet. The shift from real to online interaction in the provision of services was initially aimed at reducing the spread of the epidemic by limiting face-to-face contact. For economists, the pandemic has been a natural experiment that can be used to investigate how rapid, unexpected, and profound changes in conditions affect the behaviour of markets, individuals, and organizations.

We will investigate how a pandemic-induced rapid switch to online adjudication in the courts in Poland influenced the efficiency of the Polish judiciary. We will employ data from Polish first-instance commercial courts (formally, these are the commercial departments of district courts, but they are commonly called commercial courts) collected in the 2018–2020 period.

This chapter consists of five sections. This introduction is followed by a literature review on judicial efficiency and e-courts. The third section describes how the judiciary of Poland adjusted to the COVID-19 reality, and the fourth section presents the data set and the empirical strategy we adopted. In the fifth part, we will describe the results. The sixth section draws final conclusions.

2 Literature Review

Because not much time has elapsed since the COVID-19 outbreak, we are not aware of any empirical studies on the performance of e-courts during the pandemic. However, there are studies highlighting other aspects of the functioning of online courts. For instance, Sourdin, Li, and McNamara,[1] compared how courts in different countries handled the pandemic. Generally speaking, the authors appreciated that justice systems switched to online dispute resolution and provided parties with access to courts even in times of emergency.

There are also case studies in the available literature discussing the transition to remote justice and the problems associated with it. The most comprehensive study of its kind was conducted by McIntyre, Olijnyk, and Pender[2] for Australia. The authors claim that the sudden shift from physical courts to remote justice has revealed several significant obstacles to this mode of justice delivery. First, public and media access to the process of justice has been restricted, because in a traditional judiciary, an interested party could be in the courtroom and observe a trial or other proceeding in its entirety. The judiciary has also been deprived of the element of prestige. For example, the effects of representative court buildings and the customs and ceremonies

[1] Sourdin et al. (2020, pp. 447–453).

[2] McIntyre et al. (2020, pp. 197–201).

associated with the work of the court (which may seem intimidating to some) were lacking. The authors also drew attention to the problem of digital exclusion: the shift of the courts to the internet has made them less accessible to the less well-off, the elderly, and those with limited technical skills. The authors also flagged the problem of biases affecting the decisions of online judges, including the so-called Zoom fatigue. In the same vein, Legg[3] drew attention to the need to ensure three fundamental principles of fair justice in e-courts: open justice, procedural fairness, and impartiality.

When discussing the impact of epidemics and remote working on efficiency, we should also mention the empirical studies so far devoted to other spheres of human activity (courts have not yet been studied in this way). Criscuolo et al.,[4] based on a survey of managers and employees in twenty-five OECD countries, found that switching to teleworking improved both the productivity of companies and the well-being of people working there. However, the research highlighted the need to invest in appropriate information technology (IT) tools and the development of employees' soft skills to match the shift to telework.

On the other hand, Yang et al.[5] showed (through a quantitative analysis of the communications of employees of one large IT corporation) that the shift to remote working in 2020 led to a reduction in the flow of information between different parts of the company, which could harm its innovation in the long run. A study by Bao et al.[6] based on data from a Chinese IT company showed that the impact of remote working on productivity is uneven, depending on the nature of the work and the personal characteristics of the employee.

In our study, we aim to contribute to the filling of the still large research gap dedicated to the impact of remote/internet working on employee productivity. To this end, we analyze how the Polish judiciary functioned during the epidemic period.

Although there is a dearth of significant empirical or econometric research on the efficiency of switching from physical to remote judicial process during the pandemic, annual court statistics reports from England and the United States seem to indicate that the move to online delivery of justice did not have a significant effect on the courts' input or output. For example, in 2018, the number of new claims in the London Commercial Court Circuit (LCCC) was 248, in 2019, there were 234 new claims, and in 2020, there were 283 new claims. There is an increase in the number of LCCC claims filed in 2020, which possibly is not a result of the pandemic but actually reflects parties shifting to the LCCC from the Commercial court.[7] The LCCC held

[3] Legg (2021, pp. 161–184).

[4] Criscuolo et al. (2021, pp. 1–36).

[5] Yang et al. (2022, pp. 43–54).

[6] Bao et al. (2021, pp. 1–15).

[7] Judiciary of England and Wales (2022, pp. 21–25). The number of claims issued in the Commercial Court in 2020 (802) has reduced slightly from 2019 (860). The number of hearings listed and heard in the Commercial Court during 2020 has remined broadly similar to previous years: 1,394 listed compared to 1,476 (there is no significant change).

300 hearings (most of them online) in 2020, compared to 306 hearings in 2019.[8] In the United States, the Delaware Court of Chancery, famously known as one of the leading global venues for corporate-related litigation, reported a quick switch to remote adjudication. There was no significant change in the number of filings compared to 2019, with 1167 cases and correspondingly 1144 cases in 2020.[9] The Netherlands Commercial Court (NCC) also reported switching to remote adjudication without a significant change in the number of filings.[10]

3 COVID-19 and the Judiciary of Poland

Poland's peripheral location and its relatively weak links with Asia (where the COVID-19 pandemic originated) meant that the first COVID-19 case in the country was reported relatively late (March 4, 2020) compared to the rest of Europe (the first European case was identified at the end of January 2020 in France). This state of affairs gave the Polish authorities some time to prepare the country for the incoming disaster.

On March 1, 2020, the Sejm (the lower house of the Parliament of Poland) began its work on the so-called COVID-19 laws (a special act to regulate the functioning of the state and the private sector in the event of an epidemic). The bill was passed one day later, and the law was signed by the President immediately thereafter. The law came into force on March 8, 2020, but it has been amended several times to adapt to the changing epidemic situation.[11]

For instance, an amendment of March 31, 2020, suspended the running of court deadlines for the duration of the epidemic. However, it soon became apparent that the epidemic would last longer than anticipated, and it was necessary to find a solution that would enable the courts to function under the new conditions. As a result, an amendment of May 14, 2020, created the legal framework for the online operation of courts. From that moment on, remote court proceedings (including hearings) were allowed in civil cases (including commercial cases) whenever physical presence in court could endanger the participants' health. As a result, teleconferencing applications replaced physical presence for the conduction of hearings in the courtroom.[12]

8 Judiciary of England and Wales (2022, p. 34).

9 Delaware Judiciary (2021, pp. 2, 21–22).

10 Van Dijk et al. (2022, p. 12).

11 Szolc-Nartowski (2020, pp. 173–174).

12 Szolc-Nartowski (2020, pp. 174–175).

4 Data Set and Empirical Strategy

4.1 Data Set

We use data provided by the Ministry of Justice of the Republic of Poland. Our data set includes 2018–2020 data from fifty-three Polish first-instance commercial courts. We have data on the number of cases received and processed by these courts, as well as the number of judges and support staff. Our data set contains data on the three main types of cases heard by Polish commercial courts at the time—full trial cases, writ-of-payment cases (processed by a simplified procedure), and "other" cases. In the period under review, these three account for 99.93% of cases submitted to the commercial courts of the first instance in Poland (Figs. 1, 2 and 3).

A quick look at the figures suffices for one to note that in 2020, there was a significant drop in the number of cases received and adjudicated by Polish commercial courts. The decrease can undoubtedly be attributed to the COVID-19 pandemic and a substantial drop in overall commercial activity caused by it. Of particular interest are the figures for cases requiring a full trial. In 2020, the courts benefited from a smaller influx of new cases, which allowed them to catch up with the backlog from previous years.

Regrettably, we do not have exact data on the number of cases adjudicated in online proceedings. We can, however, assume that in 2020, there was at least the possibility of conducting judicial activities via the internet—we make use of this fact in this chapter. A detailed description of the data can be found in the study's appendix.

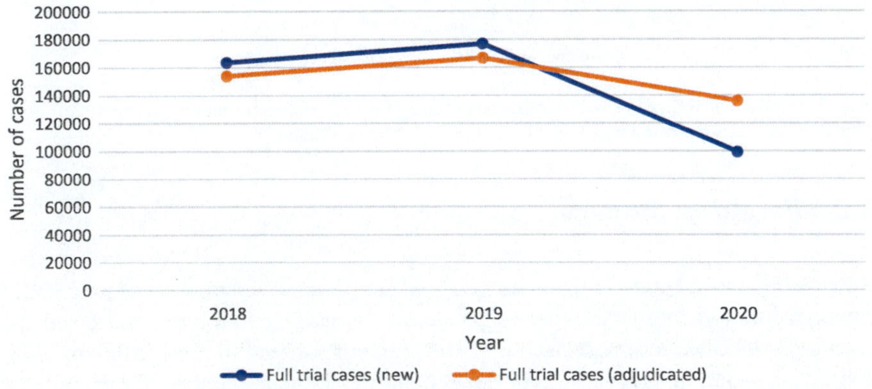

Fig. 1 Number of full trial cases received and adjudicated by Polish first-instance commercial courts (2018–2020). *Source* Ministry of Justice of the Republic of Poland

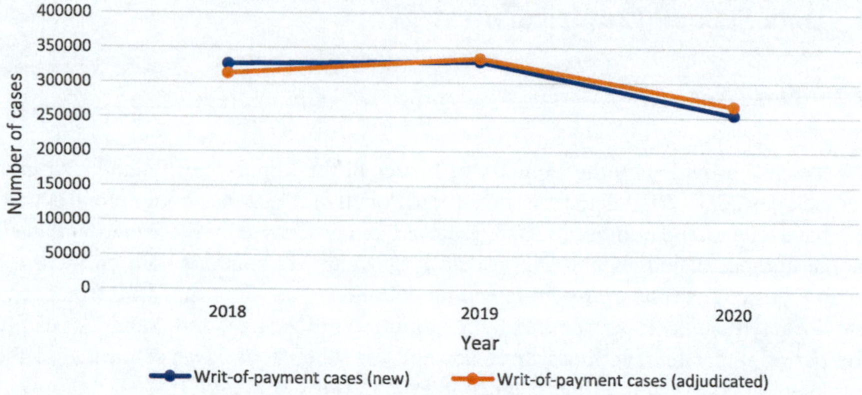

Fig. 2 Number of writ-of-payment cases received and adjudicated by Polish first-instance commercial courts (2018–2020). *Source* Ministry of Justice of the Republic of Poland

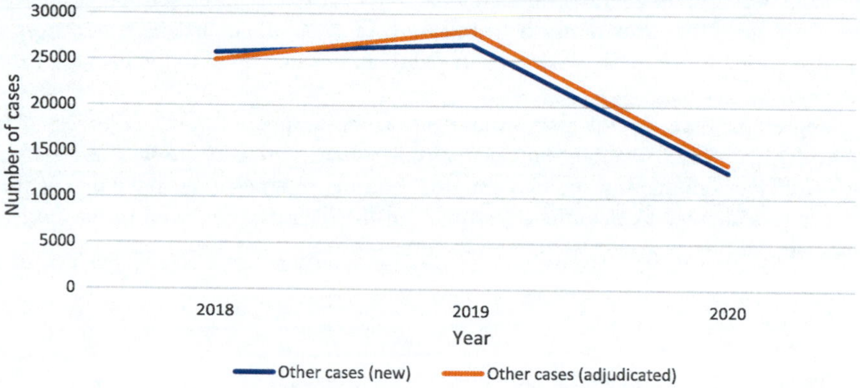

Fig. 3 Number of "other" cases received and adjudicated by Polish first-instance commercial courts (2018–2020). *Source* Ministry of Justice of the Republic of Poland

4.2 Empirical Strategy

As stated in the introduction, this study's goal is to determine whether the procedural changes induced by the COVID-19 pandemic (switching to e-courts) affected the operation of Polish commercial courts. The previous subsection showed that in 2020, there was a significant decrease in the demand for judicial justice—the number of cases received (and the workload of judges) dropped in response to the pandemic waves. Consequently, it would not be justifiable to compare only the number of cases adjudicated in the examined years. For this reason, we decided to exploit the concept of judicial efficiency, which is a measure of how well the court is doing in turning inputs (cases on the docket, judges) into outputs (cases adjudicated). In the study, we use two strategies to measure efficiency and find factors affecting it: data envelopment analysis (DEA) and stochastic frontier analysis (SFA).

4.2.1 Data Envelopment Analysis

Our DEA approach has two stages. In the first stage, we use DEA to gauge the performance of commercial courts. For every year and each court, an efficiency score is assigned, which is a variable ranging from 0 to 1 describing how well the court performs in adjudicating the cases it receives. In the second stage, we treat the efficiency score as a dependent variable and use panel econometrics to find factors that may increase or decrease the court's performance.

Data envelopment analysis is a nonparametric method used to estimate production frontiers; it was developed by Charnes, Cooper and Rhodes[13] and applied for the first time to investigate judicial performance by Lewin, Morey and Cook[14] and Kittelsen and Førsund.[15] The main advantage of this method for our study is its simplicity—it does not require making any assumptions regarding production function. The use of a nonparametric approach saves us the need to investigate the interdependence between case types that may decrease the performance of a court.

Charnes, Cooper and Rhodes stated that the efficiency of a decision-making unit (DMU) could be expressed as a maximal ratio of weighted outputs to weighted inputs, with the condition that no efficiency score can be higher than 1 (the efficiency score equal to 1 is assigned to the best-performing unit). Hence, the problem can be expressed as follows:

$$\max h_0 = \frac{\sum_{r=1}^{s} u_r y_{r0}}{\sum_{i=1}^{m} v_i x_{i0}}$$

subject to the following constraints:

$$\frac{\sum_{r=1}^{s} u_r y_{rj}}{\sum_{i=1}^{m} v_i x_{ij}} \leq 1; \; j = 1, \ldots, n$$

$$v_r, v_i \geq 0; \; r = 1, \ldots, s; \; i = 1, \ldots, m.$$

In these formulas, y and x denote outputs and inputs (respectively), and u and v can be interpreted as output and inputs weights that are fixed across all DMUs.

---

13 Charnes et al. (1978, pp. 429–444).

14 Lewin et al. (1982, pp. 401–411).

15 Kittelsen and Førsund (1992, pp. 277–306).

Given the fact that in the field of the judiciary, the inputs (usually staff and caseload) are not determined by the court itself, the "best" court is the one that manages to generate the largest output (number of cases adjudicated). We use an output-oriented two-stage DEA process with constant returns to scale.

One of the most decisive choices to be made in DEA analysis is correctly selecting inputs and outputs used in the model. For outputs, we follow the concept predominant in the available literature and use the number of cases resolved by a given court each year. Therefore, every court has three types of output corresponding to three types of commercial cases analyzed in the study.

The choice of inputs in previous studies employing DEA methodology to analyze courts of law is less unambiguous, as different sets of inputs were used in individual studies. However, it can be considered typical to treat judges as the critical input factor in the judiciary because, for a court to perform its role, their existence is necessary. Several studies include auxiliary judicial staff and the budget allocated for courts and their ICT equipment in the inputs group. Moreover, a few studies also include the caseload (e.g., the number of cases waiting to be adjudicated).[16] Following these notions, we use four inputs: the caseload of three case types analyzed in the study and the number of judges. The outputs are, unsurprisingly, the three types of cases as they were adjudicated.

As stated above, the first stage of our research enables us to generate an efficiency index for every court in question each year. The second stage builds upon these indices and uses the parametric approach to find factors affecting the efficiency of a given court in a given year. To achieve this objective, we use two-way panel models to control individual effects for each court and year and track efficiency changes that may have arisen due to the COVID-19 pandemic and subsequent changes. We employ two specifications (for the descriptions of the variables, see the appendix):

$$efficiency_{nt} = \beta_0 + \beta_1 apj_{nt} + \beta_2 cpj_{nt} + \beta_3 cpj_{nt} + u_n + \lambda_t + \varepsilon_{nt}$$

In the second stage of our study, we make the efficiency index (calculated for every court and year) dependent on a set of explanatory variables: number of assistants per judge (*apj*), number of civil servants per judge (*spj*), and legal clerks (*cpj*). Moreover, we use individual effects (u) to capture courts' unobserved traits, and we use time variables (λ). This last variable is of particular importance. Its value and statistical significance for 2020 allow us to answer the question of the impact of moving the courts online on efficiency.

Both specifications are first estimated using standard two-way panel models (with time effects and fixed and random individual effects) with White-corrected robust errors clustered by the court. Afterwards, a series of two-way tobit models is calculated to accommodate the fact that the efficiency index, by definition, ranges from 0 to 1. The tobit models are also estimated using both fixed and random individual effects.

[16] E.g. Deyneli (2012, pp. 477–493).

4.2.2 Stochastic Frontier Analysis

The DEA-plus-tobit approach presented in the previous subsection allows us to reach some conclusions, but it has one significant drawback. Because we treat judges as the input, we are precluded from determining whether the number of judges affects the number of cases adjudicated. To tackle this problem, parametric methods are required.

In the parametric part of the study, we use stochastic frontier analysis (SFA), a methodology developed by Aigner et al.[17] The dependent variable here is the production frontier (i.e., the maximal number of cases that can be resolved by a court endowed with a given number of judges and cases on the docket), not the expected mean output. The SFA model can be used to find the determinants of inefficiencies in the performance of courts (i.e., the difference between their production frontier and their actual output). In our model, the frontier part is determined using the numbers of new cases, pending cases, and judges, following Bełdowski, Dąbroś and Wojciechowski.[18] All variables are used in logarithms so they can be interpreted in terms of elasticity, and the number of cases is augmented by one before logarithmization.[19]

This strategy allows us to obtain inefficiency terms that are further explained using three types of auxiliary judicial staff and time variables, which are of particular interest in this study. Our SFA regressions have the following specification (for descriptions of the variables, see the appendix):

$$Resol_{nit} = \beta_0 + \beta_1 * New_{nit} + \beta_2 * Pending_{nit} + \beta_3 * Judges_{nt} - u_{nit} + v_{nit}$$

$$v_{nit} \sim N\left(0, \sigma_v^2\right)$$

$$u_{nit} = f(\lambda_t)$$

In this model, n stands for courts, i stands for case group, t stands for time, v_{nit} stands for random errors, and u_{nit} standards for inefficiency terms that are further explained as a function of auxiliary staff and time effects. As our data set can be characterized by a large N (53) and small T (3 years), we estimate our models using the Wang-Ho[20] estimator to tackle the plausible issue of accidental parameters.

---

[17] Aigner et al. (1977, pp. 21–37).

[18] Bełdowski et al. (2020, pp. 179–184).

[19] This is done to avoid the problem of nonexistence of ln(0).

[20] Wang and Ho (2010, pp. 286–296).

Table 1 Courts' efficiency distributions

	N	Mean	S.D.	Min	1Q	Median	3Q	Max
Entire time frame	159	0.95	0.05	0.80	0.93	0.96	1.00	1.00
Year 2018	53	0.95	0.04	0.82	0.92	0.95	0.99	1.00
Year 2019	53	0.97	0.03	0.87	0.94	0.98	1.00	1.00
Year 2020	53	0.94	0.05	0.80	0.92	0.95	1.00	1.00

5 Estimation Results

5.1 *Data Envelopment Analysis*

As stated above, in the first part of our empirical study, we use DEA methodology (assuming constant returns to scale) to calculate efficiency indices for the Polish first-instance commercial courts. The summary efficiency results for the entire time frame and single years are shown below (Table 1).

At first glance, we cannot reach a definite conclusion about the significant efficiency impact of the pandemic-induced changes in the operation of Polish first-instance commercial courts. The efficiency distribution for the year 2020 is very similar to the one for the entire time frame of this study. However, to properly evaluate the claim, we employ panel and tobit regressions (since the value of the efficiency factor is limited from 0 to 1); the results are shown below (Table 2).

The second-stage regression results show that 2020 (compared to 2018) did not bring statistically significant changes in the efficiency of Polish commercial courts. Instead, a significant increase in overall efficiency was observable in 2019 (in which there were no changes to the way the courts operated). A positive relationship between the number of civil servants and efficiency is also evident in some regressions. This outcome, however, is not robust.

5.2 *Stochastic Frontier Analysis*

As stated in the previous section, stochastic frontier analysis allows us to analyze the determinants of maximal potential output (the production possibility frontier) and factors contributing to the court's inefficiency. Hence, we can investigate how the 2020 changes in court operation affected courts' efficiency in dealing with particular case types (Table 3).

Table 2 Determinants of courts' efficiency (panel models)

	(1)	(2)	(3)	(4)
	Panel FE	Panel RE	Tobit FE	Tobit RE
Year 2019	0.021***	0.021***	0.028***	0.026***
	(0.01)	(0.00)	(0.01)	(0.01)
Year 2020	−0.0021	−0.0024	−0.0020	−0.0029
	(0.01)	(0.01)	(0.01)	(0.01)
Assistants per judge	−0.063	−0.049*	−0.086*	−0.056
	(0.04)	(0.03)	(0.05)	(0.04)
Clerks per judge	−0.033	−0.035	−0.036	−0.038
	(0.05)	(0.03)	(0.06)	(0.05)
Civil servants per judge	0.025	0.028*	0.032	0.035**
	(0.02)	(0.01)	(0.02)	(0.02)
Constant	0.93***	0.92***	0.92***	0.92***
	(0.04)	(0.02)	(0.03)	(0.03)
N	159	159	217	217
R2_within	0.18	0.18		

One, two and three stars indicate significance at the 10%, 5%, and 1% levels

Table 3 Determinants of courts' output and inefficiency (SFA)

	(1)	(2)	(3)
	Full-trial cases	Writ-of-payment cases	Other cases
	b/se	b/se	b/se
Frontier			
New cases (in log)	0.33***	0.76***	0.81***
	(0.03)	(0.03)	(0.02)
Pending cases (in log)	0.59***	0.11***	0.19***
	(0.05)	(0.01)	(0.02)
Judges (in log)	0.21***	0.055	0.079*
	(0.06)	(0.04)	(0.05)
Inefficiency term			
Year 2019	0.29	0.035	−0.43
	(63.91)	(5.65)	(28.38)
Year 2020	0.71	0.52	0.22
	(130.33)	(66.34)	(10.52)
N	159	159	157

One, two and three stars indicate significance at the 10%, 5%, and 1% levels

The SFA models estimated for individual case types also do not confirm the claim that the courts' move to remote case adjudication in 2020 affected their efficiency. The parameters defining the relationship between years and inefficiency for all three case types are statistically insignificant. The results for the frontier function are intuitive and consistent with previous studies: we see that the maximal number of cases adjudicated depends on the number of cases received and pending from the previous years. Moreover, the number of judges is positively correlated with the number of full trial cases adjudicated (which is not surprising, as this type of trial requires significant involvement by the judge).

The results obtained through the two methodological procedures are consistent with each other. We did not detect any efficiency gains for Polish first-instance commercial courts in 2020 when the courts were forced to adopt online proceedings due to the pandemic. However, this result does not mean that online provision of justice is a dead end with respect to enhancing judicial efficiency. It should be noted that with each technology, time is required to become familiar with it—in 2020, we could observe the early stage of the steep tail of the learning curve. Finally, it should be kept in mind that 2020 was a year of general disorder caused by the global epidemic shock.

6 Conclusions

In this chapter, we analyzed data on the operation of Polish first-instance commercial courts in the years 2018–2020 to examine how a COVID-19—induced switch to online operations affected their efficient adjudication performance. To achieve this goal, we used the nonparametric DEA and parametric SFA approaches, and we found no significant efficiency changes in the pandemic year 2020. This leads to a preliminary conclusion that the move to remote adjudication did not improve courts' performances.

The results, however, should be accepted with caution. The switch to online operations was sudden and unexpected. It resulted from the rapid spread of a dangerous disease. It was not the fruit of a previously announced and planned reform. Therefore, it is possible to argue that the lack of improved efficiency was due to confusion arising from the abrupt change. The courts suddenly had to adapt to the new technology and did so with some initial difficulties.

For the reasons cited above, our study is preliminary. It will need to be repeated as more data for subsequent years and micro data on individual cases become available.

Appendix

Appendix 1 Variables description

Log full-trial cases adjudicated	The number of all full-trial cases adjudicated by a Polish commercial court in a given year (in logarithm)
Log full-trial new cases	The number of all full-trial cases received by a Polish commercial court in a given year (augmented by one and in logarithm)
Log full-trial pending cases	The number of all full-trial cases pending from previous years in a Polish commercial court in a given year (augmented by one and in logarithm)
Log writ-of-payment cases adjudicated	The number of all writ-of-payment cases adjudicated by a Polish commercial court in a given year (in logarithm)
Log writ-of-payment new cases	The number of all writ-of-payment cases received by a Polish commercial court in a given year (augmented by one and in logarithm)
Log writ-of-payment pending cases	The number of all writ-of-payment cases pending from previous years in a Polish commercial court in a given year (augmented by one and in logarithm)
Log other cases adjudicated	The number of all other cases adjudicated by a Polish commercial court in a given year (in logarithm)
Log other new cases	The number of all other cases received by a Polish commercial court in a given year (augmented by one and in logarithm)
Log other pending cases	The number of all other cases pending from previous years in a Polish commercial court in a given year (augmented by one and in logarithm)
Log judges	The average number of judges in a given bankruptcy court in a given year (in logarithm)
Assistants-to-judges ratio	The average number of assistants [asystenci] per judge in a given court in a given year
Civ. servants-to-judges ratio	The average number of civil servants [urzędnicy] per judge in a given court in a given year
Legal clerks-to-judges ratio	The average number of legal clerks [referendarze] per judge in a given court in a given year

Appendix 2 Summary statistics

Variable	N	Mean	S.D.	Min	1Q	Median	3Q	Max
Log full-trial cases adjudicated	159	7.6	0.77	6.09	7.04	7.52	8.08	10.14
Log full-trial new cases	159	7.54	0.81	6.01	6.88	7.4	8.04	10.28
Log full-trial pending cases	159	7.25	0.91	5.53	6.6	7.21	7.79	10.33
Log writ-of-payment cases adjudicated	159	8.22	0.85	6.71	7.61	8.13	8.75	11.07
Log writ-of-payment new cases	159	8.21	0.85	6.52	7.57	8.18	8.74	11.09
Log writ-of-payment pending cases	159	6.09	1.23	3.09	5.25	6.03	6.81	9.34
Log other cases adjudicated	159	5.47	1.04	0	4.88	5.56	6	8.82
Log other new cases	159	5.45	1.03	0	4.81	5.5	5.99	8.8
Log other pending cases	157	3.97	1.09	0	3.3	3.97	4.53	7.38
Log judges	159	1.73	0.72	−0.14	1.23	1.69	2.19	3.85
Assistants-to-judges ratio	159	0.38	0.15	0.04	0.26	0.36	0.47	1.01
Civ. servants-to-judges ratio	159	1.81	0.39	1.19	1.53	1.75	2	3.65
Legal clerks-to-judges ratio	159	0.21	0.15	0	0.08	0.2	0.3	0.59

References

Aigner D, Lovell KCA, Schmidt P (1977) Formulation and estimation of stochastic frontier production function models. J Appl Economet 6:21–37

Bao L et al (2021) How does working from home affect developer productivity?—A case study of Baidu during COVID-19 pandemic. Sci China Inf Ser 65(April):1–15. https://doi.org/10.1007/s11432-020-3278-4 (last access 18 Aug 2022)

Bełdowski J, Dąbroś Ł, Wojciechowski W (2020) Judges and court performance: a case study of district commercial courts in Poland. Eur J Law Econ 50(1):171–201. https://doi.org/10.1007/s10657-020-09656-4 (last access 18 Aug 2022)

Charnes A, Cooper WW, Rhodes E (1978) Measuring the efficiency of decision making units. Eur J Oper Res 2(6):429–444. https://doi.org/10.1016/0377-2217(78)90138-8 (last access 18 Aug 2022)

Criscuolo C et al (2021) The role of telework for productivity during and post-COVID-19: results from an OECD survey among managers and workers. OECD productivity working paper series, 31

Delaware Judiciary (2021) The Delaware Judiciary: 2020 annual report

Deyneli F (2012) Analysis of relationship between efficiency of justice services and salaries of judges with two-stage DEA method. Eur J Law Econ 34(3):477–493. https://doi.org/10.1007/s10657-011-9258-3 (last access 18 Aug 2022)

Judiciary of England and Wales (2022) Business and property courts: the commercial court report 2020–2021 (including the Admiralty Court Report)

Kittelsen SAC, Førsund FR (1992) Efficiency analysis of Norwegian district courts. J Prod Anal 3:277–306.https://doi.org/10.1007/BF00158357 (last access 18 Aug 2022)

Legg M (2021) The COVID-19 pandemic, the courts and online hearings: maintaining open justice, procedural fairness and impartiality. Federal Law Rev 49(2):161–184. https://doi.org/10.1177/0067205X21993139 (last access 18 Aug 2022)

Lewin AY, Morey RC, Cook TJ (1982) Evaluating the administrative efficiency of courts. Omega 10(4):401–411. https://doi.org/10.1016/0305-0483(82)90019-6 (last access 18 Aug 2022)

McIntyre J, Olijnyk A, Pender K (2020) Civil courts and COVID-19: challenges and opportunities in Australia. Altern Law J 45(3):195–201. https://doi.org/10.1177/1037969X20956787 (last access 18 Aug 2022)

Sourdin T, Li B, McNamara DM (2020) Court innovations and access to justice in times of crisis. Health Policy Technol 9(4):447–453.https://doi.org/10.1016/j.hlpt.2020.08.020 (last access 18 Aug 2022)

Szolc-Nartowski B (2020) Coronavirus and the justice system in Poland. Access Justice East Eur 3(2–3):172–175. https://doi.org/10.33327/AJEE-18-3.2-3-n000034 (last access 18 Aug 2022)

van Dijk F et al (2022) The decline in commercial court cases in The Netherlands: 2001–2020 (Issue 2)

Wang HJ, Ho CW (2010) Estimating fixed-effect panel stochastic frontier models by model transformation. J Economet 157(2):286–296. https://doi.org/10.1016/j.jeconom.2009.12.006 (last access 18 Aug 2022)

Yang L et al (2022) The effects of remote work on collaboration among information workers. Nat Hum Behav 6(1):43–54. https://doi.org/10.1038/s41562-021-01196-4 (last access 31 Aug 2022)

Ido Baum is a Senior Lecturer of Law at the Haim Striks Faculty of Law, College of Management-Academic Studies (COLMAN), and Director of the Louis Brandeis Institute for Society Economy and Democracy at COLMAN. His fields of interest include Corporate Law, Securities Regulation, Economic Analysis of Law, Competition, Civil Procedure and Media Law.

Jarosław Bełdowski is an Assistant Professor at the Warsaw School of Economics, Department of International Comparative Studies. His fields of interest include New Institutional Economics, Law and Economics, Law and Finance.

Łukasz Dąbroś is a PhD student at the Warsaw School of Economics, Collegium of Economic Analysis. Fields of Interest: Law and Economics, Institutional Economics, Growth Economics, Labour Economics, Economic Policies.

Tax Administration Toward Digitalization in the COVID-19 Environment—Case Study Bosnia and Herzegovina

Law and Economics of e-Tax Administration

Lejla Ramić

Abstract The COVID-19 pandemic, as an unprecedented global health and economic crisis, has shaken digital resilience in general, and on the government side in particular. Pandemic circumstances have caused a slowdown in economic activity and, at the same time, introduced us to the momentum of accelerated digitalization. Among other things, economic policy makers had two key economic policies, monetary and fiscal, at their disposal, in order to ensure the necessary stabilization of the economy and amortization of the negative consequences of the crisis on business activities. Speaking of fiscal policy, the special burden of the crisis was in the field of ensuring the integrity of the tax system and yielding tax revenue. In this context, tax administrations have faced, on the one hand, the potentially accelerated digitization of work and, on the other hand, the pressure of having to ensure the highest possible degree of tax compliance in a situation that, due to its characteristics, presented an additional risk for tax fraud. The situation has become more complicated in developing countries, such as Bosnia and Herzegovina, which has a deep-rooted bureaucratic system and fights hard for public trust while trying to solve the problem of collecting enough tax revenue for the basic functions of the state. This chapter examines how the COVID-19 pandemic affected the process of digitalization of tax administrations with the specific aim of determining whether Bosnia and Herzegovina, as a developing country with a commitment to membership in the European Union, has seized momentum and accelerated the degree of digitalization of tax administrations, especially the Indirect Taxation Authority. In order to meet the set research goal, the first part of the chapter will present a theoretical framework of the economic analysis of the digitalization of the tax administration. The second part of the chapter will provide a comparative analysis of the situation and perspectives of digitalization of the tax administrations from 32 member administrations based on the research of the Organization for Economic Cooperation and Development published in 2021 with special reference to the impact of the pandemic. In the third and last part of the chapter, based on the empirical research and desk analysis, the

L. Ramić (✉)
University of Sarajevo, Sarajevo, Bosnia and Herzegovina
e-mail: l.ramic@pfsa.unsa.ba

K. Mathis and A. Tor (eds.), *Law and Economics of the Digital Transformation*, Economic Analysis of Law in European Legal Scholarship 15,
https://doi.org/10.1007/978-3-031-25059-0_6

author seeks to answer the fundamental research question of whether the COVID-19 pandemic accelerated the process of digitalization of tax administration in Bosnia and Herzegovina in which the stage of digitalization is generally low and which can be seen as a sludge in the digitalization process.

Keywords e-Tax administration · Digitalization of tax administration · COVID-19 and digitalization · Economic analysis of digitalization · OECD: digital resilience in the COVID-19 environment · e-Tax administration in Bosnia and Herzegovina · Effectiveness · Digital acceleration · Innovative technologies in tax collection

1 Introduction

For most countries today, the digital economy, based on digital technologies, entrepreneurship, knowledge, and intangible assets, is a model for achieving economic growth. Therefore, an important feature of the digital economy is digitization and intensive use of information. This way of growth poses new challenges for economic policy makers, including holders of economic and political powers in the field of tax policy. The dynamics of economic and technological development require permanent changes in the modelling of the tax system, with different regulatory challenges being identified in the areas of direct and indirect taxes. Digitalization in the tax framework is the direction chosen by countries that seek to reduce the gap between projected and generated tax revenue as much as possible and to generally improve the work of the tax administration. At the same time, "the ability to raise tax revenue is crucial for the functioning of any state."[1] Issues of structure and the yielding of tax revenue are always under discussion. In this regard, the effectiveness and efficiency of the tax administration are at stake. The COVID-19 pandemic, as an unprecedented global health and economic crisis, brought new challenges for the tax administration in terms of potentially accelerated digitization of work and ensuring the highest possible degree of tax compliance in a situation that, due to its characteristics, presents an additional risk for tax fraud. But one expectation from the tax administration remained unchanged. It is about securing tax revenue,[2] because "tax collection has been the main source (90%) of revenue for states all over the world".[3]

From the perspective of developing countries, where the tax gap is pronounced, in addition to the impact on tax revenue due to the economic lockdown in the COVID-19 pandemic, the revenue side of the tax is often affected by factors such as the informal labour market, small businesses, and limited banking systems.[4]

[1] Basri et al. (2021).

[2] IMF. Fiscal Affairs. Challenges in Forecasting Tax Revenue—Special Series on Fiscal Policies to Respond to COVID-19.

[3] Fragoso (2020), p. 10.

[4] Ibid.

Given these challenges, improving the tax revenue side can be done by "increasing tax rates, reducing tax breaks, expanding the tax base, improving enforcement, and levying new taxes."[5] One view is that raising tax rates alone to increase revenue will be ineffective unless governments first invest in improving administrative tax capacity.[6] However, on the one hand, raising tax rates is not an option in pandemic circumstances where taxpayers lack resources and need tax breaks. On the other hand, other measures such as expending the tax base, reducing tax breaks, or levying new taxes fall within the domain of conceptual changes in tax policy, for which it is necessary to conduct a regulatory impact assessment. In that context, and understanding the pandemic as an accelerator, the process of digitalization of the work of the tax administration was an inevitable and logical move for the tax administration. Overall, the digitalization process can improve the work of the tax administration and reduce the gap between projected and collected tax revenue—the tax gap.

This significant change that digitalization can bring in the field of tax revenue growth and securing better tax compliance was a motivating factor in writing the chapter. This chapter consists of a theoretical framework of the economic analysis of the digitalization of the tax administration with a comparative analysis of the situation and perspectives of digitalization of the tax administrations from 32 member administrations based on the research of the Organization for Economic Cooperation and Development published in 2021 with special reference to the impact of the COVID-19 pandemic. In the example of Bosnia and Herzegovina (BiH), as a developing country committed to EU membership, empirical research and desk analysis seek to answer the fundamental research question of whether the COVID-19 pandemic accelerated the process of digitalization of tax administration in a country with deep-rooted bureaucracy in which the stage of digitalization is generally low.

2 Economic Analysis of Digitalization of Tax Administration

Digitalization of tax administration is a complex and dynamic process, which, due to its importance, should minimize the chance of errors while emphasizing system security. At the same time, the digitalization of the tax administration implies better compliance, lower costs, and increased efficiency. Although the focus can often be on tax policy makers, the burden of implementation in practice is on the tax administration. In order to examine the cause-and-effect relationship between an adequate tax system framework and its implementation, it is important to identify current opportunities and the (under) capacity of the tax administration.

In addition to current efforts to adequately integrate the digital economy into tax flows, the COVID-19 pandemic has prioritized the issue of digitalization of tax administration. In response to the serious decline in economic activity caused by the

---

[5] TPC (2020).

[6] Besley and Persson (2014).

COVID-19 pandemic, economic policy makers used tax policy as an instrument of necessary stabilization of the economy and amortization of the negative consequences of the crisis on business activities and tax compliance. The assessment of the success of tax measures depends on several factors and determinants, and one of the key factors is the effectiveness of work and the readiness of the tax administration to adapt to pandemic conditions to avoid additional procedural obstacles for taxpayers. Digital agility of the tax administration in the current circumstances is important, on the one hand, for meeting the requirements of commodity in the administrative-political principle of fulfilling tax obligations and, on the other hand, for adapting the administration to the conditions of the digital economy for its fair participation in financing public expenditures.

At the beginning of the COVID-19 crisis, maintaining the continuity of the tax administration and the effective implementation of tax measures was crucial to preserving the integrity of the tax system. At the same time, pandemic circumstances have shaken earlier digital resilience and indicated that digitization of the work of the tax administration enables a significant increase in efficiency, transparency, as well as a redirection of work from simple data processing of taxpayers to digital data processing and proactive improvement of compliance, policies, and efficiency, thus formalizing the era of automation using algorithms. Digitalization in the tax framework is a direction, which, thanks to the unlimited possibilities of technology, opens new possibilities such as blockchain technology and ensuring better VAT compliance. Some countries have been quick to adopt new technologies and others, including the United Kingdom and the United States, have been more cautious.[7]

What are the benefits of the digitalization of the tax administration?

> Digital technology in tax administration not only offers lower transaction costs, but also allows innovation in tax policy.[8]

As Bas Jacobs pointed out, digitalization can help alleviate information constraints in two ways[9]:

1. Digitalization can help relax information constraints through better ways to verify the true economic outcomes of taxpayers.
2. Digitalization can allow governments to implement a more sophisticated tax system.

Following the aforementioned benefits and opportunities for tax system innovation, the evolution of the digital roadmap has enabled the use of sophisticated technologies. Such an example is the potential use of blockchain technology in diverse tax areas. Namely, blockchain technology is becoming recognized as a tool to ensure a greater degree of transparency in the harmonization of taxpayers with tax obligations. The possibility of blockchain technology is reflected in the real-time reporting

---

[7] Chen et al. (2017), p. 139.

[8] Ibid., p. 114.

[9] Bas (2017), p. 26.

system and in the authenticity of the recorded data.[10] These benefits would allow tax administrations to collect real-time tax revenue, eliminating the need for intermediaries, such as companies, in the collection of VAT revenue and for the notification of the VAT transactions. Speaking in the context of better VAT compliance, existing systems in which companies are intermediaries are prone to human error and are time-consuming.[11] Summarizing the use of blockchain technology, for example, in the VAT field, an authorized private blockchain would be created, in which only the relevant tax administrations "could access information on all the transactions that trigger the payment of VAT."[12] One of the start-up projects that are underway and seeks to use blockchain technology to combat VAT fraud is the Netherlands-based startup Summitto. Real-time reporting software has been created that allows companies to register their invoices and declare VAT, and the confidentiality of information is guaranteed. So, speaking in medias res, digitalization can enable better tax enforcement and more efficient tax systems. Tax compliance is one of the segments that stand out in the digitalization process. Namely, Bas Jacobs indicates in his paper that digitalization holds the promise of improving the tax enforcement technology of the government.[13] He views the possibilities of digitalization in the context of compliance risk in the field of direct and indirect taxes. He also identifies eight proposals to improve the equity efficiency trade-off by designing more efficient tax systems—more efficient in the sense that distributional objectives can be achieved with lower tax rates and thus lower efficiency costs.[14]

The digitalization of the work of the tax administration, on the one hand, has clear economic benefits. However, on the other hand, these economic benefits should be weighed in relation to "horizontal equity, privacy concerns and avoiding abuse of state powers".[15] In addition to the above risks, another perspective that must be considered is that the digitalized tax system should not provide additional incentives or motivation to cheat.[16] An example from the Netherlands points to the risks of using an algorithm and emphasizes the importance of using the right safeguards in an automated system. Namely, the Dutch tax authority had used a self-learning algorithm to spot suspected benefits fraud.[17] The system was launched in 2013 with the aim of eliminating fraud in benefits at an early stage. Based on audit reports, the focus of the tax administration was found to be on people with "non-Western appearance", while having "Turkish or Moroccan nationality was a particular focus."[18] Dual nationality and low income were high-risk indicators, and citizens had no way to find out if they

[10] Collosa (2021).

[11] Ibid.

[12] Ibid.

[13] Ibid.

[14] Bas (2017), p. 51.

[15] Ibid.

[16] Ibid., p. 9.

[17] Available at https://www.politico.eu/article/dutch-scandal-serves-as-a-warning-for-europe-over-risks-of-using-algorithms/ (last access 09 September 2022).

[18] Ibid.

were on the list or to defend themselves. A huge damage was done for which the Dutch privacy agency fined the tax administration "€2.75 million in December 2021 for the unlawful, discriminatory, and therefore improper manner in which the tax authority processed data on the dual nationality of childcare benefit applicants".[19] In addition to the specified penalty, an additional penalty from the country's privacy regulator for the tax administration is possible for several violations of the GDPR. Also, in February 2020, the District Court of The Hague ruled that the use of the System Risk Indication Algorithm, a legal instrument used to detect fraud in areas such as benefits, allowances, and taxes, was inconsistent with Article 8 of the ECHR.[20] The Court stated that the Netherlands has an obligation, in accordance with Article 8, to strike a balance between the right to respect for private life and the benefits of using new technologies to prevent and combat fraud.[21]

Is improving tax administration more effective than raising tax rates?

A study conducted in Indonesia on the example of corporate income tax aimed to determine whether improving tax administration is more effective than raising tax rates. Authors of the study have shown that "developing country governments can increase tax revenue through both enhanced administration and increases in tax rates. But they also imply, at least in the case of medium-sized firms, that improving administration can have a particularly dramatic effect in increasing revenue."[22]

What advantage do developing countries have in the rapidly evolving digital agenda of tax administrations, especially in the use of prosperous blockchain technology? Well, they are in a "pole position as they can build from scratch without hindrance from legacy systems".[23] Of course, because of the cost of developing new technologies, already developed technologies are more feasable for developing countries. However, to take full advantage, the vision and determination of the holders of economic and political powers are necessary.

The economies of developing countries, such as BiH, rely on deep-rooted bureaucratic systems and fight hard for public trust while trying to solve the problem of collecting enough tax revenue for the basic functions of the state. The problems of the gray economy and the non-compliance of taxpayers with tax obligations are often discussed in public discourse. These problems of developing countries are further complicated by the circumstances caused by the COVID-19 pandemic. On the one hand, there are pressures to secure yield tax revenue, and on the other hand, digitalization processes have begun in the sluggish general administration, which is facing a lack of funds and trained staff. In such circumstances, the risks posed by digitalization such as security, privacy and state abuse of power may come to the fore.

---

[19] Ibid.

[20] Available at https://www.loc.gov/item/global-legal-monitor/2020-03-13/netherlands-court-prohibits-governments-use-of-ai-software-to-detect-welfare-fraud/ (last access 09 September 2022).

[21] Ibid.

[22] Basri et al. (2021).

[23] Jurgen (2018).

In the following chapters, I will present and analyze how the COVID-19 pandemic affected the digitalization process of the tax administration to determine whether the pandemic can be considered an accelerator of the digitalization process.

3 COVID-19 as an Accelerator of the Digitalization Process

In the recent past, several steps have been taken to find an adequate response to the challenges of fast-growing digitalization. In this context, it is important to highlight the work of the Organization for Economic Cooperation and Development (hereinafter: OECD), which has approached the development of a number of strategic documents, thus making the digital economy one of the main objectives of the OECD. OECD documents present proposed solutions at the international level that have been the subject of positive and negative criticism and whose applications have deviated to a greater or lesser extent. Following the topic of the chapter, I will analyze one of the most recent OECD reports on the digitalization of tax administrations. The work of tax administrations in the COVID-19 environment influenced the usual course of the process in all areas, including difficulties in dealing with paper-based communications and forms, physical audits, taxpayer contacts and some aspects of systems maintenance.[24] The OECD report "Tax Administration: Digital Resilience in the COVID-19 Environment",[25] which included 32 member administrations[26] in a digital resilience survey, pointed out that:

- from the outset, it became clear that the digitalization of tax administrations could significantly help in dealing with the crisis
- at the same time, the move to a remote working environment and the development of new digital services was a challenging one and did not come without risks
- tax administrations have effectively addressed the challenges and often at a very quick pace
- experiences during the crisis have influenced tax administrations' future strategies and ways of engaging with taxpayers.

The report, among other things, provides an overview of the role of the digitalization of tax administrations in dealing with the COVID-19 crisis and looks at five different areas: taxpayer services; compliance risk management; remote working; IT systems; and support for the wider government.

When it comes to taxpayer services, and some of the key things highlighted in the digitization research, selected tax administration interactions with taxpayers have

[24] OECD (2021) Digital Resilience in the COVID-19 Environment.

[25] Ibid.

[26] Argentina, Australia, Austria, Belgium, Brazil, Canada, Chile, Denmark, France, Germany, Greece, Hong Kong (China), Hungary, Indonesia, Ireland, Israel, Japan, Latvia, Lithuania, Malaysia, Mexico, New Zealand, Poland, Portugal, Romania, Russia, the Slovak Republic, South Africa, Spain, Sweden, Switzerland, and the United States.

shown that there are still a large number of taxpayers who continue to use non-digital communication and service offerings, such as paper-based inquiries or in-person visits, where communication has been much more difficult during the crisis.[27] This is despite the fact that a large number of tax administrations in recent years have expanded their digital communication channels and service offerings. Paper-based communication has caused difficulties in the COVID-19 environment for 60% of administrations. As pointed out in the research, close to half of the administrations estimated that they shifted 75% or more percentage of communications from paper to digital. The change in the manner of communication between the administration and the taxpayer required the following changes to be made: legislation changes, rule changes to accept e-signature, rule changes to accept scanned documents and other changes to the administrative rules. Also, in-person meetings of taxpayers and tax administrations have been replaced with virtual meetings using digital service channels.

In the domain of compliance risk, COVID-19 circumstances are very likely to have led to a higher risk for tax evasion and fraud. Therefore, it was necessary to adapt to the new situation using digital tools. Although a notable part of compliance activity has been shifted to non-human interventions, a significant number of tax officials are still involved in the processes.[28] When it comes to field audits, the use of digital tools such as electronic access to documents and remote interviews were evaluated positively in the COVID-19 environment, which indicates the possibility of their further use. Also, close to 60% of the administrations expanded the application of innovative technology such as by using data science/analytics techniques, artificial intelligence, robotic process automation, and digital identification technologies to help ensure compliance and identify tax evasion/fraud. As noted earlier, positive experiences in using digital tools and innovative technology have been important in the field of compliance risk and encourage further use.

Speaking about remote work, the possibilities for the transition to remote work were different. In the first place, remote work requires the readiness of the administration for such a way of working, and then technical and personnel preconditions for remote work. As pointed out, not every administration was prepared for this sudden move, and some had trouble providing staff with the necessary IT equipment or remote access to the internal IT environment.[29] Certain functions could not be carried out remotely at the beginning of the crisis, but this does not necessarily mean that the administrations were not operational.[30] However, despite their best efforts, around 80% of administrations reported that certain functions could not be carried out remotely.[31] In order to make remote work possible, IT support was necessary,

[27] OECD (2021) Digital Resilience in the COVID-19 Environment.

[28] Ibid.

[29] Ibid.

[30] Ibid.

[31] Ibid.

and it was determined that while IT maintenance and support was not an issue at the beginning of the crisis, it has become one due to the prolongation of the crisis.[32]

In the domain of IT systems, the role of IT support has taken on extremely important dimensions, and at the same time the responsibility for enabling uninterrupted work and functioning. Such a scope of responsibility stems from the fact that "any failure in those systems may have far-reaching consequences (such as reputation damage, increased tax compliance risks, and taxpayer distrust) particularly when they cannot be fixed within short timeframes."[33]

- About one-third of administrations experienced outages related to internal IT systems, i.e., systems used by an administration for its business operations and internal communication,
- One-quarter of administrations experienced outages related to external IT, i.e., systems which are used by taxpayers and other stakeholders to receive services or to engage with the administration.

Consequently, greater investment in IT infrastructure is needed to reduce the risk of similar or/and the same disruptions.

The last domain of OECD research relates to support for the wider government. Namely, the tax administrations, despite all their own challenges, were given additional competencies in the provision of wider government support, such as support to other government agencies in providing financial assistance and providing information to other government agencies. With additional responsibilities, the tax administration faced the problem of a lack of additional resources, both financial and human, which consequently meant a reorganization within the available capacities. Overall, this led to additional pressure on human resources and the need for accompanying amendments to the framework to enable these processes.

Based on the presented, it is possible to conclude that:

- the COVID-19 pandemic certainly accelerated digitalization and forced the tax administration to adapt quickly to the new circumstances of work and functioning
- in the context of the COVID-19 pandemic, the interaction between taxpayers, and the tax administration has largely gone from non-digital to digital
- in the domain of compliance risk, the use of digital tools was evaluated positively in the COVID-19 environment, which indicates the possibility of their further use
- greater investment in IT infrastructure is needed to reduce the risk of the interruption of the functioning of the IT system
- overall, the need for additional financial and human resources is obvious.

[32] Ibid.

[33] Ibid.

4 Tax Administration in Bosnia and Herzegovina

The way of organizing the tax administration in BiH reflects the complex organization and division of competencies in the field of taxation. The competence for collecting indirect taxes has been transferred to the state level by an agreed transfer of competencies between the entities, i.e., the Indirect Taxation Authority has been established. The entities, RS and FBiH, and BD BiH have jurisdiction over direct taxes. At the entity level, the FBiH Tax Administration and the RS Tax Administration operate. At the level of BD BiH, within the Directorate for Finance, the Tax Administration operates.[34] When it comes to the organizational scheme, the Tax Administration of the Federation of BiH is organized at two levels, at the level of the Central Office based in Sarajevo and at the level of ten (10) cantonal tax offices with associated tax offices (73 offices).[35] On the other hand, the Tax Administration of Republika Srpska is organized into Headquarters, Regional Centers, Regional Units, and Temporary Offices. Specifically, this means 7 regional centers, 48 regional units, and 9 temporary offices[36] (Fig. 1).

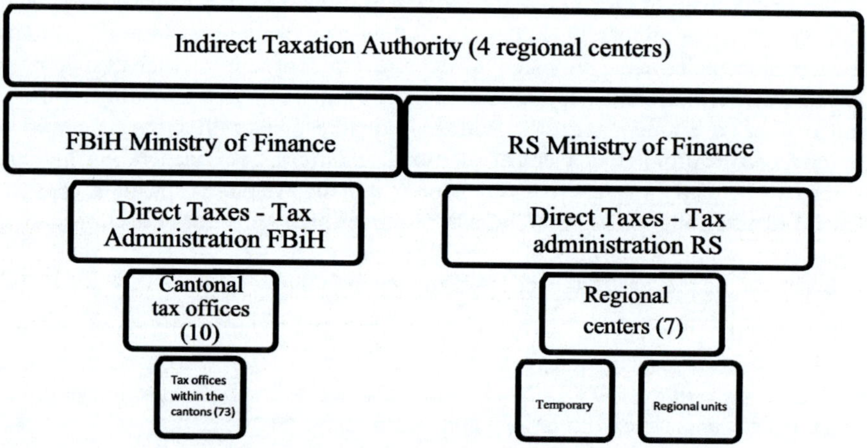

Fig. 1 Organizational chart of the tax administration in BiH

In the rest of the chapter, based on the desk analysis, the work of the entity tax administrations in pandemic circumstances will be presented with a brief overview of the general stage of digitalization in BiH and its development during the pandemic. The focus will be on the degree of digitalization of the Indirect Taxation Authority in the field of indirect taxation based on desk analysis and empirical research.

34 Bearing in mind the previous research in this area, as well as the possibilities of research in terms of available data, the focus of further analysis is on the entities.

35 Available at http://www.pufbih.ba/v1/stranica/12 (last access 09 September 2022).

36 Available at https://poreskaupravars.org/opste/organizaciona-struktura/ (last access 09 September 2022).

4.1 The Scope of Digital Transformation in BiH

Prior to the COVID-19 pandemic, the inevitable digitalization of private and public sectors towards digital business models began. "Governments around the world had been making digital advances, although at an uneven pace."[37] Surely the pandemic has significantly affected the digital transformation and rapidly introduced private and public companies in the digital age. The previously initiated transformation of tax administrations into digital business models for greater efficiency, affordability, and lower costs has become a conditio sine qua non in this time of pandemic. Customer expectations for digital and mobile experiences are pushing governments to embrace the digital transformation as fully as their constituents and commercial enterprises have.[38]

When it comes to BiH, the COVID-19 pandemic has slowed down and hampered the work of entrepreneurs across the country and pointed to the need for the rapid digital transformation of the domestic industry, which has lagged world markets for years.[39] The domestic economy is still failing to leverage new technologies and innovations to strengthen competitiveness, create new products, and open new markets.[40] The Association for Digital Transformation in BiH has published a Study on the Digital Transformation of Companies in BiH for 2021, in which the level of digital transformation in BiH was assessed as low to moderate, stating that BiH has great room for progress in terms of technology and digitalization.[41] The situation is no different in the field of e-government. In fact, there is an inevitable correlation. The degree of digitalization of the public administration determines the way companies operate.[42] The financing of reform activities in the e-government is done mainly through donor funds, without allocating budget funds for that purpose.[43] The dynamics of digitalization following strategic plans are not monitored in practice, so the realization of certain goals in the previous Revised Action Plan began only in 2018 when the plan expired.[44] "According to the latest reports prepared for the Revised Action Plan in the field of eGovernment, about 60% of activities have been implemented. This mainly refers to the introduction of IT in internal processes

[37] Sullivan et al. (2021).

[38] Ibid.

[39] Available at https://www.digitalnaekonomija.ba/bs-Latn-BA/articles/2/pandemija-ukazala-na-potrebu-brze-digitalne-transformacije-preduzeca-u-bih (last access 09 September 2022).

[40] Ibid.

[41] The Association for Digital Transformation in BiH (2021) Study on the Digital Transformation of Companies in BiH for 2021 pp. 87–95, available at https://www.udt.ba/wp-content/uploads/2021/11/Studija_final.pdf (last access 09 September 2022).

[42] Public Administration Reform Coordinator's Office (2022) https://parco.gov.ba/2022/04/12/digitalizacija-u-bih-na-niskom-nivou-i-u-privatnom-i-javnom-sektoru/ (last access 09 September 2022).

[43] Ibid.

[44] Ibid.

in public administration (use of mail communication, limited introduction of DMS systems, systems such as eSessions, etc.)."[45]

4.1.1 A Brief Overview of BiH's Development During the Pandemic

In the draft report of the Directorate for Economic Planning on the development of BiH,[46] in 2020, macro stability in BiH was not considered significantly endangered. Data from the BH Statistics Agency show that the pandemic negatively affected the movement of gross domestic product, especially in the second and third quarters of 2020, and the overall decline in GDP in 2020 amounted to 3.2%. According to available data from the Agency for Statistics of BiH, in 2020, there was a decline in economic activity of 3.2% compared to 2019. BiH's public indebtedness indicator (as a share of GDP) has increased from 31% in 2019 to 35% in 2020. What is important is that it remains within the Maastricht criterion that ranks BiH among moderately indebted countries. The fiscal goal of BiH is to strengthen fiscal stability and its sustainability as a major factor in overall macroeconomic stability, along with strengthening economic activity and economic competitiveness.

4.2 *Desk Analysis of the Digital Services of Entity Tax Administrations During the Pandemic*

Based on the desk analysis of the tax administrations at the entity level, both administrations have introduced the possibility of providing electronic services for taxpayers. In accordance with the Report on the work of the Tax Administration of the FBiH for 2020,[47] the following was done in the field of digitalization:

- access of taxpayers to bookkeeping cards on the tax administration server
- implementation of a web service for reviewing paid contributions by employers, insured for the needs of extra-budgetary funds
- adaptation of the information system of the tax administration for the application of a new way of collecting and processing data from fiscal devices, enabling the receipt, processing, and review of individual fiscal invoices
- electronic submission of income tax return, tax balance, withholding return and supporting documents
- improving the filing of the annual income tax return for all taxpayers who earned income from only one source, was achieved by automatically filling in the annual income tax return.

---

45 Ibid.

46 DEP (2021) Report on the development of BiH for 2020 (proposal).

47 Presentation of the Report on the work of the FBiH Tax Administration for 2020, available at http://pufbih.ba/v1/public/upload/files/PRESS%20%20konferencija%202020%20%20prezentovano.pdf (last access 09 September 2022).

- sending text messages to taxpayers and external users within the nPIS application.

Comparing the report of the tax administration from 2020 and 2021, the Report from 2021[48] recorded a new electronic possibility, namely the electronic submission of applications for all taxpayers who have not yet submitted applications electronically.

When it comes to material resources, based on the Report on Financial Audit of the FBiH Tax Administration,[49] the FBiH Budget for 2020 approved funds in the amount of 50,746,819 BAM to the FBiH Tax Administration, and the Amendments to the FBiH Budget for 2020 approved funds at 47,882,082 BAM (decrease by 2,864,737 BAM). The structure of expenditures consists of salaries, contributions, and compensation of employees (78.45%), expenditures for materials, small inventory, and services (10.67%), expenditures for the purchase of fixed assets (1.80%), employer's contributions and other contributions (7.24%) and other current expenditures (1.84%). In expenditures for the purchase of fixed assets, the most significant amount relates to the purchase of computer equipment (155,254 BAM), electronic equipment (155,014 BAM), licenses and software (413,222 BAM).[50] The resources for IT infrastructure, according to the report, are modest.

The report on the work of the RS Tax Administration[51] states the improvement of communication with taxpayers by introducing new electronic services, which enable communication without direct contact, i.e., information without the taxpayer coming to the premises of the Tax Administration. Also, electronic submission of all tax returns is enabled, and from December 2019, taxpayers can electronically submit applications for the issuance of certificates, tax refunds, rebooking, and other types of applications. As of January 1, 2017, all payers of income, i.e., payers of contributions, are obliged to submit monthly withholding tax returns exclusively in electronic form, signed with an electronic signature. The importance of these changes has been confirmed in pandemic circumstances, especially concerning the area of electronic filing of tax returns and registration of applications. In 2020, taxpayers were continuously invited to use electronic services as much as possible in the working conditions caused by the COVID-19 pandemic. Although the report does not contain a specific chapter on improving the IT administration system, the importance of electronic services is mentioned in several places in the report. Therefore, the tax administration in the field of collection of tax revenue stated that the tax revenue collected

---

48 Presentation of the Report on the work of the FBiH Tax Administration for 2021, available at http://pufbih.ba/v1/public/upload/files/Prezentacija%20rada%20PU%20FBiH%20za%202021%20god%2001_11_%202022_(1).pdf (last access 09 September 2022).

49 Report on Financial Audit of the FBiH Tax Administration for 2020, available at https://www.vrifbih.ba/wp-content/uploads/2021/08/FR_2020_PUFBiH_Izvjestaj_Konacan_09082021.pdf (last access 09 September 2022).

50 Ibid.

51 Report on the work of the RS Tax Administration for 2020, available at https://poreskaupravars.org/wp-content/uploads/2021/08/Izvjestaj-o-radu-Poreske-uprave-za-2020.pdf (last access 09 September 2022).

was sufficient, having in mind the pandemic circumstances, at the same time emphasizing that this trend in the collection was certainly influenced by the improvement of electronic services to taxpayers.

In accordance with the Report on Financial Audit of the RS Tax Administration for 2020,[52] total expenditures and expenses are stated in the amount of 35,742,719 BAM, within fund 01 (32,692,344 BAM) and fund 02 (3,050,375 BAM). Within fund 01, the item expenditures for professional services includes computer program maintenance services (5,400 BAM), computer and office maintenance services (75,287 BAM), and license maintenance costs (932,140 BAM). On the other hand, within fund 02, the item expenditures for professional services includes, among other things, maintenance of licenses (495,079 BAM) and computer services (23,400 BAM). Also, expenditures for the purchase of computer equipment were incurred from both funds (01 – 428.599 BAM and 02 – 239.952 BAM) and expenditures for the purchase of computer programs (317,259 BAM) and licenses (195,336 BAM) from fund 02. The value of the property was increased, among other things, with the purchase of computer equipment in the amount of 668.551 BAM. According to the report from 2019,[53] the value of the property was increased by computer equipment in the amount of 726.212 BAM. Therefore, in 2019, a larger investment in computer equipment was recorded. However, in both analyzed years, more significant investments were recorded.

According to the available reports on the work of the entity tax administrations, I conclude that maintaining the integrity of the tax system was a priority. The focus is on presenting digital services to taxpayers, with no record of the use of digitalization benefits such as better tax compliance, creating innovative tax policies etc. The possibilities of electronic communication between taxpayers and the tax administration have been introduced and expanded, i.e., that paper-based communication is changing with electronic services. The mentioned change in the way of working with taxpayers has significantly facilitated work in pandemic conditions, and at the same time brought the use of electronic services closer to taxpayers. Also, the tendency of the administration to introduce greater process automation wherever possible is evident. It is necessary to provide more sufficient funds to meet IT infrastructure needs, but problems with sufficient funds are also characteristic of other countries, as highlighted in the results of the OECD research. However, based on this desk analysis, bringing this level of digitization of work into the context of OECD research results means that the dynamics of digitalization are slower.

---

[52] Report on Financial Audit of the RS Tax Administration for 2020, p. 14, available at https://www.gsr-rs.org/static/uploads/report_attachments/2021/04/15/RI022-21_Lat.pdf (last access 09 September 2022).

[53] Report on Financial Audit of the RS Tax Administration for 2019, p. 21, available at https://www.gsr-rs.org/static/uploads/report_attachments/2020/04/24/RI003-20_Lat.pdf (last access 09 September 2022).

4.3 Work of the Indirect Taxation Authority in Pandemic Circumstances and the Challenges of Digital Transformation

4.3.1 A Summary of the Most Important Digital Services Before the Pandemic

The pre-pandemic beginnings of digital transformation for the Indirect Taxation Authority date back to 2017, i.e., to December 1, 2017, when the adopted amendments to the rulebook enabled taxpayers to electronically submit applications for value added tax and excise applications, starting from the tax period January 2018. Thus, the Indirect Taxation Authority introduced e-VAT. Taxpayers in this system primarily have access to their data kept in the Unified Register of Indirect Taxpayers as well as to data from the tax card, which allows them to see their registered tax returns, tax payments and the like.[54] Taxpayers are left with the option of using the e-VAT service. As pointed out, taxpayers for whom registration is not performed ex officio have the possibility of electronic registration through the Indirect Taxation Authority portal.[55] However, the process of registering new indirect taxpayers has not been digitized. Namely, the Rulebook on Registration and Entry in the Unified Register of Indirect Taxpayers establishes the forms that are required for registration and these forms are not intended for electronic completion. Also, the submission of customs declarations was digitized before the pandemic. Furthermore, preconditions have been created for the New Computerized Transit System-NCTS, which is a trans-European customs information system, which enables the exchange of data between customs authorities and economic operators through an electronic data exchange system.[56] Therefore, some progress has been made with plenty of room for improvement.

4.3.2 Report on the Work of the Indirect Taxation Authority in 2020 and 2021

As stated in the annual report, the problems caused by the COVID-19 pandemic in economic, trade, and service activities in BiH also had a negative effect on the area of indirect taxes. In such circumstances, the priority of the Indirect taxation authority functioning was to protect people's health, which required organizing a special way of working for employees while ensuring the regular conduct of all authority business processes.

---

[54] Available at: http://www.new.uino.gov.ba/bs/e–PDV (last access 09 September 2022).

[55] Ibid.

[56] NCTS. Available at: http://www.new.uino.gov.ba/bs/NCTS (last access 09 September 2022).

The annual report from 2020,[57] among other things, identified the challenges of working in a COVID-19 environment. The Indirect Taxation Authority has determined the following:

- all necessary business processes were adjusted to the new situation. In this regard, the employees of the Information Technology Sector continuously provided technical support in the organization of numerous seminars, workshops, and training for employees of the Management Board, which were held online via video links and applications such as Microsoft Teams, Cisco WebEx, Zoom, and the like;
- in the field of information technology during 2020, the planned activities in the public procurement procedure related to the provision of license renewal and maintenance services for software for the needs of the Indirect Taxation Authority have been completed;
- representatives of the IT Sector actively participated in the work of the Commission for drafting the Rulebook on issuing qualified digital signatures.

The Indirect Taxation Authority, in the context of digitalization of the functioning of the Administration, pointed out the following problems:

- insufficient financial resources for conducting professional education of employees and taxpayers of indirect taxes;
- IT equipment does not have satisfactory performance;
- inadequate equipment of border crossings and customs terminals.
- Completed and ongoing processes when it comes to the digitization of work are:
- in the reporting period, the ITA successfully completed the process of obtaining ISO certification: ISO 9001:2015 (Quality Management System), ISO 20000-1: 2018 (IT services management system), ISO 22301:2019 (Business Continuity Management System) and ISO 27001:2013 (Information Security Management System);
- all activities related to the project "Data exchange of four tax administrations" (Sarajevo, Tuzla, Mostar, Banja Luka) funded by the EU Delegation were implemented, so that the equipment was installed in accordance with the purpose and plans of the IT Sector;
- implementation of the capital project NCTS in BiH, which involves the exchange of data between customs authorities and economic entities through an electronic data exchange system[58];
- from October 1, 2020, a reporting portal for internal users was launched, which enables users to prepare reports related to data from the customs information subsystem;
- an e-customs portal for external users was tested, and the latest version was installed, which was adapted for viewing on various devices. As of October 1, 2020, the external e-customs portal was launched, which currently contains data

[57] Report on the work of the Indirect Taxation Authority for 2020. Available at: http://www.new.uino.gov.ba/bs/Plan%20rada (last access 09 September 2022).

[58] Implementation of the capital project approved by the Decision of the Council of Ministers of BiH, Official Gazette no. 90/13.

on the customs tariff, data on the type of documents required for certain types of goods and informative calculation of duties for selected tariff numbers.

Significant activities from the annual report for 2021 are[59]:

- continued implementation of phase 5 of the capital project NCTS
- activities continued within the project of upgrading the existing telephone exchange to improve the work of the Help Desk and customer support for indirect taxpayers, to start using the Help Desk
- certain changes have been made in the customs information subsystem for 2022
- changes have been made to applications (Risk information database), or application development activities have continued (application on paid administrative fees, Ekonomat etc.)
- after the successful certification, formal and legal conditions were created for the Administration to submit a request and for the Decision of the Ministry of Transport and Communications of BiH to become accredited and registered as a qualified certifier in BiH
- the e-records of the book of incoming and outgoing invoices have been successfully implemented

When it comes to capital expenditures in 2020, based on Report on Financial.

Audit of the Indirect Taxation Authority,[60] the procurement of customs and tax software was mentioned. However, the report stated that it was not an upgrade but maintenance. This consequently means that it is not about capital expenditures. The report cites the results of IT audits, noting that there are certain shortcomings in the areas of, inter alia, staffing, public procurement, Oracle licenses, NCTS systems, new tax software, and telecommunications network.[61]

According to the report of the Indirect Taxation Authority, I can conclude that certain capital projects leading to the digital business model have been started with the simultaneous identification of insufficient human and technical capacities, which are imperative in implementing the digital transformation process.

4.3.3 Results of the Conducted Research on the Degree of Digitalization of the Work of the Indirect Taxation Authority

For the purposes of this chapter, a survey was conducted in the Indirect Taxation Authority with the aim of determining the manner and dimensions of the digitalization process under the work conditions during the COVID-19 pandemic. The qualitative research consisted of 27 questions, of which six were open-ended, and the remaining

[59] Report on the work of the Indirect Taxation Authority for 2021, available at http://www.new.uino.gov.ba/bs/Plan%20rada (last access 09 September 2022).

[60] Report on Financial Audit of the Indirect Taxation Authority for 2020, available at http://www.revizija.gov.ba/Content/OpenAttachment?Id=d2120ba3-087f-4c18-aed9-af7ce0e65649&langTag=bs (last access 09 September 2022).

[61] Ibid, pp. 47–48.

21 were closed-ended questions. The research questions were created based on the report of the Organization for Economic Cooperation and Development (OECD) on the challenges of indirect taxation in the digital economy and the work of the tax administration in the conditions caused by the COVID-19 pandemic. In addition to the research, I conducted a semi-structured interview with representatives of the Indirect Taxation Authority on research-related issues.

In response to the research questions, three departments of the Indirect Taxation Authority participated, namely: Sector for business services, Sector for taxes, and Sector for information technologies.

Digital Transformation Strategy

The analyzed OECD research shows that the pandemic has caused changes in strategic documents on digitalization by changing the scope and dynamics of digitalization. The Indirect Taxation Authority has not adopted a digital transformation strategy. The stated reason is that digital transformation is included in the general strategy of the Indirect Taxation Authority. When asked whether changes have been made regarding the dynamics of digital transformation in working conditions caused by the COVID-19 pandemic, the answer was no. Even though the new circumstances, bearing in mind the comparative dimension, required changes in the dynamics of digitalization and the structure of investments listed in the strategic documents, in the Indirect Taxation Authority, this was not the case.

The Level of Digitalization Before the Pandemic Versus The Current Level of Digitalization

The Indirect Taxation Authority estimated the level of digitalization before the pandemic at 70–80% (Fig. 2). More specifically, this percentage of 70–80% includes the submission of customs and tax returns, internal and external communication, and digitalization of business processes. The assessment of digitalization is extremely high, bearing in mind that some of the underlying processes are not digitized. In accordance with the previous, the process of registration of taxpayers has not been digitized, nor has any form of process automation been introduced, nor has the use of any digital tool in inspections been presented. At the same time, digitization of data has not been done on a large scale. Bearing in mind the circumstances concerning the stated level of digitalization, I consider that it does not completely correspond to the stage of digitalization of the Indirect Taxation Authority.

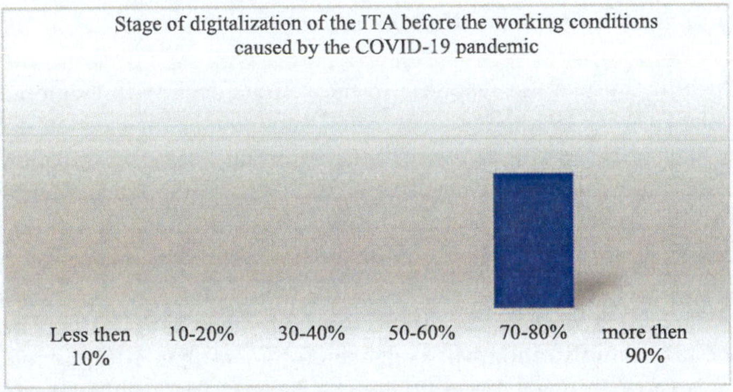

Fig. 2 Stage of digitalization before the COVID-19 pandemic

On the topic of digitalization in working conditions caused by the pandemic, the current level of digitalization of work is estimated at the same high 70–80% (Fig. 3). The above data indicate that the level of digitalization in the pandemic has not increased although the COVID-19 pandemic has generally been confirmed as an accelerator of digital transformation. The stagnation on the same level of digitalization before and during the pandemic is surprising, given that a new form of work has been introduced – remote work. However, the introduced new form of work did not cause data digitization on a large scale due to, as stated by the Indirect Taxation Authority, security, and confidentiality standards. Also, in the circumstances of the pandemic, digital tools were not introduced in the conduct of inspections, nor were any other steps made when it comes to digitization. Therefore, the momentum of the COVID-19 pandemic has not been used as an accelerator for the digitization process in the work of the Indirect Taxation Authority.

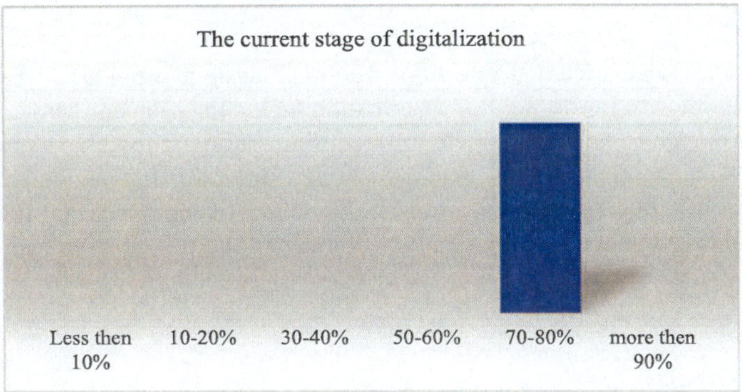

Fig. 3 The current stage of digitalization of the ITA

Continuity of Work in Pandemic Conditions

As previously mentioned, in response to the serious decline in economic activity caused by the COVID-19 pandemic, economic policy makers used tax policy as an instrument of necessary stabilization of the economy and amortization of the negative consequences of the crisis on business activities and tax compliance. Maintaining the continuity of the tax administration and the effective implementation of tax measures were crucial to preserving the integrity of the tax system. In this sense, one of the questions in the research referred to the operational threat to the work of the Indirect Taxation Authority in working conditions caused by the COVID-19 pandemic. The work of the tax administration was endangered by less than 10%, which indicates that there were no significant discontinuities in the work that would negatively affect the integrity of the system and the implementation of measures (Fig. 4).

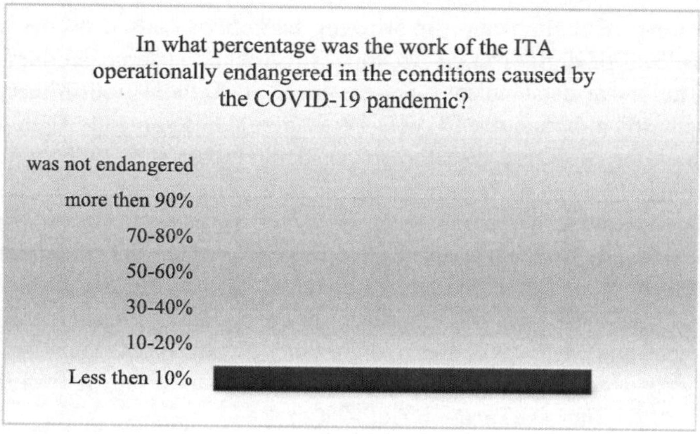

Fig. 4 Operational functionality in pandemic circumstances

The survey also included questions about IT system providers. The Indirect Taxation Authority in the field of information technology depends on an external service provider. Also, in the field of electronic services for taxpayers, the tax administration depends on an external service provider. It was stated that the dependence on the external system did not lead to problems and that the external service provider enabled, without major technical difficulties, uninterrupted work in pandemic circumstances.

Taxpayer Services

The taxpayer services and ways of communication with taxpayers, which can be proactive and reactive under the conditions of work during the pandemic, were a crucial part of the tax system. The Indirect Taxation Authority stated that telephone communication with taxpayers dominated (Fig. 5). The reason why telephone communication dominated may be the overall low level of digitalization of taxpayers who themselves were digitally challenged by the onset of pandemic circumstances. On the other hand, the availability of communication channels may be an additional reason. Namely, on the website of the tax administration for communication with taxpayers, the info email address and info telephone line are displayed without indications of the possibility of using web chat, mobile applications, social media etc. However, according to the tax administration, there is still a large percentage of paper-based communication. Also, the presence of paper-based communication, despite the available digital tools, was recorded to a significant extent in the research of the OECD. In the working conditions caused by the pandemic, paper-based communication was not a simple task. A paper-based communication requires in-person communication, which has been hampered by measures to prevent the spread of the COVID-19 virus.

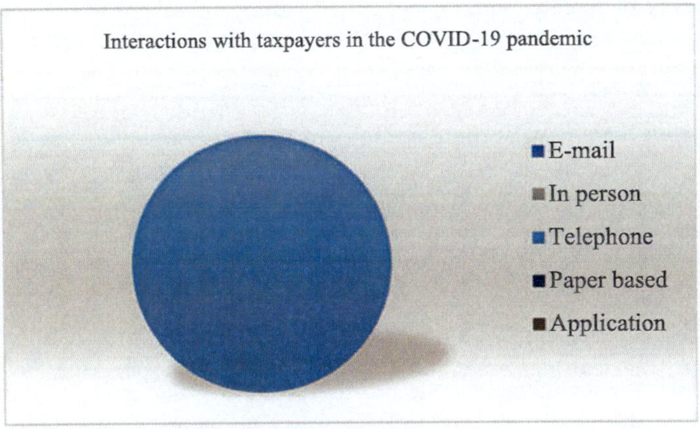

Fig. 5 Dominant form of communication with taxpayers

On a positive note, the tax administration estimated that 70–80% of in-person communication has been replaced by digital communication. Also, it was estimated that the electronic form of communication with the tax authorities was sufficient. Based on this analysis, it remains for the Indirect Taxation Authority to develop other digital forms of communication with taxpayers. At the same time, for the digital form of communication with taxpayers to come to life, it is, on the one hand, necessary to provide legal preconditions that are currently impossible due to the lack of political consensus at the state level. One of the key legal preconditions is an e-signature, whose implementation in BiH has been stagnant for years. On the other hand, greater use of digital communication channels implies the accompanying growth of the degree of digitalization of taxpayers.

Remote Working

For remote work, the key indicator was the readiness of the tax administration and the technical preconditions for such work. Prior to the onset of pandemic circumstances, there was no possibility of remote work in the Indirect Taxation Authority. In the new circumstances, this became a necessity. The tax administration estimated the presence of remote work at 50–60%, which leads to the conclusion that a high percentage of work took place in remote mode. Given that the work of the tax administration was operationally less than 10% compromised and that remote work was introduced at a rate of 50–60%, it can be stated that the tax administration effectively responded to the challenges. However, remote work was difficult in the tax administration. Namely, reasons of a security nature made it difficult to work from home and the related fact that the digitization of data was not performed. When asked about the efficiency of the work of tax officials, the answer was that there were no major oscillations. Therefore, it is not surprising that, after measures to prevent the spread of the COVID-19 virus were lifted, remote work remained no longer an option. Conclusions about the possibility of remote work do not differ significantly from the research of the OECD.

Application of Innovative Technologies

In pandemic circumstances, and in the context of indirect taxes, taxpayer behavior has changed significantly due to the lockdown that followed. Changes in behavior and in the market caused oscillations on the revenue side. At the same time, the situation was changing rapidly, making uncertainty one of the basic characteristics. The analyzed research conducted by the OECD stated that "the risk of tax evasion and fraud during the pandemic is highly likely to have increased. This results from a number of factors, including that: the situation is fast-moving; there is great potential for misinformation or confusion; and there may be reduced controls in place."[62] As an additional form of ensuring taxpayers' compliance with their obligations, tax administrations have introduced digital tools. Although the use of digital tools carries security risks, their use by tax administrations during the pandemic was still positively assessed. However, the Indirect Taxation Authority has not introduced digital tools in the conduct of inspections, nor has it introduced process automation and/or the use of artificial intelligence. The inspection is performed exclusively in-person (Fig. 6). In the field of customs control, during 2021, in the fixed part of the plan, 432 of the planned 600 controls were performed (72%). In the variable part of the plan, 318 controls were performed out of the planned 400 (80%). In the work report,[63] the reason for the impossibility of realizing the planned total number of controls in the fixed part of the plan is cited as the lack of a sufficient

[62] OECD (2021), Digital Resilience in the COVID-19 Environment.

[63] Report on the work of the Indirect Taxation Authority for 2021, p. 14, available at http://www.new.uino.gov.ba/bs/Plan%20rada (last access 09 September 2022).

number of executors, especially in RC Banja Luka (out of the planned nine executors, four performed the work), as well as the consequences of temporary incapacity of employees due to illness. In 2021, the Audit and Control Department realized 9% more controls than the planned number, since 6,649 controls were planned, and 7,262 controls were performed. When it comes to complete controls, 4,672 complete controls were planned, and 5,271 complete controls were performed, which means that the percentage of implementation of complete controls is higher by 13% than the planned number. In the reporting period, 8% more controls were performed compared to the same period in 2020.[64] The Department for the Control of Large Taxpayers is in the period 01.01–31.12.2021. Performed 1,301 controls, which is 7.07% less than the planned number for the reporting period for which a total of 1,400 controls of all types were planned (compared to the annual plan). In the reporting period, 3.42% more controls were realized compared to the same period in 2020. When it comes to complete controls, 630 controls were planned for the reporting period, and 631 complete controls were performed, or 0.16% more than planned and 22.76% more compared to the same period last year, when they were performed. 514 complete controls.[65] Problems in the functioning of organizational control units arose because of prolonged effects of the COVID-19 virus and the average age structure of inspectors (frequent absences due to illness) as well as because of the lack of the required number of employees and limited additional employment to fill the systematized number of employees.[66] These reasons can be understood as a limiting factor in the use of digital tools, especially the age structure of inspectors, but at the same time a motivating and crucial factor in improving inspections through digital tools.

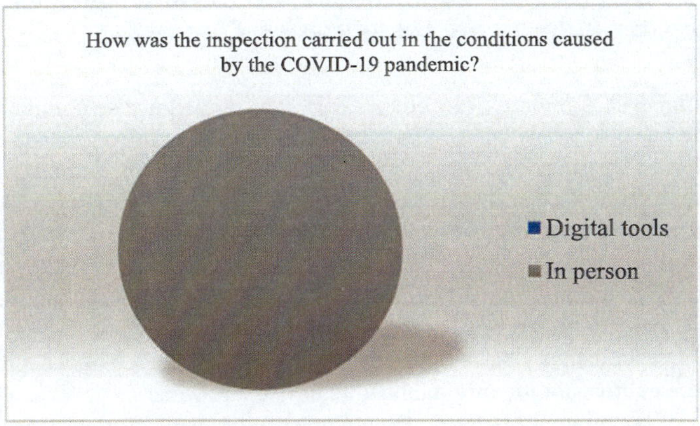

Fig. 6 Inspection and digital tools

---

[64] Ibid.

[65] Ibid.

[66] Ibid.

IT Capacities

The lack of sufficient funds and investment in IT is a remark that was made before and during the pandemic. In the research, the Indirect Taxation Authority pointed out that during the pandemic circumstances, there was no expansion of IT capacity or additional investments. This problem was also pointed out in the work reports along with the problem of a lack of educated staff. In addition to the difficulties in ensuring legal preconditions, the lack of funds for IT infrastructure and trained staff is an additional obstacle in the way of digitalization of the work of the tax administration.

Comparing the results of the research of the OECD and the research results from the Indirect Taxation Authority, I conclude that tax administrations faced similar difficulties despite varying degrees of digitalization. Some of the common difficulties and identified characteristics are:

- the lack of sufficient funds and investment in IT and the lack of educated staff,
- the ability to work from home depended on technical and human preconditions but at the same time on security protocols,
- in the crisis, efforts were made to prevent security breaches that would jeopardize the integrity of the tax system,
- the presence of paper-based communication, despite the available digital tools, was recorded to a significant extent,
- a significant number of tax officials are still involved in audit processes.

4.4 *Can Bosnia and Herzegovina's Fiscal Federalism Be Seen as Sludge in the Digitalization Process?*

The Dayton Peace Agreement establishes BiH as a sovereign state composed of two entities and one district, with the Federation of BiH entity, on the one hand, structured decentrally in a way that it is composed of 10 cantons and 79 municipalities with the existence of a three-tier fiscal system, while on the other hand, the Republika Srpska entity is structured centrally in a way that is composed of 56 municipalities with a two-tier administrative body. In addition to the two entities, the Brčko District of BiH has some autonomy in the field of direct and indirect taxes. When it comes to modeling fiscal federalism in BiH, the BiH Constitution does not provide concrete solutions but establishes a basis for modeling with a high degree of decentralization in which the entities are the original bearers of fiscal powers.[67]

Factors of tax policy in BiH are: the complexity of levels of government, decentralization, weak central government, and the asymmetric structure of entity governments. The transfer of competencies in the field of indirect taxation has strengthened the fiscal capacity at the state level, but it still is not sufficient. The lack of quality macroeconomic governance makes the criticism of the existing model more

---

[67] Keil (2013), p. 168.

pronounced. The transfer of competencies to the state does not mean isolation from the influence of the entities, but on the contrary—the entities have retained a certain type of influence on the indirect taxation policy through their representatives on the Indirect Taxation Authority Board.[68] The regulation of direct taxes, including social contributions, remained under the exclusive competence of the entities. In such a division of competencies, in a relatively small market, unfair tax competition has emerged.

The policy of fiscal equalization is not a fundamental principle of fiscal federalism in BiH, because the distribution of revenue to lower levels is done by the entities on the basis of their own regulations. Therefore, the distribution system takes place on two levels, the vertical distribution of indirect taxes and the distribution of direct taxes directed by the entities. The key coordinating body for fiscal policy is the Fiscal Council, which is not exclusively a financial institution. The work of the Fiscal Council is not isolated from political interests, which jeopardize its coordinating role. The work of the Fiscal Council is suitable for blockades due to the voting mechanism, according to which, for decisions to be legally valid, at least five members of the Fiscal Council and at least one representative of the constituent peoples in BiH must vote for them.[69]

Bearing in mind the previously stated, the parallel digitalization of tax administrations at three organizational levels and sub-organizational levels in a small country such as BiH require significant monetary expenditures, which is ironic given the key trade-off of digitalization.

In order to decide whether fiscal federalism can be perceived as sludge, it is necessary to analyze the previously mentioned factors and determinants of fiscal federalism in correlation with political relations in BiH. The current political blockades of state-level institutions make it impossible to pass legislation that is a conditio sine qua non in the field of digitalization. Some examples are[70]: the Indirect Taxation Authority started the digital transformation in 2014, and in 2021 it was certified to issue a digital signature[71]; the condition for BiH's accession to the European paperless transport system with the use of an electronic transport declaration is a change in legislation – the deadline was June 1, 2021, a new deadline has been set for August 1, 2022. Also, in an interview with the tax administration it was pointed out that the adoption of the Rulebook on the issuance of qualified digital signatures was not done due to blockades at the state level. This constellation of relations leads to slow digitalization, and even determining the state and perspectives of digitalization in the existing legal framework is complex.[72]

---

[68] Ramić (2020), p. 14.

[69] Article 4 of the Law on the Fiscal Council of BiH. Official Gazette no. 63/08.

[70] Available at http://www.new.uino.gov.ba/bs/Search/elektronsk/1/8 (last access 09 September 2022).

[71] Laws defining the use of electronic signatures and electronic documents have been enacted at the level of BiH, but also at the level of the entities and the Brčko District.

[72] The Association for Digital Transformation in BiH (2021), p. 16.

Certainly, BiH is not the only country with a complex tax system, but in the current constellation, fiscal federalism does not make digitalization simple and easy. In BiH, digitalization was supposed to be a factor in the integration and the true creation of a single market. Of course, to achieve this, digitalization needs be on the political agenda as a significant issue.

Bringing the previous elaborate context in connection with digitalization, it is justified to ask the question of the impact of regulation, lack of political consensus, and potential abuse in this domain. Therefore, fiscal federalism in the constellation of political relations does not facilitate the digitalization process but represents an additional obstacle. For the current degree of digitalization of tax administrations, not everything can be attributed to fiscal federalism, but it should also be attributed to the sluggishness and lack of determination of tax administrations on the path of digital transformation, as well as the lack of funds for IT infrastructure and educated staff.

5 Conclusion

The pandemic has introduced us to the accelerated (r)evolution of digital transformation in the private and public sectors. As pointed out in the theoretical framework of this chapter, digital transformation of tax administrations, among other mentioned things, can reduce the asymmetry of information between the tax administration and taxpayers and, in accordance with that, ensure a higher degree of tax compliance. Also, the digitalization of tax administrations can enable a more innovative tax policy.

However, the benefits of the digital transformation and a better tax compliance in the context of BiH have not been exploited. A desk analysis of the entity tax administrations in the circumstances of the pandemic showed that maintaining the integrity of the tax system was a priority. The focus is on presenting digital services to taxpayers. But, bringing this level of digitization of work into the presented comparative perspective means that the dynamics of digitalization are slower.

On the other hand, based on the desk analysis and empirical research, the momentum of the COVID-19 pandemic has not been seized and there was no accelerated degree of digitalization of the Indirect Taxation Authority in BiH, which was the primary focus of this chapter. In other words, during the pandemic, data digitization was not performed, nor was the use of digital tools in the field of inspection and supervision started, nor was process automation/the use of algorithms introduced. In addition to the above and bearing in mind the estimated degree of digitalization before and during the pandemic, I consider that this does not completely correspond to the stage of digitalization of the Indirect Taxation Authority.

Certain capital projects leading to the digital business model have been started before the pandemic with the simultaneous identification of insufficient human and technical capacities. The reason why pandemic circumstances were not used for accelerated digitalization can also be found in the limitations that existed earlier, such as legal preconditions. Furthermore, the lack of sufficient funds and investment in

IT is a remark that was made before and during the pandemic. During the pandemic circumstances, there was no expansion of IT capacity or additional investments. Also, the problem of the lack of educated staff in correlation with the high average age structure of employees, e.g., inspectors, was pointed out. Bearing in mind the comparative dimension, the same needs have been identified and these are: (a) greater investment in IT infrastructure to reduce the risk of interruption of the functioning of the IT system and (b) additional financial and human resources.

Besides the aforementioned factors of slow digitalization, fiscal federalism in the constellation of political relations does not facilitate the digitalization process but represents an additional obstacle. For the current degree of digitalization of tax administrations, not everything can be attributed to fiscal federalism, but also to the sluggishness and lack of determination of tax administrations on the path of digital transformation.

References

Bas J (2017) Digitalization and taxation. In: Gupta S et al (eds) Digital revolutions in public finance. International Monetary Fund, pp 25–57

Basri C, Felix M, Hanna R, Olken B (2021) Tax administration vs. Tax rates: evidence from corporate taxation in Indonesia. Am Econ Rev 111(12)

Besley T, Persson T (2014) Why do developing countries tax so little? J Econ Perspect 28(4)

BiH Directorate for Economic Planning. Report on the development of BiH for 2020 (proposal). http://www.dep.gov.ba/razvojni_dokumenti/izvjestaji/Archive.aspx?langTag=bs-BA&template_id=140&pageIndex=1. Last Accessed 31 Oct 2022

Chen J, Grimshaw S, Myles G (2017) Testing and implementing digital tax administration. In: Gupta S et al (eds) Digital revolutions in public finance. International Monetary Fund, pp 113–145

Collosa A (2021) Can blockchain improve VAT collection? Part 2. CIAT. https://www.ciat.org/ciatblog-blockchain-para-mejorar-la-recaudacion-del-iva-parte-2/?lang=en. Last Accessed 31 Oct 2022

Fragoso T (2020) Tax Harmonisation in the EU intelligent tax administration. dGen 4–45. https://uploads-ssl.webflow.com/601814030e1e39d44b52570b/601814030e1e3960165257d8_Tax-HarmonisationEU.pdf. Last Accessed 31 Oct 2022

Indirect Taxation Authority—e-VAT. http://www.new.uino.gov.ba/bs/e–PDV. Last Accessed 31 Oct 2022

Indirect Taxation Authority—news. http://www.new.uino.gov.ba/bs/Search/elektronsk/1/8. Last Accessed 31 Oct 2022

International Monetary Fund. Fiscal affairs. Challenges in forecasting tax revenue—special series on fiscal policies to respond to COVID-19

Jurgen G (2018) Introducing blockchain technology to the world of tax. Medium. https://medium.com/@jurgeng/an-introduction-to-blockchain-technology-tax-567e536767ec. Last Accessed 31 Oct 2022

Keil S (2013) Multinational federalism in BiH. Ashgate Publishing Limited, Farnham

Netherlands: court prohibits government's use of AI software to detect welfare fraud. https://www.loc.gov/item/global-legal-monitor/2020-03-13/netherlands-court-prohibits-governments-use-of-ai-software-to-detect-welfare-fraud/. Last Accessed 31 Oct 2022

New Computerized Transit System-NCTS. http://www.new.uino.gov.ba/bs/NCTS. Last Accessed 31 Oct 2022

OECD (2021) Digital resilience in the COVID-19 environment. https://www.oecd.org/coronavirus/policy-responses/tax-administration-digital-resilience-in-the-covid-19-environment-2f3cf2fb/#section-d1e809. Last Accessed 31 Oct 2022

Politico Dutch scandal serves as a warning for Europe over risks of using algorithms. https://www.politico.eu/article/dutch-scandal-serves-as-a-warning-for-europe-over-risks-of-using-algorithms/. Last Accessed 31 Oct 2022

Public Administration Reform Coordinator's Office (2022). https://parco.gov.ba/2022/04/12/digitalizacija-u-bih-na-niskom-nivou-i-u-privatnom-i-javnom-sektoru/. Last Accessed 31 Oct 2022

Ramić L (2020) Fiscal federalism between theory and practice in Bosnia and Herzegovina. In: Šarčević E (ed) Bosanskohercegovački federalizam. Foundation Public Law Centre, pp 118–158

Report on Financial Audit of the FBiH Tax Administration for 2020. https://www.vrifbih.ba/wp-content/uploads/2021/08/FR_2020_PUFBiH_Izvjestaj_Konacan_09082021.pdf. Last Accessed 31 Oct 2022

Report on Financial Audit of the Indirect Taxation Authority for 2020. http://www.revizija.gov.ba/Content/OpenAttachment?Id=d2120ba3-087f-4c18-aed9-af7ce0e65649&langTag=bs. Last Accessed 31 Oct 2022

Report on Financial Audit of the RS Tax Administration for 2019. https://www.gsr-rs.org/static/uploads/report_attachments/2020/04/24/RI003-20_Lat.pdf. Last Accessed 31 Oct 2022

Report on Financial Audit of the RS Tax Administration for 2020. https://www.gsr-rs.org/static/uploads/report_attachments/2021/04/15/RI022-21_Lat.pdf. Last Accessed 31 Oct 2022

Report on the work of the FBiH Tax Administration for 2020. http://pufbih.ba/v1/public/upload/files/PRESS%20%20konferencija%202020%20%20prezentovano.pdf. Last Accessed 31 Oct 2022

Report on the work of the FBiH Tax Administration for 2021. http://pufbih.ba/v1/public/upload/files/Prezentacija%20rada%20PU%20FBiH%20za%202021%20god%2001_11_%202022_(1).pdf. Last Accessed 31 Oct 2022

Report on the work of the Indirect Taxation Authority for 2020. http://www.new.uino.gov.ba/bs/Plan%20rada. Last Accessed 31 Oct 2022

Report on the work of the Indirect Taxation Authority for 2021. http://www.new.uino.gov.ba/bs/Plan%20rada. Last Accessed 31 Oct 2022

Report on the work of the RS Tax Administration for 2020. https://poreskaupravars.org/wp-content/uploads/2021/08/Izvjestaj-o-radu-Poreske-uprave-za-2020.pdf. Last Accessed 31 Oct 2022

Sullivan M et al (2021) Accelerated digital government. Deloitte. https://www2.deloitte.com/xe/en/insights/industry/public-sector/government-trends/2021/digital-government-transformation-trends-covid-19.html. Last Accessed 31 Oct 2022

Tax Policy Center (2020) Briefing book. https://www.taxpolicycenter.org/briefing-book/what-options-would-increase-federal-revenues. Last Accessed 31 Oct 2022

The Association for Digital Transformation in BiH (2021) Study on the digital transformation of companies in BiH for 2021. https://www.udt.ba/wp-content/uploads/2021/11/Studija_final.pdf. Last Accessed 31 Oct 2022

The FBiH Tax Administration. http://www.pufbih.ba/v1/stranica/12. Last Accessed 31 Oct 2022

The pandemic pointed to the need for rapid digital transformation of companies in BiH. https://www.digitalnaekonomija.ba/bs-Latn-BA/articles/2/pandemija-ukazala-na-potrebu-brze-digitalne-transformacije-preduzeca-u-bih. Last Accessed 31 Oct 2022

The RS Tax Administration. https://poreskaupravars.org/opste/organizaciona-struktura/. Last Accessed 31 Oct 2022

Lejla Ramić is a Senior Teaching and Research Assistant, Department of Legal and Economic Sciences at the Univeristy of Sarajevo—Faculty of Law, Obala Kulina bana. Her fields of interest include Law and Economics, Tax Law, Digital Economy and Taxation, Economic Analysis of Law, Law of Economic System, Competition Law and Securities Law.

Part IV: Copyright Law

Digitalization: On the Way to a New Copyright Architecture?

Rolf H. Weber

Abstract The digitalization not only impacts the financial markets or the supply chains but also the intellectual property rights framework. Copyright-protected works are suitable to be digitized in the form of a token and then be licensed or transferred on the distributed ledger technology. Such an architecture does have efficiency benefits, but some weaknesses (limited scope of involved persons, enforcement) can also not be overlooked.

Keywords Distributed ledger technology · Law is code · Licensing management · Regulatory technology · Registries · Royalties' management

1 Introduction

The advent of the distributed ledger technology (DLT) has again confronted the legal system with new technological challenges. After Lessig's notion "code is law"[1] received widespread attention, the digitalization now tends to lead to the inverse notion "law is code".[2] If transactional relations with normative contents are expressed in the form of digital assets and smart contracts, DLT (for example, Blockchain) becomes the relevant "regulatory technology" that can be used both to define and to incorporate (traditional) legal or contractual frameworks into code.

Such kind of "regulatory technology" is not only suitable in the field of financial markets and supply chains, but also in the context of intellectual property rights. The DLT platforms can create a transparent and (arguably but in practice not completely) immutable (unchangeable) chain of information. Since the technology provides a

[1] Lessig (1999, p. 3).
[2] Weber (2018, p. 705).

R. H. Weber (✉)
University of Zurich, Zürich, Switzerland
e-mail: rolf.weber@rwi.uzh.ch

K. Mathis and A. Tor (eds.), *Law and Economics of the Digital Transformation*, Economic Analysis of Law in European Legal Scholarship 15,
https://doi.org/10.1007/978-3-031-25059-0_7

history of ownership, the rights holder is prevented (at least in theory) from a third-party claim contesting the ownership. While intellectual property rights are suitable to be registered on a DLT platform, the relevant processes might become more cost-effective and faster as well as more accurate and secure.

Considering these advantages, efforts have been undertaken to make DLT platforms fruitful for the intellectual property rights field; amongst others, the concerned UN body, namely the World Intellectual Property Organization in Geneva, tackled the relevant topics.[3] Concrete legislation, however, has so far not been issued by any country.

As outlined hereinafter, the DLT has the potential to influence the copyright architecture and environment. The code is suitable to assume the function of an instrument that designs normative rights and obligations. Smart contracts add a layer of security that can be used to provide licenses or obtain royalties. In substance, copyright law attempts to introduce "artificial scarcity" by granting exclusive rights in the realm of information by prohibiting (or constraining) the reproduction of creative works without the consent of the corresponding rights holders; the actual enforcement of the exclusive rights can potentially be based on technological means and not on court decisions.[4]

First, this contribution looks at the law and technology intersections from a general perspective; in particular, similar and divergent functions are identified and based thereon, the challenges caused by the use of codes are analysed. Then, the major part of the contribution addresses the crucial elements of a new copyright architecture. Since technology allows to enforce the rules irrespective of an underlying legal provision, the regulatory framework must be adapted to the changed environment. Specific regulatory issues in the copyright context are the establishment of special registries, the implementation of a licensing management, the provision of fair remuneration (royalties' management), and the enforcement measures of copyright. A particular focus is laid on the discussion of the benefits and limits of a new copyright architecture. The contribution concludes with an overall assessment and a look into the crystal ball.

---

[3] See https://www.wipo.int/wipo_magazine_digital/en/2020/article_0002.html (last access 26 July 2022); for a general overview of relevant topics in the context of the patents' and the trademarks' registration that will not be discussed in detail hereinafter see Singh and Tripathi (2019, p. 41 et seqq.); Gürkaynak et al. (2018, p. 855 et seqq.).

[4] See also below Sect. 3.5 and de Filippi and Hassan (2016, p. 8).

2 Law and Technology

2.1 Functional Approaches

From a theoretical perspective, law is a structural system since it contains information issued by the regulator and addressed to the concerned part of society.[5] The substance of law is condensed into normative rules containing information that has a guiding or even coercive effect. Since law expresses behaviour-oriented normative expectations, it can be said that information transported by law is a special type of communication requesting the actual addressees to take note of its substantive contents.[6]

From an L&E perspective, law can also introduce a set of incentives or reward systems for people to act in a desirable way; the stricter form is a system of punishment or sanctions for those who do not behave in a compliant manner.[7] Through either approach, people's motivations are affected, like by a carrot or a stick.[8] The incentive regulation is an important element of the L&E understanding since such an approach can stimulate market competition.[9]

Similarly, as in the case of law, technology has the capacity to influence the behaviour of individuals since it provides a means for people to do things that they would be unable to do otherwise (for example, communicating through a phoneline), but it also dictates the way in which these things could or even must be done.[10] However, technology (in contrast to law) does not leave the individuals with the free discretion to choose the best course of action since it usually relies on rigid rules and technical features.

Already more than 20 years ago, Lawrence Lessig coined the notion "code is law".[11] According to his perception, code will eventually become the "supreme law of cyberspace".[12] The meaning of this notion has been that code would exercise the function of an important regulatory lever used to shape activities (particularly in cyberspace) in ways that often extend beyond the law.[13] In the meantime, however, the new technologies are also able to turn law into code,[14] leading to the notion "law is code" or "law as code".[15]

---

5 For a general overview see Weber (2017a, p. 253 et seqq.).

6 See for example Black (2001, p. 103 et seqq.).

7 See for example Braithwaite (2002, p. 12 et seqq.).

8 de Filippi and Wright (2018, pp. 193–194).

9 See Posner (2014, pp. 472–473) and below Sect. 4.

10 de Filippi and Wright (2018, p. 194).

11 Lessig (1999, p. 3).

12 Lawrence Lessig, The Code Is the Law, *The Industry Standard*, April 9, 1999, http://tech-insider.org/berkman-center/research/1999/0409.html (last access 26 July 2022).

13 For an early analysis see Benkler (2011, pp. 721 et seqq.).

14 de Filippi and Hassan (2016, p. 9).

15 Weber (2018, p. 705).

As a consequence, with DLT and associated smart contracts, legal and contractual provisions can be translated into simple and deterministic code-based tools that will be automatically executed by the underlying infrastructure.[16] Thereby, technical rules could increasingly assume the same role and functionality as legal rules.[17] DLT-based protocols and smart contracts have the potential to model or even to represent laws and, as a consequence, embed them directly into the fabric of a DLT-based network in order to ensure the automatic execution and ex-ante enforcement of such rules.[18]

These developments have become a new discussion topic in academia, mainly conducted under the heading of "lex cryptographica".[19] As the "traditional" concept of regulation by code, lex cryptographica also purports to regulate individuals by introducing a specific set of affordances and constraints embedded directly into the technological system.[20] But lex cryptographica distinguishes itself from code-based regimes insofar as it operates autonomously, i.e. independently of any government or other centralized authority.[21] However, as with code, lex cryptographica is never found by coincidence; it is only ever made on purpose, and only ever made by those who are able to impose such kind of law on the society.[22]

2.2 *Challenges of Code*

The process of transposing laws into code cannot be implemented without any problems. In first instance, not all laws are suitable to be easily translated into code since normative rules are written in natural language, which is, by its very nature, inherently flexible and ambiguous. In contrast, technology follows quite strict infrastructural conditions. In addition, if DLT-based rules evolve to become personalized, fundamental notions of universality, equality, and non-discriminatory treatment are at risk of not being complied with in an appropriate manner.[23]

Partly, legal rules are called "wet code" and technical rules "dry code" due to their different characteristics.[24] In particular, normative provisions generally aim at accounting for a variety of contingencies that are not always foreseeable by the legislature. If legal rules are drafted in a broad and open-ended manner, adaptable for a variety of contexts, the formalization into code eventually is impossible or even distorts the meaning of these rules by making them less flexible and unable to adapt to unforeseen situations.

---

[16] de Filippi and Wright (2018, pp. 194 and 201).

[17] Weber (2018, p. 705).

[18] de Filippi and Wright (2018, p. 196).

[19] de Filippi and Wright (2018 pp. 203 and 207 et seqq.).

[20] See also Benkler (2011, p. 721 et seqq.).

[21] de Filippi and Wright (2018, p. 207); see also Weber (2018, p. 705).

[22] Lessig (2006, p. 6).

[23] See also de Filippi and Wright (2018, pp. 199 and 202).

[24] de Filippi and Hassan (2016, p. 9).

Furthermore, the code or the described "regulatory technology" is often not "neutral".[25] The DLT must be qualified as a technical artefact, which inevitably has both political and social implications. The technology is not equipped to replace the democratic debate necessarily taking place within the legislative branch: "While the legal system implements a series of policies and procedures for society to collectively agree upon the type of rights and obligations that people ought to comply with, technical rules can be unilaterally imposed by software builders and device producers, without following any democratic debate."[26] Therefore, from a socio-cultural perspective, it is important to understand the consequences of having legal provisions drafted or elaborated as code. From a theoretical point of view, laws cannot (and should not) be entirely and exclusively defined through technological processes.[27]

For example, contract law and copyright law encompass a series of legal safeguards, that might either invalidate the contract and make it non-enforceable (i) if certain formalities are not fulfilled (for example, legal capacity, mutual consent, fair use, etc.) or (ii) if public interests are prevailing the individual position of a rights holder (for example, in case of unconscionability, of undue influence, or of coercion). Even if such legal safeguards are not specifically incorporated into the contractual or copyright framework, their application is mandatory by law.[28]

Finally, it is also important to understand the consequences of having legal and contractual provisions being designed or elaborated as code. In the past, legal rules have always been drafted by humans and for humans.[29] Therefore, law must find ways to regulate the code in order to limit its disruptive potential in the hands of irresponsible code designers. Otherwise, law is at risk of losing a part of its democratic legitimacy and its guiding social functions.[30] In other words, the delicate process of transposing legal rules into technical rules has an important and to be factored impact on the legal system as such and on the way how society thinks about law.[31]

3 New Copyright Architecture

Based on these general observations, having assessed the chances and challenges of the new regulatory technology ("code rules") that need to be kept in mind hereinafter, the following question must be addressed in the main part of the contribution: why does it make sense to elaborate on the design of a new copyright architecture? To tackle this question, several arguments should be considered.

---

[25] Weber (2018, p. 705); De Filippi and Hassan (2016, p. 8).

[26] De Filippi and Hassan (2016, p. 10).

[27] Weber (2018, p. 705).

[28] De Filippi and Hassan (2016, p. 10).

[29] Weber (2018, p. 705); de Filippi and Hassan (2016, p. 11).

[30] See Lessig (2006, p. 6).

[31] Weber (2018, p. 706).

In the overall copyright context, different elements of the rights management may be represented by cryptographic measures on a DLT infrastructure. Relying on a specific registry of digitized assets, smart contracts are suitable to automate and standardize copyright-related transactions, for example, by authorizing the use and exploitation of copyright-protected contents.[32] The new technological architectures[33] allow for the implementation of a quite different protection regime as far as organization, use of tokenized values, and remuneration for copyright-protected works are concerned. In practice, a number of applications in the domain of copyright already exist, mainly in the online music sector.[34] In addition, during the last few months, the term "Non-fungible Tokens" (NFT) came into the spotlight; NFTs are created for commercializing pieces of art in a digital way and with easier investment conditions.[35]

3.1 From Digital Rights Management Systems to "Regulatory Technology"

For several years already, content providers have been relying on technical means, for example, digital rights management (DRM) systems to restrain the way in which content can be accessed, used or reused. In particular, a set of technical rules was introduced as a complement to the normative provisions of copyright law.[36] However, the traditional technical measures have often been subject to hacking attacks and, therefore, were not very successful, i.e. reality has shown that it was not easily possible to transpose legal rules into technical rules.[37]

With the newest technological developments, it has become possible to establish a hypothetical DLT-based DRM system. The objective of copyright law consists in the creation of "artificial scarcity" by introducing exclusive rights in the context of specific forms of information.[38] In particular, the reproduction of creative works without the consent of the corresponding rights holders is prohibited or constrained. Since it is quite easy to produce an identical copy of a digital work, a rights management system remains important after the creation of the work; for example, a digital camera or a work processor can generate a token at the time the work is expressed

---

[32] Bodó et al. (2018, p. 312).

[33] Notwithstanding the fact that today usually the term "new" is used it should not be overlooked that the changes in the copyright architecture have already been discussed in the early days of the Internet; see for example the seminal contribution of Elkin-Koren (1997, p. 1155 et seqq.).

[34] Bodó et al. (2018, p. 319).

[35] To the NFT in particular see below Sect. 3.6.

[36] de Filippi and Hassan (2016, p. 8).

[37] For further details see the thorough analysis of Bechtold (2004, p. 323 et seqq.).

[38] de Filippi and Hassan (2016, p. 8).

and, subsequently, the rights holder is able to establish a record of rights management information for the protected content.[39]

As more and more transactional relations are implemented in the form of a smart contract (in contrast to a legal contract), the DLT technology progressively acquires the status of a "regulatory technology", i.e. a technology that allows enforcing the applicable rules irrespective of whether or not there exists an underlying legal rule.[40] Apart from contractual relations (such as sale and purchase), the new "regulatory technology" is particularly suitable in the field of copyright law.[41]

The new technologies are broadening the room for manoeuvring for authors, artists, and other copyright owners to implement individually oriented protection regimes. As a consequence, disintermediation affects incumbents at various levels, for example, (i) the publishers and music labels, (ii) the collective management organizations, and (iii) the online platforms.[42] In a DLT architectural environment, the rights holders do not need to employ any of the Hollywood organizations anymore, but they have the possibility to enter into direct (contractual) relations with the public.[43]

By leveraging the transparency and immutability of the DLT, it has become possible to restore the unicity and transferability of digital works, for example, by linking every digital copy to a particular token on the DLT. Tokens can represent a copy of a protected work or a record of information for protected content.[44] "Owners" of copyright are therewith enabled to associate these tokens with a particular set of rights to their digital works and to trade them in the same way as they would trade digital tokens.[45] In other words, the terms and conditions for accessing protected works can be expressed in smart contracts, which are linked to DLT-based payment systems.[46]

As mentioned, copyright "owners" are in a position to establish direct relationships with the public. By using smart contracts for implementing the terms and conditions that enable the users to have access to the protected works and (in parallel) by using digital currencies that put the "debtor" in a position to make micro-payments to the relevant rights holder, a new copyright architecture is realized.[47] By automatically obtaining a license that is able to "unlock" certain functionalities of the work, copyright is becoming part of the new "regulatory technology".[48]

---

39 Bodó et al. (2018, p. 315).

40 de Filippi and Hassan (2016, pp. 9–10).

41 Weber (2018, p. 705); Bodó et al. (2018, p. 319 et seqq.).

42 Bodó et al. (2018, p. 317).

43 Weber (2018, p. 706).

44 Bodó et al. (2018, p. 315).

45 de Filippi and Hassan (2016, p. 9).

46 Weber (2018, p. 705).

47 To the remuneration issue see below Chap 3.4.

48 Weber (2018, p. 705).

A new copyright architecture makes it necessary to address several specific issues. A possible approach could be to discuss private ordering, registries, rights management information, and fair remuneration.[49] Hereinafter, a slightly different approach is chosen, distinguishing between (i) registries, (ii) licensing management, (iii) royalties' management, and (iv) digital enforcement.

3.2 *Registries*

The first element of a new copyright architecture is the implementation and availability of a registry that properly reflects the legal positions of the rights holders, i.e. they must have the possibility to register the (exclusive) rights in a secure and transparent way.

So far, the legal framework in the copyright environment is very fragmented, leading to a lack of (legal) interoperability.[50] Notwithstanding the fact that international treaties have existed since the conclusion of the Berne Convention in 1886, national laws are still quite relevant for many aspects of copyright protection. For instance, apart from the different notions of exhaustion (national, regional, international), an important distinction in the legal systems concerns the creation of a registry: In contrast to the registries guaranteeing the protection of patents and trademarks in accordance with their terms, corresponding copyright registries do not exist in many (if not most) countries, particularly not in civil law countries.[51]

This lack of coherence as far as registries are concerned could be overcome by DLT-based infrastructures, exercising a similar function of allocating a digital asset to an individual. By using a DLT-based infrastructure, a tamper-proof chain of evidence for copyright ownership can be established since the next block retains the original hash value linking to the earlier block(s). Furthermore, the original copyright date can be stored in the block's data. In the passive form, DLT-based registries are able to record rights management information as a time-stamped entry that anyone is able to consult; in the active form, rights reflected in DLT-based registries are tokenized assets, and rights holders are account holders.[52]

The (preferable) active form of a DLT-registry allows the exploitation of protected works without the need to involve any intermediaries. The holder of the rights (usually represented by a token) would be in control of the digital asset and be able to transfer, license, track the use, check the execution of the corresponding payment, and enforce the rights against third persons based on the accompanying smart contract. In other words, the exploitation in the digital realm would "only" be dependent on registration in the digital ledger. Such a registry is not considered to constitute a prohibited

---

[49] This approach has been chosen by Bodó et al. (2018, p. 320 et seqq.).

[50] To the term "legal interoperability" see Weber (2014, p. 6).

[51] For more details see Bodó et al. (2018, pp. 320–321).

[52] See Bodó et al. (2018, p. 324) with references to engaged private organizations.

formality under international law, particularly not a violation of Article 5(2) of the Berne Convention.[53]

The DLT-based registries could also help to find the author of an orphan work (i.e. a protected creation that does not have an identified rights holder or at least not a locatable rights holder): A combination of smart contracts with a DLT-registry would enable the automatic licensing of these works, including other licensed creations and even works in the public domain with a special system of dedication reflecting public interests.[54]

However, several challenges exist: (i) The costs for the implementation of a copyright-related registry are relatively high, i.e. at least an individual (for example, an artist) needs quite substantial incentives to realize such an infrastructure. (ii) A practically important and not yet fully clarified problem concerns the aspect of the supervision of the rights' entries. Can and does the provider of a DLT-based registry check whether the registration is done by the real owner of the copyright-protected work? And how can a wrong entry be corrected? For these reasons, not many DLT-based infrastructures in the copyright environment exist in practice for the time being.

3.3 *Licensing Management*

A combination of smart contracts with a DLT-based registry could enable the automatic licensing of protected works. Such a system would facilitate the management of copyright, as a DLT-based registry can create and open up completely new markets for the rights holders by way of smart contracts.[55] The ownership or at least the control of the protected work is secured[56]; rights holders (for example, artists) can directly exploit the protected works without relying on any third parties (publishers, music labels).

A DLT-based registry makes it easier and more cost-efficient to coordinate the licensing management as well as to cooperate with other players (for example, in case of numerous stakeholders in the music industry owning a "piece" of music, such as songwriters, performers, record companies). The licensing management is less based on the traditional notion or quality of "ownership" than on the factual control of data; an open "sharing" of data would limit the scope of the commercial exploitation possibilities of copyright-protected works. Therefore, in addition, the licensing management requires a substantial amount of coordination both on-chain,

---

53 van Gompel (2013, p. 1439).

54 To this issue which cannot be discussed in further detail see Bodó et al. (2018, pp. 325–327 with further references).

55 Gürkaynak et al. (2018, p. 857).

56 See above Sect. 3.1.

and between on- and off-chain transactions in order to avoid conflicting claims on the same work.[57]

An additional specific problem consists in the possibility of conflicting claims on the same protected work: A DLT-registry is able to safeguard the validity and provenance of the already available, i.e. "listed" information. However, it cannot assess or check the validity of new information to be put into the system.[58] For such a situation, appropriate dispute settlement instruments need to be installed (or programmed into the code) in advance.[59]

Apart from the mentioned challenges, it is also important to tokenize the copyright-protected work in a technologically proper way. Only under this condition, the original can be distinguished from copies. For example, in the case of a digital art piece, the original is created and tokenized by the artist; copies (for example, by photographic means) are not protected originals and might also have a lower quality.

In the meantime, several initiatives have already been initiated in this context, for example, the Open Music Initiative (OMI) by the Berklee College of Music in Boston (Mass.). This initiative aims to build an open-sourced platform with a shared protocol, based on cryptography, distributed consensus, and interoperability with existing and future systems. Instead of building a simple repository of ownership and attribution, OMI establishes a system working with both open and proprietary sourced data.[60] OMI builds a database in the form of a DLT with the objective of solving the proper identification of the rights holders.[61]

Another initiative is the Ujo Creators Portal: The Ujo platform is running on the Ethereum blockchain and its stated goal is to enable artists to be paid directly by the users.[62] According to its own description, Ujo has the ability to rewire the music industry by better serving the needs of the artists through the decentralized technical infrastructure. But some questions remain unanswered, for example, how to delete music and how to recover lost accounts.[63]

3.4 Royalties' Management

A DLT-based infrastructure of copyright holders is also able to ensure the creator's fair remuneration. Three types of royalties' management regimes are to be considered: (i) the infrastructure can enable payments similar to those already taking place through existing platforms; (ii) it may open up uses currently licensed through statutory or

[57] Bodó et al. (2018, pp. 322 and 328).

[58] Bodó et al. (2018, p. 328).

[59] For further details see Schmitz and Rule (2019, p. 103 et seqq.).

[60] See http://www.thembj.org/2016/08/berklees-open-music-initiative/ (last access 26 July 2022).

[61] Gürkaynak et al. (2018, p. 859).

[62] See https://ujomusic.com (last access 26 July 2022).

[63] Gürkaynak et al. (2018, p. 859).

compulsory licenses and collective rights management schemes; (iii) it may provide greater transparency, especially from the perspective of authors and performers.[64]

If the remuneration is fully based on the DLT and on smart contracts, payment must be made in cryptocurrencies that allow the execution of micropayments by many users for many uses. In principle, the royalties' management on the DLT-based infrastructure excludes "traditional" payment means and thereby a not neglectable part of society. This consequence makes it probable that DLT solutions will be combined with off-chain transactions in practice.

First practical applications are already existing, for example, the already described Open Music Initiative and the Ujo Creators Portal,[65] apart from the fact that some artists have established individual DLT solutions. Using smart contracts containing the terms and conditions for having access to the protected works and providing for the payment with digital currencies appears to be an elegant and efficient solution. Royalties can be foreseen on the whole exploitation chain (without exhaustion). However, if "only" the use of protected works on a DLT-infrastructure is possible, the number of users will be limited since not everybody might be willing and/or able to pay by way of cryptocurrencies. As a consequence, additional (traditional) payment methods are required to increase the market penetration.

3.5 *Enforcement of Copyright*

For copyright to have any legal meaning, the rights holder must be able to enforce the rights effectively. In the case of a DLT-based infrastructure, the enforcement is possible through the execution of the technical mechanisms.[66] Since the DLT implements "artificial scarcity" at the level of each individual file, copyright "owners" become able to directly enforce their rights to technological means. Insofar, the technical code indeed replaces the legal instruments. The trust in the technological design of the DLT infrastructure replaces the normative framework.[67]

However, as already mentioned, a dispute about the entitlement can occur, particularly if two persons claim to be the entitled owner of a protected work. The risk for such a situation is prevalent if the provider of the copyright registry is not verifying the entitlement at the time of registration of copyright-protected work. In case of a contested entitlement, a dispute settlement by way of an oracle and a subsequent arbitration library must take place.[68]

A special issue consists the fight against counterfeits. A solution might be possible with the integration of the supply-chain information, for example, unique barcodes,

---

[64] Bodó et al. (2018, p. 329).

[65] See above Sect. 3.3.

[66] See above Sect. 3.1 and de Filippi and Hassan (2016, p. 8).

[67] For the notion of trust in the blockchain context see the study of Werbach (2018).

[68] For further details see Weber (2017b, nos. 42 et seqq.).

QR codes, or RFID (Radio Frequency ID).[69] However, these technical means are more suitable for patent and trademark protection than for copyright protection.

As outlined, the enforcement is confronted with difficulties if the entitlement of a protected work is contested, particularly if doubts exist in respect of the correctness of an entry in the DLT-based registry. A similar challenge is given if a dispute regarding the licensing or royalties framework is occurring. Particularly in cross-border situations, it could become difficult to "find" the responsible defendant and the competent court if the dispute is not settled by way of an automated arbitration library. A similar challenge can occur if the exhaustion of the exploitation of a copyright-protected work is not clearly designed in the code of the smart contract; the existing exhaustion rules are not aligned to the technological means allowing to code an unlimited exhaustion, and the new Copyright Directive of the European Union does not contain any rules to this aspect.[70]

3.6 *Non-fungible Tokens in Particular*

With the advent of the token "industry" the idea came up to digitize art works in the form of non-fungible tokens (NFT). The basic idea is to link every digital copy of a copyright-protected work to a particular token on the DLT. The creation of tokens not only makes it possible to commercialize digital art but also to split a high value ("expensive art") into divided smaller participations that can be more easily placed in the public.

If a token should be commercially successful, it must represent a digital value; often, however, in practice, NFT are also issued in the form of an originality certificate having a "pure" evidence function.[71] The issuance of NFT is not necessarily linked to the described new copyright architecture in a direct way; therefore, art exploitation by way of NFT is not discussed in detail hereinafter.

Recently, the NFT market has experienced a few high price auctions not always based on real economic values. In particular, the digital art work called "Everydays: The First 5000 Days" by the creator Mike William reached the price of USD 70 Mio. If NFT do not only represent the originality of a copyright-protected work (evidence function), the tokenization facilitates the transferability of the respective assets, i.e. the licensing and the royalties' management becomes more efficient.[72] But the aforementioned challenges in connection with the reliance on the DLT-based registry remain unchanged,[73] and some copyright questions (for example, regarding the minting and the scope of the transferred rights) still need to be tackled; for

69 Gürkaynak et al. (2018, p. 860).

70 Directive (EU) 2019/790 of 17 April 2019 on copyright and related rights in the Digital Single Market, JO 2019 L 130/92 of 17 May 2019.

71 See Weber (2022, p. 488); Aref et al. (2021, p. 387).

72 Aref et al. (2021, p. 385 et seqq.)

73 See above Sect. 3.2.

example, contractual arrangements in respect of the contents of usage rights appear to be recommendable.[74]

4 Benefits and Limits of a New Copyright Architecture

The DLT infrastructure generally improves efficiency and reduces costs. This effect particularly plays a role in connection with the design of the copyright architecture. The tokenization of the rights to have access to and use digital works constitutes an exemplary case for an L&E approach[75] since copyright protection is an innovation driver and incentivizes civil society to invest time and money into the creation of works.[76]

Furthermore, through virtual processes, the exploitation of copyright-protected works can determine the scope of the functionalities, such as access, reproduction, or even remix of a digital copy. The protected "information" could be stored on the DLT infrastructure and be combined with smart contracts offering certain rights such as restricting playback to legitimate owners or executing licensing and royalties agreements in real time.[77] In addition, DLT-architectures for copyright could lead to multi-territorial licensing policies and enhanced legal certainty for creators while providing effective dispute resolution mechanisms.

The modern technological developments (for example, DLT) equally have the potential to reduce ambiguities and also "grey areas" in the normative context since traditional legal drafting is usually (or even almost always) not as precise as the technical rules.[78] Therefore, a reduction of the need for canons of construction and other textual interpretation techniques can be expected, leading to cost savings and higher efficiency.

Some problems, however, should not be fully overlooked and constitute limits of the copyright architecture: in particular, the fragmentation, as far as the legal position of rights holders is concerned, remains unchanged since many claims in the copyright framework still are subject to national legislation.[79] A further "disadvantage" consists in the fact that a "pure" DLT framework limits the number of potential participants since not everybody is able or willing to accept a fully digitized regime with cryptocurrencies. However, in contrast to some statements in the literature,[80]

---

[74] For further details see Weber (2022, p. 489 et seqq.); Aref et al. (2021, p. 396 et seqq.); Hoeren and Prinz (2021, pp. 570–571).

[75] Gürkaynak et al. (2018, p. 857).

[76] See Posner (2014, p. 412 et seqq.); for an early L&E analysis see already Landes and Posner (1989, p. 325 et seqq.).

[77] Rivière (2018, p. 7).

[78] de Filippi and Hassan (2016, p. 10).

[79] Bodó et al. (2018, pp. 320–321).

[80] Gürkaynak et al. (2018, pp. 858–859).

consumer protection laws might not be relevant in most instances since the copyright holder in a fully decentralized infrastructure is usually not a commercial entity selling a standardized good to a consumer, i.e. the user of the protected work.

5 Outlook

As experience has shown during the last 20 years, digital rights management systems did not really function in practice. The implementation of distributed ledger technology schemes appears to be more promising: digital tokens are able to establish a regime that puts the "owner" or "controller" of the tokenized values in a position to exercise power over the licensing management of copyright-protected works. Due to its decentralized structure, the DLT architecture allows copyright owners (artists) to control the exploitation of their rights in an extensive manner.

A possible future path paved by DLT could be designed in a way that rights holders make their protected works available on a DLT infrastructure, creating a quasi-immutable record of initial ownership and using smart contracts to automate the exploitation as far as the protected works are concerned; furthermore, the conditions of transfers as well as the remuneration can be executed on the same platform as the distribution of works.[81] However, different enforcement challenges should not be underestimated, particularly if the provider of the DLT-based registry does not exercise specific supervisory functions in respect of the rights' entry.

In a nutshell, even in view of all the challenges of a crystal ball, the forecast may be ventured that copyright-based practices have already changed and will continue to change the copyright architecture, namely from a scarcity- and exclusivity-oriented monetization model to a controlled access-oriented system. The new regulatory technology offers the rights holders the possibility to gain and execute more options for the commercialization of their copyright protected works.

Nevertheless, a full replacement of the "real world" in the copyright environment does not seem to be realistic; moreover, on-chain and off-chain transactions (as well as the interconnectivity of the two regimes) and the existing streaming services might remain relevant. Therefore, parallel rights and exploitation regimes are to be expected in the future.

References

Aref M, Fábián L, Weber S (2021) Digitale Originale dank NFTs? GesKR 2021:385–399
Bechtold S (2004) Digital Rights Management in the United States and Europe. Am J Comp Law 52:323–382
Benkler Y (2011) Networks of power, degrees of freedom. Int J Commun 5:721–755

[81] Bodó et al. (2018, p. 333).

Black J (2001) Decentring of regulation: understanding the role of regulation and self-regulation in a 'post-regulatory' world. Curr Leg Probl 54:103–146

Bodó B, Gervais D, Quintais JP (2018) Blockchain and smart contracts: the missing link in copyright licensing? Int J Law Inf Technol 26:311–336

Braithwaith J (2002) Rewards and Regulation. J Law Soc 29:12–26

Elkin-Koren N (1997) Copyrights in cyberspace—rights without laws. Chicago-Kent Law Rev 73:1155–1201

de Filippi P and Hassan S (2016) Blockchain technology as a regulatory technology: from code is law to law is code. First Monday 21/12:1–16. http://firstmonday.org/ojs/index.php/fm/article/view/7113/5657. Last access 26 July 2022

de Filippi P, Wright A (2018) Blockchain and the law. Harvard University Press, Cambridge, Mass

Gürkaynak G et al (2018) Intellectual property law and practice in the blockchain realm. Comput Law Secur Rev 34:847–862

Hoeren T, Prinz W (2021) Das Kunstwerk in Zeitalter der technischen Reproduzierbarkeit—NFTs (Non-Fungible Tokens) in rechtlicher Hinsicht, Computer und Recht 2021:565–572

Landes WM, Posner RA (1989) An economic analysis of copyright law. J Leg Stud 18:325–363

Lessig L (1999) Code and other laws of cyberspace. Basic Books, New York

Lessig L (2006) Code 2.0. Basic Books, New York

Posner R (2014) Economic analysis of law, 9th edn. New York, Wolters Kluwer

Rivière JM (2018) Blockchain technology and IP—investigating benefits and acceptance in governance and legislations. Jr Manage Sci 3(1):1–15

Schmitz AJ, Rule C (2019) Online dispute resolution for smart contracts. J Dispute Resolut 2019:103–125

Singh BP, Tripathi AK (2019) Blockchain technology and intellectual property rights. J Intellect Proper Rights 24:41–44

van Gompel S (2013) Copyright formalities in the internet age: filters of protection or facilitators of licensing. Berkeley Tech Law J 28:1425–1458

Weber RH (2014) Legal interoperability as a tool for combatting fragmentation. Global Commission on Internet Governance, Paper Series No. 4, Chatham House, London

Weber RH (2017a) The role of law in constituting financial markets. J Int Bank Law Regul 32:253–260

Weber RH (2017b) Leistungsstörungen und Rechtsdurchsetzung bei Smart Contracts. Jusletter Weblaw of 4 December 2017

Weber RH (2018) Rose is a rose is a rose is a rose—what about code and law? Comput Law Secur Rev 34:701–706

Weber RH (2022) Non-fungible tokens—a new (legal) phenomenon in the crypto universe Sic 487–496

Werbach K (2018) The blockchain and the new architecture of trust. The MIT Press, Cambridge MA

Rolf H. Weber is a Professor of International Business Law at the University of Zurich and practicing attorney-at-law in Zurich. His fields of interest include Information Technology and Internet Law, Competition Law and International Finance and Trade Law.

A Digital Single Market, First Stop to the Metaverse: Counterlife of Copyright Protection Wanted

Danny Friedmann

Abstract Directive 2019/790 prepares the EU's copyright system for a Digital Single Market. Its implementation of a de facto strict liability for platforms has led to an increased need for automatic content recognition, which in turn has caused an increased need for sufficient safeguards of unauthorized but legal use that falls under an exception or limitation. This chapter is focusing on how to provide this breathing space for copyrighted works, especially in view of the emergence of the metaverse.

Keywords Copyright · Metaverse · Exceptions and limitations · Fair use · Automatic content recognition · AI filter · OCPPS · Platforms · Stakeholder dialogue

1 Introduction

Baudrillard has prophesied the fusion of the real and fictional worlds into a hyper-realistic reality.[1] The tokenization of physical art via NFTs and the metaverse are the capricious harbingers of the merger between the real and digital worlds.[2] This transformation is hastened on the one hand by the digitalization of reality and on the other hand by the imposition of digital layers and objects in a virtual or augmented reality in combination with the Internet of Things. This will ineluctably lead to a

[1] Baudrillard (1983).

[2] Chen and Friedmann (2023).

D. Friedmann (✉)
Associate Professor of Law, Peking University School of Transnational Law, University Town, Nanshan District, Shenzhen 518055, China
e-mail: dannyfriedmann@stl.pku.edu.cn

K. Mathis and A. Tor (eds.), *Law and Economics of the Digital Transformation*, Economic Analysis of Law in European Legal Scholarship 15,
https://doi.org/10.1007/978-3-031-25059-0_8

Cambrium-like explosion[3] of the use and abuse, but also unauthorized but legal parodic and transformative use, of copyrighted works.

In 2014, this Author foresaw the end of safe harbours and the arrival of strict liability for online service providers (OSPs),[4] by extrapolating existing trends such as the unscalability of the manual enforcement of alleged online infringements. These developments have manifested themselves in different jurisdictions such as China,[5] and most prominently, at least de facto, in the EU under the Directive 2019/790 on Copyright in the Digital Single Market.[6] Because of the strict liability, de facto or *de jure*, OSPs are incentivized to over-enforce by implementing pre-upload filtering systems (automated content recognition) to avoid any risks of liability.[7] This, in combination with a central repository, could have a strong chilling effect on the use of copyrighted works, despite fair use, fair dealing, or exceptions and limitations available in the respective jurisdictions. Building upon the "fair use by design"-concept of Niva Elkin-Koren,[8] this chapter explores how artificial intelligence can be used to implement exceptions or limitations.

Section 2 will give a brief overview of the evolution of the copyright *acquis* in the US and EU, in regard to platforms, discuss the implications of strict liability in an era of massive online use and infringements, which already has pushed and, *a fortiori*, will push platforms in the metaverse in the direction of automatic, scalable solutions, which on their turn, will increase the need for sufficient safeguards of unauthorized but legal use that falls under an exception or limitation.

Section 3 introduces the implications of the metaverse in regard to intermediary liability of copyright infringement and the need for "breathing space" for users and experimenting. Section 4 explores the safeguards for legitimate use of content, which includes exceptions and limitations.

Building on Elkin-Koren's "fair use by design"-concept, Sect. 5 provides the prerequisites for designing algorithmic exceptions or limitations, and whether automated content recognition tools should be qualified as "high risk AI" under the proposed Artificial Intelligence Act, and incentives against over-blocking.

This is followed by Sect. 6, which provides the conclusions.

---

[3] The Cambrian explosion was an event approximately 541 million years ago in the Cambrian period when most major animal phyla appeared in the fossil record. In first years of the Millennium there was an explosion of a diversity of new species of social media: Facebook (February 2004), YouTube (February 2005), Twitter (March 2006) and Instagram (October 2010), etc.

[4] Friedmann (2014).

[5] Friedmann (2020).

[6] Directive (EU) 2019/790 of the European Parliament and of the Council of 17 April 2019 on copyright and related rights in the Digital Single Market PE/51/2019/REV/1 OJ L 130, 17.05.2019, p. 92–125. Effective on 6 June 2019. Available at: https://eur-lex.europa.eu/eli/dir/2019/790/oj (last access 12 July 2022).

[7] A glimmer of hope in this respect is provided by *Lenz v. Universal Music Corp.*, 801 F.3d 1126 (9th Cir. 2008).

[8] Elkin-Koren (2017a).

2 Evolution of the Copyright *Acquis* in the US and EU

The Agreement on Trade-Related Aspects of Intellectual Property Rights (TRIPs) was adopted in 1994.[9] It provides, in particular, protection against copyright infringement of works fixed in tangible mediums of expression. In 1995, commercial internet service providers started to sell subscriptions to consumers. Copyright holders were not protected against copyright infringements that spread across the internet. To counter this problem, and to usher the TRIPs members into the internet era, the "WIPO Internet Treaties" were adopted in 1996.[10] Article 8 WIPO Copyright Treaty obliges its members "to provide to authors of literary and artistic works the enjoyment of the exclusive right of authorizing any communication to the public of their works, by wire or wireless means, including the making available to the public of their works in such a way that members of the public may access these works from a place and at a time individually chosen by them."[11] Making available to the public is technology-neutral[12] and covers all formats in which a work may be digitally communicated, including downloads, streams, and any other existing or future-developed methods of online transmission.

2.1 DMCA and Fair Use

The US did not explicitly implement the "making available to the public" provision. A combination of exclusive rights, including the distribution, public display, and public performance rights, were deemed to cover the full range of conduct encompassed by the "making available" right.[13] To implement the "WIPO Internet Treaties" in regard to technological measures[14] and rights management information,[15] the US Congress passed the Digital Millennium Copyright Act (DMCA) in 1998. However, Title II of the DMCA, introduced a notice-and-takedown mechanism in combination with a limitation of the liability in regard to copyright infringement of OSPs, which was followed by many jurisdictions, including the EU. An important argument for introducing safe harbour provisions was to stimulate the growth of the

[9] Agreement on Trade-Related Aspects of Intellectual Property Rights. Annex 1C of the Marrakesh Agreement Establishing the World Trade Organization, signed in Marrakesh, Morocco on 15 April 1994, and came into effect on 1 January 1995.

[10] Article 8 WIPO Copyright Treaty, adopted on 20 December 1996, and came into effect on 6 March 2002. Articles 10 (Right of Making Available of Fixed Performance) and 14 (Right of Making Available of Phonograms) WIPO Performances and Phonograms, adopted on 20 December 1996, and came into effect on 20 May 2002.

[11] Article 8 WIPO Copyright Treaty 1996.

[12] Ginsburg (2014).

[13] APPENDIX 21. Executive Summary: "The Making Available Right in the United States" by the U.S. Copyright Office, Hazard Jr (2021).

[14] Article 11 WIPO Copyright Treaty. Article 18 WIPO Performances and Phonograms Treaty.

[15] Article 12 WIPO Copyright Treaty. Article 19 WIPO Performances and Phonograms Treaty.

e-commerce industry and limit the risks of OSPs so that they would be willing to invest in their infrastructure and services. Under the DMCA, if OSPs expeditiously remove, or disable infringing material if they have actual or constructed knowledge of infringing activity,[16] they will be exempted from direct and indirect liability of copyright infringement.[17] OSPs that receive a financial benefit directly attributable to the infringing activity, where they had the right and ability to control such activity,[18] will be held vicariously liable for copyright infringement. If an OSP receives a notice of specific infringing material,[19] it establishes actual knowledge, and thus needs to expeditiously take down or block access to the material. The OSP needs to notify the user that uploaded material was removed or disabled.[20] If a user sends a counter-notification, implying that the work was not infringing, the OSP will inform the person who sent the notification that it will replace the removed material or cease disabling access to it in 10 business days.[21] Between 10 and 14 business days, after the receipt of the counter-notice, the removed material will be replaced, unless the right holder makes it clear that he or she will file an action seeking a court order to restrain the user from engaging in infringing activity.[22] If the sender of the notice-and-takedown knowingly materially misrepresented that the material was infringing, the OSP can hold him or her liable for misrepresentation.[23]

The DMCA's safe harbour provisions, in combination with a weak monitor obligation, have led to perverse incentives for OSPs to look the other way or be wilfully blind,[24] to shift the burden of monitoring the servers of their platform to copyright holders even though OSPs are technically in the best position to do so. The DMCA obliges OSPs to monitor "to the extent consistent with a standard technical measure",[25] that has been developed pursuant to a broad consensus of copyright owners and service providers in an "open, fair, voluntary, multi-industry standards process; is available to any person on reasonable and non-discriminatory terms; and does not impose substantial costs on service providers or substantial burdens on their systems or networks."[26]

---

[16] § 512(c)(1)(A) DMCA.

[17] § 512(c)(1)(C) DMCA.

[18] § 512(c)(1)(B) DMCA.

[19] The one sending a notice-and-takedown request, needs to include "[a] statement that the complaining party has a good faith belief that use of the material in the manner complained of is not authorized by the copyright owner, its agent, or the law." § 512(c)(3)(A)(v) DMCA. In addition, the sender should provide "[a] statement that the information in the notification is accurate, and under penalty of perjury, that the complaining party is authorized to act on behalf of the owner of an exclusive right that is allegedly infringed." § 512(c)(3)(A)(vi) DMCA.

[20] § 512(g)(2)(A) DMCA.

[21] § 512(g)(2)(B) DMCA.

[22] § 512(g)(2)(C) DMCA.

[23] § 512(f) DMCA.

[24] *Viacom Intern., Inc. v. YouTube, Inc.*, 676 F.3d 19 (2nd Cir. 2012).

[25] § 512(m)(1) DMCA.

[26] § 512(i)(2) DMCA.

However, even with the safe harbours in place, copyright holders continued to sue OSPs for alleged direct or indirect liability of copyright infringement, because it is very difficult to identify and sue a direct infringer that resides in the US jurisdiction and has sufficient financial means for compensation.[27] In contrast, OSPs can be easily traced, are predominantly located in the US, and have sufficient funds. As social media took off, OSPs were receiving progressively more notice-and-takedown requests. So much so that they were getting overwhelmed and removed or blocked material without any thorough human review, or started to apply automatic content recognition tools, that did an ever more accurate job in detecting and identifying unauthorized content. These tools did not take fair use into account. Unauthorized by a copyright holder does not automatically mean unauthorized by law, because copyright protection is not absolute. In the US, the doctrine of fair use, codified in § 107,[28] can be used as an affirmative defence against claims of copyright infringement. Since it is an affirmative defence, or even a right, as the 9th Circuit held in *Lenz v. Universal Music Corporation* in 2016,[29] the burden of proof rests with the defendants of the claim of copyright infringement. In *Lenz*, according to the majority of the 9th Circuit, the user needs to prove, if the right holder claimed to have taken fair use into account before the takedown, that the right holder did not himself/herself believe that the use in question cannot be qualified as fair use.[30] Thus, this double negation means that the right holder did not take fair use into account, although he or she knew it was fair use.

Judge Smith's partial dissent proposed a lower burden for the defendant: the user could show misrepresentation by the right holder pointing to the insufficiency of the plaintiff's fair use analysis procedure.[31] Fair use does not have bright-line rules, and the decisions are case-specific.[32] § 107 provides four factors that courts can consider.[33] These factors are not exhaustive and the courts can use more or

---

[27] Friedmann (2014).

[28] 17 U.S. Code § 107.

[29] "Fair use is not just excused by the law, it is wholly authorized by the law." *Lenz*, 1151.

Copyright Law—Digital Millennium Copyright Act—Ninth Circuit Requires Analysis of Fair Use Before Issuing of Takedown Notices—*Lenz v. Universal Music Corp.*, No. 13–16,106, 2016 WL 1,056,082 (9th Cir. Mar. 17, 2016), reh'g en banc denied, id., 129 HARV. L. REV. 2289. Available at: https://harvardlawreview.org/wp-content/uploads/2016/06/2289-2296-Online.pdf (last access 12 July 2022).

[30] According to the majority decision: "Though Lenz argues Universal should have known the video qualifies for fair use as a matter of law, we have already decided a copyright holder need only form a subjective good faith belief that a use is not authorized." *Lenz*, 1153.

[31] "Universal [Music Corp.] admittedly did not consider fair use before notifying YouTube to take down Lenz's video. It therefore could not have formed a good faith belief that Lenz's video was infringing, and its notification to the contrary was a knowing material misrepresentation." *Lenz*, 1158.

[32] In *Monge v. Maya Magazines, Inc.*, Milan Smith, judge of the 9th Circuit, called fair use the "most troublesome" doctrine in the law of copyright. "This is neither a mechanistic exercise nor a gestalt undertaking, but a considered legal judgment." *Monge v. Maya Magazines, Inc.*, 688 F.3d 1164 (9th Cir. 2012), 1183.

[33] § 107 provides the following 4 factors:

fewer factors. In his influential article "Towards a Fair Use Standard", Pierre Leval described that of the four factors, the first factor is the soul of fair use,[34] and that the assessment of the degree of transformativeness has become the main doctrine since the 1990s in the US.[35] Parody would fall under the first factor of purpose and character of the use. The paradox of parody in regard to the third factor is that the parodist has to take enough of the work to make clear which work is being ridiculed, but not too much. The Supreme Court of the US clarified in *Campbell v. Acuff-Rose Music* in 1994,[36] that a parody could take the heart out of a work. Other questions posed under this factor are whether the work is non-commercial or educational.

The second factor assesses the nature of the copyrighted work; does the work predominantly consist of facts or ideas, or original expression? And was the work already released or published? The third factor concerns the amount and substantiality of the portion taken (*de minimis*). The fourth factor measures the effect of the use upon the potential market[37]; does it supersede the use of the original?[38]

2.2 *From Under-Enforcers to Over-Enforcers*

In both the US and EU, there has been a trend from the under-enforcement of copyrighted works by OSPs, using no automated content recognition tools or those that provide many false negatives, to over-enforcement and using automated content recognition tools that provide false positives, not taking into account fair use in the US or exceptions and limitations in the EU.

2.2.1 Over-Enforcement in the US

Urban and Quilter investigated the notice-and-takedowns in the US under the DMCA. They found that nine percent of all complaints were statutorily insufficient, 30 percent of DMCA notices appeared to present an obvious question for the courts, and that no less than 57 percent of DMCA notices referred to competitors.[39] In 2010, Lawrence

(1) the purpose and character of the use, including whether such use is of a commercial nature or is for nonprofit educational purposes;

(2) the nature of the copyrighted work;

(3) the amount and substantiality of the portion used in relation to the copyrighted work as a whole; and

(4) the effect of the use upon the potential market for or value of the copyrighted work.

[34] Leval (1990), p. 1116.

[35] Leval (1990), p. 1111.

[36] *Campbell v. Acuff-Rose Music*, Inc., 510 U.S. 569 (1994).

[37] Compare this with the wording of the second step of the three-step test in Article 13 TRIPs.

[38] Leval (1990), p. 1125.

[39] Urban and Quilter (2005).

Lessig uploaded a presentation on YouTube about content collaboration by illustrating different dances that were added to the song Lisztomania by the music group Phoenix. Liberation Records owns Lisztomania's rights in Australia, but asserted its rights internationally via YouTube Content ID. Lessig and Liberation Records settled. The latter agreed that Lessig's use was fair use under US law and fair dealing under Australian law, and that it would pay Lessig for the harm it caused.[40]

Lumen (formerly Chilling Effects) observed that increases in total notice volume and the number of URLs per notice appear to be linked to a significant degree in the rise of the use of automated techniques for sending and receiving notices. This trend seems to have taken off in early 2012.[41]

In 2016, William Fisher used some sound fragments in a YouTube video of between 15 and 40 s of cover versions of Jimi Hendrix' Little Wing by Stevie Ray Vaughan and Santana, to give examples of compulsory music licensing for his CopyrightX course. The video was blocked by YouTube Content ID, on behalf of Sony Music.[42] The latter agreed with Fisher that the fragments were used for educational purposes, which in the US could be part of fair use.[43]

The research by Urban, Karaganis, and Schofield in 2017 pointed out more problems with takedown requests. It was at a time when most individual OSPs still did not deploy automatic content recognition tools.[44]

In 2017, the Takedown Project's coding engine revealed that only 34% of the DMCA notices actually raised copyright issues, while 66% pertained to other claims such as libel or privacy, which for the researchers raised serious concerns regarding the integrity of online copyright enforcement, specifically that the removal and blocking of access to online materials took place without any legal oversight, allowing some notice senders to misuse the system to restrict the availability of content online.[45]

In 2018, Sony Music asked Facebook to block James Rhodes' video playing the first Partita of Johann Sebastian Bach. Eventually, Sony Music realized that it did not own the copyright of Bach.[46]

With the deployment of ever more advanced and cheaper automatic content recognition tools, OSPs in the US switched from being under-enforcers to over-enforcers of copyright law, going from false negatives to false positives. The automatic content recognition tools only focused on whether the content is authorized, not whether it is legal, ignoring fundamental rights.

---

[40] EFF (27 February 2014).

[41] Star E van der (20 August 2014).

[42] Star E van der (17 February 2016). See also: Penney researched the chilling effect of the existence and use of takedown enforcement systems have on the freedom of speech and inclusiveness of Twitter and Wikipedia users from an empirically-grounded anthropological perspective. Penney (2019).

[43] Resnikoff (18 February 2016).

[44] Urban, Karaganis, and Schofield (22 March 2017).

[45] Bar-Ziv and Elkin-Koren (2017).

[46] EFF (4 September 2018).

2.2.2 Over-Enforcement in the EU

What happened in the US, also happened in the EU. Article 3 of the Directive 2001/29/EC "Copyright in the Information Society",[47] which protects the right of communication of works to the public and the right to make other subject-matter available to the public, implemented the equivalent obligation of Article 8 WIPO Copyright Treaty.[48] The combination of safe harbour provisions and the prohibition against general monitoring of Articles 14 and 15 Directive 2001/29/EC, respectively, led to a sense of false security provided by information society service providers (ISSP), as OSPs are called in the EU, and insufficient enforcement of the rights of copyright holders. Nevertheless, ISSPs were being sued for indirect liability of copyright infringement. In order to prevent this, they started using automatic content recognition tools and they started to over-enforce, just as their US counterparts.

In 2004, the Dutch organisation Bits of Freedom uploaded a work to ten Dutch ISSPs of the Dutch author *Multatuli* (pseudonym of Eduard Douwes Dekker), who died in 1887, with the explicit disclaimer that the work is in the public domain.[49] Subsequently, Bits of Freedom let a "mystery copyright holder" request the ISSPs to take down the work, which resulted in seven out of ten ISSPs taking down the allegedly infringing material.[50]

2.3 *EU Copyright Acquis and Exceptions or Limitations*

Fair use is not part of the copyright *acquis* in the EU, although scholars such as Hugenholtz and Senftleben advocate for a more open interpretation of some of the provisions of the copyright *acquis*.[51] Article 5 Directive 2001/29/EC provides some

[47] Directive 2001/29/EC of the European Parliament and of the Council of 22 May 2001 on the harmonisation of certain aspects of copyright and related rights in the information society, OJ L 167, 22.6.2001, p. 10–19. Available at: https://eur-lex.europa.eu/legal-content/EN/TXT/?uri=celex:32001L0029 (last access 12 July 2022).

[48] Article 8 WIPO Copyright Treaty, adopted on 20 December 1996.

[49] In the Netherlands, the term of a copyright is 70 years after the death of the author: thus $1887 + 70 = 1957$.

[50] Nas (27 October 2004).

[51] Hugenholtz and Senftleben (29 February 2012).

à la carte exceptions and limitations,[52] where "quotations for purposes such as criticism or review"[53] are subject to conditions. Moreover, in order to apply these exceptions and limitations, they have to comply with the three-step test.[54] Thus, these optional exceptions and limitations can only apply in certain special cases, which do not conflict with a normal exploitation of the work or other subject-matter and do not unreasonably prejudice the legitimate interests of the right holder.[55] The jurisdictions in the EU chose different exceptions and limitations. This resulted in a patchwork of regulations, which was not conducive to promoting a single market. This made it also more difficult for providers of automatic content recognition tools to take the particular exceptions and limitations of each of the jurisdictions of the EU into account. An additional problem was the perceived "value gap", a mismatch between, on the one hand, the value that some digital platforms extract from content, and on the other hand, the meagre revenues returned to the copyright holders. The remuneration that YouTube was prepared to pay to the copyright holder for a song that was unauthorizedly uploaded, was much lower than, for example, the remuneration that Spotify[56] was prepared to pay for an unauthorizedly uploaded song to a copyright holder. Some interest groups, such as the International Federation of the Phonographic Industry (IFPI), were successful in lobbying the Members of the European Parliament about the need to bridge this value gap.[57] It also became clear that e-commerce and OSPs no longer needed more incentives to invest and develop their business and that the profusely growing platforms could carry some liability in case of copyright infringement.

2.3.1 Directive 2019/790

The controversial Article 13, which was renamed Article 17 Directive 2019/790,[58] aims to promote the digital single market, bridge the value gap, and protect the interests of its stakeholders in a fair and balanced way. Article 17 Directive 2019/790

[52] The term "exceptions and limitations" reflects both the common law and the continental European concept of copyright protection. Senftleben (2010a). AG Verica Trstenjak described the Information Society Directive as a compromise that takes into account the different legal traditions and legal views in the Member States of the EU. C-467/08, *Padawan*, Opinion AG, 21 October 2010, ECLI:EU:C:2010:264, para. 41. Available at: https://curia.europa.eu/juris/document/document.jsf?text=&docid=83635 (last access 12 July 2022).

[53] Article 5(2)(d) Directive 2001/29/EC states that quotations for purposes such as criticism or review, can be used as an exception or limitation, "provided that they relate to a work or other subject-matter which has already been lawfully made available to the public, that, unless this turns out to be impossible, the source, including the author's name, is indicated, and that their use is in accordance with fair practice, and to the extent required by the specific purpose.".

[54] Article 5.5 Directive 2001/29/EC.

[55] Article 5.5 Directive 2001/29/EC.

[56] IFPI (2018).

[57] Awbi (25 April 2018).

[58] Directive (EU) 2019/790, supra n 6.

refers to the use of content by an online-content sharing service provider (OCSSP). Article 2(6) Directive 2019/790 provides a definition for this special category of ISSPs:

> a provider of an information society service of which the main purpose or one of the main purposes is to store and give the public access to a large amount of copyright-protected works or other protected subject matter uploaded by its users, which it organises and promotes for profit-making purposes and excludes some categories of internet society providers.[59]

Article 17(1) Directive 2019/790 states that EU member states shall provide that an OCSSP performs an act of communication to the public or an act of making available to the public when it gives the public access to copyright-protected works or other protected subject matter uploaded by its users.[60] Therefore, the OCSSP shall obtain an authorisation from the right holders referred to in Article 3(1) and (2) Directive 2001/29/EC,[61] for instance, by concluding a licensing agreement, in order to communicate to the public or make available to the public works or other subject matter. Such a license includes acts by users when they are not acting on a commercial basis or where their activity does not generate significant revenues.[62]

When an OCSSP performs an act of communication to the public or making available to the public, the safe harbour of Article 14 Directive 2000/31/EC on E-Commerce[63] does not apply.[64] If no authorisation is granted, OCSSPs shall be held liable, unless the OCSSPs demonstrate that they have (a) made best efforts to obtain an authorisation,[65] (b) made, in accordance with high industry standards of professional diligence, best efforts to ensure the unavailability of specific works and other subject

---

[59] Excluded from this definition are providers of services, such as not-for-profit online encyclopedias, not-for-profit educational and scientific repositories, open source software-developing and-sharing platforms, providers of electronic communications services as defined in Directive (EU) 2018/1972, online marketplaces, business-to-business cloud services and cloud services that allow users to upload content for their own use. Article 2(6) Directive 2019/790, last para.

[60] According to the Guidance of the European Commission, the acts of communication to the public and making content available in Article 17(1) Directive 2019/790 should be understood as also covering reproductions necessary to carry out these acts. EU member states should not provide for an obligation on OCSSPs to obtain an authorisation for reproductions carried out in the context of Article 17. Communication from the Commission to the European Parliament and the Council Guidance on Article 17 of Directive 2019/790 on Copyright in the Digital Single Market, COM/2021/288 final, 4 June 2021, IV(I) para. 2. Available at: https://eur-lex.europa.eu/legal-content/EN/TXT/?uri=CELEX:52021DC0288 (last access 12 July 2022).

[61] Directive 2001/29/EC of the European Parliament and of the Council of 22 May 2001 on the harmonisation of certain aspects of copyright and related rights in the information society, OJ L 167, 22.6.2001, p. 10–19. Available at: https://eur-lex.europa.eu/legal-content/EN/TXT/?uri=celex:32001L0029 (last access 12 July 2022).

[62] Article 17(2) Directive 2019/790.

[63] Directive 2000/31/EC of the European Parliament and of the Council of 8 June 2000 on certain legal aspects of information society services, in particular electronic commerce, in the Internal Market, OJ L 178, 17.7.2000, p. 1–16. In effect 17 July 2020. Available at: https://eur-lex.europa.eu/legal-content/EN/ALL/?uri=celex:32000L0031 (last access 12 July 2022).

[64] Article 17(3) Directive 2019/790.

[65] Article 17(4)(a) Directive 2019/790.

matter for which the right holders have provided the service providers with the relevant and necessary information[66]; and (c) in any event acted expeditiously, upon receiving a sufficiently substantiated notice from the right holders, to disable access to, or to remove from their websites, the notified works or other subject matter, and made best efforts to prevent their future uploads in accordance with point (b).

Thus, obtaining a license has preference under Directive 2019/790,[67] followed by removing and blocking access to infringing works in accordance with high industry standards of professional diligence and preventing future uploads. Article 17(4)(b) and (c) Directive 2019/790 by "best efforts" clearly imply the use of automatic content recognition and pre-upload filtering. Because, besides closing shop, what other methods remain to ensure the respective unavailability and prevention of future uploads of specific works? In *YouTube and Cyando*, the CJEU already imposed a kind of "best efforts" approach, which could help avoid liability: "putting in place the appropriate technological measures that can be expected from a reasonably diligent operator in its situation in order to counter credibly and effectively copyright infringements on that platform."[68]

It seems that most right holders of musical works,[69] photography, and the visual arts,[70] due to the relatively low production costs and the chance of relatively high repeat consumption, are inclined to make use of the licensing regime, while right holders of audiovisual works[71] and literary works (audiobooks)[72] are more interested in blocking, because of their relatively high production costs and low chances of repeat consumption.

In order to see whether the OCSSP complied with Article 17(4) Directive 2019/790, proportionality is taken into account.[73]

Article 17(6) Directive 2019/790 provides a specific liability regime for OCSSPs that are younger than three years and have a revenue below EUR 10 million. They are not bound by Article 4(b) Directive 2019/790, which imposes pre-upload filtering to unsure unavailability of infringing content. The hope is that this would lower the bar for innovative new platforms. If these relatively young OCSSPs with relative financial means have less than five million unique visitors, they are required to make their best efforts to obtain an authorisation under Article 17(4)(a), and they have to comply with the notice-and-takedown obligation under Article 17(4)(c) first part. If these OCSSPs have more than five million unique visitors, they are subject to the

---

[66] Article 17(4)(b) Directive 2019/790.

[67] Unusual that copyright law promotes this. "Opting-out from a legal licence, implied by a remuneration, is not usual in copyright law, but the [Copyright in the Digitial Single Market] CDSM Directive is not short of atypical legal mechanisms." Dusollier (2020).

[68] Joined Cases C-682/18 and C-683/18, *YouTube and Cyando*, Judgment of the Court (Grand Chamber), 22 June 2021, ECLI:EU:C:2021:503, para. 84. Available at: https://curia.europa.eu/juris/liste.jsf?num=C-682/18 (last access 12 July 2022).

[69] HADOPI (2020), 118.

[70] HADOPI (2020), 115.

[71] HADOPI (2020), 119.

[72] HADOPI (2020), 117.

[73] Article 17(5) Directive 2019/790.

same obligations of best efforts to obtain an authorisation and notice-and-takedown as OCSSPs with a smaller audience, but in addition, they also need to comply with the obligation to avoid future uploads of notified works under Article 17(4)(c) second part (staydown). However, one can doubt how one can effectively keep certain infringing works of a platform without pre-upload filtering.

Article 17(7) Directive 2019/790 clarifies that the cooperation between OCSSPs and copyright holders may not result in pre-upload filtering of non-infringing works, including works covered by an exception or limitation (see Sect. 4). The exceptions and limitations of Article 5 Directive 2001/29/EC were optional for the EU member states, and were subject to conditions in regard to quotation, criticism, and review. In contrast, Article 17(7) Directive 2019/790 makes at least the use for the purpose of quotation, criticism, review, caricature, parody, or pastiche mandatory without any conditions. This is a valuable contribution to bringing the digital single market closer.

Article 17(8) Directive 2019/790 confirms that member states shall still not impose any general monitoring obligation, in the same vein as Article 15 Directive 2000/31/EC.[74] However, the interpretation of "specific monitoring obligation" has been broadened to not only identical but also equivalent cases.[75] OCSSPs not only need to ensure the unavailability of specific works under Article 17(4)(b) Directive 2019/790, but also remove uploads (takedown) under the first part of Article 17(4)(c), and to prevent their future uploads (staydown) under the second part of Article 17(4)(c) Directive 2019/790.

Article 17(9) Directive 2019/790 obliges EU member states to impose that OCSSPs put in place an effective and expeditious complaint and redress mechanism, if they do not agree with an uploaded work blocked, removed, or disabled of access. Decisions to disable access to or remove uploaded content shall be subject to human review. Whether this will be practicable depends on the number of these complaints, which have until now been relatively low.

The proposal of the Digital Services Act (DSA) adds more detailed regulation about the notification requirements of the complaint and redress mechanism.[76] In addition, EU member states must ensure that out-of-court redress mechanisms are available.

Article 17(9) Directive 2019/790 underlines that legitimate uses (authorized uses, uses of works in the public domain, or uses under exceptions or limitations) need to be taken into account (see Sect. 4). An improvement is that OCSSPs have to inform their users in their terms and conditions that they can use works and other subject matter

---

[74] Article 15 Directive 2000/31/EC.

[75] C-18/18, Judgment of the Court (Third Chamber) of 3 October 2019 (request for a preliminary ruling from the Oberster Gerichtshof—Austria)—*Eva Glawischnig-Piesczek v Facebook Ireland Limited*, 3 October 2019, ECLI:EU:C:2019:821, para. 19. Available at: https://curia.europa.eu/juris/documents.jsf?num=C-18/18 (last access 12 July 2022).

[76] Proposal for a Regulation of the European Parliament and of the Council on a Single Market For Digital Services (Digital Services Act) and amending Directive 2000/31/EC, COM/2020/825 final, 15.12.2020. Available at: https://eur-lex.europa.eu/legal-content/en/TXT/?uri=COM:2020:825:FIN (last access 12 July 2022).

under exceptions or limitations. Of course, the efficacy of this provision depends on how these terms and conditions are communicated. The inclusion of this provision underlines the democratic public function of these "platforms of expression".[77]

Article 17(10) Directive 2019/790 obliges the European Commission, in cooperation with the EU member states, to organize stakeholder dialogues as of 6 June 2019. These stakeholder dialogues shall discuss best practices for cooperation between OCSSPs and right holders, taking fundamental rights such as the use of exceptions and limitations into account (see Sect. 4). OCSSPs shall provide adequate information on the functioning of their practices in regard to licensing, pre-upload filtering, notice-and-takedown, and staydown.[78] Taking the results of the stakeholders' dialogue into account, the European Commission was obliged to issue guidance on Directive 2019/790, and did issue an illuminating one.[79]

2.3.2 DSA *Lex Generalis* for Directive 2019/790

Since Article 17 Directive 2019/790 provides *lex specialis* rules in regard to required copyright moderation by OCSSPs, one needs to first look if this directive is covering the relevant subject matter. If not, or if it is not sufficiently detailed, the DSA[80] could play a role once it is approved.[81] Article 7 DSA (draft) provides "no general monitoring or active fact-finding obligation":

> No general obligation to monitor the information which providers of intermediary services transmit or store, nor actively to seek facts or circumstances indicating illegal activity shall be imposed on those providers.

Recital 28 DSA (draft) makes it clear that this does not concern monitoring obligations in a specific case and does not affect orders by national authorities in accordance with national legislation, consistent with the conditions established in the DSA. "Nothing in this Regulation should be construed as an imposition of a general monitoring obligation or active fact-finding obligation, or as a general obligation for providers to take proactive measures in relation to illegal content." Thus, pre-upload

77 European Declaration on Digital Rights and Principles for the Digital Decade, joint declaration by European Parliament, the Council and the European Commission, COM(2022) 28 final, Brussels, 26 January 2022, Chapter IV, 5, available at https://ec.europa.eu/newsroom/dae/redirection/document/82703 (last access 12 July 2022).

78 Article 17(4) Directive 2019/790.

79 Communication from the Commission to the European Parliament and the Council Guidance on Article 17 of Directive 2019/790 on Copyright in the Digital Single Market, COM/2021/288 final, 4 June 2021. Available at: https://eur-lex.europa.eu/legal-content/EN/TXT/?uri=CELEX:52021DC0288 (last access 12 July 2022).

80 Recital 28 DSA. Proposal for a Regulation of the European Parliament and of the Council on a Single Market For Digital Services (Digital Services Act) and amending Directive 2000/31/EC COM/2020/825 final, 15.12.2020. Available at: https://eur-lex.europa.eu/legal-content/en/TXT/?uri=COM:2020:825:FIN (last access 12 July 2022).

81 Peukert et al. (2022) p. 1.

filtering can only take place after the copyright holder has made it clear which of its content should not be uploaded.

3 The Metaverse and Copyright Enforcement

The evolution of the internet can be characterised as different iterative versions of the Web.[82] Before 1999, the internet can be characterised as Web 1.0, providing basically "read-only" functionality: viewing and linking. Encyclopaedia Britannica online is an example of this static web.[83] The most used business application of Web 1.0 was shopping carts, which led to the.com boom and bust in 2000 and 2001.

Web 2.0 (participation) can be characterized by the possibility to read, write, and publish. As of 1999, Web 2.0 started with LiveJournal and a slew of other user-generated content.

Wikipedia is an example of a Web 2.0 application, where users can participate in content creation. Since 2003, when Facebook (February 2004), YouTube (February 2005), Twitter (March 2006), and Instagram (October 2010) appeared on the social media stage, and the network effects took off, the manual copyright enforcement became impossible. After the "second AI winter" between 1988 and 1995,[84] the filter technology started to make use of the improvements in AI, with the deep learning revolution starting in 2012, as a branch of machine learning that models high level abstractions in data by using a deep graph with many processing layers.[85] As the number of users of social media exponentially increased due to network effects, so did the number of notice-and-takedown requests. As discussed above, safe harbour provisions, in the EU and US have given perverse incentives for OSPs to look the other way. Despite the safe harbours, the OSPs were still being sued by the copyright holders. In order to avoid court cases and the possibility of being held secondarily liable for copyright infringement, OSPs started to increasingly rely on AI-powered filter technology to enforce the protection against online copyright infringement.

For the emerging iteration of the internet, Berners-Lee pleads for a read-write-execute web, which he calls semantic web,[86] where data in web pages are structured and tagged in such a way that they can be read by computers. According to others, the functionality of Web 3.0 can be characterized as decentralized via blockchains. These points of view are not mutually exclusive and are compatible with the probable elements of the metaverse, as pointed out below.[87] One can argue that the pandemic, the appreciation of the value of data, and the push for a coinless society will help speed up the arrival of the metaverse.

---

[82] Economist (29 January 2022).

[83] Berners-Lee (March 1989).

[84] Schuchmann (13 May 2019).

[85] LeCun, Bengio and Hinton (2015).

[86] Berners-Lee (2000).

[87] Parisi (23 October 2021).

The evolution of the internet towards the metaverse is in full swing. Even though it is impossible to predict what it will look like, it seems there is some consensus about its contours. The definition of Metaverse Roadmap 2009–2025 seems to be still valid:

> The Metaverse is the convergence of 1. virtually enhanced physical reality and 2. physically persistent virtual space. It is a fusion of both, while allowing users to experience it as either.[88]

In 2021, Parisi added a bit more flesh to the bones of the concept by providing seven rules of the metaverse (notice that Parisi writes metaverse with a reverential capital letter, just as was done with the word "internet", until Wired dropped the capital in 2004[89]):

1. Rule: There is only one Metaverse;
2. Rule: The Metaverse is for everyone;
3. Rule: Nobody controls the Metaverse;
4. Rule: The Metaverse is open;
5. Rule: The Metaverse is hardware-independent;
6. Rule: The Metaverse is a Network;
7. Rule: The Metaverse is the Internet.[90]

3.1 Potentiality of the Metaverse

The metaverse will cater for omnifarious activities: work, social, games, and entertainment. The idea is that you can be whoever you want to be, which invites people to experiment with their identity. Even though the metaverse[91] is still a Fata Morgana,[92] there seems to be some consensus that it will encompass the existing internet and create an open, inclusive, persistent, interoperable network that provides Extended Reality, which could include digital twins of physical objects, that can be experienced multi-sensorily, and that it makes, at least partly, use of decentralized technology. The metaverse will intensify and amplify the challenges of the current internet that copyright holders, OSPs (ISSPs and OCSSPs), and users are already facing in regard to the automatic protection of copyright and fundamental rights such as freedom of expression.

---

[88] Metaverse Roadmap (2009), p. 4. See also Ravenscraft (25 November 2021).

[89] West and Karsten (1 June 2016).

[90] In the beginning, the word internet was capitalized, now that is not too common. The same can be expected from the metaverse. Parisi (23 October 2021).

[91] Metaverse is a term coined in Snow Crash by Stephenson (1992). A similar concept was introduced as the Oasis, by Cline in Ready Player One, a novel in which people gather in the Oasis. Cline (2011), which inspired the launch of Facebook's Oculus Rift. Stephen Spielberg made the book into a movie in 2018.

[92] Fata Morgana is an optical phenomenon where mirages significantly distort the object or objects on which they are based, often such that the object is completely unrecognizable.

> In that Empire, the Art of Cartography attained such Perfection that the map of a single Province occupied the entirety of a City, and the map of the Empire, the entirety of a Province. In time, those Unconscionable Maps no longer satisfied, and the Cartographers Guilds struck a Map of the Empire whose size was that of the Empire, and which coincided point for point with it.[93]

Like in the Borgesian story, the potentiality of the metaverse[94] is to let the map and the territory[95] coincide. Humans seem to accept this merger of natural and virtual reality as a new kind of reality. One can argue that this is similar to the way we perceive the physical world: even though matter has at one moment wave-like and the next moment particle-like properties,[96] our senses, nevertheless, perceive this wave-particle duality as a solid reality. Nick Bostrom poses the intriguing question of whether our reality is a computer simulation by a posthuman society that is doing an "ancestor-simulation".[97] Whether that is the case or not, our generation of humans seems driven towards simulating its own reality using Virtual Reality (VR), Augmented Reality (AR), and Mixed Reality (MR).

An example of VR is Google Maps: where one can zoom in, parachute an avatar in a street, and see through its eyes the Street View and move from A to B. An example of AR is the mobile game Pokémon Go, where a cartoon-figure based on a squirrel is superimposed on the screen of a mobile that is depicting what the camera sees, so that these Pokémons can be "collected" by the player of this game. A mixture of VR and AR is called Mixed Reality (MR). An example is the extra layers that can be imposed on Google Maps for restaurants or traffic. Extended Reality (XR) includes all experiences possible on the continuum of VR and AR.[98]

According to the Metaverse Roadmap 2009–2025, the metaverse will evolve somewhere along two continua: augmentation-simulation and external-intimate. Along these continua, one can distinguish 4 quadrants: virtual worlds (simulation + intimate); mirror worlds (simulation + external); augmented reality (augmentation + external); and lifelogging (augmentation + intimate).[99]

3.1.1 Virtual Worlds

In some of the virtual worlds within the metaverse, it is very likely, if we extrapolate existing trends, that users will be able to create and monetize virtual property; from avatars to virtual buildings and virtual influencers.[100] In one of the first virtual worlds

---

93 Borges (1946).

94 Acronym of meta (transcendent) and verse (universe).

95 Houellebecq (2012).

96 Davis (27 July 2012).

97 Bostrom (2003).

98 In other words: XR includes VR, MR, and AR.

99 Metaverse Roadmap (2009), p. 4.

100 No casting bureau, no model. Virtual influencers can represent a brand for the right demographics. Rasmussen (17 March 2022). See also, Rasmussen (14 October 2021).

called Second Life, users retain some ownership rights over the objects, land, and other assets acquired in that virtual world. Virtual worlds have become an important place for entertainment. Several artists have performed via their avatar, like Ariana Grande[101] in one of the virtual worlds.[102] A clip from a Star Wars film had its premiere in Fortnite in 2021.[103] Virtual worlds were also the refuge in pandemic times for weddings, graduation ceremonies, etc.

John Perry Barlow declared in 1996 that the laws of cyberspace would be independent from the jurisdictions of states: "Your legal concepts of property, expression, identity, movement, and context do not apply to us. They are all based on matter, and there is no matter here."[104] The last 25 years have demonstrated that Barlow's vision is romantic and that virtual worlds are not evolving in this direction. Then again, the Maldives, Malta, and the Philippines opened virtual embassies in 2007 in Second Life. In 2022, Barbados opened an embassy in Decentraland, a virtual world on the blockchain.[105]

Developers of virtual worlds will probably seek copyright protection for software and any other original or creative content, virtual object, and graphics relating to the underlying program. Depending on the end-user licence agreements (EULAs), users can create virtual objects that, if they are original (independently created with a modicum of creativity and in the US also fixed in a tangible medium), are eligible for copyright protection.

According to Russo and Risch, users will not be held liable for copyright infringement due to their role in creating virtual worlds except in cases where "(1) strikingly similar or nearly identical copying occurs for virtual worlds and virtual objects that simulate the real world and real objects or (2) substantial similarity exists for unique virtual worlds and unique virtual objects."[106] Developers of virtual reality platforms "often create only the virtual world's skeleton, encouraging players to create new material that the developers integrate into the game space."[107] If there are disputes over who owns the copyright, Beausoleil suggested co-authorship as a possible solution,[108] as demonstrated by the 3rd Cir. in *Williams Electronics, Inc. v. Arctic Intern, Inc.* in 1982.[109] Also, in the US, a user can invoke the fair use defence, she or he does not have to make clear that the use "genuinely and substantially benefited the

101 Kreps (7 August 2021).

102 Travis Scott's concert in "Fortnite", on 23 April 2020, had an audience of 12 million people. Lil Nas X, a rapper, performed as an avatar in the virtual world Roblox in November 2021. Economist (13 March 2021).

103 Economist (11 May 2021).

104 Barlow (8 February 1995).

105 James Cooper poses the interesting question whether the Vienna Convention on Diplomatic Relations is applicable to embassies of sovereign nations in virtual worlds. Cooper (21 January 2022).

106 Russo and Risch (1993).

107 Reuveni (2007).

108 Beausoleil (2017), p. 4.

109 *Williams Electronics, Inc. v. Arctic Intern, Inc.*, 685 F.2d 870, 875 (3d Cir. 1982).

public," instead she or he only needs to show that the use "could have benefited the public marginally."[110]

3.1.2 Mirror Worlds

Mirror worlds are informationally enhanced virtual models or "reflections of the physical world.[111] Or "software [that] puts the world in a shoebox", as David Gelernter put it in the subtitle of his book "Mirror Worlds".[112] A mirror world of a city could, for example, provide information at different levels. "As low-level data flows in at the bottom, the big picture comes into focus on top."[113] Mirror worlds are able to provide a deep, live picture, can use agents ("knowbots" that work on behalf of human sponsors), record history (possibility to replay what happened), and experiences at different levels.[114] Google Earth is an example of a mirror world, which stores, analyses, and manages data and associated attributes that are spatially referenced to the Earth. Street View of Google Maps,[115] is recorded with film cameras, or 3D models of cities, recorded with laser scans.[116] Appropriating a real-world copyrighted object into such a mirror world could be qualified as copyright infringement.[117] A case in point is Formula 1, which did not renew the grant of its license for the use of its intellectual property rights in the cryptocurrency game Animoca Brands' F1 Delta Time game. Players of the game bought F1 assets as NFTs and will lose them.[118] If Animoca Brands did not deactivate these virtual assets, it would lead not only to a breach of contract but also to intellectual property infringement (probably trademark and copyright infringements).

Article 5(3)(h) Directive 2001/29/EC provides freedom of panorama of use of works, such as works of architecture or sculpture, made to be located permanently in public places, which is an optional exception or limitation for EU member states. This has led to a *smörgåsbord* of regulation: in some EU member states, the use of objects in public spaces falls under copyright infringement, while other member states have introduced the exception and limitation of Article 5(3)(h) Directive 2001/29/EC to varying degrees.

---

[110] *Rubin v. Brooks/Cole Pub. Co.*, 836 F. Supp. 909, 916 (D. Mass. 1993).

[111] Metaverse Roadmap (2009) p. 9.

[112] Gelernter (1992).

[113] Gelernter (1992), p. 27.

[114] Gelernter (1992), pp. 28–30.

[115] Similar to Street View of Google Maps was Amazon's BlockView from 2004–2006, which was a kind of upgrade to yellow pages. The investments in sending cars with cameras to register all street views are not relevant in regard to copyright. Sweat of the brow is not copyrightable. *Feist Publications, Inc., v. Rural Telephone Service Co.*, 499 U.S. 340 (1991).

[116] Hobson (18 July 2014).

[117] Chheda (2005).

[118] Hayward (16 March 2022).

It seems that a metaverse that incorporates mirror cityscapes, should have the freedom of panorama, so that the builders of those virtual buildings will not be sued by the architects of the physical buildings for such use.[119] Merely annotating the mirror worlds would probably lead to fewer chances of copyright infringement. "Digital twins" broadly interpreted, can also mean the online profiles with which the users of platforms de facto pay for the use of the services of these platforms.[120] It can also mean the digital replicas of physical assets,[121] processes or systems, which can use real-time data from various sources, such as sensors placed in the physical twin. Simulations can be rendered, and analytics can be applied using machine-learning.[122] Catherine Simpson points out that in order to avoid copyright issues, the drafters of contracts also need to consider the digital twin.[123] It also must be avoided that the digital twin becomes the perfect blueprint for copyright infringers of the physical counterpart.[124]

3.1.3 Augmented Reality

AR depends on the further development of intelligent materials and the "smart environment" networked computational intelligence embedded in physical objects: "everyware",[125] and spaces.[126] Mark Weiser introduced the concept of ubiquitous computing,[127] that will be invisibly woven into the fabric of our lives, via cloud computing, sensors, and networks of the Internet of Things (IoT) using Radio-Frequency Identification (RFID), etc., and the design of "calm technology" that allows technology to move from the periphery to the centre and back.[128] Special glasses that can project extra information if necessary, can augment reality with, for example, a road map.

3.1.4 Lifelogging

Keeping a diary transposed to the era of the metaverse is lifelogging. Lifelogging is the capture, storage and distribution of everyday experiences and information for objects and people.[129] Google Glasses that could provide AR and lifelogging failed

[119] Moore (22 December 2021).
[120] Mack (8 January 2019).
[121] Economist (13 November 2021).
[122] Simpson (2020).
[123] Simpson (2020).
[124] Bird & Bird (10 November 2020).
[125] Greenfield (2006).
[126] Metaverse Roadmap (2009), p. 12.
[127] Weiser (September 1991).
[128] Weiser and Brown (21 December 1995).
[129] Metaverse Roadmap (2009), p. 14.

because it was expected to lead to privacy issues and copyright infringement, for example, if someone forgets to switch off his Google Glasses in a cinema, and then later shares his day's experience with a friend.[130] Bill Gates referred to the evidentiary value of a documented life.[131]

3.2 *Immersive Experiences*

Immersive experiences can be achieved through the use of headsets, which display 3D images and block out the "real world," while tracking the user's head movements so that the displayed images seem to exist in a 360-degree environment.[132] For example, Oculus Rift's head-mounted display ("HMD") contains sensors that detect the orientation and tilt of the user's head.[133] The multiverse, with its immersive experiences, will probably lead to an explosion of creativity. A simulation of surfing in the ocean, while trying to escape sharks, torpedoes, and drones could include works eligible for copyright infringement beyond the piracy of audio-visual or software works. A special haptic suit and gloves can simulate the feeling of water and temperature against the user's body, while the user is standing on a special board. The specific composition of a choreography of stimuli, including visual, aural, kinetic, and the sense of space (proprioception), and perhaps even the olfactory (smell)[134] and gustatory (taste)[135] of the ocean, could be eligible for copyright protection.[136]

3.3 *Places to Experiment*

Socially, the metaverse might invite users to experiment with their identity,[137] role play, and self-expression. According to the Metaverse Roadmap, this might lead to new perspectives on social norms around gender, ethnicity, species, social class,

---

[130] Davis (1 April 2014).

[131] Gates et al. (1995).

[132] Wheatley (2017).

[133] Grubb (6 August 2014).

[134] Scents can be encoded onto a digital file and decoded into a scent again by making use of a scent printer. Friedmann (2015).

[135] For example, taste can be simulated by stimulating certain areas of the tongue with a weak electric current. Matchar (15 August 2018). See also: Yen (undated).

[136] For comparison: The choreography of fountains, light, color and music was eligible for copyright protection in China. See *Beijing Water Design Technology Co., Ltd. v. West Lake Management Office and Zhongke Hengye Company*. Beijing Intellectual Property Court, upheld the decision by the Haidian District People's Court, which decided that there was copyright infringement. See, Yuan (19 July 2018).

[137] Virtual identity fluidity seems possible. Jenkins raises the question whether racial fluidity would be socially acceptable. Jenkins Jr (18 January 2022).

etiquette, and group values and goals.[138] David Brin suggested using different zones in cyberspace, which would invite some users to experiment: "Creating one or more commercially distinct zones within cyberspace, which people can visit to test and grow familiar with these payment schemes, while sampling therein some truly distinct and original entertainment experiences they can find nowhere else."[139]

Brin's suggestion of allowing micropayments[140] would be an interesting alternative for using users' data as a business model in connection to ever more precise advertisements. However, this seems out of the question in the omniscient metaverse, where there is no information loss.

3.4 *Predecessors of the Metaverse*

The predecessors of the metaverse, virtual worlds such as Fortnite, Decentraland, Minecraft, and Roblox,[141] demonstrate some of the potential that the metaverse could offer and what concomitant challenges this would bring for copyright holders, platform holders and users. Users can create avatars expressing the identity in which they want to manifest themselves, and objects such as virtual land[142] and architecture,[143] cars,[144] etc. For example, there is a virtual version of the Starcourt Mall from the Netflix series "Stranger Things" in Roblox but also Fortnite. Roblox provides programs that let users build and monetise three-dimensional games and experiences. Examples include: "Piggy", which is a user-created horror game inspired by "Peppa Pig", a cartoon; and programmes based on "Squid Game", a Netflix series.[145] These examples make clear that the risk of copyright infringement cases is not imaginary. In May 2021, one user resold a virtual copy of a Gucci handbag for around US$4,100.[146] However, if virtual creations were made by avatars that have AI aspects built into

[138] Metaverse Roadmap (2009), p. 8.

[139] Brin (1998) A Future for Copyright?

[140] Brin (1998) An Economy of Micropayments?

[141] Many companies want to be part of the metaverse. Fortnite, made by Epic Games, has more than 300 million players worldwide. Roblox has 47 m gamers who spend 3 billion hours a month on its platform. Economist (22 January 2022).

[142] There has been a steep rise in the prices paid for virtual property. Smaller parcels that fetched around US$20 apiece when the virtual world Decentraland launched in 2017, can now sell for as much as US$100,000. Economist (1 January 2022).

[143] ONE Sotheby's International Realty and Voxel Architects, along with general contractor and NFT collector Gabe Sierra, are introducing the first ever "MetaReal" mansion that includes a real-world home and a virtual counterpart in the Sandbox (https://metaverse.properties/buy-in-the-sandbox/ (last access 12 July 2022), which is a virtual world that calls itself the metaverse. Reynolds (5 January 2022).

[144] In July 2021, Ferrari uploaded a virtual version of one of models into Fortnite for players to drive around. Economist (20 November 2021).

[145] Economist (20 November 2021).

[146] Economist (20 November 2021).

them, these creations will be deemed AI creations[147] instead of human creations, and may not be allowed copyright protection,[148] but could still be protected under trademark law. Big fashion brands, such as Gucci, Dolce & Gabbana, and Burberry all show or sell virtual versions of their goods in virtual worlds. In its art district, Sotheby's, a real-world auction house, has opened a virtual gallery in Decentraland.[149] The US footwear and apparel company Nike has filed with the US Patent and Trademark Office for some of its famous trademarks, such as "Nike", "Jordan", the swoosh logo, and the slogan "Just Do It" in respect of the following goods and services: classes 9, 35, and 41 of the WIPO Nice Classification system.[150] This demonstrates that companies such as Nike see a future for selling virtual versions of their goods. Unauthorized copies of such branded virtual items can obviously lead to trademark and, if they are original, copyright infringement cases. When trademark holders are not able to rely on their trademarks because there might be no confusion as to the source of the virtual good or because of an absolute ground for refusal,[151] an alternative method to stop the unauthorized use would be to file a claim for copyright infringement. But in such cases, exceptions and limitations should come into play.

3.5 The End of Walled Gardens?

Lack of interoperability has prevented users from using copyrighted works on other devices. For example, iBooks of Apple could not be accessed on a Kindle of Amazon. One of the tenets of the metaverse is interoperability. This would make it possible for users to move their avatars or other virtual assets between virtual worlds and

[147] Lehot and Allen (1 December 2021).

[148] The Compendium of U.S. Copyright Office Practices states a work may be copyrightable (i) if it is eligible for copyright protection in the United States, (ii) if the work has been fixed in a tangible medium of expression, (iii) if the work was created by a human author, (iv) if the work constitutes copyrightable subject matter, and (v) if the work contains at least a minimum amount of creative authorship that is original to the author. Perlmutter (2021).

[149] Economist (1 January 2022).

[150] Class 9: Downloadable virtual goods, namely, computer programs featuring footwear, clothing, headwear, eyewear, bags, sports bags, backpacks, sports equipment, art, toys and accessories for use online and in online virtual worlds. Class 35: Retail store services featuring virtual goods, namely, footwear, clothing, headwear, eyewear sports bags, backpacks, sports equipment, art, toys and accessories for use online; on-line retail store services featuring virtual merchandise, namely, footwear, clothing, headwear, eyewear, bags, sports bags, backpacks, sports equipment, art, toys and accessories. Class 41: Entertainment services, namely, providing on-line, non-downloadable virtual footwear, clothing, headwear, eyewear, bags, sports bags, backpacks, sports equipment, art, toys and accessories for use in virtual environments. Saint Island (undated). WIPO Nice Classification. Available at: https://www.wipo.int/classifications/nice/en/ (last access 12 July 2022).

[151] Article 7 Regulation (EU) 2017/1001 of the European Parliament and of the Council of 14 June 2017 on the European Union trade mark, ELI: http://data.europa.eu/eli/reg/2017/1001/oj (last access 12 July 2022).

be able to use different interfaces for the same virtual property.[152] It is expected that merging these fragments of the internet into one metaverse will be a formidable challenge. China also invests in the metaverse.[153] Perhaps an organization such as the Internet Corporation for Assigned Names and Numbers (ICANN) could take on the coordination of the different parts of the metaverse and their interoperability.[154] The rise of interoperability increases the scale and speed of the spread of works without the authorization of the right holders. Then again, a central repository in such a constellation might be established, so that the different platforms in the metaverse can use automated content recognition tools to see whether a work matches with a work on the central repository,[155] before the work is uploaded to or created on the platform. In this respect, it becomes of crucial importance that these tools learn to consider exceptions and limitations, fair use or fair dealing in their filter decisions as well. One can imagine that a central repository becomes a voluntary copyright register with rights management information functionality. Those that upload their works to the central repository first get a timestamp and will be presumed to be the authors.[156] At this point in time, if this central repository were on the blockchain, it would be prohibitively expensive to upload works.[157] Instead, the Interplanetary File System (IPFS) could be used. This is a protocol and peer-to-peer network for storing and sharing data via a distributed file system with the goal of providing permanence to the internet.[158] One can think of a constellation whereby once the works are on the central repository, the works are not visible to anyone other than platforms. Authors could use the rights management information function of such a central repository by indicating to platforms if they want to block or monetize after publication. It is also possible for authors to instruct the platforms to allow their works to be used in certain ways that go beyond the exceptions or limitations. A licensing system, such as Lessig's Creative Commons (CC), shows a possible solution. CC has three layers: human-readable, lawyer readable, and machine-readable.[159] CC's voluntary formalities are not prohibited under the influential Article 5(2) Berne Convention for the Protection of Literary and Artistic Works, and are incorporated in Article 9(1) TRIPs. Stef van

152 Virtual worlds syndication. Metaverse Roadmap (2009), p. 7.

153 Li Z et al. (30 October 2021).

154 ICANN is an American multistakeholder group and nonprofit organization responsible for coordinating the maintenance and procedures of several databases related to the namespaces and numerical spaces of the Internet, ensuring the network's stable and secure operation. Available at: https://www.icann.org/ (last access 12 July 2022).

155 Automated content recognition uses various techniques, including hashing, watermarking, fingerprinting, AI-based/Enhanced content recognition. EUIPO (2020).

156 In such a scenario, the ownership of the copyright could be disputed out-of-court and in court.

157 Chen and Friedmann (submitted 2022), p. 4.

158 IPFS (undated).

159 "Human readable" uses intuitive icons and words, such as BY (attribution), SA (share-alike), NC (non-commercial), and ND (no derivative works). "Lawyer readable" provides the legal code. "Machine readable" enables automatic enforcement. Licensees may copy, distribute, display and perform the work and make derivative works and remixes based on it only if they give the author or licensor the credits (attribution) in the manner specified by these. Creative Commons (undated).

Gompel makes the case that the challenges for copyright in the dominant digital realm warrant legislative reform, which might include formalities.[160] An assessment of each factor makes it clear that formalities could be conducive for all protagonists of the tough love triangle: copyright holders, OCSSPs, and users. The author could indicate how he or she wants the platforms to monetize or block the work, after its publication.

3.6 Dark Potential of the Metaverse

When the right balance is not struck, the result of the metaverse can become anaemic. If users want to express themselves via a Spiderman avatar, it should be made possible, even in return for some micropayment for a license. If one wants to use a Spiderman avatar and exaggerate certain features, then the avatar would become a "caricature", which falls under an exception or limitation. This should be allowed without the fear of being blocked, which would have a chilling effect on creativity.

Machine learning deployed by current social media, such as Facebook, had, already a decade ago, the uncanny ability to predict when people get into an amorous relationship,[161] when a woman is pregnant,[162] or someone's sexual orientation,[163] based on their online behaviour. This possibility to monitor, manipulate, and monetize users,[164] will be incomparably higher on the metaverse than on the current social media. The risk is that subliminal and supraliminal techniques will be used that respectively go under and above the threshold of the users' consciousness but still influence them.[165]

Because of its interoperability, the technology of the metaverse is able to keep tracking you. Because of its equipment that makes immersive experiences possible, the technology is able to determine where the gaze lingers, when the pupil dilates, the facial expressions, heart and respiration rate, galvanic skin responses, etc. Where true name registration failed in the past, the metaverse will be able to detect, identify and authenticate anyone based on their multi-factor unique profiles.

As a counterweight, breathing space is required for the metaverse, so that it will truly reach its potential in regard to creativity, inclusiveness, and diversity, especially given its public function. In other words, to avoid the metaverse becoming anaemic, it should have sufficient safeguards for exceptions and limitations.

---

160 Van Gompel (2010).

161 Ferenstein (15 February 2014).

162 Hill (16 February 2012).

163 Kosinski et al. (2013).

164 Rosenberg (22 December 2021).

165 Neuwirth (2022).

4 Safeguards for Legitimate Use of Content

Copyright is an intellectual property right. Article 17(2) Charter of Fundamental Rights of the EU[166] obliges member states of the EU to protect intellectual property. According to this syllogism, copyright needs to be protected by the members of the EU. However, the protection of copyright is not absolute. This fundamental right needs to be balanced with other fundamental rights, such as Article 11 Charter of Fundamental Rights of the EU, which prescribes the freedom of expression and information, and Article 13 Charter of Fundamental Rights of the EU; freedom of the arts and sciences. The EU members are also members of the European Convention on Human Rights and Fundamental Freedoms (ECHR),[167] and have to comply with Article 10 ECHR; freedom of expression. But they have to balance this with Article 1 Protocol to the Convention for the Protection of Human Rights and Fundamental Freedoms[168]; protection of property, which the EU members also signed and ratified, and which arguably implies intellectual property.

Elkin-Koren argues that "users are not passive recipients of creative works but constitute an input in the creative process."[169] Virtues of users' rights include enhancing human capital; productive and transformative use[170]; and generating meaning.[171]

An ideal copyright system incentivizes authors to create works, protects and enforces these works, but also gives sufficient rights to users and follow-on authors to the unauthorized but legal use of the works if that use falls within fair use, fair dealing[172] or an exception or limitation. The scholarship of especially Lessig[173] and Boyle,[174] respectively, covered the need for free use, fair use, and the public domain.

166 Charter of Fundamental Rights of the European Union, OJ C 326, 26.10.2012, p. 391–407. Available at: https://eur-lex.europa.eu/legal-content/EN/TXT/?uri=CELEX:12012P/TXT (last access 12 July 2022).

167 Convention for the Protection of Human Rights and Fundamental Freedoms, Rome, open for signature on Rome, 4 November 1950, entered into force on 3 September 1953. Available at: https://www.echr.coe.int/documents/convention_eng.pdf (last access 12 July 2022).

168 Protocol to the Convention for the Protection of Human Rights and Fundamental Freedoms, Paris, opened for signature, on 20 March 1952, entered into force on 18 April 1954. Available at: https://www.echr.coe.int/documents/convention_eng.pdf (last access 12 July 2022).

169 Elkin-Koren (2017b), p. 146.

170 Elkin-Koren (2017b), p. 143.

171 Elkin-Koren (2017b), p. 144.

172 Fair Dealing can be found in Common Law jurisdictions such as the UK §§ 29 and 30 Copyrights, Designs and Patents Act 1988 UK and Hong Kong §§ 38, 39, 41A and 54A Copyright Ordinance. Fair dealing with a copyrighted work is not infringing if the dealing is for a purpose specifically stated in the act. Canada is moving from Fair Dealing to the Fair Use direction. Geist (2013).

173 Lessig (2004), Lessig (2008).

174 Boyle (2008).

The emergence of technological measures and rights management information mandated by the "WIPO Internet Treaties",[175] led to §§ 1201[176] and 1202[177] of the DMCA. This set of access control technologies for restricting the use of proprietary hardware and copyrighted works in combination with mobile internet and cloud computing[178] have made it possible for copyright holders to monetize their works not by selling copies but by providing contractual services, which keeps these works out of reach of fair use, fair dealing, or exceptions or limitations.[179]

4.1 Mandatory and Optional Exceptions or Limitations

Article 17(7) Directive 2019/790 states that the cooperation between OCSSPs and right holders should not result in the prevention of legitimate works uploaded by users. The legitimate use of works by users is when they hold the relevant rights, when the work is in the public domain, or when the use is an exception or limitation to copyright and related rights.

For the first time, the users of OCSSPs can rely on the mandatory exceptions or limitations of quotation, criticism, review, caricature, parody, or pastiche. This is a step in the right direction; however, the exceptions or limitations of Article 5 Directive 2001/29/EC are still optional for EU member states. Besides the mandatory exceptions or limitations of Directive 2019/790, it is very difficult for OCSSPs and all other ISSPs to take into consideration the specific sets of exceptions or limitations for each of the 27 jurisdictions of the EU. Therefore, harmonisation of all exceptions or limitations at the EU level would be very welcomed.

---

[175] WIPO Internet Treaties include the WIPO Copyright Treaty and WIPO Performances and Phonograms Treaty. Articles 11 and 12 WIPO Copyright Treaty, adopted on 20 December 1996, and came into effect on 6 March 2002. Articles 18 and 19 WIPO Performances and Phonograms Treaty, adopted on 20 December 1996, and came into effect on 20 May 2002.

[176] 17 U.S.C. § 1201.

[177] 17 U.S.C. § 1202.

[178] The first mention of the concept of the "cloud" was in 1996. Dan Ciuriak, On the Metaverse, Web3 and Prospering in the Digital Transformation (December 21, 2021). Commentary, in Chinese Views of Non-traditional Security 13(1), December. Saint Pierre Center for International Security (SPCIS), Guangzhou. Available at: https://papers.ssrn.com/sol3/papers.cfm?abstract_id=3991217 (last access 12 July 2022).

[179] Elkin-Koren (2017b), p. 136.

4.2 Stakeholder Dialogues

At the 6th and latest Stakeholder Dialogue in Etterbeek, Belgium, on 10 February 2020,[180] there was a distinct difference of opinion between especially users' organizations on the one hand, and the representatives of right holders on the other hand about the main route of ensuring fundamental rights. The first group held that fundamental rights were an *ex ante* issue. Thus, when users try to upload works without the authorization of the right holders, which is nevertheless legal, because the use falls under an exception or limitation, right holders and OCSSPs should take this into consideration when making the decision to block a work from being uploaded. The latter group held that fundamental rights were an *ex post* issue. Thus, that users could make use of the complaint and redress mechanism if they believed that the work that was blocked was an exception or limitation.

The users' organizations also advocated a system similar to the one proposed by a group of copyright scholars,[181] where users will be informed that the work they tried to upload matches a reference work, to a certain degree (percentage given), according to the party that had sent the reference work (presumed copyright holder) to the OCSS. The user will then get the opportunity to flag the use as legal if he or she believes that that work falls under an exception or limitation, after each of the six exceptions and limitations is clarified with an example. If the right holder still wishes to remove or disable access to the content, he or she must explain why the use in question is *prima facie* an infringement, and why it is not conceivable that the content falls under an exception or limitation.[182]

According to a proposal by media company Studio71,[183] only if the copyright holder learns that the work is equivalent or identical to the reference work (via automated content recognition) or if it is known that the work is time-sensitive,[184] the copyright holder could "push a red button", so that the work could still be blocked without human review.

The users' organizations argued that there is a need for solutions to prevent or reduce abusive claims (typically when a claimant does not actually hold the rights) and reliable rights information.

In contrast, the rights holders argued that Directive 2019/790 is a balanced law that should not be tinkered with. It was argued that since automated content recognition software is not capable of taking context of use into account, so it cannot distinguish between infringing use and use that falls within an exception or limitation, the work should first be blocked. Then it is up to the user to make use of the complaint and redress mechanism of Article 17(9) Directive 2019/790, and send a counter notice, after which the right holder will make a decision to either agree with the claim that

[180] European Commission (10 February 2020).

[181] Quintais et al. (11 November 2019).

[182] Quintais et al. (11 November 2019), para. 26.

[183] Presentation Studio 71. Available at: https://ec.europa.eu/newsroom/dae/document.cfm?doc_id=64796 (last access 12 July 2022).

[184] Pre-released music or films or live or recent broadcasts of sports events.

there was an exception or limitation and de-block the content, or to not agree on this point and continue to block the work. In addition, the right holders argued that it was not up to the European Commission to initiate a discussion of possible changes. The representative of the European Commission responded that Article 17(10) Directive 2019/790 mandated the Commission, in cooperation with the Member States, to discuss best practices for cooperation between OCSSPs and right holders, during stakeholder dialogues.

The respective solutions favoured by users' rights groups and right holders seem both flawed. On the one hand, to allow users to flag use as an exception or limitation, and also allow OCSSPs to use the "red button" to continue to block the work, and thereby undo the action of the user, seem vulnerable to the abuse of both parties, but more importantly require human review, and thus is not scalable.

On the other hand, in case of an exception or limitation, OCSSPs will standardly block each use if it matches a reference work, and only after the user makes use of the complaint and redress mechanism, the OCSSP unblocks the works. However, only a very small percentage of users makes use of this complaint and redress mechanism, since they are either intimidated by the complexity of the procedure or are fearful of legal action, or perceive it as useless.[185] Making the complaint and redress mechanism more streamlined and user friendly might not be in the OCSSPs' interest since it would lead to more complaints which require more human reviews.

Users' rights organisations also urged for more transparency in regard to why content is blocked or removed.

The HADOPI report demonstrated that 33 percent of French internet users had shared third party content (audio and video); 13 percent of these users have had an upload blocked for copyright infringement; 56 percent of them have challenged the last block that they encountered; 58 percent of these challenges have resulted in the content being reinstated. This is 1.4 percent of all French internet users, or about 700,000 individuals, who have been wrongfully blocked at least one time.[186] It is probable that similar results can be measured throughout the EU, which would lead to a few million individuals that have been wrongfully blocked.

4.3 *Sufficient Safeguards Against Over-Blocking*

In regard to the use of automated means by various intermediary service providers, the DSA draft does not provide precise requirements and limits.[187] Advocate General (AG) Henrik Saugmandsgaard Øe provided more clarity in his opinion on C-401/19 *Republic of Poland v European Parliament and Council of the European Union.*[188]

[185] HADOPI (2020), p. 90.

[186] Based on statistics of the HADOPI report: Communia (10 February 2020).

[187] Peukert et al. (2022), p. 11.

[188] C-401/19, *Republic of Poland v European Parliament, Council of the European Union,* Opinion of Advocate General Saugmandsgaard Øe, 15 July 2021, ECLI:EU:C:2021:613. Available at:

In this case, Poland asked the CJEU for a preliminary ruling on whether the monitoring and filtering obligations of Article 17(4)(b) and (c) Directive 2019/790 are circumscribed by sufficient safeguards to minimize the impact on the freedom of expression.

The AG argued that *ex ante* blocking of content uploaded by users of a platform is allowed if it concerns information that was already established as being illegal (by a court) or that is manifestly illegal ("obvious from the outset").[189] The AG pointed to the CJEU in *Eva Glawischnig-Piesczek v Facebook Ireland Ltd.*,[190] a case about an injunction against a defamatory post, pertaining to Directive 2000/31/EC. The CJEU linked the scope of identical or equivalent content to the lack of a need to carry out any additional human assessments,[191] and instead could rely on automatic monitoring and filtering that the CJEU interpreted to fall under the specific monitoring obligation.[192] The AG held that paragraphs (4)(b) and (4)(c) of Article 17 Directive 2019/790 are compatible with the Charter of Fundamental Rights,[193] provided that those obligations are circumscribed by sufficient safeguards to minimize the impact of such filtering on that freedom.[194] In this respect, the CJEU followed the AG's point of view.[195]

In C-401/19, the European Parliament and the Council of the EU asserted that OCSSPs are private operators and, therefore, may freely choose the information they wish to see disseminated using their services. Therefore, they may decide to filter and block content. "Even if this were to constitute an 'interference' with the freedom of expression of users, that interference, in any event, would not be attributable to the EU legislature."[196] This argument can be criticized since many a platform performs the important public function indispensable to the democratic process.[197] Chapter IV of the European Declaration on Digital Rights and Principles for the Digital Decade of 2022 states:

---

https://curia.europa.eu/juris/document/document.jsf?docid=244201&doclang=en (last access 12 July 2022).

[189] C-401/19, *Republic of Poland v European Parliament, Council of the European Union*, Opinion of Advocate General Saugmandsgaard Øe, 15 July 2021, ECLI:EU:C:2021:613, para. 198. Available at: https://curia.europa.eu/juris/document/document.jsf?docid=244201&doclang=en (last access 12 July 2022).

[190] C-18/18, supra n 75.

[191] C-18/18, supra n 75, para. 19.

[192] C/18/18, supra n 75, para. 46.

[193] C-401/19, *Republic of Poland v European Parliament, Council of the European Union*, Provisional text Opinion of Advocate General Saugmandsgaard Øe, 15 July 2021, ECLI:EU:C:2021:613.

[194] Opinion on C-401/19, para. 6.

[195] C-401/19, *Republic of Poland v European Parliament, Council of the European Union*, Provisional test Judgment of the Court (Grand Chamber), CJEU of 26 April 2022, ECLI:EU:C:2022:297, paras 63, 69, 82 and 92. Available at: https://curia.europa.eu/juris/document/document.jsf?text=&docid=258261&doclang=en (last access 12 July 2022).

[196] Opinion on C-401/19, para. 81.

[197] A widely noted and characteristic feature of the digital age is the democratization of information production, and therefore the democratization of opportunities to speak and express one's self. Jack M Balkin, 'Old-School/New-School Speech Regulation', 127:8 Harvard Law Review 2014, 2304.

> Very large online platforms should support free democratic debate online, given the role of their services in shaping public opinion and discourse.[198]

This joint declaration includes "taking measures to tackle all forms of illegal content in proportion to the harm they can cause, and in full respect of the right to freedom of expression and information, and without establishing any general monitoring obligations."[199]

The main question is whether a violation of the freedom of expression by the excessive or arbitrary filtering and blocking measures is proportional to its goal of protecting copyright.[200]

The AG pointed to the risk of over-blocking in order to avoid any risk of liability.[201] *A fortiori*, because of Article 17(4) Directive 2019/790, OCSSPs bear the burden of proof to demonstrate that they have made "best efforts" to prevent infringing content from being uploaded. Logically, the risk of liability is relative to the amount of content to which they provide access.

Also, in *YouTube and Cyando*, the CJEU obliged ISSPS "as soon as they actually obtained knowledge or awareness of illegal information, act expeditiously to remove or to disable access to that information, and must do so with due regard to the principle of freedom of expression."[202] The wording can be criticized because if exceptions or limitations apply, the information cannot be illegal. Still, these paragraphs make clear that exceptions or limitations need to be taken into account in the assessment after there is a match with a reference work.

The AG referred to the exceptions or limitations of Article 5(3) Directive 2001/29/EC, and Article 17(7)(a) and (b) that include uses that are creative reappropriations such as memes, film reviews, misappropriation, and other types of content for entertainment or education, which are abundant on those services and which, moreover, may in themselves constitute works which, often, are "transformative".[203]

The same AG Saugmandsgaard Øe, held in the Opinion on *YouTube and Cyando* in 2020, that over-removal would pose an obvious problem in terms of freedom of expression.[204]

---

[198] European Declaration on Digital Rights and Principles for the Digital Decade, joint declaration by European Parliament, the Council and the European Commission, COM(2022) 28 final, Brussels, 26 January 2022, Chapter IV, 5, available at https://ec.europa.eu/newsroom/dae/redirection/document/82703 (last access 12 July 2022).

[199] European Declaration on Digital Rights and Principles for the Digital Decade, joint declaration by European Parliament, the Council and the European Commission, COM(2022) 28 final, Brussels, 26 January 2022, Chapter IV, 5, available at https://ec.europa.eu/newsroom/dae/redirection/document/82703 (last access 12 July 2022).

[200] Opinion on C-401/19, para. 97.

[201] Opinion on C-401/19, paras 141–142.

[202] *YouTube and Cyando*, paras 113 and 116.

[203] Opinion on C-401/19, para. 145.

[204] Opinion *YouTube and Cyando*, para. 189.

In C-401/19, the AG put it succinctly: "automatic content recognition tools detect *content* and not copyright *infringement*."[205] For the latter, one needs to take exceptions or limitations into account. Poland held that in the application of exceptions or limitations to copyright, Article 17(7) Directive 2019/790 is more wishful thinking than an effective safeguard.[206] The AG explained that Article 17(4)(b) and (c) and Article 17(7) Directive 2019/790 apply simultaneously. Importantly, the AG held that "[t]he interpretation that that content could be systematically blocked *ex ante*, provided that users could obtain its reinstatement *ex post*, [was in his opinion], far from being the most natural way of understanding that wording."[207] The AG interpreted the Recitals 66 and 70(1) Directive 2019/790 in such a way that OCSSPs need to enable uploads of use that fall under exceptions or limitations.[208] According to the *travaux préparatoires*, users' rights and the complaint and redress mechanism were separated into distinct provisions.[209]

The AG also referred to *Scarlet Extended*[210] and *SABAM*,[211] where the filtering focused on unauthorized content led to a collateral effect that is too great for the fundamental rights.[212] OCSSPs have two cumulative obligations: they must seek to prevent the uploading of content which unlawfully reproduces the works and other protected subject matter identified by right holders, while not preventing the making available of content which lawfully reproduces that subject matter.[213]

5 Designing Algorithmic Exceptions or Limitations

Automated content recognition, deployed by OCSSPs, under Article 17(4)(b) and (c) Directive 2019/790, makes use of machine learning algorithms that are trained to recognize certain content. This section will explore whether it is possible to let the algorithm distinguish between the unauthorized and illegal use of content and unauthorized but legal use of content. In other words, can it detect exceptions or limitations? In the second part of this section, the question is posed whether AI used in automated content recognition should fall under the category "high risk AI", so that certain precautionary measures would become mandatory.

205 Opinion on C-401/19, para. 148.

206 Opinion on C-401/19, para. 166.

207 Opinion on C-401/19, para. 172.

208 Opinion on C-401/19, para. 174.

209 Opinion on C-401/10, para. 175.

210 C-70/10, *Scarlet Extended*, Judgment of the Court (Third Chamber) of 24 November 2011, ECLI identifier: ECLI:EU:C:2011:771, para 52. Available at: https://eur-lex.europa.eu/legal-content/EN/TXT/?uri=CELEX:62010CJ0070 (last access 12 July 2022).

211 C-360/10, *SABAM*, Judgment of 16 February 2012, EU:C:2012:85, para. 50. Available at: https://curia.europa.eu/juris/documents.jsf?num=C-360/10 (last access 12 July 2022).

212 Opinion on C-401/10, para. 186.

213 Opinion on C-401/10, para. 191.

5.1 Setting the Parameters

One could train an algorithm via machine learning to figure out patterns to distinguish between infringing and non-infringing content. However, this system will lead to black box results[214] that are moreover dynamic,[215] based on its data feed. This lack of *ex ante* transparency and explainability leads to legal uncertainty and unpredictability.

In the EU context, based on exceptions or limitations under Article 17(7) Directive 2019/790, one could feed that algorithm data based on settled case law, but also synthetic data.[216] This would enable the stakeholders to set the parameters and test the algorithms via simulations whether they will detect unauthorized but legal uses based on exceptions or limitations within the desired bandwidth, after graduating from the sandbox, throughout its lifecycle.

Therefore, a system could be devised, in the same vein as the concept of algorithmic fair use of Elkin-Koren,[217] to set up the parameters for an algorithmic exceptions or limitations recognition system from scratch so that the considerations become and remain transparent and that the algorithm fluctuates within a bandwidth. In C-401/10, the AG Saugmandsgaard Øe also suggested incorporating parameters in automatic content recognition tools, which help distinguish between what seems manifest and what is ambiguous. This may vary according to the types of protected subject matter and types of exceptions or limitations in question.[218] Thresholds will have to be determined above of where automatic blocking of content is justified and below of where the application of an exception is reasonably conceivable.

5.2 Protected Subject Matter

As pointed out above, depending on the production costs, a movie that has not yet launched in cinemas needs to be filtered without much room for exceptions or limitations, while a musical work is dependent on micropayments of royalties and advertisements during repeat use leaves more possibility. The nature of the work is also relevant. In the US, this falls under the second fair use factor, which assesses whether a work is predominantly based on facts/ideas or original expressions. Plagiarism detection software uses algorithms that can distinguish between facts and original expressions, probably based on the frequency of certain words or phrases, and will provide the percentages and ratio, and are thus useful to make this distinction as part of the second fair use factor's assessment. The nature of a work is also determined by whether the work is published or not. The algorithm can compare the work with

[214] Pasquale (2015).

[215] Bathaee (2018).

[216] Synthetic data is artificial data generated with the purpose of preserving privacy, creating training data for machine learning algorithms. Dilmegani (15 July 2020).

[217] Elkin-Koren (2017a).

[218] Opinion on C-401/10, para. 211.

a list of published works, such as the register of the Library of Congress or another central repository.

5.3 *Automated Exceptions and Limitations Recognition*

Article 17(7) Directive 2019/790 states:

> Member States shall ensure that users in each Member State are able to rely on any of the following existing exceptions or limitations when uploading and making available content generated by users on online content-sharing services:
>
> (a) quotation, criticism, review;
>
> (b) use for the purpose of caricature, parody or pastiche.

In addition, there is a variety of exceptions and limitations in force in each of the member states of the EU under Article 5(3) Directive 2001/29/EC. Beside the exceptions and limitations of Article 17(7) Directive 2019/790, OCSSPs need to take the respective combinations of exceptions and limitations per EU jurisdiction into account of Article 5(3) Directive 2001/29/EC. It is challenging for developers of automated content recognition tools to produce 27 different versions that take into account the mishmash of exceptions and limitations in the EU jurisdictions. The 6 mandatory exceptions and limitations for OCSSPs are the low-hanging fruit that can be tackled first, especially quotation, criticism, and review.

5.3.1 Quotation, Criticism and Review

> Quantity has a quality all its own.[219]

This exception is not defined in the copyright *acquis*. However, Article 5(3)(d) Directive 2001/29/EC provides a little bit more information:

> quotations for purposes such as criticism or review, provided that they relate to a work or other subject-matter which has already been lawfully made available to the public, that, unless this turns out to be impossible, the source, including the author's name, is indicated, and that their use is in accordance with fair practice, and to the extent required by the specific purpose;

In the opinion on *Pelham*, the AG Maciej Szpunar wrote that quotation must be for purposes such as criticism or review.[220] But he noticed that many quotations, in particular artistic quotations, such as musical quotations, are not for purposes of

---

[219] Misattributed it to Clausewitz, Lenin, Stalin, and Brezhnev, but mostly to Stalin. Klang (16 September 2016).

[220] C-476/17, *Pelham and Others*, Opinion of Advocate General Szpunar, 12 December 2018, ECLI:EU:C:2018:1002, para. 64 Available at: https://curia.europa.eu/juris/document/document.jsf?text=&docid=208881 (last access 12 July 2022).

criticism or review, but pursue other objectives. In the AG's opinion, "the quotation must enter into some kind of dialogue with the work quoted."[221] It seems that the drafters of Article 17(7)(a) Directive 2019/790 have taken notice: quotation, criticism, and review are now listed as separate exceptions or limitations that might all be part of the same group, where part of a work is extracted to refer to that work in another work.

What is lacking in Article 5(3)(k) Directive 2001/29/EC, in the case of caricature, parody or pastiche, is the explicit requirement that attribution is given to the author of the work that was used, just as in Article 5(3)(c) Directive 2001/29/EC for a quotation, review or criticism. All member states of the EU are members of the Berne Union, and have to comply with Article 6*bis*(1) Berne Convention for the Protection of Literary and Artistic Works, which includes: "the author shall have the right to claim authorship of the work".[222] Attribution could be given by adding the name of the author, and preferably a link to the author's website, as meta-data of the work, for example, as part of the YouTube post, or as an annotation in the video, visible to the audience of the caricature, parody or pastiche.

A series of ratios of quotations in relation to the complete works seem to be a first step that can help constitute the parameters for an algorithm. This way, an algorithm could consult a repository of works to see whether the quotation matches a work. If the right holder made clear in the content management system of the repository that it allows use that goes beyond the parameters for quotation, the algorithm could check whether the use meets that right holder's more lenient parameters. If the right holder's work was published, but the right holder indicated that it does not authorize any use, the algorithm needs to check whether the use would be nevertheless legal if it matches the parameters of the exceptions or limitations.

What are reasonable parameters? For example, how many seconds of a song can one quote? The CJEU in *Pelham*[223] made clear that in regard to a well-known song, one can prevent another person from taking a sample of an approximately 2-s rhythm sequence from a phonogram. However, in that case, the distinctive sample was played in a loop, so one has to multiply the 2 s by the times that the sample was played in the destination song. A factor in *Pelham* was whether the fragment in the destination song was recognizable to the ear.[224] An assumption could be made that the more popular the source song is, which an algorithm can derive from its performance in the music charts, the more chance that the fragment will be recognized.

If one uses a 10 s fragment of the men's 100 m of 2009, which was won by Usain Bolton in 9.58 s, it is obviously too big a quotation for the genre. The Italian Supreme

[221] C-476/17, *Pelham and Others*, Opinion of Advocate General Szpunar, 12 December 2018, ECLI:EU:C:2018:1002, para. 64 Available at: https://curia.europa.eu/juris/document/document.jsf?text=&docid=208881 (last access 12 July 2022).

[222] Berne Convention for the Protection of Literary and Artistic Works of 1886. Paris Act, 24 July 1971. Available at: https://wipolex.wipo.int/en/text/283693 (last access 12 July 2022).

[223] C-476/17, *Pelham and Others*, Judgment of the Court (Grand Chamber) of 29 July 2019, ECLI:EU:C:2019:624. Available at: https://curia.europa.eu/juris/liste.jsf?num=C-476/17 (last access 12 July 2022).

[224] C-476/17, para. 72.

Court made clear that the quotation exception only applies to partial reproductions of works, never to works in their entirety.[225]

Quotation is similar to the third fair use factor in the US: amount and substantiality, which relatively is the easiest to determine. If one of the formalities for copyright holders was that for each work, the amount and substantiality of the taking above the minimal amount and substantiality could be clarified, this would make pre-upload filtering relatively effortless.

In a more ambitious system of exceptions and limitations or fair use system, the jurisdiction could set rules for the maximum level of amount and substantiality, which could be dynamic. For example, the more the work is coming towards its expiration date, the higher the amount and substantiality of the work that can be shared. Or, after the copyright holder has earned a certain amount of revenues, the amount and substantiality can increase. Or the opposite, if the copyright holder did not earn sufficient revenues, the amount and substantiality could increase. The latter rule could avoid spoilage, which is when a work remains unused or underused.[226]

5.3.2 Caricature

Article 5(3)(k) Directive 2001/29/EC does not provide any explanation of what a caricature, parody or pastiche is, and neither does Article 17(7)(b) Directive 2019/790.

The plain meaning of a caricature is an exaggeration by means of often ludicrous distortion of parts or characteristics.[227] Distortions can be measured by algorithms in a quantitative manner. This can be an important factor in determining whether something is a caricature. The degree to which a work was distorted depends on how transformative the work will be experienced by a human reviewer as comic or grotesque. Additional factors could be the context where the caricature is used, is it to illustrate a news item or opinion piece?

5.3.3 Pastiche

According to the dictionary Merriam-Webster, a pastiche is "a literary, artistic, musical, or architectural work that imitates the style of previous work."[228] It seems that this use is similar to a caricature. But where most salient characteristics of an original work are distorted as a caricature, the style of the original work is copied,

---

225 Rosati (13 March 2022).

226 Benjamin Damstedt applied the anti-spoilage proviso of John Locke's Chapter 5s Treatise of Government. Damstedt (2003).

227 Merriam-Webster, dictionary "caricature". Available at: https://www.merriam-webster.com/dictionary/caricature (last access 12 July 2022).

228 Merriam-Webster, dictionary "pastiche". Available at: https://www.merriam-webster.com/dictionary/pastiche (last access 12 July 2022).

but not the story, image or melody. In other words, one can write any book in a Dickensian style, any image in the style of Vincent van Gogh, or any melody in the style of Johann Sebastian Bach. Since algorithms can learn how to make the next Rembrandt,[229] they are also able to distinguish between the original and a pastiche.

5.3.4 Parody

The meaning and scope of parody must be determined by considering its usual meaning in everyday language, while also taking into account the context in which it occurs and the purposes of the rules of which it is part.[230] The plain meaning of parody is to evoke an existing work while being noticeably different from it and, secondly, to constitute an expression of humour or mockery.[231] Parody is not subject to the condition that it should display an original character of its own.[232] Recital 31 Directive 2001/29/EC states that a parodist should strike a fair balance between the copyright holder and the freedom of expression.[233] The CJEU in *Deckmyn* makes it clear that EU member states that have introduced that exception under Directive 2001/29/EC need to uniformly implement the exception in a harmonized manner.[234]

A parody is paradoxically taking enough of the original work that the audience understands the reference, and not too much, because then the audience will be confused and might think that the parody is the original work. The US Supreme Court case *Campbell v. Acuff-Rose* in 1994 explained that "taking the heart of the original and making it the heart of a new work"[235] is not excessive, and also commercial parody can weigh in favour of fair use.[236] It is not clear whether the CJEU would come to a similar conclusion. But either way, parody is much harder for algorithms to identify than the other exceptions and limitations. The concept of letting candidate parodists indicate their intent of the use via flagging, as proposed by the copyright scholars,[237] could be a factor that the algorithm weighs in. In addition, one could consider a link-back obligation to refer to the author of the reference work, so that

[229] The Next Rembrandt (undated) Can The Great Master Be Brought Back To Create One More Painting. Available at: https://www.nextrembrandt.com/ (last access 12 July 2022).

[230] *Deckmyn*, para. 19.

[231] *Deckmyn*, para. 20.

[232] *Deckmyn*, para. 33.

[233] Recital 31, Directive 2001/29/EC.

[234] *Deckmyn*, para. 16. C-467/08, *Padawan*, Judgment of the Court (Third Chamber), 21 October 2010, ECLI:EU:C:2010:620, para. 36. Available at: https://curia.europa.eu/juris/document/document.jsf?text=&docid=83635 (last access 12 July 2022); C-435/12, ACI Adam and Others, Judgment of the Court (Fourth Chamber), 10 April 2014, EU:C:2014:254, para. 49. Available at: https://curia.europa.eu/juris/document/document.jsf?text=&docid=150786 (last access 12 July 2022).

[235] *Campbell v. Acuff-Rose Music, Inc.*, 510 U.S. 569 (1994).

[236] *Ibid.*

[237] Quintais et al. (11 November 2019).

the public can take note from both the parodic and reference work in an adversarial way.[238]

The first fair use factor in the US is the purpose and character of the use, to comment upon, criticize, or parody. It is challenging to provide parameters for this factor, especially in case of parodic and transformative use. After the software (a framework of different machine learning algorithms) is trained with sufficient data from judge-made decisions about transformativeness, it could figure out what the artificial neurons should be computing so that it would learn the most accurate function mapping from the input (the original works and the alleged transformative works) to the output (the court decisions).[239] Whether use is of a commercial nature or for non-profit educational purposes can also be inferred from the context in which the work is placed: are their advertisements, and is the work behind a paywall to get access? Non-profit educational institutions could be registered and listed and thus relatively easily checked by an algorithm.

5.4 *Who Will Set the Parameters?*

In the US, Elkin-Koren[240] applied Lessig's motto that "code is law"[241] to algorithmic fair use, and proposed that the fair use needs to be designed with reasonable standards. "[T]he process may further involve translating each of the four [fair use] factors into legal specifications or rules, assigning weights to each, and analysing the relationship between the different factors based on the case law."[242] She pointed to the possibility that algorithms can enrich themselves with external data,[243] and suggested that in some cases there is still a need for human supervision.[244] Dan Burk wrote that "the design values embedded in automated systems become embedded in public behaviour and consciousness."[245] Thus, algorithmic fair use could perpetuate the biases and "altering the fair use standard it attempts to embody."[246] The need to design algorithms that avoid biases is relevant for algorithmic exceptions or limitations as well. Especially, since they are, to put it in Lessig's words, the "architectures of control".[247]

[238] Danny Friedmann, Trade Marks and Social Media, Cheltenham: Edward Elgar Publishing 2015, pp. 221, 316 and 330.

[239] Based on Andrew Ng's framework of deep learning, "AI For Everyone", Coursera. Available at: https://www.coursera.org/learn/ai-for-everyone/home/welcome (last access 12 July 2022).

[240] Elkin-Koren (2017a).

[241] Lessig (2006).

[242] Elkin-Koren (2017a), p. 1095.

[243] Elkin-Koren (2017a), p. 1095.

[244] Elkin-Koren (2017a), p. 1098.

[245] Burk (2019), p. 285.

[246] *Ibid.*

[247] Lessig (2006), pp. 38 et seq.

Should the process of setting the parameters of filter technology be left to the OCSSPs and copyright holders, taking the users' interest organizations' perspectives into account, as Article 17(10) Directive 2019/790 prescribes? Or are these parameters too important to be left to a private ordering? The AG Saugmandsgaard Øe held that such solutions could be defined by private parties under the supervision of public authorities in a transparent way.[248] The stakeholder dialogues of Article 17(10) Directive 2019/790, between the European Commission, representatives of OCSSPs, copyright holders and users' rights organizations seem to be an adequate forum for this.

The AG agrees that, in conformity to the proposal by the copyright scholars,[249] the solution of pre-upload filtering that takes exceptions or limitations into account could be coupled with a mechanism allowing users to flag at the time of uploading or immediately after the work was blocked as falling under an exception or limitation.[250] Such a solution assumes that after flagging, the content will be manually reviewed by the OCSSP. As the number of users that flag their use as an exception or limitation is growing, a human review might not be feasible, since it is not scalable. Therefore, in the long term, pre-upload filtering that takes exceptions or limitations into consideration seems to be in the best position to solve the problem. After the parameters are set, if a user would like to upload content because she or he thinks it falls under an exception or limitation, but the use does not meet the parameters, she or he can either apply for a license or make use of the complaint and redress mechanism.

5.5 *Automated Content Recognition Should be Qualified High-Risk*

In April 2021, a proposal for an Artificial Intelligence Act (AIA) was introduced,[251] which is a kind of product safety law, not aimed at end-users. The proposed AIA uses a pyramid of risks and provisions to mitigate these risks. The highest level of risk is "unacceptable risk". This is regulated by Titel II (Article 5) of the proposed AIA. It includes "AI systems used by public authorities, or on their behalf, for social scoring purposes".[252] The second level on the pyramid is "high risk" and is regulated by Title III (Article 6) of the proposed AIA. It is relevant to AI systems that create an

[248] Opinion on C-401/10, para. 212.

[249] Quintais et al. (11 November 2019).

[250] Opinion on C-401/10, para. 211.

[251] Proposal for a Regulation of the European Parliament and of the Council Laying Down Harmonised Rules on Artificial Intelligence and Amending Certain Union Legislative Acts, COM/2021/206 final, 21 April 2021. Available at: https://eur-lex.europa.eu/legal-content/EN/TXT/?uri=CELEX:52021PC0206 (last access 12 July 2022).

[252] In China, there is a link between IP enforcement and social score. The PRC Social Credit System and IP Protection, SIPS, 4 April 2019. Available at: https://sips.asia/knowledge/legislation-and-policy/the-prc-social-credit-system-and-ip-protection/ (last access 12 July 2022).

adverse impact on people's safety or their fundamental rights.[253] In the Briefing of the EU Legislation in Progress, the European Parliament observed that "AI systems may jeopardise fundamental rights such as the right to non-discrimination, freedom of expression, human dignity, personal data protection and privacy."[254] However, the proposed AIA does not explicitly classify the problem of OCSSPs or other ISSPs that use AI to filter content that is being uploaded without taking exceptions or limitations into account as high risk.[255] However, the European Commission will assess the need for amendment of the list in Annex III once a year after the entry into force of the act.[256] The Opinion of the European Committee of the Regions (CoR)[257] recommended that Recital 1 AIA draft will be amended to include "fundamental rights of citizens" as the purpose of the regulation.[258] However, the CoR did not explicitly refer to automated content recognition tools deployed by platforms.

Access to and enjoyment of essential private services and public services and benefits[259] is another reason for an AI system to be qualified as high-risk. This seems very relevant in regard to automated content recognition that can adversely impact fundamental rights, if it does not take exceptions or limitations into account; especially since OCSSPs provide essential private services with a public function.

According to the definition of law enforcement in the draft AIA, it means activities related to "prevention, investigation, detection or prosecution of criminal offences or the execution of criminal penalties, including the safeguarding against and the prevention of threats to public security."[260] Blocking content would at least be in line with the broader concept of law enforcement. AlgorithmWatch, an advocacy organisation, criticized the proposed AIA for not using the notion of automated and

[253] Annex III Articles 6(2)(6) Article 7(1)(b) AIA draft.

[254] Artificial Intelligence Act, Briefing EU Legislation in Progress, European Parliament, COM(2021)206 21 April 2021. Available at: https://www.europarl.europa.eu/RegData/etudes/BRIE/2021/698792/EPRS_BRI(2021)698792_EN.pdf (last access 12 July 2022).

[255] For comparison, AI systems used in education or vocational training, notably for determining access or assigning persons to educational and vocational training institutions or to evaluate persons on tests as part of or as a precondition for their education should be considered high-risk. Recital 35 AIA draft. AI systems used in employment, workers management and access to self-employment, notably for the recruitment and selection of persons, for making decisions on promotion and termination and for task allocation, monitoring or evaluation of persons in work-related contractual relationships, should also be classified as high-risk. Recital 36 AIA draft.

[256] Article 84 AIA draft.

[257] The European Committee of Regions (CoR) is an assembly of local and regional representatives that provides sub-national authorities (i.e. regions, counties, provinces, municipalities and cities) with a direct voice within the EU's institutional framework. Available at: https://cor.europa.eu/en (last access 12 July 2022).

[258] Opinion of the European Committee of the Regions—European approach to artificial intelligence—Artificial Intelligence Act (revised opinion) (2022/C 97/12) 28 February 2022. Available at: https://eur-lex.europa.eu/legal-content/EN/TXT/HTML/?uri=CELEX%3a52021AR2682&from=EN (last access 12 July 2022).

[259] Annex III Article 6(2)(5) AIA draft.

[260] Article 3(40) AIA.

algorithmic decision-making (ADM) systems that capture more precisely the socio-economic impact of AI systems on individuals and society.[261] One can argue that automated content recognition tools also fall in this category since decisions are made on whether content is blocked.

Including automated content recognition tools in the high-risk category would mean that the system needs to conform throughout its life-cycle to pre-set parameters.[262] High-risk systems would have to comply with a range of requirements, particularly on risk management, testing, technical robustness, data training and data governance, transparency, human oversight, and cybersecurity.[263] In this regard, providers, importers, distributors and users of high-risk AI systems would have to fulfil a range of obligations. Providers established outside the EU will have to appoint an authorized representative in the EU to ensure the conformity assessment, establish a post-market monitoring system and take corrective actions as needed.[264]

Title III requires an *ex ante* conformity assessment,[265] verifying whether the requirements set out will match the results, before the algorithms are deployed on the market. Then, when the system is being used, the risks that may emerge need to be evaluated if the system is used with its intended purpose and under conditions of reasonably foreseeable misuse.[266] After use of the AI system, there needs to be post-market monitoring[267]: to proactively collect and review experiences gained from the use of AI systems for the purpose of identifying any need to immediately apply any necessary corrective or preventive actions.[268]

The European Commission proposed that EU member states, or the European Data Protection Supervisor, could establish a regulatory sandbox: a controlled environment that facilitates the development, testing and validation of innovative AI systems (for a limited period of time) before they are put on the market.[269] Machine learning can be qualified as a dynamic[270] "black box".[271] To ensure that such systems provide results during their life-cycle that are within the bandwidth set by the EU, one could argue that the conformity assessment and quality management for high-risk AIs is necessary to safeguard that they take fundamental rights, such as exceptions or limitations into account.

An alternative for blocking or disabling unauthorized use is the manipulation of a platform so that the number of visitors that is able to see a "contested" uploaded

261 AlgorithmWatch (August 2021).

262 Article 9 AIA draft.

263 Articles 8–15 AIA draft.

264 Article 25(1) AIA draft.

265 Articles 3(20) and 19 AIA draft.

266 Article 9(2)(b) AIA draft.

267 Articles 9(2)(c) and 61 AIA draft.

268 Article 3(25) AIA draft.

269 Article 53 AIA draft.

270 Bathaee (2018).

271 Pasquale (2015).

post decreases.[272] The opportunity is that this might be harmless in case the use of a work is unauthorized and illegal. The threat is that it would be used in case of unauthorized but legal use. This topic requires more attention.

5.6 Regulation of AI

Until around 2004, self-regulation of digital ethics did not seem to be a bad idea.[273] Luciano Floridi showed that this did not work out as planned, and he pleads for *dura lex, sed lex digitalis* (hard law, but digital law).[274] Eric Schmidt, ex-CEO of Alphabet and visiting innovation fellow at Massachusetts Institute of Technology, has been critical of EU policy on AI, which he qualified as "regulation first", which in his opinion would stifle innovation. Schmidt held that the proposed AIA,[275] with transparency, explainability, and documentation[276] requirements, would be a huge setback. According to Schmidt, the biggest 20 AI companies in the world are from the US or China, and none from the EU.[277] French President Emmanuel Macron held that the US' AI regulation is excessively lax and China's AI regulation is over-restrictive[278] and over-centralized.[279] Instead, Macron advocated for EU global standards that embody EU values,[280] just as the General Data Protection Regulation set a global standard in regard to privacy. In the same vein, one can argue that due to the "Brussels effect",[281] the rest of the world might follow.

272 Goldman (2021).

273 Floridi (2021), p. 619.

274 Floridi (2021), p. 622.

275 Haeck (31 May 2021).

276 Recital 38 AIA draft.

277 Joint Interview—Digital Bridge with Cédric O and Eric Schmidt | Politico AI Summit, 31 May 2021. Available at: https://www.youtube.com/watch?v=tNv5IG7z-uE&t=2093s (last access 12 July 2022).

278 Then again, China obliges platforms to enable their users to switch off the platform's recommendation algorithm, taking their well-being into account. Art 17 Regulations on the Administration of Internet Information Service Algorithms Recommendation "provide users with options that are not tailored to their personal characteristics, or provide users with a convenient option to turn off the algorithmic recommendation service." Regulations on the Administration of Internet Information Service Algorithms Recommendation have been reviewed and approved at the 20th office meeting of the State Internet Information Office on 16 November 2021, and have been approved by the Ministry of Industry and Information Technology, Ministry of Public Security, and State Administration for Market Regulation, and will come into force on 1 March 2022. Available at: http://www.cac.gov.cn/2022-01/04/c_1642894606364259.htm (last access 12 July 2022); Romero (9 March 2022).

279 Rosemain (24 May 2018).

280 Rosemain (24 May 2018).

281 "Brussels effect", refers to the process of unilateral regulatory globalisation caused by the EU de facto externalising its laws outside its borders through market mechanisms. Bradford (2020).

One can argue that it is easier to detect an enumerated and narrowly delineated list of exceptions or limitations via algorithms than fair dealing or fair use. However, it seems that the civil law jurisdictions in the EU have at least some of the same open-endedness of the fair dealing and fair use systems of common law jurisdictions. Hugenholtz and Senftleben have advocated the re(introduction) of more flexibility in the EU copyright regime. They hold the need for more openness in copyright law "almost to be self-evident in this information society of highly dynamic and unpredictable change."[282] The US, with its open-norm fair use system, has shown that this has been beneficial for the creative and technology industries: certain new uses, for example, home recording using the videocassette recorders, were considered fair use and have led to the innovation of time-shifting for consumers and the genesis of the movie rental industry.[283]

Senftleben et al. argued convincingly that the international three-step test in the Berne Convention for the Protection of Literary and Artistic Works, TRIPs, and WIPO Internet Treaties, etc., was designed to accommodate multiple legal systems, including the common law copyright tradition of fair dealing and fair use. The three-step test includes inherent flexibilities such as the subjective terms: "special," "normal," and "unreasonably". Despite the 2013/2014 Public Consultation on the Review of the EU Copyright Rules, which explicitly addressed the need for more flexibility, Directive 2019/790 did not provide further interpretations on the three-step test.[284] Recital 6 Directive 2019/790 provides the following rendition of the three-step test:

> The exceptions and limitations provided for in this Directive seek to achieve a fair balance between the rights and interests of authors and other rightholders, on the one hand, and of users on the other. They can be applied only in certain special cases that do not conflict with the normal exploitation of the works or other subject matter and do not unreasonably prejudice the legitimate interests of the rightholders.

The first sentence of Recital 6 is the only but important innovation, acknowledging the rights of users. Ultimately, the CJEU will have to interpret it. So far, it seems that the EU created what Senftleben called the "worst case scenario",[285] where a closed-catalogue of limitations is combined with an open test that can only further restrict the scope of what is allowed.[286] Quotation, criticism, review, caricature, parody, and pastiche are "certain special cases", so the first step of the test is not a problem. One could interpret the second step of the test "do not conflict with the normal exploitation of the work", as "does it supersede the use", as Leval proposed for the fourth fair use factor.[287] Such situations are arguably "identical or equivalent" cases, which

[282] Hugenholtz and Senftleben (29 February 2012).

[283] *Sony Corp. of America v. Universal City Studios, Inc.*, 464 U.S. 417 (1984).

[284] Senftleben M (2017), pp. 232–233.

[285] Senftleben M (2010b), pp. 528, 539 and 550.

[286] Senftleben points to that limitations and exceptions might be narrowly circumscribed (and thus provide legal certainty) in domestic legislation, they may further be restricted by invoking the three-step test. Senftleben (2021).

[287] Pierre Leval, Toward a Fair Use Standard, 103 HARV. L. REV. (1990), p. 1125.

can be blocked without any intervention, according to the CJEU in *Glawischnig-Piesczek*.[288] One can argue that the third step of the test "unreasonably prejudice the legitimate interests of the right holders", is already incorporated in the design of the parameters.

5.7 Incentive Against Over-Enforcement

According to Burk, copyright enforcement algorithms generally make a decision to remove content without taking user privileges or exceptions into account.[289] In *Lenz v. Universal Music Corp.*,[290] the 9th Circuit demonstrated the risks involved for right holders and OSPs of an unbalanced enforcement system that does not take unauthorized but legal use of content into account. Stephanie Lenz posted a twenty-nine-second clip of her toddler dancing to the Prince song "Let's Go Crazy", which can be heard in the background of the video clip.[291] Universal Music Corp. manually detected unauthorized use of music and sent a notice and takedown request to YouTube, which expediently removed the content. The Electronic Frontier Foundation (EFF) represented Lenz *pro deo* against Universal Music Corp.[292] *Lenz* is a break from *Ringgold v. Black Entm't Television, Inc.*,[293] where the 2nd Circuit held that a poster depicted in the background of a TV series was not fair use. The US case *Lenz* is a cautionary tale for right holders and OCSSPs in the EU who use automatic content recognition systems that do not take exceptions or limitations into account.

The 9th Circuit panel in *Lenz* amended its original opinion by reducing the opinion from 39 to 32 pages. The following relevant passage was also deleted: "We note, without passing judgment, that the implementation of computer algorithms appears to be a valid and good faith middle ground for processing a plethora of content while still meeting the DMCA's requirements to somehow consider fair use."[294] It seems the judges of the appellate court had second thoughts about the feasibility of algorithmic fair use. Five years after *Lenz*, in 2022, one can argue that AI technology has significantly improved, while the costs have dropped.

Matthew Sag inventoried the copyright holders' reaction to *Lenz*: from investing more resources into ensuring notice quality, automating some aspects of fair use consideration, to accepting the increased risk of liability and continuing with their

---

[288] C-18/18, supra n 75, para. 19.

[289] Burk (2019) 290. Available at SSRN: https://ssrn.com/abstract=3076139 (last access 12 July 2022).

[290] *Lenz v. Universal Music Corp.*, 801 F.3d 1126 (9th Cir. 2008).

[291] The video was put back online after Lenz successfully petitioned YouTube. "Let's Go Crazy" #1. Available at: https://www.youtube.com/watch?v=N1KfJHFWlhQ (last access 12 July 2022).

[292] *Lenz v. Universal*, Electronic Frontier Foundation. Available at: https://www.eff.org/cases/lenz-v-universal (last access 12 July 2022).

[293] *Ringgold v. Black Entm't Television, Inc.*, 126 F.3d 70 (2d Cir. 1997).

[294] Cullins (17 March 2017).

current practices.[295] Ensuring notice quality seems most desirable, but it is highly probable because of the sheer numbers of notice-and-takedown requests that OSPs will feel compelled to automate their systems to be able to distinguish between infringing (unauthorized and illegal) and non-infringing (unauthorized and legal) use of content.

5.8 *Hard Law to Create Soft Law*

Most parts of Directive 2019/790 can be qualified as hard law, according to Article 288 TFEU,[296] "[which] shall be binding in its entirety and directly applicable in all Member States."[297] Article 17(10) Directive 2019/790, however, provides an instruction of the Commission to start using stakeholder dialogues. Thus, this instruction is hard law, but the outcome of the stakeholder dialogue is soft law.[298] The objective is to discuss best practices for cooperation between OCSSPs and right holders. The European Commission shall, in consultation with OCSSPs, users' rights organisations, and other relevant stakeholders and taking into account the results of the stakeholder dialogues, issue guidance on the application of this Article, in particular regarding the cooperation referred to in Article 17(4) Directive 2019/790, about "best practices" in obtaining authorization, high industry standards of professional diligence" in pre-upload filtering (Article 17(4)(b)), takedowns (first part Article 17(4)(c)), and staydowns (second part of Article 17(4)(c)). Special account shall be taken of the need to balance fundamental rights and of the use of exceptions or limitations. For the purpose of the stakeholder dialogues, users' rights organisations shall have access to adequate information from OCSSPs on the functioning of their practices with regard to Article 17(4) Directive 2019/790.

The Stakeholder Dialogues organized by the European Commission had participants from platforms, organizations of rights holders and users, mapping out existing practices related to the use of copyright-protected content by OCSSPs in cooperation with copyright holders, as well as gathering user experiences. The first of six Stakeholder Dialogues[299] was held on 15 October 2019, and the last on 10 February

---

295 Sag (2018) Internet Safe Harbors and the Transformation of Copyright Law, 93 NOTRE DAME L. REV., pp. 499 and 534.

296 Article 288 Treaty on the Functioning of the European Union (ex Article 249 TEC), OJ C 326, 26.10.2012, pp. 171–172. Available at: https://eur-lex.europa.eu/legal-content/EN/TXT/?uri=CELEX:12012E288 (last access 12 July 2022).

297 Article 288 Treaty on the Functioning of the European Union (ex Article 249 TEC), OJ C 326, 26.10.2012, pp. 171–172. Available at: https://eur-lex.europa.eu/legal-content/EN/TXT/?uri=CELEX:12012E288 (last access 12 July 2022).

298 Senden's definition of soft law: "Rules of conduct that are laid down in instruments which have not been attributed legally binding force as such, but nevertheless may have certain (indirect) legal effects, and that are aimed at and may produce practical effects." Senden (2004).

299 The first Stakeholder Dialogues was held in Brussels on 15 October 2019; the second Stakeholder Dialogue was held in Brussels on 5 November 2019; the third Stakeholder Dialogue was held in

2020. The outcome of the discussions would feed into the European Commission's guidance on the application of Article 17, referred to in the Directive 2019/790.[300] The guideline, based, for an important part, on the opinion on C-401/19,[301] left open the possibility that it needs to be revised if the CJEU decision in C-401/19 derogated from the AG's Opinion. However, this is not the case since the CJEU followed the AG's Opinion.[302]

6 Conclusions

It is said that with the investments in new virtual worlds, mirror worlds, augmented realities, and lifelogging tools, the metaverse inches ineluctably closer – that it might touch all aspects of our lives. It is expected that the interoperability of the metaverse will lead to a cornucopia of creativity and copyrighted works that can be encountered, purchased, and traded across platforms. The copyrighted works promise unprecedented immersive experiences for users, but at the same time, they will expose users' sensorial profiles that make them vulnerable to monitoring, manipulation, and monetization at a much deeper level than was ever possible by the social media of Web 2.0. To counter this encroaching dystopia, the metaverse needs to enable a counterlife with sufficient breathing space: where users can experiment and express themselves in creative ways, using authorized works, using public domain works and using works without authorization in legal ways that fall under exceptions and limitations. It is expected that the metaverse will be omniscient, and using a central repository in combination with automated content recognition, platform providers and right holders could prevent the unauthorized but legal use of a work from being uploaded. This would lead to a sterile desert of staleness. Safeguards for fundamental rights are needed *a fortiori* in the metaverse, as they are in the Digital Single Market, the first stop towards the metaverse. Article 17 Directive 2019/790 has made some steps in the right direction by pointing out the importance of fundamental rights in an era when AI is taking over the human copyright enforcement for OCSSPs.

Etterbeek on 25 November 2019; the fourth Stakeholder Dialogue in Brussels was held 16 December 2019; the fifth Stakeholder Dialogue was held in Le Charlemagne on 16 January 2020; and the sixth Stakeholder Dialogue was held in Etterbeek on 10 February 2020. See European Commission (10 February 2020).

[300] Communication from the Commission to the European Parliament and the Council Guidance on Article 17 of Directive 2019/790 on Copyright in the Digital Single Market, COM/2021/288 final, 4 June 2021. Available at: https://eur-lex.europa.eu/legal-content/EN/TXT/?uri=CELEX:52021DC0288 (last access 12 July 2022).

[301] C-401/19, *Republic of Poland v European Parliament, Council of the European Union*, Opinion of Advocate General Saugmandsgaard Øe, 15 July 2021, ECLI:EU:C:2021:613. Available at: https://curia.europa.eu/juris/document/document.jsf?docid=244201&doclang=en (last access 12 July 2022).

[302] CJEU decision on C-401/19, supra n 195.

There are two main visions of taking exceptions and limitations into account. The first is the *ex post* way, endorsed by representatives of right holders: first unauthorized use of works is blocked or disabled from access. If users do not agree with this, they can make use of the complaint and redress mechanism. The second is the *ex ante* way, advocated by users' organizations: unauthorized use of works can only be blocked without further contextualization during the uploading process if they are identical or equivalent to a reference work. In any other scenario, users can upload a work without authorization, after they have flagged that the work falls under one of the exceptions or limitations. AG Saugmandsgaard Øe preferred the latter option, and, in the absence of a CJEU decision at the time, the Guidance to Directive 2019/790, in regard to Article 17(4)(b) and (c), followed the AG's well-considered Opinion. The relevance of the guidance has significantly increased after the CJEU decided to follow the AG's Opinion.[303]

Instead of blocking or disabling access to a work, platforms can manipulate the number of people that can visit a contested uploaded work. When this use is unauthorized but legal, the loss of traffic to that post degrades the fundamental right of the freedom of expression.

For the first time, the exceptions or limitations: quotation, criticism, review, caricature, parody, or pastiche have become mandatory in case of OCSSPs in the whole "Digital Single Market", this makes one set of parameters for all 27 EU member states possible.

EU member states have an obligation under Article 6*bis* Berne Convention that the author shall have the right to claim authorship of the work. For a caricature, parody or pastiche, the work has been transformed, but it builds upon the original. Therefore, a requirement in the Directive 2019/790 or Directive 2001/29/EC to refer to the author of the original work would be desirable. This would attest to an adversarial system, so that the public can learn about the caricature, parody, or pastiche on the one hand and reference work on the other hand.

Elkin-Koren proposed that algorithmic fair use can be designed. The US, where social media platforms were developed and which has an advanced filter technology industry, is developing a feasible solution for its fair use system. If this is possible for a system with open norms, *a fortiori*, it will be possible for EU member states with less flexible norms. The Stakeholder Dialogues of Article 17(10) Directive 2019/790 provide a good *forum* to set the parameters for the algorithmic exceptions or limitations. If this were coupled with the "high risk AI" precautionary measures of the AIA draft, that would be implemented before and during the lifecycle of the AI, the results of the automatic content recognition tools could stay within the set bandwidth in regard to exceptions or limitations, thereby safeguarding fundamental rights.

Due to network effects, very large platforms with private ownership will have to take responsibility as democratic *fora*, where users should be able to express themselves.

---

[303] CJEU decision on C-401/19, supra n 195.

As AG Saugmandsgaard Øe makes clear, there is "[n]o zero risk, in regard to pre-upload filtering."[304] It is the price to pay for a Digital Single Market where users can express their creativity, which in turn leads to a thriving ecosystem for users, copyright holders, OCSSPs, and a thriving AI filter industry, clearing the way for a metaverse that respects fundamental freedoms.

References

AlgorithmWatch (August 2021) Draft AI Act: EU needs to live up to its own ambitions in terms of governance and enforcement. Submission to the European Commission's Consultation on a Draft Artificial Intelligence (AI) Act. https://algorithmwatch.org/en/wp-content/uploads/2021/08/EU-AI-Act-Consultation-Submission-by-AlgorithmWatch-August-2021.pdf. Last Accessed 12 July 2022

Awbi A (25 April 2018) IFPI slams "value gap" in new Global Music report. PRS for Music. https://www.prsformusic.com/m-magazine/news/ifpi-slams-value-gap-in-new-global-music-report/. Last Accessed 12 July 2022

Barlow JP (8 February 1995) A declaration of the independence of cyberspace. EFF. https://www.eff.org/cyberspace-independence. Last Accessed 12 July 2022

Bar-Ziv S, Elkin-Koren N (2017) Behind the scenes of online copyright enforcement: empirical evidence on notice & takedown. Connecticut Law Rev 50. https://ssrn.com/abstract=3214214. Last Accessed 12 July 2022

Bathaee Y (2018) The artificial intelligence black box and the failure of intent and causation. Harvard J Law Technol 31(2):913. https://jolt.law.harvard.edu/assets/articlePDFs/v31/The-Artificial-Intelligence-Black-Box-and-the-Failure-of-Intent-and-Causation-Yavar-Bathaee.pdf. Last Accessed 12 July 2022

Baudrillard J (1983) Simulacra and simulation. In: SF Glaser (Transl), Michigan, p 83

Beausoleil L (2017) Copyright issues and implications of emerging virtual reality technologies. Boston College Intellectual Property and Technology Forum December 2017, 4. http://bciptf.org/wp-content/uploads/2017/12/Lauren-Beausoleil-F17.pdf. Last Accessed 12 July 2022

Berners-Lee T (March 1989) Information management: a proposal. CERN. https://www.w3.org/History/1989/proposal.html. Last Accessed 12 July 2022

Berners-Lee T (2000) Weaving the web, weaving the web, the original design and ultimate destiny of the World wide web by its inventor Tim Berners-Lee, with Mark Fischetti, HarperCollins Publishers 2000. Chapter 14

Bird & Bird (10 November 2020) Legal implications of digital twins in the supply chain. https://www.twobirds.com/en/insights/2020/global/legal-implications-of-digital-twins-in-the-supply-chain. Last Accessed 12 July 2022

Bostrom N (2003) Are you living in a computer simulation? Philos Q 53(211):243–255. https://www.simulation-argument.com/simulation.pdf. Last Accessed 12 July 2022

Boyle J (2008) The public domain: enclosing the commons of the mind. Yale University Press. https://scholarship.law.duke.edu/faculty_scholarship/2708. Last Accessed 12 July 2022

Borges JL (1946) On exactitude in science. In: Hurley A (Trans) Collected fictions. https://kwarc.info/teaching/TDM/Borges.pdf. Last Accessed 12 July 2022

[304] Opinion on C-401/10, para. 216.

Bradford A (2020) The Brussels effect: how the European Union Rules the World. Oxford University Press, Oxford. *passim*

Brin D (1998) The transparent society: will technology force us to choose between privacy and freedom? Basic Books, New York

Burk D (2019) Algorithmic fair use. Univ Chicago Law Rev 86:283, 290. SSRN. https://ssrn.com/abstract=3076139. Last Accessed 12 July 2022

Chen J, Friedmann D (2023) Jumping from Mother Monkey to Bored Ape: the value of NFTs from an Artist's and intellectual property perspective. Asia Pacific Law Rev 31(1). *passim*. http://ssrn.com/abstract=4213536 (last access 08 September 2022)

Chheda T (2005) Intellectual property implications in a virtual reality environment. J Marshall Rev Intell Prop L 4:483, 493–494. https://repository.law.uic.edu/cgi/viewcontent.cgi?article=1077&context=ripl. Last Accessed 12 July 2022

Cline E (2011) Ready player one. Crown Publishing Group, *passim*

Communia (10 February 2020) Article 17 stakeholder dialogue, How to safeguard users' rights. Brussels, 9. https://ec.europa.eu/newsroom/dae/document.cfm?doc_id=64795. Last Accessed 12 July 2022

Cooper J (21 January 2022) Towards the Metaverse: first thing we do, let's grill all the lawyers. The Hill. https://thehill.com/opinion/technology/590319-towards-the-metaverse-first-thing-we-do-lets-grill-all-the-lawyers?rl=1. Last Accessed 12 July 2022

Creative Commons (undated) Creative Commons Licenses. https://creativecommons.org/share-your-work/licensing-types-examples/. Last Accessed 12 July 2022

Cullins A (17 March 2017) "Dancing Baby" appeals court decision stands minus the "Fair Use" algorithms. https://www.hollywoodreporter.com/thr-esq/dancing-baby-appeals-court-decision-876557. Last Accessed 12 July 2022

Damstedt B (2003) Note, limiting locke: a natural law justification for the fair use doctrine. Yale E LJ 112:1179, 1179

Davis T (2012) Explainer: what is wave-particle duality. The Conversation. https://theconversation.com/explainer-what-is-wave-particle-duality-7414. Last Accessed 12 July 2022

Davis W (1 April 2014) Google Glass is already causing legal experts to see problems. ABA J. https://www.abajournal.com/magazine/article/google_glass_is_already_causing_legal_experts_to_see_problems. Last Accessed 12 July 2022

Dilmegani C (15 July 2020) Synthetic data generation: techniques, best practices & tools. AI Multiple. https://research.aimultiple.com/synthetic-data-generation/. Last Accessed 12 July 2022

Dusollier S (2020) The 2019 directive on copyright in the digital single market: some progress, a few bad choices, and an overall failed ambition. Common Market Law Rev 57(4):1015. https://ssrn.com/abstract=3695839. Last Accessed 12 July 2022

Economist (13 March 2021) Will Roblox's thriving virtual economy make it the next meme stock? https://www.economist.com/business/2021/03/13/will-robloxs-thriving-virtual-economy-make-it-the-next-meme-stock. Last Accessed 12 July 2022

Economist (11 May 2021) What is the metaverse? https://www.economist.com/the-economist-explains/2021/05/11/what-is-the-metaverse. Last Accessed 12 July 2022

Economist (13 November 2021) Companies want to build a virtual realm to copy the real world. https://www.economist.com/business/2021/11/13/companies-want-to-build-a-virtual-realm-to-copy-the-real-world. Last Accessed 12 July 2022

Economist (20 November 2021) The video-game industry has metaverse ambitions, too. https://www.economist.com/business/the-video-game-industry-has-metaverse-ambitions-too/21806341. Last Accessed 12 July 2022

Economist (1 January 2022a) Virtual-property prices are going through the roof. https://www.economist.com/business/2022a/01/01/virtual-property-prices-are-going-through-the-roof. Last Accessed 12 July 2022a

Economist (22 January 2022b) Big tech's supersized ambitions. https://www.economist.com/leaders/2022b/01/22/big-techs-supersized-ambitions. Last Accessed 12 July 2022b

Economist (29 January 2022) Will web3 reinvent the internet business? https://www.economist.com/business/2022/01/29/will-web3-reinvent-the-internet-business. Last Accessed 12 July 2022

EFF (27 February 2014) Lawrence Lessig settles fair use lawsuit over phoenix music snippets. https://www.eff.org/press/releases/lawrence-lessig-settles-fair-use-lawsuit-over-phoenix-music-snippets. Last Accessed 12 July 2022

EFF (4 September 2018) Sony finally admits it doesn't own bach and it only took a bunch of public pressure. https://www.eff.org/takedowns/sony-finally-admits-it-doesnt-own-bach-and-it-only-took-public-pressure. Last Accessed 12 July 2022

Elkin-Koren N (2017a) Fair use by design. UCLA L Rev 64:22. https://ssrn.com/abstract=3217839. Last Accessed 12 July 2022

Elkin-Koren N (2017b) Copyright in a digital ecosystem: a user rights approach. In: Okediji R (ed) Copyright law in an age of limitations and exceptions. Cambridge University Press, Cambridge, pp 132–168

EUIPO (2020) Automated content recognition—discussion paper phase 1: "Existing technologies and their impact on IP". https://euipo.europa.eu/tunnel-web/secure/webdav/guest/document_library/observatory/documents/reports/2020_Automated_Content_Recognition/2020_Automated_Content_Recognition_Discussion_Paper_Full_EN.pdf. Last Accessed 12 July 2022

European Commission (10 February 2020) Sixth meeting of the stakeholder dialogue on Article 17 of the Directive on Copyright in the Digital Single Market. https://digital-strategy.ec.europa.eu/en/events/sixth-meeting-stakeholder-dialogue-article-17-directive-copyright-digital-single-market. Last Accessed 12 July 2022

Ferenstein G (15 February 2014) Predicting love and breakups with Facebook data. TechCrunch. https://techcrunch.com/2014/02/14/facebook-love-data/.

Floridi L (2021) The end of an era: from self-regulation to hard law for the digital industry. Philos Technol 34:619. https://link.springer.com/content/pdf/. https://doi.org/10.1007/s13347-021-00493-0.pdf. Last Accessed 12 July 2022

Friedmann D (2014) Sinking the safe harbour with the legal certainty of strict liability in sight. J Intell Property Law Pract 9(2):148–155

Friedmann D (2015) EU opens door for sound marks: will scent marks follow? J Intell Property Law Pract 10(12):931–939. https://ssrn.com/abstract=2717940. Last Accessed 12 July 2022

Friedmann D (2020) Oscillating from safe harbor to liability: China's IP regulation and omniscient intermediaries. In: Frosio G (ed) The Oxford handbook of online intermediary liability. OUP, Oxford, pp 277–294. https://ssrn.com/abstract=2969807. Last Accessed 12 July 2022

Gates B, Myhrvold N, Rinearson P (1995) The road ahead. Viking, Chapter 12. Crit Iss

Geist M (2013) The copyright pentology: how the Supreme Court of Canada shook the foundations of Canadian Copyright Law, UOP

Gelernter D (1992) Mirror worlds: or the day software puts the universe in a shoebox...how it will happen and what it will mean. OUP, New York

Ginsburg J (2014) Comment letter on the right of making available 2. http://copyright.gov/docs/making_available/comments/docket2014_2/Jane_Ginsburg.pdf. Last Accessed 12 July 2022

Goldman E (2021) Content moderation remedies. Michigan Technol Law Rev 28:31–36. https://ssrn.com/abstract=3810580. Last Accessed 12 July 2022

Greenfield A (2006) Everyware: the dawning age of ubiquitous computing. New Riders, Berkeley

Grubb J (6 August 2014) Everything you need to know about the Oculus Rift. Venture Beat. https://venturebeat.com/2014/08/06/everything-you-need-to-know-about-the-oculus-rift/. Last Accessed 12 July 2022

HADOPI (28 April 2020) Rapport CSPLA/HADOPI/CNC: Vers une application effective du droit d'auteur sur les platformes numérique de partage: Etat de l'art et propositions sur les outils de reconnaisance des contenus, 118. https://hadopi.fr/sites/default/files/sites/default/files/ckeditor_files/CSPLA_Hadopi_Mission_Report_Content_Recognition_Tools_ENG.pdf. Last Accessed 12 July 2022

Haeck P (31 May 2021) Ex-Google boss slams transparency rules in Europe's AI bill. Politico. https://www.politico.eu/article/ex-google-boss-eu-risks-setback-by-demanding-transparent-ai/. Last Accessed 12 July 2022

Hayward A (16 March 2022) Licensed Formula 1 Ethereum NFT game is shutting down. Decrypt, 16 March 2022. https://decrypt.co/95176/licensed-formula-1-ethereum-nft-game-is-shutting-down. Last Accessed 12 July 2022

Hazard Jr JW (2021) Copyright law in business and practice, Revised edn, September 2021 Update, 2

Hill K (16 February 2012) How target figured out a teen girl was pregnant before her father did. Forbes. https://www.forbes.com/sites/kashmirhill/2012/02/16/how-target-figured-out-a-teen-girl-was-pregnant-before-her-father-did/?sh=6fe5ebf86668. Last Accessed 12 July 2022

Hobson B (18 July 2014) 3D-scanning technology will enable cities to exist in "both a virtual and a physical form. Dezeen Mini Front. https://www.dezeen.com/2014/07/18/movie-william-trossell-scanlab-3d-scanning-virtual-model-cities/#. Last Accessed 12 July 2022

Houellebecq M (2012) The map and the territory. Bowd G (Trans) Knopf, New York

Hugenholtz PB, Senftleben M (29 February 2012) Fair use in Europe: in search of flexibilities. https://ssrn.com/abstract=2013239. Last Accessed 12 July 2022

IFPI (2018) Fixing the value gap. Global music report 2018 State of the Industry, 26. https://www.fimi.it/kdocs/1922703/gmr-2018-ilovepdf-compressed.pdf (last access 08 September 2022)

IPFS (undated) How IPFS works? https://ipfs.io/#how. Last Accessed 12 July 2022

Jenkins Jr HW (18 January 2022) Progressives vs. the metaverse. Wall Street J. https://www.wsj.com/articles/progressives-vs-the-metaverse-facebook-zuckerberg-virtual-reality-social-media-identity-politics-11642542878. Last Accessed 12 July 2022

Klang M (16 September 2016) Quantity has a quality all its own. Klangable. http://klangable.com/blog/quantity-has-a-quality-all-its-own/. Last Accessed 12 July 2022

Kosinski M, Stillwell D, Graepel T (2013) PNAS 110:15. https://www.pnas.org/. https://doi.org/10.1073/pnas.1218772110. Last Accessed 12 July 2022

Kreps D (7 August 2021) Watch Ariana Grande's 'Rift Tour' event on 'Fortnite'. Rolling Stone, 7 August 2021. https://www.rollingstone.com/music/music-news/ariana-grande-rift-tour-event-fortnite-watch-1209152/. Last Accessed 12 July 2022

LeCun Y, Bengio Y, Hinton G (2015) Deep learning. Nature 521:436–444 (2015). https://doi.org/10.1038/nature14539. Last Accessed 12 July 2022

Lehot L, Allen N (1 December 2021) Live, work and play in a legal metaverse: preparing for a new online existence. IP Watchdog. https://www.ipwatchdog.com/2021/12/01/live-work-play-legal-metaverse-preparing-new-online-existence/id=140614/. Last Accessed 12 July 2022

Lessig L (2004) Free culture—how big media uses technology and the law to lock down culture and control creativity. Penguin Press, New York. https://www.researchgate.net/publication/5149684_Free_Culture_How_Big_Media_Uses_Technology_and_the_Law_to_Lock_Down_Culture_and_Control_Creativity (last access 08 September 2022)

Lessig L (2006) Code: and other laws of cyberspace, version 2.0, 2nd Revised edn. Basic Books

Lessig L (2008) Making art and commerce thrive in the hybrid economy. Bloomsbury Academic. https://textbookequity.org/Textbooks/Remix.pdf. Last Accessed 12 July 2022

Leval P (1990) Toward a fair use standard. Harv L Rev 103:1105

Li Z, Li M, Zhang LS, Han YF (30 October 2021) 元宇宙与国家安全 (The Metaverse and National Security). China Institutes of Contemporary International Relations, Modern Academy Report, 30 October 2021. Chinese at: http://www.cicir.ac.cn/NEW/opinion.html?id=d568c9de-d8d3-4cf3-9e86-6b2ded4fdc49. Last Accessed 12 July 2022

Mack O (8 January 2019) Who owns your digital twin? Not you—and here's why that's a massive problem. Opinion, Newsweek. https://www.newsweek.com/who-owns-your-digital-twin-not-you-heres-why-thats-massive-problem-opinion-1451991. Last Accessed 12 July 2022

Matchar E (15 August 2018) Using electric currents to fool ourselves into tasting something we're not. Smithsonian Mag, 15 August 2018. https://www.smithsonianmag.com/innovation/using-electric-currents-to-fool-ourselves-into-tasting-something-were-not-180970005/. Last Accessed 12 July 2022

Metaverse Roadmap (2009) Pathways to the 3D web. A cross-industry public foresight project, 4. https://www.metaverseroadmap.org/MetaverseRoadmapOverview.pdf. Last Accessed 12 July 2022

Moore S (22 December 2021) Law in the metaverse. Forbes. https://www.forbes.com/sites/schuylermoore/2021/12/22/law-in-the-metaverse/?sh=e9865e245d13. Last Accessed 12 July 2022

Nas S (27 October 2004) The multatuli project, ISP notice & take down. Bits of Freedom. https://www-old.bof.nl/docs/researchpaperSANE.pdf. Last Accessed 12 July 2022

Neuwirth RJ (2022) The EU artificial intelligence act: regulating subliminal AI systems. Routledge, London, p 17

Parisi T (23 October 2021) The seven rules of the metaverse. Medium. https://medium.com/meta-verses/the-seven-rules-of-the-metaverse-7d4e06fa864c. Last Accessed 12 July 2022

Pasquale P (2015) The black box society. Harvard University Press. *passim*

Penney J (2019) Privacy and legal automation: the DMCA as a case study 22:1 STLR 412. https://papers.ssrn.com/sol3/papers.cfm?abstract_id=3504247. Last Accessed 12 July 2022

Perlmutter S (2021) Compendium of the U.S. copyright office practices, 3rd edn, Chapter 300, para. 309. https://www.copyright.gov/comp3/chap300/ch300-copyrightable-authorship.pdf. Last Accessed 12 July 2022

Peukert A, Husovec M, Kretschmer M, Mezei P, Quintais JP (2022) European Copyright Society comment on copyright and the digital services act proposal. ECS 1. https://europeancopyrightsocietydotorg.files.wordpress.com/2022/01/2022-01-17-ecs-comment-on-copyright-and-the-digital-services-act-proposal-4.pdf. Last Accessed 12 July 2022

Practice UC Berkeley Public Law Research Paper No. 2755628. https://ssrn.com/abstract=2755628. Last Accessed 12 July 2022

Quintais J et al (11 November 2019) Safeguarding user freedoms in implementing Article 17 of the copyright in the digital single market directive: recommendations from European Academics. https://ssrn.com/abstract=3484968. Last Accessed 12 July 2022

Rasmussen M (14 October 2021) Virtual transhuman Ruby 9100M talks about her new Adidas collaboration. Virtual Humans. https://www.virtualhumans.org/article/virtual-transhuman-ruby-9100m-speaks-about-her-new-adidas-collaboration. Last Accessed 12 July 2022

Rasmussen M (17 March 2022) Why PUMA chose virtual influencers to advertise their new Kosmo Rider Shoe. Virtual Humans. https://www.virtualhumans.org/article/why-puma-chose-virtual-influencers-to-advertise-their-new-kosmo-rider-shoe. Last Accessed 12 July 2022

Ravenscraft E (25 November 2021) What is the metaverse, exactly? Wired. https://www.wired.com/story/what-is-the-metaverse/. Last Accessed 12 July 2022

Resnikoff P (18 February 2016) Sony Music decides Harvard's copyright lecture isn't illegal after all. https://www.digitalmusicnews.com/2016/02/18/breaking-sony-music-backs-down-on-harvard-university-copyright-claim/. Last Accessed 12 July 2022

Reuveni E (2007) On virtual worlds: copyright and contract law at the dawn of the virtual age. 82 Ind LJ 261, 272

Reynolds E (5 January 2022) ONE Sotheby's is selling the first real-world home through the metaverse using NFT technology. Forbes. https://www.forbes.com/sites/emmareynolds/2022/01/05/one-sothebys-is-selling-the-first-real-world-home-through-the-metaverse-using-nft-technology/?sh=60c173653471. Last Accessed 12 July 2022

Romero A (9 March 2022) China has pioneered a law to empower people over algorithms, it's unprecedented in the world. OneZero. https://onezero.medium.com/china-has-pioneered-a-law-to-empower-people-over-algorithms-70b29ba6285f. Last Accessed 12 July 2022

Rosati E (13 March 2022) Italian Supreme Court says that the quotation exception in copyright law only applies to partial reproductions of works, never to works in their entirety. https://ipkitten.blogspot.com/2022/03/italian-supreme-court-says-that.html. Last Accessed 12 July 2022

Rosemain M (24 May 2018) Wary of China, Macron urges Europe to set tech regulation standards. Reuters. https://www.reuters.com/article/us-france-tech-macron-idUSKCN1IP28I. Last Accessed 12 July 2022

Rosenberg L (2021) Regulate the metaverse, why regulation is important and urgent. Medium. https://medium.com/predict/regulating-the-metaverse-7c893ed00865. Last Accessed 12 July 2022

Russo J, Risch M (1993) The law of virtual reality—law firm computer law group LLP Attorneys Palo Alto, California Computer Law Group, LLP. http://www.computerlaw.com/Articles/The-Law-of-Virtual-Reality.shtml. Last Accessed 12 July 2022

Sag M (2018) Internet safe harbors and the transformation of copyright law. Notre Dame L. Rev 93:499, 534 Saint Island (undated) trademark protection in the metaverse. https://papers.ssrn.com/sol3/papers.cfm?abstract_id=2830184 (last access 08 September 2022)

Schuchmann S (2019) History of the second AI winter. Toward data science. https://towardsdatascience.com/history-of-the-second-ai-winter-406f18789d45. Last Accessed 12 July 2022

Senden L (2004) Soft law in European Community Law. Hart Publishing 111

Senftleben M (2010a-I) The international three-step test, a model provision for EC fair use legislation. 1 JIPITEC 76, para. 53. https://www.jipitec.eu/issues/jipitec-1-2-2010/2605 (last access 12 July 2022a)

Senftleben M (2010b-II) Bridging the differences between copyright's legal traditions—the emerging EC fair use doctrine. J Copyright Soc U.S.A. 57:528, 539 and 550. https://ssrn.com/abstract=1723902 (last access 12 July 2022b)

Senftleben M (2017) The perfect match—civil law judges and open-ended fair use provisions. Am Univ Int L Rev 33(1):231–286. https://ssrn.com/abstract=3002275. Last Accessed 12 July 2022

Senftleben M (2021) EU copyright 20 years after the InfoSoc Directive—flexibility needed more than ever. https://ssrn.com/abstract=4001482. Last Accessed 12 July 2022

Simpson C (2020) The challenges and legal implications of digital twins, Fenwick Elliott. https://www.fenwickelliott.com/research-insight/annual-review/2020/challenges-legal-implications-digital-twins. Last Accessed 12 July 2022

Stephenson N (1992) Snow crash. Bantam Books US. *passim*

Urban J, Quilter L (2005) Efficient process or chilling effects—takedown notices under Section 512 of the Digital Millennium Copyright Act. Santa Clara Computer & High Tech. L.J. 22:621

Urban J, Karaganis J, Schofield B (2017) Notice and takedown in everyday

van der Star E (20 August 2014) Google asked to remove 1 million pirate links per day. TorrentFreak. https://torrentfreak.com/google-asked-to-remove-1-million-pirate-links-per-day-140820/. Last Accessed 12 July 2022

van der Star E (17 February 2016) YouTube copyright complaint kills Harvard Professor's copyright lecture. Torrent Freak. https://torrentfreak.com/youtube-copyright-complaint-kills-harvard-professors-copyright-lecture-160217/. Last Accessed 12 July 2022

van Gompel S (2010) Formalities in the digital era: an obstacle or opportunity? In: Bently, Suthersanen U, Torremans P (eds) Global copyright: three hundred years since the statute of Anne, From 1709 to cyberspace. Edward Elgar, pp 395–424. https://ssrn.com/abstract=1986827. Last Accessed 12 July 2022

Weiser M (September 1991) The computer for the 21st century. Sci Am. https://www.ics.uci.edu/~corps/phaseii/Weiser-Computer21stCentury-SciAm.pdf. Last Accessed 12 July 2022

Weiser M, Brown JS (21 December 1995) Designing calm technology. Xerox PARC. http://pages.cpsc.ucalgary.ca/~saul/wiki/uploads/CPSC7018108/Designing%20Calm%20Technology.pdf. Last Accessed 12 July 2022

West D, Karsten J (1 June 2016) Associated press style change marks growth of "internet" and "web". Brookings. https://www.brookings.edu/blog/techtank/2016/06/01/associated-press-style-change-marks-growth-of-internet-and-web/#:~:text=Capitalization%20of%20internet%20and%20web,to%20capitalize%20the%20word%20today. Last Accessed 12 July 2022

Wheatley A (2017) Copyright protection in virtual reality. Inform Counsel 8:1–2. Available at: https://decrypt.co/95176/licensed-formula-1-ethereum-nft-game-is-shutting-down. Last Accessed 12 July 2022

Yen C-C (undated) Virtual cocktail Keio-NUS CUTE Center. Available at: https://cutecenter.nus.edu.sg/projects/virtual-cocktail.html. Last Accessed 12 July 2022

Yuan SG (19 July 2018) Fountain ordered to play a different tune. China Daily. https://www.chinadaily.com.cn/cndy/2018-07/19/content_36604073.htm. Last Accessed 12 July 2022

Danny Friedmann is an Assistant Professor of Law at the Peking University School of Transnational Law. Room 513 Peking University School of Transnational Law, University Town, Nanshan District, Shenzhen, China. His fields of interest include Intellectual Property Law (Trademark Law, Geographical Indications, Copyright Law, Patent Law), Consumer Law, Ethics and the Law.

Deepfakes, Copyright and Personality Rights an Inter-Disciplinary Perspective

Kalpana Tyagi

Abstract This chapter concentrates on unsupervised learning, the recent rise of deepfakes, the potential role of copyright and related rights, exceptions and limitations therein, and personality rights to ensure a balanced application of the technology. Using inter-disciplinary insights from law and the technical literature, this chapter takes a holistic view on the uptake, adoption, and the future of deepfakes. Considering the centrality of personality rights to deepfakes, this chapter also explores the potential foundations of an EU-wide personality rights framework. It crucially examines the future acceptance of deepfakes, and considers the potential role of the blockchain technology to prevent the apocalypse of a potential infodemic following the widespread prevalence of deepfakes.

Keywords Deepfakes · Privacy rights · Generative adversarial network (GAN) modelling · Blockchain technology · Variational autoencoders (VAE) · EU copyright · Personality rights

1 Introduction

The divide between true and false, real and imaginary, has never been so thin. The emergence of big data and Artificial Intelligence (AI) has turned science fiction into a mundane reality. Consider the recommendations on Youtube and Netflix that well align with the content that one would like to consume, but of whose existence one was unaware until it popped up as a recommendation by the platform. The promise of AI has been around since the 1970s. However, it was the uptake of big data and cloud computing, that enabled the potential of AI to actually be harnessed into real world applications. The rise in computing power meant that data could now be used as food for these networks to feed on and learn from. Deep learning, so far, has largely been supervised learning, meaning that AI feeds on the data to learn from

K. Tyagi (✉)
Maastricht University, Maastricht, Netherlands
e-mail: k.tyagi@maastrichtuniversity.nl

K. Mathis and A. Tor (eds.), *Law and Economics of the Digital Transformation*, Economic Analysis of Law in European Legal Scholarship 15,
https://doi.org/10.1007/978-3-031-25059-0_9

and perform certain tasks. The Next Rembrandt project, where the system was fed with hundreds of works of the great painter Rembrandt Van Rijn to learn and create a work of art, is one such notable example.[1] The Next Rembrandt project is one of the many well-recognized contributions of supervised learning. In supervised learning, the AI is fed with lots of data. In the Big Data debate 1.0, the question was one of having a large volume of data. In other words, the volume, that is the quantity of data, was just as important as the other three v's of data. The rise of the Big Data 2.0 seems to have changed the dynamics of the debate. The focus is increasingly on the second "v" that is the "value" of data. For deepfakes, impressive results could already be achieved with lots of good quality data. However, what was required for this one was availability of abundant data.[2] The algorithms trained on this raw data over time before they became adept at performing a particular task. Supervised learning, it seems, is now well-developed or at least on a promising trajectory of growth. There, however, remains another field of deep learning and neural networks that remain under-explored. This is the area of unsupervised learning. It is this area of unsupervised learning, the recent rise of deepfakes, and what role, if any, this could play for copyright and related rights, as well as personality rights, that are the key focus of this article. Using inter-disciplinary insights from law and technical literature, this article takes a holistic view on the uptake, adoption, and the future of deepfakes.

The chapter is organized as follows. Section 2 presents an overview of unsupervised learning, emerging technologies in the field and how it has contributed to the recent uptake of deepfakes. Section 3 evaluates whether deep-faked creations are copyright-protected. Section 4 maps the personality rights framework, contemplates cases wherein copyright and personality rights may be in discord, and explores the potential foundations of an EU-wide personality rights framework. Section 5 examines the future acceptance of deepfakes, and considers the potential role of the blockchain technology. Section 6 concludes, and offers a road map for further research.

2 Technology Behind Deepfakes

The four v's of data drive and promote the big data revolution. These are "volume", "value", "variety", and "veracity".[3] In "supervised deep learning", the volume of data remains just as (if not more) important as the other three v's of big data. Unsupervised learning, however, disrupts this dynamic.

Whereas supervised learning remains controlled and directed by human intervention; in unsupervised learning, the machines learn on their own accord. For

[1] The project is available here https://www.nextrembrandt.com/ (last access 10 October 2022) Dutch Digital Design (2018).

[2] Thies et al. (2018, p. 2).

[3] Technology Advice (2021).

supervised learning, the four v's of big data—volume, value, variety, and veracity—remain central to produce meaningful outputs.[4] For unsupervised learning, however, the volume of data diminishes in significance. The emergence of some recent technologies has contributed to this trend, and has made a notable contribution to help deepfakes go mainstream. These technological innovations include the rise of the generative adversarial network (GAN) modelling and the variational autoencoders (VAEs).

Ian Goodfellow, currently senior scientist at Google, invented the GAN technology. In this technology, the system is deliberately fed with both correct as well as incorrect inputs. The system learns to identify incorrect inputs by comparing them with the correct inputs. These are respectively referred to as generative neural network and discriminative neural network.[5] Whereas the generative neural network creates the "noise", the discriminative neural networks assess the veracity or correctness of those inputs against the training data.[6] This process is much more data efficient than the hitherto supervised learning. In supervised learning, the system is fed with large volumes of accurate data, and trained to perform a particular task. Following the GAN model, unsupervised learning efficiently and quickly trains the system to perform a range of tasks with a higher level of efficiency.[7]

The second technological innovation that has contributed to the rapid uptake of the deepfakes is the Variational autoencoders (VAEs). VAEs, simply put, are mathematical representations of an image. A smiling face, for example, can be allocated a certain precise value. This, technically speaking, is referred to as a discrete value. The certainty with which a person may (or may not) have this expression on his face is indicated in the form of a range, that is a probability distribution.[8] These signals are then encoded and decoded as they are assigned to the images (see Fig. 1 infra).[9]

More recently, scientists at the Max Planck Institute and Stanford University developed the first ever "real-time facial re-enactment of a monocular target video sequence".[10] The "realistic renderings" of the image as a video sequence are an impressive aspect of this technological innovation (see Fig. 2 infra).

The technology promises to disrupt virtual reality, augmented reality, and live teleconferencing. In this technology, the scientists capture a live video from the source (such as through live streaming on a webcam) and re-enact it on a downloaded monocular video clip which is the target (for example, a video from Youtube or Vimeo or Mediasite).[11] The relevance of these technological innovations for a legal discourse on deepfakes is that this means that it is now possible to create a real-time high-quality

[4] For an early discussion on Big Data, *see* Schönberger and Cukier (2013) 74 ff. For a non-technical discussion on the different Vs of Big Data, *see* Williamson (2015).

[5] Kan (2018).

[6] Kan (2018).

[7] Giles (2018).

[8] Kan (2018).

[9] Jordan (2018).

[10] Thies et al. (2018).

[11] Thies et al. (2018, pp. 6–8).

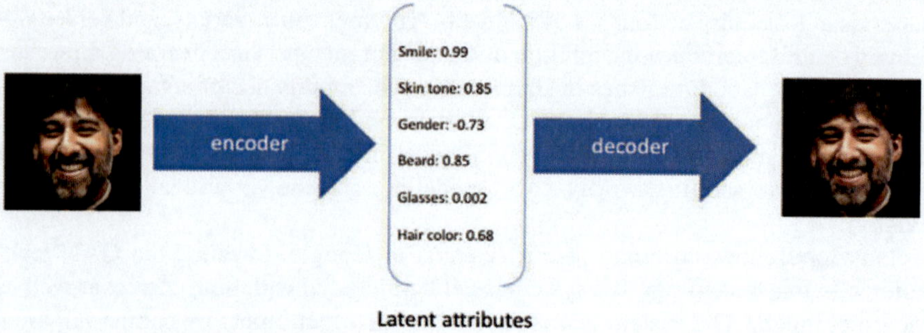

Fig. 1 Encoding and decoding images

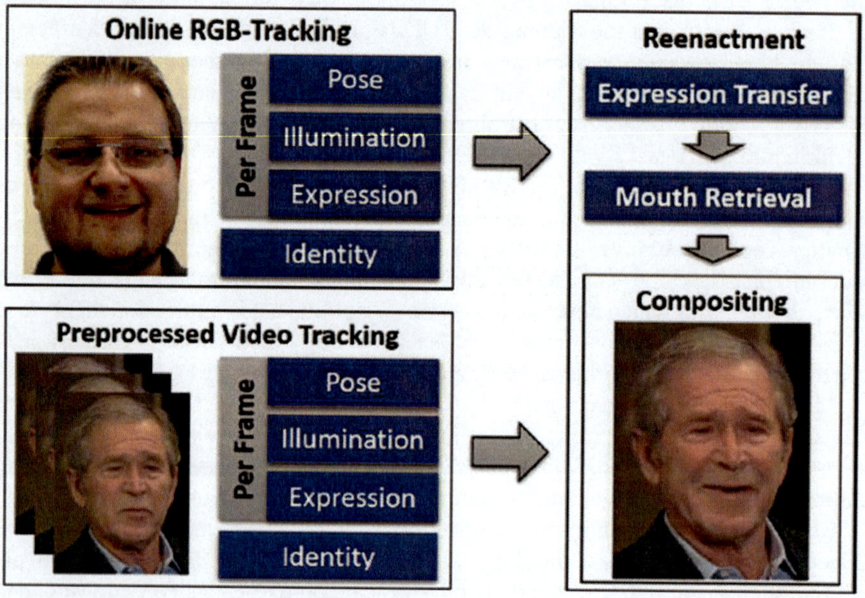

Fig. 2 Real-time facial reenactment[12]

deepfake at moderate costs. On a positive note, this also means that it is now possible to deliver, in real-time, the same content in different languages with different facial expressions, taking into account, the cultural and linguistic diversities of the target audience. This offers the possibility to deliver more personalized messages to distinct target audiences in their vernacular languages.

While on the one hand, the rise of deepfakes facilitates the delivery of more personalized content, on the other, it also enhances the danger of mischief. Consider a deepfake video, where a politician is shown to be saying something or performing

[12] Thies et al. (2018, p. 3).

a certain act, that he had never said or done in the first place. Neither an outright prohibition nor a free reign is a suitable response. Excessive regulation of deepfakes may frustrate our march towards Industry 4.0. This observation is also endorsed by the EU Regulation on Artificial Intelligence. The question then is, if (the deepfake) technology presents an opportunity and a challenge, can the technology also offer some solutions to insulate the potentially harmful effects of deepfake technology? We return to this issue in Sect. 5, where we discuss the cryptography-based blockchain technology as a potential remedy to resolve the dilemma flowing from unwelcome deepfakes.

3 Deepfakes, Copyright and Personality Rights

Meskys et al. divide deepfakes into the following four use categories: creation of valuable content (1), original and creative deepfakes (2), revenge porn (3) and political campaigns (4).[13] To appreciate the advantages and disadvantages associated with them, let us illustrate the content and import of each of these types of deepfake.

Deepfakes may contribute to sales and marketing efforts of a small start-up firm. Consider, for example, a neighborhood boutique that offers personally customized dresses. The boutique sets up a website with a global reach. Considering the high price of the dresses, prospective customers may first want to try the dress, and see whether it fits them and suits their silhouette. A deepfake app may help customers virtually try these attires, and make a more effective purchase decision.[14] It may also boost the sales and visibility of the individual entrepreneur, and thereby positively contribute to trade and commerce.

Deepfakes may also involve humour or parody. Consider the Tom Cruise deep fakes that went viral on TikTok in 2021. In some of the videos, Cruise is seen eating a lollipop only to find a chewing gum in the center of lollipop and question his own wisdom (!); whereas in another, he is evidently drunk and stumbling and mumbling in a high-end clothing and apparel store.[15]

In 2016, shortly before the US presential election, a website reported that thousands of fake ballots were sitting in a warehouse ready to swing the election results in Ohio. This created a huge uproar as it created fears amongst the citizens that the elections may, after all, be rigged. It was not long before that, that a follow-on exposé revealed that both the image, and the person who had unearthed these so-called "fake" ballots, were a deepfake.[16]

In the case of deep-faked revenge porn, sexually explicit images and videos are made available by an acrimonious former partner. These deep-faked images and videos involve an element of originality as images are transformed and shown to

---

[13] Meskys et al. (2020, p. 25).

[14] Ajder (2019).

[15] Metz (2021).

[16] Blitz (2018, pp. 64–65).

perform an act that may not have been performed in reality. Such deepfakes may not only be an encroachment on one's personal and intimate sphere, they may also carry serious negative long-term repercussions for one's personal and professional life. What is worse is that over 85% of the time, women are at the receiving end of the deep-faked porn videos,[17] and in that sense technology may unwittingly end up negating our march towards the United Nations' Sustainable Development Goal no. 5 which is gender equality.

Whereas deepfakes for revenge porn and politics raise substantial ethical concerns and call for a re-think on whether IP protection should be more carefully tailored to deepfakes. Deepfakes used to create valuable content, such as for marketing and/or a personalized social message in vernacular languages are certainly creative, original and call for a more balanced discussion on the debate.[18] There is another nuanced dimension to the debate on the regulation of deepfakes. This relates to the concerns regarding the regulation of free speech. An outright prohibition may, in addition, also imply regulating speech and expression. Such a regulation is an anti-thesis to the fine fabric of democracy, freedom of expression, and trust. This brings us to the following three questions. First, are deepfakes protected by copyright? Second, what role can exceptions and limitations play in balancing the debate on deepfakes? Third, how does one balance the interplay between freedom of expression and the IP-protection, or in other words, are distinct rights needed in the charter of fundamental rights, in the context of deepfakes?

A nuanced discussion also calls for a "clear distinction" between copyright—(Sect. 3 *infra*) and personality rights-related issues in the deepfake technology (Sects. 3.1 and 4 *infra*).[19]

3.1 Deepfakes and Copyright and Related Rights

The first and perhaps the most fundamental question is whether deep-faked works can benefit from copyright protection. Deepfakes can be highly creative, and involve substantial technical innovation. Can such creations, then qualify as copyright-protected works? To benefit from copyright protection, the following two conditions must be met. First, there must be a work; and second, it must be original in the sense that it is the author's own intellectual creation. According to Article 2(1) of the Berne Convention, "Literary and artistic works" shall include "every production in the literary, scientific and artistic domain" irrespective of its "mode or form of expression".[20] Prior to the *Infopaq* decision of the Court of Justice of the European Union (CJEU), the meaning and threshold for originality within the meaning of the 2001 Information Society Directive remained elusive. What was this threshold for

---

[17] Langguth et al. (2021, p. 8).

[18] Meskys et al. (2020, p. 25).

[19] Drexl et al. (2020, p. 7, para. 23).

[20] Berne Convention (1886, as amended on September 28, 1979).

protection? Was the threshold of originality "infused with some degree of personhood theory", and, thus, a "reflection of the traditional Continental notion based on the personality of the author"?[21] Or was the test closer to the UK's "skill, labour and judgment", which would mean that a work is an author's creation, "simply" if s/he did not copy the work from another source?[22] The *Infopaq* decision cleared these doubts as it harmonized the meaning and concept of originality in the Information Society Directive.[23] In Infopaq, the CJEU eloquently stated that work could be deemed original if it is "the author's own intellectual creation".[24] Elaborating on "author's own intellectual creation", the CJEU found that in the case of a newspaper article, this was evident from "the form, the manner in which the subject is presented and the linguistic expression".[25] In *Eva Maria Painer*, the Court went a step a further to explain the meaning of the expression "author's own intellectual creation". In the case of a portrait photograph, the photographer has the choice to clearly express his personality by choosing and combining different elements, such as "the background, the subject's pose and the lightning".[26] In the process of making such distinct creative and technical choices, the author of a photograph "can stamp the work created with his 'personal touch'".[27]

Considering that we are talking about works created by the use of apps, it may be useful to add that the author contemplated is a human author. The authorship of the work created, belongs to a human being. Gathering from the international conventions, most notably the Berne Convention, case law on both sides of the Atlantic as well as academic commentary on the subject, it seems largely settled that the author must be a human being. Ginsburg makes a comparative study of different legal systems, such as the UK and the US (common law) and France and the Netherlands (continental civil law, *droit d'auteur* traditions), and identifies a common thread in terms of the definition of authorship—in each one of these systems, the author contemplated of is a human being.[28] Thus, across the jurisdictions "the romantic [human] author sits monolithically at the core of copyright law".[29] More recently, in a *Second Request for Reconsideration for Refusal to Register a Recent Entrance to Paradise*, the Copyright Review Board rejected Stephen Thaler's request to register an AI-generated image. Stephen Thaler had earlier created a Device for the Autonomous Bootstrapping of Unified Sentience (DABUS). DABUS is an AI-device that can autonomously create new works.[30] Thaler created an algorithm called

[21] Judge and Gervais (2009–2010, p. 375) et seqq.

[22] Judge and Gervais (2009–2010, p. 375) et seqq.

[23] Case C-5/08 Infopaq International (2009).

[24] Case C-5/08 Infopaq International (2009) at para. 37.

[25] Case C-5/08 Infopaq International (2009) at para. 44.

[26] Case C-145/10 Eva-Maria Painer (2011) at paras 90–91.

[27] Case C-145/10 Eva-Maria Painer (2011) at paras 91–92.

[28] Ginsburg (2003, p. 1063).

[29] Bridy (2012, p. 4); *See also* reference to works of Jaszi, Matha Woodmansee and Mark Rose therein.

[30] Sims (2021).

"Creative Machine" that generated the work "A Recent Entrance to Paradise". He requested the US Copyright Review Board for the registration of the said work. Both the US Copyright Office in the year 2019, and its Review Board more recently in 2022, rejected Thaler's request for registration as the author and owner of said AI-generated work on the grounds that human authorship was clearly a pre-requisite for copyright.[31]

Provided that deep-faked work is original, and is the result of a human author's own intellectual creation, they are copyright-protected. Even the most popular deepfake apps, such as Wombo, Reface and MyHeritage, require human input.[32] In each of the resulting deep-faked creations, the human author who offers his input, such as the selection of personalities, choice of attire or background, shall be deemed as the author.

In a deep-faked video, an individual is seen performing an act that he did not quite engage in. This involves an element of originality. The threshold for originality is not particularly high, it is sufficient that there is an element of originality. Following Infopaq,[33] Painer[34] and Levola Hengelo,[35] in the EU, works that have an author's personal touch are deemed original. In the United States, following Feist publication, a work that has a "modicum of creativity" is sufficient to benefit from copyright protection.[36] In the four different cases concerning deepfakes, referred to in Sect. 2 *supra*, each of the works has an element of originality. The subjects in the image or the video are seen to be engaging in an act that they did not perform in reality. This involves an element of originality. Moreover, as the threshold is not particularly high, so long as the work carries an author's intellectual input, it merits copyright protection. The content in each one of these cases involves manipulation of the original content to create a wrong narrative, a false version of the reality, quite distinct from the actual original content.[37] In the case of deep-faked news, these too may be copyright protected. News items cannot be allowed copyright protection. As per Article 1(8) of the Berne Convention, news items or "miscellaneous facts" that have the "character of mere items of press information" do not benefit from the protection afforded by the Convention. However, press articles and editorial commentaries may benefit from the protection provided they meet the threshold for originality. Copyright does not protect news, but the manner of communication, in other words, the narration of the news and information.[38] Considering that fake news involves an element of originality, as they depict an event that did not quite take place, they too may, merit copyright protection.

[31] United States Copyright Office, Copyright Review Board (2022).

[32] Beebom (2022).

[33] Case C-5/08 Infopaq International (2009).

[34] Case C-145/10 Eva-Maria Painer (2011).

[35] Case 310/17 Levola Hengelo BV (2018).

[36] Feist Publications, Inc. (1991).

[37] Bonadio et al. (2021, p. 448).

[38] Bonadio et al. (2021, p. 451).

The traditional view on exceptions and limitations identifies them as the contour that circumscribes the general protection afforded to the right holders. In other words, copyright and related rights offer the creator an exclusive set of economic and moral rights. If anyone uses those works, without taking the requisite authorisation from the right holder, and/or without paying him adequate remuneration, s/he is deemed to be an infringer. Once an infringement of an author's rights has been established, the follow-up question is whether the right holder can benefit from any exception and limitations (E&Ls). In the European Union, Article 5 of the 2001 Information Society Directive offers a closed ended list of twenty E&Ls. With the exception of the exception for transient use (under Article 5(1) of the Directive), the other 19 exceptions and limitations are optional in nature. The use of the word "optional" means that Member States enjoy the discretion to implement or refrain from implementing these nineteen exceptions in their national legislation. However, should they choose to implement these other nineteen exceptions, these E&Ls cannot go beyond the limits prescribed in the Information Society Directive.[39] In the context of deepfakes, the quotation exception and the parody exception may be the most relevant E&L to escape the liability of infringement.

As per Article 5(3)(k) of the InfoSoc Directive, Member States may introduce an exception for "caricature, parody or pastiche". The opinion of the CJEU in the Deckmyn case is insightful in order to understand the scope (and limitations) of this parody exception. In the said case, a calendar by Johan Deckmyn was found offensive by some, as the calendar depicted the mayor of Ghent throwing coins on people of colour and people covered in veils. The work was reminiscent of the famous must-read Dutch children's comic book *Suske & Wiske*. The successors of the creator of the comic series, Willy Vandersteen, and holding companies in charge of *Suske & Wiske* brought copyright infringement proceedings before the Belgian courts. As the matter reached the Court of Appeals of Brussels, it decided to rest the proceedings and refer a set of questions dealing with parody exception to the CJEU.[40]

The CJEU was of the opinion that parody was "an autonomous concept of EU law".[41] This implies that Member States have a freedom to implement or not to implement the parody exception. However, should they choose to implement one such E&L, it must have a uniform and consistent interpretation within the meaning of Article 5(3)(k) of the Directive. As regards the other questions dealing with the scope of such an exception, the Court was of the following view.

> [...] the essential characteristics of parody, are, first, to evoke an existing work, while being noticeably different from it, and secondly, to constitute an expression of humour or mockery. The concept of 'parody' within the meaning of that provision, is not subject to the conditions that the parody should display an original character of its own, other than that of displaying noticeable differences with respect to the original parodied work; that it could reasonably be attributed to a person other than the author of the original work itself; that it should be related to the original work itself or mention the source of the parodied work.

---

[39] Case C-476/17 Pelham GmbH (2019), Case C-516/17 Spiegel Online (2019) and Case C-469/17 Funke Medien NRW GmbH (2019).

[40] C-201/13 Johan Deckmyn (2014).

[41] C-201/13 Johan Deckmyn (2014) at para. 17.

The quotation exception is one of the most fundamental and universally recognized exception in copyright law. Article 10 of the Berne Convention allows Member States to offer a quotation exception. To benefit from such an exception, the work should have been "lawfully made available to the public".[42] The quotation should not exceed what is required and should be compatible with fair practice.[43] Article 5(3)(d) of the InfoSoc Directive offers the Member States to introduce a quotation exception. As per the Directive, the quotation should concern a work that has been available lawfully, and should ideally mention the source and the author's name. Further, such a use must be in accordance with "fair practice, and to the extent required by the specific purpose".[44] In *Pelham*, wherein the issue concerned a two-second sample played in a repeated loop, the CJEU was of the opinion that in order to benefit from the quotation exception, the user must have "the intention of entering into a 'dialogue' with [the] work".[45]

A notable contribution of the three decisions *Pelham, Funke Medien and Spiegel Online*, all delivered by the CJEU on the same day, is that, following these decisions, exceptions and limitations are now seen as user rights, and, therefore, merit safeguard from the perspective of fundamental rights.[46] The threads weaving a balance between the right to freedom of creative expression in Article 11 and the right to intellectual property first surface in the Deckmyn case.[47] These three decisions further strengthened this perspective on balancing the fundamental right of expression against the original right holder's exclusive economic and moral rights.

A change in perspective has also changed the narrative. As "positive user rights", the role of these exceptions and limitations in terms of their contribution to follow-on creativity cannot be underestimated.[48] To summarize this section, copyright protection, provided the conditions for protection are met, may be afforded to these deepfake works. They may also generally benefit from the quotation and the parody exception, provided the above-referred conditions are met. This must, however, be balanced against the competing rights as referred to in the Charter of Fundamental Rights (CFRs) that have attained constitutional status in the EU, following the 2009 Lisbon Treaty entering force.[49]

---

[42] Article 10(1) Berne Convention.

[43] Article 10(1) Berne Convention. Case C-145/10 Eva-Maria Painer (2011) at paras 119–120.

[44] Article 5(3)(d) InfoSoc Directive (2001).

[45] Case C-476/17 Pelham GmbH (2019) at para. 71. For a critical discussion on the exception, *see* Tyagi (*forthcoming* 2023).

[46] Frosio and Geiger (2022), pp. 21–24.

[47] Rosati (2015, p. 511).

[48] Tyagi (2021).

[49] Kokott and Sobotta (2012, p. 111).

4 Deepfakes and Personality Rights

The mix of the internet and deepfakes can be a lethal challenge to law enforcement. Deepfakes involve the creative manipulation of images and videos. This means that individuals may oftentimes be a reluctant actor in a deep-faked work. What is worse, they may even be unaware of the deep-faked work. By the time they come to know of its existence, the work may already have been widely dispersed. The damage to one's personality and sometimes even the society at large, in such a case, can be borderless, irreversible and irretrievable. Discussion on personality rights and privacy is, therefore, highly suitable to construct the complete IP rights framework. Personality rights are the least harmonized among different kinds of rights.

What makes the situation complex is that deepfakes, in a certain sense, work like the pharmaceutical industry. In the world of pharma, the doctor prescribes the drug, the pharmacy sells it, the patient uses the drug, and the national health authorities re-imburse it. The prescriber, the user, and re-imbursement authority are three different sets of individuals and enterprises. The case of deepfakes, remarkably, is not very different. The consumer of a deep-faked video is different from the creator of the video, who in turn has morphed and deep-faked another image or video. The fact that images, voice, data, and other audio-visual contents are involved means that in addition to copyright, privacy laws and personality rights may also be involved. The consumer, the creator of the original video or image, the creator of deepfake and the individuals depicted in these videos or images are often distinct parties and they may often times be unrelated and unknown to each other. This means that while viewing a deeply morphed image or a video, the consumer may be unable to empathize with the target of these deep-faked creations.

This brings the issue of personality rights and their relationship with deepfakes center stage. Preferences vary amongst individuals as regards the sharing of their images. For some, sharing an image may be the equivalent of "stealing their soul", whereas others may cherish public scrutiny of all aspects of their "personhood, even the most intimate ones".[50] It may be useful to add here that the image is but one aspect of the personality rights. Other aspects may include name, signature, and other attributes that uniquely identify an individual.

According to the Black's Law Dictionary (7th edition, 1999), "intellectual property" is.

1. A category of intangible rights protecting commercially valuable products of the human intellect. The category comprises primarily trademark, copyright, and patent rights, but also includes trade-secret rights, publicity rights, moral rights, and rights against unfair competition.
2. A commercially valuable product of the human intellect, in a concrete or abstract form, such as a copyrightable work, a protectable trademark, a patentable invention, or a trade secret.

---

[50] Synodinou (2014, p. 182).

Also, the question is, under what circumstances or situations will the image of an individual be protected? To benefit from protection, "[clear and categorical] identification of the person" is a pre-requisite.[51] This implies that the use of look-alikes or atypical characteristics that identify a certain celebrity with certainty may be deemed as an infringement of their image rights.[52]

Referring to Black's Law Dictionary, McCarthy and other leading dictionaries, the United States Court of Appeals for the Third Circuit, recently established that "personality rights" should be deemed as intellectual property.[53] In the US, publicity rights were first clearly established with the decision of *Haelan Laboratories Inc. v. Topps Chewing Gum Co.*[54] In the said case, some baseball players had entered into a contract with Haelan Laboratories, a gum manufacturer, to offer the latter an exclusive right to use their images on baseball cards. Some of these players then also entered a contract with a competing Chewing Gum company, giving them the right to use their image on their product. The Court was of the opinion that by entering into an exclusive contract with Haelan, the baseball players had transferred their alienable property right for the use of their image on baseball cards exclusively to Haelen. The right of publicity in the US has since undergone significant evolution, and is increasingly viewed as an alienable right. In light of this commodification, scholars call for the need to take "non-economic concerns" into account to ensure that the interests of all—"those who seek to commercialize their identities and those who do not" are equally protected.[55] Interestingly, the EU with its *droit d'auteur* tradition offers a more fertile ground for one such framework, wherein the balance between commercial and non-commercial interests can be adroitly maintained.

In Europe, divergences across Europe exist as regards the protection of personality rights. The civil law tradition protects images based either on the right to privacy or on the right to personality.[56] In the UK, images are protected by the law of "torts of breach of confidence and of passing off".[57] There is no specific legislation dealing with image rights, as they are known more popularly in the UK. Courts seem to engage in a balancing exercise between the right to privacy on the one hand, and the freedom of expression on the other. In the EU, to this day, we do not have a harmonized personality law. Likewise, in the US, publicity laws are a "web of 'disparate' state laws".[58]

---

[51] Synodinou (2014, p. 183).

[52] Synodinou (2014, p. 183).

[53] Karen Hepp (CoA 2022), pp. 20–22.

[54] Haelan Laboratories Inc. (2nd Circuit 1953).

[55] Rothman (2012, p. 220).

[56] Synodinou (2014, p. 183).

[57] Synodinou (2014, p. 183).

[58] Opinion of Cowen in Karen Hepp (CoA 2022, p. 16).

4.1 *Copyright and Personality Rights: Does One Prevail Over Another?*

There may be instances when copyright and personality rights are in conflict. Consider, for instance, a case, where a photographer has captured an image on the camera without the person's consent. Following *Painer*, it is evident that a photograph, provided it has the author's "personal touch" is copyright-protected. But what happens when the photograph is taken without an individual's consent? Whose interests—the photographer's or the individual's—prevail in such a case? The decision by the Paris court is insightful in this regard. In a case before the French courts, the photographer Juan had taken photographs of his ex-girlfriend and given them his artistic touch to transform them into creative works of contemporary art. As Juan's work met the threshold for copyright protection, they were copyright-protected. However, his girlfriend objected to the use of her image, particularly those of an intimate nature. The Court looked at the two interests at stake—of Article 10 of the European Convention of Human Rights on the one hand, and of the artist and Article 8 on the other. Whereas Article 10 refers to the freedom of expression and information, Article 8 guarantees privacy. On a balancing of the two rights, the Court was of the opinion that even though Juan's works were undoubtedly creative in expression, the respect for his girlfriend's right to privacy merited priority, as she had evidently not given her consent to the use of her intimate images for public display.[59]

Personality rights may, thus, be seen as an "informal" and "external limitation" on copyright law.[60] In *Vereinigung Bildender Kunstler*, Austrian painter Otto Mühl presented his work "Apocalypse" at an art exhibition. The painting was provocative as it showed mixed figures with faces of famous personalities transposed over naked bodies. An aggrieved Austrian politician who was depicted in these paintings requested an injunction to prohibit the presentation of the painting in public on the basis of Section 78, Urheberrechtsgesetz,[61] the Austrian Copyright Act.

> **Bildnisschutz § 78** (1) Bildnisse von Personen dürfen weder öffentlich ausgestellt noch auf eine andere Art, wodurch sie der Öffentlichkeit zugänglich gemach werden, verbreitet werden, wenn dadurch berechtigte Interessen des Abgebildeten oder, falls er gestorben ist, ohne die Veröffentlichung.
>
> (2) Die Vorschriften der §§ 41 und 77, Absatz 2 und 4, gelten entsprechend.

As per the said provision, images of persons may neither be publicly exhibited nor made available, in case it may adversely affect their legitimate interests. The said provision also protects the interest of the deceased by ensuring that a close relative must first give his/her authorization. The Austrian Courts granted the request for an injunction. When the matter reached the European Court of Human Rights (ECtHR), the key consideration was whether, following a balancing of different interests under consideration, the national court had trumped the artist's freedom of expression as

[59] Virginie G/Juan F Paris TGI (10 January 2013).

[60] Synodinou (2014, p. 189).

[61] Urheberrechtsgesetz, Bildnisschutz § 78.

provided in Article 10 of the Convention. The Court answered in the affirmative and stated thus:

> 38. In sum, having balanced Mr. Meischberger's personal interests and taking account of the artistic and satirical nature of his portrayal, as well as the impact of the measure at issue on the applicant association, the Court finds that the Austrian courts' injunction was disproportionate to the aim it pursued and therefore not necessary in a democratic society within the meaning of Article 10 § 2 of the Convention.[62]

How does one reconcile the above two notable decisions—the first by the *Paris Tribunal de grande instance*, the Court of major instance, and the second by the ECtHR? Possibly central to the decision of the French court was that, whereas the artist Juan's girlfriend may have given her consent to be photographed and agreed to be present on some public occasions, this was insufficient to subsequently manoeuvre those photographs that were particularly intimate in nature. The ECtHR, on the other hand looked at the totality of the circumstances, and took the "satirical nature of [the artist's] portrayal" of the political situation into account. On a finer reading of the two, it emerges that the courts seem to engage in a balancing exercise, and evaluate the interest of the different parties. Overall, this implies that the question of which of the two sets of interests may outweigh the other in a given case is highly fact-specific and contextual in nature.

4.2 *Droit Moral*: The Thread that Weaves Copyright and Personality Rights

The French law on personality rights is "characterised by a dualistic approach",[63] something more closely aligned with the duality in copyright law. In copyright law, there exists a duality of moral and economic rights. Likewise, in the French tradition, a person's image is seen to have two dimensions—an extra-patrimonial and a patrimonial aspect; unlike the US tradition of "an exclusive autonomous image right encompassing both dignity and property interests".[64]

French tradition most distinctly brings out the relationship between copyright and personality rights. In the continental law tradition, the "personhood theory" means that the personality of the author remains center stage. In the French *droit d'auteur* tradition, in addition to the economic rights, the *droit moral* remains central to copyright.[65] *Droit moral* offers four different protection rights, though it may be useful to clarify here that not every civil law tradition may equally recognize each

[62] Case of Vereinigung Bildender Künstler (2007) at para. 38.

[63] Synodinou (2014, p. 184).

[64] Synodinou (2014, p. 184).

[65] Germain (2017, p. 9).

one of these four rights.[66] These four rights are—first, "right to publication"; second, "right to paternity"; third, "right to integrity" and fourth, the "right to withdrawal".[67]

Amongst the foregoing four dimensions of *droit moral*, the "right to integrity" is that fine silk thread that weaves our discussion on copyright and personality rights, and offers a promise to have a *sui generis* European-level personality rights tradition. Right to integrity means that the author can proscribe any unapproved changes to his works. In the French *droit moral* tradition, these rights are inalienable and perpetual. The strict nature of *droit moral* tradition is best illustrated by the famous John Huston case. The French *Cour de Cassation*, the highest French Court, found that even though the Turner Company had legally acquired the rights of performance, it could not colourize John Houston's classic film shot in black and white.[68] Approvingly citing the decision of the judges in the first instance, the *Cour de Cassation* found that John Houston's "great fame" came from his distinct ability to bring things in black and white colour, which in turn "enabled him to create an atmosphere according to which he directed the actor and selected the backdrops".[69] The Court also went on to take note of the fact that despite the wide availability of colour film techniques at the time, Huston went on to shoot "Asphalt Jungle" in black and white. This choice, in the opinion of the Court, was no coincidence, it was rather a "deliberate aesthetic choice, according to a process which its authors considered best suited to the character of the work".[70] In light of the foregoing, the colourization of the film, without authorization either from the author or from his heirs, was deemed to be a "violation of the creative activity of its makers, even if" it was done for "commercially obvious reasons" and satisfied "the expectations of a certain public".[71]

It emerges that *Droit moral* could form the normative basis of a pan-EU personality rights framework. The droit d'auteur regime is driven by Hegel's "personhood theory". Within this framework, a work is a reflection of an author's personality. This is also evident from the jurisprudence of the CJEU, as discussed above. In *Painer*, the CJEU was of the opinion, that for copyright protection, it is sufficient that the work has the author's "personal touch". To have a true pan-European EU-wide framework for personality rights, "patrimonial right of personality" can formulate one such basis.[72] In one such framework, one may identify the "celebrity's persona as a shell", and thereby, "an external embodiment of personal traits" distinguishable from the person's "inalienable internal sense of self".[73] This also more closely aligns with the German approach, wherein the courts have referred to an innate inner self of an individual that is reflected in his personality.

[66] Pettenati (2000, p. 429).

[67] Pettenati (2000, p. 429). See also references therein.

[68] Turner Entertainment Co. (1994).

[69] Turner Entertainment Co. (1994) at para. 9 on p. 6.

[70] Turner Entertainment Co. (1994) at para. 9 on p. 6.

[71] Turner Entertainment Co. (1994) at para. 10 on p. 6.

[72] Synodinou (2014, pp. 192–193).

[73] Synodinou (2014, pp. 192–193).

5 Blockchain and Deepfakes

Despite all their creative promises, deepfakes carry the potential to emerge as a challenge for law enforcement. This may be particularly true for fake news and deep-faked revenge porn, two of the more dangerous facets of deepfakes. How does one avert this situation? AI, the technology behind deepfakes, at least in its current state, has its limitations. The question is, if technology presents a challenge, can technological innovation also present a solution? Here, a reference to blockchain may be helpful. Blockchain has been proposed as a promising solution to detect deepfakes. Blockchain is a cryptography-based solution, and therefore, it does not suffer from similar limitations as the AI-technology.[74] To offer a sound policy recommendation, it may be useful to distinguish between different types of blockchains and to ascertain, which particular types of blockchain technology have a greater chance of successful commercial application and acceptance across industries.

Blockchain may be defined as a decentralized ledger of a cryptography-based solution, wherein transactions are time-stamped. The technology solves the problem of "trust" as each transaction is hash-tagged and carries valuable metadata, such as the time of the transaction.[75] A given blockchain comprises a range of blocks. Each block carries the value and the relevant data of the transaction. In addition, the block is time-stamped, which suggests the exact time at which the transaction was validated. The block also comprises the value of the earlier block, and a nonce.[76] A nonce is a unique random number that distinctly verifies a given hash.[77] The process ensures the integrity of the blockchain. What makes blockchain distinct from other traditional methods of record keeping is that each node in the ledger is distinctly stamped, in other words hash-tagged, and each copy has a duplicate ledger copy that can directly interact with every other node in the chain.[78] The technology found rapid uptake in the pharmaceuticals sector, wherein the challenge of counterfeit medicines remains a key concern.[79] The COVID-19 pandemic further added impetus to the pharma sector's rapid uptake of the technology.[80] The value of the blockchain technology likewise offers a worthwhile remedy to consider for the digital value chains. A digital solution such as blockchain, may, in fact, be even easier to implement in a digital ecosystem, such as deepfakes.

The distributed nature of the blockchain architecture ensures that one no longer requires a trusted third party to intermittently intervene and authenticate the transactions in the blockchain. This entire process is consensus-based, and in case of disagreement, a "fork" may emerge in the chain.[81] Decentralization, transparency

---

[74] Langguth et al. (2021, p. 7).

[75] Pierro (2017).

[76] Nofer et al. (2017, p. 183).

[77] Nofer et al. (2017, pp. 183–184).

[78] Rashid et al. (2021, pp. 1048–1049).

[79] McCauley (2020).

[80] McCauley (2020).

[81] Rashid et al. (2021, pp. 1048–1049).

and immutability of the blockchain are the frequently cited reasons for its promise to disrupt traditional value chains.[82] However, it emerges that the technology is not without its limitations. As an example, one needs to do away with expressions such as "immutable" as is currently widely used in the discourse on the blockchain technology.[83] In the case of the US-based Distributed Autonomous Organization (DAO), for instance, a certain crowd-funded project developed a bug. A hacker quickly identified this bug and stole over US$ 60 million, about 40% of the crowd-funded money, to his personal account.[84] It may, thus, be more judicious to suggest blockchain as a near-immutable or more befittingly, "temper resistant" ledger of transactions. This means that though blockchain retains its potential to offer a decentralized, temper-resistant ledger of time-stamped transactions, its limitations must also be kept in sight.

Preliminary findings indicate that a private or permissioned-blockchain will drive the acceptance of the technology.[85] A private blockchain is based on the Byzantine fault tolerance, which, as Satoshi Nakamoto first suggested, differs fundamentally from the technology used in public ledger-based bitcoin technology. Byzantine General problems are solved by pre-determined participants in the permissioned model.[86] In other words, in such a model, participants are no strangers to each other, as in the case of a permissionless public ledger.

This means that blockchains may present a potential remedy to address deepfakes in a permissioned ecosystem. In other words, a remedy from blockchain, though promising, may still have its limitations. To address this gap, one may also need to look at digital literacy and awareness of deepfakes to counter the threat of infodemic posed by deepfakes.

6 Conclusion, Recommendations and the Road Ahead

Scalable solutions in the digital world require substantial sunk costs in terms of research and development (R&D). For the private sector, financing schemes such as venture capital are an important mode of funding. The resource-constrained public sector, however, has limited funding options. Moreover, there are diverging interests at force in the public and the private sector. Whereas, as once coined by Milton Friedman, profit is the only business of the business; justice, equity, and rule of law remain top concerns for a democratically-elected government.

The rise of the GAFAM (Google, Apple, Facebook, Amazon and Microsoft)—that has on the one hand contributed to the rapid adoption of digital technologies and that also remains one of the key contributors to deepfakes—has brought these delicate

[82] Rashid et al. (2021, pp. 1048–1049).

[83] Yaga et al. (2018).

[84] Tyagi (2018).

[85] Tyagi (2018).

[86] Zhang (2020, p. 115).

questions of balancing economic growth, digitalization, and democracy center-stage. Here, the concept of misinformation and manipulating misinformation merits attention. It is, therefore, imperative to keep account of manipulating information and misinformation and how deepfakes may offer an impetus to the same. As the technical discussion in Sect. 2 above indicates, data is the food on which neural networks feed. With technical advances such as GAN and RGB Videos (Sect. 2 *supra*), even though the volume of data may no longer drive the next wave of Schumpeter's creative destruction, data, nonetheless, retains significance even in an unsupervised learning environment. This brings complex issues of text and data mining into consideration, an issue that I discuss elsewhere. Considering the scope of this article, I focused on copyright and personality rights-related issues.

As the foregoing discussion elucidates, an outright prohibition of technological innovation is neither desirable nor the optimum. Whereas deepfakes for revenge porn and politics raise substantial ethical concerns and call for a re-think on whether IP protection should be available; deepfakes used to create valuable content, such as for marketing, and original and creative deepfakes may call for a more balanced discussion on the debate.[87] As the creation of original and creative deepfakes and valuable content involves copyright and personality rights related issues, they remain the focus of this article. This is, in the opinion of the author, the first step towards the design of a holistic regulatory framework for deepfakes. Whereas personality rights may be defined by national borders, internet is borderless. The CJEU had the opportunity to encounter this borderless nature of personality rights-related issues on the internet, in the case of *eDate Advertising GmbH v. X* and *Oliver Martinez v. MGN Ltd.* In both the cases, the CJEU found that individuals retained the right to bring forth a case in the Member States, wherein they had their "center of interests".[88] To avert such a potential case of forum-shopping, the article deliberates on the *droit moral*-based pan-EU personality rights framework. The second part of this article, further develops the contours of this droit moral-driven framework.[89] In addition, the issue of secondary liability of platforms too gains center-stage, an issue that remains central to the follow-up article.

References

Ajder A (2019) Japanese startup uses GANs to generate deepfake fashion models. Medium. https://medium.com/sensity/tracer-newsletter-11-06-05-19-japanese-startup-uses-gans-to-generate-deepfake-fashion-models-ba5d4b1b6690. Last access 04 August 2022

Beebom (2022) 10 best deepfake apps and websites you can try for fun. Beebom. https://beebom.com/best-deepfake-apps-websites/. Last access 04 August 2022

Blitz MJ (2018) Lies, line drawing, and (Deep) fake news. 71 Oklahoma Law Rev 59

[87] Meskys et al. (2020, p. 25).

[88] Synodinou (2014, p. 195).

[89] Tyagi (2022).

Bonadio E, Lucchi N, Policino O (2021) Fake news and copyright. Queen Mary J Intellect Prop 11(4):444–468

Bridy A (2012) Coding creativity and the artificially intelligent author. Stanf Technol Law Rev 5

Drexl J et al (2020) Comments of the max Planck institute for innovation and competition on the draft issues of the world intellectual property organization on intellectual property policy and artificial intelligence. WIPO, Geneva

Dutch Digital Design (2018) The next rembrandt project: bringing the old master back to life. Medium. https://medium.com/%40DutchDigital/the-next-rembrandt-bringing-the-old-master-back-to-life-35dfb1653597. Last access 04 August 2022

Frosio G, Geiger C (with the contribution of Fedunyshyn K) (2022) Taking fundamental rights seriously in the digital services act's platform liability regime. Eur Law J. https://papers.ssrn.com/sol3/papers.cfm?abstract_id=3747756. Last access 04 August 2022

Germain CM (2017) Don't steal my recipe! a comparative study of French and U.S. Law on the protection of culinary recipes and dishes against copying. In: Presented at Juris Diversitas annual conference, Law & Food: La Cuisine Juridique (July 9–12, 2017 Lyon, France) and Southeastern Association of Law Professors (SEALS) annual meeting (August 2018 Fort Lauderdale Fl). https://papers.ssrn.com/sol3/papers.cfm?abstract_id=3393891. Last access 04 August 2022

Giles M (2018) The GANfather: the man who's given machines the gift of imagination. MIT Technol Rev

Ginsburg JC (2003) The concept of authorship on comparative copyright law. De Paul Law Rev 52:1063

Jordan J (2018) Variational autoencoders. Data Sci Jeremy Jordan. https://www.jeremyjordan.me/variational-autoencoders/. Last access 04 August 2022

Judge EF, Gervais D (2009–2010) Of silos and constellations: comparing notions of originality in copyright law. Cardozo Arts Entertain Law J 27:375

Kan E (2018) What the heck are VAE-GANs? towards data science. https://towardsdatascience.com/what-the-heck-are-vae-gans-17b86023588a. Last access 04 August 2022

Kokott J, Sobotta C (2012) The charter of fundamental rights of the European union after Lisbon. 2012 RRDE 5:93–111

Langguth J et al (2021) Don't trust your eyes: image manipulation in the age of deep fakes. Front Commun 6:1–12

Mayer-Schönberger V, Cukier K (2013) Big Data: a revolution that will transform how we live, work and think. John Murray Hachette, UK

McCauley A (2020) Why BigPharma is betting on blockchain. Harv Bus Rev. https://hbr.org/2020/05/why-big-pharma-is-betting-on-blockchain. Last access 04 August 2022

Meskys E et al (2020) Regulatory deep fakes: legal and ethical considerations. J Intellect Prop Law Pract 15(1)

Metz R (2021) How a deepfake Tom Cruise on TikTok turned into a very real AI company. CNN Bus. https://edition.cnn.com/2021/08/06/tech/tom-cruise-deepfake-tiktok-company/index.html. Last access 04 August 2022

Nofer M et al (2017) Blockchain. Bus Inf Syst Eng 59(3):183–190. https://doi.org/10.1007/s12599-017-0467-3.pdf. Last access 04 August 2022

Next Rembrandt Project. https://www.nextrembrandt.com/. Last access 04 August 2022

Pettenati LA (2000) Moral rights of artists in an international marketplace. Pace Int Law Rev. 12(2)

Pierro MD (2017) What is the blockchain? Comput Sci Eng 19(5)

Rashid MM, Lee SH, Kwon KR (2021) Blockchain technology for combating deepfake and protect video/image integrity. J Korea Multimed Soc 24(8):1044–1058

Rosati E (2015) Just a laughing matter? why the CJEU decision in *Deckmyn* is broader than parody. Common Market Law Rev 52(2):511–529

Rothman JE (2012) The inalienable right of publicity. Loyola legal studies Paper No. 2012-46. 101 Georgetown Law J 185 https://papers.ssrn.com/sol3/papers.cfm?abstract_id=2174646. Last access 04 August 2022

Sims D (2021) US judge rules only humans, not AI, can get patent. TechSpot. https://www.techspot.com/news/91110-court-ruling-uspto-cannot-issue-patents-artificial-intelligence.html. Last access 04 August 2022

Synodinou T (2014) Image rights and copyright law in Europe: divergences and convergences. Laws 3(2):181–207

Thies J et al (2018) Face2Face: real-time face capture and reenactment of RGB videos. Commun ACM 62(1):96–104

Tyagi K (2018) Touch of disruption. IBLJ. https://www.researchgate.net/publication/327646364_A_Touch_of_Disruption. Last access 04 August 2022

Tyagi K (2021) Sampling the "soul of music" in the 4th industrial revolution: a comparative and inter-disciplinary perspective. Research Gate. https://www.researchgate.net/publication/355978852_Sampling_the_'soul_of_music'_in_the_4_th_Industrial_Revolution_A_Comparative_and_Inter-disciplinary_perspective. Last access 04 August 2022

Tyagi K (2022) Deepfakes and personality rights: looking through the glass of copyright and trademarks. To be presented at European Policy for Intellectual Property (EPIP). https://epip2022.org/about-epip/. Last access 04 August 2022

Tyagi K (2022) Sounds of sampling in the 4th industrial revolution: what role for exceptions and limitations? 39 ATRIP Research Book Edward Elgar

Technology Advice (2021) The 4 Vs of Big Data: complete 2022 guide. https://technologyadvice.com/blog/information-technology/the-four-vs-of-big-data/. Last access 04 August 2022

Williamson J (2015) Getting a big data job for dummies. Wiley, Oxford

Yaga D et al (2018) Blockchain technology overview. U.S. Department of Commerce: National Institute of Standards and Technology 8202. https://doi.org/10.6028/NIST.IR.8202. Last access 04 August 2022

Zhang Y (2020) Blockchain. In: Shen X, Lin X, Zhang K (eds) Encyclopedia of wireless networks. Springer

Part V: Competition Law

Innovation in High-Tech Mergers: Should Competition Law Bother?

Alexandra Telychko

Abstract The analysis of the adverse effects of a merger on competition has recently changed. While for years, competition authorities have focused primarily on the effects of a merger on prices, the impact on output, or the creation or strengthening of a dominant position in a given market, they are now examining the effects of a merger on innovation. According to the author's analysis, which begins by explaining the peculiarities of high-tech industries, the notion of "innovation", and the rationale for merger control, this system can only establish its effectiveness by applying the same standards of proof of the pro- and anti-competitive effects of a merger.

Keywords Consumer welfare · EU competition law · Future markets · High technology · High technology industries · Innovation · Merger control · Merger efficiency · Impediment to effective competition · Technology market

1 Introduction

Big tech companies are supposed to make the world a better place by bringing technology and innovation[1] to the masses. However, what makes them unique and beloved by some, also makes them the absolute evil to others: these companies are likely to be big and to focus exclusively on their profits while neglecting the

[1] The term "innovation" can be used in different contexts to denote either a process or an outcome. To avoid confusion, this chapter uses the term "innovation activities" to refer to the process, while the term "innovation" is limited to outcomes.

A. Telychko (✉)
Faculty of Law, University of Geneva, Geneva, Switzerland
e-mail: oleksandra.telychko@unige.ch

K. Mathis and A. Tor (eds.), *Law and Economics of the Digital Transformation*, Economic Analysis of Law in European Legal Scholarship 15,
https://doi.org/10.1007/978-3-031-25059-0_10

well-being and privacy[2] of consumers. In other words, they are "BAADD: big, anti-competitive, addictive and destructive to democracy".[3]

This could explain the mistrust and scrutiny of the European Commission (Commission) when it is called upon to decide on a merger[4] between high-tech[5] companies. Its mandate—formulated in fairly simple terms[6] but still difficult to implement—is to prevent a concentration that "significantly impede[s] effective competition in the common market or in a substantial part of it, in particular as a result of the creation or strengthening of a dominant position".[7] The analysis consists of

---

[2] This chapter will not address the issue of data exploitation by Big Tech companies (Alphabet (Google), Amazon, Apple, Meta (Facebook), Microsoft), nor the regulation of data protection practices, nor the interrelation between data protection and competition. For more information, see for example the following cases (non-exhaustive list): Italian Competition Authority, "Google" Case A552, (press release of 14 July 2022); "Amazon's Marketplace", UK Competition and Market Authority (press release of 6 July 2022); Case 50972, "Google Privacy Sandbox", UK Competition and Market Authority (commitment decision issued and case closed on 11 February 2022); Google-Adtech and Data-related practices (Case AT.40670), opened by the Commission on 22 June 2021; Facebook leveraging (Case AT.40684), opened by the Commission on 4 June 2021; "Meta's use of data", UK Competition and Market Authority, investigation opened on 4 June 2021; "Proceeding against Google based on new rules for large digital players (Section 19a GWB)—Bundeskartellamt examines Google's significance for competition across markets and its data processing terms", Bundeskartellamt (press release of 25 May 2021); "In the Matter of Facebook, Inc., a corporation", Federal Trade Commission (FTC), order of 28 April 2020; Google/Fitbit (Case M.9660), Commission decision of 17 December 2020; Case 1:20-cv-03010, U.S. Department of Justice (DOJ) and 10 State Attorneys General v Google to Restore Competition in the Search and Search Advertising Markets, complaint filed on 20 October 2020; Apple—App Store practices—music streaming (Case AT.40437), initiated by the Commission on 16 June 2020; Apple—App Store practices—e-books/audiobooks (Case AT.40652), initiated by the Commission on 16 June 2020; Amazon Marketplace (Case AT.40462), initiated by the Commission on 17 July 2019; Google Android (Case AT.40099), Commission decision of 18 July 2018 (appeal by Google currently pending before the General Court of the Court of justice of the European Union (CJEU); Google Search (Shopping) (Case AT.39740), Commission decision of 27 June 2017, confirmed by the General Court of the CJEU judgment of 10 November 2021); Microsoft/LinkedIn (Case M.8124), Commission decision of 6 December 2016.

[3] How to Tame the Tech Titans, The Economist (18 January 2018), retrievable under: www.economist.com/leaders/2018/01/18/how-to-tame-the-tech-titans (last access 07 October 2022).

[4] Council Regulation (EC) No 139/2004 of 20 January 2004 on the control of concentrations between undertakings (European Merger Regulation) [2004] OJ L 024, refers to the control of a "concentration", which includes, inter alia, mergers, joint ventures, and share acquisitions which lead to acquiring control over the target company. The terms "mergers", "mergers and acquisitions" and "concentrations" are used interchangeably throughout this chapter.

[5] High-tech is an abbreviation of high technology. For the purposes of this chapter, the term "high-tech" industry refers to manufacturing industries based on their high level of technology intensity (research and development (R&D) expenditure/value added), using the Statistical Classification of Economic Activities in the European Community (NACE Rev. 2) at the 3-digit level for group compilation.

[6] European Merger Regulation, Article 2(2).

[7] Under European competition rules, a dominant position is one in which an undertaking or group of undertakings would be able to behave to an appreciable extent independently of its competitors, its customers and, ultimately, its consumers (Definition given by the European Court of Justice (ECJ) in Hoffmann-La Roche Case 85/76 [1979] ECR 461 and confirmed in subsequent judgments).

ensuring that technology titans will not use their market power to protect or increase their market dominance to the detriment of consumer welfare.[8]

> In its assessment of mergers, the Commission carries out a balancing of interests. In theory, when assessing non-horizontal mergers, the Commission will consider both the possible anti-competitive effects arising from the merger and the possible pro-competitive effects stemming from substantiated efficiency benefiting consumers. The Commission examines the various chains of cause and effect with a view to ascertaining which of them is the most likely. The more immediate and direct the perceived anti-competitive effect of a merger, the more likely the Commission is to raise competition concerns. Likewise, the more immediate and direct the pro-competitive effects of a merger, the more likely the Commission is to find that they counteract any anti-competitive effects.[9]

The approach is similar in the case of horizontal mergers:

> In order to assess the foreseeable impact of a merger on the relevant markets, the Commission analyses its possible anti-competitive effects and the relevant countervailing factors such as buyer power, the extent of entry barriers and possible efficiency put forward by the parties.[10]

In practice, however, the situation resembles that of a prosecutor's obligation to investigate for and against the accused in an impartial manner. Oddly enough, the scales always tip in one direction.

Furthermore, there is no adequate and widely accepted theoretical or legal framework for innovation assessment in merger review, which is problematic both from the point of view of the principle of legality[11] and from the point of view of legal certainty[12] for all parties involved. It is not clear what innovation is (the Commission never defines it in its analysis), at what stage of the merger control innovation is to be analysed, or what means and degree of proof are required (both from the Commission and from the merging parties). Thus, as things stand, companies large and small should expect increased transactional uncertainty and be prepared to articulate

---

[8] Certain mergers may weaken competition by providing a means of segmenting markets or gaining significant market power, notably if they lead to the creation or strengthening of a dominant position (European Merger Regulation, Article 2(3)). This can result in increased concentration, reduced economic efficiency, reduced innovation, higher prices, lower quality and reduced consumer welfare (Ezrachi 2021, p. 445).

[9] Commission "Guidelines on the assessment of non-horizontal mergers under the Council Regulation on the control of concentrations between Undertakings" [2008] OJ C 265/07 (Guidelines on the assessment of non-horizontal mergers), para. 21.

[10] Commission "Guidelines on the assessment of horizontal mergers under the Council Regulation on the control of concentrations between undertakings" [2004] OJ C 031 (Guidelines on the assessment of horizontal mergers), para. 12.

[11] The principle of legality, a corollary of the rule of law, requires that the actions of the (European) administration be carried out in accordance with the law. According to European Convention, Charter of Fundamental Rights of the European Union [2000] OJ C 364/1, Article 52(1) sentence 1: "Any limitation on the exercise of the rights and freedoms recognised by this Charter must be provided for by law and respect the essence of those rights and freedoms."

[12] The concept of legal certainty—one of the general principles of European law recognised by the CJEU, Duff and Others, case C-63/93 [1996] para. 31—means that the law must be clear and precise and that its legal implications must be foreseeable.

the pro-competitive factors driving their investment, development and acquisition decisions.

In this chapter, we will focus on the Commission's assessment of the pro- and anti-competitive effects of high-tech mergers on innovation. In its prospective analysis of the negative impact of the merger on innovation, the Commission seems to assume that merging firms will necessarily decrease their R&D budgets after the merger,[13] thereby reducing their incentives to innovate and inevitably harming competition. Looking at the relevant market, the Commission also analyses the impact of the merger on the incentives and ability to innovate of the merged firm's competitors.

Logically, on the other side of the scale, the analysis of efficiency as a positive consequence of mergers should be done in the same way, i.e. by applying the same standard for evaluating and predicting innovation and innovation efforts. Alas, this does not seem to be the case, as the companies involved in the merger never seem to be able to claim the future innovation(s) as a post-merger efficiency, due to the forward-looking nature of the analysis, as the efficiency in question cannot be verified at the stage of the analysis.[14] How is it then that the Commission is able to verify (to use its own terminology) the absence of future innovation due to the merger, when no positive innovation efficiency alleged by the parties can be verified due to their uncertain nature?

This clear divergence in the Commission's approach to innovation due to the double standard of taking into account the pro- and anti-competitive effects of mergers on innovation must be addressed.

The analysis here focuses in particular on mergers in the high-tech sector[15] that have been notified[16] to the Commission and in which the Commission has in some

---

[13] According to the Commission, the transaction, which brings together, under a single owner, competing clinical research programmes that seek to address the same unmet medical needs is likely to diminish competition in innovation by reducing the R&D efforts of the notifying parties, see Novartis/GlaxoSmithKline Oncology Business (Case M.7275), Commission Decision of 18 March 2015, para. 104. The same reasoning applies to a transaction, prior to which the parties had significant research lines and products under development that target the same product markets. According to the Commission, the transaction would reduce competitive innovation between the parties, leading to the abandonment, postponement or redirection of competing lines of research and products under development. In addition, the transaction raised the question of the likelihood of a significant impediment to effective competition with respect to the parties' incentive to innovate in the areas in which they operated and the risk of a significant reduction in the overall level of competition and, therefore, product innovation in the industry in question—Dow/DuPont (Case M.7932), Commission Decision of 12 October 2017, para. 1955.

[14] See Chap. 5, Merger Efficiency: A Losing Game.

[15] See n 6 earlier. For the purposes of this chapter, when we refer to high-tech industries, we are considering industries classified under NACE code C.26 (manufacture of computers, electronic and optical products) and C.30.3 (manufacture of air and spacecraft and related machinery). Although traditionally the manufacture of basic pharmaceuticals and pharmaceutical preparations is considered part of high-tech manufacturing, we purposely exclude them from our analysis.

[16] Only concentrations that have a "Union dimension" are notifiable to the Commission under Article 4(1) of the European Merger Regulation. Article 1 of the European Merger Regulation sets out the numerical thresholds for establishing EU jurisdiction. Concentrations that do not have a Union dimension are subject to the merger laws of the Member States.

way analysed innovation.[17] This chapter, however, does not address the ongoing debate on killer acquisitions.[18]

The analysis begins with a background on the characteristics of high-tech industries, the rationale for merger control and the concept of innovation (2). This is followed by an analysis of the relevant market (3), which is then followed by an assessment of the anti-competitive effects (4), which turns out to follow a completely different logic than (5) the analysis of the pro-competitive effects of the merger on innovation.

2 Background

2.1 High Technology Industries

2.1.1 Definition of High Technology

There is no single definition of high-tech industries. The OECD and Eurostat classify industries into low-,[19] medium–low,[20] medium high,[21] and high technology[22] based on a comparison of their technological intensity (R&D expenditure/value added). Using a similar methodology, the OECD also defines high-tech products[23] and patents.[24]

---

[17] As of 20 June 2022, 272 mergers in the high-tech sector have been notified to the Commission. Of the published decisions, 58 analyse innovation in some way, of which we have selected the 26 most salient. For an overview of the decisions analysed, see the table in the Appendix.

[18] "Killer acquisitions", i.e. transactions that have the purpose or effect of terminating overlapping R&D projects, are currently the subject of debate, particularly with respect to the ability of merger control laws to identify and prevent such deals. See in particular the study by Cunningham et al. (2018), which focuses on the pharmaceutical sector and argues that mergers in research-intensive industries not only reduce the innovation efforts of the merged entities, but also have a negative impact on the innovation spending and efforts of rivals; Organisation for Economic Co-operation and Development (OECD) (2020), Commission et al. (2019).

[19] The low-technology industries are (i) paper printing, (ii) textiles and clothing, (iii) food, beverages and tobacco, and (iv) wood and furniture.

[20] The medium–low-technology industries are (i) rubber and plastic products, (ii) shipbuilding, (iii) other manufacturing, (iv) non-ferrous metals, (v) non-metallic mineral products, (vi) fabricated metal products, (vii) petroleum refining, and (viii) ferrous metals.

[21] The medium–high-technology industries are (i) scientific instruments, (ii) motor vehicles, (iii) electrical machinery, (iv) chemicals, (v) other transport equipment, and (vi) non-electrical machinery.

[22] The high-tech industries are (i) aerospace, (ii) computers and office machinery, (iii) electronics and communications, and (iv) pharmaceuticals.

[23] Products are considered high-tech according to calculations of R&D intensity by product group (R&D expenditure/total sales).

[24] Patents are considered high technology or biotechnology based on the International Patent Classification (IPC), eighth edition. The following technical fields are defined as high-tech IPC groups:

High technology is advanced, knowledge-intensive technology that increases the value of a product or process to the consumer, in the sense that the consumer gets better quality, lower costs, or easier use of products compared to outdated technology.[25]

2.1.2 Characteristics of High Technology

High technology is characterised by high scientific intensity and a high degree of market,[26] technological,[27] and competitive uncertainty.[28] In addition, the rapid evolution of technology leads to rapid obsolescence and explains the shortening of the life cycle.

High-tech industries tend to grow faster than low-tech industries. This is because, economically, thanks to productivity gains and increased demand, a much larger share of their output is sold at prices that decline significantly over time; thus the high-tech industries grow disproportionately in terms of volume.[29]

2.1.3 High Barriers to Entry and Expansion

The high-tech industry is characterised, among other things, by high barriers to entry, i.e. entry into these industries often requires large upfront R&D expenditures,[30] lengthy innovation activities, and production often has low marginal costs (the cost of supplying another unit).[31]

(i) aviation, (ii) communication technology, (iii) computer and commercial automation equipment, (iv) lasers, (v) micro-organisms and genetic engineering, and (vi) semiconductors, according to Eurostat, Glossary: High-tech, retrievable under: https://ec.europa.eu/eurostat/statistics-explained/index.php?title=Glossary:High-tech (last access 07 October 2022); According to a study by the U.S. Bureau of Labor Statistics to classify high-tech industries, a high-tech industry is defined by the presence of four factors: (i) a high proportion of scientists, engineers, and technicians; (ii) a high proportion of R&D employment; (iii) the production of high-tech products, as specified in a Census Bureau list of advanced technology products; and (iv) the use of high-tech production methods, including the extensive use of high-tech capital goods and services in the production process, Hecker (2005, p. 58).

[25] Serediuk and Vdovychenko (2018, p. 315).

[26] Market uncertainty refers to ambiguity about the type and extent of customer needs that can be met by a particular technology, Mohr (2000, p. 247).

[27] Technological uncertainty is "not knowing whether the technology—or the company providing it—can deliver on its promise to meet specific needs", Mohr (2000, p. 247).

[28] Competitive volatility refers to changes in the competitive landscape: which firms are one's competitors, their product offerings, the tools they use to compete. Innovations by entrants and incumbents can render older technologies obsolete, and as a result, the mortality rate of firms in high-tech industries can be high, contributing to competitive volatility.

[29] Von Furstenberg (1986, p. 43).

[30] Many high-tech companies spend 10% or more of their revenues on R&D, Gilbert (2020, pp. 13–14), referring to reports of the US National Science Foundation.

[31] Gilbert (2020, p. 16).

In the Commission, barriers to expansion or entry can take various forms.

- Legal or regulatory barriers can have a direct effect on the conditions of entry and/or the positioning of operators in the relevant market. These may include legal or regulatory barriers, such as tariffs or quotas, licensing procedures, territorial restrictions, safety and security standards, and other legal requirements in regulated sectors, or company-specific (dominant) advantages, such as economies of scale and scope, privileged access to key inputs or natural resources, important technologies, or a well-established distribution and sales network.[32]
- Structural barriers to entry arise from differing cost or demand conditions that determine asymmetric conditions between incumbents and entrants, hindering or preventing the latter from entering the market. High structural barriers can also be found when the market is characterised by absolute cost advantages or substantial economies of scale and/or network effects, capacity constraints and/or high sunk costs. The (dominant) firm's behaviour may also create barriers to entry, for example, where it has made significant investments that entrants or competitors would be expected to match, or where it has entered into long-term contracts with its customers that have appreciable foreclosure effects. Persistently high market shares may be an indication of barriers to entry and expansion.[33] Structural barriers may also exist where the provision of a service requires a network element that cannot be technically duplicated or whose duplication is not economically feasible.[34]

The Commission has pointed out that in innovation-driven markets characterised by constant technological progress, such as electronic communications markets, barriers to entry may become progressively less relevant. In such markets, competitive constraints often arise from threats from potential innovative competitors not currently in the market. Therefore, the potential for overcoming barriers to entry over the relevant time horizon should also be considered when identifying relevant markets for possible *ex ante* regulation.[35]

2.1.4 Role of IP

In high-tech industries, a company's IP, whether patented or in the form of non-patented know-how, is extremely important to the competitive potential of market

---

32 Guidance on the Commission's enforcement priorities in applying Article 82, para. 17; Commission Recommendation on relevant product market within the electronic communications sector, para. 10.

33 Guidance on the Commission's enforcement priorities in applying Article 82, para. 17; Commission Recommendation on relevant product market within the electronic communications sector, para. 9.

34 Ibid.

35 Commission Recommendation on relevant product market within the electronic communications sector, para. 11.

players.[36] Therefore, a company's products, technologies, customer base, data, and innovation capability are what makes it an attractive merger partner. Yet, a combination of leading manufacturers that are competitors or operate in different markets can lead to the combination of large IP portfolios, with a potential risk of restricting access to important cutting-edge technologies.[37]

Interestingly, however, design patents, related to the aesthetic design of a functional article, generally do not constitute a barrier to entry or limit innovation.[38]

2.2 *Innovation*

2.2.1 Definition of Innovation

Innovation activities—which refer to the process—include all developmental, financial and commercial activities undertaken by a company and intended to result in an innovation.[39]

Innovation processes are very difficult to predict, and the constantly changing technological and business environment challenges competition authorities to accurately assess innovation.[40] Because innovation is a pervasive, heterogeneous, and multifaceted phenomenon, a clear and concise definition of innovation and related concepts is needed to accurately measure and interpret firms' innovation activities and to establish a common standard of reference.[41]

---

[36] Boeing/McDonnell Douglas (Case M.877), Commission decision of 30 July 1997, para. 102.

[37] Idem.

[38] Lenovo/Motorola Mobility (Case M.7202), Commission decision of 29 July 2014, paras 22 and 55.

[39] OECD/Eurostat (2018, p. 20). For other definitions of innovation, see: Dosi (1988, p. 222), for whom innovation is the search for, discovery of, experimentation with, development of, imitation of, and adoption of new products, new production processes, and new organisational structures. For O'Sullivan and Dooley (2009, p. 3), innovation is the process of making changes, large and small, radical and incremental, to products, processes, and services that result in the introduction of something new to the organisation that adds value to consumers and contributes to the organisation's knowledge stock. For Christensen (2013, p. xiii), innovation means a change in one of the technologies, with the help of which an organisation transforms labour, capital, materials, and information into more valuable products and services. McKinley et al. (2014, p. 91), define innovation as any new product, service, or production process that deviates significantly from previous product, service, or production process architectures. Nahm (2014, p. 9), defines innovation as the process, used by firms to develop, master, and commercialise new product, service, and production process designs. It includes the process used to introduce new and improved technologies and practices to commercial markets. Tidd and Bessant (2014, p. 3), describe innovation as the process of introducing a new idea that creates widespread or long-term change. Mukhtar (2016, p. 47), views innovation as an interactive process to bring value to the market. In many cases, this process is initiated by a technological breakthrough from a research activity, which is followed by other activities such as manufacturing and marketing.

[40] Schreiber (2021, p. 291).

[41] OECD/Eurostat (2018, p. 68).

According to the concept of creative destruction, developed by Schumpeter,[42] the innovator creates new ways to produce goods or services or entirely new industries but, in doing so, destroys something else, often the competitive position of a rival firm. Innovation thus creates and destroys at the same time, with the prospect that the value of the creation will exceed that of the destruction.[43]

A business innovation—the outcome—is a new or improved product or business process (or a combination thereof) that differs significantly from the firm's previous products or business processes and that has been introduced on the market or brought into use by the firm.[44]

A new product, service, method or way of doing business is considered innovative if no one has ever launched or tried something similar. In other words, the product or service does not exist and no one knows about it. It must be something truly unique to the company's market or market segment.

2.2.2 Components of Innovation

The key components of innovation, as they relate to competition law and economics in general, are knowledge,[45] novelty, implementation, and value creation.[46] Moreover, as the very definition of innovation shows,[47] the difference between the new product or service and the one already on the market and used by consumers must be significant for them to be considered innovative.

However, one must keep in mind the components of innovation resulting from intellectual property (IP) law.

---

[42] Schumpeter (2008, p. 83). Schumpeter also insisted that this creative destruction was a much more important competitive force than the traditional concept of price competition, contrary to the conventional view of neoclassical economics (pp. 84–85).

[43] Swann (2009, p. 12).

[44] OECD/Eurostat (2018, p. 20).

[45] R&D is one of many activities that can generate innovations, or through which knowledge useful for innovation can be acquired. Other methods of acquiring potentially useful knowledge include market research, engineering activities to evaluate process efficiency and market surveys, OECD/Eurostat (2018, p. 46).

[46] Every innovation implies the likely intention to pursue some form of value creation (or preservation) by the actors responsible for it (OECD/Eurostat 2018, pp. 47–48). Value is thus an implicit objective of innovation, but it cannot be guaranteed ex ante because the outcomes of innovation are uncertain and heterogeneous. According to Dosi (1988, p. 222), innovation involves a fundamental element of uncertainty. This is not simply the absence of all relevant information on the occurrence of known events, but more fundamentally it means that (i) there are technical–economic problems whose resolution procedures are unknown, and (ii) that it is impossible to trace precisely the consequences to action. Almost by definition, what is being sought cannot be known precisely before the very activity of research and experimentation, so that the technical (and, even more, commercial) results of innovation efforts can hardly be known ex ante. Certainly, whenever innovative activities are undertaken by profit-motivated agents, they must also involve some perception of untapped technical and economic opportunities. However, these perceptions and beliefs rarely involve detailed knowledge of possible events, states of the world, input combinations, and product characteristics.

[47] "New or improved product or business process (or combination thereof) that differs significantly from the firm's previous products or business processes".

Take, for example, inventions, which are the basis of innovation. An invention is a new solution to a technical problem and can be protected by patents. The criteria for obtaining a patent are defined in national IP laws and may differ from country to country. But in general, to obtain a patent, an inventor must demonstrate that his technology is new (novel), useful, and not obvious to someone working in the field concerned.

Novelty with Respect to Potential Uses

The invention must be new to merit legal protection. An invention is considered new when it is not already part of the state of the art, which includes everything that has been made public in writing, orally, by use or by any other means, anywhere in the world, before the date of the patent application.

Novelty can be both objective and subjective. Some characteristics of a new product or service can be measured objectively, such as energy efficiency, speed or material strength. On the other hand, subjective characteristics, such as satisfaction, user-friendliness or the emotional experience of the user, may be more difficult to measure. In addition, novelty may be inherently subjective because users may assign different priorities to specific attributes, e.g. one group of users may place a higher priority on the ease of use of a cell phone, while a second group might prioritise its technical performance.[48]

Industrial Application and Actual Use

For an invention to be considered an innovation, it must be manufacturable or applicable in some commercial sector. The requirement for implementation is an essential characteristic of innovation that distinguishes it from inventions, prototypes, new ideas, etc.[49]

Non-obviousness

The solution to a problem is considered inventive if, based on the current state of the art, it is not obvious to a person skilled in the art. The use of another type of material instead of the usual type (e.g. the use of aluminium instead of steel) is obvious to a person skilled in the art and therefore does not constitute an inventive development.

[48] OECD/Eurostat (2018, p. 47).

[49] OECD/Eurostat (2018, p. 47).

An indication of an inventive step is the unexpected quality of a product or the surprising effect of a process.[50]

2.2.3 Drivers of Innovation

Innovation is an important factor in improving productivity and business performance. A variety of factors influence the incentives and ability of firms to innovate. Some of these factors are internal and reflect either the characteristics of the firm or the decisions made by the firm. Other factors are external and shape the general business environment in which firms operate (such as customs and trade regulations).

Four types of business capabilities are relevant for assessing the innovation performance of firms:

- The resources controlled by a firm, including its own workforce, physical and intangible assets (comprising knowledge capital), accumulated experience in conducting business activities, and available financial resources. Access to the resources of affiliated firms for firms that are part of a business group and those of partners and collaborators may also be relevant.[51]
- The general management capabilities of a firm, including a firm's competitive strategy and capabilities related to the management of innovation activities.[52]
- The skills of the workforce and how a company manages its human capital, as people are the most important resource for innovation since they are the source of creativity and new ideas.[53]
- The ability to develop and use technological tools and data resources, the latter being an increasingly important source of information for innovation.[54]

2.3 *Rationale for Merger Control*

The main objective of competition policy is to maintain the competitive process in the market, not as an end in itself, but as a means to maximise consumer welfare,[55] one of the main objectives of European competition policy.[56] Consequently, merger control aims to identify transactions that are detrimental to competition and to block

---

[50] Swiss Federal Institute of Intellectual Property, Guide for Innovative and Creative Minds, Patents Protection Requirements, retrievable under: https://www.ige.ch/en/intellectual-property/guide/patents/protection-requirements (last access 07 October 2022).

[51] OECD/Eurostat (2018, p. 104).

[52] OECD/Eurostat (2018, p. 106).

[53] OECD/Eurostat (2018, p. 115).

[54] OECD/Eurostat (2018, p. 117).

[55] Whish and Bailey (2021, p. 859).

[56] Commission Communication "Notice: Guidelines on the application of Article 81(3) of the Treaty" [2004] OJ C 101/97, para. 13; Guidelines on the assessment of horizontal mergers, para. 8.

or modify them. But merger control is not only about preventing future abuses: it is also about maintaining competitive markets that lead to better outcomes for consumers.[57]

One of the ways[58]—and the most effective one—to avoid the outright prohibition of a potentially anti-competitive merger is to divest a business, an asset or other rights.[59] This allows assets to be redistributed, thus avoiding the accumulation of market power in the hands of a single economic agent.

A key feature of merger control is that it is necessarily forward-looking: a competition authority has to consider whether a merger will have adverse effects on competition in the future.[60] Since mergers must be notified to the competition authority and cleared before they can be implemented, the substantive analysis is entirely prospective.[61]

To decide on the impact of a merger is to predict future behaviour. This necessarily means that merger control is partly theoretical. Therefore, a competition authority that decides to challenge a merger must have a theory of competitive harm as to why the market will function less well for consumers in the future than before the merger. However, it would not be acceptable for the authority to oppose a merger solely on the basis of theory or mere speculation.[62]

There is nothing illegal about merger activity, and the market for corporate control, in which firms compete for the right to acquire and manage businesses, is an important feature of a market economy. Just as the right to sell one's business rewards the risk taken, the effort and the innovation developed by an entrepreneur. It follows that the competition authority should be required to produce evidence showing how its theory of competitive harm applies to the merger.[63] In addition, the competition authority should also be required to demonstrate that the market will be less competitive after the merger than it would have been without the merger: in other words, the authority will not only have to predict the likely outcome of the merger, but also consider the counterfactual, i.e. the situation if the merger had not taken place.

---

[57] Whish and Bailey (2021, p. 859), Këllezi (2010, p. 16); on this point see Gencor v Commission Case T-102/96 [1999] para. 106.

[58] Other remedies include the removal of links with competitors, commitments to grant access to key infrastructure, networks, and key technologies such as patents or interoperability obligations.

[59] AB InBev/SAB Miller (Case M.7881), Commission decision of 19 June 2017; Këllezi (2010, p. 13), Williamson (1987, p. 116 et seqq).

[60] Whish and Bailey (2021, p. 860); See ECJ Commission v Tetra Laval BV Case C-12/03 P [2005], para. 42.

[61] The competition authorities intervene at two different times: ex post to sanction cartels and abuses of dominant positions (within the meaning of articles 101 and 102 of the Treaty on the Functioning of the European Union [2012] OJ C 326/01 (TFEU), or ex ante, beforehand, to prevent anti-competitive mergers (European merger regulation).

[62] General Court of the CJEU, Hutchison/Telefonica, Case T-399/16 [2020] upheld the validity of the Commission's theories of harm, but concluded that the Commission had not demonstrated a "significant impediment". See e.g. para. 118: "The Commission is required to produce sufficient evidence to demonstrate with a strong probability the existence of significant impediments following the concentration" to block a merger that does not create a dominant position.

[63] Whish and Bailey (2021, pp. 860–861).

2.4 *Commission's Merger Control Methodology*

Once the Commission has jurisdiction over a merger, Article 2 TFEU requires it to determine whether the merger significantly impedes effective competition (SIEC). The burden of proof lies with the Commission, which must provide convincing evidence that a merger is incompatible with the internal market.[64] According to the Court of Justice, there is no presumption that a merger is (in)compatible with the internal market[65]; rather, the Commission must adopt a decision on the basis of "its assessment of the economic outcome attributable to the merger which is most likely to ensue".[66]

In order to determine whether the merger with an EU dimension may have anti-competitive effects, the Commission proceeds according to the following steps: (i) identifying the market(s) concerned by the merger[67]; (ii) identifying the type of potential anti-competitive effect generated depending on the type of merger[68]; (iii) determining whether the merger is the cause of the potential anti-competitive effect[69]; (iv) determining whether the anti-competitive effects are counteracted by pro-competitive efficiency generated by the same merger[70]; and (v) determining whether the parties can undertake commitments that would eliminate the anti-competitive effects.[71]

64 See ECJ, Commission v Tetra Laval BV Case C-12/03 P [2005] paras 37–51; General Court of the CJEU, Deutsche Lufthansa AG v Commission Case T-712/16 [2018] paras 32–45.

65 General Court of the CJEU, Bertelsmann A.G. and Sony Corporation of America v Impala, Case C-413/06 P [2008], para. 48; Court of First Instance of the CJEU, General Electric v Commission, Case T-210/01 [2005] para. 61.

66 General Court of the CJEU, Bertelsmann A.G. and Sony Corporation of America v Impala, Case C-413/06 P [2008] para. 52; see also General Court of the CJEU, Cisco Systems v Commission, Case T-79/12 [2013] para. 47, rejecting the assertion that the Commission would have to prove beyond reasonable doubt that a merger does not give rise to competition concerns.

67 Commission Notice on the definition of the relevant market for the purposes of Community competition law [1997] OJ C 372/05 (Notice on the definition of the relevant market), para. 2.

68 Guidelines on the assessment of non-horizontal mergers, para. 28; Guidelines on the assessment of horizontal mergers, para. 12.

69 Guidelines on the assessment of horizontal mergers, para. 89; In CJEU, France v Commission, Cases C-68/94 and C-30/95 [1998] the Court of Justice held that there must be a causal link between the merger and the deterioration of the competitive structure of the market for the European Merger Regulation to apply.

70 European Merger Regulation, recital 29.

71 European Merger Regulation, Article 6(2) and Article 8(2); Commission Notice on remedies acceptable under Council Regulation (EC) No 139/2004 and under Commission Regulation (EC) No 802/2004 [2008] OJ C 267/01, para. 2.

3 Market Definition

The standard procedure in a merger control case consists of first[72] defining a relevant market[73] and then calculating market shares, which provide useful information about the market power of the companies involved, the competitive constraints they face,[74] and generally an overview of market concentration.

The definition of the relevant market includes both the product market aspect and the geographic market, the latter being essentially global in the case of the high-tech industry, given the mere presence of a handful of producers in the world.

Competition authorities have defined a method for identifying market boundaries, called the hypothetical monopolist test or Small but Significant Non-transitory Increase in Price (SSNIP) test.[75] The objective of this test is to identify the smallest set of products in a geographic area for which a hypothetical monopolist or monopsonist[76] could exercise market power, i.e. profitably raise its price above competitive levels.[77]

It should be noted, however, that the standard SSNIP test is inapplicable in markets where technology companies do not charge nominal prices to users.[78] As a result, competition authorities and courts have to fall back on qualitative methods to assess demand substitution, often focusing on similarities between product characteristics. This method, far from perfect, underestimates functional substitutions that transcend product differences. This is particularly the case in the Commission's *Facebook/WhatsApp* decision, in which traditional communication services such as SMS

[72] A correct definition of the relevant market is a prerequisite for any assessment of the effect of a merger on competition: CJEU, France v Commission, Cases C-68/94 and C-30/95 [1998] para. 143; subsequent judgments have regularly repeated this point, for example General Court of the CJEU, Spar Österreichische Warenhandels v Commission, Case T-405-08 [2013] para. 116; General Court of the CJEU, HeidelbergCement AG and Schwenk Zement v Commission, Case T-380/17 [2020] para. 293.

[73] According to the Notice on the definition of the relevant market, para. 7: "A relevant product market comprises all those products and/or services which are regarded as interchangeable or substitutable by the consumer, by reason of the products' characteristics, their prices and their intended use."

[74] Notice on the definition of the relevant market, para. 2 and para. 13. Firms are subject to three main sources of competitive constraints: demand substitutability (paras 15–19), supply substitutability (paras 20–23) and potential competition (para. 24).

[75] Notice on the definition of the relevant market, paras 14–18.

[76] In economics, a monopsony is a market structure in which a single buyer substantially controls the market as the primary purchaser of goods and services offered by many potential sellers. Microeconomic monopsony theory assumes that a single entity has market power over all sellers as the sole buyer of a good or service. This is similar to the power of a monopolist to influence the price for its buyers in a monopoly, where many buyers have only one seller of a good or service at their disposal.

[77] The reasoning behind this approach is that if a hypothetical monopolist cannot profitably raise its price, it is not a true monopolist. In particular, this means that a significant portion of its customers might respond to the price increase and switch to another product.

[78] Petit (2020, p. 22).

were not really taken into account when assessing the competitive constraints on WhatsApp.[79]

There are many sources of information that help competition authorities to get a clear picture of the relevant market: (i) precedents from previous cases or other jurisdictions[80]; (ii) information from market participants, such as competitors, distributors, customers, or industry experts[81]; (iii) the parties' internal business documents[82]; (iv) in some circumstances, past events – such as sudden changes in the price of an input or the entry or exit of suppliers[83]; (v) and more sophisticated tools, including price correlation, critical loss, and price/margin concentration analysis.

3.1 *Market Definition in High-Tech Industries*

Although high-tech markets come in many shapes and sizes,[84] many share common characteristics that can make the market definition exercise difficult.[85]

To define the relevant market, the Commission takes into account, among other things, the characteristics of the product and its intended use (in order to determine possible substitutes), consumer preferences, the functioning and specificity of the production, sale and distribution of the products concerned, etc.[86]

In order to refine the assessment of the degree of market power held by a company, other important elements are taken into account: barriers to entry and potential competition or countervailing buyer power, but also criteria that are specific to a given company or sector, such as the advantage of having significant financial power or holding a product portfolio.

Where innovation plays an important role, competition authorities consider a range of firms' innovation efforts to define relevant markets and more accurately assess the effects on competition.

---

[79] Facebook/WhatsApp (Case M.8228), Commission decision of 17 May 2017.

[80] It is up to the competition authority to determine whether the precedents are still applicable or whether, on the contrary, market conditions have changed since the previous decisions or are different in other countries.

[81] For this reason, competition authorities usually send targeted requests for information and organise hearings.

[82] It is always revealing to learn from parties whom they consider to be their direct competitors, provided, of course, that these documents are authentic and not prepared for investigation.

[83] Such events can shed light on how customers have reacted to price increases in reality, making the SSNIP test more than a theoretical hypothesis.

[84] While our analysis does not address digital markets, it should be noted that their multisided nature (where outcomes between different markets are linked), and the fact that services are provided for free (effectively having a price of zero), pose an additional challenge in defining the relevant market.

[85] See Chap. 2.1 High-technology industries, notably "Characteristics of High Technology" and "High Barriers to Entry and Expansion".

[86] Some competition experts have begun to question the primary role traditionally played by market definition, and, in particular, the Notice on the definition of the relevant market, a tool that has not been updated since its introduction in 1997.

To determine the relevant market and account for the stage of product development and the form and structure of the innovation in question, four distinct approaches can be identified in the literature and decision-making practice: technology markets (Sect. 3.2), future markets (Sect. 3.3), innovation markets (Sect. 3.4), and innovation spaces, an alternative concept developed by the Commission.

3.2 Technology Markets

Technology markets are relatively well established in policy practice and soft law,[87] although they are not addressed by the Notice on the definition of the relevant market. These markets view technology as a commercialised intermediate product resulting from a successful innovation. The technology itself is thus seen as the result of an innovation that can then be sold in the market as a stand-alone product, such as a licensable intellectual property right.[88]

Technology markets can also be defined for areas where only the potential for future use of the technology exists and where it would then be likely to be commercialised, and in cases where the technology is not actually commercialised but where the lack of commercialisation constitutes an abuse (e.g. cases of refusal to supply).[89]

3.3 Future Markets

The concept of future markets is intended to capture possible competition in a future product or service market (e.g. under the assumptions that R&D activities are observable and predictable to a reasonable extent, but that future products cannot be associated with existing product markets because of some uncertainty about the results of R&D, uncertain substitutability with existing products, or a longer time to market). This means that there are no established companies but only potential entrants for a market that may develop in the future. Future markets are not a highly conceptualised phenomenon and they appear only sporadically in case law, but they have been

[87] E.g. U.S. DOJ/FTC Antitrust Guidelines for Licensing of Intellectual Property [2017] (U.S. Antitrust Guidelines for Licensing of Intellectual Property) retrievable under https://www.justice.gov/atr/IPguidelines/download (last access 07 October 2022), para. 3.2.2: "Technology markets consist of the intellectual property that is licensed and its close substitutes—that is, the technologies or goods that are close enough substitutes to constrain significantly the exercise of market power with respect to the IP that is licensed. When rights to IP are marketed separately from the products in which they are used, the agencies may analyse the competitive effects of a licensing arrangement in a technology market."; Commission Communication "Guidelines on the applicability of Article 101 of the Treaty on the Functioning of the European Union to horizontal co-operation agreements" [2011] OJ C 11/1 (EU Guidelines on horizontal co-operation agreements), paras 116–118.

[88] Directorate General for Competition (DG Competition) (EC) et al. (2021, p. 112).

[89] DG Competition (EC) et al., p. 112.

developed by the literature as an alternative to address the drawbacks of the concept of innovation markets.[90]

In several cases, the Commission has identified markets for products or services that have not yet been provided, on the basis that there is clear customer demand for the product and a reasonable likelihood that the product will be available in the foreseeable future.[91] For example, in *Allied Signal/Honeywell*, the Commission found a future market because one of the merging parties had announced its intention to develop a product and the Commission's market research established that there would be a clear demand for that product.[92]

3.4 Innovation Markets and Innovation Spaces

"Innovation markets" is a broader category that focuses more on R&D capabilities and efforts rather than on specific future or new products. Decision practice shows that anti-competitive practices may arise in the early stages of innovation processes, when few reliable forecasts can be made about future products, competition, or prices, but companies invest heavily in R&D in a similar field and may therefore exert competitive pressure on each other. Even if these firms are not currently competing in the same market, their merger could, for example, remove important competitive constraints. The literature, guidance from competition authorities, and case law use various terms

---

[90] See Chap. 3.4 "Innovation Markets and Innovation Spaces"; DG Competition (EC) et al. (2021, p. 112).

[91] A distinction can be made between competition in current goods, future goods (i.e. new markets), and pure research. The Commission has identified a number of "emerging" markets, including portals (Vodafone/Vivendi/Canal Plus (Case JV.48), Commission decision of 20 July 2000); online music (Vivendi/Canal+/Seagram (Case M.2050), Commission decision of 13 October 2000, para. 15 and paras 26–32, and AOL/Time Warner (Case M.1845), Commission decision of 11 October 2000, para. 26), interactive video networks (Alcatel/Thomson Multimedia/JV (Case M.2048), Commission decision of 26 October 2000, para. 16), one-stop integrated broadband content supply via the Internet (AOL/Time Warner (Case M.1845), Commission decision of 11 October 2000, para. 35), bottled water in Norway (Orkla/Volvo (Case M.582), Commission decision of 20 September 1995, para. 39), Internet book sales in Spain (Bertelsmann/Planeta/BOL Spain (Case JV.24), Commission decision of 3 December 1999, para. 26), as well as the collection of spent catalytic converters, the equipping/pounding of these converters, and the extraction of precious metals from the catalysts (Rhône-Poulenc/Engelhard (Case M.615), Commission decision of 23 October 1995, para. 25).

[92] AlliedSignal/Honeywell (Case M.1601), Commission decision of 1 December 1999, paras 57 and 58.

to describe this competition in innovation efforts. These terms include "innovation markets" or "R&D markets",[93] "innovation activity", "innovation rivalry" or "innovation/R&D efforts", and "R&D poles or innovation competition".[94]

"Innovation spaces" is a related term used to describe a broader area or domain (but, at least according to the Commission, this concept is not explicitly a "market")[95] in which firms have been innovation competitors in the past and are likely to continue to be in the future.

When the Commission is concerned that a merger will reduce the parties' incentive to innovate, thereby potentially depriving consumers of the benefits of new or improved products, it may define innovation markets.[96]

However, one might question whether this is an artificial exercise, as the real concern is the potential reduction of competition in the market for the new or improved product.[97]

For instance, in *Airbus/SITA*, the notifying parties submitted that, given the emergence of some of the markets of the joint venture and the innovation that drives them, there may not be any existing product market definition, since many of the intended products are still in development. The Commission, however, did not deem it necessary to take a final position as regards product markets, since, irrespective of the exact definition, the transaction did not raise competition concerns.[98]

3.5 Analysis of the Case Law

Two trends emerge from the analysis of the selected decisions: (i) the Commission, considering that innovation contributes to the evolutionary nature of the market, sometimes relativises the weight to be given to market shares; (ii) it does, however, give greater weight to financially self-sufficient firms, a quality that will enable them to develop innovations on the market.

---

[93] A term that the Commission explicitly takes from the U.S. Antitrust Guidelines for Licensing of Intellectual Property when discussing innovation competition in Dow/DuPont (Case M.7932), Commission decision of 12 October 2017 (para. 346), although the term (and concept) of "R&D market" was already used by the Commission in Glaxo Wellcome/Smithkill Beecham (Case M.1846), Commission decision of 8 May 2000, para. 174.

[94] DG Competition (EC) et al. (2021, p. 112).

[95] For example, in Bayer/Monsanto (Case M.8084), Commission decision of 14 December 2018, para. 1023, the Commission found that innovation should not be considered as a market in its own right, but as an entry activity for downstream product markets. If the innovation ultimately leads to products competing in these markets, the assessment of competition in innovation cannot be directly conflated with the relevant downstream product markets.

[96] Lindsay and Berridge (2017, p. 167).

[97] Nevertheless, the Commission regularly examines the loss of innovation competition in pharmaceutical mergers. See Ciba-Geigy/Sandoz (Case M.737), Commission decision of 17 July 1996, paras 101–106; Glaxo Wellcome/SmithKline Beecham (Case M.1846), Commission decision of 8 May 2000, paras 70–72, 175–178, 194, 195 and 222.

[98] Airbus/SITA (Case M.3657), Commission decision of 27 January 2005, para. 11.

3.5.1 Innovation as a Criterion Influencing the Competitive Landscape on the Market

Thrane & Thrane/Nera

In the *Thrane & Thrane/Nera* case,[99] the Commission emphasised the role of innovation in defining the competitive landscape in the market.

Indeed, once the market shares were defined, the Commission put them into perspective, considering that they overestimated the parties' market position, given the rapid development and evolution of technology. It appeared that innovation plays a very important role in these markets and that despite the presence of the most advanced high-end products on the market, the new technologies under development could quickly weaken their market position.[100]

Western Digital Ireland/Viviti; Seagate Technology/The HDD Business of Samsung Electronics

Two transactions in the hard disk drive industry were evaluated at the same time but separately: *Seagate/Samsung*[101] and *Western Digital/Viviti*,[102] the latter being notified one day later. Thus, in an identical manner (literally), before analysing the relevant market, the Commission presented the innovation and technology trends in the HDD sector, which is characterised by significant technological advances and rapid product life cycles.[103]

According to the Commission, in general, the HDD industry's innovation efforts are aimed at (i) extending the life of current technologies (incremental innovation) and (ii) new enabling technologies.[104] The interoperability inherent in the industry—through standard HDD interfaces—allows customers to substitute any manufacturer's product with a competing disk. This factor has helped spur incremental innovation to improve drive capacity, head or media design, or architecture and mechanical engineering, among others.[105]

---

99 Thrane & Thrane/Nera (Case M.4465), Commission decision of 21 March 2007.

100 Ibid., para. 45.

101 Seagate/HDD Business of Samsung (Case M.6214), Commission decision of 19 October 2011.

102 Western Digital Ireland/Viviti Technologies (Case M.6203), Commission decision of 12 August 2013.

103 Western Digital Ireland/Viviti Technologies (Case M.6203), Commission decision of 12 August 2013, para. 94; Seagate/HDD Business of Samsung (Case M.6214), Commission decision of 19 October 2011, para. 66.

104 Western Digital Ireland/Viviti Technologies (Case M.6203), Commission decision of 12 August 2013, para. 96; Seagate/HDD Business of Samsung (Case M.6214), Commission decision of 19 October 2011, para. 68.

105 Western Digital Ireland/Viviti Technologies (Case M.6203), Commission decision of 12 August 2013, para. 97; Seagate/HDD Business of Samsung (Case M.6214), Commission decision of 19 October 2011, para. 69.

Because of the relatively short product cycles, it is important for HDD manufacturers not only to be first to market or to bring a similar product to market soon after, but also to strive to reach volume production quickly for each new size of the disk to take maximum advantage of the temporary lead on a given product.[106]

3.5.2 Financial Self-sufficiency

General Electric/Honeywell

In the *General Electric/Honeywell* case,[107] when assessing market shares, the Commission took into account sources of financing as a proxy for future innovation. It was considered that since aftermarket revenues were the main source of cash that financed the development and marketing of new engines, these finances influenced the innovation efforts for future generations of engines, and thus the likely future competitive position of the company. The Commission has therefore deduced a direct correlation between increased aftermarket revenues and a company's chances of remaining competitive in the future.[108]

The Commission continued its analysis as follows. Because the aerospace industry is characterised by long lead times, i.e. large gaps between investment in new projects and return on investment, companies in this sector must rely heavily on their own internal cash flow to finance development and innovation.[109]

General Electric (GE) is fortunate to have a financial arm, GE Capital, that has "enormous internal financial resources", contributing about half of GE Corporation's consolidated revenues and managing more than 80% of GE's total assets.[110]

GE's financial strength through GE Capital is undeniably a great competitive advantage, particularly because, unlike any other company, GE is able to take more risk in product development programmes, and absorb product failures without jeopardising its future ability to compete and develop new products in an industry characterised by long-term investment, a quality the Commission has described as essential.[111]

Thus, it is worth noting that the Commission views the fact of having an in-house financial force for future innovation development positively. In short, having a constant source of revenue to access cash on first demand is a good thing. The company could then devote this unconditional funding (only) to the development and

---

106 Western Digital Ireland/Viviti Technologies (Case M.6203), Commission decision of 12 August 2013, para. 99; Seagate/HDD Business of Samsung (Case M.6214), Commission decision of 19 October 2011, para. 71.

107 General Electric/Honeywell (Case M.2220), Commission decision of 3 July 2001.

108 Ibid., para. 79.

109 Ibid., para. 110.

110 If GE Capital were a stand-alone company, it would (at the time of the analysis) rank alone in the top 20 of the Fortune 500 (para. 107).

111 Ibid., para. 110.

commercialisation of new products and possibly to the absorption of the financial damage resulting from possible strategic mistakes. In our opinion, financial self-sufficiency could increase the chances of a merger being approved.

UTC/Goodrich

The Commission came to a similar, but less radical, conclusion in its analysis of the *UTC/Goodrich* merger.[112] The market investigation revealed that the R&D expenditures that companies allocate to specific programmes are essential in order to remain competitive in the power generation market and that IP rights are used by companies to protect know-how developed in power systems.[113]

A company's ability to innovate in the power generation is therefore based on its accumulated R&D expenditures, which are also dependent on the revenues generated by past generator sales.[114]

4 Commission Analysis of the Anti-competitive Effects of Mergers in the High-Tech Sector

In its substantive analysis of the anti-competitive effects of mergers in the high-tech sector, the Commission sometimes takes into account the characteristics of the industry, which is fuelled by innovation, and where any reduction in innovation and any coordinated effect are impossible (Sect. 4.1). It also considers the opposite case, where an innovator, although recent, is able to exert considerable pressure on the market (Sect. 4.2). The Commission recognises the role of IP rights in promoting innovation (Sect. 4.3), but it also looks at innovation from other perspectives. There appears to be a direct (and logical for the Commission) link between the financial strength of a merged entity and the reduction of innovation among its competitors (Sect. 4.4). It sometimes concludes that the merger of two innovative firms can lead to a reduction in innovation among competitors, who would no longer have a development partner (Sect. 4.5). The race to innovate also sometimes takes on a political tinge (Sect. 4.6), especially when a state openly commits to maintaining the level of investment and guaranteeing future innovations.

112 UTC/Goodrich (Case M.6410), Commission decision of 26 July 2012.

113 Ibid., para. 312.

114 Ibid.

4.1 *Perpetual Innovation Preventing Its Reduction and Coordinated Effects*

4.1.1 Alcatel/Finmeccanica/Alcatel Alenia Space and Technology

In the analysis of possible collusive behaviour, the characteristics of the market may play a role. Indeed, in the *Alcatel/Finmeccanica/Alcatel Alenia Space & Technology* case,[115] the Commission interestingly came to the conclusion that in the space markets in question, characterised by innovation and complex technologies, collusive behaviour was unlikely.[116]

4.1.2 Axalto/Gemplus

In the analysis of the *Axalto/Gemplus* merger,[117] the Commission's investigation of the SIM card chip market showed that the two merging companies were, prior to the transaction, constraining each other because they were the main innovators. The new entity and its main competitors would nevertheless retain a strong incentive to innovate. Indeed, according to the Commission, the ability to innovate is strategic in the market in question because manufacturers of innovative SIM cards—like those of computer chips—immediately achieve their margins in the first year following the launch of a new product. After this initial period, prices drop dramatically as more and more competitors are able to supply the product.[118]

In contrast, market players that do not innovate are offering low-end "commodity" products with very low margins. Thus, not all competitors are equivalent and not all products can be considered as differentiated, which is particularly true for SIM cards where innovation plays a more crucial role, in particular because, *inter alia*, customers of SIM cards producers (i.e. mobile telecom operators) generally seek to improve their offering by providing new products and services.[119]

In this context, according to the Commission, the parties would have no incentive to reduce their R&D efforts. On the contrary, the merged entity would be able to reallocate R&D capacity in such a way that the number of R&D projects after the merger would probably be higher than that of the two companies before the merger.[120]

The market investigation and the review of the parties' internal documents of the parties confirmed that the parties would retain a strong incentive to innovate, both

---

[115] Alcatel/Finmeccanica/Alcatel Alenia Space and Technology (Case M.3680), Commission decision of 28 April 2005.

[116] Ibid., para. 112.

[117] Axalto/Gemplus (Case No M.3998), Commission decision of 19 May 2006.

[118] Ibid., para. 50–52.

[119] Ibid.

[120] Ibid., para. 53.

in the short and long term. In particular, several telecom operators welcomed the merger as they expected it to lead to more and faster innovation.[121]

In view of these elements, the Commission concluded that the proposed transaction would not have a negative impact on innovation.[122] We welcome this analysis which seems to us quite reasonable, as it takes into account the particularities of the market.

4.1.3 Seagate/Maxtor

In the *Seagate/Maxtor* case,[123] market participants indicated that some head suppliers (used in hard drives) were sometimes able to offer newer, more innovative technology, especially when the drive producer's internal offerings tended to focus on larger, low-margin, slightly older products. On the other hand, the existence of new third-party component technology is prompting vertically integrated hard drive producers to innovate in their own component production. Thus, according to the Commission, competition between integrated and non-integrated head manufacturers drives innovation in both cases,[124] yet another reasoning with which we agree.

4.1.4 Lite-On/PBDS

We find it interesting, if not amusing, to read the Commission's decision in the *Lite-On/PBDS* case from 2007[125] in 2022, when it speaks of the disk industry as being characterised by a high degree of innovation and very dynamic technological advances that occur in short cycles.[126]

The Commission had considered that CD-ROM, DVD-R, COMBO and CD-RW would be phased out over the next two to three years, which has indeed happened. On the other hand, the Commission had expected substantial growth for DVD-RW and the new Blu-ray and HD-DVD technologies.[127]

It rightly considered that innovation cycles were very, very short, often less than a year. In addition, vendors of optical data-storage disk drives (ODD) seemed to be able to adapt quickly to any new technology.[128]

The Commission had noted that the pace of innovation appeared to be continuing and cited the need for vendors to adapt quickly to new and evolving standards.[129]

[121] Ibid.

[122] Ibid., para. 54.

[123] Seagate/Maxtor (Case M.4100), Commission decision of 27 April 2006.

[124] Ibid., para. 39.

[125] Lite-On/PBDS (Case M.4502), Commission decision of 16 February 2007.

[126] Ibid., para. 34.

[127] Ibid., para. 29.

[128] Ibid.

[129] Ibid., para. 35.

What the Commission could not predict with its crystal ball, however, is the total collapse of the market with the widespread demise of CDs, DVD, and Blu-ray disks.

4.1.5 Acer/Packard-Bell

In the analysis of the *Acer/Packard-Bell* merger,[130] the Commission considered that it was unlikely that the major PC vendors would be able to agree on the terms of coordination after the merger: there would remain many competitors with asymmetric market shares, products were differentiated, the industry was very dynamic, and none of the parties could be considered innovators or price takers.[131] In addition, there was insufficient transparency (supply agreements were negotiated individually) and customers or competitors could undermine any attempt at coordination.[132]

4.1.6 Ericsson/STM

In its analysis of the joint venture between *Ericsson and STM*,[133] the Commission found that effective coordination seemed unlikely in this market, which had several characteristics that prevented coordination. These include differentiated products, long-term contracts, infrequent tenders and a large volume of individual tenders, asymmetric market shares of the players after the joint venture, significant buyer power of customers and the importance of innovation in the market.[134]

The sector was characterised by the strong countervailing buying power of a few customers (manufacturers of wireless handsets). In the event of coordination, they could respond by sourcing themselves through development or sponsoring a new entry. In an innovation-driven market, this could happen in particular if market players tend to compete with each other and innovate less.[135]

The Commission's market research has, in fact, shown that any attempt to coordinate behaviour would be unsustainable. Moreover, if collusion were to occur, especially with Qualcomm, it would directly affect Sony Ericsson as a customer, Ericsson being one of the joint venture's parent companies.[136]

---

130 Acer/Packard Bell (Case M.4979), Commission decision of 27 February 2008.

131 Ibid., para. 40.

132 Ibid.

133 Ericsson/STM/JV (Case M.5332), Commission decision of 25 November 2008.

134 Ibid., para. 129.

135 Ibid.

136 Ibid.

4.1.7 Panasonic/Sanyo

In the *Panasonic/Sanyo* merger,[137] the Commission's investigation concluded that the Li-Ion battery market was growing rapidly and was characterised by a high rate of innovation. There were, at the time of the analysis, a significant number of players active in the Li-Ion battery market with sufficient spare capacity. In addition, new competitors were entering and continuing to enter the market and gaining substantial market shares.[138] The proposed transaction, therefore, did not raise serious doubts on the market(s) for portable Li-Ion batteries.

4.1.8 Toshiba/Fujitsu HDD Business

In the acquisition of *Fujitsu's HDD business by Toshiba,*[139] given the relatively high levels of concentration in the sector, the Commission examined whether the proposed transaction could raise competition concerns due to coordinated effects.[140]

However, the industry had characteristics of rapid innovation and bidding markets, making it unlikely that HDD suppliers could agree on coordination terms. In addition, the level of concentration among HDD buyers appeared to be high, and buyers often placed large volume orders, which had the incentive to make coordination unviable.[141]

4.1.9 Thermo Fisher/Dionex Corporation

In the merger of *Thermo Fisher/Dionex Corporation,*[142] the Commission analysed the risks of the merged entity exercising market power.

It was considered that the market players (from Nano-LC and MS) that could be affected by a possible foreclosure strategy were already integrated. Even in the hypothetical case where the merged entity would limit the interoperability of its Nano-LC and MS devices, the presence of other significant integrated competitors will continue to exert a significant competitive constraint on the merged entity. The fact that the Nano-LC and MS markets are subject to continuous innovation also limits the ability of any market participant to engage in a foreclosure strategy.[143]

---

137 Panasonic/Sanyo (Case M.5421), Commission decision of 29 September 2009.

138 Ibid., para. 88.

139 Toshiba/Fujitsu HDD Business (Case M.5483), Commission decision of 11 May 2009.

140 Ibid., para. 37.

141 Ibid.

142 Thermo Fisher/Dionex Corporation (Case M.6126), Commission decision of 13 May 2011.

143 Ibid., para. 81.

4.1.10 Harris Corporation/L3 Technologies

In case *Harris Corporation/L3 Technologies,*[144] in its competitive assessment of horizontal coordinated effects, the Commission considered that for several of the devices analysed, the transaction would not give rise to coordinated effects because innovation is an inherent feature of the markets, making coordination impossible.

First, the Commission held that the lack of product homogeneity made implicit coordination impossible, especially in a bidding market. Second, the relevant markets were not transparent, as it was essentially a bidding market, which makes such implicit collusion inherently implausible. Third, the market is driven by innovation, given the technological characteristics of the products. This characteristic also rules out the possibility of implicit and sustained coordination over a significant period of time.[145]

4.2 *Promising Innovator Able to Eliminate a Significant Competitive Force*

4.2.1 Varian/Agilent

In the merger of *Varian and Agilent,*[146] the latter was considered to have developed a very reliable technology, well received by customers and an immediate competitive force in the market. Although Agilent was an entrant, it was already considered to have considerable competitive pressure in the market.[147]

In addition, Agilent was considered to be one of the top three GC–MS instrument suppliers in terms of quality, specifications, service/training and price by the vast majority of customers. Therefore, these attributes, combined with its reputation and instrument reliability, allowed it to overcome potential barriers to successful entry and expansion into a related market.[148]

Although the area under analysis was experiencing significant growth, the likely entry of new competitors in this market had to occur in a timely manner and be sufficient to deter or counteract any potential anti-competitive effects of the proposed transaction, which the Commission found unlikely.[149]

---

[144] Harris Corporation/L3 Technologies (Case M.9234), Commission decision of 21 June 2019.

[145] Ibid., paras 183–185 with respect to night vision devices; paras 242–245 with respect to image intensification tubes; paras 353–355 with respect to the handheld video data links and handheld tactical air-to-ground communication devices used by ground forces markets.

[146] Agilent/Varian (Case M.5611), Commission decision of 20 January 2010.

[147] Ibid., para. 95.

[148] Ibid., para. 98–99.

[149] Ibid., para. 99.

Thus, in light of the above, the Commission concluded that the proposed transaction was likely to result in the elimination of a significant competitive force in the market in question.[150]

4.2.2 Intel/McAfee

In the *Intel/MacAfee* merger,[151] the Commission dwelt at length on the analysis of innovation in the different markets.

Quoting its own 2009 decision on Intel, the Commission recalled that innovation was, together with price, one of the main drivers of demand in this sector (CPU transistors), which is characterised by the speed of innovation. In these circumstances, the very high R&D and production costs can usually only be recouped if new inventions can be sold before the competitor responds with a more innovative product,[152] given that CPU transistor density typically doubles every 18 months or so.[153]

The Commission also analysed the (relatively low) barriers to entry[154] and the barriers to expansion, which appeared to be significant,[155] as several key factors contribute to this, including brand recognition, the range of products, services and support, confidence that the company will continue to innovate, and the need to have an extensive threat detection system and threat intelligence database in order to be competitive.[156]

The Commission then analysed the security (anti-virus) market, which is globally characterised by rapid, intense, and necessarily continuous innovation,[157] thus requiring security software vendors (SSVs) to invest in innovation.[158]

In order to justify its high R&D budgets, which were much higher than those of its competitors, Intel invoked the need to support larger product portfolios and customer bases. According to Intel, SSVs with smaller R&D budgets would be able to compete effectively by focusing their efforts on narrower product portfolios and concentrating on specific customer segments and/or security threats. This argument did not convince the Commission, which, while acknowledging the possibility for a security software vendor to bring a competitive product to market on the basis of limited R&D programmes, concluded that these companies tend to focus on a narrow set of applications. For this reason, and given their less stable market position, these start-ups will generally not be considered viable suppliers to corporate customers.[159]

---

[150] Ibid., para. 100.

[151] Intel/McAfee (Case M.5984), Commission decision of 26 January 2011.

[152] Ibid., para. 97.

[153] Ibid., para. 99.

[154] Ibid., para. 100.

[155] Ibid., para. 101.

[156] Ibid., para. 102.

[157] Ibid., para. 112.

[158] Ibid., para. 110.

[159] Ibid., paras 110–111.

The Commission had a series of post-merger concerns related to (i) a degradation of interoperability between Intel's hardware and security solutions, on the one hand, and competitors' products on the other, and (ii) possible technical bundling/tying and commercial bundling strategies in general.[160]

McAfee's competitors have alleged a reduction in revenue, leading to the exit of some of them from the market. Although the Commission explicitly stated that the price consequences remained unclear at this stage, it aligned itself with the allegations of McAfee's competitors that innovation and choice would be reduced.[161]

The Commission considered that McAfee, however, would be shielded from innovation competition by interoperability and thus would have no incentive to continue investing in innovative products. If McAfee were the only security vendor with full access to Intel interoperability, it would become the preferred security solution for any Intel customer. Competitors would then have to consolidate, retreat into niche markets, or disappear. In either scenario, consumer choice would be heavily impacted.[162]

The Commission, therefore, found that the effects of an interoperability barrier imposed by Intel were likely to be significant in the markets for endpoint security and CPU/chip sets, in particular with respect to innovation and choice.[163]

In the security software market, it was interesting to observe the comments of McAfee's competitors: while some of them argued that choice would be ultimately reduced, security software prices would be driven down, reducing the funds available for R&D and future innovation, others indicated that, on the contrary, innovation could be fostered by such a strategy.[164]

In light of the above, the Commission still found a possible foreclosure of SSVs, raising serious doubts as to the compatibility of the proposed transaction with the internal market.[165]

4.2.3 Airbus/Safran JV

In its analysis of the creation of a joint venture between *Airbus and Safran*,[166] the Commission considered that if Airbus were to adopt a customer foreclosure strategy, this would likely result in an alternative supplier of Hall effect thrusters in Europe leaving the market or at least preventing it from entering it successfully, thus reducing innovation.[167] This was also confirmed by a supplier of satellite propulsion subsystems, according to whom the 'transaction would have led to less innovation in the

[160] Ibid., para. 124 ff.

[161] Ibid., para. 167.

[162] Ibid., paras 166–167.

[163] Ibid., para. 172.

[164] Ibid., para. 214.

[165] Ibid., para. 218.

[166] Airbus/Safran/JV (Case M.7353), Commission decision of 26 November 2014.

[167] Ibid., para. 370.

market' because it would 'lead other potential suppliers to either leave the market or reduce development programmes or the creation of new products. This would impact global competitiveness and innovation in Europe.'[168]

In addition, Safran's main competitors in the supply of Hall effect thrusters would have higher costs. As a result, the price of Hall thrusters would increase, which would have a negative impact on the price of the downstream satellite prime contractor market.[169]

On the basis of the above and the evidence available, the Commission concluded that the transaction raised serious doubts as to its compatibility with the internal market as regards access to the satellite market for suppliers of Hall thrusters.[170]

4.3 *Role of IPR in Promoting Innovation*

Although the following developments are not revolutionary in themselves, nor are they specific to high-tech mergers, we find it appropriate to note them.

4.3.1 Axalto/Gemplus

In the *Axalto/Gemplus* case,[171] the Commission considered that innovation was an important factor in the competition between smart card manufacturers and, therefore, IP rights played a crucial role.[172]

In order to ensure a sufficient return on inventions or technological development and thus preserve *ex ante* incentives for innovation, IP rights give the innovator an exclusive right to exploit the invention or development.[173] Since the objective of IP policy is also to facilitate the diffusion of innovation, the relationship between IP rights and competition law should not be seen as a contradiction, since both IPR legislation and competition rules are meant to promote innovation in the interest of consumers.[174]

---

[168] Ibid.

[169] Ibid., para. 371.

[170] Ibid., para. 372.

[171] Axalto/Gemplus (Case M.3998), Commission decision of 19 May 2006.

[172] Ibid., para. 55.

[173] Ibid., n. 14.

[174] Ibid.

4.3.2 Thermo Fisher Scientific/Life Technologies

In the *Thermo Fisher Scientific/Life Technologies* merger,[175] the Commission's market investigation revealed that most customers and competitors consider IP rights to play an important role in the markets for the supply of magnetic beads.[176]

Indeed, new competitors face high barriers to innovation and small companies do not have the capacity to innovate due to the lack of access to IP rights. A new company starting to manufacture magnetic beads would not be free to operate since the known processes are already covered by the patent portfolios of existing companies.[177]

In addition, in this decision, we find the discussion of factors contributing to a successful merger interesting. Competitors and customers of the merging companies expressed the important caveat that the gene modulation business can only be viable and competitive in the hands of certain purchasers with experience in the life sciences. Indeed, only an acquirer with such experience and background can overcome potential barriers to customer acceptance and can offer manufacturing expertise as well as quality control and assurance. In addition, global sales and distribution assets are needed to be an effective competitive force. Only such players seem to be able to integrate the business (which they acquire) into their existing structures, and can ensure that it remains innovative and successful in introducing new products in this rapidly emerging field of molecular biology.[178]

4.4 *(Questionable) Correlation Between Future Revenue Streams and Future Innovation*

The Commission seems to be saying that if the merged firm has the financial strength for the development projects to guarantee a constant source of revenue, its competitors will automatically have less future revenue available to them and, therefore, will innovate less. We get the impression that the Commission believes that there is a limited amount of future revenue to be shared between companies. However, we believe that the success of one does not mean the failure of the other. Both are possible, but not automatic.

In the *General Electric/Honeywell* merger,[179] the Commission reiterated,[180] that future revenues are necessary to finance future product development expenses, encourage innovation and allow for a potential leapfrogging effect.[181]

---

[175] Thermo Fisher Scientific/Life Technologies (Case M.6944), Commission decision of 26 November 2013.

[176] Ibid., para. 247.

[177] Ibid.

[178] Ibid., para. 400.

[179] General Electric/Honeywell (Case M.2220), Commission decision of 3 July 2001.

[180] See the discussion of this case in the Commission's analysis of the relevant market (Chap. 3.5).

[181] General Electric/Honeywell (Case M.2220), Commission decision of 3 July 2001, para. 347.

Whereas in the relevant market analysis, the Commission saw GE's financial strength, through GE Capital, as a competitive asset, this asset became a burden, which weighed heavily in the conclusion that the merged entity would be dominant.[182] The financial strength and vertical integration of GE/Honeywell is certainly a good thing, says the Commission, allowing it, among others, to launch new platforms and promote their own products.[183] This is not the case for their competitors, who will not be able to place their products on these new platforms, delaying their cash flow and depriving them of the return necessary to finance future investments and innovation.[184]

Moreover, GE's financial strength could, among other things, be used to boost the merged company's R&D efforts in areas of intense competition and ultimately discourage rivals from competing and being innovative.[185]

As a result of the integration of Honeywell into GE, competitors will be deprived of future revenues generated by sales of the products and their spare parts and will therefore be progressively marginalised and unable to fund innovation expenditures and outperform the merged entity by any means. The foreclosure will lead the merged entity's competitors to reassess the reason for their presence (in the market) and to make the economically rational decision to withdraw from competitions where the addition of GE products to Honeywell would leave them no realistic chance of winning.[186]

We almost get the impression that GE/Honeywell's efforts to launch a platform would be futile because they would deprive their competitors of future revenues generated by product sales on these future (not yet existing) platforms. And no one wonders why competitors would not seek revenue elsewhere. While a company in a dominant position certainly bears a special responsibility,[187] we deplore the implied universal responsibility to ensure the success of its competitors.

Indeed, we support the idea that some large technology companies can simultaneously be large market players and competitive businesses.[188] Those who want to remain successful and maintain their position must necessarily take risks and continue to innovate. However, the success of the merging companies is certainly not due to the Commission's injunctions to innovate more and do a better job.[189]

Thus, competition for technology companies is a form of pressure in itself. And this competition comes from everywhere: from companies outside the product and

---

[182] Ibid., para. 346.

[183] Ibid., para. 344.

[184] Ibid.

[185] Ibid., para. 479.

[186] Ibid., paras 480–482.

[187] Guidance on the Commission's enforcement priorities in applying Article 82, paras 1 and 9.

[188] Petit (2020, p. 32).

[189] We generalise that all merging companies are successful because notification is triggered by a significant turnover, just as a takeover or the creation of a joint venture is usually based on an existing or predictable success.

service markets that they serve alone, but also from all other companies, markets, or indeterminate industries.[190]

4.5 *Elimination of a Potential Innovation Partner*

When two innovative companies merge, the merger may lead to the elimination of one (or more) product development partner(s) for competitors, thus depriving them of a potential innovation partner.

In *General Electric/Honeywell*,[191] GE already had a dominant position in large commercial aircraft engines, a position which the Commission believes would be strengthened post-merger. Indeed, Honeywell would no longer be a partner in the development of More Electrical Engine Aircraft for its competitors. GE would thus be the only engine manufacturer able to develop innovations in the framework of this project. As this project was to be decisive for future competition on this market, GE would have been the first, if not the only, to benefit from the innovation.[192]

Thus, according to the Commission, the further weakening of competing engine manufacturers would have strengthened GE's dominant position and ultimately harmed competition.

4.6 *State as a Guarantor of Innovation*

4.6.1 Dassault Aviation/TASA/Thales

The promise, or rather the guarantees offered by a State for its continued innovation efforts are sometimes worth their weight in gold.

Indeed, in its analysis of the acquisition of joint control of *Thales by Dassault Aviation and TSA*,[193] the Commission analysed the concerns raised by third parties regarding a possible reduction in investment and innovation due to the vertical integration of Dassault Aviation and Thales activities. However, the French Ministry of Defence has stated that "as these are military products, innovation in the areas concerned is the responsibility of the States and the operation will therefore have no effect on this point".[194]

---

[190] Petit (2020, pp. 32 and 60).

[191] General Electric/Honeywell (Case M.2220), Commission decision of 3 July 2001.

[192] Ibid., paras 417 and 418.

[193] Dassault Aviation/TSA/Thales (Case M.5426), Commission decision of 10 Mars 2009.

[194] Ibid., para. 78.

In view of these elements, the Commission considered that the vertical integration of the activities of Thales and Dassault Aviation was not such as to raise serious doubts on the markets concerned.[195]

4.6.2 ASL/Arianespace

The Commission's investigation revealed that at the time of *ASL's acquisition of Arianespace*,[196] almost all satellite manufacturers were heavily subsidised by public funds and that innovation began with military/institutional projects.[197]

Indeed, in both Europe and the United States, satellite R&D is not driven by the commercial segment. All the R&D activities of all the major satellite manufacturers are largely subsidised by public funds, and the major innovations, both in terms of communications and optics, are generally driven by military and institutional contracts. The results of the R&D only lead to applications in the commercial segment after some time.[198]

In the particular case of the United States, the parties argued that a significant part of the innovations offered by U.S. satellite manufacturers was financed by the military budget and that this allowed U.S. satellite manufacturers to develop innovative communication solutions that were then transferred to telecommunication satellites.[199]

With this funding, satellite manufacturers will continue to innovate, even though their commercial satellite order rates are relatively low.[200]

5 Merger Efficiency: A Losing Game

5.1 Efficiency Gains: The Raison d'Être of Mergers

Mergers generally result in some positive effects or efficiency gains. Often, the potential efficiency is the very reason for the merger in question. If, at some point, companies decide to join forces, it is because they expect to gain an economic advantage, which will allow for the external growth of the company. Ideas flow, know-how is shared and synergies are created when companies join forces, allowing them to expand their product and service offerings and consequently increase profits.

195 Ibid., para. 79.

196 ASL/Arianespace (Case M.7724), Commission decision of 11 December 2017.

197 Ibid., para. 302.

198 Ibid., paras 303 and 306.

199 Ibid., paras 304 and 306.

200 Ibid., para. 306.

Efficiencies can be static or dynamic. Dynamic efficiencies are synergies that enable firms to improve their performance, whether in terms of cost, quality, service or new product development, on a potentially continuous basis. Dynamic efficiencies include: (i) learning-by-doing,[201] (ii) upgrading management,[202] (iii) combining complementary distribution or marketing assets,[203] (iv) elimination of duplicative R&D,[204] (v) R&D economies of scale and scope,[205] (vi) joint exploitation of intellectual property,[206] (vii) better allocation of R&D risk and investment,[207] (viii) better

[201] Learning by doing means that companies get better at what they do by gaining experience in that area. Over time, they can learn new ways to minimise their costs or improve their products.

[202] One claim (somewhat controversial in the literature and empirical studies, see in particular McGuckin and Nguyen 1995) is that dynamic efficiency gains occur when the acquiring firm has an excellent management team that replaces the target firm's inferior team, resulting in sustained performance improvement.

[203] Some vertical mergers can bring together complementary assets so that products reach consumers faster. This includes opportunities such as improved product distribution logistics due to the combined company's greater geographic coverage, or combining a company with a strong R&D programme with a company whose forte is marketing.

[204] If the two merged companies devote resources to the same research, there is clear potential for cost savings and dynamic efficiency if the merged company uses these savings to fund other innovation efforts. However, although both companies were trying to achieve the same end result, they may have conducted their research in different ways. Because one method may be better than the other, it may be appropriate to keep the two programmes separate and fund both rather than risk eliminating the wrong programme. It is therefore important to verify that the two allegedly duplicated research projects are in fact duplicated, not only in terms of purpose but also in terms of method.

[205] When the research programmes of two companies are combined, their R&D assets can accomplish more than they would have if the programmes had remained separate. For example, one programme may benefit from access to a certain piece of equipment or technology owned by the other company's laboratory that the first company would have found too expensive to purchase on its own. Or it may be that a new research tool, useful to both programmes, is worth purchasing when neither company would have purchased it on its own. Another possibility, and probably the most common, is that the two companies have complementary R&D assets and can reduce transaction costs by merging.

[206] In general, a licensing agreement will be sufficient to make better use of the intellectual property. In some cases, however, a merger may be the only arrangement to persuade a company to share its IP with another company. The IP owner may feel that its IP is more valuable than anyone else's, for example, and so may insist on royalties that no other company is willing to pay. It may also feel that allowing another company to use its IP is potentially dangerous because it will allow the licensee to innovate more, which will eventually replace the licensed technology.

[207] If both parties to the merger are profitable, they can afford to take more risks and invest more in R&D. Not only can these initial investments be spread over a broader revenue and income base, but any potential failure will be more easily absorbed by the merged company.

IP enforcement,[208] (ix) access to increased financial resources for funding R&D,[209] and (x) the Schumpeter effect.[210]

Static efficiencies, on the other hand, enable improvements that occur only once, such as economies of scale in production. Over time, the benefits of dynamic efficiencies may outweigh those of static efficiencies, even if the latter are initially larger.[211]

Yet some argue that not all efficiencies are necessarily relevant to the merger review, making an important distinction between efficiencies based on simple economies of scale and true merger synergies.[212] For economies of scale can also, at least in principle, be achieved unilaterally through organic growth, so they may not be specific to a merger in this sense.[213]

At the same time, mergers often bring many benefits to consumers: new, better, more effective or more efficient products or services than those already on the market are available in sufficient quantity and variety at lower prices.

Of course, it may be that the real reason why companies want to merge is to increase their market power and thus be able to restrict output and increase prices. But this risk is mitigated by the procedures in place, notably when competition authorities regularly request copies of company documents (both internal and from outside advisors) setting out the commercial reasons for a particular transaction.

208 Smaller firms are less likely than larger firms (i) to protect their IP in the first place, and (ii) to have the resources to fund legal actions to protect their IP. Therefore, when a merger improves the ability of the merging parties to enforce their IP portfolios, their incentives to innovate may also increase.

209 When companies' financial resources are combined, they can undertake more research projects. As a larger entity, the combined firm may have better access to capital markets or borrow (more) money at lower interest rates, thus undertaking more research projects in general. If so, it may invest more in its research equipment, facilities and personnel. It may also be willing to fund projects with a slightly lower expected return than the individual parties would have been willing to fund. In addition, if the merger involves a large, cash-rich company and a smaller, research-oriented company with little capital, the purpose of the merger may have been to fund the work of the smaller company—especially if the larger company understands and values the potential value of the smaller company's ideas.

210 There may be a very general efficiency of innovation associated with mergers that significantly increase concentration. According to Schumpeter, market power stimulates innovation. In short, this theory argues that firms with market power tend to innovate more than firms without market power, but that any market power is temporary due to the process of creative destruction through innovation.

211 OECD (2007, p. 9).

212 Niels et al. (2016, p. 350), Farrell and Shapiro (2001, p. 687).

213 Ibid.

5.2 *Commission's Framework for Analysis of Efficiencies*

The Commission applies a strict consumer welfare criterion: efficiency gains must be so large that they offset any price increases. In other words, the test requires that the efficiency be passed on to consumers. The Commission's guidelines require that the efficiencies "benefit consumers, be merger specific and be verifiable", these three conditions being cumulative.[214]

The burden of proof for efficiency lies with the merging parties, and the Commission's role is to verify the claimed efficiency and assess whether they are sufficient to offset any potential price increase. This burden is extremely heavy. This is evidenced by the fact that the Commission and the Court of Justice consistently refuse to consider the parties' efficiency claims in the absence of objective or convincing evidence in this regard.

The problem is not only that the Commission is hostile to efficiencies, but that it may be difficult to measure the efficiencies themselves. It may be very hard to determine prospectively whether a merger will result in static efficiencies relative to the anti-competitive effects it is believed to cause. Dynamic efficiencies pose an even greater measurement problem than static efficiencies, because dynamic effects will occur—if at all—over several periods and can be more abstract in nature than static effects.[215]

Several types of complications can arise when trying to assess dynamic efficiencies. First, the so-called apples-to-oranges comparison problem. A merger may lead to higher prices soon after it occurs, but it may also lead to dynamic efficiencies that have positive non-price effects (e.g. benefits from new or improved products) in the longer term. This puts competition authorities in the difficult position of having to compare different concepts over different periods, and possibly in two or more different markets with different consumer groups. This is because it is difficult, if not impossible, to know how many quality improvements or how many new products are needed for some customers to offset a given expected price increases affecting other customers.[216]

Another complicating factor is the inherent uncertainty of the innovative activity with respect to its cost, timing, and the likelihood and magnitude of its commercial success, the difficulties in measuring the innovation itself, the problem of conceptually transforming innovation into some measure of welfare, and the asymmetry of information between the merging parties and the Commission.[217]

In *Ryanair Holdings Plc v Commission*,[218] Ryanair argued that the Commission had committed a manifest error in assessing Ryanair's claim that the merger would

---

[214] Guidelines on the assessment of non-horizontal mergers, para. 53; Guidelines on the assessment of horizontal mergers, paras 78, 86–88.

[215] OECD (2007, p. 9).

[216] Ibid., p. 10.

[217] Ibid.

[218] General Court of the CJEU, Ryanair v Commission, Case T-342/07 [2010].

lead to efficiency.[219] The General Court rejected the argument and merely cited the Commission's Guidelines on the assessment of horizontal mergers, and determined whether it had applied them correctly. In essence, the Commission explains in paragraph 76 of its Guidelines that the efficiencies induced by a merger may outweigh the effects on competition and potential harm to consumers that would otherwise have occurred. In its assessment of a merger, the Commission takes into account all relevant factors, including the development of technical and economic progress, as set out in the assessment criteria in Article 2(1) of the European Merger Regulation. In other words, and to summarise, this approach means that there is no 'efficiency defence'—if the merger leads to a SIEC, it cannot be saved on efficiency grounds.

5.2.1 Benefit to Consumers

The efficiencies must be substantial and timely and must benefit consumers in the relevant markets where competition concerns are likely to arise.[220]

Efficiencies may take the form of (i) lower prices, although cost reductions that result simply from a reduction in output do not qualify[221]; (ii) new or improved products or services, for example, through R&D or innovation[222]; (iii) increased output and a subsequent reduction in prices, which would reduce the incentive for a firm in an oligopolistic market to act in a coordinated manner.[223] In any event, there must be an incentive to pass on efficiencies to consumers, and the Commission will be more sceptical when the merger leads to a monopoly or a very high degree of market power.[224]

With respect to the claim of cost savings, the Commission distinguishes between the impact of variable and fixed cost savings. It is generally accepted that efficiencies that result in reductions in variable or marginal costs are more likely to be relevant to the assessment of efficiencies than reductions in fixed costs. However, in dynamic markets, where innovation is important, fixed cost savings may also have a dynamic impact on (quality-adjusted) prices if these fixed cost savings lead to faster price erosion and/or faster quality increases.[225]

---

[219] Ibid., paras 386–443.

[220] Guidelines on the assessment of horizontal mergers, para. 79.

[221] Ibid., para. 80.

[222] Ibid., para. 81.

[223] Ibid., para. 82.

[224] Ibid., para. 84.

[225] Western Digital Ireland/Viviti Technologies (Case M.6203), Commission decision of 12 August 2013, para. 1015.

5.2.2 Merger Specificity

Efficiencies must directly result from the notified merger and must not be achievable through less anti-competitive alternatives; the burden of proof lies with the notifying parties.[226]

5.2.3 Verifiability

Efficiencies must be verifiable so that the Commission can be reasonably certain that they are likely to occur, with the burden of proof on the parties to produce the relevant information in good time.[227]

In *Ryanair Holdings Plc v Commission*, the Court stated that "efficiency claims are verifiable if they give rise to a reasonable certainty that the efficiencies are likely to materialise and to be sufficiently large to outweigh the potential harm to consumers of the merger".[228] In the contested decision, the Commission had indeed stated that Ryanair's claimed efficiencies appeared to be very optimistic and that Ryanair had not presented any objective or convincing evidence in this regard, other than a general reliance on Ryanair's more ruthless management style.[229] And the Court accepted in full the Commission's analysis that the efficiencies would not benefit consumers, were not specific to the merger, and were not verifiable.

The question naturally arises as to the validity (and insurmountable burden of proof) of an efficiency argument in future or innovation markets.

5.3 *Commission's Analysis of Efficiencies Based on Its Case Law*

Whether it is a coincidence or an entrenched policy, the efficiency defence argument almost never seems to be accepted.

Either the Commission looks at the efficiency, but rejects it outright.[230] Or the Commission examines it, takes it into consideration, and on one occasion even concludes that the savings in products and services would benefit consumers and

[226] Guidelines on the assessment of horizontal mergers, para. 85.

[227] Ibid., paras 86–88; General Court of the CJEU, Deutsche Börse v Commission, Case T-175/12 [2015] para. 362.

[228] General Court of the CJEU, Ryanair v Commission, Case T-342/07 [2010] para. 411.

[229] Ryanair/Aer Lingus (Case M.4449), Commission decision of 17 December 2016, para. 1133.

[230] Inco/Falconbridge (Case M.4000), Commission decision of 4 July 2006, paras 529–550.

that they were merger-specific and verifiable,[231] but ends up prohibiting the mergers anyway.[232]

Sometimes (although rarely) the Commission does accept the efficiencies claimed by the parties, although we wonder whether the Commission would not have approved the mergers in question unconditionally anyway.[233]

With regard to the analysis of mergers in the high-tech sector in particular, the following can be said: of the 26 decisions analysed, in 7 the efficiencies were discussed, in 25 the merger was approved, of which only in one precisely because of the efficiencies.

We can only reiterate how much of a gap there is in the analysis conducted by the Commission. The promotion of innovation is elevated to the highest rank as a competition concern, especially post-merger. At the same time, against all logic, this same innovation, a positive thing, never seems to be able to be claimed as an efficiency resulting from a merger.

5.3.1 Axalto/Gemplus

Interestingly, in the *Axalto/Gemplus* case,[234] the parties invoked price efficiency, which the Commission seems to have accepted as it is, without necessarily checking whether the cumulative conditions were met.[235] The merger was indeed approved, but rather because of the commitments and conditions entered by the parties, not due to the expected efficiencies.

In particular, in internal documents, the parties claimed that the new entity would benefit from lower prices on raw materials, mainly chips, because the price paid by a card manufacturer to its chip supplier depends on the number of chips purchased. Most of the parties' customers agreed with this allegation, expecting that the transaction would not hinder their ability to negotiate competitive supply terms. In particular, many customers expected that the transaction would lead to an acceleration of price decreases due to the announced efficiencies.[236]

---

231 GE/Alstom (Case M.7278), Commission decision of 8 September 2015, paras 1362–1363.

232 Deutsche Börse/NYSE Euronext (Case M.6166), Commission decision of 1 December 2012, paras 1133–1342, upheld on appeal General Court of the CJEU, Deutsche Börse v Commission, Case T-175/12 [2015] para. 362; UPS/TNT Express (Case M.6570), Commission decision of 30 January 2013: the Commission's decision was annulled on appeal to the General Court on procedural grounds in General Court of the CJEU, United Parcel Service v Commission, Case T-194/13 [2017]. The case is currently pending on appeal by the Commission, CJEU, Commission v UPS, Case C-265/17 P; Hutchison 3G UK/Telefonica UK (Case M.7612), Commission decision of 11 May 2016, paras 2337–2608.

233 Korsnäs/Assidomän Cartonboard (Case M.4057), Commission decision of 12 May 2006, paras 57–64; TomTom/Tele Atlas (Case M.4854), Commission decision of 14 May 2008, paras 238–250; Nynas/Shell/Harburg Refinery (Case M.6360), Commission decision of 2 September 2013, paras 443–474.

234 Axalto/Gemplus (Case M.3998), Commission decision of 19 May 2006.

235 Ibid., para. 48.

236 Ibid.

The Commission concluded that in light of these considerations, no negative price impact was expected as a result of the proposed transaction. Thus, there was no potential negative effect that needed to be addressed, hence the relative weight given to efficiencies by the Commission in this case.

5.3.2 Western Digital Ireland/Viviti Technologies

In the *Western Digital Ireland/Viviti Technologies* merger,[237] the parties alleged five types of expected efficiencies,[238] including (i) improved market position to compete vigorously with Seagate and Toshiba; (ii) greater and faster product development at lower prices due to the combination of the parties' R&D resources; (iii) significant expected savings in operating expenses, including through economies of scale (including savings on operating expenses of more than $400 million); (iv) reduction in overlapping factory overheads; (v) reduction in capital costs through better utilisation of existing assets and consolidation of equipment suppliers; (vi) reduction in production costs and consequently reduction in the cost of goods sold through the use of internally produced components; (vii) possibility to increase internal production of these components, thereby reducing the premium paid for them from third party suppliers; (viii) potential for further vertical integration.

Before presenting its analysis, the Commission set the tone and a foretaste of its conclusion[239] by noting a series of inconsistencies regarding the nature and extent of the claimed efficiencies, including the lack of particularly compelling evidence of their impact on consumers.[240] The Commission concluded that the efficiencies were

[237] Western Digital Ireland/Viviti Technologies (Case M.6203), Commission decision of 12 August 2013.

[238] Ibid., paras 990–995.

[239] Ibid., para. 1037.

[240] Ibid., paras 999–1002.

not verifiable,[241] were not specific to the merger,[242] and that the merger would not have provided a consumer benefit.[243]

5.3.3 ASL/Arianespace

In the case of *ASL's acquisition of Arianespace*,[244] the parties argued that the transaction would lead to several efficiencies in the launch services sector, which would benefit satellite operators and manufacturers,[245] including a certain financial gain (amount redacted),[246] cost reductions as well as synergies in distribution networks, since Arianespace's global commercial networks could be used to promote ASL's product portfolio.[247]

In addition, the parties argued that the transaction is an integral part of the Ariane 6 programme and that the objectives of Ariane 6 will not be achieved if the integration between development and operation is not implemented,[248] an argument that the Commission had accepted when analysing the creation of the Arianespace joint venture.[249]

The parties have, *inter alia*, submitted an economic study, which presents an efficiency claim that any potential negative effects on rival satellite manufacturers arising from the parties' incentive to bundle their products would be overcompensated

---

[241] Ibid., paras 1004–1007. According to the Commission, the parties' efficiency claims were rather general in nature, and the indication that efficiencies should start to materialise in 2011 (the year of the Commission's analysis of the transaction)—speculative. The parties tried to rely on their experience with recent acquisitions while submitting a numerical prognosis of the cost savings—to no avail. In the Commission's view, the figures submitted were, by their nature, "extremely aggregated", the accuracy of which was neither verifiable nor credible. The Commission stated that quantitative or other detailed evidence should have been presented to clearly explain how the efficiency calculations were made.

[242] Ibid., paras 1008–1013. The efficiencies submitted by the parties also failed to pass the test of merger specificity, as they did not provide concrete evidence, in particular with respect to the type of complementarities that each of the merging firms brings to the table (including the reasons why the parties would not achieve the same result by mere co-operation between them). The Commission found it "extremely unlikely that many of the other elements of the efficiency claims are entirely, if not totally, merger-specific", such as incentives to increase efficiency, improve quality and reduce inventories. They would, according to the Commission, also be present in the absence of the merger.

[243] Ibid., paras 1014–1036. The Commission analysed both the expected fixed and variable cost reductions and was not convinced by the parties' claims. The estimates alleged by the parties were not credible and were not related to any possible benefit to consumers resulting from the merger.

[244] ASL/Arianespace (Case M.7724), Commission decision of 20 July 2016.

[245] Ibid., para. 436.

[246] Ibid., para. 437.

[247] Ibid., para. 438.

[248] Ibid., para. 439.

[249] Airbus/Safran/JV (Case M.7353), Commission decision of 26 November 2014, paras 174 and 175.

by the removal of the partial elimination of double margins, i.e. the vertical efficiency arising from the transaction.[250]

According to the parties, given the very strong competitive constraints imposed by SpaceX and other innovative players, Arianespace has no choice but to immediately reduce the cost of launch services and pass on the economic gains resulting from the transaction to customers.[251]

Not surprisingly, the Commission considered that the efficiencies alleged by the parties were not sufficiently substantiated. In particular, the only documentary evidence regarding the efficiency claims consisted of [...] (type and name of document redacted), which the Commission was not able to verify.[252] And the Commission concluded that the information provided did not, therefore, meet the standards required by the non-horizontal guidelines, namely that it must be verifiable in addition to being specific to the concentration and likely to be passed on to consumers.[253]

The Commission therefore concludes that, without prejudice to the existence or not of such efficiencies by the parties, they cannot be taken into account.[254]

5.3.4 Siemens Healthineers/Varian Medical Systems

In the analysis of the compatibility of the acquisition of *Varian by Siemens Healthineers*[255] with the internal market, in particular as it relates to the markets for imaging and radiotherapy, due to bundling practices, the notifying party has argued that the transaction will lead to efficiency for customers, resulting in lower prices and the availability of new innovative products in a faster and more efficient way.[256]

Many customers confirmed this claim, pointing out that the transaction could indeed lead to efficiencies (lower prices). More generally, they expected the transaction to result in innovation benefits for customers. For example, one customer noted that the transaction could lead to "increased product development", while another customer expected the production of "new features in the Siemens/Varian portfolio that will benefit patients". Overall, they expected the deal to "have the main effect of driving technological innovation", which will ultimately benefit "oncology patients in the EU".[257]

Regrettably, the Commission did not conduct a systematic efficiency analysis in this case. It simply concluded that on the basis of the evidence at hand, and taking into account the results of the market investigation, the transaction was not likely to

---

[250] ASL/Arianespace (Case M.7724), Commission decision of 20 July 2016, para. 441.

[251] Ibid., para. 442.

[252] Ibid., para. 443.

[253] Ibid.

[254] Ibid., para. 444.

[255] Siemens Healthineers/Varian Medical Systems (Case M.9945), Commission decision of 19 February 2021.

[256] Ibid., para. 122.

[257] Ibid., para. 130.

raise serious doubts as to its compatibility with the market in the relevant markets for imaging and radiotherapy, due to bundling practices.[258] Indeed, it would have been really interesting to see a concrete analysis of the claimed efficiency gains as in that the merger would lead to innovations, which were, furthermore, confirmed by industry members.

6 Conclusion

In its assessment, competition law provides for a balancing of competitive harm and efficiency, either explicitly (as in the case of Article 101 TFEU) or implicitly (for example, the European Merger Regulation or Article 102 TFEU). In practice, such balancing exercises prove difficult, partly because it is a challenge to quantify competitive harm and efficiencies, both of which are linked to innovation, in a comparable manner, and partly because litigation strategies will encourage authorities to downplay harm or efficiencies depending on whether the case is headed towards clearance or rejection of the merger.

The cases analysed demonstrate that the current merger analysis framework is inherently incapable of balancing the harm and efficiency that arise from innovation. Indeed, even if efficiencies could be proven and quantified (which is rare in itself), no balancing is possible when competitive harm is established and cannot be mitigated by the remedies offered by the parties. In fact, the EU merger control framework does not provide for balancing at all: as soon as an acceptable efficiency is identified, the presumption of harm is reversed, and there is, therefore, no finding of a SIEC. This situation is clearly unsatisfactory from a policy perspective.

The result is that such an approach creates different standards of proof for harm and efficiency: there is a presumption of harm from a merger on innovation and a presumption of absence of efficiency gains from future innovations

Appendix—Summary Table of the Analysed European Commission Merger Cases in High-Technology Industries

[258] Ibid., para. 131.

Decision date	Case	Industry	Theory of harm	Efficiency	Cleared	Challenged?
01.12.1999	**M.1601** Allied Signal/Honeywell Merger between AlliedSignal Inc. and Honeywell Inc., both U.S. firms AlliedSignal is a manufacturing company operating in the aerospace, automotive and engineered materials (i.e. polymers, speciality chemicals and electronic materials) sectors Honeywell develops and supplies advanced technology controls and products, systems and services for homes and buildings, industrial applications and the aerospace industry	C.30.3—Manufacture of air and spacecraft and related machinery	The Commission's in-depth investigation raised serious doubts as to the creation or strengthening of a dominant position (CSDP) in certain avionics product markets through technical bundling and withholding of information due to the overlapping activities of undertakings. See in particular paras 101–103 and para. 114	"As long as such technical integration does not lead to foreclosure effects, improved technical interoperability may generally be considered to be in the interest of customers…" (para. 112)	**Yes**, both in the EU and in the U.S., **subject to substantial conditions** (paras 125 et seq.)	No
03.07.2001	**M.2220** General Electric/Honeywell Proposed acquisition by General Electric Co. of Honeywell Inc Markets for aero-engines, avionics and other aircraft components and systems	C.28.11—Manufacture of engines and turbines, except aircraft vehicle and cycle engines; C.26.51—Manufacture of instruments and appliances for measuring, testing and navigation; C.20.16—Manufacture of plastics in primary forms	CSDP The Commission's in-depth investigation showed that GE alone already held a DP in the markets for jet engines for large commercial aircraft and large regional aircraft, a position that would have been further strengthened after the merger. The investigation also showed that Honeywell was the leading supplier of avionics and non-avionics products, as well as corporate jet engines and engine starters	The Commission asserted that GE had not presented any efficiency resulting from the merger	**No, in the EU**, since remedies proposed by GE were insufficient to resolve the competition concerns **Yes, in the U.S**	**Yes,** T-210/01, General Electric Company vs Commission, Judgment of the Court of First Instance, 14.12.2005 The Court of First Instance upheld the prohibition of the acquisition of Honeywell by GE

(continued)

(continued)

Decision date	Case	Industry	Theory of harm	Efficiency	Cleared	Challenged?
28.04.2005	**M.3680** Alcatel/Finmeccanica/Alcatel Alenia Space & Technology Creation of two JVs resulting from Alcatel merging its space activities with those of Alenia Spazio and Telespazio, and engineering company Finmeccanica Alcatel is a French industrial company that produces telecommunication equipment, satellites, and space subsystems and provides space-related services Finmeccanica is an Italian state controlled diversified engineering company that produces satellites and subsystems and provides satellite-based services such as space mission management	C.30.3—Manufacture of air and spacecraft and related machinery	The Commission's investigation did not find that the JV of Alcatel Space/Alenia Spazio JV could foreclose competing satellite prime contractors and integrators or have a negative effect on satellite users. Indeed, both companies face credible competitors for satellite systems and related equipment However, the market investigation showed that the combination of the merging parties' activities would lead to an almost uncontested market position for tracking and telemetry control systems and radar altimeters, which are key parts used on satellites	No	**Yes, with conditions and obligations**	No

(continued)

(continued)

Decision date	Case	Industry	Theory of harm	Efficiency	Cleared	Challenged?
19.05.2006	**M.3998** Axalto/Gemplus Axalto, a Dutch company, acquired Gemplus, based in Luxembourg Both companies produce and sell smart cards used for cell phones, payments and identification, as well as related products and services The parties also provide products and services related to the administration of already issued SIM cards. SIM card administration is performed through Over-the-Air (OTA) platforms, which allow mobile operators to control a SIM card without a physical connection	C.26.2—Manufacture of computers and peripheral equipment	SIEC Based on its market investigation, the Commission concluded that, despite the strong positions of the two companies, the transaction would not lead directly to higher prices or a reduced pace of innovation However, the Commission also found that the merged entity would have had both the ability and the incentive to undermine the position of its competitors, given that the transaction would combine two important IP portfolios. In addition, the Commission had identified serious risks of compatibility of OTA platforms with competing card manufacturers	The merging parties have claimed expected efficiencies that have been confirmed by their customers (para. 48)	**Yes**, the parties have undertaken (i) to license the patent portfolio of the combined entity and (ii) to provide third parties with the necessary interoperability information to ensure the compatibility of their cell phone SIM cards with the technology of the combined entity	No

(continued)

(continued)

Decision date	Case	Industry	Theory of harm	Efficiency	Cleared	Challenged?
27.04.2006	**M.4100** Seagate/Maxtor Merger between Seagate and Maxtor Seagate, based in the United States, designs, manufactures and markets hard drives worldwide for a variety of uses. It also produces thin-film recording media and read/write heads that are used in its hard drives Maxtor, also based in the United States, is a global supplier of hard disk drives for a variety of uses, including desktop computers, servers and consumer electronics applications, and is also active in the production of recording media for its own hard disk drives	C.26.2—Manufacture of computers and peripheral equipment	SIEC The Commission took into account, inter alia, the following factors: (i) the practice of regular supply of HDDs to customers, who can easily switch suppliers; (ii) competition with eight other HDD manufacturers, who face relatively low barriers to entry in neighbouring HDD markets; (iii) the possibility of expanding existing capacities in the various HDD markets without significant costs and delays; (iv) the high rate of innovation in the market, short product life cycles and a continuous decline in prices The merger will not lead to a significant reduction of the component markets if the merging parties increase their in-house production of components	Efficiency gains were not claimed	**Yes**	No

(continued)

(continued)

Decision date	Case	Industry	Theory of harm	Efficiency	Cleared	Challenged?
28.04.2007	**M.4465** Thrane & Thrane/Nera Acquisition of Nera Satcom AS by Thrane & Thrane A/S Thrane & Thrane, the Norway-based acquirer, is active in the development, production and sale of equipment for terrestrial, maritime and aeronautical satellite communications, based on Inmarsat satellite systems. It also produces and sells radio communication equipment. It is also one of the designated distributors of airtime for Inmarsat's next generation satellites in the terrestrial communications sector Nera, the Dutch target company, is active in the development, production and sale of terminals and earth stations for mobile terrestrial and maritime satellite communications	C.26.51—Manufacture of instruments and appliances for measuring, testing and navigation	SIEC The Commission concluded that the merged entity would not be able to increase its prices profitably, as the terminals produced by the parties are subject to competition from terminals produced by other manufacturers The market investigation showed that there are a number of competitors capable of developing and supplying maritime terminals The market investigation also revealed that the competitive landscape is likely to change in the foreseeable future due to technological developments in the market for terminals addressing more complex communication needs, namely the introduction of terminals capable of providing broadband services	Efficiency gains were not claimed	**Yes** in the EU, Norway and Spain in October 2006 Initially following a request for information from the UK Office of Fair Trading, the merger was notified in the UK in October 2006. The OFT subsequently referred the case to the Commission, which acquired jurisdiction to assess the merger in December 2006	No

(continued)

(continued)

Decision date	Case	Industry	Theory of harm	Efficiency	Cleared	Challenged?
16.02.2007	**M.4502** Lite-On/PBDS Proposed entry of Lite-On into Philips & BenQ Digital Storage Corporation (PBDS). Under the proposed transaction, Lite-On would replace BenQ as a shareholder, while Philips NV would retain its shares Lite-On, a Taiwanese technology company, is active in computers, communication products, consumer electronics and optical data storage disk drives for personal computers PBDS of Taiwan is active in the development, design, marketing and sales of optical data storage disk drives for personal computers. With the proposed acquisition, Lite-On would replace BenQ as the controlling shareholder of PBDS, while Philips would remain the other controlling shareholder	C.26.2—Manufacture of computers and peripheral equipment	SIEC The Commission's examination showed that the horizontal overlap between the activities of Lite-On and PBDS in the supply of ODD PCs would not give rise to competition concerns and that the combined entity would continue to face several strong, effective competitors The Commission also analysed the effects on the branded aftermarket (i.e. retail sales as opposed to sales to original equipment manufacturers) in which Philips is active. The Commission concluded that there would be no risk of substantial strengthening of the new entities' position in any of these markets and that customers would continue to have alternative and competing sources of supply	Efficiency gains were not claimed	**Yes**	No

(continued)

(continued)

Decision date	Case	Industry	Theory of harm	Efficiency	Cleared	Challenged?
27.02.2008	**M.4979** Acer/Packard Bell Acer to acquire Packard Bell Acer, based in Taiwan, is a global supplier of PCs and related products, including notebook and desktop PCs, servers and storage, LCD monitors and high-definition TVs Packard Bell, headquartered in the Netherlands, is a European supplier of desktop computers, notebooks and digital entertainment solutions	J.62.0—Computer programming, consultancy and related activities; C.33.20—Installation of industrial machinery and equipment; C.26.4—Manufacture of consumer electronics; C.26.51—Manufacture of instruments and appliances for measuring, testing and navigation	SIEC The Commission's examination showed that the proposed merger would lead to horizontal overlaps for desktops and notebooks, both for professionals and consumers, at the EEA and national level. However, the market would remain competitive post-merger in all segments of the PC sector with well-established alternative suppliers such as Hewlett-Packard, Dell, Fujitsu-Siemens, Toshiba, Sony and Lenovo	Efficiency gains were not claimed	**Yes**	No
21.01.2009	**M.5332** Ericsson/STM/JV Creation of a JV between Ericsson Mobile Platforms (EMP), and ST-NXP, the wireless semiconductor business of STMicroelectronics Ericsson (Sweden) is active in the field of telecommunication products, ranging from networks and multimedia solutions to business services and other communication products such as cell phones. It is the ultimate parent company of EMP STMicroelectronics (Netherlands) is active in the supply of semiconductors, ranging from individual components to complex integrated systems and complete electronic platform solutions. It is the ultimate parent company of ST-NXP, a company active in semiconductors for mobile telecommunications	C.26.3—Manufacture of communication equipment; C.26.4—Manufacture of consumer electronics	SIEC The Commission's market investigation found that the creation of the joint venture would not raise horizontal competition concerns in the markets for wireless platforms and wireless semiconductors The parties were also active in vertically related markets. The joint venture would result in the creation of an integrated platform provider by combining ST-NXP's semiconductor activities with EMP's platform design activities. However, the Commission's investigation did not reveal any competition concerns in this respect either	Efficiency gains were not claimed	**Yes**	No

(continued)

(continued)

Decision date	Case	Industry	Theory of harm	Efficiency	Cleared	Challenged?
28.09.2009	**M.5421** Panasonic/Sanyo Acquisition of Sanyo by Panasonic, subject to conditions Panasonic Corporation, based in Japan, is primarily engaged worldwide in the development, manufacture and sale of a wide range of audio-visual and communication products, home appliances, electronic components and devices, including batteries and industrial products Sanyo Electric Co. Ltd., based in Japan, is primarily engaged in the development, manufacture and sale of consumer products, commercial equipment, electronic components including batteries and industrial logistics and maintenance equipment worldwide	C.27.2—Manufacture of batteries and accumulators; C.26.4—Manufacture of consumer electronics; C.26.11—Manufacture of electronic components	SIEC The Commission's investigation identified competition concerns in a number of battery markets where the merged entity would have a significant market share The Commission also investigated a number of consumer electronics markets, such as camcorders and flat-screen TVs, where both Panasonic and Sanyo are active. The Commission's investigation revealed that in many cases the eventual increase in market share was limited and that the merging parties were generally not considered each other's closest competitor. In addition, the merged entity would continue to face competitive pressure from a number of players in each of the relevant markets	Efficiency gains were not claimed	**Yes**, subject to conditions	No

(continued)

(continued)

Decision date	Case	Industry	Theory of harm	Efficiency	Cleared	Challenged?
10.03.2009	**M.5426** Dassault Aviation/Thales Acquisition of Thales by Dassault Aviation and TSA Dassault Aviation, a public limited company under French law, is active in the space sector and in the civil aviation (business aircraft) and military (combat aircraft, flight simulators) sectors TSA, a holding company wholly owned by the French State, has no operational activities. It holds a 26.56% stake in Thales, also a French company, which is active in satellites and associated subsystems, aeronautical equipment for civil and military aircraft, air defence systems, military communication systems and maritime security equipment and systems	C.30.3—Manufacture of air and spacecraft and related machinery	SIEC The Commission's investigation ruled out any risk of distortion of competition that might result from a combination or vertical integration of the parties' activities, as there would remain credible alternative suppliers on the markets after the transaction The Commission also considered that the French Ministry of Defence would have a say in the selection process of component manufacturers for these products, so the transaction would not restrict the access of Thales's competitors to products manufactured by Dassault Aviation. In addition, the selection processes for military equipment manufacturers are part of long-term programmes that will not be affected by the proposed transaction	Efficiency gains were not claimed	**Yes**	No

(continued)

(continued)

Decision date	Case	Industry	Theory of harm	Efficiency	Cleared	Challenged?
11.05.2009	**M.5483** Toshiba/Fujitsu HDD Business Toshiba acquires Fujitsu's HDD business Toshiba Corporation, of Japan, manufactures and markets a wide range of high-tech electronic and electrical products, including hard disk drives, including various types of mobile hard disk drives and various electronic products that use these hard disk drives The HDD Business of Fujitsu Limited, also of Japan, includes Fujitsu's global assets and subsidiaries in the production, design, sales, research and development of hard disk drives, including 2.5-inch mobile hard disk drives and 2.5- and 3.5-inch enterprise hard disk drives, excluding Fujitsu's development and production of hard disk drive media, heads and components	C.26.2—Manufacture of computers and peripheral equipment	SIEC The Commission considered that although the transaction would make the merged entity the largest producer of mobile HDDs in terms of market share, the HDD market is competitive and the transaction would therefore not give rise to competition concerns in these markets Post-transaction, Toshiba will continue to face significant competitors in a market where technological advances are relatively rapid, resulting in short product life cycles	Efficiency gains were not claimed	**Yes**	No

(continued)

(continued)

Decision date	Case	Industry	Theory of harm	Efficiency	Cleared	Challenged?
20.01.2010	**M.5611** Agilent/Varian Acquisition of Varian by Agilent Agilent Technologies Inc. and Varian Inc are both U.S.-based and active in the design, development, manufacture and sale of bioanalytical measurement products, including analytical and life science instruments, as well as related services, consumables and software	C.26.51—Manufacture of instruments and appliances for measuring, testing and navigation	SIEC The Commission identified competition concerns in each of the markets for instruments used to detect and quantify molecular and atomic components in a given sample. The proposed transaction would bring together close competitors in some of the identified markets, resulting in the combined entity holding significant market shares The proposed transaction would also result in the elimination of a significant competitive force in one identified market (triple quad GC–MS instruments). Varian already had significant market shares in this market and, although a recent entrant, Agilent has also rapidly gained significant influence and competes closely with Varian in this market	Efficiency gains were not claimed	**Yes**, subject to conditions	No

(continued)

(continued)

Decision date	Case	Industry	Theory of harm	Efficiency	Cleared	Challenged?
26.01.2011	**M.5984** Intel/McAfee Acquisition of McAfee by Intel Intel is the leading U.S. manufacturer of CPUs, the core chip in a computer, and chipsets, which are used in industries such as computing and communications, and are among the most important components of computers. Intel also develops digital computing technology platforms, which combine various types of hardware and software McAfee is a U.S.-based security technology company that designs and develops security products and services to protect Internet-connected devices from malicious content	J.62—Computer programming, consultancy and related activities; C.26.1—Manufacture of electronic components and boards	The Commission was concerned that competing computer security products could be foreclosed from the market, given Intel's strong presence in the worldwide markets for computer chips and chipsets. In particular, the Commission was concerned that the merged entity would be very likely to embed its own security solutions in its chips and chipsets, thereby creating interoperability problems with regard to competitors' CPUs, which would need access to them in order to develop new solutions	The Commission analysed the efficiencies of the merger in terms of complementing the commitments. Both were likely to eliminate the competition concerns identified, as they were designed to maintain interoperability between the merged entity's products and those of their competitors, thereby ensuring equal competition between the parties and their competitors	**Yes**, subject to conditions	No

(continued)

(continued)

Decision date	Case	Industry	Theory of harm	Efficiency	Cleared	Challenged?
27.06.2011	**M.6126** Thermo Fisher/Dionex Corporation Acquisition of Dionex by Thermo Fisher U.S.-based Thermo Fisher Scientific Inc. produces analytical instruments, scientific equipment, consumables, software and services for research, analysis, discovery and diagnosis Dionex Corporation is a U.S.-based manufacturer of liquid chromatography instruments (particularly ion chromatography), sample preparation systems, consumables and software for chemical analysis	C.26.51—Manufacture of instruments and appliances for measuring, testing and navigation	SIEC The Commission's review showed that the combination of Thermo Fisher's and Dionex's activities will not lead to competition concerns in any of the relevant markets The Commission's investigation also showed that the combined entity will not have the ability or incentive to restrict the interoperability of its Nano-LC instruments or mass spectrometry instruments with those of its competitors The Commission therefore concluded that the transaction would not raise competition concerns	Efficiency gains were not claimed	**Yes**	No

(continued)

(continued)

Decision date	Case	Industry	Theory of harm	Efficiency	Cleared	Challenged?
23.11.2011	**M.6203** Western Digital Ireland/Viviti Technologies Western Digital acquires Hitachi's hard drive business Western Digital (WD), a U.S.-based company, designs, develops, produces and sells hard drives, SSDs, external hard disk drives (XHDDs) and media players. WD also produces key hard drive components, such as read/write heads and media Hitachi Global Storage Technologies (HGST), renamed Viviti Technologies, is a wholly owned subsidiary of Hitachi, Ltd. of Singapore. It develops and manufactures hard disk drives and SSDs, under the XHDD brand, and also produces key hard disk drive components such as heads and media	C.26.2—Manufacture of computers and peripheral equipment	SIEC The Commission's extensive review found that there are distinct global markets for hard disk drives based on their form factor and their end use. The Commission also identified a separate market for XHDDs, which is downstream of HDDs In the markets for 3.5″ desktop HDDs and consumer electronics HDDs, the merged entity will only face competition from the recently merged Seagate/Samsung. This is a problem because, for security of supply reasons, most customers in these markets buy their HDDs from several suppliers	The parties alleged a series of expected efficiencies. The Commission rejected all of them in full, as the parties failed to prove that the claimed efficiencies were verifiable, specific to the merger or that the merger will benefit customers	**Yes**, subject to conditions	No

(continued)

(continued)

Decision date	Case	Industry	Theory of harm	Efficiency	Cleared	Challenged?
10.05.2012	**M.6214** Seagate Technology/The HDD Business of Samsung Electronics Seagate Technology acquires Samsung's hard drive business Seagate Technology (USA) is a worldwide manufacturer of branded hard drives, SSDs and external drives. Its businesses are vertically integrated upstream in the manufacture of key components, such as heads and media Samsung Electronics's HDD business (Korea) produces branded hard drives and external drives. Samsung's HDD business is not vertically integrated upstream in the manufacture of components. Samsung's SSD business will not be transferred to Seagate	C.26.2—Manufacture of computers and peripheral equipment	SIEC The main impact of the transaction is in the markets for 3.5″ desktop HDDs and 2.5″ mobile HDDs, where the investigation revealed that Samsung is not a particularly strong competitor. There would remain three strong suppliers in the 3.5″ desktop market (the merged entity, WD and Hitachi Global Storage Technologies), and four strong suppliers in the 2.5″ mobile drive markets (the three plus Toshiba). With at least 3 suppliers, customers will retain sufficient options to switch suppliers. The Commission also found that the elimination of Samsung is not likely to lead to a risk of coordination between the remaining HDD suppliers	Efficiency gains were not claimed	**Yes**	No

(continued)

(continued)

Decision date	Case	Industry	Theory of harm	Efficiency	Cleared	Challenged?
09.03.2012	**M.6381** Google/Motorola Mobility Google to acquire Motorola Mobility Google is a provider of Internet search and online advertising services. It also provides a number of additional online services and software products. Google's revenues are primarily derived from online advertising and, to some extent, from mobile online advertising. Google also develops and makes available an open source mobile operating system called Android Motorola Mobility is a provider of mobile devices (smartphones and tablets), set-top boxes, end-to-end video solutions and cable broadband access solutions	C.26.30—Manufacture of communication equipment; J.61—Telecommunications; J.61.20—Wireless telecommunications activities	SIEC The Commission's investigation showed that Android contributes to the diffusion of Google's other services and, given Google's basic business model of distributing its online and mobile services and software to the widest possible audience, it is therefore unlikely that Google would restrict the use of Android only to Motorola The Commission also concluded that the proposed transaction would not significantly change the current market situation with regard to access to SEPs held by Motorola Finally, the Commission found that Google would not be able to use Motorola's SEP to obtain preferential treatment for its services, including search and advertising	Efficiency gains were not claimed	**Yes**	No

(continued)

(continued)

Decision date	Case	Industry	Theory of harm	Efficiency	Cleared	Challenged?
26.07.2012	**M.6410** UTC/Goodrich United Technologies to acquire Goodrich aerospace equipment company United Technologies Corporation (UTC) is a U.S.-based company active in the production of a wide range of high-technology products and support services for the building systems and aerospace industries worldwide Goodrich Corporation is a U.S.-based company engaged in the production and sale of systems and services to the aerospace, defence and security industries worldwide	C.30.3—Manufacture of air and spacecraft and related machinery	SIEC The Commission examined the competitive effects of the proposed acquisition in various affected markets and concluded that the transaction would not raise competition concerns in any of them	Efficiency gains were not claimed	**Yes**, subject to conditions	No

(continued)

(continued)

Decision date	Case	Industry	Theory of harm	Efficiency	Cleared	Challenged?
26.11.2013	**M.6944** Thermo Fisher Scientific/Life Technologies Acquisition of Life Technologies by Thermo Fisher Thermo Fisher Scientific Inc. is a U.S. company active in the production and supply of analytical instruments and laboratory consumables (e.g. reagents) in virtually all areas of experimental science, including life sciences, chemistry and physics. Thermo Fisher also operates a strong multi-brand scientific distribution business, Fisher Scientific Life Technologies Corp. is a U.S.-based manufacturer of analytical instruments and laboratory consumables for the life sciences, where it is the global market leader	C.26.51—Manufacture of instruments and appliances for measuring, testing and navigation	SIEC The investigation showed that the transaction, as initially notified, would have significantly reduced competition in the production and supply of (i) cell culture media and sera, (ii) gene deletion products and (iii) polymer-based magnetic beads These concerns were based on the large combined market shares of the merged entity and the presence of significant barriers to entry, namely (i) the considerable time and investment required to establish the necessary track record and reliability as a supplier, (ii) the limited availability of the required equipment (blood), but also (iii) the presence of IP rights, technical know-how and established commercial relationships	Efficiency gains were not claimed	**Yes**, subject to conditions	No

(continued)

(continued)

Decision date	Case	Industry	Theory of harm	Efficiency	Cleared	Challenged?
26.11.2014	**M.7353** Airbus/Safran/JV Aerospace and defence JV between Airbus and Safran Airbus Group N.V. of the Netherlands is active in the aerospace and defence industry. Its activities include the design, manufacture and worldwide sale of civil space launchers, launch vehicle subsystems and equipment, satellites, satellite subsystems and equipment. Airbus is also active in strategic and tactical missiles Safran S.A. of France is active in aerospace propulsion, aircraft equipment, defence and security. Its activities include the production of liquid and solid propellant engine propulsion systems for launch vehicles and electric propulsion systems for satellites. Safran is also active in strategic and tactical missile propulsion	C.30.30—Manufacture of air and spacecraft and related machinery; C.25.40—Manufacture of weapons and ammunition	Significant impact on competition The Commission examined the competitive effects of the proposed transaction and concluded that, as initially notified, it would have significantly reduced competition in the supply of satellites and spacecraft Indeed, the JV would have an incentive to exclude or limit access of Airbus's competitors to a number of important components The transaction could also have led to exchanges of confidential information concerning satellites and their components between the joint venture and Airbus, to the detriment of competitors	The parties did not present a defence based on expected efficiency per se. Instead, they have indicated that the reason behind the creation of the JV was to generate efficiencies and rationalise costs in the new Ariane 6 programme, which both the European Space Agency (ESA) (para. 175) and the Commission's investigation have confirmed (para. 174)	**Yes**, subject to conditions	No
20.07.2016	**M.7724** ASL/Arianespace Acquisition of Arianespace by ASL Arianespace is a French company that provides satellite launch services to private and institutional satellite operators Airbus Safran Launchers (ASL) is a 50/50 JV between Airbus and Safran that manufactures the Ariane launcher	C.30.30—Manufacture of air and spacecraft and related machinery	Potential flows of sensitive information The Commission was concerned that the transaction could lead to sensitive information flows between Airbus and Arianespace, to the detriment of competing satellite manufacturers and launch service providers. These potential information flows could lead to less competitive bidding and less innovation in the satellite and launch service markets	The parties alleged a series of efficiencies, all of which were rejected in full by the Commission (paras 436 to 444)	**Yes**, subject to conditions	No

(continued)

(continued)

Decision date	Case	Industry	Theory of harm	Efficiency	Cleared	Challenged?
29.05.2019	**M.8858** Boeing/Safran/JV (auxiliary power units) Creation of a joint venture by Boeing and Safran for the production of auxiliary power units The joint venture will manufacture APUs which provide electrical power to the aircraft when the engines are shut down The Boeing Company, a U.S.-based company, designs, manufactures and sells commercial aircraft and defence, space and security systems The French company Safran S.A. designs, manufactures and sells aerospace systems and aerospace and defence equipment	C.30.30—Manufacture of air and spacecraft and related machinery; C.33.16—Repair and maintenance of aircraft and spacecraft	No particular theory of harm The Commission concluded that the proposed acquisition would not raise any competition concerns The overlaps between Safran and the JV are limited: Safran manufactures APUs for military aircraft and helicopters, while the joint venture will manufacture APUs mainly for large commercial aircraft Secondly, the Commission found that despite Boeing's strong position in the manufacture of large commercial aircraft, the transaction is unlikely to lead to the foreclosure of competing APU suppliers from the market for commercial aircraft APUs. In fact, the transaction will lead to the creation of an entrant in this market	Efficiency gains were not claimed	**Yes**	No

(continued)

(continued)

Decision date	Case	Industry	Theory of harm	Efficiency	Cleared	Challenged?
21.06.2019	**M.9234** Harris Corporation/L3 Technologies Harris Corporation to acquire L3 Technologies Harris Corporation, based in the United States, is a global aerospace and defence technology company that provides products, systems and services for defence, civilian government and commercial applications L3 Technologies, based in the United States, is an international aerospace and defence systems company that provides intelligence, surveillance and reconnaissance, communications and electronics systems for military, homeland security and commercial aviation customers	C.26.3—Manufacture of communication equipment; C.26.7—Manufacture of optical instruments and photographic equipment; C.27.9—Manufacture of other electrical equipment; C.25.4—Manufacture of weapons and ammunition	SIEC With respect to night vision devices, the Commission found that Harris Corporation and L3 Technologies compete directly in the markets for image intensified night vision devices and image intensified tubes. The proposed transaction, as originally notified, would have significantly reduced competition in these markets, leading to higher prices and reduced choice for ministries of Defence, commercial customers and others As regards portable video data links, the Commission concluded that the proposed merger would not give rise to any competition concerns, as the merged entity would continue to face a number of credible competitors	Efficiency gains were not claimed	**Yes,** subject to conditions	No

(continued)

(continued)

Decision date	Case	Industry	Theory of harm	Efficiency	Cleared	Challenged?
19.02.2021	**M.9945** S Healthineers/Varian Medical Systems Acquisition of Varian by Siemens Healthineers Siemens A.G., headquartered in Germany, is a globally active technology group focused on various fields, including medical technology and digital healthcare services. Its subsidiary Siemens Healthineers provides healthcare solutions and services worldwide, including medical imaging solutions Varian, headquartered in the United States, is a global provider of medical devices and software solutions for the treatment of cancer and other conditions with radiation therapy and other advanced treatments	C.26.60—Manufacture of irradiation, electromedical and electrotherapeutic equipment	SIEC The Commission was concerned that the transaction, as originally notified, would lead to the foreclosure of competitors in the markets for (i) the provision of medical imaging solutions, as well as (ii) the provision of radiotherapy solutions. This could occur through the degradation of interoperability (i) between Siemens Healthineers's imaging solutions and third-party radiation therapy solutions, as well as (ii) between Varian's radiation therapy solutions and third-party medical imaging solutions. The foreclosure of competitors resulting from the acquisition would therefore likely have led to a reduction in product choice and a loss of innovation to the detriment of customers and patients	The parties claimed efficiencies for customers in terms of lower prices and the availability of new innovative products in a faster and more efficient way (para. 122), which had been confirmed by their customers (para. 130). The Commission approved the transaction without conducting a systematic analysis of the efficiencies (para. 131)	**Yes**, subject to conditions	No

(continued)

(continued)

Decision date	Case	Industry	Theory of harm	Efficiency	Cleared	Challenged?
20.05.2021	**M.10059** SK Hynix/Intel's Hand and SSD Business Acquisition of Intel's NAND and SSDs business by SK Hynix Intel Corporation's (U.S.) NAND and SSDs business is active in the manufacture and sale of products using the NAND flash memory SK Hynix Inc. of the Republic of Korea designs and manufactures memory storage devices such as DRAM (Dynamic Random Access Memory), NAND flash memory and NAND-based SSDs, as well as CMOS (Complementary Metal Oxide–Semiconductor)	C.26.2—Manufacture of computers and peripheral equipment	SIEC The Commission concluded that the proposed acquisition would not give rise to any competition concerns, given the limited horizontal overlaps and the limited effects resulting from the vertical relationships between the companies In addition, the Commission found no concerns regarding the companies' activities in neighbouring markets, as the companies would not have the ability and/or incentive to engage in exclusionary practices, and even if they did, there would be no appreciable effect on the markets	Efficiency gains were not claimed	**Yes**	No

References

Christensen C (2013) The innovator's dilemma: when new technologies cause great firms to fail. Harvard Business Review Press, Boston

Commission et al (2019) Competition policy for the digital era. Publications Office

Cunningham C, Ma S, Ederer F (2018) Killer acquisitions. J Polit Econ 129(3):649–702

DG Competition (EC) et al (2021) Support study accompanying the evaluation of the Commission Notice on the definition of relevant market for the purposes of Community competition law, Final report, Luxembourg

Dosi G (1988) The nature of the innovative process. In: Dosi G et al (eds) Technical change and economic theory. Pinter Publishers, London, NY, pp 221–238

Ezrachi A (2021) EU competition law: an analytical guide to the leading cases, 7th edn. Bloomsbury USA

Farrell J, Shapiro C (2001) Scale economies and synergies in horizontal merger analysis. Antitrust Law J 68(3):685–710

Gilbert R (2020) Innovation matters: competition policy for the high-technology economy. The MIT Press

Hecker D (2005) High-technology employment: a NAICS-based update. Monthly Labor Rev (U.S. Dept. of Labor and U.S. Bureau of Labor Statistics) 128(7):57–72

Këllezi P (2010) Les mesures correctives dans les cas de concentrations d'entreprises et d'abus de position dominante, Collection munichoise du droit de la concurrence européen et international, Max Planck Institute for Intellectual Property, Competition and Tax Law, Stämpfli, Bern, LGDJ, Paris/Bruylant/Bruxelles

Lindsay A, Berridge A (2017) The EU merger regulation: substantive issues. Sweet and Maxwell

McGuckin R, Nguyen S (1995) On productivity and plant ownership change: new evidence from the longitudinal research database. Rand J Econ 26:257–276

McKinley W, Latham S, Braun M (2014) Organizational decline and innovation: turnarounds and downward spirals. Acad Manag Rev 39:88–110

Mohr J (2000) The marketing of high-technology products and services: implications for curriculum content and design. J Mark Educ 22(3):246–259

Mukhtar D (2016) Implementation of technology driven policy initiatives in emerging economies: the case of Malaysia's Commercialization of Research and Development Fund, Doctoral dissertation, Nottingham Trent University

Nahm J (2014) Varieties of innovation: the creation of wind and solar industries in China, Germany, and the United States. Massachusetts Institute of Technology, Cambridge

Niels G, Jenkins H, Kavanagh J (2016) Economics for competition lawyers, 2nd edn. Oxford University Press

OECD (2007) Dynamic efficiencies in merger analysis

OECD (2020) Start-ups, killer acquisitions and merger control. Retrievable under https://www.oecd.org/daf/competition/start-ups-killer-acquisitions-and-merger-control-2020.pdf. Last Access 10 Oct 2022

OECD/Eurostat (2018) Oslo manual 2018: guidelines for collecting, reporting and using data on innovation, 4th edn, the measurement of scientific, technological and innovation activities. OECD Publishing, Paris/Eurostat, Luxembourg

O'Sullivan D, Dooley L (2009) Applying innovation. SAGE Publications Inc

Petit N (2020) Big tech and the digital economy: the moligopoly scenario. Oxford University Press

Schreiber M (2021) Regulating innovation. In: Mathis K, Tor A (eds) Law and economics of regulation. Economic analysis of law in European legal studies

Schumpeter J (2008) Capitalism, socialism and democracy. Harper Perennial Modern Thought, New York

Serediuk T, Vdovychenko Y (2018) Common features and distinctions between high technology and innovation. Baltic J Econ Stud 4(5):315–319

Swann P (2009) The economics of innovation: an introduction. Edward Elgar, Cheltenham, UK/Northampton, MA, USA
Tidd J, Bessant J (2014) Strategic innovation management. Wiley
von Furstenberg G (1986) High-tech industries and economic growth. Bus Econ 21(3):43–45
Whish R, Bailey D (2021) Competition law, 10th edn. Oxford University Press, Oxford, UK
Williamson O (1987) The economics of antitrust: transaction cost considerations. In: Blackwell B (ed) Antitrust economics: mergers, contracting, and strategic behavior

Alexandra Telychko is a Lecturer, Geneva School of Economics and Management; Research and Teaching Assistant, PhD candidate, Faculty of Law, University of Geneva. Uni Mail. Her fields of interest include Competition Law (Merger Control), Intellectual Property, Law and Economics, Law and Technology.

Innovation as a Competitive Constraint on Online Platforms in European Competition Law: The Industry Life Cycle and Dominant Designs in Digital Markets

Lisanne M. F. Hummel

Abstract Although market power in platform-mediated markets seems to be ubiquitous, in some cases it may be short-lived due to innovation. Innovation can make an undertaking redundant or an entrant fuelled by innovation can take away market power of established undertakings. European competition law struggles to distinguish between these two situations. The theory of the industry life cycle and the concept of dominant design might help to understand when market power is a persisting problem and when innovation may make market power short-lived. All industries follow a similar pattern, where the emergence of a dominant design is the key turning point, signifying when innovation is no longer a competitive constraint. In abuse of dominance and merger control cases this theory might help in different ways to inform our assessments of several competitive constraints on online platforms.

Keywords EU competition law · Market power · Dominant position · Competitive constraints · Online platforms · Big tech · Digital markets · Dominant design · Industry life cycle · Economic analysis · Innovation · Disruption · Law and technology · Schumpeterian competition · Merger control · Abuse of dominance · Market shares · Dynamic efficiencies · Killer acquisitions · Digital markets act

1 Introduction

The market power of big tech companies has been the subject of many debates and different regulatory responses. There are concerns that big tech companies have become gatekeepers on digital markets, making their positions unassailable. Yet, big tech companies themselves do not agree and find that their markets are characterized "by innovation, rapid change, and disruptive technologies" and state that they "face changing technologies, shifting user needs, and frequent introductions of rival

L. M. F. Hummel (✉)
Utrecht University, Utrecht, Netherlands
e-mail: l.m.f.hummel@uu.nl

K. Mathis and A. Tor (eds.), *Law and Economics of the Digital Transformation*, Economic Analysis of Law in European Legal Scholarship 15,
https://doi.org/10.1007/978-3-031-25059-0_11

products and services."[1] Their businesses may be disrupted by an innovation at any moment, and consequently, there is no need to worry about their current market power.

At the heart of these statements lies the Schumpeterian argument that competition primarily occurs through cycles of innovation, rather than through static price or output competition. Undertakings compete for temporary dominance of the market through the introduction of new generations of technology. That is, firms do not compete simultaneously for a share of the market, but sequentially for the market as a whole.[2]

Competing for the market is especially apparent in industries where big tech companies operate. Big tech companies have several platforms and with those platforms operate in platform-mediated markets such as operating systems, app stores, online marketplaces and search engines. These markets have strong increasing returns and positive feedback loops alternatives.[3] Increasing returns are caused among others by network effects. Users are attracted to platforms with many other users and when a critical mass of users is reached, the market tips toward the platform, leaving no room for alternatives.[4] Another source for increasing returns is the collection and use of big data and the creation of software and artificial intelligence, which can give rise to economies of scale. The presence of such strong increasing returns can limit the number of viable competitors and even create a tendency to tip toward monopoly. These increasing returns may lead to competition being for the market rather than in the market.[5]

This Schumpeterian competition for the market causes issues for European competition law assessments. European competition law focuses on static efficiencies, meaning that competition is assessed at a certain point in time. In contrast, dynamic efficiencies, such as innovation are difficult to integrate in these assessments because they are ever-changing. Especially in platform-mediated markets, the uncertainty inherent to innovation causes problems for European competition because static analyses of the market may offer an unreliable indicator of the future.[6] Static analyses are especially an issue for the competitive assessments where innovation may play a constraining role, such as the assessment of market power and the theories of harm involving small nascent start-ups and innovations.

In this chapter I will question how European competition law can integrate innovation as a competitive constraint on online platforms' market power in platform-mediated markets, which I will answer in Sect. 5. To answer that question, I will first discuss in Sect. 2 European competition law's struggles to deal with the uncertainty that innovation brings to platform-mediated markets. In economic theory, there has

---

[1] Meta, Annual Report (2021, p. 7); Alphabet, Annual Report (2021, p. 10).

[2] Katz and Shelanski (2007, p. 4).

[3] Crocioni (2008, pp. 468–469); Katz and Shapiro (1994, p. 93); OECD (2020a, p. 17).

[4] Crocioni (2008, pp. 468–4690); Katz and Shapiro (1994, p. 93); OECD (2020a, p. 17).

[5] Katz (2021, pp. 1–2).

[6] OECD (2020b, p. 9).

been a move from static theory to a dynamic theory of markets. It has been theorized that all markets follow a similar pattern of development, where innovation is initially a competitive constraint but stops constraining market power when a dominant design emerges. I will explore this theory and its relevance to online platforms in Sect. 3. This pattern of innovation and the concept of dominant design can inform market power assessments in European competition law but also the issues we have encountered in European competition law with killer acquisitions and countervailing powers to big tech companies (Sect. 4).

2 Market Power and Innovation in European Competition Law

European competition law focuses on static efficiencies, which are measured at a certain point in time. This stands in stark contrast to dynamic efficiencies, denoting the potential of change or innovation in a market (Sect. 2.1). Innovation is inherently uncertain and unpredictable and therefore often given a less significant role in European competition law cases. In both abuse of dominance and merger control cases, this focus on static efficiencies poses a problem when it comes to platform-mediated markets. For platform-mediated markets, the Commission and the CJEU are struggling to grasp the uncertainty that is inherent to innovation and the Schumpeterian argument of innovation as a competitive constraint (Sects. 2.2 and 2.3).[7]

2.1 *Static Efficiencies v Dynamic Efficiencies*

European competition law has recently been driven by static efficiencies, which means that undertakings and consumers are observed at a particular point in time.[8] The focus on static efficiencies have made the state of competition and the effect of potential abuses or concentrations more measurable. However, simultaneously, the importance attached to static efficiencies gives an incomplete representation of reality. Static efficiencies focus on the most efficient result as it relates to output, price, and costs, which can be calculated by using allocative efficiency and productive efficiency.[9] A market achieves allocative efficiency when all resources are allocated to their highest valued use.[10] When there is productive efficiency, it is not possible to produce a given quantity of output at a lower cost.[11] For these efficiencies, it

[7] This section is an adaptation from the paper submitted to the EU Antitrust: Hot Topics & Next Steps International Conference, 24–25 January in Prague, Czechia.

[8] OECD (2012, p. 12).

[9] OECD (2012, p. 12).

[10] Kolasky and Dick (2003, p. 242).

[11] OECD (2012, p. 13).

is assumed that the technology with which goods are produced is also assumed to be fixed, or, not subject to change.[12] This is at odds with what we observe in platform-mediated markets, which are constantly subject to change.

Dynamic efficiencies are more closely related to a potential of change in technology, as they denote the ability of an undertaking and its incentives to introduce new products or processes of production or to improve existing ones.[13] The effects of dynamic efficiencies are displayed over time by showing the best combination of production factors considering how they might be improved.[14] Dynamic efficiencies rather than static efficiencies reflect the changes and uncertainty in platform-mediated markets.

2.2 Determining Market Power

Determining market power is relevant to abuse of dominance and merger control cases. To determine whether an undertaking has a dominant position in European competition law, the Commission examines the competitive structure of the market, and in particular the competitive constraints imposed by actual competition, future entry and exit or potential competition, and countervailing buyer power.[15] The existence of a dominant position derives in general from a combination of these factors which, taken separately, would not necessarily be determinative for the assessment of a dominant position.[16]

However, from these factors, the actual competition as measured by market shares is important in determining that an undertaking has a dominant position.[17] An undertaking holding a market share of more than 40% will be presumed dominant but additional factors like barriers to entry will have to be observed to conclusively establish dominance.[18] Very large market shares of more than 50% "are in themselves, and save in exceptional circumstances, evidence of the existence of a dominant position".[19]

In sum, market power is assessed using certain and predictable competitive constraints, focusing on the assessment on static efficiencies. Market shares as a

[12] OECD (2012, p. 12).

[13] OECD (2012, p. 14).

[14] Costa-Cabral (2018, p. 313); OECD (2012, p. 14).

[15] Guidelines 102 TFEU, paras 13–24.

[16] United Brands (1978, paras 65–66); Hilti (1991, para. 90); Gøttrup-Klim (1994, para. 47); Telefonica (2012, para. 148).

[17] Hilti (1991, para. 90); Imperial Chemical Industries (2010, paras 255–256); Telefonica (2012, para. 148).

[18] Communication of the Commission on article 82, para. 15.

[19] Hoffmann-La Roche (1979, para. 41); Solvay (2009, para. 277); Imperial Chemical (2010, paras 256 and 259).

key factor show the current competition on the market. The question is how innovation—which is said to potentially constrain market power—is considered in this market power assessment.

2.3 *Innovation Constraining Market Power*

Although innovation cannot be overlooked as it may constrain big tech companies' power, innovation is awarded a limited role in the assessment of market power in European competition law in abuse of dominance and merger control cases. Innovation is difficult to unite with static efficiencies. Innovation is inherently unpredictable, uncertain, and complex, whereas static efficiencies assume a certain level of stability.[20]

2.3.1 Innovation as a *General* Constraint on Market Power

Innovation can constrain an undertaking's market power in various ways. The introduction of a new technology, product or service class may constrain the power of an undertaking. Yet, we do not always know what type of innovation may constrain the power of an undertaking. For example, in the 1990s we would not have known the impact of the Internet on brick-and-mortar stores. I call this the impact of innovation as a general constraint, since the innovation is largely undefined as are the effects and the timeline of the effects. Besides the impact of an undefined innovation, a specific competitor with a new product or service can also constrain the power of an undertaking, which I call innovation as a specific constraint. Keeping with the e-commerce example, we can now say that Amazon (in the US) or more national e-commerce market places (such as Bol.com in the Netherlands) constrain the market power of brick-and-mortar stores.

Innovation as a general constraint on market power can be considered in abuse of dominance and merger control cases. In both types of cases, market power plays a prominent role and therefore the constraint that innovation may place on that market power is relevant. While market shares are the basis of the assessment of market power, the Commission and the CJEU have always nuanced the importance of market shares when assessing market power as "a substantial market share as evidence of the existence of a dominant position varies from market to market according to the structure of these markets [...]."[21] Market shares may not be an accurate proxy for market power when innovation constrains the market power of an undertaking.

---

[20] OECD (2012, p. 12).

[21] Case 85/76 *Hoffmann-La Roche v Commission* (1979) ECR I-00461, paras 39–41; AKZO (1991, para. 60); Case T-30/89 *Hilti v Commission* (1991) ECR II-1439, paras 90–92; Case T-340/03 *France Télécom v Commission* (2007) ECR II-107, para. 100.

However, in previous cases on big tech companies, market shares have nearly always been a decisive factor in determining that an undertaking has a dominant position.[22]

Although innovation may constrain the market power of big tech companies, this is rarely considered in abuse of dominance cases. In Google Shopping the Commission held that a dominant position can still be determined based on market shares, as the "fast-growing market does not show signs of marked instability during the period at issue and, on the contrary, a rather stable hierarchy is established".[23] Subsequently, market shares and barriers to entry and expansion were used to determine that Google had a dominant position and innovation as a competitive constraint was therefore not a factor to refute these indicators of market power.[24] The CJEU confirmed this decision.[25]

In merger control, concentrations that significantly impede effective competition are not allowed, in particular if this is the result of the creation or strengthening of a dominant position.[26] This makes the assessment of a dominant position only a subset of the broader assessment of significant impediments to effective competition. It is also different from abuse of dominance cases as it is a forward-looking assessment where the Commission compares the pre- and (estimated) post-merger competitive conditions.[27] Post-merger market shares can only be an estimation of what is expected after the merger. This means that market shares in merger control are inherently less important as other factors may also significantly impede effective competition and as the market will necessarily change following the merger.

The CJEU and the Commission therefore more readily accept other competitive constraints such as innovation in the assessment of competitive conditions in merger control. Innovation is seen as a competitive constraint on undertakings that leads to market shares not being indicative of market power and, therefore, of lasting damage to competition.[28] The fact that an undertaking has high pre- or post-merger market shares can be made insignificant by other market conditions such as the instability of a market due to innovation or low entry barriers combined with a heterogeneous market character with growth, innovation and technological change.[29] The problem with these assessments is that we cannot predict the future of innovation.

---

[22] Case T-612/17 *Google and Alphabet v Commission* (Google Shopping), ECLI:EU:T:2021:763, para. 54; Case AT.40153—E-Book MFNS and related matters) OJ C 264, 11.8.2017, pp. 7–10, para. 58; Case AT.40099—Google Android C/2018/4761 OJ C 402, 28.11.2019, pp. 19–22, para. 439.

[23] Commission Decision *Google Shopping* 4444 [2017] OJ C9/11, para. 267.

[24] Commission Decision *Google Shopping* 4444 [2017] OJ C9/11, Sects. 6.2.1 and 6.2.2.

[25] Case T-612/17 *Google and Alphabet v Commission* (*Google Shopping*), ECLI:EU:T:2021:763.

[26] Articles 2(2) and (3) Merger Regulation.

[27] Articles 2(1)(b) Merger Regulation.

[28] Case T-79/12 *Cisco Systems v Commission* (CFI, 11 December 2013), para. 69.

[29] Case IV/M.68 Tetra Pak/Alfa Laval (1991) OJ L 290/35; Case COMP/M.2256—Philips/Agilent Health Care Technologies, paras 31–32; Case COMP/M.2609—HP/Compaq, para. 39, paras 31–32; Case No COMP/M.6281—Microsoft/Skype, C(2011) 7279, paras 78 and 99; Case T-79/12 *Cisco Systems v Commission* (CFI, 11 December 2013), paras 61 and 65.

The forward-looking assessments in merger control therefore always have a certain level of uncertainty, reducing the credibility of the assessment.

2.3.2 Innovation as a *Specific* Constraint

The CJEU and the Commission may consider innovation as a specific competitive constraint on undertakings in abuse of dominance and merger control cases by using the concept of potential competition. In abuse of dominance cases, the potential competition doctrine is considered in the sense that the existence of potential competition determines the economic strength and therefore the dominant position of an undertaking. In merger control, the doctrine of potential competition can also constitute a theory of harm, where acquiring a potential competitor might not be allowed as it harms competition by removing an important competitive constraint.

The concept of potential competition does not immediately relate to innovation but considers *in general* how potential competitors exert a competitive constraint on undertakings. Yet, when a potential competitor is fueled by innovation, innovation can indirectly be considered as a competitive constraint on the dominant position of an undertaking. Potential competitors can only impose a competitive constraint if their entry is likely, timely and sufficiently swift to deter the exercise of substantial market power in abuse of dominance cases or to deter or defeat any potential anti-competitive effects of the merger.[30] Barriers to entry are assessed for the likelihood of entry, for the timeliness of entry (entry should take place within two years) and be of sufficient scope and magnitude to deter or defeat the anti-competitive effects of the merger.[31] These time limits mean that the Commission and the CJEU can only consider innovative potential competitors to a limited extent.

Killer acquisitions are closely related to the doctrine of potential competition and pose a specific problem for merger control in digital platform-mediated markets where big tech companies operate. In a killer acquisition, the acquiring undertaking aims "to discontinue the development of the targets' innovation projects and pre-empt future competition".[32] With a killer acquisition, an undertaking takes pre-emptive action against or tries to prevent Schumpeterian or innovation competition, where a new innovative entrant might wipe out their market power or dominant position.

While killer acquisitions are closely related to the theory of harm on potential competition, there is an important difference.[33] In a killer acquisition theory of harm, it is not only competition that is killed, but also the product itself. In contrast, a

---

30 Article 82 (now 102 TFEU) Guidance, pp. 5–18, paras 68–69.

31 Saint-Gobain/Wacker-Chemie/NOM, para. 184; Alcoa/Reynolds, paras 31–32, 38; Tetra Pak/Alfa Laval, Sect. 3.4.

32 OECD (2020b, p. 9).

33 Nascent acquisitions constitute a whole category of acquisitions of young firms with products or services whose competitive significance remains highly uncertain (OECD, p. 10). Alternative theories of harm might include vertical theories of harm in which the acquired product might grow into a key input that allows input foreclosure in downstream markets. They might also include conglomerate theories of harm in which the acquired product might grow into a complement that

potential competition theory of harm is less specific in that it simply requires that the potential competitive threat be removed or "killed" while the product itself may live on, for example as a non-aggressive product line or an input in the acquirer's product.[34] From the 175 acquisitions by Google, Amazon, Facebook, Amazon, and Microsoft over a three-year period, in 105 cases the brand of the target firms was discontinued within a year of the acquisition.[35] Yet, very few acquisitions by digital platforms were examined by the Commission.

The EU has a mandatory notification system, where mergers need to be notified if they meet EU thresholds. If a merger does not meet the thresholds, it does not mean that it will avoid merger control but it may face merger control in each of the EU's member states.[36] There is also a referral mechanism, which enables the Commission to review a merger that does not meet the thresholds at the request of the parties, the national competition authorities, or its own initiative under certain conditions. Through this referral mechanism, the Facebook/WhatsApp merger was reviewed, despite WhatsApp's low turnover at the time. Similarly, the Apple/Shazam merger was referred to the Commission after a request by several Member States.[37]

Despite the referral mechanism, an enforcement gap has been signaled for acquisitions of highly valued targets with no or limited turnover, or in other words, for killer acquisitions.[38] The Commission is aiming to close that gap without amending the Merger Regulation. At the time of this writing, the proposal for the Digital Markets Act includes the introduction of an "obligation to inform about concentrations" in Article 12 of the DMA, meaning that gatekeepers need to inform the Commission of all its acquisitions. The goal of this provision is to enable the Commission to review gatekeepers status' as well as the possibility to adjust the list of core platform services provided by a gatekeeper.[39] The notifications will also provide information that is crucial to monitoring broader contestability trends in the digital sector.[40]

Only notifying the Commission of concentrations, does not mean that the Commission will have jurisdiction to assess these concentrations. The turnover thresholds are still in place and some acquisitions by gatekeepers or big tech companies even fall below national thresholds. The DMA was therefore quickly followed by a new Guidance on article 22 of the Merger Regulation.[41] With this new Guidance, the Commission will welcome referrals from Member States of concentrations even

might be bundled or tied to the incumbent's product in order to exclude rivals (OECD, killer acquisitions, p. 10).

[34] OECD (2020b, p. 10).

[35] OECD (2020b, p. 14).

[36] EU Jurisdiction notice, para. 127.

[37] OECD (2020b, p. 18).

[38] OECD (2020b, p. 18).

[39] Rec. 31 DMA.

[40] Rec. 31 DMA.

[41] See Guidance Art. 22 Merger Regulation. This amendment purports simply to change the Commission's approach to mergers but in essence preventing a tedious change in the Merger Regulation (which requires unanimity).

where there is no national jurisdiction in the first place. The reasoning behind this change in enforcement priorities are transactions in the digital and pharma sectors that have escaped review by both the Commission and the Member States.[42] The Commission emphasizes that the Guidance is aimed at those concentrations where the turnover of at least one of the undertakings concerned does not reflect its actual or future competitive potential. This would include, for example, cases where the undertaking is a start-up or recent entrant with significant competitive potential that has yet to develop or implement a business model generating significant revenues (or is still in the initial phase of implementing such business model), is an important innovator or is conducting potentially important research; is an actual or potential important competitive force.[43] It is to be expected that the Commission will hear from a merger or acquisition through the notification obligation in article 12 of the DMA. The Commission may then invite specific Member States to refer the merger of acquisitions to the European Commission, which might lead to more killer acquisitions being reviewed in the European Union.

The mere fact that more acquisitions of big tech companies will be reviewed by the Commission, will not solve the problem of killer acquisitions. The problem with killer acquisitions is that it is difficult for the Commission and the CJEU to distinguish between anti-competitive concentrations and competition on the merits. In some cases, the acquisition of a smaller undertaking is merely a sign of a well-functioning competitive market, as the competitive process eliminates those undertakings that are unviable. These undertakings might exit the market by seeking a takeover. However, in other cases, the acquisition of a smaller undertaking is the elimination of a competitive threat and thereby significantly impedes competition. It is difficult to distinguish between the two types of acquisitions. The question therefore remains whether the European Commission has the tools to determine when an acquisition consists of competition on the merits and when it significantly impedes competition.

2.3.3 Interim Conclusion: Innovation as a Competitive Constraint in European Competition Law

In sum, innovation as a competitive constraint on market power is considered more readily in merger control than in abuse of dominance cases. For both types of cases, potential competition might be an avenue to explore when considering innovation as a constraining power. However, this can only be considered when there is a potential innovative entrant (and not a broad innovation) constraining power within a specific period. The static nature of European competition law therefore remains a problem, as innovation is inherently uncertain and unpredictable, reducing the value of the forward-looking assessments of market power in merger control. When looking at killer acquisitions, this problem becomes even more apparent as it is difficult to

[42] Rec. 10 Art. 22 Guidance.

[43] Rec. 19 Art. 22 Guidance.

distinguish between pro- and anti-competitive acquisitions. European competition law's assessments of innovation fit within its framework of static efficiencies as it does not consider complex effects of innovation by limiting its impact to foreseeable consequences.

To consider innovation, which is inherently uncertain and unpredictable, in European competition law, a further analysis of innovation is needed. Maybe innovation is not as uncertain and unpredictable as we might think but there is a certain pattern to innovation. In the next section I will discuss how economics and innovation studies have discovered an innovative pattern over several industries, which might also be applicable to platform-mediated markets. Understanding the theory behind this pattern might eventually inform and nuance market power assessments in European competition law.

3 Dominant Designs in Online Platforms

Innovation studies have tried to move beyond static efficiencies by looking at the patterns of innovation in industries. The emergence of a dominant design is the key turning point in that pattern when innovation stops constraining market power. Online platforms also follow this pattern, which can inform and nuance European competition law concepts of market power and innovation by identifying a dominant design. (Sect. 3.1). A dominant design emerges when at least 50% of the market has the same design. However, only a majority measure is insufficient to determine there is a dominant design. The design also needs to be the archetype of the product in both the user and the designer imagination and provide an answer to the need of many people by freezing the socio-economic context (Sect. 3.2).

3.1 The Industry Life Cycle and Dominant Designs

Dynamic efficiency or innovation shows that markets are not stable and do not necessarily reach an equilibrium but there is a degree of change. This change can be visualised by a dynamic pattern, which all industries follow, called the industry life cycle. The phases are roughly the same across industries: the start-up phase, the growth phase, the maturity, and the decline phase. Customer demand starts out limited in the start-up phase and then slowly gains traction, attracting other undertakings to the market in the growth phase. In the maturity phase customer demand stagnates, which leads to a shake out of undertakings and thus consolidation in the market. In the decline phase, customer demand declines in favour of a new industry. Profitability and market characteristics depend on the phase of the industry.[44]

The competitive constraint of innovation on undertakings also varies with these market phases.[45] After a technological breakthrough, in the start-up and growth phase, there are many competitors that market many distinctive designs of a product. For example, when the automobile was brought to the market, undertakings introduced automobiles with different engines, steering wheels, clutches, and materials. The companies that market these designs compete on innovation and try to persuade the most customers to use their design.[46] Competition at this stage is marked by competition on innovation.[47]

Online platforms also start with this start-up phase or era of experimentation, where innovation is a competitive constraint on the power of online platforms. Taking the development of mobile operating systems as an example, we currently have two dominant mobile operating systems: Apple's iOS and Google's Android.[48] Until Apple and Google opened their mobile operating systems to third party app developers, different manufacturers, such as Nokia, Blackberry and Samsung, had introduced various devices with various operating systems that differed from each other since the introduction of the smartphone in 2000.[49] At that point innovation imposes a competitive constraint, as new designs are often and quickly introduced in the market and gain some traction among customers.

This phase of uncertainty and innovation as a competitive constraint ends with the establishment of a dominant design. Although the definition of dominant designs has varied over time, a dominant design is the successful design which is widely adopted and changes the nature of competition, driving out other competitors.[50] The emergence of a dominant design means that future technological progress consists of incremental improvements elaborating the standard, meaning that subsequent design are so similar that disruption seems unlikely.[51] Innovation therefore stops being a competitive constraint on the core platform and undertakings switch to price competition.[52] For example, once Google introduced a mobile operating system open to third parties, other undertakings either copied the design (e.g. Apple) or left the market (e.g. Symbian).[53] Dominant designs tend to remain stable for long retention

[44] Porter (1980). See also LMF Hummel (2022). Dominant positions or dominant design? In Conference Proceedings of Antitrust: Hot Topics & Next Steps International Conference, 24–25 January in Prague, Czechia.

[45] Tushman and Murmann (1998); Utterback and Abernathy (1975).

[46] Anderson and Tushman (1990, pp. 606 and 610); Utterback and Abernathy (1975, p. 641); Tushman and Murmann (1998, p. 10).

[47] Anderson and Tushman (1990, p. 611).

[48] Taleby et al. (2017, p. 31).

[49] Markovic et al. (2018, p. 6).

[50] Sidak and Teece (2009, p. 604); Murmann and Frenken (2006, p. 932).

[51] Anderson and Tushman (1990, p. 613).

[52] Anderson and Tushman (1990, p. 613).

[53] Taleby et al. (2017, p. 31).

periods in a relatively concentrated market, which then enters the maturity stage in the industry life cycle.[54]

This process has been the same for search engines, a different platform-mediated market. For example, in the 1990s, many search engines entered the market with diverse ways of categorizing and searching the Internet. Dominant positions were taken over by new entrants with an innovation quite frequently until Google Search entered the market with its PageRank algorithm.[55] Google Search became the dominant platform design, which comprises a stable technological architecture of core components.[56] The core platform has a community of organizations and individuals that produce goods and services value on the core platform.[57] The dominant platform is the core platform and the community depending on the platform is the ecosystem or the periphery.[58] Google Search, for example, has advertisers, businesses and users depending on the search engine.

The emergence of a dominant design on the core platform leads to a shake out of undertakings in the market of the core platform.[59] A shake-out means that the market consolidates and competition on the core platform market diminishes. Usually, one or two undertakings become dominant, such as Google Search became dominant in the search engine market. With a dominant design, users are no longer persuaded to switch to alternative designs because of network effects, switching costs and market tipping. Users are attracted to platform with many other users and when a critical mass of users is reached, the market tips toward the platform, leaving no room for alternatives.[60] New entrants in the market are not different or "special" enough to overcome the costs that users occur when switching to alternatives, such as losing connections with other users or learning how a new platform works.[61] For example, DuckDuckGo offers a privacy-respecting alternative to Google Search but is not able to compete with the high quality and user-friendliness of Google Search, leaving users to remain with Google Search.[62] Innovations are therefore no longer a competitive constraint on the market power of undertakings.

In the periphery of the core platform an opposite movement takes place: a shake-in. A shake-in means that where core platforms leave the market, the number of complementor firms in the periphery of the platform increases.[63] Complementor firms are attracted to stable core platforms, as they face steep learning curves and increased development costs with every notable change to the core platform.[64] For

[54] Sidak and Teece (2009, p. 604).

[55] Buganza and della Valle (2010, p. 47).

[56] Zeijen and others, forthcoming.

[57] Moore (1996).

[58] Kenney et al. (2021, p. 1).

[59] Porter (1980).

[60] Crocioni (2008, pp. 468–469); Katz and Shapiro (1994, p. 93); OECD (2020a, p. 17).

[61] Fan and Suh (2014).

[62] Hollingsworth (2020).

[63] Ozalp et al. (2018, p. 1205); Zeijen and others, forthcoming.

[64] Ozalp et al. (2018, p. 1205).

example, if Amazon Web Services (AWS) as a cloud service changes its system fundamentally, complementors such as Netflix[65] and Spotify need to change the services to continue running them on AWS or if Apple changes its operating system, all app developers need to change their apps. Stable core platforms with a dominant design benefit complementor firms.[66] When it became clear that Google and Apple were the dominant platform designs, more app developers dared to invest in their platforms.[67]

Complementors in the periphery of the core platform can still innovate after the emergence of a dominant design. For example, if AWS as a cloud service is a dominant design, the companies depending on AWS such as Spotify and Netflix, can still innovate and design their own products and services. Complementors design and develop their own functionality within the boundaries that the core platform gives them. This means that even when a dominant design has emerged on the core platform level and innovation is no longer a competitive constraint on the market power of core platforms, more significant changes can still be expected in the periphery of the product.[68] In the periphery of the platform, innovation can therefore still be a competitive constraint on the companies in the periphery of platform, such as app developers.

In sum, a dominant design is the key turning point for innovation as a competitive constraint on online platforms. Before a dominant design emerges, innovation makes the future trajectory of the market uncertain and unpredictable. A new undertaking can enter the market at any time with an innovation and take over the market. After a dominant design has emerged, this is less likely to happen and innovation is no longer a competitive constraint on the core platform. Yet, it can still constrain the complementor firms that operate in the periphery of the core platform.

3.2 *Determining the Emergence of a Dominant Design*

If the emergence of a dominant design is the key turning point for using innovation as a competitive constraint, it is important to know how to determine when we can speak of a dominant design. A dominant design has emerged if most designs in the market are the same. The notion of a majority of designs can be defined empirically by using either a threshold (e.g., 50, 40, 30, 20% market share) or a variety measure (such as

[65] Interesting to note about dominant designs in platform-mediated markets. In principle in digital markets, a dominant design means that there is a dominant company due to network effects and other economies of scale. However, originally this was not the case. The Ford Model T was a dominant design but was copied by many different companies, which competed with Ford. This can also happen in digital markets when we look at Netflix. Netflix is a dominant design but many similar video-on-demand-platforms keep entering the market (HBO, Apple, Amazon Prime, Disney, and so on) by copying the Netflix design.

[66] Impact Assessment Report Digital Markets Act (2021).

[67] Markovic et al. (2018, p. 6).

[68] Zeijen and others, forthcoming.

the Herfindahl index).[69] To determine whether a dominant design has emerged, it is not the market shares of an undertaking that needs to be measured but the market shares of the design.

Using only the empirical calculation of market shares has been regarded as oversimplified and insufficient to determine the existence of a dominant design.[70] This criterion has therefore been expanded with three further characteristics to know whether a dominant design has emerged. Besides a 50% market share of the dominant design, the design needs to be the archetype of the product in both the user and the designer imagination, the design needs to provide an answer to the need of many people and the winning design freezes the socio-economic context.[71] For example, Google Search answered nearly all needs of people using search engines and other search engines changed to Google's single search bar design. This froze the socio-economic context and changed innovation from disruptive to incremental innovations.[72]

Using a combination of these three criteria is also important because a dominant design can be best viewed as a continuum instead of a binary state: it is not that there is or is not a dominant design but there can be a dominant design to a certain extent.[73] This means that a design can be dominant in an industry to different extents.[74] This could entail that when most of these factors point towards a dominant design, innovation might no longer pose a competitive constraint.

The industry life cycle can inform and nuance the current static image of market power assessments in European competition law. By determining the phase of the market, innovation as a competitive constraint can be either integrated in the assessment of market power or not. In the industry life cycle, the turning point for innovation as a competitive constraint seems to be the emergence of a dominant design. If the Commission would adopt this approach, it would essentially adopt the approach of the Cisco judgment. For online platforms, before a dominant design, innovation is a competitive constraint on the core platform. After a dominant design emerges, the competitive constraint of innovation is no longer exerted on the core platform but on the periphery of the platform, which in turn flourishes because of the stability of the core platform.

---

[69] Murmann and Frenken (2006, p. 944).

[70] Anderson et al. (1997); Murmann and Frenken (2006, p. 944).

[71] Anderson et al. (1997).

[72] Buganza and della Valle (2010, p. 47).

[73] Murmann and Frenken (2006, p. 944).

[74] Murmann and Frenken (2006, p. 944).

4 Implications for European Competition Law

European competition law struggles to integrate innovation in its assessments due to its unpredictable and inherently uncertain nature. It is difficult in European competition law assessments to distinguish between the situation where innovation will affect the market power of big tech companies and the situation where it will not. Identifying in which phase of the industry life cycle the relevant market is and whether a dominant design has emerged, can clarify when and when not to consider innovation as a competitive pressure (Sect. 4.1). A dominant design on the core platform level also has consequences for merger control cases. This is specifically true when it concerns the ecosystem of the platform, which will flourish following the emergence of a dominant design (Sect. 4.2).

4.1 Dominant Designs in Abuse of Dominance Cases

European competition law currently looks at market power at one point of time in abuse of dominance cases. This is a static assessment of market power and innovation. Innovation is inherently dynamic, unpredictable, and uncertain. Identifying the broader pattern of the market and identifying whether a dominant design has emerged or not can help integrate innovation as a competitive constraint in European competition law.

Identifying the market phase can show to what extent we should value market shares in market power assessments. When the Commission determines market shares, it can simultaneously identify the market phase of the relevant market. The turning point is the emergence of a dominant design, which needs to comprise at least 50% of the designs in the market. The design also should be perceived as the archetype of the product in both the user and the designer imagination, answers the need of many people and freezes the socio-economic context.[75] These elements can be determined by using market and customer surveys. If none or just one of these elements is present, a dominant design has not yet emerged and innovation should be considered in the market power assessment. This means that the Commission and the CJEU should attach less value to market shares than after a dominant design has emerged, as has been done by the Commission and the CJEU in merger control cases.[76] If a majority of these elements are present, a dominant design has emerged and the CJEU and the Commission can use this to attach less value to innovation in the market power assessment. The industry life cycle or the concept of a dominant design is not the holy grail for assessing the constraining influence of innovation on market power but might be an element to consider.

For abuse of dominance cases, using the industry life cycle and the emergence of a dominant design can be a complementary factor for the CJEU and the Commission to

[75] Anderson et al. (1997).

[76] *Cisco v Commission*, para. 69.

determine if and if so, how to consider innovation in its assessment. When a dominant design has not been established, innovation could be a factor to consider in the market power assessment. Market power or a dominant position can be constrained by innovation and other factors need to therefore play a more prevailing role in assessing market power. For example, innovation in a general broad sense or innovative potential competitors as a competitive constraint could be considered. As markets may remain in the pre-dominant design state over several years—as we have seen in the case of operating systems and search engines—this might imply that the two-year threshold for potential competitors needs to be extended. After a dominant design has emerged, innovation is less likely to constrain market power due to the stability of the dominant core platform design and the CJEU and the Commission might be less inclined to consider innovation as a competitive constraint.

4.2 Dominant Designs in Merger Control Cases

For merger control, the industry life cycle and the concept of dominant design can inform the market power assessment in the same way as in abuse of dominant cases. The CJEU and the Commission have previously considered innovation as a competitive constraint on market power in specific cases. However, the concept of dominant design and the overall pattern of the industry life cycle might still be valuable for the assessment of market power. Once a dominant design has emerged, innovation should be awarded a less significant role in the market power assessment. Determining the market phase and whether a dominant design has emerged can be done by using market and customer surveys. The concepts might nuance or clarify why innovation is a competitive constraint in some cases, whereas in others it is not.

The fact that a dominant design has emerged, can be beneficial for the complementors that are dependent on the core platform and the rest of the ecosystem revolving around the core platform. These complementors are certain where to invest their money and know that they can build their business on the platform. This confirms the "rule" in competition law that an undertaking that has a dominant position is "not itself a recrimination but simply means that [...] the undertaking concerned has a special responsibility not to allow its conduct to impair genuine undistorted competition on the common market".[77] The dominance of a core platform is simply how the market works. Yet, in platform-mediated markets, it can also be observed that once a dominant platform design emerges, complementors become increasingly dependent on these dominant (online) platforms. The turning point of an emerging dominant design therefore might also signify the need for a closer scrutiny abuses of dominance and mergers. Undertakings inside and outside of the ecosystem of the core platform are then more vulnerable to abuse or killer acquisitions.

[77] *Michelin v Commission*, para. 57.

4.2.1 Dominant Design and Killer Acquisitions

In a killer acquisition theory of harm, it is not only competition that is killed, but also the product itself. In contrast, a potential competition theory of harm is less specific in that it simply requires that the potential competitive threat be removed or "killed" while the product itself may live on. The DMA combined with the new Guidance on Art. 22 of the Merger Regulation will ensure that more acquisitions by big tech companies will be reviewed. Yet, the fact that mergers and acquisitions will be notified, does not mean that the Commission and the CJEU have a theory of harm to assess these mergers and acquisition. It is still difficult to distinguish between situations in which innovation exerts a competitive pressure and when removing that pressure through an acquisition might be anticompetitive. The concept of dominant design might guide these decisions.

Whether a dominant design has emerged can be visualized on a spectrum. On the one end, there is the situation where there is no dominant design at all and undertakings compete on innovation. On the other end, a dominant design has emerged and there is no real competition for a new design. In the middle of the spectrum, a dominant design is emerging, and a shakeout of the market is slowly occurring. Where a market is on the spectrum can be determined using the four criteria for a dominant design: the design comprises at least 50% of the market, it should be perceived as the archetype of the product in both the user and the designer imagination, it answers the need of many people, and it freezes the socio-economic context.[78] If none of the criteria is fulfilled, the market is at the first end of the spectrum: there is no dominant design. If all criteria are fulfilled, a dominant design has fully emerged.

When the market transitions from one side of the spectrum (no dominant design) to the other side of the spectrum (a dominant design), a shake out occurs. This situation can be identified when just one or two of the criteria are fulfilled, acquisitions are a natural movement in the development of markets when a shakeout occurs. This shake out means that undertakings acquire other undertakings with similar designs. The less efficient competitors are taken over by the undertakings with a dominant design, as their designs become less attractive and less used by users and complementors. When a market is in this transition period, it might mean that it is not so much a killer acquisition but a natural shakeout of the market. This is a natural movement in the market, which does not cause any anti-competitive harms. However, once a dominant design has fully emerged, this motive for taking over a competing design might no longer be present.

The dominant design concept also shows that after a dominant design fully emerges for an online platform with an ecosystem, it seems unlikely that there will be a new competitor on the core platform level. If a platform acquires a new-and-upcoming design, which is gaining some ground in the market after a period of

---

[78] Anderson et al. (1997).

stability, the dominant design provides no explanation for the acquisition.[79] After such a dominant design emerges, it might be more likely that the motive for the acquisition is to kill the competing product or design. The dominant design only provides an explanation for the acquisition if the acquired undertaking is already stagnating or declining in its number of customers and therefore poses no threat to the acquiring undertaking.

4.2.2 Complementor Countervailing Power

Following the theory on dominant designs, innovation will not be able to be a countervailing power to the core platform once a platform has "won" the market, or in other words, has a dominant design. However, a stable core platform leads to benefits for complementors in the ecosystem. These complementors start growing in size and power once they know where to invest and in turn, they may become a countervailing power to the core platform.

There are some undertakings in the ecosystems of big tech companies that are starting to constrain the power of big tech companies. For example, in 2020 in the US, Epic Games updated its Fortnite app with a new feature that allowed consumers to pay Epic directly for in-app currency at a discount, rather than paying traditionally via Apple's App Store payment mechanism. Offering the option enabled Epic to skirt App Store rules that demanded payments go through the App Store payment system, paying a 30% fee in the process.[80] As was to be expected, Apple pulled the game from the App Store for violating the App Store guidelines within hours of the update's appearance. Similarly, Google also pulled the game from the Google Play Store, though on Android, the game was still available via third-party stores and from Epic directly.[81] The disagreement led to a court case, where it was confirmed that Apple was not a monopoly, and that Epic was not able to demonstrate Apple was engaging in monopolistic behavior. There was no evidence of other critical factors that would be considered antitrust behavior, such as barriers for entry and decreasing innovation in the market. Yet, Epic did achieve one goal: it will no longer be forced to abide by Apple's anti-steering policies, preventing them from saying there's other payment mechanisms available to consumers. In the court case, the judge acknowledges that Epic Games (as a complementor in the ecosystem) was not a small undertaking itself: "As a major player in the wider video gaming industry, Epic Games brought this lawsuit to challenge Apples control over access to a considerable portion of this submarket for mobile gaming transactions."[82] Both Epic and Apple appealed the judgment.

---

[79] It should be noted here that this is a still oversimplified representation of the analysis that could aid European competition law. There is a difference between horizontally competing designs, vertically competing designs and designs that have the ability to form a completely new market.

[80] Neely (2020a).

[81] Neely (2020b).

[82] *Epic Games v Apple Inc.*, 493 F. Supp. 3d 817 (N.D. Cal. 2020).

Interesting from this "Epic-battle" is the broader ramifications it had in both the uprising of complementors in the ecosystem and the subsequent regulatory responses. This initial battle between Epic and Apple attracted attention of other antitrust authorities, as Epic filed complaints in both Australia and the European Union with the European Commission and national antitrust authorities closely watching the Epic v Apple case as well.[83] Epic also joined forces with other complementors in the Apple ecosystem that were suffering from the Apple in-app commission rules and anti-steering provisions. Epic allegedly contacted other companies in a matter of weeks to try and create a so-called "coalition" of Apple critics.[84] The list of companies included Spotify, who came out in support of Epic's legal action shortly after it was filed. Spotify at that time was already engaging Apple via an antitrust complaint since 2019.[85] On September 29 2020, the Coalition for App Fairness was formed by several big-name app developers, among which Epic. The non-profit aims to highlight issues developers face when developing for the App Store.[86]

As we now know, the European Commission proposes in the DMA that Apple should allow for alternative app stores.[87] It also seems that anti-steering provisions will no longer be allowed, as per the DMA gatekeepers should allow business users to communicate and promote offers including under different conditions to end users acquired via the core platform service or through other channels, and to conclude contracts with these end users regardless of whether for that purpose they use the core platform services of the gatekeeper or not.[88]

In sum, once a dominant design has emerged complementors can grow their business on a stable core platform. This means that on the one hand complementors are dependent on the core platform but on the other hand—in time—can also become a countervailing power to the core platform. While this type of countervailing power is not considered in European competition law often (as, for example, countervailing buyer power), it might be worth examining whether this should happen in the future. As was the case with Epic as well, these complementors can also become "major players" that are not to be underestimated.

5 Conclusion

Innovation brings uncertainty and unpredictability to the market. Undertakings do not compete simultaneously for a share of the market, but sequentially for the market as a whole. This uncertainty is especially prominent in platform-mediated markets,

---

83 Epic Games (2021); Owen (2020); Busvine (2020); Reuters (2020).

84 Wingfield (2020).

85 Gallagher (2019).

86 Neely (2020c).

87 Article 6 (1) c DMA, Commission proposal.

88 Article 5 c DMA, Council proposal. I have used the wording in the Council proposal as it is better worded than the Commission's proposal.

where big tech companies with online platform compete for several markets at once. Innovation and the uncertainty it brings to markets poses a problem for European competition law, which focuses on static efficiencies that are measured at a certain point in time. The question therefore arises how European competition law can integrate innovation as a competitive constraint on online platforms' market power in platform-mediated markets.

Innovation studies move beyond static theories and conceptualize a more dynamic theory, the industry life cycle. The industry life cycle shows that all industries follow a similar pattern, where the emergence of a dominant design is the key turning point in when innovation is no longer a competitive constraint. It is this more dynamic theory that the CJEU and the Commission could use to both *nuance and inform* the role of innovation used in abuse of dominance and merger control cases. These theories will not replace the market power assessment but it could support the current assessments of market power.

How can the CJEU and the Commission use the industry life cycle and the concept of a dominant design to inform their current assessments? Before a dominant design has emerged, market power may be short-lived as innovation constrains it by letting a new undertaking suddenly taking over. Before the emergence of a dominant design, innovation could be a factor to consider in the market power assessment. However, after a dominant design has emerged, innovation is less likely to constrain market power.

The emergence of a dominant platform design can also have consequences for the ecosystem surrounding the online platform. Undertakings in the ecosystem of the core platform are dependent on the core platform. Once a dominant platform design emerges, it is unlikely that an alternative core platform will emerge. On the one hand, this makes the undertakings in the ecosystem very vulnerable for abuse by the core platform. On the other hand, stability of the core platform is beneficial to the undertakings in the ecosystem since they know where to invest their capital for a more certain future. Undertakings are subsequently able to grow and may become a countervailing power to the core platform as well, such as Epic is now constraining Apple's power in the App store market. European competition law could in the future consider both this vulnerability as well as this potential countervailing power.

In no way do I mean to claim that using the industry life cycle or dominant designs will completely solve the disconnect between the static nature of European competition law and the dynamic nature of innovation. However, it does seem clear that European competition law is currently not fully equipped to deal with innovation in its market power assessments. While there is no definitive answer as to how European competition law should integrate innovation in its assessments, the industry life cycle and dominant designs might be a first step in the direction of dealing with the dynamic force of innovation in the static analyses of European competition law.

References

Jurisprudence

Judgment of the Court of Justice 14 February 1978, *United Brands and United Brands Continentaal v Commission*, (Case 27/76), ECLI:EU:C:1978:22, paras 65 and 66
Judgment of the Court of Justice of 13 February 1979, *Hoffmann-La Roche v Commission* (Case 85/76), ECLI:EU:C:1979:36, paras 38–41
Judgment of the Court of Justice of 9 November 1983, *Michelin v Commission*, (C-322/81), ECLI:EU:C:1983:313, para. 30
Judgment of the Court of Justice of 3 July 1991, *AKZO v Commission*, (C-62/86), ECLI:EU:C:1991:286, para. 60
Judgment of the Court of Justice of 15 December 1994, *Gøttrup-Klim e.a. Grovvareforeninger v Dansk Landbrugs Grovvareselskab*, (C-250/92), ECLI:EU:C:1994:413, para. 47
Judgment of the Court of 2 April 2009, *France Télécom v Commission*, (C-202/07), ECLI:EU:C:2009:214, para. 100
Judgment of the Court of 4 June 2009, *T-Mobile Netherlands and Others*, (C-8/08), ECLI:EU:C:2009:343, paras 38 and 39
Judgment of the Court of First Instance of 12 December 1991, *Hilti v Commission*, (Case T-30/89), ECLI:EU:T:1991:70, paras 90–92
Judgment of the Court of First Instance of 29 June 1995, *Solvay v Commission*, (T-57/01), ECLI:EU:T:1995:115, para. 277
Judgment of the Court of First Instance of 25 March 1999, *Gencor v Commission*, (T-102/96), ECLI:EU:T:1999:65, paras 247–263
Judgment of the Court of First Instance of 25 June 2010, *Imperial Chemical v Commission*, (T-66/01), ECLI:EU:C:2010:221, paras 255–256 and 259
Judgment of the Court of First Instance of 29 March 2012, *Telefonica v Commission*, (T-336/07), ECLI:EU:C:2013:852, para. 148
Judgment of the Court of First Instance of 11 December 2013, *Cisco Systems v Commission*, (T-79/12), ECLI:EU:T:2013:635, para. 69
Judgment of the Court of First Instance of 10 November 2021, *Google Shopping v Commission*, (T-612/17), ECLI:EU:T:2021:763, paras 54 and 156
Epic Games v Apple Inc., 493 F. Supp. 3d 817 (N.D. Cal. 2020)

Commission decisions

Commission decision COMP/M.2256 pursuant to Article 6(1)(b) of Council Regulation No 4046/89, *Philips/Agilent Health Care Technologies*, SG(2000)D/286492, paras 31–32
Commission decision COMP/M.2609 pursuant to Article 6(1)(b) of Council Regulation No 4046/89, *HP/Compaq*, SG (2002) D/228300, para. 39
Commission Decision of 19 July 1991 declaring the compatibility with the common market of a concentration (Case No IV/M068 – Tetra Pak/Alfa-Laval) Council Regulation (EEC) No 4064/89, *OJ L 290, 22.10.1991*, pp. 35–43
Commission Decision of 4 December 1996 declaring a concentration to be incompatible with the common market and the functioning of the EEA Agreement (Case No IV/M.774 – Saint-Gobain/Wacker-Chemie/NOM) (Council Regulation (EEC) No 4064/89), *OJ L 247, 10.9.1997*, pp. 1–46, para. 184
Commission Decision of 3 May 2000 declaring a concentration to be compatible with the common market and the EEA Agreement (Council Regulation (EEC) No 4064/89) (Case No COMP/M.1693 — Alcoa/Reynolds), *OJ L 58, 28.2.2002*, pp 25–55, paras 31–32 and 38

Commission decision COMP/M.6281 pursuant to Article 6(1)(b) of Council Regulation No 139/2004, *Microsoft/Skype*, C(2011)7279, paras 78 and 99
Commission Decision of 03/10/2014 declaring a concentration to be compatible with the common market (Case No COMP/M.7217 – FACEBOOK / WHATSAPP) according to Council Regulation (EC) No 139/2004, *OJ C 7239, 03.10.2014,* para. 99
Commission Decision of 11/03/2008 declaring a concentration to be compatible with the common market and the functioning of the EEA Agreement (Case No COMP/M.4731 – Google/DoubleClick), *OJ C 184, 02.10.2007*
Commission Decision of 4 May 2017 relating to a proceeding under Article 102 of the Treaty on the Functioning of the European Union and Article 54 of the EEA Agreement (Case AT.40153 — E-Book MFNS and related matters) (notified under document C(2017) 2876), *OJ C 264, 11.8.2017*, pp 7–10, para. 58
Commission decision of 27 June 2017 relating to a proceeding under Article 102 of the Treaty on the Functioning of the European Union and Article 54 of the EEA Agreement (Case AT.39740 — Google Search (Shopping)) (notified under document number C(2017) 4444), *OJ C 9, 12.1.2018*, pp 11–14, para. 267
Commission Decision of 18 July 2018 relating to a proceeding under Article 102 of the Treaty on the Functioning of the European Union and Article 54 of the EEA Agreement (Case AT.40099 — Google Android) (notified under document C(2018) 4761) 2019/C 402/08 C/2018/4761, *OJ C 402, 28.11.2019*, pp 19–22, para 439

Regulations, Guidelines and Communication

Council Regulation (EC) No 139/2004 of 20 January 2004 on the control of concentrations between undertakings (the EC Merger Regulation), *OJ L 24 29.1.2004*, pp 1–21
Guidelines on the assessment of horizontal mergers under the Council Regulation on the control of concentrations between undertakings. *OJ C 31, 5.2.2004*, pp 5–18
Communication from the Commission – Guidance on the Commission's enforcement priorities in applying Article 82 of the EC Treaty to abusive exclusionary conduct by dominant undertakings, *OJ C 45, 24.2.2009*, pp 7–20
Commission Staff Working Document. Executive Summary of the Impact Assessment Report Accompanying the document Proposal for a Regulation of the European Parliament and of the Council on contestable and fair markets in the digital sector (Digital Markets Act), COM(2020) 842 final, SEC(2020) 437 final, SWD(2020) 363 final

Literature

Alphabet (2022) Annual Report 2022. https://abc.xyz/investor/static/pdf/20220202_alphabet_10K.pdf?cache=fc81690. Last access 25 July 2022
Anderson P, Tushman ML (1990) Technological discontinuities and dominant designs: a cyclical model of technological change. Quarterly 35(4)
Anderson P, Tushman ML, O'Reilly C (1997) Technology cycles, innovation streams and ambidextrous organizations. In: Anderson P, Tushman M (eds) Managing strategic innovation and change. Oxford University Press. https://www.hbs.edu/faculty/Pages/item.aspx?num=803. Last access 25 July 2022
Buganza T, della Valle E (2010) The search engine industry. In: Ceri S, Brambilla M (eds) Search computing: challenges and directions, p 319

Busvine D (2020) Apple-Epic row being closely watched by German antitrust chief (Reuters, 2 September 2020). https://www.reuters.com/article/us-apple-epic-games-germany-idUSKBN25T1QS. Last access 25 July 2022

Costa-Cabral F (2018) Innovation in EU competition law: the resource-based view and disruption. Yearbook Eur Law 37:305–343. https://doi.org/10.1093/yel/yey019(lastaccess25July2022)

Crocioni P (2008) Leveraging of market power in emerging markets: a review of cases, literature, and a suggested framework. J Compet Law Econ 4(2):449–534. https://doi.org/10.1093/joclec/nhm018. Last access 25 July 2022

Epic Games (2021) Epic game files EU antitrust complaint against apple. https://www.epicgames.com/site/en-US/news/epic-games-files-eu-antitrust-complaint-against-apple. Last access 25 July 2022

Fan L, Suh YH (2014) Why do users switch to a disruptive technology? an empirical study based on expectation-disconfirmation theory. Inform Manage 51(2):240–248. https://doi.org/10.1016/j.im.2013.12.004. Last access 25 July 2022

Gallagher W (2019) Spotify accuses Apple of anti-competitive practices in Europe over App Store restrictions. Apple Insider. https://appleinsider.com/articles/19/03/13/spotify-accuses-apple-of-anti-competitive-practices-in-europe-over-app-store-restrictions. Last access 25 July 2022

Gregory Sidak J, Teece DJ (2009) Dynamic competition in antitrust law. J Compet Law Econ 5(4):581–631. https://doi.org/10.1093/joclec/nhp024. Last access 25 July 2022

Hollingsworth S (2020) DuckDuckGo versus google: an in-depth search engine comparison. https://www.searchenginejournal.com/google-vs-duckduckgo/301997/#close. Last access 25 July 2022

Hummel LMF (2022) Dominant design or dominant positions? In: Conference proceedings EU antitrust: hot topics and next steps international conference, 24–25 January in Prague, Czechia

Katz ML (2021) Big tech mergers: innovation, competition for the market, and the acquisition of emerging competitors. Inf Econ Policy 54. https://doi.org/10.1016/j.infoecopol.2020.100883. Last access 25 July 2022

Katz ML, Shapiro C (1994) Systems competition and network effects. J Econ Perspect 8

Katz ML, Shelanski HA (2007) Mergers and innovation. http://www.usdoj.gov/atr/. Last access 25 July 2022

Kenney M, Bearson D, Zysman J (2021) The platform economy matures: measuring pervasiveness and exploring power. Soc Econ Rev. https://doi.org/10.1093/ser/mwab014. Last access 25 July 2022

Kolasky W and Dick A (2003) The merger of guidelines and the integration of efficiencies into antitrust review of horizontal mergers. Antitrust J 17:207–225. http://law.bepress.com/wilmer/art31. Last access 25 July 2022

Markovic M, Draskovic N, Gnjidic V (2018) Product innovation, process innovation and competitive lessons from consumer electronics industry. Ann DAAAM Proceed Int DAAAM Sympo 29(1):0004–0008. https://doi.org/10.2507/29th.daaam.proceedings.001. Last access 25 July 2022

Meta (2022) Annual Report 2021. https://d18rn0p25nwr6d.cloudfront.net/CIK-0001326801/14039b47-2e2f-4054-9dc5-71bcc7cf01ce.pdf. Last access 25 July 2022

Moore JF (1996) The death of competition: leadership & strategy in the age of business ecosystems. Harper Collins

Murmann JP, Frenken K (2006) Toward a systematic framework for research on dominant designs, technological innovations, and industrial change. Res Policy 35(7):925–952. https://doi.org/10.1016/j.respol.2006.04.011. Last access 25 July 2022

Neely A (2020a) Epic skirts Apple's 30% commission fee by implementing "direct" payments. Apple Insider. https://appleinsider.com/articles/20/08/13/epic-skirts-apples-30-commission-fee-by-implementing-direct-payments. Last access 25 July 2022

Neely A (2020b) Apple pulls Fortnite from App Store for sidestepping commission fee. Apple Insider. https://appleinsider.com/articles/20/08/13/apple-pulls-fortnite-from-app-store-for-sidestepping-commission-fee. Last access 25 July 2022

Neely A (2020c) Coalition for App Fairness unites developers to fight Apple's App Store fees and policies. Apple Insider. https://appleinsider.com/articles/20/09/24/coalition-for-app-fairness-unites-developers-to-fight-apples-app-store-fees-and-policies. Last access 25 July 2022

OECD (2012) The role of efficiency claims in antitrust proceedings 2012. http://www.oecd.org/daf/competition/. Last access 25 July 2022

OECD (2020a) Merger control in dynamic markets

OECD (2020b) Start-ups, killer acquisitions and merger control

Owen M (2020) Epic Games brings "Fortnite" fight with Apple to Australia's courts. Apple Insider. https://appleinsider.com/articles/20/11/17/epic-games-brings-fortnite-fight-with-apple-to-australias-courts. Last access 25 July 2022

Ozalp H, Cennamo C, Gawer A (2018) Disruption in platform-based ecosystems. J Manage Stud 55(7):1203–1241. https://doi.org/10.1111/joms.12351. Last access 25 July 2022

Porter ME (1980) Industry structure and competitive strategy: keys to profitability. Financ Anal J 36(4):30–41. https://doi.org/10.2469/faj.v36.n4.30. Last access 25 July 2022

Taleby M, Li Q, Rabbani M, Raza A (2017) A survey on smartphones security: software vulnerabilities, malware, and attacks. Int J Adv Comput Sci Appl 8(10). https://doi.org/10.14569/ijacsa.2017.081005. Last access 25 July 2022

Tushman ML, Murmann JP (1998) Dominant designs, technology cycles, and organization outcomes. Acad Manage Proceed 1–33

Utterback JM, Abernathy WJ (1975) A Dynamic model of process and product innovation. Int J Manage Sci 3(6):639–656

Wingfield N (2020) Epic games seeks to form coalition of apple critics. Information. https://www.theinformation.com/articles/epic-games-seeks-to-form-coalition-of-apple-critics. Last access 25 July 2022

Zeijen A et al (forthcoming) Dominant platform designs and industry lifecycles in platform-mediated industries

Lisanne M. F. Hummel is a PhD candidate in EU competition law at Utrecht University. Her fields of interest include EU competition law, Big Tech, Digital Markets, Innovation, Law and Technology.

Part VI: General and Global Perspectives

Rules and Nudging as Code: Is This the Future for Legal Drafting Activities?

Rute Saraiva

Abstract In the advent of a risk society in which even a more conservative area such as the Law begins to understand, transfer and use technology, in addition to regulating it, with blockchain potential in terms of contracts or artificial intelligence with chatbots for legal advice. Also, voices are being raised in favour of machine-consumable legislation and intelligent nudging, in order to increase legislative effectiveness, efficiency and transparency, thus enhancing compliance at a lower cost thanks to greater simplicity, lower error rate, clarity, accessibility and accountability. The traditional models of drafting and applying legislation were constructed to be used in a non-digital environment, especially because of the underlying hermeneutics process, although it may be interpreted and transformed in a more automatic and operational way in certain topics such as taxing or social security. Nevertheless, the cost required to understand and comply is often disproportionate comparing with the benefit of compliance. Therefore, there seems to be a language gap between production and consumption of legal rules. A (new) solution for this problem may lie in machine-consumable legislation, i.e. transforming legal text, concepts and rules (e.g. procedures, requirements and exemptions) into code that can be read, understood and interacted with by specific software. Also (legal) nudging can benefit from a more technological approach, by helping simplifying and making behaviour more automatic in the "right" direction. The digital world is already well aware of the power of nudging. It is time for the law and policy makers to grasp or at least look at similar instruments. The challenge to overcome the legal language and implementation disparity with technology in a digital era, which is still at an embryonic stage, despite its potential, presents several obstacles, from legal conservatism and a tendency towards inertia, to issues of legal certainty and the loss of humanism. Thus, this chapter intends, beyond a survey of the state of the art of rulemaking and nudging as code, to understand how it could work, its advantages and pitfalls, preferential areas of application, caution and limits in its implementation.

R. Saraiva (✉)
University of Lisbon Law School, Alameda da Universidade, 1649-014 Lisbon, Portugal
e-mail: rutesaraiva@fd.ulisboa.pt

K. Mathis and A. Tor (eds.), *Law and Economics of the Digital Transformation*, Economic Analysis of Law in European Legal Scholarship 15,
https://doi.org/10.1007/978-3-031-25059-0_12

Keywords Accountability · Algorithmic law · Artificial intelligence · Better legislation · Data-driven law · Efficiency · Governance · Government-as-a-platform · Human rights · Innovation · Law in natural language · Legal interpretation · LegalTech, RegTech and SupTech · Machinable-consumable legislation · Nudging · Personalization · Rule-as-code · Separation of powers · Translation gap · Transparency

> Thus when a man takes on absolute power, he first thinks of simplifying the law. In such a state one begins to be more affected by technicalities than by the freedom of the people, about which one no longer cares at all. – Montesquieu

1 Introduction

Advances and technological leaps accelerated in recent decades, having left marks on society with impacts on human and social behaviour and, consequently, on Law, in a context of globalization and transformation, in a trend of creative destruction. Two major lines of influence can be observed in the legal world: on the one hand, in the Law of Technology and, on the other, in the Technology of Law. The first deals with a myriad of new formal, substantive, procedural and adjective legal problems arising from the introduction and use of new technologies in social life. The second focuses on the development of technological information and communication tools that can and are increasingly used in the professional daily life of jurists, from the lawyer to the judge. However, in this new context, not only is a new profile of legal professionals necessary, but their training must be rethought, particularly in Law Schools.[1] Furthermore, the legislative process itself, from policy-making to the application of norms, whether by the Administration, the courts or individuals, must be revisited and reconsidered in the light of the inevitable and unstoppable socio-economic digitalization, considering the noble functions of Law in society: instrumental, constitutional, political, democratic, expressive and symbolic.[2]

Therefore, in the advent of a risk and information society in which even a more conservative area such as the Law begins to understand, transfer and use technology, in addition to regulating it, with blockchain potential in terms of contracts or artificial intelligence with chatbots for legal advice. Also, voices are being raised in favour of machine-consumable legislation and intelligent nudging, in order to increase legislative effectiveness, efficiency and transparency, thus enhancing compliance at a lower cost thanks to greater simplicity, lower error rate, clarity, accessibility and accountability.

The traditional models of drafting and applying legislation were constructed to be used in a non-digital environment, especially because of the underlying hermeneutics process, although it may be interpreted and transformed in a more automatic and

---

[1] About this topic, Saraiva (2020).

[2] Voermans (2009, pp. 61–62).

operational way in certain topics such as taxing or social security. Nevertheless, the cost required to understand and comply is often disproportionate comparing with the benefit of compliance. Therefore, there seems to be a language gap[3] between production and consumption of legal rules.

A (new) solution for this problem may lie in machine-consumable legislation, i.e. transforming legal text, concepts and rules (e.g. procedures, requirements and exemptions) into code that can be read, understood and interacted with by specific software, turning traditional law into legal micro-directives.[4] Also (legal) nudging can benefit from a more technological approach, by helping simplifying and making behaviour more automatic in the "right" direction, mainly by augmenting the scale and the personalization with precision nudging through machine learning, AI (Artificial Intelligence) and open data.[5] The digital world is already well aware of the power of nudging. It is time for the law and policy makers to grasp or at least look at similar instruments as an additional tool boosted by technology.[6]

The challenge to overcome the legal language and implementation disparity with technology in a digital era, which is still at an embryonic stage, despite its potential, presents several obstacles, from legal conservatism and a tendency towards inertia, to issues of legal certainty and the loss of humanism. Thus, this chapter intends, beyond a survey of the state of the art of rulemaking and nudging as code, to understand how it could work, its advantages and pitfalls, preferential areas of application, caution and limits in its implementation.

2 No Country for Old Men: The Need for New Law-Making

2.1 It's a New e-Day

It is a truism to say that the world has been evolving extremely fast in recent decades, largely on the back of technological innovations and growing transversal macro-digitization, despite differences in pace depending on latitude or sector.

In fact, on the ride of technology, with the massification and omnipresence of the internet, smartphones, apps and social media and the development of AI and machine-learning, some disruptive trends are reinforced on an institutional system based on physicality. On the one hand, in parallel with the deepening of the Digital Economy (and even digital social relations), there is a phenomenon of dematerialization and disintermediation of the economy, with electronic commerce and financial products and services being paradigmatic. On the other hand, there is increased and flexible mobility with the facilitated circulation of production factors and citizens,

3 The terminology varies from author to author, with frequent terms such as language gap, translation gap and hermeneutics gap.

4 Eliot (2021a).

5 On personalized nudging, for all, Hrnjic and Tomczak (2019), Mills (2020).

6 Franco (2019), Greveler (2017).

boosted by the globalization and progress in transport, technology and in international understandings on minimizing barriers to movement (cf. WTO). In addition, there is a "capitalism of intangibles",[7] with these factors (e.g. intellectual and industrial property, data, software, know-how) representing a growing share of the world's wealth, gradually replacing land, equity and securities.

Now globalization, digitization, dematerialization and mobility are correlated with legislative competition, including international tax competition, despite an observable phenomenon of legal mimicry, sometimes with legal transplants and enhanced in various sectors by the more or less harmful "subliminal" and expressive power of soft law,[8] with States seeking to either protect themselves or to gain competitive advantages. Such may cause, on the one hand, a race to the bottom, and, on the other hand, phenomena of rule/treaty/jurisdiction shopping and law arbitrage, particularly in view of the inadequacy of the connection elements, largely based on the physical dimension of territoriality both for the residence or domicile and the source (and permanent establishment), as identified by the OECD BEPS project, in the search for a digital taxation to accompany the digitization of markets and taxpayers. This type of behaviour in addition reveals an inversion of the power relationship between the State and the citizens, in which the latter, as a result of increased mobility and digitization, choose which jurisdiction they want to be connected with, instead of the more established passive solution.[9]

Hence, some authors question themselves about the loss or fragmentation of state sovereignty, namely in terms of traditional functions and prerogatives of the State, such as the tax component,[10] especially given that an increase in multilateralism is observed (whether through phenomena of international cooperation or integration regional) and also the emergence of new actors, such as society and civil platforms, markets or multinationals. Regardless of the answer to this question, not least because international self-binding is as well, in essence, an expression of sovereignty, the doctrine[11] seems to be generically inclined to identify the inadequacy of a classical State based on physicality and very bureaucratized, namely regarding one of its oldest functions and most relevant power, law-making, in the face of an accelerated, changeable, fluid, complex, interconnected and interdependent reality, with constant passages between areas, levels, jurisdictions, languages and legal traditions. As paradigmatic examples, attention should be paid to the environmental, energy or financial areas, which, due to their transversality and globality, cross legislative and regulatory ecosystems.

---

[7] Rosado Pereira (2021, p. 40).

[8] In certain areas, such as the environment or financial markets, soft law proves to be a true hard law or hoft law and encourages a functional understanding of the sources of law and serves as an engine for legal and regulatory development and a tendency to harmonize the various legal systems. Saraiva (2015), Brummer (2011).

[9] Calçada Pires (2018, p. 410).

[10] Rosado Pereira (2021, pp. 45–470), Calçada Pires (2018, pp. 27 et seqq.).

[11] For all, Mohun and Roberts (2020, pp. 8 et seqq.).

This mismatch explains, on the one side, a state and, in particular, a legislative power under pressure and, on the other, an increase in distrust of public authorities and the expansion of a phenomenon of fake news and conspiracy theories linked to incorrect and/or creative interpretations and perceptions of the Law,[12] conditioning the beliefs and attitudes of citizens and addressees of the rules and helping to explain the rise of populist movements.

It seems, therefore, that it is time for a new era of Law, an era of consent and information, through the gathering of technological and volitional means for this endeavour.[13]

2.2 *Mind the Gap*

Despite efforts around the world, in particular in developed countries, of digital transition and updating of the State and of its various functions and powers, there is still a breach between the digitization of the State, especially regarding the rule-making dimension, and society, associated with a phenomenon of status quo bias and greater ballast and less flexibility in the face of changes in public institutions, largely shaped by their institutional and traditional weight.

2.2.1 Old School Rules

Taking the Portuguese example, a country of the OECD and the EU, part of the Civil Law family, the main legal source has long been, and continues to be, the law (in a formal sense). Now, an analysis of the Portuguese legal system, particularly legistic and legislative, quickly reveals that, despite some ameliorations, it proves to be quite conservative and complex and that, fundamentally, it maintains a business-as-usual logic in which laws emerge as the default solution to solve any identified social problem.

Indeed, and considering the disruptive example of the Covid-19 pandemic, several lessons can be learned with the case of the Portuguese legislature[14]:

1. The inadequacy and rigidity of the existing legal framework. Despite the somewhat imaginative interpretation and application of certain pre-existing legislation, such as the biweekly reiteration of the state of emergency or the use of the Civil Protection Law and the Public Health Law, its limitation was evident, all the more

[12] Mohun and Roberts (2020, p. 7).

[13] Eliot (2021b).

[14] In general, with better regulation concerns, especially in terms of risk, during the pandemic, see: OECD Regulatory Policy Outlook 2021 https://www.oecd.org/gov/regulatory-policy/oecd-regulatory-policy-outlook-2021-38b0fdb1-en.htm (last access 05 May 2022); and OECD Regulatory Policy and the COVID-19 Crisis https://www.oecd.org/gov/regulatory-policy/reg-covid-19-activities.htm (last access 05 May 2022).

so as the Civil and, later, the Constitutional Court were recognizing its misuse.[15] Furthermore, there was a gap between the legislator's intention in creating those diplomas and rules and their concrete implementation in cases not previously considered;

2. The moroseness and complexity of the legistic and legislative process and the interconnection between areas of application and laws. Early on, it was realized that there were no adequate rules to deal with the pandemic, namely with the restriction or suspension of fundamental rights and the imposition of new duties, such as the duty of isolation, and that a new health emergency law and a constitutional review—namely with regard to the declaration of a State of emergency—would be necessary. Now, despite this evidence, today, more than two years after the beginning of the pandemic in Portugal, neither of the two is even drafted, because of the always complicated need for parliamentary agreements and diplomacy between constitutional bodies, the requirement to hear a multiplicity of experts and stakeholders, and because of requests for legislative restraint (which ironically did not happen during this period, quite the contrary) due to the difficulty of the topic and to avoid weak solutions made under pressure, without the due distance or study (including impact assessment), pushing therefore the problem forward, especially as the salience of the pandemic diminishes;
3. If some new solutions take time to emerge from political discourse, the covidian period proved to be prodigal in the multiplication of legislation, regulation, and bureaucratization, from the definition of restrictive measures (often already prethought and built before the hearing of "specialists"), with changes almost every two weeks, to support for families and companies, including the redefinition of State tasks. Thus, not only is it considered, in a very paternalistic way, that it is up to the State to solve each and every problem, but that the law is the solution of all evils, its elaboration and publication functioning as a placebo that, even if not feasible or adequate, calms both its addressees and gives the (false) sense of duty fulfilled to the State, especially when supported, even if in a "pro forma" exercise, by the opinion of experts. Other options that could, in the specific context, be more efficient, such as economic instruments, nudges and ruling-without-rules solutions[16]—assuming that it is appropriate to intervene—, are not properly considered, with costs in terms of welfare;
4. The Covid-19 episode only highlights an old trend of "legislarrhea", "regularrhea" and bureaucracy,[17] in which diplomas and procedures are becoming more complex, lengthy and interconnected, with an increasing radius of action, touching almost all aspects of life in society. Just remember that there is (unnecessary) legislation on quality standards for bananas (including shape) or the musical

[15] For all, about Covidian normative production in Portugal and its limits: Lanceiro (2020a, b), Violante and Lanceiro (2020a, b), Botelho (2020a). Regarding constitutional considerations, among others: Botelho (2020b, pp. 9–57), Reis Novais (2020), Reis Novais and Nogueira de Brito (2020), Melo Alexandrino (2020), Costa Gonçalves (2020).

[16] Lorini and Moroni (2020).

[17] Voermans (2009, p. 78). On quantitative data on legislative production in Portugal, Rodrigues (2018).

band in bullfights[18] or that financial activity and financial instruments only had a handful of articles in the 1888 commercial code and, today, in addition to three national diplomas with hundreds of provisions for banking, securities and insurance, in the process of consolidated review, it is necessary to attend to countless international and European rules of direct application;

5. In the Portuguese case, part of the enormous flow of legislation, due to the technical-scientific nature of the basic problem, involved the consultation of expert committees and working groups (for example, on education, health, models, risk, behaviour), gradually evolving into government requests for the definition of public policy guidelines. However, although consulting the opinions and recommendations of these more or less inorganic structures, we may observe that political and later legal decisions do not always reflect the options proposed by specialists. They unveil the correct option of the decision to be, in the end, political (and informed), because of its democratic legitimacy and macro and integrated vision which has to weigh multiple interests that are not necessarily convergent. However, despite the goodness of the transparency of the consultation process (although with some advances and setbacks), this generates among the citizens some misapprehension regarding the decisions taken and designed since they diverge, totally (e.g. closing schools in March 2020) or partially (e.g. degree and pace of restrictions and their lifting) of those pointed out by the experts. In other words, there is a visible gap between "science", public policies, their regulation and finally their application, increasing the noise in terms of comprehension and interpretation and showing a misalignment between the intentions initially declared and those revealed in the implementation;
6. The inadequacy, complexity, interconnection of matters and proliferation of rules leads to a gap and even a handicap between the elaboration of rules and their publication and application by public services and agencies and by private agents. The implementation is not always feasible or enforceable or yet consistent with the legislator's initial intention. The Portuguese law on telework passed during this pandemic phase is paradigmatic: it has caused huge headaches both for private actors (bosses and workers), and for the Public Administration itself and its employees, in the implementation of the definition, calculation and payment of costs added to the worker for reasons of teleworking and in its (un)expected tax implication. Remember also the support for the lay-off in a first phase, whose opacity generated requests below the expected and budgeted, or, ridiculously, the imposition of certified tests for access to certain activities, which, given their scarcity, slowness and above all, onerousness, forced an administrative "desk" interpretation with the acceptance of self-tests provided they were carried out or supervised by an employee of the activity in question (with several, for example restaurant owners, refusing to assume the role of health inspection agents, in addition to the fact that, given the high number of establishments in the country, assessment of compliance would, by definition, be derisory);

[18] Silveira (2018, p. 179).

7. The reasons mentioned above explain, in themselves, the difficulty of not only not knowing for sure which rules are in force, but also their interpretation and the understanding of the "real" intention of the legislator on the part of their final addressees. In the intricate web of resolutions and Covidian decrees, not always published in a consolidated way, with references to other diplomas (even if with hyperlinks) and with the presentation of the mere amended paragraphs, it was easy to see that government officials and supervisory authorities sometimes did not acknowledge what was in effect, and thus less did citizens or companies. The interpretation, often made according to the need to confront reality and fringe cases that were not initially addressed (e.g. sale of alcohol during the night period by online companies; relevant area of the commercial establishment for the purposes of opening or closing), was different depending on the public and private agents, in a true "desk law" (e.g. commercial associations; police authorities; municipal entities; social services; health authorities). If at times it gained some authentic dimension from diploma to diploma every 15 days with corrections and clarifications during its revision, at other times it generated costly disagreements, not only for the addressees of the rules (e.g. due to increased transaction costs, inefficient allocation of resources, sanctions for non-compliance, freezing of activity, loss of support for not grasping the eligibility or calculation criteria), but also for the State itself (e.g. non-compliance and misalignment with its objectives, increased inspection costs, misallocation of resources);
8. It is easy to see that the ubiquity, complexity and onerousness of regulations, with incomprehensible and impracticable rules, have boosted the intermediation of jurists (as liberal professionals or as members or workers of public, private or social institutions), who, together with journalists and traditional and social media, served as translators of the legislative intent, streamlining the understanding of the norms for their recipients. Often, law firms, together with trade and professional associations, released newsletters with interpretative clarifications, sometimes in line with the official version released in the meantime by the authorities (in view of the interpretative doubts that were raised during the implementation process), others trying to seek to condition the interpretation to the interests of the sector. In other words, there is intermediation and agency of legislative interpretation by multiple stakeholders, which translates into the potential for misalignments between the legislator's intent and the final application of the rules and an increased burden for end users, with costs in terms of confidence in the State and legal security, with the potential for conspiracy theories, populism and resistance to law enforcement;
9. Finally, it was observed, as a rule, an effective implementation of normative provisions, even the restrictive and suspensive ones of fundamental rights (though most likely unconstitutional), and the compliance behavior of the majority of their addressees (who incidentally, in several cases, as in the obligation of masking or confinement, behaviorally anticipated the rules), hence verifying the importance of the alignment between the social rules, which can work as nudges, and

the adopted legal norms. Therefore, one should consider, in the adhesion and enforcement of the Law, the power of social acceptability and normativity.[19]

This illustrative example shows that the legislator is under constant high pressure to legislate fast and well, in time, quantity and quality. That is, legislation must be created and implemented in good time, taking into account an enormous amount of data, and must be proportionate (necessary, adequate and not excessive), effective, efficient, equitable and generating welfare gains. On the other hand, norms must be accessible and well communicated in order to be well understood and applied. Finally, they must be coherent and certain, yet sufficiently adaptable to a real context that is constantly changing.

However, in the face of this Herculean challenge, the general assessment is of failure and difficulty in the traditional model of legisprudence and legislation to accompany reality and citizens with increased expectations and scrupulous, who assume a relationship of greater parity with the State, as "clients" and "consumers" of legislative services,[20] demanding greater competence (with fewer errors, costs and delays and higher levels of productivity), consistency, transparency, accountability and closer and more personalized treatment.

Indeed, it is often observed that, as demonstrated by the case of Covid-19 law, there is an inconsistency and misalignment between policy-making and rule-making because, more often than not, they are processes carried out separately, with no institution having a holistic view of the whole process. After all, either the law is a mere by-product of policy-making or it is its trigger for needing adjustments or a more comprehensive treatment or, still, it is its limit and parameter for revealing, during its implementation, impacts that were not anticipated and also greater complexity, due, in particular, to the high degree of interconnection between matters (and, therefore, legal and regulatory diplomas).[21] In other words, a divorce is to be expected between the needs felt at the time of the legislative process (and the corresponding political will) and the needs revealed by reality at the time of application (sometimes much later), namely because of variables not previously identified or by fringe cases that do not fit perfectly into the established rules.

In this way, three main problems, which will tend to worsen with the acceleration of socio-economic digitization, can be identified in terms of the current state of legisprudence and legislative activity[22]:

1. Divorce between language and application;
2. Complexity;
3. Inefficiency.

Let us start with the first one.

---

19 Franco (2018).

20 Cabugueira (2020, p. 11).

21 Mohun and Roberts (2020 pp. 93–94).

22 Mohun and Roberts (2020 pp. 32 et seqq.).

Lost in Translation: The Divorce Between Language and Enforcement

The current legislative process has been trying to be schematized according to three major models: a linear and sequential model, in which the procedural stages from the identification of the problem to be addressed to the implementation and evaluation of the norms follow one another on a regular basis; a circular model functionally succeeding the political cycle[23]; and a model, now more consensual, of non-linear and contextual evolution, depending on the actors involved and their interactions, as well as on anchoring processes.[24] Regardless of its conceptualization, the legislative process goes through several relatively stagnant phases that involve actors with different interests, methodologies and working methods (experts, policy makers, legal firms—centralized or sub-contracted, government officials, parliamentarians and regulatory agencies, implementing agencies and end users), with various moments of translation (of terminology, concepts, semantics) and interpretation, i.e. "rulemaking is thus not just a technocratic exercise—rules are a manifestation of power, and so is their interpretation and application."[25]

The hermeneutic dimension cannot therefore be forgotten, all the more so since, at the present time, it is multi-level and multi-institutional, which gives rise to growing problems of alignment and errors between the legislator's will and its implementation by the end users, and therefore of judgment and decision, especially in a context of celerity and legislative massification. For the purposes of defending the Rule as Code (RaC) and its conceptualization from the beginning of the legal process, let us point the fact that several firms and activities, individually, with a greater or lesser support of "translators" and in-house legal interpreters or subcontractors, transform into code certain rules traditionally elaborated in natural language and in a human-readable format (e.g. tax, financial, social support, urban planning and building regulations, eligibility or calculation) to be read and used by machines (computers) in order to ensure their best and broadest compliance. Just remember invoicing or payment software with automatic application of tax rules, including for withholding purposes, in legally established cases. Or, for example, the practice, often verified with delivery services, particularly public ones, of the existence of a "Desk Law", which results from the interpretation and consequent misaligned application of norms with the legislative intent or from subsequent changes by the administrative services, who repeat endlessly what they have always done, losing in time the origin of that translation. The recent "Russiagate" at Lisbon City Council is paradigmatic, in which, under the automated procedures of decades, without its modernization in the face of the new data protection legislation or its updated interpretation and with a later established loss of the historical root of those judgments and decision, personal information of protesters who gathered in front of the Russian embassy in Lisbon was sent (in addition to many other situations of data sharing with other entities) to the Russian authorities, putting them in danger. The Municipality was convicted

---

[23] Cabugueira (2020, p. 10).

[24] Mohun and Roberts (2020 pp. 29–30).

[25] Mohun and Roberts (2020, p. 30).

and fined in circa one million euros for more than two hundred violations, the final amount having been mitigated because of the pandemic.[26]

There is therefore the risk of misinterpretations of the true legislative intent and of non-compliance costs proportional to the various levels of translation and interpretation and to the scale of dissemination and application of the final software or of "desk" interpretation. Thus, an integrated and systematic approach to RaC, which simultaneously accompanies the human-readable law process, can help to identify critical moments and potential problems in translation and interpretation, minimizing (but not totally eliminating) misalignments and the inherent costs, including in terms of legal certainty.[27]

In other words, there is opacity in the legislative process, even if democratic and participatory, since its hermeticity and successive hermeneutic complexity tend to distance the interpretation and the final code from its origin, especially since mere changes in punctuation or the intervention of an elite of law firms in the elaboration of draft legislation (whether integrated into working groups, or as advisors, or even as turnkey drafters of diplomas) can introduce noise in the hermeneutic and implementation exercise and generate distrust regarding the State, due to the perception of intentionality of interpretive ambiguity, benefiting those who wrote or helped to write the rules (namely favouring clientele or being paid to provide an interpretive opinion for clarification). In Portugal, where the parliamentary legislative process is more complex than the governmental one,[28] as it involves more actors, legislative initiatives of more diverse origins and more intricate approval procedures, three relatively controversial and mediatic cases exemplify the perception of this misalignment of interests and wills and the consequent narrative of lack of transparency and capture of the legislative process.[29]

Firstly, the holding of a parliamentary inquiry commission, in 1993, convened to ascertain the veracity of a journalist's allegations that someone connected to the legislature had been paid to change a comma in a certain diploma in order to favour a minister. In the end, it was not possible to prove (or disprove) the allegations.

---

[26] https://expresso.pt/sociedade/2022-01-14-russiagate-camara-municipal-de-lisboa-multada-em-mais-de-um-milhao-de-euros (last access 12 May 2022).

[27] Waddington (2019, p. 46), Mohun and Roberts (2020, p. 34).

[28] Assembleia da República (2020, pp. 9, 11–13).

[29] Recall other historic American cases related to the change of commas in a process of legislative review, such as the one referring to the Ulysses S. Grant tariff law, whose list of exemptions went from "fruit-plants, tropical and semi-tropical for the purpose of propagation or cultivation" to "fruit, plants, tropical and semi-tropical for the purpose of propagation or cultivation", thus exempting the fruits and creating a loss of two million dollars in tax revenue collection. Also a comma in a regulation allowed Oakhurst Dairy truck drivers to receive millions for unpaid overtime. The regulation provided: "The canning, processing, preserving, freezing, drying, marketing, storing, packing for shipment or distribution of: (1) Agricultural produce; (2) Meat and fish products; and (3) Perishable foods." Now, without the comma after "shipment", the expression "packing for shipment or distribution" refers to a single activity. After all, truck drivers do not pack food and therefore these exemptions do not apply to them. Cf. https://www.newyorker.com/culture/culture-desk/a-few-words-about-that-ten-million-dollar-serial-comma?mbid=social_facebook (last access 05 May 2022).

Secondly, an opinion from the Transparency Commission of the Assembly of the Republic admits that deputies who receive a 10% increase in their salary under the exclusivity regime can also hold positions in different entities as long as they do not receive any remuneration. However, the 2019 Remuneration Statute of Holders of Political Positions would have been written in the opposite direction, with the interpretative difference residing in the placement of a comma.[30] Finally, the correspondence between the lawyers of a public manager and the Minister of Finance raised doubts when the approved diploma that amended the statute of the Public Manager largely coincided with the proposals of the law firm, ending up benefiting its client by exempting the managers of the Portuguese public bank, Caixa Geral de Depósitos, of the Statute.[31]

In this context of opacity, there is also the difficulty for the end user to access the rules, even when published online, yet because of their volume and subsequent modifications (introduced manually), and in understanding, on the one hand, the scope of the changes considering the intent of the legislator and, on the other hand, the extent of interactions and reverberations between pieces of legislation. In fact, and as recently seen in Portugal during the pandemic, few diplomas were republished in a consolidated way, generating insecurity and confusion regarding the rules in force.

Furthermore, as Portugal belongs to several international organizations, the translation gap problem is aggravated because legal texts are not always officially translated into Portuguese. Think, for example, of the OECD Model Convention in the 2017 version. Thus, if these texts present "Whereas", it will be a good practice to keep or adapt them, translate them and integrate them as preambles to national legislation diplomas in order to ensure that the legislative intent is clearer, since they provide important information on the reasoning of the provisions adopted and help a more accurate interpretation of the national legislation, which is bounded by the directive,[32] especially when, in particular the laws of the Assembly of the Republic, in Portugal, do not usually have (due to legisprudence rules—which is paradoxical) preambles or Whereas.[33]

Even within the European Union, despite the official translation into all Members' languages, and in various formats, even machine-readable, webpages with information on the history of the legislative process and associated initiatives are not always in Portuguese. Worse, especially in financial legislation and regulation, the so-called second level European regulations (i.e. development) are discussed and written in English, which later raises problems of translation and qualification of conceptual innovations, especially as some concepts are of Common Law with little transferability and systematic integration within Civil Law frameworks. This is, in fact,

[30] https://www.publico.pt/2021/06/12/politica/noticia/virgula-lei-permite-deputados-acumularem-funcoes-empresas-1966154 (last access 05 May 2022).

[31] https://eco.sapo.pt/2017/02/16/os-escritorios-de-advogados-podem-fazer-leis/ (last access 05 May 2022).

[32] Silveira (2021).

[33] Assembleia da República (2020, p. 13).

one of the problems linked to frequent practices of copy-pasting European directives for domestic law, sometimes creating complex problems of interpretation and application.[34] For example, a frequent issue is the synonymous use of license and authorization in European Law but which, in Portugal, legally correspond to two different types of permits.[35]

Despite the *iuris tantum* presumption that we all know and correctly interpret the Law (after all, "ignorance or misinterpretation of the Law does not justify the lack of compliance with it, nor does it exempt people from the sanctions established therein", as established, namely, in article 6 of the Portuguese Civil Code), it is actually not humanly possible, within a framework of limited rationality, due to the ubiquity and legal massification, to correctly master the entirety of the applicable Law and, consequently, apprehend all its rights, duties and prerogatives. When we do not know the rules of the game or when we do not have "legal translators", like lawyers, to support us, we do not have the means and accessibility to smartly navigate the legal system. This, naturally, uncovers a problem of inequality in access to Law and creates perceptions of unequal treatment of different social groups, thus eroding trust in the State and in institutions and values, including Law, Justice and Democracy.[36]

Do not infer that we argue that the move towards an early, systematic, strategic and deliberate RaC proposal is the magic panacea for all these problems, all the more so as there will continue to be several levels, stages and multi-stakeholders, in a fast changing world, and that the rules must therefore maintain flexibility to continue to be interpreted and applied in dynamic contexts that may distance themselves from the original causes and intentions of the rules.[37] At this moment, we just want to emphasize that the RaC project can be an important step in the identification and, above all, in the assumption of the interpretative gap, helping to reduce it and, thus, increase legal literacy, trust and alignment with the institutions, creating a kind of traceability mechanism for the legislative intent, the interpretation, and origin and application of norms, in order to better navigate the complexity of the legislative process.

Complexity

Certain subjects, due to their novelty, enhanced interconnection with other areas and technicality, are complex by nature, especially in a context of rapid socio-economic and technological change. Think about areas such as the environment, energy, climate change, financial markets, social media, the sharing economy or bio and nanotechnology. The temptation to legislate and regulate in an optimal way sometimes leads

---

[34] Silveira (2021).

[35] See, for example, Directive 2010/75 on industrial emissions. Silveira (2021).

[36] Mohun and Roberts (2020, p. 35).

[37] Barraclough et al. (2021, pp. 1, 42 et seqq.), moderate optimism about RaC, especially regarding the translation gap, and argue that legislation can be written in code but should not be. Code should be subordinate to Law, even if written in parallel.

to efforts to write great diplomas and codes, which imply the study and analysis of Comparative Law and the best historical and foreign solutions. In the end, this results in the best anachronistic Law, with a tendency towards crystallization and inertia and, therefore, tending to be inadequate. On the other hand, quick legislative solutions, without great weighting or cost–benefit and impact analysis, can, in turn, in an attempt to correct problems or calm society, generate difficulties and errors in their implementation and even perversions. Remember the Portuguese telework law.

In other words, the risk anticipated is that, in the search for a cutting-edge Law, sometimes through legal transplants, it will be inoperative because it is inappropriate to the reality and tradition of the host State. Moreover, as it is a long process of maturation and construction, the solution found ends up being the best Law of the past with a tendency towards a certain immobility, due to the moral risk and natural tendency towards inertia, with the consequent outdated and crystallization, fatal above all in very technical and dynamic fields.[38]

It is therefore important to rethink in a systematic and holistic way the processes, procedures and methodologies of legislating, namely not losing sight of the interconnections between matters, thus avoiding legislation by separate segments. Remember the tendency that still exists in European law to legislate and regulate (and even "federalize") in a parallel and almost stagnant way the banking, capital and insurance market, not to mention money laundering, even in the face of increasingly more integrated markets, with hybrid financial instruments (e.g. Credit Default Swaps), financial conglomerates, FinTech, the trend towards the universal banking and allfinance model, the expansion of the practice of cross-selling and the phenomena of bancassurance, assurebanque, assurefinance and unit-link. One way to globally renew and reconsider the form and the legislative instruments can be found in the inspiration given by International Environmental Law, which, in a flexible way but also better prepared for the need for rapid adaptations without losing the backbone and lines of force of the legislative intent and the origin of the norms, resorts to framework conventions, very participated and involving in its construction and drafting multidisciplinary and multitaskers teams and the contributions of multiple stakeholders. These "umbrella" conventions have a hard core of principles and definition of the organizational architecture and a more plastic and easily revised part for the more technical and procedural elements, always imbued with the values previously and above defined. This also allows the central function of evaluating the potential transversal impacts of the built rules network and foreseeing possible requirements for adjustments.

In terms of complexity, there is also a problem with the language and terminology used, often with a level of legal technicality, especially using Latin expressions, which becomes incomprehensible to the layman, who therefore needs a translator. Added to this is some ambiguity (intentional or not)[39] allied, among others, to indeterminate or non-legal concepts (e.g. the concept of climate emergency in the new Portuguese

[38] Saraiva (2015).

[39] According to Ma and Wilson (2021, p. 111): "While syntactic uncertainties are often inadvertent, semantic uncertainties are often deliberate."

Climate Law). In fact, to make matters worse, the terminology sometimes varies intra and inter-diploma, aggravating the problem of legal uncertainty, as well as the conceptual framework. Furthermore, to exacerbate the misunderstanding of lay people, there are implicit rules (for example, *a fortiori*) taken from other rules.

Inefficiency

The scarcity of resources, including in the State, requires a judicious allocation, even more so when considering the essential nature of the legislative and regulatory function and its cascading and spillover effects. Now, from what has been written, it can easily be inferred that, in a context of a risky digital society, inefficiencies both in the production and in the consumption of rules result from a classic and rather sticky system of legislating. Consider the high transaction costs with the duplication of translation and interpretation tasks and the inherent problems in misinterpretations throughout the process, namely with the frequent need for a last-line interpreter (usually a lawyer/jurist) who, expensively, helps to ensure compliance, and a team that transforms the business rules into code and inserts it manually and individually into the firm's work-flow or activity or service delivery.

In addition, myopia as to the appropriate means of application at the time of drafting reveals a mismatch between what is desired and what is feasible or adequate to the specific situation and context. As an example, consider, from the perspective of developing or less developed countries, the reputational pressure and market access pressure for the adoption of the Basel rules on banking prudential matters or the successive models of the double taxation convention of the OECD countries that benefit capital-exporting and, therefore, developed countries. Or recently, in Portugal, the amendment to the procedural law, establishing several impediments for judges to be able to carry out the instruction or judgment of a case. However, given the reduced number of judges compared to the number of cases, there is a fear of a domino effect of successive impediments that pushes crime cases to family or civil courts.[40] That is, the divorce between the drafters' vision and the application's reality feeds costly inefficiencies and dynamites trust in institutions. Finally, the question that arises, in the first line, is how will it be possible to legislate well today with a system that is still analogue, in a digital world?

2.2.2 Fast and Furious 3.0

Although the Law is increasingly dealing with technological matters, it has not used it to systematically and holistically integrate this knowledge into its own creation

[40] https://expresso.pt/sociedade/2022-03-12-Justica-Conselho-Superior-de-Magitsratura-tenta-travar-caos-anunciado-nos-tribunais--E-A-responsabilidade-E-de-uma-lei-parlamentar--b809ce70 (last access 05 May 2022).

and implementation, in the most diverse sectors of State powers and functions. Even so, efforts towards modernization and digitalization are gradually being observed.

From Analogue Government to Digital Government

Gradually, all over the world, although at different speeds, efforts are being made to move from a paper-based, closed, self-centred State with watertight operations and services to a Digital State, using Information and Communication Technologies (ICT), in a phenomenon of dematerialization, disintermediation, debureaucratization, acceleration and personalization of the public response. New trends such as Open Data, Open Government and Government as a Platform contribute to this transition, which passes through an intermediate stage of e-Government.

The Open Data movement puts information in an open and accessible format, which later makes it possible that, in addition to being at least machine-readable, the data can be converted into knowledge that enhances the development of social and economic innovation. Furthermore, it increases transparency in the markets and in the Administration and, consequently, their accountability, ultimately benefiting the State itself. In fact, it has been evolving towards an Open Government, a broader figure than a Digital Government, which indicates a structural culture of innovation, participation, transparency and accountability, especially when combined with a conception of a Government as a Platform, insofar as the Administration intentionally assumes itself as a provider of (big) public data and as an infrastructure for others to use, thus favouring, in the first line, the innovation of private actors and academies, that, later, will end up reverberating positively in the State.

Currently, in most OECD countries, although with asymmetries, progress has already been made to a more or less high level of e-Government, with a gradual shift to ICT, including AI, online accessibility and user centre with some websites, such as the electronic Diário da República (e-Official Gazette), in Portugal, as an official legal publication, online services and systems, revealing a partial paradigm shift in the search for greater operational efficiency.[41] In a different way, a true Digital Government requires a systematic, transversal, structural and procedural intervention of the State's culture, with a user and data driven logic and the refoundation of State functions based on ICT, with the support of Government as a Platform and Open Government trends. In this context, a deliberate RaC policy may have greater legitimacy and acceptance, not being a mere experimental curiosity or an uprooted activity exposed to the misunderstanding and distrust of the citizens.

In this path of growing and unavoidable digitalization of Law and the State, we already find several initiatives in the various functions and duties of the State and in the public and private legal world. RaC, in its broad conception of simultaneous creation of human-readable and machine-consumable legislation and regulation from

---

[41] Comparing the degree of digitalization of countries, especially in terms of Open Government: https://www.oecd.org/gov/digital-government/open-government-data.htm (last access 05 May 2022).

the moment of its political intention and of its normative drafting, as will be seen later, is the last stronghold of this trend, despite the centrality of the legislative power and function in a rule of law.

LegalTech: 1984 2.0?

The daily life of law firms and lawyers has been affected in the past by the introduction of typewriters and the telephone.[42] The introduction of computers, printers, photocopiers, fax, internet, e-mails, video calls, videoconferences or electronic signatures has decidedly changed routines and tasks, accelerating them, concentrating them or, on the contrary, multiplying them, facilitating or complicating them,[43] but above all dematerializing them and trying to increase their efficiency with cost reduction, precision, verifiability and agility and optimizing processes and reorganizing tasks.[44] Subsequently, the so-called LegalTech or LawTech has been developed: platforms, information and communication technology services and software for lawyers,[45] namely for day-to-day management, invoicing and accounting, document storage, legislative, jurisprudential and doctrinal research or support in due diligence processes or in the elaboration or automatic filling of contracts.[46] Furthermore, there are electronic "one-stop shops" and websites where all types of drafts of legal transactions, disputes (for example, very frequent for road traffic offences), applications, procedural documents, online divorces or wills can be downloaded.[47]

But LegalTech continues to evolve,[48] with innovations such as jurimetrics, peer-to-peer platforms, big data,[49] automation or AI,[50] using no-code tools[51] but also increasingly complex algorithms that overcome the limitations of searches by keywords,[52] and machine learning systems to allow advances in terms of research and analysis and their application to case prediction, legal arguments,[53] risk management, decision making, dispute resolution and supporting clients to understand, review and even prepare legal documents, in a role reversal in relation to the traditional model of

---

42 See here, Saraiva (2020).

43 Hino and Cunha (2013, pp. 6–7).

44 Hino and Cunha (2013, pp. 5–6), Cunningham et al. (2018, pp. 26 et seqq.).

45 In Portugal, see JVRIS® or iManage.

46 Eliot (2021c).

47 Take, for example, the famous LegalZoom that allows any user to create customized legal documents, such as wills, divorces or trademark applications, without ever having a lawyer present.

48 For all, Green (2019).

49 Goldberg and Miller (2011), Devins et al. (2017), with a very critical position regarding the impact of Big Data on legal daily life.

50 Eliot (2021d).

51 Eliot (2021e).

52 Baron (2011, p. 11).

53 For all, Eliot (2021f).

consultancy and advocacy.[54] In Portugal, for example, similarly to what has been verified in other countries, technology based on AI is being developed and refined, with IBM launching Watson Assistant, a legal assistance tool, adapted to the Portuguese reality, which makes searches on the requests of its interlocutors and learns from them, using a supercomputer, and which may also be used to predict the probability of success of a judicial process, based on a statistical forecast of the decisions of the Courts of Appeal and the Supreme Court stored in a repository of decisions with more than 300 thousand decisions of the Portuguese superior courts, in a format capable of being read by AI. Some large firms already use these tools in certain areas, such as mergers and acquisitions, in which these instruments enable quick massive document analysis, search for keywords, categorize them or understand which jurisdiction they are subject to. In other words, it seems that the legal work will be less and less "manual" and mechanical and more and more "intellectual" and creative, especially with the definition and construction of strategies, project management and analytical capacity for interpreting data. Therefore, customary tasks of lawyers, especially by young interns and junior lawyers and associates, will tend to be replaced by "robots" or will be forced to adapt.[55]

The potential of LegalTech raises, however, in addition to considerations about the future of the legal professions, questions about its proper regulation, including possible conflicts of interest when AI mechanisms are lawyers for both sides.[56]

If there are sites that allow, in minutes, the provision of legal services such as those exemplified above, whenever admitted in some jurisdictions, it is important to define rules, in the name of legal certainty and the defence of "clients", for example regarding the type, structure, organization and characteristics of providers (e.g. number of lawyers required, insurance, liability).

On the other hand, the security of customer data, namely stored in clouds, raises concerns, especially as several cases of hacking to law firms have been reported, as well as the exponential dimension of the damage caused by technology due to the speed gained with automatism, allowing, in seconds, the accomplishment of countless tasks and, therefore, errors.

In short, the automation and dematerialization of legal work are here to stay, raising new questions.

Total Recall: New Business Models

In a scenario of disruption of the legal professions associated with LegalTech, three typical attitudes can emerge: to give up and change professions; business as usual,

[54] For all, Vermeulen (2017), Fenwick et al. (2017, pp. 6–7).

[55] Fenwick et al. (2017, pp. 36–37), Remus and Levy (2016), Bennion (2016). In the United States there is another trend: outsourcing these tasks to offices in countries such as India, where costs are lower but where mental issues among young lawyers are increasing and aggravating. Thomson (2008, pp. 16–17), Flood (2011, pp. 11–12).

[56] Eliot (2021g).

trying to stay afloat with (less and less) customers who also resist change; to seek, in a logic of entrepreneurship, new business models, either through new structures and organizations, or through new activities that traditionally do not involve a lawyer or jurist, in an increasingly decentralized and networked society.

In fact, the cost of technological investment, namely in AI tools, accentuates the cleavage between "large" law firms that now have a CIO (Chief Innovation Officer) or equivalent,[57] and the more old-fashioned firms and, in particular, individual practice, which has an impact on the structure of the legal market[58] and on the reinforcement of a Schumpeterian competition logic for those who want to survive, thus forcing constant updating and innovation.

For example, more and more "boutique" offices are emerging, which not only try to differentiate themselves, in terms of competition of the legal matters or areas they work (e.g. Technology Law, Patents, Sharing-Economy, Data Protection, Blockchain, Smart contracts, software and hardware contracts, electronic commerce, electronic disputes, e-administration, electronic proof—E-discovery) but also the way in which they provide their services, namely virtual law firms[59] (although the Orders continue to favour the lawyer-client face-to-face relationship) and the type of activities they carry out, especially project management, through teamwork and networking.[60] Along these lines, new legal professionals should, in addition to the traditional mission of consultant, assume the role of architects and designers, setting up legal platforms based on connection, matchmaking, collaboration and management of networking and virtual work of legal and non-legal professionals,[61] namely in a logic of advising (not necessarily physical) open organizations, with new organizational forms and governance structures.[62] Furthermore, they can even move towards a lawyers-as-coders business model,[63] which has been generating debate, between potentialities and fears,[64] or generating predictive coding,[65] for managing and reviewing the data they need for their cases.

It can also be seen that the demand itself and the consequent model of supply of legal and related services tends to change, as a result of technological advances. In Portugal, in 2018, a Portuguese start-up launched Lawra, a platform that allows any citizen to quickly find and get in touch with a lawyer. It was eventually suspended, due to the Bar Association's reservations about the potential violation of the prohibition of publicity of defenders and the confidentiality of contacts. However, the technological and social pressure will hardly be able to be stopped in relation to this type of solutions.

---

57 Fenwick et al. (2017, p. 4).

58 Koo (2007, pp. 5–6).

59 Fenwick et al. (2017, pp. 13–14).

60 Vermeulen (2017), Fenwick et al. (2017, pp. 10–11; 2018, pp. 13–14).

61 Hogemann (2018, p. 108).

62 Vermeulen (2017).

63 Eliot (2021h).

64 Eliot (2021h).

65 Christian (2020).

The entrepreneurship of legal professionals is boosted by the countless opportunities that technology brings and that they should be able to identify and seize, especially through careful planning of their business model, thinking strategically, defining stages and evaluating progress, specializing and building partnerships, which may not involve being part of a typical organization of jurists and lawyers,[66] fostering networking, not only to attract new clients but also to retain them.

On the other hand, given the opportunities created by the increasing digitalization and a translation gap phenomenon, business opportunities and commercial initiatives arise to transform into code and automate the rules that end users will have to apply, making their use faster, more accurate, and less costly due to scale gains and lower non-compliance costs. Thus, several companies turn to and rely on Business Rules Management Systems, software programs, created generally on an entity-by-entity basis, which facilitate the interpretation and application of business rules that must be complied with, and which have multidisciplinary teams behind them.

12 Angry Men Versus TechJustice

Technology is also not at the doorstep of courts and conflict resolution in general, namely arbitration solutions or more or less formalized mediation. The terminology varies, for example, technological or electronic Justice,[67] E-Justice, Cyberjustice or TechJustice.[68]

In simple terms, its progress and subsequent study have focused on four sectors: Online Dispute Resolution[69]; Open Data; AI[70]; and Electronic Filing (e-Filling) or Process Management Systems.[71]

The digitization and computerization of documents and electronic judicial cases allow, among others, easier contact with Justice, letting the parties and their legal representatives to have access anywhere to their case via the internet, or that acts and procedural documents, such as subpoenas and notifications, can be submitted remotely, reducing costs or allowing the payment of court fees through ATMs. However, this can have consequences in terms of legal arguments, increasing, for example, the number of citations and footnotes in jurisprudential decisions or impacting on the quality of justice by granting phenomena of decision-making copy paste (which, by the way, already exists in some rulings).[72]

---

66 Canick (2014, pp. 667–668).

67 Machado et al. (2008, pp. 21–23), Santos (2005, pp. 82–109).

68 Pointing problems with studies on this subject: Dias et al. (2019, p. 8).

69 Pointing problems in terms of the quality of the rulings despite the increase in efficiency, Webb (2019, p. 10).

70 For example, Eliot (2021ab, ac).

71 Dias et al. (2019, p. 3).

72 Webb (2019, p. 10), Richmond (2013).

Also worth mentioning is the possibility of having testimonies by videoconference, speeding up justice and ensuring greater efficiency, or the electronic draw of cases for judges that promotes greater transparency.

In Portugal, the Citius application/portal,[73] created by the DGAJ (General Directorate of the Administration of Justice) to enhance dematerialization and simplification of acts and processes in justice, is used in the procedural management in the Judicial Courts and by the Public Ministry, in spite of the frequent criticisms pointed out mainly by magistrates and lawyers. The Citius application covers five main areas: Procedural management for judicial secretariats and the Public Ministry; Access and delivery of procedural documents by lawyers and solicitors; Injunctions; Procedural management by judicial magistrates; and Procedural management by public prosecutors.

However, the technological revolution of Justice is more profound with the anticipation of algorithms to replace, in some situations, the judges, with documents written in machine-readable code, such as self-imposing smart contracts, and foreseeable robot-judges with capabilities to detect dishonesty[74] and deflect decisions made by human judges under the influence of biological, social or emotional distortions.[75] In the United States, there are magistrates using computer tools to measure the penalty (revealing, moreover, a discriminatory bias against the black minority)[76] or to assess the probabilities of a suspect's recidivism, as well as algorithms to decide cases for traffic violations, or decisions, as in the case of State v. Loomis, in the Wisconsin Supreme Court,[77] in which the Court accepts the help of the COMPAS system—an algorithm for analysing the risk of the accused—even though the methodology used is incomprehensible to the judges and the defendant, this still does not violate the accused's right to due process at all times. In several countries, complex instruments are applied to predict the probability of success of a given judicial ruling. In Brazil, in turn, the Federal Supreme Court[78] announced the use of technology to examine the admissibility of some of the appeals and the Court of Justice of the State of Minas Gerais has been instituting several technological tools, with and without the use of AI, namely three robotics projects for repetitive tasks: Agile, which detects a disproportionate increase in the distribution of cases in the districts or in the court itself; Radar, which uses Elastic Search technology to study, almost in real time, large amounts of data contained in digital documents, such as procedural documents; and an automated tool for automatic recording and transcription of audio generated during trial

---

73 https://www.citius.mj.pt/portal/default.aspx (last access 05 May 2022).

74 Eliot (2021i).

75 Eliot (2021j).

76 Webb (2019, p. 8), Spielkamp (2017).

77 State v. Loomis, Wisconsin Supreme Court Requires Warning Before Use of Algorithmic Risk Assessments in Sentencing. Recent Case: 881 N.W.2d 749 (Wis. 2016). https://harvardlawreview.org/2017/03/state-v-loomis/ (last access 05 May 2022); Kouroutakis (2021, pp. 7–8).

78 Coelho and Allemand (2014).

sessions. Even so, some Brazilian doctrine[79] raises doubts on constitutionality, especially in view of the use of black box algorithms in decision-making, for violation of constitutional procedural guarantees such as contradictory and ample defence.

As a result, matters of fact and Law, discussed in Court, also reveal the weight of technology and of new types of illicit acts such as e-crime[80]: discovery, production and use in court of information created and stored by computer, including the procedure for processing, cost allocation, inadvertent waiver of privileges, document repositories, computer forensics, data preservation, email, social media and smartphone analysis, forensic experts, technology witnesses and evidentiary challenges, as not to mention, on the one hand, the use of technology as a source of evidence (e.g. DNA analyses, polygraph, colposcope and ending up in Neurolaw), but, on the other hand, its use to present evidence in hearings (e.g. digital animations, graphic representations, videos), with potential impacts on the judge's and jury's perception and interpretation of the case.[81]

Communication beyond justice operators, streamlined with intranet networks and other information and communication tools, especially between citizens and the Courts, is also changing with technological advances, whether through telephone lines, websites, automatic kiosks, computerized attendance terminals or electronic public information systems with information on the judges' agenda, rooms and session times.[82]

In the area of justice, other fields have also been undergoing changes. As a paradigmatic example, it is worth remembering, in Portugal, the electronic offer of various services such as: Firm-in-an-hour; Online company; Commercial Registration on the Internet; Permanent certificate; Simplified business information; Online Application for Registration of Trademarks and Patents; Online publication of corporate acts; On-the-Spot Branch; Born Citizen; Ready House; Association on Time; Inheritance Desk; Divorce Desk with Sharing or Single Car Document.[83] Other services are also starting to gain interest, such as the use of AI for translation in the context of legal proceedings, replacing expensive solutions that are not always easy to obtain from human interpreters and translators,[84] or in the statistical and analytical treatment of jurisprudential decisions, for the purposes of prediction but also to determine the state of justice.[85]

---

[79] Marques and Nunes (2018, p. 9).

[80] Yadav (2016, p. 13).

[81] Webb (2019, p. 9).

[82] Santos (2005, pp. 94–95).

[83] Machado et al. (2008), Dias et al. (2019, pp. 2–3).

[84] Eliot (2021k).

[85] Eliot (2021l).

E-Administration

The wish for a modernized, fast, efficient, effective, less bureaucratic and informed Administration is very old, now seeing in technology an opportunity for reform, so its digitization (and associated necessary security) has been successively deepened, for example, in Portugal,[86] by the SIMPLEX and SIMPLE+ Programmes, both for internal purposes and in telematic relations with the administrators. Therefore, on the one side, efficiency gains are sought in the internal functioning of the administrative machine and, on the other, the transformation of the paradigm of Public Administration is in place passing from a self-centred approach to an Administration more oriented towards the citizen, able to provide quality services and information, at any time, and tailored to the users. Like other legal-political areas, such as regulation, justice or advocacy and legal advice, new technologies are beginning to be integrated into the Administration, from digitalization and virtualization of several proceedings to chatbots and automated decision systems based on AI and machine learning.[87]

In this way, in order to enhance and extend access to the Administration, there has been a focus on a user-centred and mobile friendly approach, tailor-made with the support of the user and available via mobile. See, as an example, the Citizen's Portal, in Portugal. Furthermore, in order to reduce costs and promote effective, transparent and accountable public management, with measurable, monitorable and scrutinized results that allow citizens to gain confidence in their institutions, an open data government and e-procurement initiatives are supported, with the help of digital platforms. But a more transparent e-Governance must also be more e-participatory. In certain areas, including local ones, citizens are already involved in the co-creative process of new policies, services or projects (e.g. participatory budgeting) thanks to the use of information technologies. However, decision-making processes, such as online voting, are still delayed, at least in Portugal.

Technoregulation, RegTech and SupTech

Technology necessarily impacts regulation and supervision, either through the omnipresence of technology in everyday life, in the most diverse sectors, such as transport, energy, telecommunications, communication, health, agriculture or the environment, or through the facilitation and mediation of technological means in a SMART (Specific, Measurable, Achievable, Realistic and Time-limited)[88] regulation that is more adequate and efficient and tends, therefore, to be more decentralized, collaborative and polycentric, combining soft and hard instruments that are not necessarily legal (e.g. economic instruments, social norms). In fact, technology not only raises questions about new ways of applying and enforcing the Law, but also about its transformative power, especially as a code, although with doubts on the loss of

[86] Mateus (2008), Marques (2016).

[87] Kouroutakis (2021).

[88] Cabugueira (2020, p. 9).

normative values for more technical regulation and supervision.[89] Moreover, in the traditional attempt to oppose technology and Law, it is expected, however, that the latter regulates and monitors the former. This will most likely mean that the Law will transform itself, despite the fact that there is often a delay between the slower (and often reactive) pace of the Law and the accelerated pace of technology, creating a problematic gap. After all, building a Law that is proof of future evolution is an ingenious and herculean challenge.

RegTech (together with FinTech) and SupTech have witnessed a growing interest and development, seeking, through the use of technology, to improve in terms of efficiency and effectiveness the implementation and compliance of regulation by both regulators and regulated, namely in terms of Electronic Know-Your-Consumer tool, Fraud Monitoring or Automatic Clearing Registry, with new processes altogether to rethink regulation and compliance.[90]

RegTech and SupTech therefore have advantages for both regulated and new business models and regulators. For the former, it allows massive cost savings[91] (e.g. automation of the more mundane compliance tasks and reduction of operational risks related to meeting compliance and reporting obligations; centralized risk management for global firms,[92] the use of the regulator as a platform,[93] and corporate governance[94]), increased opportunities for emerging FinTech start-ups, IT and advisory firms, with the development of new products and services and incentives to trade off data for faster market entry, and the ability to release excess regulatory capital.[95] For the second, it ensures more granular, effective and faster supervision of markets and market participants with continuous monitoring providing close to real-time insights with new flows of information and because their internal reporting processes are significantly enhanced. This improves predictive supervision and ensures adequate implementation of constantly evolving rules. This further ensures the means to move towards a proportionate risk-based approach and small risk of regulatory capture, although needing to develop systems to deal with massive data, cybersecurity and the "de-skilling" of the personnel because of atrophy or attrition.[96] In short,

> RegTech and SupTech help to ensure financial stability, fight financial crime, and promote good market conduct, competition, financial inclusion, and innovation. The adoption of RegTech and SupTech can also have positive spillovers on market efficiency, consumer welfare, and governance. These stem from their potential to lower transaction costs for

---

[89] Webb (2019, pp. 11–13).

[90] Enriques (2017) distinguishes between four different RegTech functions: Operations RegTech, ComplianceTech, OversightTech, and PolicymakingTech. Barefoot (2020a).

[91] On the costs of compliance in the financial sector, EBA (2021a, b), Miguel and Algarvio (2019), Barefoot (2019, pp. 14 et seqq.).

[92] Aziz and Dowling (2018).

[93] Snow (2019, pp. 9, 29).

[94] Packin (2017, p. 210).

[95] Financial Stability Board (2020, pp. 7–8), Gurung and Perlman (2018, p. 1).

[96] Arner et al. (2016a, b, pp. 6–7; 2015, pp. 38 et seqq.), Castri et al. (2018, pp. 13–15, 31).

individuals and firms seeking to enter the financial service market, as well as their ability to reduce information asymmetries between regulator, providers, and consumers.[97]

Given these benefits, it is not surprising that SupTech is a strategic priority for an increasing number of authorities, especially in areas of regulatory reporting, data management, misconduct analysis and microprudential supervision.[98] Actually, European Banking Authority (EBA) has anticipated the MDMER (Model-Driven Tech-Driven Machine Executable Regulations)[99] after the 2017 TechSprint conducted by the Financial Conduct Authority (FCA) and the Bank of England (BoE).[100] Furthermore, other different authorities and experts have discussed the future so that, "by 2024, information to be publicly released under EU financial services should be disclosed in standardized and machine-readable formats", adding that "in a digital context, the Commission intends to ensure that regulated information is provided in electronic machine-readable formats."[101] Also, the Financial Stability Board (FSB), the FSI (Financial Stability Institute) and the SEC (Securities and Exchange Commission) refer to the use of SupTech strategies, including the development of data strategies, availability of AI technologies, and emergence of machine-readable data.[102]

As an example, remember the Apiax initiative in building digital solutions to manage complex regulation or codified approaches to compliance by design, with software programmed with technical, ethical, regulatory, legal and compliance standards. These solutions are born as a result of top-down institutional demand due to post-crisis increased costs of compliance, additional data reporting and disclosure, data science developments and regulators' efforts to enhance efficiency of supervisory tools, moving from a Know-Your-Customer to a Know-Your-Data approach,[103] and have the potential for application in a wide range of contexts, forcing a paradigm shift in regulation, especially with the increased use of AI.[104]

Furthermore, they necessarily imply ab initio the individual interpretation and translation of the rules that have traditionally been created in a human-readable format, which, on the one hand, considering the actual state-of-the-art, requires monitoring by multidisciplinary teams that include jurists, and, on the other hand, when not dealing with authentic interpretations, interpretive errors may occur, with non-compliance effects proportional to the scale of their dissemination,[105] boosted by an

[97] Castri et al. (2018, p. 1).

[98] Financial Stability Board (2020), Gurung and Perlman (2018), Barefoot (2020a, pp. 11 et seqq.).

[99] EBA (2020). See also for EBA, EBA (2018, 2021a, b).

[100] https://www.fca.org.uk/events/techsprints/model-driven-machine-executable-regulatory-reporting-techsprint (last access 01 August 2022).

[101] European Commission (2020).

[102] Financial Stability Board (2020), Financial Stability Institute (2020), Bauguess (2017).

[103] Arner et al. (2016b, pp. 79–86; 2017, p. 9).

[104] Arner et al. (2016a, pp. 6–7, 48).

[105] Waddington (2019, p. 24), Mohun and Roberts (2020, p. 67).

overconfidence in technology and an underestimation of risks.[106] The same, incidentally, is valid for the phenomenon of model driven regulation, for example worked in the BoE and the FCA's Digital Regulatory Reporting Project, in which an attempt is made to architect a conceptual, logical and/or open source model that captures the regulation in question, which can then be transformed into a machine-consumable format.[107]

However, do not withdraw from here, similar to what will be discussed about RaC, that RegTech and SupTech are the silver bullet. In addition to resistances and barriers that have to be broken, such as questions of legitimacy, accountability, interests of workers or of certain service providers that tend to concentrate power, not only can technology be used to frustrate regulatory compliance (anti-RegTech), as it does not completely avoid undesired and unethical business or corporate governance practices. Moreover, technology can hinder human input and judgment in the governance and risk management decision processes, and many of the RegTech's automation and efficiency gains may be offset by the expanded regulatory requirements and the need for better technology and specialized staff.[108] In short, despite significant advantages, challenges, risks, and pitfalls of "the rise of the machines" must be taken care of, so as not to pervert the potential of RegTech and SupTech, including in terms of governance, ethics and meta-regulation, seeking to solve tech problems before policy and legal questions.[109]

3 Terminator 3: The Rise of the Machines

3.1 Desperately Seeking for Better Legislation

The concern to legislate and regulate well has, in the last twenty or so years, worried the legislating bodies all over the world, namely through the definition of unique criteria and rules for the writing of normative acts, taking into account the nature and local legal tradition and its interconnection with other legal systems.

In Portugal, for example, the area of legistics has been the subject of increasing research,[110] inserted in the broader theme of the quality of legislation, i.e. to theorise

[106] Among the risks of RegTech and SupTech are over reliance on this technological tools, skills and resourcing problems, due integration in internal processes, cyber risk, reputational risk, data quality issues and the potential for limited transparency or "explainability" in the design and outputs of tools. Financial Stability Board (2020, pp. 9–10).

[107] Mohun and Roberts (2020, p. 67), Box 5.3.

[108] Packin (2017, pp. 194, 211 et seqq.), EBA (2021a, b, pp. 6, 32 et seqq.), Micheler and Whaley (2020, pp. 349–377), Barefoot (2020a, pp. 42 et seqq.).

[109] Barefoot (2020b, p. 89).

[110] It is worth noting the work carried out by the Research Centre for Public Law of the Faculty of Law of the University of Lisbon, in particular in the search for the definition of criteria, standards and common rules for legislation drafting for Portuguese speaking countries and regions, but which

ways of producing "good laws",[111] although it is not part of the traditional curricula of law schools. There have been several attempts to create an action guide, especially after the theme was boosted by the Sutherland Report in 1992,[112] but above all by the Mandelkern Report[113] and the deepening effort on Better and Smart Regulation within the EU,[114] the OECD[115] and the World Bank.[116] At issue is not the merit of the legal act but rather its quality, that is knowing how legal rules may be drafted with the respect of the principles of proportionality, transparency, simplicity, certainty, accessibility, accountability and subsidiarity when transmitting the intention of the political decision-maker. Traditionally, the study of better legislation drafting is divided into four different but complementary topics: (i) the study of legal sources system, both in a legal and political component, but with a growing concern over other instruments than command and control typical solutions; (ii) "material"

---

also has been focusing on RaC and the use of AI in legislation drafting. http://www.icjp.pt/cidp/investigacao/4463/projectos/11619 (last access 05 May 2022).

[111] Blanco de Morais (2007, p. 70).

[112] The Sutherland report ("The internal market after 1992: meeting the challenge") of 1992s (1992) 2044. For the follow up of the report, inter alia, the European Commission's Communication SEC (1992) 2277 and COM (1993) 361 def.

[113] Mandelkern Group on Better regulation, Final Report (2001). https://www.smartreg.pe/reportes/Mandelkern%20Report%20on%20Better%20Regulation%202001.pdf (last access 05 May 2022).

[114] Since the Sutherland report, several scholars and policy makers, such as Koopmans, Piris and Timmermans, felt the need to study and ask for proper quality standards for European legislation. For all on European Better Legislation, Voermans (2009). See also, inter alia, the report of the Molitor group (Report of the Group of Independent Experts on Simplification of Legislation and Administration, COM (1995) 288 final/2, of 21 June 1995); the White Paper on European Governance COM (2001) 428 final; the EU Commission's Action Plan on Better law-making COM (2002) 275 final; followed by the Action Plan for simplifying and improving the regulatory environment COM (2002) 278 final; A strategic review of Better regulation in the European Union (Common Better regulation Strategy, for short) launched in a Commission communication of 14 November 2006 COM (2006) 689; The European Commission's REFIT programme—making EU law simpler, less costly and future proof; the Commissions Fit for Future Platform (F4F); the Commission's Communication Better regulation for better results—An EU agenda COM/2015/0215 final; the Commission's Communication Better regulation: taking stock and sustaining our commitment COM/2019/178 final; and the 2021 Better regulation: Joining forces to make better laws. See https://ec.europa.eu/info/law/law-making-process/planning-and-proposing-law/better-regulation-why-and-how_en (last access 05 May 2022); and for the Better regulation: guidelines and toolbox https://ec.europa.eu/info/law/law-making-process/planning-and-proposing-law/better-regulation-why-and-how/better-regulation-guidelines-and-toolbox_en (last access 05 May 2022). Furthermore, in 2015, the Commission established the Regulatory Scrutiny Board, an independent body of Commission officials and experts who review impact assessments and selected evaluations.

[115] See for instance OECD (2002, 2011); on OECD Recommendations and Guidelines on Regulatory Policy since 1995 to 2021 see https://www.oecd.org/gov/regulatory-policy/recommendations-guidelines.htm (last access 05 May 2022); and https://www.oecd.org/gov/regulatory-policy/#d.en.194409 (last access 05 May 2022); including behavioural insights: https://www.oecd.org/gov/regulatory-policy/behavioural-insights.htm (last access 05 May 2022).

[116] See The Better Regulation for Growth (BRG) Programme launched in 2007 by the Dutch Ministry of Foreign Affairs, the UK Department for International Development (DFID) and the investment climate advisory services (IC) of the World Bank Group. World Bank (2010a, b).

rules for legislation drafting fundamentally concerned with methodological aspects, the sequence of steps of the legal process and the set of basic principles regarding public discussions, consultations and hearings; (iii) "formal" rules for drafting legislation that envision the definition and implementation of rules and good practices regarding the drafting exercise and (iv) legislative impact assessment which foresees evaluating if the proposed piece of legislation is the fittest to address the issues at stake (*ex ante* evaluation) or if the outcomes of the enforcement of a piece of legislation match those initially envisaged by the legislator and what are their impacts in that subject and beyond (*ex post* evaluation).[117]

Thus, in Portugal,[118] which registered a rapid and significant qualitative leap in this matter,[119] one should remember the "lei formulário",[120] as well as the work of the Commission for Legislative Simplification, created under the XV Constitutional Government[121]; the Technical Committee of the Strategic Programme for the Quality and Efficiency of the Government's Normative Acts, which operated between 2003 and 2006 under the Presidency of the Council of Ministers[122]; the working group created in the Assembly of the Republic in the IX Legislature, which allowed the establishment of its legal rules, such as the guide of Legal Rules to Observe in the Drafting of Normative Acts of the Assembly of the Republic, approved in 2008; and the norms that, until 2015, were part of the Regulations of the Council of Ministers, contained in the Guide to Good Legal Practices of the XXI Constitutional Government, which, however, are no longer provided for therein and which are now included in the annex to Decree-Law no. 169-B/2019, of December 3, which approves the organization and functioning regime of the XXII Constitutional Government. In 2020, the Portuguese legislative bodies, together with the services of the Parliament, decided, in the interest of having common rules for all entities that produce normative acts, to review their rules, adapting them to the needs felt with the publication of the Legal Guide for the Elaboration of Normative Acts.[123]

These efforts, associated with a deliberate project to develop an e-Government and a digital transition for the modernization of the Administration (with a specific ministry), involve a series of projects and programmes over the last twenty years, such as SIMPLEX or the umbrella programme Legislar Melhor (Better Law Making Programme),[124] with the special and differentiating intervention in the development

[117] It will not be discussed here whether there are similarities and differences between the regulatory quality approach and the legislative quality approach, taking into account the purposes and expressions of the Law pursued. Terms will be used interchangeably throughout the text. See Voermans (2009, pp. 67–68). See also, Hildebrandt (2018).

[118] With data until 2009, OECD (2009).

[119] OECD (2009, p. 16).

[120] Law No. 74/98, of November 11, on the publication, identification and form of diplomas, amended by Laws No. 2/2005, of January 24, 26/2006, of June 30, 42/2007, of August 24th and 43/2014, of July 11th.

[121] Resolution of the Council of Ministers No. 29/2001, of 9 March.

[122] Order No. 12017/2003, of 25 June, and Order No. 26748/2005, of 19 December.

[123] Assembleia da República (2020).

[124] Approved by Council of Ministers Resolution No. 63/2006, of 18 May.

of Better Regulation in Portugal by CEJUR (the legal centre of the Presidency of Council of Ministers in charge of the Legislar Melhor Programme) and SEMA (Secretary of State for Administrative Modernisation), despite their lack of resources.[125] Under the latter's purview, some significant progress has been made, such as: no paper publication of the Diário da República (Official Gazette), its electronic edition now having official value and assuming itself as a public service with universal and free access[126]; creation of the Normative Acts Control System (SCAN) for the purpose of automated monitoring, using an electronic system, of the activity of administrative regulation of legislative acts, in order to control compliance with the legal requirements of regulation, as well as monitoring the timeliness transposition of European directives[127]; creation of the Simplex Test, the first technical instrument for assessing the normative impact available to the Government to assess, in a preventive way, the administrative burden of governmental normative acts, before their effective application.[128]

As a matter of fact, in terms of assessment of normative impact, there has been considerable progress, similarly to other countries. Among others, are included the following initiatives, mainly under the auspices of the Directorate-General for Justice Policy, of the Ministry of Justice: the Simplegis Programme,[129] started in 2010, aimed to simplify and clarify the Portuguese legal system, through access from citizens and firms to the legal instruments and through their better application, and it developed, with the support of the ICJP/CIDP of the University of Lisbon Law School, advanced preparation actions in legislative evaluation in order to train all the Ministries with permanent multidisciplinary teams qualified to carry out legislative assessment exercises both *ex ante* and *ex post*; and the Custa Quanto? Programme, an experimental model that has become definitive[130] for the prior assessment of legislative impact, especially on people's lives and on the activities of firms, which translates into an institutionalized system to identify, measure and estimate, based on criteria and standardized parameters, in a systematic way and at an early stage of the legislative procedure, the burdens arising from the legislation.[131]

The Assembly of the Republic, for its part, does not normally carry out normative impact studies, but with the entry into force of the legal framework for the assessment of the gender impact of normative acts,[132] all bills and proposals submitted to Parliament must be accompanied by a prior gender impact assessment prepared under the terms of that legal framework. As for the draft laws, the Assembly of the

---

125 Mohun and Roberts (2020, p. 17).

126 Decree-Law No. 116-C/2006, of June 16.

127 Resolution of the Council of Ministers No. 197/2008, of 30 December.

128 Resolutions of the Council of Ministers No. 64/2006, of 18 May, and No. 198/2008, of 30 December.

129 Resolution of the Council of Ministers No. 77/2010, of 11 October, amended by Declaration of Rectification No. 36/2010, of 10 December. For all, Ettner and Silveira (2014).

130 Council Resolution No. 74/2018, of 8 June; OECD (2017), UTAIL (2018).

131 Resolution of the Council of Ministers No. 44/2017, of 24 March. See Egídio et al. (2018).

132 Law No. 4/2018, of February 9.

Republic requires that they be accompanied, as far as possible, in abbreviated form, by a description of the social, economic, financial and political situations to which they apply, by informing on the benefits and the consequences of its application and a review of current legislation on the subject. The Government committed itself, under the terms of paragraph 2 of article 6 of Decree-Law no. 274/2009, of 2 October, to send to the Portuguese Parliament, in the case of draft laws, "copy (…) of opinions or contributions resulting from direct consultation with entities whose consultation is constitutionally or legally mandatory and which have been issued in the course of the Government's legislative procedure."[133]

Despite developments in terms of legislative impact, barriers to its full effectiveness remain.

> The difficulties that practitioners find when implementing impact assessment (…) are: 1st lack of political support and commitment because the process is time consuming and may jeopardise political goals and the effectiveness of the intervention; 2nd lack of technical expertise in the public sector; 3rd lack of data mechanisms (in quality and quantity), and the resistance to create data centers and to implement self-learning; 4th lack of flexibility and capacity to adapt creating regulatory lags and regulatory delays; 5th lack of transparency which undermines accountability and hampers stakeholder engagement19. All the previous will put in stress the capacity for regulation to have quality, to be fit for purpose, fit for future and resilient.[134]

Finally, in this regard, it should be noted that, despite notable progress in the legal field, in Portugal, on the one hand, there are no "nudge units" with policy-making and law-making bodies, contrary to what is observed in other parts of the world, such as the US, UK or Singapore, nor is there a deliberate, systematic and integrated consideration[135] of replacing (unnecessary) legislative instruments and rules with alternative solutions, more efficient and effective in certain contexts, in particular more or less sophisticated and tailor-made nudges for the concrete problem,[136] such as disclosure[137] or social norms, including AI support.[138] On the other hand, there have not yet been any RaC initiatives or experiences, as in France, New Zealand, Australia, Denmark, or Estonia despite the fact that national publications on the subject can already be found, especially by researchers working at the ICJP/CIDP, who have been collaborating in the legisprudence programmes.[139] This does not mean, however, that

[133] Assembleia da República (2020, p. 12).

[134] Cabugueira (2020, p. 13).

[135] It should be noted that the absence of a political-legislative position on the use of nudging can raise questions of constitutionality and legitimacy of its use, especially since several nudges do not need a legal command to be applied, depending on the discretion of the administrative decision (e.g. establishment, by default, of photocopies on both sides, with lower quality printing or use of an identification card to make prints and copies; or thermostat at 19 °C).

[136] Franco et al. (2021, pp. 4–20).

[137] Amariles (2020, p. 287), Loewenstein et al. (2013), Barefoot (2019, pp. 10–11), also noting the pitfalls of disclosure.

[138] Franco (2019), Hrnjic and Tomczak (2019).

[139] Franco (2019), Lanceiro (2019), Cabugueira (2020); International conference "Do androids dream of legislative drafting? The use of AI and new technologies in legislative drafting" by the Institute for Legal and Political Sciences/Lisbon Centre for Research in Public Law School/University

electronic tools are not used in the drafting of Portuguese legislation. The Covid 19 pandemic has, in fact, potentiated its usage, mainly by adopting a fully electronic procedure for the approval, including the

> e-filing to present drafts to be submitted for governmental approval, ii) electronic sending of an agenda of the meetings where drafts are to be considered for approval and draft versions of the proposed laws, iii) electronic sending of the approved bills to the President of the Republic and iv) the electronic signature of the ministers and electronic promulgation by the head of state after approval[140] and v) the electronic publication, speeding the publication when compared with the traditional paper format.

In short, in Portugal, as in most countries, the issues surrounding a better law are predominantly centred around legislative quantity and quality, in an effort to reduce bureaucracy, and enhance simplification, clarification and assessment of regulatory impact, without revisiting methods, procedures and legislative processes and, therefore, not approaching the legislative process in its entirety and in a systematic, integrated and holistic way. Although intertwined with the issue of machine-consumable law and RaC, the approach of better legislation is neither to be confused nor summarized with those projects, which are instrumental and have a specific purpose to achieve better law in a digitalization context.[141]

3.2 *A Law for All Seasons: The Rule as Code Project*

The design of proportional rules, in its triple aspect of necessary, adequate and not excessive, that are clear, accessible, efficient and effective requires time and transversal technical knowledge. Its poor (qualitative and quantitative) construction, dissemination and implementation have added costs not only for the normative system and for the credibility of the State and the Law, but also economic and social costs, above all, as has been mentioned, in a context of inadequacy to a risk and information society. Thus, proposals for an effort of transversal change in the legislative process have emerged in recent years, even if with older roots,[142] taking advantage of the ICTs, including AI, for a new paradigm of RaC, which, although not the panacea for all problems and presenting challenges and limits, can be a fundamental piece in the progress towards a truly Digital State, promoting efficiency, effectiveness and

---

of Lisbon School of Law, the Korea Legislation Research Centre and the International Association of Legislation, University of Lisbon School of Law (June 7, 2019).

140 Silveira (2018, p. 181).

141 Barraclough et al. (2021, pp. 2, 18 et seqq.).

142 Recall the initiatives of Computational Law as a branch of Legal Informatics, which can be found in 1960 at the I Conference on National and Electronic Law, in the work of Allan and Engholm in 1978 or by Sergot et al. in 1986, with proposals for computerization of the Law and the automation of legal analysis in order to reduce the complexity of Law and increase its understanding and efficiency, using data structures representative of legal content in computerized format that can be processed without the need for human legal experts. Allan and Engholm (1978, pp. 380–412), Sergot et al. (1986, pp. 370–386).

equity, and to bring legislators, interpreters, applicators and citizens closer, increasing the knowledge and understanding of Law, in a qualitative approach beyond Lessig's Code as Law,[143] entering a new phase in the relationship between Law and Technology.[144] To be successful, this initiative must be: (i) deliberate (and not the reactive, non-programmed or implicit result of an evolution due to the context, namely by the action of private parties with the creation of hybrid artefacts/legal rules),[145] that is, an explicit choice, assumed and discussed, to accommodate legislative traditions; (ii) strategic, integrated in the broader movement of digitization of the State, Open Government and Better Law; and (iii) systematic, i.e. integrated and supported.[146] This is the only way to ensure its legitimacy and acceptability, particularly socially, avoiding the risk of mistrust and rejection, especially considering the perception of the coercive power of the legislature and the close State/citizen connection underlying it.

In this sense,

> Rules as Code is not a specific technology. Rather, it is an approach to creating and delivering better, machine consumable rulesets, with the objective of enabling the automated or semi-automated application of rules in a way that provides: i) better services that help users understand and apply laws, more easily and effectively; ii)more transparency, traceability and auditability in how rules are applied. The central part of Rules as Code is the process of drafting and publishing rules in legislation, regulation, and policy in both human and machine-consumable languages (code) so they can be read and used by computers. (…) Ideally, the Rules as Code approach encompasses the simultaneous co-drafting of the human-readable and machine-readable versions of the ruleset, to enable the alignment of the intent of policy drafters and the logical constraints of coding. These two versions can then be published together.[147]

In other words, from this perspective, RaC is not just a mere output as a codified version of machine-readable and consumable rules, as this broader definition would include private and individual RegTech, LegalTech solutions for transforming business rules and other rules into software, late in the legislative process and without prerogatives of authority. Nor is it limited to the mere automation of norms, as it aims (although not to be confused with) better Law and better efficiency and transparency in interpretation and application, in addition to maintaining the version in natural language and recognizing that there are norms that, by their very nature, (in particular with a necessary degree of discretion), are not capable of being transformed into a program code.[148]

---

143 Lessig (2000a, b, 2006).

144 On the comparison and transition from Code-as-Law (hetero-imposed by private/unknown entities on public and private entities) to Law-as-Code (self or co-imposed by the State on public and private entities), for all: Hassan and de Filippi (2016; 2017, p. 89). Introducing ameliorations to code-as-law under the form of a new concept—digisprudence: Diver (2020, 2022). Also on this matter, Eliot (2021m).

145 Amariles (2020, p. 299).

146 Mohun and Roberts (2020, p. 13).

147 Sousa (2021a).

148 Waddington (2020, p. 180). Barraclough et al. (2021, p. 152), discussing if RaC is an output, a process or something else.

The simultaneous production of rules in human and machine format allows mutual influence, namely through the identification of rules that are less clear and difficult to enforce, that raise problems in their writing in code, as it guarantees isomorphism (or rather, intends to guarantee) between the two languages, with equally authentic and equivalent versions, thus making the rules valid for everyone (humans and machines) and easier to access, understand and implement as they do not depend on transformations, translations and interpretations by teams disconnected from the legislative intent.[149]

Now, as we can see from what has been exposed and which should be underlined again, RaC presents a dimension of precocious, deliberate, systematic, strategic and authoritative production, seeking, if not to transform the entire legislative process (revolutionizing it), at least to improve (evolving) it,[150] including lowering costs for legislators and end-users.[151] "RaC, conceptualized in this way, is about changing *when, how, by and for whom* rules are made. It moves beyond enhancing existing workflows and processes, and requires deeper and deliberate examination of every part of the rule making process."[152] In other words, RaC thus has a double valence: "The first is Lessig's concept of a regulatory mechanism: that computer code can substitute for law or other forms of regulation. The second aspect is as an anti-regulatory mechanism: a tool to minimize the costs of law that certain groups will use to their advantage",[153] in order to massively decrease their compliance costs.

In short, "RaC can be seen as part of the ongoing movement to digital government, fitting with, shaped by and in some ways a result of existing reform agendas",[154] integrating and enhancing its main lines of force, namely:

- "Data-driven public sector: RaC makes one of the government's biggest data sets, its rules, available for public use and consumption, and allows for existing data to be used more effectively in rulemaking, for example, through enhanced *ex ante* modelling of policy effects.
- Open by default: machine-consumable versions of rules should be open to the public, for their consumption and use, as well as scrutiny and understanding (...).
- Government as a platform: RaC remakes a core function of government, rule-making, and exposes it as a public resource which enables collaboration with, and third-party value creation by, citizens, businesses and other government entities.
- Digital by design: RaC represents a recognition that machines are a major consumer of government rules, and there exists a need to design for their needs as well as for those of humans.

---

[149] Mohun and Roberts (2020, p. 19).

[150] Mohun and Roberts (2020, p. 17).

[151] Morris (2020) goes even further and states that "the Rules as Code argument is one that applies to all rules, not only laws. (...) The principles of Rules as Code could—and I argue *should*—be applied to contracts, organizational policies, or even the rules of your favourite board game."

[152] Mohun and Roberts (2020, p. 18).

[153] Wu (2003, p. 682).

[154] Mohun and Roberts (2020, p. 62).

- User-driven: RaC can be used to better meet the needs of the public, by helping to improve citizen and business' understanding of their rights and responsibilities through public sector service delivery based on coded rules.
- Proactive: RaC should increase the speed of government service delivery and improve the responsiveness of the rulemaking process. It may also increase the government's ability to rapidly achieve transformative reforms. If rules are digital and linked, changes can be more rapidly affected and enforced."[155]
- It should be noted, however, that some initiatives and processes, some already raised above, are confused with RaC, even because of the interchangeable use of denominations, but they must be distinguished from it.[156] This does not mean that they have less dignity or value, only that they do not coincide with RaC, although they may have common points and serve as an inspiration for this proposal to deepen the digitization of the legislating power.

3.2.1 Legaltech, RegTech and New Business Models

Without repeating what has already been discussed above in this regard and taking into account the *supra* definition of what is intended with the RaC project, it is easy to see that the increasingly frequent experiences of Legaltech, RegTech and new business models can be distinguished from RaC by three orders of reason: on the one hand, because they are not deliberate, systematic or integrated initiatives; on the other hand, because they tend to happen in the final phase of the legislative project, after the publication in human-readable format, which is manually and individually transformed into code consumable by computers for compliance purposes; lastly, because they are seldom of public origin and, therefore, fail the authority of interpretation.

3.2.2 Electronic Procedures and Tools and Online Digital Publication

Electronic procedures reduce costs, increase efficiency and allow for more secure procedures, by avoiding unnecessary paper. Furthermore, they allow a better tracking and comprehension of amendments and versions of proposed drafts and deliver more accurate statistical data. In addition, online digital publication of approved laws and regulations in official gazettes shortens the delays and offers more accurate and transparent information on which laws are in force.[157] Official electronic publications are nowadays done in several formats. Some of them, like PDF documents, are hardly machine readable. Others like XML are machine readable but not consumable, although they provide tools to better sort wanted information through enhanced web search engines and hyperlinks (which can find amendments, revoked bills, connected laws). In sum, these solutions, part of an e-government, are once again too short and

[155] Mohun and Roberts (2020, p. 63).

[156] Waddington (2020, p. 180), even points out that "there is no unified line on what 'Rules as Code' means (or even whether it is the best label to use)."

[157] Silveira (2018, pp. 182–183).

distant from a simultaneous drafting of human-readable and machine-consumable legislation, which indicts that computers are still not seen as real end-users.[158]

After all, there is still a lack of adequate and accurate technology to generally and easily process and convert human natural language into code, although some products are trying it but with limitations, including depending heavily on human interdisciplinary teams, even though AI and machine-learning may assume in the future larger roles.

3.2.3 Machine-Readable Versus Machine-Consumable

The terms machine-readable and machine-consumable are often used synonymously. However, in technical terms, they present two different levels of digital integration.

The machine-readable format, which cannot be confused with a mere digital format (for example, a PDF document cannot be automatically read by the computer), allows information to be processed and understood with little or no human intervention without loss of semantic meaning. The machine-consumable format, on the other hand, goes a step further: not only is the information known and understood, but it also allows for compliance, namely enabling calculations or checking eligibility and criteria. That is, the rules, in code with which the software can interact, are triggered by the automatic processing of computer systems.

In comparison with RaC, if machine-readable legislation does not advance in automated operation, machine-consumable legislation is a fundamental instrument for the RaC project, which, more than a simple legislative format, reflects a more ambitious agenda of amendment of the legislating paradigm, reducing, from the root, in an early and authoritative way, the translation gap of norms.

3.3 Machine-Consumable Experiences

It is not intended here to make an exhaustive or in-depth treatment of all machine-consumable legislation experiences around the world. We only would like to show that, on the one hand, it is not science fiction and, on the other hand, the potential but also the limits of these initiatives that have been developed both at governmental and academic[159] levels as tests and engines of a change in the legislative paradigm.[160]

Thus, we can find codification efforts in New Zealand,[161] Australia, Estonia, Denmark, France, UK, Germany and Canada, most of them being developed by

158 Mohun and Roberts (2020, p. 24).

159 Especially, https://www.cohubicol.com/ (last access 05 May 2022).

160 For all, Mohun and Roberts (2020, pp. 67 et seqq.), Sousa (2021b). Rules as Code projects around the world, in Rules as Code Handbook, https://github.com/Rules-as-Code-League/RaC-Handbook/wiki/7.1-Rules-as-Code-projects-around-the-world (last access 05 May 2022).

161 Barraclough et al. (2021).

central governments[162] and applied in limited sectoral aspects such as taxation, social support or reporting obligations. Similar to what is also seen in international organizations such as the OECD[163] and the EU,[164] many of these projects mainly have a learning dimension and seek to increase knowledge about the process, application, its advantages and disadvantages or its potential evolution, for example as to its constitutional implications in terms of separation of powers and democratic legitimacy,[165] the (legal) nature of the code parallel to norms in natural language,[166] its principles and framework, its script and operationalization or its communication strategy.

In a brief appreciation of the results of these initiatives, it is observed that they are still preliminary and sectoral trials. In other words, no State or Organization uses the RaC in a systematic, integrated and transversal way, focusing on sectors of greater operationality, revealing a pragmatic approach. In fact, opting for sectors that are potentially more suitable for machine-consumable legislation may be a strategy, given the probabilities of success, to be able to extend the new paradigm to other less obvious areas and, thus, progressively expand, in a more sustained and consolidated way, coding to the entire law-making process. However, this path can fail for two main reasons. On the one hand, this sectoral approach can generate a patchwork and asymmetrical system, with imbalances and resistance. On the other hand, by starting with matters that are susceptible to codification, possible limits and pitfalls associated with machine-consumable legislation may be minimized and underestimated, thus eroding the value of the RaC due to lack of preparation, critical prognosis, unbiased diagnosis and holistic vision and by possibilities of capture (namely of private companies interested in the development of this type of technology).

From the evaluation of these experiences, it is also verified that they are implemented only in developed countries and with significant advances in administrative modernization, in the construction of an E-Government and in the path of a digital State. This indicates that the costs, know-how and technologies required are still too expensive and, therefore, not usable broadly and massively, requiring more solid and reliable institutions that guarantee the sustainability, reliability, accountability and transparency of the process. However, by increasing the scale of application,

---

162 In the British case, the Digital Regulatory Reporting Project, based on a model driven regulation that can be transformed into programmatic language, is led by the Bank of England and the Financial Conduct Authority.

163 See as paradigmatic Mohun and Roberts (2020), this report being just one among many from the OECD around the themes of better legislation and state digitization. In this matter, as in the context of the EU, its collaboration with the Observatory of Public Sector Innovation (OPSI) stands out.

164 For all, https://joinup.ec.europa.eu/collection/better-legislation-smoother-implementation/news/rules-code-opsi-cohubicol (last access 05 May 2022); and https://joinup.ec.europa.eu/collection/better-legislation-smoother-implementation/digital-ready-policymaking (last access 05 May 2022).

165 Barraclough et al. (2021, pp. 3, 9, 58).

166 Barraclough et al. (2021, pp. 3, 154 et seqq.), against the legal nature of the code mainly because it calls into question the separation of powers, even when drafting in parallel. In favour, Mohun and Roberts (2020, pp. 26–32). Showing differences between text and code-driven rules but still recognising their normativity, Hildebrandt (2020a, pp. 69–70, 72 et seqq., 77–79; 2020c, pp. 10 et seqq.).

marginal costs will fall, not only due to technological developments but also due to competition with and between private parties, which will allow for greater dissemination of machine-consumable legislation and of the RaC project. Furthermore, if international organizations such as the World Bank adopt the machine-consumable regulation project, then, in a top-down approach, it will be easier for the code to be disseminated worldwide.

In fact, the involvement of international and supranational organizations in the development and implementation of RaC can be strategic for what seems to be an unavoidable move towards machine-readable and machine-consumable legislation.[167] In addition to international and supranational support (of studies, administrative, technical, technological and financial), it promotes a systematic and transversal approach to the digitization of legislating power, which not only has advantages in national but also international terms, as it allows the reduction of legislative barriers, with the establishment of international principles and standards and increases the scale, reducing costs, and the interoperability so necessary in a globalized and digital world.

These experiences underline the importance of multidisciplinary approaches and of teams with members belonging to various sectors, institutions and administrative levels, with multi-step processes that allow the construction of the code in a cohesive and coherent way, through the identification and selection of key concepts, their interrelationships, common denominators, decision trees and logic mapping. In this way, at each step, it is possible, through the dialectic between the different actors of the team, to identify ambiguities, gaps, margins of discretion and practical problems of interpretation and translation.

Finally, it should be noted that almost all of the initiatives carried out so far are not truly RaC but tests, especially since they have been transforming pre-existing human-readable rules into machine-consumable rules, therefore not operating early, in the two simultaneous formats, from the initial legislative impulse, which makes upstream insights difficult, such as realizing which rules can and should be codified and how, in practice, to manage and operationalize the elaboration of consumable digital rules by computers.

Despite all these limitations, these attempts serve for learning purposes, not only in terms of better operationalization, but also in terms of a preliminary cost–benefit analysis to determine the goodness of proceeding on the RaC path.

[167] Mohun and Roberts (2020, pp. 93 et seqq.). Considering the three potential future scenarios regarding RaC, although not necessarily successful, in either case, progress is made in a more or less coordinated and balanced way towards the emergence and consolidation of machine-readable and consumable legislation phenomena.

3.4 *To Operationalize Machine-Consumable Legislation and RaC*

The operationalization of machine-consumable legislation and RaC, that is, the passage from theory to practice, involves, on the one side, technical and technological decisions and, on the other, epistemological and methodological choices.

In the first case, there is still no precise and reliable technology for automatic and universal translation from natural language to code. Several options have been tested and the debate about what type (authenticity, provenance, quality, quantity, ownership and consent) of data,[168] programming language, technical parameters, rules engine, or use of AI remains alive.[169]

In practice, manual coding solutions are being tested, such as smart contracts and blockchain, software libraries and Application Programming Interfaces (APIs). If there are already some attempts at semantic translation technologies, they are still far from being sufficient and automatic.[170] Other hypotheses involve the creation of authoritative, open source and agnostic models of legislation, with setting parameters for the regulatory content, which end-users can then convert entity-by-entity into a machine-consumable format adaptable to their technical systems.[171] France went a little further, trying to develop a specific purpose language for RaC, Catala.[172]

In doctrine, it is discussed, which of the programming languages is the best: an imperative system more focused on action (such as Java) or declarative closer to traditional legal rules (such as HTML or SQL), or a general or specific purpose language. They all have advantages and disadvantages and on a case-by-case basis may be more or less suited to the needs of machine-consumable legislation and RaC.[173] Looking at the current scenario, there are multiple solutions instead of the privileged resource to a language, namely Excel,[174] Blawx,[175] RaaP or Oracle Intelligent Advisor.[176] That is, for now, one-code-language-does-not-fit-all or no language seems like an obvious choice.

As for the second set of operationalization problems, unavoidable questions arise such as: who is responsible for the production of machine-consumable legislation?;

---

[168] Snow (2019, pp. 5–7), points out that there may be problems with the use of technology, especially AI, in regulation, if the data is narrow, unrepresentative, imbalanced. Data abuse and privacy issues, as well as monopoly formation, auditability and regulatory arbitrage can also be strong challenges. Also, Amariles (2020, pp. 280 et seqq.).

[169] Mohun and Roberts (2020, pp. 79 et seqq.).

[170] Mohun and Roberts (2020, p. 74). On technical issues, for all, Nay (2018).

[171] Example of proposal: Cvejic et al. (2021).

[172] Ma and Wilson (2021, pp. 124–125).

[173] Mohun and Roberts (2020, pp. 80 et seqq.).

[174] For all, Waddington (2021).

[175] Morris (2020).

[176] Mohun and Roberts (2020, pp. 84–86), Waddington (2019, pp. 35–36; 2020, p. 181).

can and should all rules be codified? What rules should be codified?; what principles should guide the machine-consumable legislation process and the broader RaC project?; what steps should be taken in this process?[177]

Regarding the first question, if we accept the fullness of the RaC project beyond machine-consumable legislation, and, therefore, with simultaneous drafting of rules in natural language and in code, both from their origin with authoritative value, then inevitably policy-making and law-making bodies at various levels should be involved, as well as public services and agencies with technical and technological knowledge and delivery services that will apply the rules, in order to form multitask and interdisciplinary teams (since there are, at the moment, very few lawyers who can code).[178]

A different but interconnected question will be whether this type of teams and services should be centralized or decentralized, but the answer will depend on several factors that will not have to do exclusively with technical issues.[179] Indeed, they will depend on political options but also on the constitutional and administrative organization of the State (e.g. federal or not, regional autonomies and local authorities), legal-administrative traditions, and existing human and technical resources.[180] In a context of globalization (and regional economic integration), one should also think, as discussed above, to what extent it would not make sense to have some degree of centralization of the codification process at the level of international and regional organizations, especially with regard to legislative acts directly applicable (such as European regulations or international conventions in non-dual systems) or to be transposed into domestic legal systems (such as European directives or conventions in dual systems). Not only would transaction costs be reduced, but the risks of translation gaps would also be decreased, in addition to alleviating problems of non-compliance by States with their international obligations, namely regulatory and legal transposition.

Assuming RaC as a deliberate project of the State, with the involvement of early codification, the participation of public bodies and services must be central. This does not mean, however, that individuals cannot play a relevant role, either as partners, including through Public–Private Partnerships (PPPs),[181] working in an integrated and coherent way with the State, or as service providers, as far as total outsourcing with the presentation of a finished legislative product in digital (and human-readable) format—which could raise doubts as to its constitutionality—, either as drafters or as software developers (competing or not with public services). This will be all the more true if we are only talking about machine-consumable rules projects, since we are

[177] Mohun and Roberts (2020, pp. 102 et seqq.).

[178] Andrews (2020).

[179] In New South Wales, "Rather than relying on a central entity to code all the relevant rules, the program set out to create the framework and technical tools required for individual teams and agencies to code rules specific to their operations. To this end, the program team (from the NSW Department of Customer Service) have developed the foundational components of a framework that will help to scale RaC efforts within NSW." Mohun and Roberts (2020, p. 87).

[180] For example, Lestré (2019) argues that the State Council should centralize the RaC project.

[181] Reis et al. (2019, pp. 247–248).

not necessarily considering either early interventions or authoritative versions of the rules. In these terms, however, there may be, in addition to contractual disagreements and imbalances in the distribution of risk in the case of PPPs,[182] dangers of capture by private interests, on the one hand, and, on the other, of commercial lock-in, therefore, with the legislative power and the State losing control over the process.[183]

As for the second question, academic research and machine-consumable legislation initiatives make it possible to determine what type of legal rules, within the existing panoply (despite the doctrinal attempts to look for common denominators and characteristics to define them in a more restricted and unitary way),[184] are most suited to their transformation into code and which may pave the way for others (if necessary and appropriate). From what has been written, it is easy to foresee that existing prescriptive rules with little or no margin of discretion, more objective and categorical and less ambiguous and open to subjective interpretations, such as referring to questions of eligibility, calculation, deductions or exemptions (such as some rules on taxing or social support), and with logical if–then-that formulations, are the best candidates in theoretical terms.[185] Likewise, more technical rules seem like good options.[186] On the contrary, norms that use indeterminate or broad concepts or that fit into sensitive (such as fundamental rights) and/or fracturing themes (such as euthanasia, abortion) present greater obstacles, on the one hand, due to the interpretative margin (sometimes intended to allow greater flexibility of the rule in different contexts and its evolution), and, on the other hand, because the controversy can generate distrust, resistance and repudiation of the codification of the rules. In the latter case, only time, will, willingness to accept norms with lower performance standards, technological advances and the significant increase in the scale of machine-consumable rules will be able to mitigate the expected opposition.[187] In the first one, the code transformation project could be a good opportunity to identify the problems of interpretation and unnecessary discretion, namely forcing us to rethink the rules, the conceptual framework and the creation of indicators and criteria that

[182] Reis et al. (2019, p. 248).

[183] Mohun and Roberts (2020, pp. 102–103).

[184] See discussions on the characteristics of legal rules, including generality, abstraction, imperativity, coercibility, and dual structure with prediction and statute, in any Introduction to the Study of Law or General Theory of Law manual.

[185] Mohun and Roberts (2020, pp. 103–104), Hildebrandt (2018). Along these lines, as it is clear from the OECD report, the Government of New South Wales has built a decision tree that integrates these elements and thus helps to make a decision on whether or not to codify rules. See also, Sousa (2021c).

[186] Yudkin (2021) points out the need for processability of legal norms. He also adds the that they should, in order to be machine-readable, algorithmized, use the information system and ensure the legality of machine—readable law. Oster (2021, pp. 108–109), goes even further, stating: "On a purely logical-syntactic level, the law thus provides exact results; there are 'right' and 'wrong' decisions. Seen from this perspective, the law is an algorithm. As such, it can easily be applied by machines." Nevertheless, semantically, "Law is thus an organism, and not merely a mechanism. On a macro-level, the law is different in kind than on a micro-level: 'the law' is more than the sum of its 'laws'."

[187] Sheppard (2021, p. 2262).

help to further densify the grey areas of the norms. This, however, does not mean that interpretation should be turned into a merely technocratic or even useless exercise, completely replacing human autonomy and discretion (not least because the RaC project provides for the simultaneous creation of rules in a double human and computerized format), or that the rules become so rigid that they hardly adapt to the contingencies of the dynamism of the real world that one wants to apprehend and regulate, being constantly a Law of the past. There will always have to be a certain trade-off between certainty, clarity vs. adaptive flexibility, innovation, and resilience,[188] which may (and should) imply that certain (necessarily) discretionary rules, even if the process is automated, should be handled manually, since they are not, by nature, computable.[189]

In practice, regarding the type of rule most suitable for digital formulation and automation, for reasons of efficiency (with economies of scale), visibility and impact, norms of repeated application and by multiple users (e.g. tax eligibility and calculation rules) should be strong candidates.

Finally, with regard to rules, between new and old, the experiences mentioned above[190] have worked with the latter, but the RaC project foresees its application to new rules for reasons of efficiency. In fact, in the same way that progress has been made in the transformation into electronic and online formats (e.g. pdf, html) of legislative acts, in parallel between new and old with the progressivity of the latter by criteria of date or relevance, nothing prevents that the same does not happen in the RaC movement.

Regarding the principles that should govern the operationalization of the process and writing in code, several were identified, both in the OECD report[191] and in national assessments of these initiatives, as is the case in Denmark,[192] although with different but complementary dimensions and partially overlapping. In the former, a concern with the definition of substantive and framing principles, in the latter a more pragmatic and operational approach to the process, including control questions at each step that should be sought to answer to ensure, in the end, a successful and adequate experience.

Indeed, the Danish Digitization Agency identifies seven principles, although it recognizes that they can be derogated from when specific considerations arise, such as the best interests of the child:

- Principle 1: Simple and clear rules (avoid ambiguous wording and multiple exceptions or special schemes);
- Principle 2: Digital communication (if mandatory for citizens and businesses to communicate with public authorities there must be legal authority for this, which should be technology-neutral);

188 Cabugueira (2020, pp. 9–10).

189 Waddington (2019, pp. 41–42).

190 See point 3.3.

191 Mohun and Roberts (2020, pp. 104–106).

192 Agency for Digitalisation (n.d.).

- Principle 3: Possibility of automated case processing (seeking to make the rules as objective as possible for automation based on the principle of legality and, in case of necessary discretion, provide for their manual treatment);
- Principle 4: Consistency across authorities (uniform concepts and reuse of data);
- Principle 5: Safe and secure data handling (high prioritisation of data security; transparency is ensured in the public data handling and citizens and firms should be offered insight into public data on themselves);
- Principle 6: Use of public infrastructure (public authorities should use existing public infrastructure to ensure the largest degree of reuse and cohesion across authorities);
- Principle 7: Prevention of fraud and errors (risk-based control and to allow effective IT application for control purposes of the correctness of data).

Considering this last principle, the OECD, which also includes security as a principle (in particular with regard to data protection and cyber-attacks),[193] goes further and proposes and strengthens a principle of appealability, that is, the possibility, at all times, of requests for review of automatic decisions not only in view of the (unavoidable) possibilities of error and fraud, but also as an instrument of legitimation, trust and transparency of the entire RaC process.

Transparency (from the perspective of citizens and end-users) is also one of the fundamental principles identified by the OECD to ensure the democratic dimension of RaC, in particular its access and understanding, and it translates into various actions that may include nudging[194] such as the explanation and public dissemination of the rules behind the code, as well as the outputs of the automation process like decision trees or concept models, the inherent reduction in the translation gap process with the decrease of interpreters involved, and even the possibility by default of public consultation and hearing on the draft code before its official publication, or the use of simulators[195] to grasp and train the contact with machine-consumable solutions, bringing citizens closer to technology, reducing their fears and, consequently, changing their beliefs and attitudes. The visibility of the rules and the underlying processes and the disclosure of the information that the system is automated, as is already evident from article 22 of the EU General Data Protection Regulation, are important to obviate problems of mistrust when errors arise, allowing not only to correct it more quickly and fairly as explaining the reasons for misapplication, obviating feelings of insecurity and conspiracy theories. Paradigmatic was, in 2021, the case of the

> software bug in [the] inmate management software used by the Arizona Department of Corrections, [that] led to hundreds of inmates being incarcerated longer than their sentence

---

[193] It is all the more sensitive if the process is in the hands of the private sector, for example, within a partnership between the State and the private sector to operationalize the codification. Reis et al. (2019, p. 248), Enriques (2017).

[194] Seeing the nudging at the service of communication and transparency in the process of translating and transforming European directives into national law (if we think about it, similar to the process of passing from human-readable to machine-consumable legislation), Franco et al. (2021).

[195] As an example of a simulator: https://mes-aides.org/ (last access 05 May 2022).

> required because the software could not interpret a 2019 amendment to sentencing laws. As the coded rules were not publicly viewable, this issue only came to light as a result of whistle-blower action.[196]

This transparency requirement is allied to three other OECD principles: traceability, accountability, and accessibility and interoperability. As for the first, it is necessary to ensure the documentation of the entire process, even so as not to lose the intention of the legislator and guarantee the isomorphy (strictly, alignment) with the natural language and also to understand and detect eventual errors (or fraud attempts).[197] However, in practice, isomorphy is mainly wishful thinking because, in fact, as it comes from the experience with European regulations with direct effectiveness in the domestic law of the Member-States, their interpretation and application gains wings depending on the context. Moreover, the interpretation of any legal norm evolves beyond the policy and law-maker's intent, taking into account the dynamics of the application reality, with a flexibility that allows norms not to rapidly become obsolete and adapt to the demands of a society in permanent mutation. In other words, the objective of RaC cannot be to have only a single normative interpretation, nor that this is eternal or a production of the past,[198] as this conflicts with the principles of legal hermeneutics, with the nature of norms and with the role of the courts as arbiters in the interpretation, especially since authentic interpretations and rulings may be overturned. In other words, the objective is above all to reduce interpretive noise and to provide coherence, aligning interests, among the various participants in the legislative and application process, increasing traceability[199] and legal certainty. Thus, the expression "translation", so often used here, must be moderate. After all,

> coded models are better understood as an interpretation of what the law requires. The fact they are computational models does not change this, even where parallel drafted. Further, in practice, most computational models will draw on a wide range of legal sources, and the notion that a single model will represent a single legal instrument is difficult to sustain.[200]

On the other hand, it is necessary to be accountable for possible errors, especially since, in addition to consistency with human-readable legislation, it is essential to guarantee the trust and authoritative nature of the code that must be published in open access and in a directly consumable version (regardless of option and technological means of end-users and service delivery).

Returning to the beginning of this work and to the answer to the last question, it follows from what has been written the need to rethink in a strategic, holistic, integrated and systematic way the relationship between policy-making and law-making,

---

196 Sousa (2021d).

197 For example, the Australasian Legal Information Institute (Austlii) platform DataLex has a proof-of-concept chatbot for interpretation and eligibility to stand for Parliament, which delivers a report that sets out its conclusion, together with the relevant rules and the evidence applied. Sousa (2021d), Mowbray et al. (2021a, b).

198 Defending code-driven rules as a normativity of the past, in contrast with text-driven rules, Hildebrandt (2020a, p. 78).

199 Barraclough et al. (2021, pp. 3–4, 45 et seqq.).

200 Barraclough et al. (2021, p. 3).

in which all stakeholders (including the hearing and participation of stakeholders, designers and service delivery),[201] at different and across levels, must communicate with each other and work together so that data, concepts, criteria and legislative and code norms are delimited in order to be used and to ensure the fit between technical solutions (and their interoperability), legislative style and application context. This requires, in addition to prototype testing,[202] iterative cooperation and *ex ante* evaluations, that successive (human and automated) systems of feedback and loops[203] are foreseen, including an *ex post* assessment of the implementation, in order to correct and adjust the code, and if interconnections with other diplomas and codes and possible or real difficulties are identified. This also ends up ensuring democratic scrutiny and safeguarding values. In other words, although steps can be identified in the legislative procedure ladder (policy-maker—rule-maker—technical coder—test—publication), more than a linear process, it pursues to establish a strongly integrated and interconnected network, mostly to guarantee greater traceability. The data accumulated and also provided by stakeholders throughout the iterative process (including their attitudes and behaviours) are used for "a 'need led approach' that should be more efficient, effective and responsive to social changes."[204]

3.5 *Nudging 2.0*

Within the scope of an effort to digitize the legislative power but also to improve Law, nudging can be an important ally at several levels.[205]

On the one hand, nudge may emerge as a more efficient and effective alternative, in some cases, to traditional legislative instruments. On the other hand, it can be incorporated into the legal codification process, either to help ensure alignment in interpretation and application, reducing unnecessary noise, or to support the distinction between norms (or parts of norms) that can be codified or not (due to their technical characteristics and content).

In the first case, in a logic of proportionality and of building better policies and law, the nudges, which may or may not be intrinsically normative (e.g. social norms and default rules vs. reminders, information or stickers), appear as an option to command and control, with the potential advantages of not being imposed and being less costly. However, it is not easy, by nature, to work massively for a wide and heterogeneous public, so their resource, although ingenious and usually cheap, is not

[201] Some countries already demand pre-drafting hearings. Cf. Kouroutakis (2021).

[202] For all: Sousa (2019a, 2021e), elaborating further and foreseeing that coding will test legal solutions per se; Waddington (2019, pp. 30–31).

[203] Waddington (2019, pp. 31–32).

[204] Cabugueira (2020, p. 18). Note that the "needed based" intervention is related to libertarian paternalism and the nudge approach to policy making.

[205] Questions related to the conceptual framework of nudge, its application or its goodness (efficiency, effectiveness, equity, social acceptability, ethical and constitutional aspects) and ideological dimension (e.g. libertarian paternalism) will not be addressed here.

always effective in a sustained and transversal way. Now, technological advances can help to increase its shaping power and scale.[206]

In fact, on the one hand, in addition to the possibility of real nudges, digital and coded nudges[207] can be used, as the private agents already do abundantly, especially on social networks and, sometimes, in a harmful way,[208] thus enhancing some psychological effects that shape behaviours.[209] On the other hand, data-driven nudges (in particular, with the extraction from the data of general prescriptions with legal effects), with the support of open data policies and big data, machine-learning or even AI,[210] allow greater precision, making the appropriate boosts and aimed at the individual characteristics of each addressee and, therefore, more effective and efficient, above all being able to be readjusted according to the dynamics revealed by the behaviours.[211] Furthermore, due to their greater adjustment to the recipient and continuous learning, they can be less paternalistic, more holistic and easily updated.[212] In this line, similarly,

> the effective content of data-driven rules depends on the dataset or machine-learning techniques used by the administration. This means citizens may in practice be subject to different rules or standards of behaviour despite the applicable law being the same. As for the latter, data-driven rules affect procedural rights by creating an inequality of arms between the administration and the citizens, and by increasing or shifting the burden of proof. For example, (…), access to the source code, let alone the full dataset used by the administration, is generally limited or unavailable, which prevents citizens from effectively exercising their rights of defence, such as being able to challenge the evidence or the rules effectively applied to them.[213]

In addition to the problem related to this potential imbalance of forces, there is also the risk of aggravating biases or behavioural lock-in, as is the case with reinforcements resulting from algorithms used by the most successful search engines or social networks. This means, therefore, that it is necessary to think about monitoring, evaluating and de-bias systems (even using counter-nudges).

Secondly, and as will be seen throughout this chapter, nudging, real or virtual, can be an instrument in the construction of machine-consumable legislation and, above all, of RaC. Here, its role (in analogue, codified or digital versions) is linked to three main aspects: (i) to ensure good communication and dissemination of the project, in order to reduce more or less irrational resistance, namely by seeking to safeguard

---

206 Risdon (2017).

207 On the definition of digital nudges, Weinmann et al. (2016, pp. 433–436), Schneider et al. (2018, pp. 67–73), Meske and Potthoff (2017, pp. 2587–2597), Mirsch et al. (2017, pp. 634–648; 2018).

208 Calling them "evil nudges", Lavi (2018). Similarly, Puaschunder (2018, pp. 87–117), Puaschunder (2017).

209 For all, on digital nudging and psychological effects, Mythili and Kiruthiga (2021), Mirsch et al. (2017, pp. 634–648), Jesse and Jannach (2021, pp. 10 et seqq.).

210 Suh (2019).

211 Mythili and Kiruthiga (2021, p. 63), Hrnjic and Tomczak (2019).

212 Porto (2022, p. 19). Calling these precision digital nudges "smart nudges", Karlsen and Andersen (2019, pp. 1–4).

213 Amariles (2020, p. 299).

transparency, accountability and appealability; (ii) to guarantee the alignment of interests and of translations and interpretations between the various actors in the legislative process, from the policy-maker, to the applicator and end-user, passing through the drafter, the law-maker and the coder, promoting larger consistency, legal certainty and traceability of the created rules; (iii) to assert a system of checks and balances throughout the legal and coding process, especially in the delimitation of rules (or parts thereof) that can and should be legislated in machine-consumable (and executable) format, thus reducing constitutional and value problems (for example, with warning boxes, default rule of opt-in for coding in certain subjects or types of norms, a digital assistant,[214] or recommender automated systems).[215]

In short, nudging, especially smart, tailor-made and digital, should be part of the external and internal architecture of the RaC project, not only as a communication tool but above all as an integral part and one of its pillars in noise reduction and guarantee of its legitimacy. Its study must therefore be in-depth, notably in a digital context, and the solutions tested (including with regard to their interaction with other nudges and instruments) and always ethically and legally guided, including in terms of privacy.[216]

4 The Good, the Bad and the Ugly: Advantages, Challenges and Pitfalls of Machine-Consumable Legislation

From the theoretical scientific research and the experiments that are being implemented with machine-consumable legislation and its *ex post* evaluation, one can guess, on the one hand, advantages in a deliberate and systematically integrated RaC strategy, especially in a world undergoing profound digital transformation, and, on the other hand, limits and risks. However, before listing and analysing them, it should be noted that these are considerations based mainly on theoretical predictions and on small, case-by-case tests. Hence an increase in scale and dissemination of their application could reveal a new balance of costs and benefits and unintended (positive and negative) consequences.[217]

---

[214] Porto (2022, pp. 13 et seqq.), preferring, in terms of disclosure, less intrusive and paternalistic nudges such as warning boxes over default rules or digital assistants.

[215] Jesse and Jannach (2021), Karlsen and Andersen (2019). Warning against recommender systems and their most probable perverse effects, Hildebrandt (2022).

[216] For all, concerning nudging digital, Meske and Amojo (2020), Karlsen and Andersen (2019, pp. 5–6), Mele et al. (2021, p. 958).

[217] Eliot (2021n, p. 2).

4.1 Goodfellas—The Benefits

From what has been written, especially regarding the inadequacy of the Administration and the legislating power to a society undergoing rapid digital transformation, as well as about the foundations of the RaC project, it is easy to infer that this proposal brings advantages, direct and indirect, for the State, society (citizens, institutions, market) and the Law.

4.1.1 Decreased Translation Gap, Adequacy and Efficiency

Without wishing to repeat the above, it should be remembered that one of the problems diagnosed is related to the successive interpretation of the norms throughout the legislative process by various actors, with the introduction of a gap between the policy intent and the effective implementation of the rules and increased transaction costs, either because the interpretation departed from the original intention (namely during the final translation by the end-users or their technical teams, particularly when the rules are codified), or because in practice the application as planned is not feasible since the norms are misaligned with reality and context.

However, in order to create machine-consumable legislation (from scratch or not)[218] with authentic and authoritative value, there must be careful planning, at the procedural, formal and substantive level, in order to, on the one hand, ensure the possible isomorphism between natural and programmatic language, as well as better drafting legislation, above all by eliminating unnecessary ambiguities[219] and discretion and, finally, to foresee and frame the assessment of its impact and the imperative of amendments, both for reasons of legal certainty, and for reasons of contextual adaptation (after all, reality is dynamic and the Law is not, and should not be, immutable).[220]

Indeed, a parallel and simultaneous writing of rules in two different formats, with a view to addressees with different characteristics and motivations, requires an iterative communication between multidisciplinary designers and coders, and a dialogue between jurists and programmers, in order to align their objectives and discourses, in an efficient and effective effort. The difference between the languages used, even in terms of underlying logic, creates difficulties in translations, aggravated by the fact that interlocutors with distinct conceptual backgrounds are also involved. Note that this is not a mere monologue in which the policy-maker and the law-maker interpellate the coder to explain their purposes. The latter, and his technical team,

[218] This implies to find or develop a user-friendly interface for drafters to easily "code" their rules themselves, during the drafting process. Sousa (2019b).

[219] Eliot (2021o, p. 3), proposes the use of AI to aid translation rather than a large-scale project to modify the language by a simpler and more precise language. Revealing the scaling potentials of the approach behind Austlii, Mowbray et al. (2021b) Representing legislative Rules as Code.

[220] Nevertheless, Hildebrandt (2020a, p. 76), considers that text-driven rules are more adaptative and revisable than code-driven rules.

also address the former to ensure that they not only correctly understand the legal concepts and the legislator's intent, but also recognize the specifics and needs of programming and code. In fact, their inputs can help to reformulate the rules to be codified, namely in their logical formulation but also in increasing their objectivity, simplicity, clarity, feasibility and limiting the multiplication of exemptions, exceptions and special regimes. Paradigmatic is the case experienced in New South Wales on encoding a provision that said a grant was payable to parents of children aged four and a half to eighteen.[221] To a human it seems, at first glance, a clear and simple rule. However, the same is not true for a computer (and inherently for the coder) that needs to know exactly what to do. Just think about doubts associated, among others, with time changes, leap years and whether it is counted from the time of birth, the beginning or the end of the day. However, in practice, the decision taken on these aspects can decide whether or not to award the scholarship and will make a difference in the lives of citizens. This situation clearly reveals the challenges in interpreting and translating even in norms that are considered clear. In fact, it ends up demonstrating the challenges but also the limits of criticism to a project of machine-consumable legislation or RaC: although these initiatives advocate simplification, objectivity and clarity of rules in order to reduce ambiguities and misinterpretations, their wording in these terms continues to present hermeneutic challenges and, therefore, requires an exercise of interpretation. In other words, neither clear, simple and objective norms (with almost or no discretion) are truly clear, simple and objective, nor does the interpretive function disappear with its transformation into code, turning interpretation and application into mere technocratic and formal acts.[222] This does not mean, on the one hand, that codifying rules (even if clear and objective) is impossible, nor, on the other hand, that with codification hermeneutics ends due to a blind subservience of the investigation of meaning to practical operationalization.

In fact, for the purpose of the present case,

> the point of RaC is not necessarily to eliminate this challenge [interpretation and translation of rules] or all ambiguity, but instead to make it visible to both implementers and policy makers (who can then decide if it is warranted or desirable). The current, linear sequence of rulemaking does not currently facilitate this and, as a result, issues such as these are not evident nor easily correctable until after the policy is implemented. Revealing these discrepancies, through RaC, may therefore help to realize outcomes that are closer to the original policy intent.[223]

In other words, more than an aim of codification, automation or a transformative panacea, the main objective of RaC is to promote an integrated and collaborative reflection between stakeholders in the legislative process, specifically between policy makers and legislators, advancing step by step in their alignment.[224]

---

[221] Waddington (2019, pp. 46–47).

[222] Ma and Wilson (2021, p. 114), by the way, highlight the difficulty over the years in moving from legislating in "legalese" to legislating in plain English, which seems to indicate the specifics (including symbolic) of legal syntax and semantics. Thus, simple rules will not necessarily be simple.

[223] Mohun and Roberts (2020, p. 34).

[224] Waddington (2020, p. 182).

Additionally, this dialogue between the policy-maker/law-maker and the coder enables legal design and better policy outcomes, since it reveals, in a more intense way, the difficulties of the creation and enforcement of the Law and highlights the need for better legislation, with upstream impacts of greater trust in institutions, given higher consideration and adequacy of legislative solutions, but also downstream with greater accessibility, transparency and comprehension of the rules, with a consequent increase in certainty regarding application with augmented compliance and, therefore, alignment between the legislator's intent and enforcement. Besides, given the bigger intelligibility, it reduces problems of inequality before the Law in which, as verified in several legal systems, those who have the best lawyers are able to benefit more from dubious rules and from interconnections that are not always obvious (e.g. aggressive tax planning). It also has the advantage of demonstrating that being a lawyer is not limited to reading or knowing the laws by heart (as is so often socially perceived) and that law schools play a fundamental role in the training of jurists. Finally, with the more precise identification of legal limitations,

> the design of code may provide a new option for specific influencing laws. It will be of the greatest importance to individuals or large, disorganized groups poorly equipped to take advantage of existing means of political influence. And as such, the code option may mean some change in the relative power of interest groups, as it makes organization slightly less important,[225] thus promoting larger fairness.

Finally, the high need for planning when legislating (both in natural language and) in code implies that, more than in a context of just human-readable legislation, attention is paid to the interconnections between rules, diplomas and regimes for coherence and terminological and conceptual consistency and for an assessment of the impacts of the new legislation on the entire legal system, as well as the possible changes that it may undergo in a conjunctural or structural way (e.g. contextual dynamism and the legal system itself). This early forecast allows for testing various scenarios in which the rules would be applied, and faster, more efficient and effective adjustments (particularly before implementation), anticipating impacts and solutions that guarantee systemic adequacy and balance between Law and the universe of enforcement.[226] In other words, using coded rules permits "regression" testing with built-in contestation[227] (i.e. test proposed rulesets against a multitude of test scenarios with an adversarial nature) in order to observe if they will operate as intended and model different legislative approaches, to get closer to the desired effect. In fact, it is easier to adjust and correct a machine than to change human attitudes, beliefs and behaviours, especially in contexts of uncertainty and risk.[228]

In short, machine-consumable legislation or RaC initiatives are valuable contributions to strengthening the digitization of the State and its adaptation to the times and trends of a dynamic society of risk and information, specifically as they allow a

[225] Wu (2003, p. 682).

[226] Sousa (2019b), Morris (2020).

[227] Hildebrandt (2018).

[228] Mullainathan (2019); presenting solutions to design fair algorithms: Zehlike et al. (2019).

reallocation of scarce resources both by the State and the private actors. Simply put, as Sousa summarizes:

> Currently, we have numerous businesses each coding their own version of the same laws. This creates the risk that translations will be incorrect or misinterpreted. In contrast, a single government-provided and assured translation, made available via Application Programming Interfaces ('APIs', which make it possible for machines to speak with one another and transact) would cut down on this needless duplication. Regulators would be able to see the rules being consumed, and the community would have certainty that the rules being used by automated systems were the correct interpretation (or even certified to be correct). A single set of government-assured coded rules would also be a boon to the private sector. They wouldn't have to devote resources into translating the rules into a form their systems could use – saving money, increasing productivity and profits and, therefore, increasing the tax base. What's more, individuals, small businesses and startups could use the APIs as well, removing expensive barriers to competition and creating a more even playing field. As a bonus, when the rules or laws change, the code can be amended and the linked systems would be updated automatically. Everyone wins.[229]

After all, at least in theory, (big) data analysis, learning algorithms and code may provide analytical and instrumental tools for better and more efficient Law and regulation, by simultaneously, being able to handle and process large amounts of information, exploit self-learning systems with alternative solutions and massify the implementation of an authoritative interpretation. Moreover, the output is more flexible, fit and resilient.

4.1.2 Consistency, Interoperability and Equity

Proactive planning, necessarily reinforced in the legislative process, given the requirement of codification, comprises the best legal practices, both material and formal, which translates, among others, into an effort of terminological and conceptual coherence, as well as the principles underlying the entire legal system. This implies, in particular, as has been mentioned, the participation of multidisciplinary teams that involve elements (or at least their hearing or consultation) from services from various State institutions (including service delivery) but also from private and social stakeholders, in order to achieve at least a terminological and conceptual harmonization that not only allows an easier identification of interconnections and impacts (especially within the legal network) but also permits greater homogeneity in the legal treatment of problems and, consequently, larger equity thanks to the increase of navigability in the legal system. For example, a different conceptual framework of what is meant by small or medium-sized firm depending on whether the diploma in question is tax, social support, commercial firms or labour law can generate perplexities, injustices and misunderstanding. Naturally, the dialogue between the several actors in the legislative process, as discussed in the previous point, allows for a better and more accurate identification of discrepancies and solutions for their management, minimization or even elimination, when possible.

[229] Sousa (2019a).

The issue of coherence and equity can be seen from another angle: with the code having an authoritative value equal to that of human-readable legislation,[230] passing from the legislative source directly to the end-user, with a centralization of the elaboration of business rules and the legislation to be applied, namely for eligibility, calculation or reporting purposes, interoperability and consistency are increased in terms of interpretation and application, thus not depending on the individual and manual translation of the rules and (expensive) teams of technicians for this purpose.[231] In other words, ensuring an authentic, traceable and centralized interpretation of the codified, shared, open and accessible rules (in open source), with data that are reusable and easily reviewed and preferably with the shared use of public infrastructures, in a Government as a Platform logic, superior compliance is ensured and costs are reduced, in terms of time and expertise in particular, thus dropping asymmetries in the application (and consequent charges for non-compliance due to misinterpretation or translation) and between users.

The increase in the scale of machine-consumable legislation, possibly boosted by the introduction of AI in the process of interpretation and transformation into code, could deepen the issues of consistency and interoperability and, thus, of equity, efficiency and effectiveness, all the more so as a process of machine-learning may allow for a better adaptation and more "personalized" and granular treatment[232] of the end-user, increasing her well-being.

4.1.3 Transparency and Accessibility

Transparency in the RaC process and in the construction and application of machine-consumable legislation is required for reasons of legitimacy, on the one hand, and, on the other, for structural reasons to the process itself.

Indeed, given the traditional myths and fears that involve the use of technology (which most do not understand or master), due to the uncertainty, risks and ignorance regarding several of its aspects and potential consequences, a clear and transparent communication strategy is appropriate, presenting the advantages and disadvantages of the solution under development and which means and principles (especially precautionary and proportionality) were found to manage eventual challenges. Lessons should be drawn, among others, from examples such as the introduction of

---

[230] Against, Barraclough et al. (2021, pp. 3, 154 et seqq.).

[231] In New South Wales, "The program also includes the development of a web form builder, which is a standard website form that connects to the government's API, extracts the questions needed to populate the specific form and presents them to the front end user. The responses are automatically sent to the API and the response is presented back to the user in a meaningful way. This will allow multiple agencies to easily create website components (i.e. eligibility engines) which all draw from a 'single source of truth'. Future plans for the programme include supporting agencies to code specific rule sets (...), as well as the development of a rules explorer (...) that allows developers to examine all rules contained in the API." Mohun and Roberts (2020, p. 87).

[232] For all on personalized law, granular rules and microdirectives, Ben-Shahar and Porat (2021), Busch and De Franceschi (2018), Casey and Niblett (2017).

transgenics and cloning in agriculture and food or, more recently, in mRNA technology in vaccines against Covid-19. Transparency is, therefore, fundamental to ensure both the democratic legitimacy and the social acceptability of this step in digitization and thus help to undo or mitigate resistance, mistrust and more or less Luddite conspiracy theories. After all, the narrative of catastrophist and Orwellian pessimism seems painful to deconstruct once installed or suggested. It follows, therefore, that once the damage to the social reputation of machine-consumable legislation is done, no matter how much rehabilitation efforts are developed, with serious information and clarification campaigns, the harm will hardly be reversible. The management of the fear of the unknown and the uncertain, in order to remove behavioural irrationality and entrenched distorted and counterproductive archetypes and heuristics, is fundamental in the policy and regulation of the codification of Law.[233] The necessary lessons must be learned from the always timeless Platonic parable of the cave, in which the light of wisdom is not assumed, by itself, as sufficient in a world of darkness, incomprehension and pre-defined mental and cultural frames.[234]

Thus, and as mentioned above, it highlights the fact that the introduction of this new legislative and regulatory format is a deliberate and strategic option of the State, which must assume and explain it. Furthermore, all interested parties should be consulted and involved, for example through public consultation, and promote the elaboration and public dissemination of studies on this matter, particularly with the support of academies and associations representing the main interests in place. However, as argued elsewhere, public involvement and participation do not constitute, despite being essential, a sufficient solution for gaining social trust and agreement with RaC. The action must be imperatively precocious and dismantle—and for that to know and understand—the wrong perceptions and stereotypes built on this purpose and what feeds scepticism and resistance. The intervention, in order to gain in efficiency and effectiveness, must be tailored to the recipients, both in terms of content and form of communication, that is, different attention and communication strategies depending on the target: general public, developed or less advanced countries, business and industrial sector, policy makers, the academic and scientific community, among others. In short, it is important to seek to comprehend and anticipate their behaviours, attitudes and beliefs as they shape both the way in which decisions are made (procedural rationality) and the content of decisions (substantive rationality), thus managing to prevent a cascading phenomenon that is self-reinforcing (and which, therefore, becomes more difficult to lock and reverse) against the encoding advance.

Recent lessons learned from studies developed by the Cultural Cognition Project at Yale University[235] may add value in the necessary preparation and adequacy of risk (and uncertainty) communication. For example, it was found that subjects tend to align themselves with positions diametrically opposed to their cultural convictions when they observe others, with whom they identify, defend opposing ideas. If there

[233] Slovic (1987, p. 236).

[234] Saraiva (2014).

[235] Kahan et al. (2008a). See also, Kahan et al. (2006, p. 5; 2007, 2008b).

is no congruent relationship between the perceived values of informants and their position on the harms and benefits of technology, cultural polarization is neutralized. This indicates that the cultural affinity heuristic (which is also determined by the need for social identification and belonging) has a greater weight than the affect heuristic. Attention to ensuring a cultural pluralism of communicators can therefore help to reduce polarization by widening the spectrum of affinities. Put another way, the messenger (especially if he is a culturally appropriate influencer) may well be more important than the message in building risk perception and messenger-shaped herd behaviour. This pluralist solution, however, resembles an arduous execution, mainly due to the natural difficulty, in this context, of generating consensus.[236] Even so, this opens the door to the correction of biases through the use of intelligent, targeted, precise and personalized nudging (by demographic categories or even finer with the support of AI), namely considering the power of social norms and the possibility (even if not total) of its alteration by the modification of expectations and beliefs, considering the dynamism of the social rules themselves (although some are more sticky) and their ability to adapt to changing and new contexts.[237]

On the other hand, *a fortiori*, similarly to what happens with the traditional legal process, specific legal rules for codification should be established and publicized and even the establishment of legislation should be considered (preferably preceded by a public consultation) about its procedures, formalities, and fundamental principles. As mentioned above, it may be a good practice to publish (online) documents and work instruments, especially the concept models and decision trees that were built. Truthful, clear and current information, as a boost, serves as an antidote to unfounded mistrust (although it makes it easier, because it is open, to resist interests)[238] but also as a measure of internal self-control and modesty for those involved in the process of creation and implementation of machine-consumable legislation. For example, feedback mechanisms between the various actors, namely between designers and implementers, between jurists and coders, allow the correction and adaptation of behaviours. Likewise, the construction and strategic salience of decision-trees, logic planning, concept-models and checklists, especially at the beginning and passage of each phase of the legislative process, help to align the interests at stake. This system of nudges can be manual or it can also be automated, mainly through reminders, cooling periods to evaluate and test the solutions found or default rules in which it is not possible to proceed to the next phase without filling them correctly with certain type of data or that determine opt-in systems for the codification of certain rules (for example more complex ones).

Furthermore, it is also important to clarify and protect the interactions with the rights (and duties), freedoms and guarantees of citizens, namely with regard to personal data, and with the functions of the State and their constitutionality (expressly regarding aspects of operationalization and division of powers). In these cases, in particular, an intelligent system of more or less automated alerts that require a review

[236] Saraiva (2014).

[237] Franco (2018).

[238] Lessig (2006, p. 327), refers a trade-off between transparency and effectiveness.

of the coding of the rule or that force it to be prepared by default in a merely human-readable mode should be established.

Transparency also emanates from the very way in which RaC is conceptualized and from the operationalization that has been devised and tested with machine-consumable legislation, since the visibility of the rules and their formation process is increased and internal and iterative debate is encouraged between multidisciplinary and multi-institutional stakeholders, *a fortiori* including public consultation solutions during the drafting process,[239] and between law-maker and coder.[240] As argued above, this interaction allows us to highlight where the "law smells"[241]: conceptual incongruities, unnecessary ambiguities and discretion, interconnections and the challenges of coordinating rules (with their positive and negative conflicts) and their feasibility and implementation, on the ground, namely of anticipating the need and direction of future changes. Consequently, the solutions found to overcome or manage them and the changes that may be made become more visible and scrutinized. Furthermore, since the code is imbued with authoritative value in everything equivalent to the corresponding human-readable legislation, there is a double certification of the rules and their comparability enhances transparency. In fact, the accessibility of the rules (shared, in open source, with less intermediation and more understandable) allows anyone to evaluate them. This accessibility, combined with interoperability, foreshadows the importance that the authoritative version published by government would need to be program-neutral as far as possible.[242]

The increased accessibility and greater proximity and navigability by the end user, namely thanks to the online availability of instruments that simulate, inform or actually apply rules on eligibility and calculation based on the codification of legal rules (e.g. social support, taxation[243]),[244] allow achieving a more agile administration because there is less noise introduced by multiple hermeneutic experts and it becomes more "massified" and "industrialized"[245] since it gains scale, celerity and disintermediation in the automation of the treatment of interpretive and semantically less controversial issues. This does not mean, once again, that a by-pass is made and the interpretive exercise and the support of specialists are dispensed, or that a movement towards greater personalization of Law, in a logic of data-driven rules (and nudges), is not also in place.

Indeed, as noted above, even "clear" norms need interpretation for their translation into another language and for their subsumption in the specific case. Furthermore, a certain level of interpretive automation (including through machine-learning) for more unanimous understanding rules frees up interpreters to deal with more complex

---

239 Sousa (2019b).

240 Against, talking about opacity and hermeneutics injustice, Hoven (2021).

241 Eliot (2021p).

242 Waddington (2020, p. 181).

243 For example, https://fr.openfisca.org/showcase/mesaides/ (last access 05 May 2022).

244 Sousa (2019b).

245 Mohun and Roberts (2020, p. 45).

and noble situations, thus optimizing their intervention.[246] In other words, there is an efficient reallocation of scarce resources (interpretative, translation, transformation and subsumption) from less complicated and controversial issues and rules to added value, ennobling the exercise of Law and consolidating legal certainty.[247] Basically, and using a metaphor, it is as if the coding were cognitive System 1, relieving System 2 and allowing it to optimize its deliberative judgment and decision resources to weight the interpretative elements in less obvious cases.[248] This, however, does not prevent errors in either system, since the interpretation, while founded, also in the automated version and in machine-learning, in the performance of men of flesh and bones, limited and subject to biological, evolutionary, cognitive, social, emotional, contextual and motivational biases, may not be adequate nor optimal, particularly in the face of ambiguity, as it, for example revealing phenomena of confirmation or hindsight biases.[249]

4.1.4 Legal Certainty

Here too, the contribution that machine-consumable legislation and a RaC project can offer in enhancing legal certainty is taken from the previous pages if appropriate precautions are taken to reduce risks and uncertainties.

The accessibility and transparency described and developed above, together with the disintermediation of interpretation, reducing the translation gap, especially with the authoritative value of the code, ensure a reduction in risk throughout the system.

Furthermore, the rise in the coding scale and the use of data, in combination with the iterative cooperation between the multidisciplinary participants (and all the more with the algorithmic and AI resource), increase the predictive power[250] in terms of the needs of legislative adjustments thanks to the resulting diagnoses of the close monitoring throughout the legislative process, the interconnections detected with other legal regimes and thematic areas and the trends of contextual changes, natural in dynamic societies. In other words, legal certainty is reinforced both by anticipating possible changes in the rules and by being able to carry out these alterations more swiftly and efficiently. Since regulated organizations have linked their business systems to APIs published by regulators and consume new rules through these, in a near future they will be able to automatically update when changes come into effect, ensuring immediate compliance.

On the other hand, the advisable deliberate and assumed character of codification, combined with a necessary tailor-made communication policy appropriate to the addressees and the issue under discussion, also promote greater confidence in the initiative, in the legislating and legislative power and, consequently, in the State.

---

[246] Mohun and Roberts (2020, p. 46).

[247] Sousa (2019b).

[248] In a similar way, Eliot (2021q).

[249] For all, Moniz Lopes and Franco (2019, pp. 47–79).

[250] Critical about the predictive power of data-driven rules, Hildebrandt (2020b, p. 3).

This should transparently include recognition of the merits but also of the limits and risks inherent to machine-consumable legislation and RaC, as well as the strategies systematically pursued to mitigate and manage any pitfalls, from nudging to regulation, through densification and operationalization of the precautionary principle used, especially since its scope varies greatly depending on the context of application.

Now, given the distrust observed regarding the use of technology in sectors that intersect with human daily life (e.g. nuclear, GMO or nanotechnology), it will not be difficult to guess movements of disproportionate resistance to the codification of the Law, particularly louds if there is not a concern of deliberate communication to clarify the project, above all due to its sovereign function and transversal impact, whether because of neophobia and structural conservatism, or because of fear of what is not understood, known or perceived as a danger, revealing an aversion to risk, or all the more because of the desire to protect interests arising from the *status quo*. By stressing and distorting the perception of risk, one can erode and invalidate, right from the start, any generalized attempt at RaC (with or without the use of AI) with the consequent (unfortunate and inefficient) influence on the regulatory agenda, with a (wrong) (re)allocation of scarce resources away from the digitization of the legislative power. Only with the integrated consideration of multiple dimensions such as effectiveness, static and dynamic efficiency, equity, social acceptability, political feasibility, cost–benefit analysis and economic-behavioural analysis of the codification of the Law will it be possible to cut and densify a precautionary principle adapted and adjusted to the circumstances, namely that it is not so broad as to destroy, from the outset, the development of the code itself, nor so restricted that it is virtually inapplicable.

Thus, the key lies in the application of the principle of proportionality to the logic of prevention, by providing the necessary flexibility to follow the requirements of the range of uncertainties. Therefore, the more intense and costly the potential damage, the lower the level of probability required to allow the cessation of the coding activity or the regulatory and supervisory public intervention that must consider the values and interests at stake, avoiding, in particular, excessive, inappropriate and unnecessary actions. Otherwise, progress and the process of creative destruction are inhibited from birth due to the excessive burden of total harmlessness, generating, in a perverse way, a kind of adverse selection in which only the least dynamic elements remain with the outdated and costly means and methodologies, with known risks, in a clear preference for the maintenance of the *status quo*, which sustains the crystallization of the inadequacy of the Administration and of the legislating power in a digital society. Furthermore, this Luddite predisposition to precaution can deprive the present generation of goods or services that not only satisfy their needs, but also do so more promptly, effectively, efficiently and equitably. This is valid not only for the possibility of machine consumable-legislation or of decision automation, but also of its development via algorithms and AI.[251]

Delaying the introduction of innovations until more information is obtained can be a long, strenuous and counterproductive journey, especially since the precaution that seeks to eliminate risks from the root creates other risks. Thus, similarly to what has

[251] Proposing a *ex ante* soft regulation of AI through nudges, Guihot et al. (2017).

been defended in other works,[252] a more restrictive formulation and conceptualization of precaution is preferred, in line with Sunstein.[253] This restrictive formulation and conceptualization of precaution shall be accompanied with an irreversible harm precautionary principle or a catastrophic harm precautionary principle that would legitimize aggressive measures only to the extent of the magnitude of the damages (intensity, extension, temporality), despite the difficulty in their accounting and valuation, which, however, does not rule out the susceptibility of requiring, if appropriate, the performance of *ex post* tests, in a monitoring logic tailored to the learning, and even *ex ante* tests in situations of well-founded distrust of extreme harmful effects, specifically ethical and legal ones. Transparency will thus be a fundamental ally in the precautionary analysis, both contributing to the reduction of risk and safeguarding legal certainty.

4.1.5 Innovation

In a context where machine-consumable legislation is seen as an investment and, consequently, as an innovative application of technology to the Law—which, by its nature, will require adaptations and new solutions—, innovation promotes innovation, both in the public and in the private sectors. This is all the more true if we consider that the codification of Law is part of a broader movement of digitization of the State that includes, in addition to the availability of online services (which may integrate engine rules for real effects or for simulating eligibility and calculation), a logic of Open Data and Open Government but also of Government as a Platform, which feed private innovation thanks to the sharing of data and the use of public infrastructures, that will, in turn, promote public innovation itself. For example, the know-how, software, applications, systems and private methodologies developed and successively deepened and improved within the scope of LegalTech, RegTech, machine-learning applied to Law and the judiciary and even RaC will have benefits for the modernization of an inadequate Administration, despite the risks of commercial lock-in, also increasing the ratio of compliance with public legislation and regulation.

Innovation in this field is, therefore, deliberate, adaptive, oriented towards specific ends (better Law, better State), tending to be anticipatory and self-feeding.[254] Even so, considering the conservatism shown by the legislature, it is necessary to try to overcome path dependencies (not least because contact with information and the empirical tendency of preference for maintaining the *status quo* with an aversion to change influence the path taken by the various stakeholders, anchoring them to certain models of thought and architecture). The path dependencies emphasize the dynamics of self-reinforcement, prolonging the conservation of sub-optimal solutions at the

---

[252] Saraiva (2009, 2014).

[253] Sunstein (2005, pp. 14–15, 35 et seqq.). With a similar opinion, Farber (2011, pp. 919–920).

[254] Mohun and Roberts (2020, pp. 48–49).

expense of better alternatives due to the perception of a certain institutional framework of reference and the high costs of paradigm modification, and lock-in situations (whether commercial or technological, mainly associated with the—high—costs of the option taken) that make it impossible or at least make changes difficult, especially in a context of a risk and information society in which leaps and disruptive changes occur. Therefore, it is necessary to encourage, mainly via nudging or soft solutions, the exploration of alternative options such as clinical trials,[255] test beds, living labs,[256] innovation hubs, incubators[257] or the (regulatory) sandboxes[258] that allow testing new challenges, business models, instruments and responses in border areas without strict regulation. Think, in particular, of the extremely fast and changing scope of FinTech and the regulatory sandbox of the British FCA or Italian supervisor.[259] Similar instruments can make it possible to test the modelling and simulation of changes in legislative policies, helping to foresee potential impacts and challenges and the reverberations in the legal system as a whole and in the solidity and trust in the State. Such solutions will be as valuable or more valuable the greater the scale of available data and machine-consumable legislation and will contribute to transparency and better Law with an anticipation of its effects. See the Leximpact simulator associated with the French OpenFisca initiative, which makes it easier for political-administrative agents to simulate the effects of tax reforms on citizens and the State budget.[260] The availability and salience of this type of tools, which could be included as a default option in the legislative procedure, could nudge policy makers and law-makers in the direction of a better Law.

The advantages listed here should not be interpreted as a complete argument to defend the thesis of the absolute goodness of a transition to a machine-consumable legislation or to the broader RaC project, or that these are the magic solution for an inadequate Administration. When it comes to the application of technology to a sovereign power, a precautionary approach must be adopted in its design and implementation, with regular monitoring of its direct and indirect impacts on the State, Law and society.

4.2 *Cape Fear—The Costs and Risks*

The combination of the use of technology—when some of which has not been fully tested or with possible unknown, ambiguous, uncertain or risky effects (such as

255 Arner et al. (2016a, b, p. 45).

256 Engels et al. (2019).

257 Barraclough et al. (2021, pp. 6, 111).

258 Snow (2019, p. 31), Arner et al. (2017, pp. 16–18), Barefoot (2020b, pp. 76–79), Barraclough et al. (2021, pp. 6, 32, 168–169).

259 https://www.fca.org.uk/firms/innovation/regulatory-sandbox (last access 05 May 2022); See also, Arner et al. (2016a, b, pp. 45 et seqq.), Grassi et al. (2020, pp. 7–8).

260 https://fr.openfisca.org/showcase/leximpact/ (last access 05 May 2022).

AI), with the exercise of sovereign power that impacts the heart of the State and its relationship with citizens and among those citizens, raises questions of evaluation of its limits, costs, and risks, both in a precautionary logic and in a cost–benefit analysis in order to consider the worth and opportunity of its adaption. When adopted, the questions of *for, if, when and to the extent necessary* provide for a preventive, mitigating and management strategy.

As already explained, given the incipient experience of machine-consumable legislation, it is not easy at this embryonic stage to anticipate with certainty the totality, breadth and interconnection between limits, burdens, and challenges. Even so, by theoretical inferences from analogous cases, mainly related to technological evolution and application, and from the experiences tested in the meantime, some theoretical and practical questions can be anticipated here, which will be divided, in a crude way (as they are closely interconnected), between technical and legal-political issues.

4.2.1 Technical Questions

The concrete operationalization of an analogue to digital legislative process and the transformation of natural language into machine-consumable legislation entails changes at various levels, from habits to procedures, planning organization, structures, design and workflows, through the choice of standards to codify, the data to work, the technology to use, sharing systems and legal methodologies (formal, material and impact assessment).

Several of these problems have been addressed above, so we refrain from returning to them, especially surrounding codifiable rules and whether new or old rules, the technological option and problems of commercial lock-in and path dependencies that lead to sub-optima choices that tend to crystallize.

In technical terms, we should add the:

> high dependence on the technical state of the information infrastructure, called in the expert environment the 'chopper problem'. Destruction or interruption of power supply to data storage and processing devices, disconnection from computer networks, including the Internet, and similar cases actually cease the very existence of machine – readable rights or minimize the functionality of information systems.[261]

Furthermore, the variation in terms of increasing the scale of code production will have transversal implications on the various issues (technical and legal-political) and constitutes, in itself, a challenge for its start-up and for its maintenance and management, as it is important to monitor its impact in terms of average costs.[262] If today, legal programming has high average costs (due to the cost of a technology and procedures under development and the incipient number of uses), it is expected that, like other technology cost curves, there will be a significant dilution of total and average costs (partly due to the lesser intervention of multiple interdisciplinary

---

[261] Yudkin (2021).

[262] Mowbray et al. (2021b).

teams), although it will be necessary to continue investing in improvements and even innovation and development in this area (which obviously cost money).

A different question is whether there will be changes as to who else bears these costs. Now, taking some public experiences in half a dozen states, in practice the conversion into code is done by private agents and supported in large part by the companies (and citizens) that resort to them to make their compliance more efficient and effective (although the overwhelming majority of the time this generating code has no guarantee of authoritative value). Assuming a RaC process, i.e. with simultaneous legislative initiative in natural language and in code, then there should be a transfer of (high) costs from the private sector to the State, reducing (massively) compliance costs for the former. However, it must not be forgotten that ensuring interoperability, making the rules accessible and easily consumable, in practice, also implies costs in adapting the existing systems.[263] However, increasing the coding scale can be an opportunity for a long-term restructuring of systems, giving them greater flexibility but also a modular logic, more compatible with constitutional and competitive values,[264] and reuse.[265]

This growth process can also be fundamental in learning about the identification, collection and processing of the necessary and adequate data, in quantity, quality and consistency, to guarantee the best code. In a logic of open data, big data and open Government, it is a delicate operation that requires specialized and expensive teams, prepared to interact and analyse the data (sometimes public, others private).

4.2.2 Legal-Political Questions

Moving forward in a consolidated manner to machine-consumable legislation forces, as noted above, means to consider issues of governance and of the best level to act and of who must take this initiative in hand, namely discussing centralization or decentralization issues (which will depend, among other, on aspects of political organization, allocation of resources and the scale of the project and the moment of creation of the code—whether early or at an implementation stage), and whether or not the new structure coincides with the legislative structures of human-readable legislation. It also asks for teams with the necessary and adequate skills and resources.

In addition, given the different system of sources of Law between diverse legal families, and between the Common and Civil Law, in particular, considerations arise, especially in Common Law, concerning the relationship between the legislature and the judiciary and the impact it suffers with the introduction of a code, namely

[263] In fact, interoperability is nowadays mostly wishful thinking since there are no "minimum standards for the logic of legislation so that all legislation as code APIs behave predictably, regardless of the platforms used. (…) most 'rules as code' platforms focus entirely on the translation of rules into code rather than taking a born digital approach to rules in the first place. Worse, most current platforms don't allow for easy and consistent API access to the rules independent from business logic, which limits the reusability of rules." Andrews (2020).

[264] Lessig (2006, p. 328).

[265] Mohun and Roberts (2020, pp. 86–87).

regarding its operationalization but also regarding the balance between powers and with the transformation of judicial rulings also into code.[266] This generates the fear, in Anglo-Saxon systems, of the judge becoming a mere enforcer of Law and solver rather than a creator and creative performer.[267] Furthermore, and following the French law 2019–222—in particular its article 33 which imposes limits on the use of judges' data, with the prohibition that they can be used, either by manual statistical processing or by algorithm, with the aim of establishing a decision-making profile for the magistrate and, thus, predicting the direction of his decisions—, it is foreseen that, *a fortiori*, similar solutions may advance in Common Law countries, in a conflict between the protection of data and privacy of judges and neutrality and independence of justice and, on the other hand, guarantees of defence, transparency and predictability of the Law.[268] The French Constitutional Council, in its decision n. 2019–778 DC, of March 21, 2019,[269] confirms the constitutionality of the rule, since it considers that its purpose is to avoid and contain the creation of litigation strategies according to the individual characteristics of the judges, which would contribute to distort the functioning of Justice by the comparability between magistrates. Thus, it seeks to ensure the functional independence of the judges in the face of a framework of public and electronically available judicial decisions (which facilitates the processing of data). In fact, the *ratio decidendi* seems to be to block or at least delay the introduction of technology, especially machine-learning algorithms, in the courts, due to fears of abuse and conditioning.[270]

These considerations, still uncertain in view of the embryonic nature of Law programming experiences, should take into account, in addition to guidelines, recommendations and manuals of legisprudence in code, the future need for the construction and adoption of a public policy and regulation on RaC.[271] Indeed,

> two analytical frameworks have to be strictly separated: the law of technology and the technology of law. This also applies to the digitalization of the law itself. 'Technology' is the realm that decides to what extent the application of the law 'can' be digitalized, that is, whether a digitalization of the law is possible. This has to be distinguished from the question to what extent the law 'may' be digitised, in other words, whether a digitalization of law would be legal. This question is located in the normative realm of the law, not in the factual realm of technology. It concerns the 'law of digitalization of the law', hence the law of digitalization,[272] or regulatory framework of RaC and machine-consumable legislation.

It should be noted that this will largely depend on the actors who will assume a leading role in this process. After all, the framework and concerns will be different if

---

266 Eliot (2021r).

267 Mohun and Roberts (2020, p. 91).

268 Eliot (2021s).

269 https://www.conseil-constitutionnel.fr/decision/2019/2019778DC.htm#:~:text=L'article%207%20a%20pour,%C3%A0%20l'%C3%A9ducation%20des%20enfants (last access 05 May 2022). See paragraphs 93 et seqq.

270 See Bragança and Bragança (2019).

271 Mohun and Roberts (2020, p. 89).

272 Oster (2021, p. 114).

the initiative, particularly technical and operational, is taken by private hands or by the State. In the first case, public regulation can/should be stronger and by rules, even for a greater guarantee of not capturing the legislative power. In the second case, a (soft) regulation should be based on principles and more on behavioural instruments, such as precision nudges and more or less intelligent speed-bumps[273] that could even be introduced in the legislative procedures and in the code itself (warnings, reminders, moments of reflection, default rules of action and operationalization) in order to promote, in a more efficient way, the intended legislative results, and the reflection on the choices made and the technological increments to be incorporated and how. It should be noted that although transparency is a way of guaranteeing the quality of the process, in practice it is not always easy to implement. Thus,

> instead, by understanding what can and cannot be done correctly when evaluating software systems, and by demanding convincing evidence that systems are operating and within the bounds set by law, society can allow the use of sophisticated software techniques to thrive while also having meaningful ways to ensure that these systems are governable. In some cases, determining compliance and effecting governance will require oversight by a competent authority, in which case software systems must create sufficient audit trails to support that oversight. (…) although current software systems pose large challenges for those who wish to understand how they operated, computer science offers a way out for software engineered to provide such assurances. One can require that software be built to allow for analysis and technical accountability. Or rather, software can be built so that we can trust, but verify.[274]

In other words, the design of the software itself can impose or nudge safeguards and debiasing by code systems.

In any case, it is important to promote the establishment of effective governance and participatory regulatory frameworks, in order to avoid the inadequacy of analogue regulatory approaches in a digital world, ensuring adaptation to the current dynamism and new challenges, considering the current capabilities of technology but providing flexibility to future disruptive advances, with requirements that are proportionate and achievable.[275]

Certain countries and organizations that are more advanced in public digitalization are seeking to regulate automatic decision-making. New Zealand has, within a wider

[273] Eliot (2021t, p. 4), Calo (2013, p. 775), classifies speed-bumps as code and not as nudge. We do not agree with this differentiation. The author defines code as “altering the physical or digital world to make certain conduct more difficult or costly”. Although by definition a nudge should not be costly (for the nudgee), it still has costs and changes the architecture of choice. Therefore, it all comes to a question of degree, in line with the difference between boosts and nudges or between, first, second and third degree nudges. For all, Hertwig and Grüne-Yanoff (2017), Baldwin (2014).

[274] Desai and Kroll (2017, p. 64).

[275] Desai and Kroll (2017, p. 6).

ecosystem and set of tools and networks,[276] an algorithm charter,[277] which includes formalized risk assessments and guiding principles and commitments, including transparency, partnership, people-driven concerns, data, privacy, ethics, human rights and human oversight. In Canada, the Government has established a set of Digital Standards, including ethical standards, to guide the development of digital government products and services, and a mandatory algorithmic impact assessment for any automated decision system.[278] In the EU, the EU General Data Protection Regulation forbids automated decisions (article 22), except in listed circumstances (e.g. explicit or legal consent) and establishes the need of implementing safeguards to the rights, freedoms and legitimate interests of the individual, including the right to appeal an automated decision to a human arbiter.

In political-regulatory terms, in fact, and in addition to a principle of transparency, it will be convenient to establish systems of accountability, of explanation of codified norms[279] and of their possible revision, introducing and enabling the quick and unencumbered appeal and review of codified norms that can be classified of errors or of source of errors, or the support, in addition to a public defender, of a public coder.[280] Thus, administrative or alternative dispute resolution processes should be considered preferentially (or at least as first-line) to address these problems, since the traditional judicial remedy can be time consuming and, consequently, inefficient. In fact, in this case, it is important not only to consider the terms of the judicial process itself (especially whether it should be a special or summary process, in particular) but also which is the best jurisdiction if a special or specialized court (e.g. constitutional court), whether a common or higher court.

It can be seen that an error in the code, due to its massification in the application, has scale effects, with high costs and consequently raises, in addition to practical issues of resolution and "undoing" the error and the wrong applications, questions of responsibility, non-contractual civil liability and to whom to impute it.

---

[276] Principles for the Safe and Effective Use of Data and Analytics (Privacy Commissioner and Government Chief Data Steward, 2018); Government Use of Artificial Intelligence in New Zealand (New Zealand Law Foundation and Otago University, 2019); Trustworthy AI in Aotearoa—AI Principles (AI Forum New Zealand, 2020); Open Government Partnership, an international agreement to increase transparency Data Protection and Use Policy (Social Wellbeing Agency, 2020); Privacy, Human Rights and Ethics Framework (Ministry of Social Development).

[277] Algorithm-Charter-2020_Final-English-1.pdf (data.govt.nz) (last access 05 May 2022).

[278] Government of Canada Digital Playbook (draft)—Government of Canada Digital Playbook (draft) (canada-ca.github.io) (last access 05 May 2022); https://canada-ca.github.io/aia-eia-js/ (last access 05 May 2022).

[279] In France, after some litigation and controversy over algorithms within the education system, the French Parliament passed the Law for a Digital Republic, Loi No. 2016-1321 "for a Digital Republique – République numérique", in October 2016, providing for the possibility for the user to claim an explanation of the algorithm functioning. Furthermore, the French Constitutional Court, in its decision No. 2018-765, ruled that the administration cannot use machine-learning algorithms for automated decision-making, because they hinder "the administration knowing the rules on the basis of which administrative decisions have essentially been made," since they autonomously "revise the rules that they apply." On this matter, Amariles (2020, pp. 283 et seqq.).

[280] Amariles (2020, p. 299).

After all, we must not forget that we are facing a new way of doing Law and that, in the face of technological developments, advances in programming and the introduction of AI in the legislative process, it may be questioned whether or not the Law obtained is still a human product, by him decided and controlled, or not, and, therefore, who should be responsible for it. Furthermore, if there is an "outsourcing" of its execution to private parties, who, for example, is responsible for the software used or for the introduction of data, and who should be held responsible, notably if the code has an authoritative value?

In Portugal, there is specific legislation on the non-contractual liability of the State, including in the legislative dimension, Law no. 67/2007, of 31 de December, which has, besides general rules, an article 15 specifically on civil liability for damages resulting from the exercise of the political-legislative function. This, however, is designed not only for abnormal damages that must be assessed on a case-by-case basis, but also for issues of illegality or unconstitutionality, and therefore conflicts between a lower norm and a higher norm, but not for legislative errors that do not involve this hierarchical conflict (e.g. bad wording of a rule that leads to the exemption or incidence of a certain taxable fact not wanted by the legislator's intention). In other words, the rule will not be adapted to translation and coding errors, so, in the Portuguese case, to proceed with machine-consumable legislation experiments with authoritative value, this law should be amended. Even so, the last paragraph of the article is interesting when it states that "when the injured parties are in such a number that, for reasons of exceptional public interest, the limitation of the scope of the obligation to indemnify is justified, this may be equitably fixed at an amount lower than what would correspond to full compensation for the damage caused", as it allows for the recognition of the potential for mass reproduction of the error.

In Australia, the courts are also trying to understand how and who will be responsible for coding errors. In 2018, namely,

> the Australian Federal Court ruled[281] that a letter from the Australian Taxation Office (ATO) advising a taxpayer of their tax debt could not be relied on, as it was automatically generated by a system and there was no 'mental' element to the decision, even though the recipient had no way of knowing that the decision was automated and the letter was system-generated. Leave to appeal to the High Court of Australia was denied, but the ATO has since taken steps to clarify the language of their communications.[282]

In other words, in this matter, it is necessary to look at the existing regime for human-readable legislation and understand, given the specifics of the codification (especially introducing private parties into the process and AI), the special redesign and adequacy needs. This interconnection between the two regimes (for human and machine-consumable legislation) is all the more important in a deliberate, systematic and early RaC initiative, due to the parallelism between the two processes and their mutual authoritative value, in order to ensure the alignment between both and thus

[281] https://www.judgments.fedcourt.gov.au/judgments/Judgments/fca/full/2018/2018fcafc0079 (last access 05 May 2022).

[282] Sousa (2021d).

not creating disproportionate distortions between end-users depending on whether they are more or less technologically sophisticated.

Behind these issues is the biggest question of the ethics of this type of initiative and its impacts on the Law,[283] upstream (e.g. in the "classical" structure of the legal rule by the necessary adjustments to the logic of the code[284]; ontology of the legislative power; separation of powers and State-citizen relationship; nature and methodology of legal interpretation)[285] and downstream (e.g. the application of the Law, not only by end-users but also by service delivery and courts, and its monitoring). This relates to what some call "computational legalism",[286] albeit in a code-as-law context. In other words, like other technologies and steps in digitalization, such as Blockchain, crypto-assets or machine-learning, there is a fear of a shift from trusting man to trusting machines, getting rid of institutional intermediaries,[287] moving towards a legal singularity emptied of uncertainty, discretion and free will.[288] Worse, it is feared that, paradoxically, instead of the contrast of computational coldness versus a reinforcement of humanism in human interventions that are still maintained, there will be an "automation" and erosion of their stronghold of humanism.[289]

In its genesis and purpose, the project of digitization of the legislative power has neither a technocratic tendency, nor a replacement or annulment of the human and evaluative component. The basic intention, although it may eventually be perverted if structured checks-and-balances measures are not taken, is that, by adapting the State to a society of risk and information, better policy outcomes and better Law can be achieved, with less noise in its successive interpretation and application. Hence, it is defended that it is a strategic, deliberate, assumed, founded and democratically

283 On the need for ethical and legal dimensions but also on their potential conflicts and whether and how they could be resolved by AI: Eliot (2021u).

284 Although the logic behind codified norms can influence the classical structure of legal rules and its characteristics, it is not obvious that it is too impactful and distorting. After all, not all rules are codable and human-readable legislation remains in natural language. Waddington (2019, p. 41).

285 On this matter: Sheppard (2021, pp. 2260, 2266), argues that: "the openness of a standard is a double-edged sword; it can make translation of its meaning into computer code difficult, but it can also make it easier to offer attractive, translation-friendly conceptions of that meaning. Proponents of automation will likely be drawn to those rule-like interpretations, so long as they are compatible enough with existing law. This complex dynamic between computer-friendliness and legal interpretation makes it troublesome for legislators to identify the variable and fixed costs of automation. (…) With time, however, technological advancement will likely drive down innovation costs, and mainstream interpretations (…) could find favor again."

286 Diver (2020, pp. 17 et seqq.; 2022, pp. 43 et seqq.), Eliot (2021v). The computational legalism characterizes itself by "ruleishness", opacity, immediacy, immutability, pervasiveness and its production by private enterprise for commercial gain, leading to an extreme form of unreflective rule-following.

287 Kirchschläger (2021a, p. 186).

288 Eliot (2021x), Markou and Deakin (2020).

289 Similarly, Eliot (2021y). However, pointing out the possibility of humanizing technology, and AI in particular, including in the identification of emotions, Eliot (2021z). Mele et al. (2021, pp. 955–956), on prompting cognition and emotion through technology.

legitimized solution and not an imposition that comes in a reactive way from the need to adapt, often without endorsement, to a changing world.

In addition, it is not intended to completely substitute the human and humanist component, although fear is perceived, in particular, when considering moving towards singularity solutions or black box algorithms. However, there, the issue is not a matter of machine-consumable legislation per se, but of technology (like any other issue involving technology, from food production to decision making), and programming errors are, in theory, not only correctable but also easier to correct and change than human behaviour, beliefs and attitudes. In fact, as systems are designed and monitored by humans[290] (and, ultimately, are built around and for them) their discretion does not disappear from the creation, interpretation and implementation of legal rules and should be ethically and legally treated.[291] Paradoxically, in fact, biases in the algorithms used, for example, in judicial or administrative decisions, most often result from the accumulation of previous biased "human" decisions and anchored in previous rulings, with poorly collected or processed data,[292] blind spots and subjectivities of the encoder, in a feedback loop,[293] thus making distortions more visible and, consequently, by this salience, motivating their correction, therefore not perpetuating "human" errors (which also exist, although the scale of their impacts may be smaller).[294] In other words, machine-learning algorithms may help against discrimination and bias: "If we use AI systems to face that mirror instead of stepping into an echo chamber or filter bubble we may improve our capability to move away from discrimination."[295]

Despite the concern of making the interpretation disappear or the emergence of a regulatory computer system that implements a single, government-determined interpretation of legal rules (with risk to rights, freedoms and guarantees, in line with the technicist simplification referred to by Montesquieu),[296] more operational and technocratic, in fact, several arguments may invalid the perceived fears: the provision of checks-and-balances, bearing in mind that there is a whole set of rules that are not "codable" and automatable and that the effort is mainly on reducing the noise of the translation gap, improving the legislative process by eliminating inconsistencies, ambiguities and unnecessary misalignments. In other words, the anticipation of the end of the interpreter and, with it, of the Law, does not seem to be expected (or even desirable).

---

[290] The New Zealand's algorithm charter expressively establishes the need to retain human oversight by nominating a point of contact for public inquiries about algorithms, providing a channel for challenging or appealing of decisions informed by algorithms and by clearly explaining the role of humans in decisions informed by algorithm.

[291] Hildebrandt (2021b, pp. 12–13), while distinguishing inherent computational bias from the unwarranted impact of unfair or wrongful bias.

[292] Pointing the problem for Artificial Intelligence to deal with prior data that were overturned: Eliot (2020).

[293] Marques and Nunes (2018, pp. 4–5).

[294] Eliot (2021w, p. 3).

[295] Hildebrandt (2021a).

[296] Waddington (2020, p. 182), Eliot (2021aa, pp. 1–2).

Thus, the process must guarantee, as has been defended, a strategy duly outlined by the political power, which requires effective governance and transparency equipped with check and balance mechanisms (including to keep humans in the loop)[297] that, similar to what already happens in natural language legislation (which thus reduces the technical opacity of the code), prevent, mitigate or manage potential abuses (including by the State) and loss of control by the legislature.[298]

This approach must be based on more multidisciplinary, theoretical and experimental studies, which combine academia and experts with actors on the ground, under the penalty of distorted and ineffective results.[299] This is all the more important as technology, often with a disruptive and rapid evolution, is frequently developed and applied taking into account short-term benefits, without great consideration for potential future reverberations, both sectoral and systemic.[300] It should be remembered, however, that the degree of digitization of the Law is, ultimately, a human and political choice. After all,

> it is the law's realm – the actions of legislators and decisions by courts – that decides to what extent its own digitalization is permissible, not the realm of technology. While it is true that law and technology exerts a mutual influence, these are nevertheless different systems. In particular, there is no 'technological determinism' on the law.[301]

In sum: "code is not law, and law is not code. Code is code and law is law."[302]

The establishment of a code of ethics,[303] as in Denmark, with the introduction of ethical principles around accountability, responsibility, justice, fairness, transparency and human rights (from an intra and intergenerational perspective),[304] can help to prevent and settle eventual conflicts, and even promote technological innovations (for example in the scope of smart nudging) to prevent abuses and deviations, given the eternal problem of dual-use (technology ambiguity) in an iterative bilateral relationship between technology and ethics, with implications for the Law itself.[305]

---

297 Pasquale (2019, pp. 5, 43 et seqq.), Oster (2021, pp. 116–117), Eliot (2021ab, pp. 1–2). Even so, the author recognizes some limitations to this possible human monitoring of AI systems: the requirement and cost of providing judges for these functions; potential confirmation bias by the magistrate of the algorithm's position; and anchoring in the position found by it. But notice that even in a reverse scenario (AI judge assessing human judge decision), Eliot defends that, for now, further levels of appeal would consist of human judges. Eliot (2021ac, pp. 1, 4).

298 Mohun and Roberts (2020, p. 101).

299 Alerting to the risk of studies on the digitization of the Administration without its participation, Reis et al. (2019, p. 242).

300 Kirchschläger (2021a, p. 187).

301 Oster (2021, p. 114). Similarly, Amariles (2020, p. 300).

302 Oster (2021, p. 117).

303 The New Zealand's algorithm charter expressively predicts in its regulation of automated decision making the role of ethics and human rights, and the Canadian regulation also includes ethical standards.

304 Kirchschläger (2021b, pp. 117 et seqq.; 2013).

305 Kirchschläger (2021a, pp. 187–189).

That is, despite the fears of erosion of interpretive and humanist values,[306] of the loss of free will (including not wanting to comply with the rules) due to their automation, the choice of low interpretive standards since they are more easily codable, or even a language shopping,[307] namely with the replacement of the values of the interpreter by those of the encoders (despite being understandable in view of the novelty), in fact, they do not constitute the intention of creating machine-consumable legislation. Nevertheless they can be foreseen as a possible perverse effect.[308] However, with due care established (political, ethical, regulatory, governance, and smart nudging, which on a case-by-case basis and in certain cases can be programmed or trained as rules for data-based systems even if operated in a neutral way),[309] and after further studies and the definition of guiding principles and framework, it seems that more than eroding traditional functions of the State, the Law and the interpreter, it is effectively sought to improve them by increasing rigor and coherence. Moreover, it should also be remembered that, on the one hand, not all rules are adequately codifiable—and even those that are, may not be deliberately so, or one may choose to escalate the parts that require nuance for human consideration[310]—, and that, on the other hand, legislation is maintained in natural language (which, in many cases, will continue to be used, especially in court). Moreover, even a codified norm requires, in order to have an authoritative value, a hermeneutic process that involves many more actors than the encoder (especially if we think about the process of simultaneous production of "human" norms and code, in the guarantee of its best possible alignment). In the end, it allows for a reallocation of interpretive and evaluative resources to aspects of superior added value. After all, private companies, in order to reduce compliance costs, already apply, in several sectors, individually and privately codified rules, with greater systemic risks than the assumption of an authoritative interpretation process in a code of rules that have their mirror in a natural language version and that free the interpreter for more complex and noble functions.

5 The Future Is Here (and Should be Politically and Legally Decided)—Final Remarks

The digitization of the State and its functions seems unavoidable in the face of exogenous pressures and the strong capacity for adaptation and incentives that the private sector presents in changing according to its needs and activities. For the time being, it does not seem feasible (or even desirable) to fully automate the Law, and not just for technological reasons. After all,

[306] Eliot (2021ad, p. 4), nevertheless reminds that AI can indeed be infused with emotion if we so desire.

[307] Ma and Wilson (2021, pp. 127–128).

[308] Sheppard (2021, p. 2266).

[309] Kirchschläger (2021b, pp. 112–113).

[310] Sousa (2019a).

> central features of existing legal systems are difficult to change, both because citizens likely perceive them to be of great benefit and because widescale revisions present challenging logistical or coordination problems.[311]

Furthermore, in addition to sensitive areas in the Law, such as those involving rights, freedoms and guarantees, there is a necessary margin of discretion in certain matters that can hardly and should not be codified.[312] Thus, machine-consumable legislation and RaC are neither ends in themselves[313] nor the silver bullet. Rather, they are a set of alternative and complementary instruments to the existing ones for an adaptation of the Law to the new times, especially to a flood of data.

A different question will be whether the State has the motivation and the means to make the digital transition in a deliberate, planned and systematic way or whether it will passively and reactively be eroded.

Various forces intervene, pulling in opposite directions. If, on the one hand, efficiency, effectiveness and adequacy drive a policy of legislative and regulatory digitalization, not least because it increases compliance and reduces unnecessary costs (with a positive impact on State revenue), on the other hand,

> the argument will be made that politicians have a democratic mandate to implement a plan in a given time-frame and should not be obstructed by procedures (like impact assessments) that are lengthy and resource consuming. Besides this political discussion, there are also the technical difficulties that come from the regulatory lag – time lag between the adoption of a new theological by the market and the regulatory adaptation to it, and regulatory delay – time lag between the creation of a new technology and the regulatory green line for its application.[314]

Although both of these can be mitigated by a new data driven and algorithmic driven regulation, hence reducing the delays, in fact, the biggest obstacle lies in the loss aversion on the part of the politicians, since RaC will inevitably involve new and more visible constraints on their ability,[315] and a strong institutional conservatism within the State and a consequent strong *status quo* bias in the form of the business-as-usual path.

The change to a data-driven, machine-learning-and-consumable legislation will not, however, be the panacea for all the problems of the State or of the legislating power and could, as we have seen, by increasing the scale, generate new challenges and pitfalls, deserving special regulatory attention. In any case, new challenges require new strategies, which means that, in order to embrace the intelligent codification (of part) of the Law, it is necessary, while taking into account the acquired experience, to embrace new instruments and methodology, such as smart, digital and precision nudging during and after the legislative process, as well as innovative tools such as data-driven, machine-learning-and-consumable legislation and regulation, in an assumed trial and error process (namely experimenting and using sandboxes

[311] Sheppard (2021, p. 2263).

[312] For example, Nay (2018, pp. 2–3), argues that it is easier to codify contracts than public law.

[313] Riazantseva (2020, p. 54).

[314] Cabugueira (2020, p. 19).

[315] Mohun and Roberts (2020, pp. 100–101).

or test beds), knowing that the options for digitizing the Law are decided politically and legislatively and not by technological determinism. In other words, it is up to the policy maker and the legislator to ensure that a Law 3.0 continues to secure its values and guiding principles, such as the separation of powers, human dignity, fundamental rights, justice, proportionality, transparency and democratic legitimacy. To the Law what belongs to the Law, to technology what belongs to technology.

References

Agency for Digitalisation (n.d.) Seven principles for digital-ready legislation. https://en.digst.dk/policy-and-strategy/digital-ready-legislation/guidances-and-tools/seven-principles-for-digital-ready-legislation/. Last accessed 12 May 2022

Allan LE, Engholm CR (1978) Normalized legal drafting and the query method. J Leg Educ 9:380–412. https://repository.law.umich.edu/articles/29. Last accessed 12 May 2022

Amariles DR (2020) Algorithmic decision systems automation and machine learning in the public administration. In: The Cambridge handbook of the law of algorithms. https://papers.ssrn.com/sol3/papers.cfm?abstract_id=3974564. Last accessed 12 May 2022

Andrew P (2020) We need to recode the rules of government https://apolitical.co/solution-articles/en/we-can-create-better-results-when-we-code-the-rules. Last accessed 12 May 2022

Arner D et al (2015) The evolution of FinTech: a new post-crisis paradigm? University of Hong Kong Faculty of Law Research Paper N. 2015/047

Arner D et al (2016a) FinTech, RegTech and the reconceptualization of financial regulation. Northw J Int Law Bus. Forthcoming. University of Hong Kong Faculty of Law Research Paper N. 2016/035. https://ssrn.com/abstract=2847806. Last accessed 12 May 2022

Arner D et al (2016b) The emergence of RegTech 2.0: from know your customer to know your data. J Financ Transform 44

Arner D et al (2017) Fintech and RegTech in a nutshell, and the future in a sandbox. CFA Research Foundation

Assembleia da República (2020) Guia de legística para a elaboração de actos normativos. https://www.parlamento.pt/ArquivoDocumentacao/Documents/AR_Regras_Legistica.pdf. Last accessed 12 May 2022

Aziz S, Dowling M (2018) AI and machine learning for risk management. https://papers.ssrn.com/sol3/papers.cfm?abstract_id=3201337. Last accessed 12 May 2022

Baldwin R (2014) From regulation to behavioural change: giving nudge the third degree. MLR 71

Barefoot JA (2019) Regulation innovation: failures and costs of consumer financial protection regulation. M-RCBG Associate Working Paper Series: 111

Barefoot JA (2020a) Digitizing financial regulation: Regtech as a solution for regulatory inefficiency and ineffectiveness. M-RCBG Associate Working Paper Series, N. 150

Barefoot JA (2020b) A RegTech manifesto: redesigning financial regulation for the digital age. Alliance for innovative regulation

Baron JR (2011) Law in the age of exabytes: some further thoughts on "information inflation" and current issues in E-discovery search. Richmond J Law Technol 9

Barraclough et al (2021) Legislation as code for New Zealand: opportunities, risks, and recommendations. New Zealand Law Foundation

Bauguess S (2017) The role of big data, machine learning, and AI in assessing risks: a regulatory perspective. SEC Keynote Address: OpRisk North America

Bennion J (2016) Are robots going to take our legal jobs? Above the law. https://abovethelaw.com/2016/06/are-robots-going-to-take-our-legal-jobs/. Last accessed 12 May 2022

Ben-Shahar O, Porat A (2021) Personalized law: different rules for different people OUP

Blanco de Morais C (2007) Manual de Legística, Critérios Científicos e Técnicos para Legislar Melhor. Verbo

Botelho C (2020a) From constitutional emergency to administrative calamity: covid-19 regulation in Portugal. In Revista derecho del estado, 29 May 2020a

Botelho C (2020b) Estados de exceção constitucional: estado de sítio e estado de emergência. In: Amado Gomes C, Pedro R (eds) Direito Administrativo de Necessidade e de Excepção, AAFDL, pp 9–57

Bragança F, Bragança L (2019) Ética e Inteligência Artificial: algumas reflexões sobre a norma francesa que proíbe análises sobre as decisões dos juízes. Perspectivas de Direito Contemporâneo

Brummer B (2011) How international financial law works (and how it doesn't). Georgetown Law J 99

Busch C, de Franceschi A (2018) Granular legal norms: big data and the personalization of private law. Draft—Forthcoming. In: Mak V et al (eds) Research handbook on data science and law. Edward Elgar. https://papers.ssrn.com/sol3/papers.cfm?abstract_id=3181914. Last accessed 12 May 2022

Cabugueira M (2020) Data and artificial intelligence for better and intelligent regulation. ULP Law Rev 14(1)

Calçada Pires R (2018) Manual de Direito Internacional Fiscal Almedina

Calo R (2013) Code, nudge, or notice? University of Washington School of Law Research Paper No. 2013-04. https://ssrn.com/abstract=2217013. Last accessed 05 September 2022

Canick S (2014) Infusing technology skills into the Law School curriculum. Cap Univ Law Rev 42

Casey AJ, Niblett A (2017) The death of rules and standards. Indiana Law J 92:1401–1447

Castri S et al (2018) Financial authorities in the era of data abundance RegTech for regulators and SupTech solutions BFA

Christian G (2020) Predictive coding: adopting and adapting artificial intelligence (AI) in civil litigation. https://ssrn.com/abstract=3530039. Last accessed 12 May 2022

Coelho M, Allemand L (2014) Processo judicial electrónico Ordem dos Advogados do Brasil, Conselho Federal, Brasília

Costa Gonçalves P (2020) Abdicação parlamentar na emergência e continuação da abdicação na calamidade. In observatório almedina, 21 de maio de 2020. https://observatorio.almedina.net/index.php/2020/05/21/abdicacao-parlamentar-na-emergencia-e-continuacao-da-abdicacao-na-calamidade/. Last accessed 12 May 2022

Cunningham A et al (2018) Disruptive technologies and legal service provision in the UK: a preliminary study

Cvejic A et al (2021) Automatic transformation of plain-text legislation into machine-readable format conference. In: The 11th international conference on information society, technology and management (ICIST 2021)

Desai DR, Kroll JA (2017) Trust but verify: a guide to algorithms and the law. J Law Technol 31(1)

Devins C et al (2017) The law and big data. Cornell J Law Public Policy 27

Dias M et al (2019) Tecnologia e Justiça: Modelo de Ciberjustiça [Versão 1.0 versus 2.0]. Encontro de Administração da Justiça – EnAJUS 2019At, Brasília

Diver L (2020) Digisprudence: the design of legitimate code, law. Innov Technol 13(2). https://ssrn.com/abstract=3650885. Last accessed 12 May 2022

Diver L (2022) Digisprudence: code as law rebooted. Edinburgh University Press

EBA (2018) Cryptotechnologies: improving regulatory compliance

EBA (2020) EBA response EC consultation on the digital finance strategy/action plan BS 2018 (Cover note—Crypto-assets)—251118.docx (europa.eu). Last accessed 12 May 2022

EBA (2021a) EBA analysis of RegTech in the EU financial sector, EBA/REP/2021/17

EBA (2021b) Study of the cost of compliance with supervisory reporting requirement (Report 15/2021). https://www.eba.europa.eu/sites/default/documents/files/document_library/Publications/Reports/2021/1013948/Study%20of%20the%20cost%20of%20compliance%20with%20supervisory%20reporting%20requirement.pdf. Last accessed 12 May 2022

Egídio M et al (2018) A avaliação de impacto no processo legislativo governamental: o caso português. Panel 3101: better regulation and its importance for citizens and companies in Portuguese-speaking countries and regions RCSL, SDJ Annual meeting, ISCTE—IUL, Lisbon, 12 September. https://ial-online.org/wp-content/uploads/2019/02/Apresenta%C3%A7%C3%A3ocustaquanto.pdf. Last accessed 12 May 2022
Eliot L (2020) Overturned legal rulings are pivotal in using machine learning and the law. AI & law: the master class series
Eliot L (2021a) Legal micro-directive amplification via artificial intelligence. AI & law, the master class series
Eliot L (2021b) Next era of american law is shaped via AI and the law. AI & law: the master class series
Eliot L (2021c) Computable contracts and AI. AI & law: the master class series
Eliot L (2021d) Quick and handy primer on AI and law. AI & law: the master class series
Eliot L (2021e) Assessing the no-code trend in the legal field and in light of AI. AI & law: the master class series
Eliot L (2021f) Legal argumentation and AI. AI & law, the master class series
Eliot L (2021g) Lawyer-client conflict of interest when AI is the attorney on both sides. AI & law, the master class series
Eliot L (2021h) Aspirations toward lawyers as coders comes under scrutiny in an AI era. AI & law, the master class series
Eliot L (2021i) The dangers of miscalculating human behavior via Robo-Judge. AI & law, the master class series
Eliot L (2021j) Judicial rulings per what the judge ate for breakfast and how AI fits. AI & law, the master class series
Eliot L (2021k) Increasing access to justice via AI-based language translation. AI & law, the master class series
Eliot L (2021l) Boosting judicial analytics via AI. AI & law, the master class series
Eliot L (2021m) Introducing digisprudence into the equation of code as law and AI. AI & law, the mater class series
Eliot L (2021n) Unintended consequences in the law and AI. AI and the law. The master class series
Eliot L (2021o) How AI intertwines with the trend toward law as code. AI & law: the master class series
Eliot L (2021p) AI aiding legisprudence via the uncovering of law smells. AI & law, the master class series
Eliot L (2021q) Think fast and think slow metacognition model applied to AI and law. AI & law, the master class series
Eliot L (2021r) AI in the law impeded due to machine readability of judicial decisions. AI & law, the master class series
Eliot L (2021s) Legal judgment predictions and AI. AI & law: the master class series
Eliot L (2021t) Using AI as a techno-regulatory enforcement tool. AI & law: the master class series
Eliot L (2021u) AI entering into the murky dualism of morality and the law. AI & law: the master class series
Eliot L (2021v) Computational legalism and the role of AI. AI & law: the master class series
Eliot L (2021w) Using AI to overcome gambler's fallacy that pervades human judges. AI & law, the master class series
Eliot L (2021x) Legal singularity and postulated ramifications. AI & law: the master class series
Eliot L (2021y) The curious paradox that AI in the law might dehumanize lawyers. AI & law: the master class series
Eliot L (2021z) Legal sentiment analysis and opinion mining using AI. AI & law: the master class series
Eliot L (2021aa) Legal simplification and AI. AI & law, the master class series
Eliot L (2021ab) When human judges judge the judging by AI judges. AI & law, the master class series

Eliot L (2021ac) When AI judges our human judges and the judgment of the courts. AI & law, the master class series

Eliot L (2021ad) The matter of judges being dispassionate and what about AI jurists. AI & law, the master class series

Engels F et al (2019) Testing future societies? Developing a framework for test beds and living labs as instruments of innovation governance. Res Policy 48(9)

Enriques L (2017) Financial supervisors and RegTech: four roles and four challenges. https://papers.ssrn.com/sol3/papers.cfm?abstract_id=3087292. Last accessed 12 May 2022

Ettner D, Silveira J (2014) Programas de Better Regulation em Portugal: o SIMPLEGIS E-pública, Revista eletrónica de Direito Público, ICJP/CIDP: 1

European Commission (2020) Communication from the Commission to the European Parliament, the Council, the European Economic and Social Committee and the Committee of the Regions EUR-Lex—52020DC0625—EN—EUR-Lex (europa.eu). Last accessed 12 May 2022

Farber DA (2011) Uncertainty. Georgetown Law J 99

Fenwick M et al (2017) Legal education in the blockchain revolution. University of St. Thomas (Minnesota) Legal Studies Research Paper N. 17-05

Fenwick M et al (2018) Legal education in a digital age: why "coding for lawyers" matters TILEC discussion paper N. 2018/033

Financial Stability Board (2020) The use of supervisory and regulatory technology by authorities and regulated institutions market developments and financial stability implications. https://www.fsb.org/2020/10/the-use-of-supervisory-and-regulatory-technology-by-authorities-and-regulated-institutions-market-developments-and-financial-stability-implications/. Last accessed 12 May 2022

Financial Stability Institute (2020) From data reporting to data-sharing: how far can suptech and other innovations challenge the status quo of regulatory reporting? https://www.bis.org/fsi/publ/insights29.htm. Last accessed 12 May 2022

Flood J (2011) Legal education in the global context challenges from globalization, technology and changes in government regulation. Report for the Legal Services Board, University of Westminster School of Law

Franco R (2018) The relevance of social norms within the context of regulatory impact assessment Panel 3101: better regulation and its importance for citizens and companies in Portuguese-speaking countries and regions RCSL, SDJ Annual meeting, ISCTE—IUL, Lisbon, 12 September 2018. https://ial-online.org/wp-content/uploads/2019/02/PPT-12-09-2018.pdf. Last accessed 12 May 2022

Franco R (2019) Will robots make it simpler? An overview on intelligent nudging and machine-readable legislation. https://ial-online.org/wp-content/uploads/2019/06/Apresenta%C3%A7%C3%A3o-Raquel-Franco.pdf. Last accessed 12 May 2022

Franco R et al (2021) Nudging as a tool—the case of the transposition of EU directives. e-Pública – Revista Eletrónica de Direito Público 8(2)

Goldberg N, Miller M (2011) The practice of law in the era of "big data"; with big data tools, the focus turns from managing the burden of large amounts of information to leveraging its value. Natl Law J

Grassi L et al (2020) Regulatory sandboxes: a catalyst for innovation in Finance. Inforbanca 120

Green J (2019) Legaltech and the future of startup lawyering. https://ssrn.com/abstract=3360174. Last accessed 12 May 2022

Greveler U (2017) Nudging the government: how open data can be used to make behavioural governance work both ways. In: Bala C, Schuldzinski W (eds) The 21st century consumer: vulnerable, responsible, transparent? Proceedings of the international conference on consumer research (ICCR) 2016. Verbraucherzentrale Nordrhein-Westfalen e.V., Düsseldorf, pp 33–46

Guihot M et al (2017) Nudging robots: innovative solutions to regulate artificial intelligence. Vanderbilt J Entertain Technol Law 20(2). https://scholarship.law.vanderbilt.edu/jetlaw/vol20/iss2/2. Last accessed 12 May 2022

Gurung N, Perlman L (2018) Use of RegTech by Central Banks and its impact on financial inclusion. https://papers.ssrn.com/sol3/papers.cfm?abstract_id=3285985. Last accessed 12 May 2022
Hassan S, de Filippi P (2016) Blockchain technology as a regulatory technology from code is law to law is code. https://arxiv.org/ftp/arxiv/papers/1801/1801.02507.pdf#:~:text=Blockchain%20technology%20reinforces%20the%20tendency,of%20thinking%20about%20the%20law. Last accessed 12 May 2022
Hassan S, de Filippi P (2017) The expansion of algorithmic governance: from code is law to law is code field actions science reports, special issue 17
Hertwig R, Grüne-Yanoff T (2017) Nudging and boosting: steering or empowering good decisions. Perspect Psychol Sci 12(6)
Hildebrandt M (2018) Algorithmic regulation and the rule of law. Philos Trans R Soc A. https://doi.org/10.1098/rsta.2017.0355. Last accessed 12 May 2022
Hildebrandt M (2020a) Code-driven law. Freezing the future and scaling the past. In: Deakin S, Markou C (eds) Is law computable? Critical perspectives of law and artificial intelligence. Hart Publishing, Oxford
Hildebrandt M (2020b) Data-driven prediction of judgment law's new mode of existence? Draft chapter in collected courses volume EUI 2019 summerschool. Oxford University Press. https://osf.io/preprints/lawarxiv/q5nrm/. Last accessed 12 May 2022
Hildebrandt M (2020c) The adaptive nature of text-driven law. J Cross-Discip Res Comput Law. https://journalcrcl.org/crcl/article/view/2. Last accessed 12 May 2022
Hildebrandt M (2021a) Discrimination, data-driven AI systems and practical reason. Eur Data Prot Law Rev 7(3):358–366
Hildebrandt M (2021b) The issue of bias the framing powers of machine learning. Draft Version. In: Pelillo M, Scantamburlo T (eds) Machine we trust. Perspectives on dependable AI. MIT Press. https://papers.ssrn.com/sol3/papers.cfm?abstract_id=3497597. Last accessed 12 May 2022
Hildebrandt M (2022) The issue of Proxies. And why EU law matters for recommender systems. Front Artif Intell. https://osf.io/preprints/socarxiv/45x67/. Last accessed 12 May 2022
Hino M, Cunha MA (2013) A Tecnologia na Prática dos Escritórios de Advocacia no Brasil. Inn: Proceedings of the nineteenth Americas conference on information systems, Chicago, Illinois
Hogemann ER (2018) O futuro do Direito e do ensino jurídico diante das novas tecnologias. Revista Interdisciplinar de Direito Faculdade de Direito de Valença 16(1)
Hrnjic E, Tomczak N (2019) Machine learning and behavioral economics for personalized choice architecture. https://arxiv.org/abs/1907.02100. Last accessed 12 May 2022
Jesse M, Jannach D (2021) Digital nudging with recommender systems: survey and future directions. https://arxiv.org/abs/2011.03413. Last accessed 12 May 2022
Kahan DM et al (2006) Affect, values, and nanotechnology risk perceptions: an experimental investigation cultural cognition project working paper N. 22
Kahan DM et al (2007) The future of nanotechnology risk perceptions: an experimental investigation of two hypotheses cultural cognition project working paper N. 46
Kahan DM et al (2008a) Biased assimilation, polarization, and cultural credibility: an experimental study of nanotechnology risk perceptions. Cultural cognition project report
Kahan DM et al (2008b) Cultural cognition of the risks and benefits of nanotechnology. Nat Nanotechnol 4(2)
Karlsen R, Andersen A (2019) Recommendations with a nudge. MDPI Technol 7(2). https://www.mdpi.com/2227-7080/7/2/45. Last accessed 12 May 2022
Kirchschläger P (2013) Human rights as ethical basis for science. J Law Inf Sci 22(2)
Kirchschläger P (2021) Ethics of blockchain technology. In: Ulshöfer G et al (eds) Digitalisierung aus theologischer und ethischer Perspektive Konzeptionen – Anfragen – Impulse, vol 22. Nomos-Verlag, Baden-Baden, pp 185–209
Kirchschläger P (2021b) Digital transformation and ethics: ethical considerations on the robotization and automation of society and the economy and the use of artificial intelligence. Nomos

Koo G (2007) New skills, new learning: legal education and the promise of technology. The Berkman Center for Internet & Society Research Publication Series, Harvard, Research Publication N. 2007-4
Kouroutakis A (2021) Legaltech in public administration: prospects and challenges. https://papers.ssrn.com/sol3/papers.cfm?abstract_id=3862557. Last accessed 12 May 2022
Lanceiro R (2019) Is artificial intelligence up to the task of legislative drafting?
Lanceiro R (2020) Breves notas sobre a resposta normativa portuguesa à crise da covid-19. Lisbon Law Rev LXI(1)
Lavi M (2018) Evil nudges. Vand J Ent Tech L 21(1)
Lessig L (2000a) Code is law: on liberty in cyberspace, Harv Mag
Lessig L (2000b) The code in law, and the law in code, lecture given at the pcForum 2000b, Phoenix, AZ
Lessig L (2006) Code, Version 2.0. Basic Books
Lestré T (2019) Do we need machinable-readable law? https://www.linkedin.com/pulse/do-we-need-machine-readable-laws-tanguy-de-lestr%C3%A9/. Last accessed 12 May 2022
Loewenstein G et al (2013) Disclosure: psychology changes everything. Harvard Public Law Working Paper N. 13–30 https://ssrn.com/abstract=2312708. Last accessed 12 May 2022
Lorini G, Moroni S (2020) Ruling without rules: not only nudges. Regulation beyond normativity. Global Jurist 20(3)
Ma M, Wilson B (2021) The legislative recipe: syntax for machine-readable legislation. Northwest J Technol Intellect Property 19(1)
Machado H et al (2008) Justiça Tecnológica: promessas e desafios, edições Ecopy, Porto
Markou C, Deakin SF (2020) Is law computable? From rule of law to legal singularity. University of Cambridge, Faculty of Law Research Paper. https://ssrn.com/abstract=3589184. Last accessed 12 May 2022
Marques AL, Nunes D (2018) Inteligência artificial e direito processual: vieses algorítmicos e os ricos de atribuição de função decisória às máquinas Revista de Processo
Marques MC (2016) A Governação Pública na Era Digital: o caso português. RIGC: XIV(27)
Mateus JC (2008) O Governo Electrónico, a sua aposta em Portugal e a importância das Tecnologias de Comunicação para a sua estratégia Revista de Estudos Politécnicos VI(9)9
Mele C et al (2021) Smart nudging: how cognitive technologies enable choice architectures for value co-creation. J Bus Res 129:958
Melo Alexandrino J (2020) Devia o direito à liberdade ser suspenso? – Resposta a Jorge Reis Novais In observatório almedina, 07 April 2020. https://observatorio.almedina.net/index.php/2020/04/07/devia-o-direito-a-liberdade-ser-suspenso-resposta-a-jorge-reis-novais/. Last accessed 12 May 2022
Meske C, Amojo I (2020) Ethical guidelines for the construction of digital nudges. In: Proceedings of the 53rd Hawaii international conference on system sciences
Meske C, Potthoff T (2017) The DINU-model—a process model for the design of nudges. In: 25th European conference on information systems (ECIS 2017), pp 2587–2597
Micheler E, Whaley A (2020) Regulatory technology: replacing law with computer code. Eur Bus Org Law Rev 21
Miguel A, Algarvio D (2019) Bits and bytes of financial regulation: the Regtech environment. Int J Bus Soc Sci 10(9)
Mills S (2020) A theory of personalised nudging: integrating heterogeneity and behavioural science into political decision-making. PhD thesis, Manchester Metropolitan University
Mirsch T, Lehrer C, Jung R (2017) Digital nudging: altering user behavior in digital environments. In: Leimeister JM, Brenner W (eds) Proceedings der 13. Internationalen Tagung Wirtschaftsinformatik (WI 2017), St. Gallen, pp. 634–648
Mirsch T et al (2018) Making digital nudging applicable: the digital nudge design method. In: ICIS 2018 proceedings. https://aisel.aisnet.org/icis2018/design/Presentations/5. Last accessed 12 May 2022
Mohun J, Roberts A (2020) Cracking the code, rulemaking for humans and machines, OECD/OPSI

Moniz Lopes P, Franco R (2019) Naturalizing interpretation: a first approach on "hardware" and "software" determinants of legal interpretation upcoming. In: Duarte D, Moniz Lopes P, Silva Sampaio J (eds) Legal interpretation and scientific knowledge. Springer

Morris J (2020) Blawx: rules as code demonstration. https://law.mit.edu/pub/blawxrulesascodedemonstration/release/1. Last accessed 12 May 2022

Mowbray A et al (2021a) Law as code: introducing AustLII's DataLex AI UNSW Law Research Paper No. 21–81. https://papers.ssrn.com/sol3/papers.cfm?abstract_id=3971919. Last accessed 12 May 2022

Mowbray A et al (2021b) Representing legislative rules as code: reducing the problems of "scaling up". https://papers.ssrn.com/sol3/papers.cfm?abstract_id=3981161. Last accessed 12 May 2022

Mullainathan S (2019) Biased algorithms are easier to fix than biased people NY Times, 6 December. https://www.nytimes.com/2019/12/06/business/algorithm-bias-fix.html. Last accessed 12 May 2022

Mythili R, Kiruthiga V (2021) A study on digital nudging and psychological heuristics effect. Int J Manag (IJM) 12(10)

Nay J (2018) Natural language processing and machine learning for law and policy texts. https://papers.ssrn.com/sol3/papers.cfm?abstract_id=3438276. Last accessed 12 May 2022

OECD (2002) Regulatory policies in OECD countries; from interventionism to regulatory governance. OECD Publishing, Paris

OECD (2009) Better regulation in Europe—Portugal. https://www.oecd.org/gov/regulatory-policy/44830175.pdf. Last accessed 12 May 2022

OECD (2011) Better regulation in Europe—the EU 15 project. https://www.oecd.org/gov/regulatory-policy/better-regulation-in-europe-the-eu-15-project.htm. Last accessed 12 May 2022

OECD (2017) Reviewing and supporting regulatory impact assessment in Portugal. https://dgpj.justica.gov.pt/Portals/31/AIN_Programas/ria-in-pt-final-draft.pdf. Last accessed 12 May 2022

Oster J (2021) Code is code and law is law—the law of digitalization and the digitalization of law. Int J Law Inf Technol 29

Packin N (2017) RegTech, compliance and technology judgement rule. Chicago-Kent Law Rev 93(1)

Pasquale F (2019) A rule of persons, not machines: the limits of legal automation. George Wash Law Rev 87(1)

Porto F (2022) Good algorithms, better rules: how algorithmic tools could revive disclosure regulation. Forthcoming. Riv. Trim. Dir. Publ

Puaschunder JM (2017) The nudging divide in the digital big data era. Int J Res Bus Econ Manag. https://papers.ssrn.com/sol3/papers.cfm?abstract_id=3007085. Last accessed 12 May 2022

Puaschunder JM (2018) Nudgital: critique of behavioral political economy. In: Proceedings of the 9th international RAIS conference on social sciences and humanities, pp 87–117. https://ssrn.com/abstract=3179017. Last accessed 12 May 2022

Reis Novais J (2020) Estado de emergência – Quatro notas jurídico-constitucionais sobre o decreto Presidencial. In observatório almedina, 19 March 2020. https://observatorio.almedina.net/index.php/2020/03/19/estado-de-emergencia-quatro-notas-juridico-constitucionais-sobre-o-decreto-presidencial/. Last accessed 12 May 2022

Reis Novais J, Nogueira de Brito M (2020) Debate – Pensar no estado de exceção na sua exigência In observatório almedina, 02 April 2020. https://observatorio.almedina.net/index.php/2020/04/02/pensar-no-estado-da-excecao-na-sua-exigencia/. Last accessed 12 May 2022

Reis Novais J et al (2019) Artificial intelligence in government services: a systematic literature review. In: Rocha A et al (eds) New knowledge in information systems and technologies. Springer, pp 241–252

Remus D, Levy FS (2016) Can computers be lawyers? Comput Lawyers Pract Law. https://papers.ssrn.com/sol3/papers.cfm?abstract_id=2701092. Last accessed 12 May 2022

Riazantseva YO (2020) Machine-readable law and its prospects in Ukraine Юридичний науковий електронний журнал: 2/2020. http://lsej.org.ua/2_2020/14.pdf. Last accessed 12 May 2022

Richmond DR (2013) Unoriginal Sin: the problem of judicial plagiarism. Ariz State Law J 45
Risdon C (2017) Scaling nudges with machine-learning. Behav Sci
Rodrigues S (2018) A análise quantitativa da lei e outras ferramentas para o exercício da cidadania Observatório da Legislação Portuguesa, Panel 3101: better regulation and its importance for citizens and companies in Portuguese-speaking countries and regions RCSL, SDJ Annual meeting, ISCTE – IUL, Lisbon, 12 September 2018. https://ial-online.org/wp-content/uploads/2019/07/Observat%C3%B3rio-da-Legisla%C3%A7%C3%A3o-Portuguesa.pdf. Last accessed 12 May 2022
Rosado Pereira P (2021) Convenções sobre Dupla Tributação no Atual Direito Fiscal Internacional Almedina
Santos BS (2005) Os tribunais e as novas tecnologias de comunicação e de informação: Sociologias 7(13)
Saraiva R (2009) A Herança de Quioto em Clima de Incerteza Análise Económica do Mercado de Emissões num Quadro de Desenvolvimento Sustentado. PhD thesis, FDUL
Saraiva R (2014) Memórias de um Átomo: nanotecnologia, percepção do risco e regulação. In: CA Gomes (coord.) Direito(s) dos Riscos Tecnológicos, AAFDL
Saraiva R (2015) Financial markets law: notes, 2nd edn. AAFDL
Saraiva R (2020) Fast & Furious 10.0: O Ensino do Direito e a Tecnologia: a aceleração forçada pela pandemia covidiana na Faculdade de Direito da Universidade de Lisboa, em especial In: Lupion R, Araújo F (eds) Direito, Tecnologia e Empreendedorismo, Editora Fi, Porto Alegre, Brasil
Schneider C et al (2018) Digital nudging: guiding online user choices through interface design. Commun ACM 61:67–73
Sergot MJ et al (1986) The British Nationality Act as a logic program. Commun ACM 29(5):370–386. http://www.doc.ic.ac.uk/~rak/papers/British%20Nationality%20Act.pdf. Last accessed 12 May 2022
Sheppard B (2021) The reasonableness machine. Boston Coll Law Rev 62(7)
Silveira J (2018) Streamlining the governmental legislative procedure. In: Innovation of legislative process. https://ial-online.org/wp-content/uploads/2019/01/7.-Streamlining-the-Governmental-Legislative-ProcedureJo_o-Tiago-Silveira.pdf. Last accessed 12 May 2022
Silveira J (2021) The copy/paste approach to transpose EU directives 2020. In: International Association of Legislation conference, organised by the General Secretariat for Legal and Parliamentary Affairs, Presidency of the Hellenic Government 12th February 2021. http://www.icjp.pt/sites/default/files/cidp/projectos/docs/copy-paste_approach_to_transpose_eu_directives_022021.pdf?724. Last accessed 12 May 2022
Slovic P (1987) Perception of risk science
Snow D (2019) Financial machine learning regulation. https://ssrn.com/abstract=3371902. Last accessed 12 May 2022
Sousa T (2019a) Why code rules? In: Rac handbook. https://github.com/Rules-as-Code-League/RaC-Handbook/wiki/2-Why-code-rules%3F. Last accessed 12 May 2022
Sousa T (2019b) Rules as code—NSW joins the worldwide movement to make better rules. https://www.digital.nsw.gov.au/article/rules-code-nsw-joins-worldwide-movement-make-better-rules. Last accessed 12 May 2022. https://github.com/Openfisca-NSW. Last accessed 12 May 2022
Sousa T (2021a) Testing and modelling using coded rules. In: Rac handbook. https://github.com/Rules-as-Code-League/RaC-Handbook/wiki/6-Testing-and-modelling-using-coded-rules. Last accessed 12 May 2022
Sousa T (2021b) Rules as code projects around the world. In: Rules as code handbook. https://github.com/Rules-as-Code-League/RaC-Handbook/wiki/7.1-Rules-as-Code-projects-around-the-world. Last accessed 12 May 2022
Sousa T (2021c) Analysing rules. In: RaC handbook. https://github.com/Rules-as-Code-League/RaC-Handbook/wiki/4.2-Analysing-rules. Last accessed 12 May 2022

Sousa T (2021d) Introduction—rules as code. In: Rules as code handbook. https://github.com/Rules-as-Code-League/RaC-Handbook/wiki/1-Introduction:-What-is-Rules-as-Code%3F. Last accessed 12 May 2022

Sousa T (2021e) Building trustworthy systems using coded rules. In: RaC handbook. https://github.com/Rules-as-Code-League/RaC-Handbook/wiki/3-Building-trustworthy-systems-using-coded-rules. Last accessed 12 May 2022

Spielkamp M (2017) Inspecting algorithms for bias. MIT Technol Rev. https://www.technologyreview.com/s/607955/inspecting-algorithms-for-bias. Last accessed 12 May 2022

Suh B (2019) Can AI nudges to make better choices? Harv Bus Rev

Sunstein CR (2005) Irreversible or catastrophic. AEI-Brookings Joint Center Working Paper N. 05-04

Thomson D (2008) Law school 2.0. In: Thomson D, Bender M (eds) Law school 2.0: legal education for a digital age

UTAIL (2018) Relatório nos termos do disposto no n.º6 da RCM n.º44/2017, 24 March. https://dgpj.justica.gov.pt/Portals/31/AIN_Programas/30012017-utail-relatorio-atividades.pdf. Last accessed 12 May 2022

van den Hoven E (2021) Hermeneutical injustice and the computational turn in law. J Cross-discip Res Comput Law. https://journalcrcl.org/crcl/article/view/6. Last accessed 12 May 2022

Vermeulen E (2017) The future of law, lawyers and law professors… and the exponential growth of disruptive technology. https://chatbotslife.com/the-future-of-law-lawyers-and-law-professors-and-the-exponential-growth-of-disruptive-technology-b5c979608c9c. Last accessed 12 May 2022

Violante T, Lanceiro R (2020a) Coping with covid-19 in Portugal: from constitutional normality to the state of emergency. In: COVID 19 and states of emergency, verfassungsblog, 12 April 2020. https://verfassungsblog.de/coping-with-covid-19-in-portugal-from-constitutional-normality-to-the-state-of-emergency/. Last accessed 12 May 2022

Violante T, Lanceiro R (2020b) A resposta à covid-19 em Portugal: da normalidade constitucional ao estado de emergência. In observatório almedina, 08 May 2020. https://observatorio.almedina.net/index.php/2020b/05/08/a-resposta-a-covid-19-em-portugal-da-normalidade-constitucional-ao-estado-de-emergencia/. Last accessed 12 May 2022

Voermans W (2009) Quality of EU legislation under scrutiny: what kind of problem, by what kind of standards? Erasmus Law Rev 2(1)

Waddington M (2019) Machine-consumable legislation: a legislative drafter's perspective—human v artificial intelligence. The Loophole 2. http://www.calc.ngo/sites/default/files/loophole/Loophole%20-%202019-02%20%282019-06-24%29.pdf#page26. Last accessed 12 May 2022

Waddington M (2020) Research note rules as code law in context. 37(1)

Waddington M (2021) Using Excel's if/and/or/not logic as a demo of "Rules as Code" for legislative drafters. https://legislativedrafter.wordpress.com/2021/09/04/using-excels-if-and-or-not-logic-as-a-demo-of-rules-as-code-for-legislative-drafters/. Last accessed 12 May 2022

Webb J (2019) Information technology & the future of legal education: a provocation Griffith J Law Hum Dign Spec Number Law Hum Dign Technol Age

Weinmann M et al (2016) Digital nudging. Bus Inf Syst Eng 58:433–436

World Bank (2010a) Better regulation for growth: governance frameworks and tools for effective regulatory reform. http://documents.worldbank.org/curated/en/958741468334887904/Better-regulation-for-growth-governance-frameworks-and-tools-for-effective-regulatory-reform-regulatory-capacity-review-of-Zambia. Last accessed 31 Oct 2022

World Bank (2010b) Institutions for regulatory governance. Washington, DC. https://openknowledge.worldbank.org/handle/10986/27880. Last accessed 12 May 2022

Wu T (2003) When code isn't law. Va Law Rev 89

Yadav JP (2016) Legal education in the era of information and communication technology: an analysis. JLJ

Yudkin A (2021) Machine—readable law: the future in the present. https://investforesight.com/machine-readable-law-the-future-in-the-present/. Last accessed 31 Oct 2022

Zehlike M et al (2019) Matching code and law: achieving algorithmic fairness with optimal transport, data mining and knowledge discovery. Forthcoming. https://papers.ssrn.com/sol3/papers.cfm?abstract_id=3470026. Last accessed 12 May 2022

Rute Saraiva is a Professor of Law and Economics at the University of Lisbon Law School, Alameda da Universidade. Her fields of interest include Behavioural Law and Economics, Economic Analysis of Law, Regulation, Law of Sustainable Development, Law and Literature.

Digital Transformation as a Reshaper of Global Trade Law

Mira Burri

Abstract This chapter explores the far-reaching effects of the digital transformation on trade and trade law. It first sketches the state of affairs under the multilateral forum of the World Trade Organization (WTO) and, second, analyzes the more deliberate regulatory responses to the challenges of digitization formulated in free trade agreements (FTAs). The focus here is placed on distinct advanced models of digital trade regulation, such as the Comprehensive and Progressive Agreement for Transpacific Partnership (CPTPP), as well as on particular forms of legal innovation, such as the new generation of Digital Economy Agreements. By looking at specific agreements, the chapter also demarcates the positioning of key stakeholders, in particular the US, the EU, and China, and contributes to the understanding of the dynamic and contentious landscape of global trade law, as reshaped by digital transformation in recent years. This chapter finally asks whether the emergent regulatory environment is adequate to match the data-driven economy and whether certain pitfalls of international cooperation and path dependencies hinder this.

Keywords Digitization · Data flows · Data-driven economy · International trade law · Free trade agreements · World Trade Organization

1 Introduction

Technological advances have triggered multiple changes with varying breadth and depth in different areas of law.[1] The legal environment itself is also often of direct relevance as to how businesses and users tap into the affordances of a particular

[1] See e.g. Brownsword and Yeung (2008); Gervais (2010); Kauffman Taskforce on Law, Innovation and Growth (2011).

M. Burri (✉)
University of Lucerne, Lucerne, Switzerland
e-mail: mira.burri@unilu.ch

K. Mathis and A. Tor (eds.), *Law and Economics of the Digital Transformation*, Economic Analysis of Law in European Legal Scholarship 15,
https://doi.org/10.1007/978-3-031-25059-0_13

technology and to what extent it ultimately becomes embedded in different societal contexts—so, in this sense, law and technology have a "dialectical",[2] mutually dependent relationship. Digitization has been commonly seen as one of the latest and perhaps most pervasive technological advances, which triggers ripples across legal domains. It is the aim of this chapter to explore the changes that the digital transformation has caused in one discrete area of international law—namely, trade law. It conceptualizes digital transformation as a reshaper of the existing regulatory regime for trade and reveals a highly dynamic, albeit fragmented, field of governance with some path dependencies but also streaks of legal innovation. The chapter begins by setting the scene and sketching how digitization has disrupted the patterns of trade by focusing on a few developments, such as servicification or the growing importance of data, that also pose a variety of challenges for trade regulation, as established in a brick-and-mortar world. It then turns to the current regulatory framework for digital trade—first, by sketching the state of affairs under the umbrella of the World Trade Organization (WTO) and second, by analyzing the more deliberate regulatory responses to digital transformation formulated in free trade agreements (FTAs). The focus here is placed on distinct advanced models of digital trade regulation—those of the Comprehensive and Progressive Agreement for Transpacific Partnership (CPTPP), the United States Mexico Canada Agreement (USMCA), the newer FTA templates of the European Union, the Regional Comprehensive Partnership Agreement (RCEP), and the Digital Economy Partnership Agreement (DEPA) as representative of a new category of Digital Economy Agreements (DEAs). By looking at specific agreements, the chapter also demarcates the positioning of key stakeholders, in particular the US, the EU, and China, and contributes to the understanding of the dynamic and contentious landscape of global trade law in the process of being reshaped by digital transformation. The chapter finally asks whether the emergent regulatory environment is adequate to match the data-driven economy and whether certain pitfalls of international cooperation and path dependencies hinder this.

2 Digital Transformation as a Reshaper of Trade

Digitization has had and continues to have multiple effects on trade—first, as an important part of globalization processes and second, as a trigger of new patterns of trade in services and goods. In 2016, the McKinsey Global Institute published an influential report on digital globalization that includes full data and econometric analyses of the changes in trade due to the advent and wide spread of digital technologies and the Internet in particular.[3] It establishes that the world has never been

[2] Cottier (2017), p. 1017.

[3] Manyika et al. (2016).

more deeply connected by commerce, communication, and travel than it is today.[4] A particularly important finding, which the chapter also underscores later, is the contribution of data flows, which exert a larger impact on growth than traditional goods flows. This is remarkable given that the world's trade networks have developed over centuries, while cross-border data flows are still relatively young a phenomenon.[5] The share of digital trade has also become significant, and approximately 12% of the global goods trade is conducted via international electronic commerce.

Also critically, some 50% of the world's traded services are already digitized,[6] as digitization enables instantaneous exchanges of virtual goods, such as e-books, apps, online games, music, or software. Digitization also renders global flows more inclusive. The near-zero marginal costs of digital communications and transactions open new possibilities for conducting business across borders on a massive scale. So, while trade was previously largely driven by advanced economies and their large multinational companies, digital platforms allow more countries and smaller enterprises to participate. Still, one trend that needs to be carefully considered is the power of the few, as network effects that are intrinsic to digital markets often trigger "winner-takes-all" scenarios.[7] Companies like *Google, Facebook, Amazon* and *Apple* have dominant positions in multiple markets and ways to leverage this dominance onto neighbouring and new markets. The vast data assets that these firms possess only make these effects stronger and may call for intervention, be it in domestic contexts to level the playing field[8] or in global contexts to ensure that radical data inequalities do not ensue.[9]

Against the backdrop of these broader trends in trade powered by digitization, there are a few distinct ones that may pose challenges to trade policy and law. We highlight two particular developments in this context: (1) the growing importance of trade in services and (2) the growing importance of data.

1. Services have been conventionally considered non-tradable across borders, as it is the nature of many services that their provision coincides with the consumption and requires the physical proximity of the service provider. Digitization changes this, and a great number of services, such as legal, computer related, and financial services, can now be provided online in part or in their entirety. As mentioned earlier, more than 50% of the world's traded services are already digitized, and this opens entirely new opportunities for global trade in services,[10] as again

[4] Admittedly the report was published before the Covid-19 pandemic; the effects of online commerce has only been enhanced during the pandemic times. See e.g. WTO (2020).

[5] Manyika et al. (2016), p. 73 and Chap. 4.

[6] Manyika et al. (2016), p. 7.

[7] See e.g. Shapiro and Varian (1999).

[8] See e.g. Ezrachi and Stucke (2016); Burri (2019). This has been reflected in recent legislative efforts of the European Union, such as the Digital Services Act and the Digital Markets Acts.

[9] See e.g. Couldry and Mejias (2019); Fisher and Streinz (2021).

[10] See e.g. Castro and McQuinn (2015); Manyika et al. (2016).

highlighted by the developments during the pandemic, which raised digitally deliverable services to nearly 64% of total services exports.[11]

Digitization also fuels the trend of "servicification", whereby there is an increase in the use, produce and sale of services.[12] This happens as some goods are traded as services: for example, while software has been typically distributed on a tangible medium, now that same software can be delivered and updated online. The same is true for trade in books, movies, and music, where trade in the physical form has been replaced by a cross-border movement of digital content. In addition, many of the newer generation of IT products, such as smartphones or video game consoles, inherently include some sort of support, continuous maintenance, or new content, which transcend the purchase of the initial product and essentially render these devices platforms for selling services.

Overall, the relationship between trade in goods and trade in services becomes more complex in the digital space. This means, among other things, that previous distinctions between goods and services are rendered obsolete and newer types of digital offers pose challenges to domestic regulation, which stems from traditional branches, such as telecommunications or media law,[13] as well as to international trade law, which operates under pre-Internet rules and classifications, as the chapter discusses below.

2. Data has certainly become the buzzword in the contemporary debates of digitally driven economic growth and innovation.[14] Enabled by a new generation of digital technologies and because of their deep embeddedness in all facets of societal life, companies increasingly capture vast amounts of information about their customers, suppliers, and operations.[15] It is often maintained in this context that data has become the "new oil".[16] And while this is not entirely a valid statement,[17] it well illustrates the new centrality of data and the dependence of modern economic activity on it.[18] Many studies and expert reports point at the vast potential of data as a trigger for more efficient business operations, highly innovative societal solutions, and ultimately better policy choices.[19] The transformative potential refers not only to new "digital native" areas, such as

---

[11] UNCTAD (2021). Notably, worldwide exports of digitally deliverable services fell by only 1.8%, while total services exports declined by 20% (an unprecedented drop since records began in 1990) (ibid.).

[12] See e.g. Kommerskollegium (2012); Lanz and Maurer (2015).

[13] We have seen regulatory reforms unfold due to convergence effects—the European Union, for instance, has adopted twice such reform packages and is now in the process of undergoing a third reform as part of its Digital Single Market Strategy. See European Commission (2015).

[14] Although there were some debates on data flows in the 1980s. See e.g. Kuner (2011); Aaronson (2015); OECD (2011).

[15] Manyika et al. (2011); Mayer-Schönberger and Cukier (2013); Burri (2019).

[16] The Economist (2017).

[17] See e.g. Daskal (2015); Burri (2019); for a fully-fledged analysis, see Scholz (2019).

[18] Manyika et al. (2011).

[19] See e.g. Manyika et al. (2011); Mayer-Schönberger and Cukier (2013); Henke et al. (2016); World Bank (2021).

search or social networking, but also to "brick-and-mortar", physical businesses, such as manufacturing, which often have remained shielded from the effects of globalization so far.[20]

In the context of trade and trade policies, the growing importance of data for the digital economy has one crucial implication: data must flow across borders. Otherwise, many of the innovations of the data economy and things that we have become accustomed to in everyday life, such as apps, the provision of digital products and services, cloud computing applications, or the Internet of Things (IoT), would not function.[21] The interdependence between cross-border data flows and digital innovation is also critical for the future, as, for instance, the development of artificial intelligence (AI) also hinges on data inputs.[22] This interdependence puts trade policy under pressure. Finding solutions, however, is not easy as the use of data opens many regulatory questions as to data sovereignty, the protection of privacy, national security, and other domestic values and interests.[23] This has also led governments to adopt a variety of instruments,[24] such as notably data localization measures,[25] that try to keep data within the country and effectively act as trade barriers.

3 Digital Transformation as a Reshaper of Global Trade Regulation

The digital transformation of trade has not occurred in a regulatory vacuum. International trade law, even without deliberate adaptation, has mattered for the regulation of trade in goods, services, and the protection of intellectual property (IP). This is not to say, however, that digital trade could be easily and without any challenges subsumed under the analogue-based rules. Indeed, quite the opposite is true, and states have sought ways to proactively address these challenges, especially in the last decade, rendering digital trade regulation one of the most dynamic governance domains. It is important to note that the changes have not occurred at the same speed and with the same scope and depth in all trade venues. As the next sections will show, legal adaptation under the multilateral forum of the WTO has been minimal, and the reform initiatives are advancing slowly. In contrast, bilateral and regional trade forums, which will be analyzed subsequently, have become a major source of new rules that directly tackle the challenge of digitally-induced transformations.

---

20 See e.g. Manyika et al. (2011).

21 See Chander (2016), p. 2; Chander (2021).

22 Irion and Williams (2019).

23 Burri and Schär (2016); Gasser (2021); Burri (2021a).

24 See e.g. USITC (2013); USITC (2014); USTR (2022).

25 Localization measures can be defined as measures that compel companies to conduct certain digital trade-related activities within a country's borders. They may include policies that require data servers to be located within the country; that require local content; government procurement preferences and technology standards that favour local digital companies. See e.g. OECD (2015).

3.1 Adaptation of the Multilateral Trade Regime

The WTO membership early recognized the implications of digitization for trade by launching a Work Programme on E-commerce in 1998.[26] This initiative to examine and, if needed, adjust the rules in the domains of trade in services, trade in goods, IP protection, and economic development was broad in scope but did not come with a concrete negotiating mandate. Over a period of twenty years, despite continued discussions, very little happened, and WTO law is still in its pre-Internet state.[27] Despite this lack of legal adaptation, WTO law is not irrelevant. As has been well-documented, the WTO is based on strong principles of non-discrimination, which can potentially address later technological developments. WTO law also often tackles issues in a technologically neutral way—for instance, with regard to the application of the basic principles of most-favoured-nation (MFN) and national treatment (NT), with regard to standards, trade facilitation, subsidies and government procurement.[28] Moreover, the WTO possesses the advantage of a dispute settlement mechanism, which on the one hand, makes WTO rules "hard" ones and, on the other hand, can potentially support the adjustment of the rules by clarifying the law and its application to new situations.[29] Indeed, a few important cases have dealt with Internet-related issues.[30]

This has, however, been hardly sufficient. A great number of critical issues have remained unresolved and exposed the disconnect between the existing WTO rules, in particular under the General Agreement on Trade in Services (GATS), and digital trade practices. A good example in this context is the question of whether previously not existing digital offerings should be classified as goods or services (and thus whether the more binding General Agreement on Tariffs and Trade [GATT] or the GATS apply)—the examples given earlier with regard to electronically delivered software or books are pertinent in this context, but one can also think further of more complex situations, such as those stemming from 3D printing.[31] Even if categorized as services, it is then difficult to say under the scope of which subsector such digital offerings would fall. Online games, for instance, as a new type of content platform, could be potentially fitted into the discrete categories of computer and related

[26] WTO (1998).

[27] Burri (2015); WTO (2018).

[28] For a fully-fledged analysis, see Burri and Cottier (2012).

[29] See e.g. Sacerdoti et al. (2006).

[30] Major GATS cases have had a substantial Internet-related element. See Panel Report, *United States—Measures Affecting the Cross-Border Supply of Gambling and Betting Services (US—Gambling)*, WT/DS285/R, adopted 10 November 2004; Appellate Body Report, *US—Gambling*, WT/DS285/AB/R, adopted 7 April 2005; Panel Report, *China—Measures Affecting Trading Rights and Distribution Services for Certain Publications and Audiovisual Entertainment Products (China—Publications and Audiovisual Products)*, WT/DS363/R, adopted 12 August 2009; Appellate Body Report, *China—Publications and Audiovisual Products*, WT/DS363/AB/R, adopted 21 December 2009; Panel Report, *China—Certain Measures Affecting Electronic Payment Services (China—Electronic Payment Services)*, WT/DS413/R, adopted 31 August 2012.

[31] See e.g. Fleuter (2016).

services, value-added telecommunications services, entertainment, or audio-visual services. This classification is not trivial at all, as it triggers very different obligations for the WTO members, the divergence in commitments being particularly radical between those for the telecommunications and the media sectors.[32]

The classification impasse is only one of many issues discussed in the framework of the 1998 WTO Work Programme on Electronic Commerce that have been left without a solution.[33] Despite its recent reinvigoration with the 2019 Joint Statement Initiative,[34] the feasibility of an agreement that will cover all the pertinent issues that the data-driven economy has brought about appears, at this point in time, limited. There is a likelihood that mostly questions around digital trade facilitation will be addressed in some sort of a plurilateral rather than a multilateral deal.[35] Against the backdrop of the still struggling multilateral trade forum and the lack of deliberate action over a period of two decades, countries have changed venues and used FTAs to address digital trade issues. The next sections look at the solutions found in these treaties with a brief overview of the developments and closer attention paid to a few newer and particularly far-reaching agreements that help us understand how digital transformation is reshaping global trade law.

3.2 Reshaping Trade Law Through Preferential Agreements

3.2.1 Overview

States have, over the years, intensely used preferential trade agreements of bilateral or regional nature, which permit giving certain preferences to the parties to the treaty beyond the WTO standards and commitments ("WTO-plus") and addressing issues outside those regulated under the WTO ("WTO-extra").[36] Important for this chapter's discussion is the fact that an increasing number of these agreements tackle digital trade. Out of the 360 plus PTAs entered into between 2000 and 2022, 203 contain provisions relevant to digital trade, and 95 have dedicated electronic commerce chapters.[37] Although the pertinent rules are very heterogeneous as to scope, level of commitments, and bindingness, it is evident that the move towards more, more detailed, and more binding provisions on digital trade has intensified significantly over the course of the past few years.[38] Even more recently, there is also a trend of adopting dedicated Digital Economy Agreements (DEAs). This regulatory push in

---

32 Weber and Burri (2012); Peng (2012); Willemyns (2019).

33 Wunsch-Vincent and Hold (2012).

34 WTO (2019b).

35 See e.g. Burri (2021b); Burri (2023).

36 See e.g. Cooper (2014); Corbin and Perry (2019).

37 This analysis is based on a dataset of all data-relevant norms in trade agreements (TAPED). See Burri and Polanco (2020) and https://unilu.ch/taped (last access 05 August 2022).

38 See Burri and Polanco (2020); Willemyns (2020).

the domain of digital trade can be explained by the increased importance of the issue over time as well as by the proactive role played by the United States, which has sought to implement its "Digital Agenda"[39] in more than a dozen agreements since 2001. The template endorsed by the US has also diffused and can be found in other FTAs.[40] Other countries, such as those that are members of the European Free Trade Area (EFTA) and a number of developing countries, are, on the other hand, still in the process of developing distinct digital trade strategies.

For the regulation of digital trade, particularly critical are the rules found in: (1) the specifically dedicated e-commerce FTA chapters; (2) the chapters on cross-border supply of services (in particular in the telecommunications, computer and related, audiovisual, financial services sectors); as well as in (3) the chapters on IP protection.[41] The focus of this article is on the e-commerce chapters, which have been the main source of new rule-making and are indicative of the increased attention trade negotiators paid to digital trade. The next sections will reveal the importance of these new rules: the shift from classic trade liberalization topics towards ones that are beyond-the-border regulation and effectively shape the domestic regimes relevant for the data-driven economy. The chapter looks more closely at the most advanced digital trade templates that have emerged only in recent years. It clusters these in four groups: (1) the CPTPP and the USMCA, which illustrate liberal, largely US-led approaches to digital trade regulation; (2) agreements that reveal the EU approach; (3) the RCEP, which reveals the position of China; and finally, (4) the recent phenomenon of DEAs, which highlights legal innovation in the area of digital trade.

3.2.2 Liberal Approaches to Digital Trade: The Comprehensive and Progressive Agreement for Transpacific Partnership and the United States Mexico Canada Agreement

The CPTPP

The Comprehensive and Progressive Agreement for Transpacific Partnership (CPTPP) was agreed upon in 2017 between eleven countries in the Pacific Rim[42] and entered into force on 30 December 2018. Despite the US having dropped out of the agreement with the start of the Trump administration, the CPTPP e-commerce chapter reflects the US efforts to secure obligations on digital trade and is a verbatim reiteration of the e-commerce chapter under the previously negotiated Trans-Pacific Partnership Agreement (TPP).

---

[39] US Congress (2001); Wunsch-Vincent (2003); Gao (2018).

[40] See e.g. Elsig and Klotz (2021).

[41] For analysis of all relevant chapters, see Burri (2017).

[42] Australia, Brunei, Canada, Chile, Japan, Malaysia, Mexico, New Zealand, Peru, Singapore and Vietnam.

The CPTPP e-commerce chapter has a broad scope of application covering "measures adopted or maintained by a Party that affect trade by electronic means".[43] A number of the chapter's provisions, as is common for many other FTAs, address some of the leftovers of the WTO E-Commerce Programme and provide for the facilitation of online commerce. In this context, Article 14.3 CPTPP bans the imposition of customs duties on electronic transmissions, including content transmitted electronically, and Article 14.4 endorses the non-discriminatory treatment of digital products, which are defined broadly pursuant to Article 14.1. Article 14.5 CPTPP goes beyond WTO-discussed issues and is meant to shape the domestic electronic transactions framework by including binding obligations for the parties to follow the principles of the UNCITRAL Model Law on Electronic Commerce 1996 or the UN Convention on the Use of Electronic Communications in International Contracts. Parties must endeavour to (1) avoid any unnecessary regulatory burden on electronic transactions; and (2) facilitate input by interested persons in the development of its legal framework for electronic transactions.[44] The provisions on paperless trading, electronic authentication, and electronic signatures complement this by securing the equivalence of electronic and physical forms.[45]

The remainder of the provisions found in the CPTPP e-commerce chapter can be said to belong to a more innovative category of rule-making that tackles the emergent issues of the data economy. Most importantly, the CPTPP explicitly seeks to restrict data protectionism. It does this by a ban on data localization measures, whereby parties cannot require from a "covered person to use or locate computing facilities in that Party's territory as a condition for conducting business in that territory".[46] In addition, there is a hard rule on data flows: "[e]ach Party shall allow the cross-border transfer of information by electronic means, including personal information, when this activity is for the conduct of the business of a covered person."[47] These provisions clearly reflect the new centrality of data for trade, as highlighted earlier, as well as the shift towards more binding forms intended to curb data protectionism.

Measures restricting digital flows or implementing localization requirements are permitted only if they are adopted to achieve a legitimate public policy objective, provided that the measure is not applied in a manner which would constitute "arbitrary or unjustifiable discrimination or a disguised restriction on trade" and does not "impose restrictions on transfers of information greater than are required to achieve the objective".[48] These non-discriminatory conditions are very similar to the general exception clauses of Article XIV GATS and Article XX GATT 1994, which are intended to balance trade and non-trade interests by "excusing" certain violations,

---

[43] Article 14.2(2) CPTPP. Excluded for the scope are (a) government procurement and (b) information held or processed by or on behalf of a Party, or measures related to such information, including measures related to its collection. Article 14.2(3) and (4) CPTPP.

[44] Article 14.5(2) CPTPP.

[45] Articles 14.9 and 14.6 CPTPP respectively.

[46] Article 14.13(2) CPTPP.

[47] Article 14.11(2) CPTPP.

[48] Article 14.11(3) CPTPP.

but their legal tests are also extremely hard to pass.[49] The CPTPP four-prong test[50] differs from the WTO norms in one significant element: while there is an exhaustive list of public policy objectives (such as the protection of public moral or public order) in the GATT and the GATS, the CPTPP provides no such enumeration and simply speaks of a "legitimate public policy objective". This certainly permits more regulatory autonomy for the CPTPP signatories; it may be linked, however, to legal uncertainty until clarified through dispute settlement.

The CPTPP also addresses forced technological transfer in digital trade by a dedicated provision on source code. Pursuant to Article 14.17, a CPTPP party may not require the transfer of, or access to, a source code of software owned by a person of another party as a condition for the import, distribution, sale, or use of such software, or of products containing such software, in its territory. The aim of this provision is to protect software companies and address their concerns about loss of IP or cracks in the security of their proprietary code; it may also be interpreted as a reaction to China's demands to access to source code from software producers selling in its market.

Further, in terms of conditioning the domestic regulatory environment, the CPTPP e-commerce chapter includes provisions, albeit in a soft law form, on consumer protection,[51] spam control,[52] net neutrality,[53] as well as newly introduced rules on cybersecurity.[54] Key in addressing and shaping the regulatory conditions for digital trade are the rules with regard to personal data protection. The CPTPP requires parties to "adopt or maintain a legal framework that provides for the protection of the personal information of the users of electronic commerce".[55] While this is an important statement, it comes with no specified benchmarks for the legal framework except for a general requirement that the CPTPP parties "take into account principles or guidelines of relevant international bodies".[56] Parties are also invited to promote compatibility between their data protection regimes by essentially treating lower standards as equivalent.[57] The CPTPP template reveals the new importance attached to data protection but also shows that under the US-led model, there seems to be a prioritization of trade over privacy rights, which can be problematic for countries sharing a different understanding of personal data protection.

---

[49] See e.g. Andersen (2015).

[50] See e.g. Greenleaf (2017).

[51] Article 14.17 CPTPP.

[52] Article 14.14 CPTPP.

[53] Article 14.10 CPTPP.

[54] Article 14.16 CPTPP.

[55] Article 14.8(2) CPTPP.

[56] Article 14.8(2) CPTPP. A footnote (6) provides some clarification in saying that: "… a Party may comply with the obligation in this paragraph by adopting or maintaining measures such as a comprehensive privacy, personal information or personal data protection laws, sector-specific laws covering privacy, or laws that provide for the enforcement of voluntary undertakings by enterprises relating to privacy".

[57] Article 14.8(5) CPTPP.

3.2.3 The USMCA

After the US withdrawal from the TPP and the politics of the Trump administration, many questions were raised as to the next steps the US would take. The renegotiated NAFTA, which is now referred to as the "United States Mexico Canada Agreement" (USMCA), confirmed that the US continues its liberal approach to the regulation of the digital economy. The USMCA has a comprehensive e-commerce chapter, which is now also properly titled "Digital Trade" and follows all critical lines of the CPTPP, creating an even more ambitious template. As a follow-up to the CPTPP model, the USMCA adopts the same broad scope of application,[58] bans customs duties on electronic transmissions,[59] and binds the parties to non-discriminatory treatment of digital products.[60] It also provides for a domestic regulatory framework that facilitates online trade by enabling electronic contracts,[61] electronic authentication and signatures,[62] and paperless trading.[63]

The USMCA follows the CPTPP model also with regard to data issues and ensures the free flow of data through a clear ban on data localization[64] and a hard rule on free information flows,[65] with the same exception possibilities.[66] Beyond these similarities, the USMCA introduces some novelties. The first one is that the USMCA departs from the standard US approach and signals that the US is willing abide by the guidelines of relevant international bodies with a specific reference to the OECD and APEC.[67] The parties also recognize key principles of data protection, which include: limitation on collection; choice; data quality; purpose specification; use limitation; security safeguards; transparency; individual participation; and accountability,[68] and aim to provide remedies for any violations.[69]

---

58 Article 19.2 USMCA.

59 Article 19.3 USMCA.

60 Article 19.4 USMCA.

61 Article 19.5 USMCA.

62 Article 19.6 USMCA.

63 Article 19.9 USMCA.

64 Article 19.12 USMCA.

65 Article 19.11 USMCA.

66 Article 19.11(2) USMCA. A footnote attached clarifies: "A measure does not meet the conditions of this paragraph if it accords different treatment to data transfers solely on the basis that they are cross-border in a manner that modifies the conditions of competition to the detriment of service suppliers of another Party". The footnote does not appear in the CPTPP.

67 Article 19.8(2) requires from the parties to "adopt or maintain a legal framework that provides for the protection of the personal information of the users of digital trade. In the development of its legal framework for the protection of personal information, each Party should take into account principles and guidelines of relevant international bodies, such as the APEC Privacy Framework and the OECD Recommendation of the Council concerning Guidelines governing the Protection of Privacy and Transborder Flows of Personal Data (2013)".

68 Article 19.8(3) USMCA.

69 Article19.8(4) and (5) USMCA.

Further, three new issues as part of the USMCA may be mentioned. The first refers to the inclusion of "algorithms", the meaning of which is "a defined sequence of steps, taken to solve a problem or obtain a result"[70] and has become part of the ban on requirements for the transfer or access to source code. The second novum refers to "interactive computer services". With regard to these, the USMCA parties pledge not to "adopt or maintain measures that treat a supplier or user of an interactive computer service as an information content provider in determining liability for harms related to information stored, processed, transmitted, distributed, or made available by the service, except to the extent the supplier or user has, in whole or in part, created, or developed the information".[71] This provision is important, as it seeks to clarify the liability of intermediaries and secures the application of Sect. 230 of the US Communications Decency Act, which insulates platforms from liability but has been recently under attack in many jurisdictions in the face of fake news and other negative developments related to platforms' power.[72] The third and rather liberal commitment of the USMCA parties regards open government data and seeks to facilitate public access to such data.[73]

The US approach towards digital trade issues has also been confirmed by the 2019 US–Japan Digital Trade Agreement (DTA), signed alongside the US–Japan Trade Agreement. The US–Japan DTA replicates almost all provisions of the USMCA and the CPTPP,[74] including the new USMCA rules on open government data,[75] source code including algorithms,[76] and interactive computer services,[77] but notably also covers financial and insurance services as part of the scope of the agreement. Overall, the CPTPP/USMCA template has been followed by a great number of FTAs, and its impact has been so augmented.[78]

---

[70] Article 19.1 USMCA.

[71] Article 19.17(2) USMCA. Annex 19-A creates specific rules with the regard to the application of Article 19.17 for Mexico, in essence postponing its implementation for three years.

[72] See e.g. Burri (2022).

[73] Article 19.18 USMCA.

[74] Article 7: Customs Duties; Article 8: Non-Discriminatory Treatment of Digital Products; Article 9: Domestic Electronic Transactions Framework; Article 10: Electronic Authentication and Electronic Signatures; Article 14: Online Consumer Protection; Article 11: Cross-Border Transfer of Information; Article 12: Location of Computing Facilities; Article 16: Unsolicited Commercial Electronic Messages; Article 19: Cybersecurity US–Japan DTA.

[75] Article 20 US–Japan DTA.

[76] Article 17 US–Japan DTA.

[77] Article 18 US–Japan DTA.

[78] See e.g. the 2016 Chile–Uruguay FTA; the 2016 Updated Singapore—Australia Free Trade Agreement, the 2017 Argentina–Chile FTA, the 2018 Singapore–Sri Lanka FTA, the 2018 Australia–Peru FTA, the 2018 Brazil–Chile FTA and the 2019 Australia–Indonesia FTA.

3.2.4 The EU Approach to Reshaping Digital Trade Law

The EU approach to digital trade has substantially developed over time. Earlier treaties, such as the 2002 agreement with Chile and the 2009 EU–South Korea FTA, did include substantial e-commerce provisions (often as part of the services chapter), but the language was still cautious, of limited scope, and largely focused on the area of cooperation activities.[79] The EU, as particularly insistent on data protection, has also sought commitments of its FTA partners to compatibility with the international standards of data protection.[80]

The 2016 EU agreement with Canada, the Comprehensive Economic and Trade Agreement (CETA), only goes a step further. The CETA includes a separate chapter on electronic commerce, but next to the ban on customs duties for electronic transmission,[81] it covers again only softer norms ensuring: (1) clarity, transparency, and predictability in the domestic regulatory frameworks; (2) interoperability, innovation, and competition in facilitating electronic commerce; as well as (3) facilitating the use of electronic commerce by small and medium sized enterprises.[82] The CETA also has a specific norm on trust and confidence in electronic commerce, which obliges the parties to adopt or maintain laws, regulations, or administrative measures for the protection of personal information of users engaged in electronic commerce in consideration of international data protection standards.[83] Yet, there are no deep commitments on digital trade; nor are there any rules on data and data flows.

In this sense, it can be underscored that for a lengthy period of time, and in divergence with the US, the European Union has been very cautious when inserting rules on data in its trade deals. It is only recently that the EU has made a step towards such rules, whereby parties have agreed to consider in future negotiations commitments related to the cross-border flow of data. Such a clause is found in the 2018 EU-Japan EPA[84] and in the modernization of the trade part of the EU-Mexico Global Agreement. In the latter agreements, the parties commit to "reassess" the need for the inclusion of provisions on the free flow of data into the treaty within three years of its entry into force. This "place-holder" is not particularly bold, but it marks the onset of a process of repositioning of the EU. The EU is indeed now willing to subscribe to a regime that endorses free data flows—a position evident in EU's currently negotiated deals with Australia, New Zealand, and Tunisia, which include norms on the free flow of data and data localization bans in their draft digital trade chapters. This repositioning and newer commitments are, however, also linked with high levels of data protection,[85] which signifies a unique position of the EU as a champion of privacy in the area of digital trade.

---

[79] See e.g. Articles 102 and 37 EU–Chile FTA.

[80] Article 7.48 EU–South Korea FTA.

[81] Article 16.3 CETA.

[82] Article 16.5 CETA.

[83] Article 16.4 CETA.

[84] Article 8.81 EU-Japan EPA.

[85] See European Commission (2018).

The EU wishes to permit data flows only if coupled with the high data protection standards of its General Data Protection Regulation (GDPR).[86] In its currently negotiated trade deals, as well as in the EU proposal for WTO rules on electronic commerce,[87] the EU follows a distinct model of endorsing and protecting privacy as a fundamental right. On the one hand, the EU and its partners seek to ban data localization measures and subscribe to a free data flow, but on the other hand, these commitments are conditioned: first, by a dedicated article on data protection, which clearly states that: "Each Party recognises that the protection of personal data and privacy is a *fundamental right* and that high standards in this regard contribute to trust in the digital economy and to the development of trade",[88] followed by a paragraph on data sovereignty: "Each Party may adopt and maintain the safeguards it deems appropriate to ensure the protection of personal data and privacy, including through the adoption and application of rules for the cross-border transfer of personal data. Nothing in this agreement shall affect the protection of personal data and privacy afforded by the Parties' respective safeguards."[89] The EU also wishes to retain the right to see how the implementation of the FTA with regard to data flows impacts the conditions of privacy protection, so there is a review possibility within three years of the entry into force of the agreement and parties remain free to propose to review the list of restrictions at any time.[90] In addition, there is a broad carve-out, in the sense that: "The Parties reaffirm the right to regulate within their territories to achieve legitimate policy objectives, such as the protection of public health, social services, public education, safety, the environment including climate change, public morals, social or consumer protection, privacy and data protection, or the promotion and protection of cultural diversity."[91] The EU thus reserves ample regulatory leeway for its current and future data protection and other measures in a way very different from the test under the CPTPP and the USMCA or that under WTO law.[92]

The current EU approach, which has been confirmed by the post-Brexit Trade and Cooperation Agreement (TCA) with the United Kingdom,[93] is interesting in

---

[86] Regulation 2016/679 of the European Parliament and of the Council of 27 April 2016 on the protection of natural persons with regard to the processing of personal data and on the free movement of such data, and repealing Directive 95/46/EC (General Data Protection Regulation), OJ 2016 L 119/1 [hereinafter GDPR].

[87] WTO (2019a).

[88] See e.g. Article 6(1) draft EU–Australia FTA (emphasis added). The same wording is found in the draft EU–New Zealand and the EU–Tunisia FTAs.

[89] See e.g. Article 6(2) draft EU–Australia FTA. The same wording is found in the draft EU–New Zealand and the EU–Tunisia FTAs.

[90] See e.g. Article 5(2) draft EU–Australia FTA. The same wording is found in the draft EU–New Zealand and the EU–Tunisia FTAs.

[91] See e.g. Article 2 draft EU–Australia FTA. The same wording is found in the draft EU–New Zealand and the EU–Tunisia FTAs.

[92] Yakovleva (2020), p. 496.

[93] Trade and Cooperation Agreement between the European Union and the European Atomic Energy Community, of the one part, and the United Kingdom of Great Britain and Northern Ireland, of the other part, OJ L [2021] 149/10. See also Irion and Burri (2022).

the way it balances the support for an open data-driven economy and, in this sense, converges with the liberal stance shared by the US and other countries like Japan, Singapore, Australia, and New Zealand, while at the same time carving out a lot of policy space for domestic values and the protection of fundamental rights, which, albeit in a different way, links to the approach of China.

3.2.5 China's Approach to Digital Trade

China currently maintains 22 FTAs with its trade partners.[94] The recent Regional Comprehensive Economic Partnership (RCEP) signed on 15 November 2020 between China, the ASEAN Members,[95] Japan, South Korea, Australia, and New Zealand is particularly important in the digital trade context, as "it showcases what China, the RCEP's dominant member state, is willing to accept in terms of e-commerce/digital trade provisions"[96] and illustrates where China stands vis-à-vis the diverging approaches of the EU and the US.[97]

While the RCEP chapter on e-commerce includes a number of provisions that imitate the CPTPP model, albeit in a soft law form, the RCEP provisions on cross-border data flows are particularly critical in the context of this chapter's discussion. In essence, the RCEP provides only for conditional data flows while preserving room for domestic policies, which well may be of data protectionist nature. So, while the RCEP electronic commerce chapter includes a ban on localization measures,[98] as well as a commitment to free data flows,[99] there are clarifications that give RCEP Members a lot of policy space and essentially undermine the impact of the made commitments. In this line, there is an exception possible for legitimate public policies and a footnote to Article 12.14.3(a), which says that: "For the purposes of this subparagraph, the Parties affirm that the *necessity* behind the implementation of such legitimate public policy *shall be decided* by the implementing Party."[100] This essentially goes against

94 For details, see People's Republic of China, Ministry of Commerce: http://fta.mofcom.gov.cn/english/fta_qianshu.shtml (last access 05 August 2022).

95 Brunei, Cambodia, Indonesia, Laos, Malaysia, Myanmar, Philippines, Singapore, Thailand and Vietnam.

96 Leblond (2020).

97 Prior to the RCEP, of all of China's 22 FTAs, 12 of them have e-commerce chapters or provisions. These are China–Cambodia FTA, China–Mauritius FTA, China–Georgia FTA, China–Australia FTA, China–Korea FTA, China–New Zealand Upgraded FTA, China–Chile Upgraded FTA, China–Singapore Upgraded FTA, China–ASEAN Upgraded FTA, China–Hong Kong Agreement on Economic and Technical Cooperation, China–Macao Agreement on Economic and Technical Cooperation and China–Taiwan Economic Cooperation Framework Agreement. Although the China–US Phase I Agreement does not have an e-commerce chapter, it contains provisions on Piracy and Counterfeiting on E-Commerce Platforms in Section E of Chap. 1: Intellectual Property. In this section, the parties seek to combat online infringement of IP, including infringement on major e-commerce platforms.

98 Article 12.14 RCEP.

99 Article 12.15 RCEP.

100 Emphasis added.

any exceptions assessment, as we know it under WTO law, and triggers a self-judging mechanism. In addition, subparagraph (b) of Article 12.14.3 says that the provision does not prevent a party from taking "any measure that it considers necessary for the protection of its *essential security interests*. Such measures shall not be disputed by other Parties."[101] Article 12.15 on cross-border transfer of information follows the same language and thus secures plenty of policy space for countries like China or Viet Nam to control data flows without further justification.

Noteworthy are some things missing from the RCEP. In comparison to the CPTPP, the RCEP does not include provisions on custom duties, non-discriminatory treatment of digital products, source code, principles on access to and use of the Internet for electronic commerce and Internet interconnection charge sharing. These are aspects that have been discussed in the context of the JSI negotiations on electronic commerce and to which China will need to agree to if admitted to the CPTPP club, according to its recently expressed wish. Yet, particularly the provisions on non-disclosure of source code and net neutrality may be a hard pill to swallow, considering the current levels of state intervention in China.

3.2.6 Legal Innovation: Digital Economy Agreements

The need to tackle digital transformations through enhanced regulatory cooperation has become evident in the last couple of years through the adoption of the so-called Digital Economy Agreements (DEAs)—a new phenomenon in the landscape of digital trade regulation. So far, five such agreements have been agreed upon: the above mentioned 2019 Japan-US Digital Trade Agreement; the 2020 Singapore-Australia DEA; the 2020 Digital Economy Partnership Agreement (DEPA) between Chile, New Zealand, and Singapore; the 2021 Korea-Singapore DEA, and the 2022 UK-Singapore DEA. It should be noted that the DEAs are in most cases linked to an existing or in parallel adopted trade agreement; only in the case of the DEPA do we have a stand-alone agreement. This section looks more closely at the DEPA to illustrate the development of DEAs.

The DEPA seeks to address the broader issues of the digital economy. In this sense, its scope is wide, flexible, and covers several emergent issues, such as those in the areas of AI and digital inclusion. The agreement, unlike other DEAs, is also not a closed deal but one that is open to other countries,[102] and the DEPA is meant to complement the WTO negotiations on e-commerce and build upon the digital economy work underway within APEC, the OECD, and other international forums. To enable flexibility and cover a wide range of issues, the DEPA follows a modular approach, including sixteen different modules.[103]

---

[101] Emphasis added. The "essential security interest" language has been endorsed by China also in the framework of the WTO electronic commerce negotiations.

[102] Article 16.2 DEPA.

[103] After Module 1, specifying general definitions and initial provisions, Module 2 focuses on "Business and Trade Facilitation"; Module 3 covers "Treatment of Digital Products and Related Issues";

The type of rules varies across the different modules. On the one hand, all rules of the CPTPP are replicated—some of the USMCA rules, such as the one on open government data[104] (but not source code), and some of the US–Japan DTA provisions, such as the one on ICT goods using cryptography,[105] have been included too. On the other hand, there are many other so far unknown to trade agreements rules that try to facilitate the functioning of the digital economy and enhance cooperation on key issues. So, for instance, Module 2 on business and trade facilitation includes, next to the standard CPTPP-like norms,[106] additional efforts "to establish or maintain a seamless, trusted, high-availability and secure interconnection of each Party's single window to facilitate the exchange of data relating to trade administration documents, which may include: (a) sanitary and phytosanitary certificates and (b) import and export data".[107] Parties have also touched upon other important issues around digital trade facilitation, such as electronic invoicing (Article 2.5); express shipments and clearance times (Article 2.6); logistics (Article 2.4) and electronic payments (Article 2.7). Module 8 on emerging trends and technologies is also interesting to mention, as it highlights a range of key topics that demand attention by policymakers, such as in the areas of fintech and AI. In the latter domain, the parties agree to promote the adoption of ethical and governance frameworks that support the trusted, safe, and responsible use of AI technologies, and in adopting these AI Governance Frameworks, parties would seek to follow internationally-recognized principles or guidelines, including explainability, transparency, fairness, and human-centred values.[108] The DEPA parties also recognize the interfaces between the digital economy and government procurement and broader competition policy and agree to actively cooperate on these issues.[109] Along this line of covering broader policy matters to create an enabling environment that is also not solely focused on and driven by economic interests, the DEPA deals with the importance of a rich and accessible public domain[110] and digital inclusion, which can cover enhancing cultural

Module 4 "Data Issues"; Module 5 "Wider Trust Environment"; Module 6 "Business and Consumer Trust"; Module 7 "Digital Identities"; Module 8 "Emerging Trends and Technologies"; Module 9 "Innovation and the Digital Economy"; Module 10 "Small and Medium Enterprises Cooperation"; and Module 11 "Digital Inclusion". The rest of the modules deal with the operationalization and implementation of the DEPA and cover common institutions (Module 12); exceptions (Module 13); transparency (Module 14); dispute settlement (Module 15); and some final provisions with regard to amendments, entry into force, accession and withdrawal (Module 16).

[104] Article 9.4 DEPA.

[105] Article 3.4 DEPA. The article also provides detailed definitions of cryptography, encryption, and cryptographic algorithm and cipher.

[106] Article 2.2: Paperless Trading; art 2.3: Domestic Electronic Transactions Framework.

[107] Article 2.2(5) DEPA. "Single window" is defined as a facility that allows Parties involved in a trade transaction to electronically lodge data and documents with a single-entry point to fulfil all import, export and transit regulatory requirements (Article 2.1 DEPA).

[108] Article 8.2(2) and (3) DEPA.

[109] Articles 8.3 and 8.4 DEPA.

[110] Article 9.2 DEPA.

and people-to-people links, including between Indigenous Peoples, and improving access for women, rural populations, and low socio-economic groups.[111]

Overall, the DEPA is a future-oriented project that well covers the broad range of issues that the digital economy impinges upon, offers a good basis for harmonization and interoperability of domestic frameworks and international cooperation, and adequately takes into account the complex challenges of contemporary data governance that has essential trade but also non-trade elements. This modular approach is not isolated and has also been followed in the Singapore–Australia Digital Economy Agreement, which next to the treaty text, regulates the modalities of cooperation through discrete Memoranda of Understandings attached to the agreement.

4 The Dynamic Landscape of Digital Trade Law: Concluding Remarks and Outlook

Digitally-induced transformations have had a deep impact on trade, and this has been reflected in global trade law as well. While the multilateral forum of the WTO as the core of international economic law and an organization with almost universal membership would be the optimal venue to address digital trade issues, so far and presumably in the near future, the WTO appears unlikely to deliver either swift or comprehensive solutions.[112] In contrast, FTAs have served as proactive regulatory laboratories in the last two decades that have, although in a fragmented manner, dealt with many of the pertinent issues and advanced a new regulatory model for digital trade. It includes a number of WTO-plus commitments and clarifies some issues that the WTO Members could not agree on. More importantly, the FTAs tackle certain WTO-extra issues that have become particularly critical in the data-driven economy. The chapter's closer examination of discrete FTAs, such as the CPTPP and the USMCA, showed the breadth of the topics covered, as well as the deep intervention of some of the agreed-upon norms, such as those related to localization bans and free cross-border data flows. The CPTPP/USMCA template, although widely diffused, is, however, not universally accepted—indeed, some countries, such as the EU Member States, have chosen a more cautious approach towards digital trade, which gives them policy space domestically and more opportunities to protect their citizens and their sovereignty.[113]

It is overall apparent that digitization has had a deep impact on global trade regulation and the governance landscape is highly dynamic with a number of evolving innovative processes, such as those under the DEAs, and a number of pronounced contestations, in particular in the area of data flows and privacy protection. The next years will show to what extent digital transformation can reshape global trade law, considering some of the path dependencies existing under WTO law (for instance,

[111] Article 11.2 DEPA.

[112] See e.g. Burri (2021b).

[113] See e.g. Burri (2021b); also Shaffer (2021).

the "all-or-nothing" approach that limits variable geometry solutions) and those of individual stakeholders (such as the EU with regard to privacy protection). There is certainly a process of institutional learning involved as well as room for new solutions, such as the DEPA, which can move us closer to finding an optimal regulatory model for the data-driven economy.

References

Aaronson S (2015) Why trade agreements are not setting information free: the lost history and reinvigorated debate over cross-border data flows, human rights and national security. World Trade Rev 14:671–700

Andersen H (2015) Protection of non-trade values in WTO appellate body jurisprudence: exceptions, economic arguments, and eluding questions. J Int Econ Law 18:383–405

Brownsword R, Yeung K (2008) Regulating technologies: legal futures, regulatory frames and technological fixes. Hart, Oxford

Burri M (2015) The international economic law framework for digital trade. Zeitschrift Für Schweizerisches Recht 135:10–72

Burri M (2017) The governance of data and data flows in trade agreements: the pitfalls of legal adaptation. UC Davies Law Rev 51:65–132

Burri M (2019) Understanding the implications of big data and big data analytics for competition law: an attempt for a primer. In: Mathis K, Tor A (eds) New developments in competition behavioural law and economics. Springer, Berlin, pp 241–263

Burri M (2021a) Interfacing privacy and trade. Case Western J Int Law 53:35–88

Burri M (2021b) Towards a treaty on digital trade. J World Trade 55:77–101

Burri M (2022) Fake news in times of pandemic and beyond: exploring of the rationales for regulating information platforms. In: Mathis K, Tor A (eds) Law and economics of the coronavirus crisis. Springer, Berlin, pp 31–58

Burri M, Cottier T (2012) Trade governance in the digital age. Cambridge University Press, Cambridge

Burri M, Polanco R (2020) Digital trade provisions in preferential trade agreements: introducing a new dataset. J Int Econ Law 23:187–220

Burri M, Schär R (2016) The reform of the EU data protection framework: outlining key changes and assessing their fitness for a data-driven economy. J Inf Policy 6:479–511

Burri M (2023) A WTO agreement on electronic commerce: an enquiry into its substance and viability. Trade Law 4.0 Working Paper No. 1/2021, forthcoming Georgetown journal of international law, vol 53

Castro D, McQuinn A (2015) Cross-border data flows enable growth in all industries. Information Technology and Innovation Foundation, Washington DC

Chander A (2021) AI and trade. In: Burri M (ed) Big data and global trade law. Cambridge University Press, Cambridge, pp 115–127

Chander A (2016) National data governance in a global economy. UC Davis legal studies research paper 495

Cooper WH (2014) Free trade agreements: impact on US trade and implications for US trade policy. Congressional Research Service Report, RL31356

Corbin L, Perry M (2019) Free trade agreements: hegemony or harmony. Springer, Berlin

Cottier T (2017) Technology and the law of international trade regulation. In: Brownsword R, Scotford E, Yeung K (eds) The oxford handbook of law, regulation and technology. Oxford University Press, Oxford, pp 1017–1051

Couldry N, Mejias UA (2019) Data colonialism: rethinking big data's relation to the contemporary subject. Telev New Media 20:336–349

Daskal J (2015) The un-territoriality of data. Yale Law J 125:326–398
Elsig M, Klotz S (2021) Data flow-related provisions in preferential trade agreements: trends and patterns of diffusion. In: Burri M (ed) Big data and global trade law. Cambridge University Press, Cambridge, pp 42–62
European Commission (2015) A digital single market strategy for Europe. COM(2015) 192 final
European Commission (2018) Horizontal provisions for cross-border data flows and for personal data protection in EU trade and investment agreements. https://trade.ec.europa.eu/doclib/docs/2018/may/tradoc_156884.pdf. Last access 05 Aug 2022
Ezrachi A, Stucke ME (2016) Virtual competition: the promise and perils of the algorithm-driven economy. Harvard University Press, Cambridge MA
Fisher A, Streinz T (2021) Confronting data inequality. international law and justice. Working Paper 1, New York
Fleuter S (2016) The role of digital products under the WTO: a new framework for GATT and GATS classification. Chic J Int Law 17:153–177
Gao H (2018) Regulation of digital trade in US free trade agreements: from trade regulation to digital regulation. Legal Issues Econ Integr 45:47–70
Gasser U (2021) Futuring digital privacy. In: Burri M (ed) Big data and global trade law. Cambridge University Press, Cambridge, pp 95–211
Gervais D (2010) The regulation of inchoate technologies. Houston Law Rev 47:665–705
Greenleaf G (2017) Free trade agreements and data privacy: future perils of Faustian bargains. In: Svantesson D, Kloza D (eds) Transatlantic data privacy relationships as a challenge for democracy. Intersentia, Antwerp, pp 181–211
Henke N et al (2016) The age of analytics: competing in a data-driven world. McKinsey Global Institute, Washington DC
Irion K, Burri M (2022) Digitaler handel. In: Kübek G, Tams CJ, Terhechte JP (eds) Handels- und Kooperationsvertrag EU/GB Handbuch. Nomos, Baden-Baden, pp 343–368
Irion K, Williams J (2019) Prospective policy study on artificial intelligence and EU trade policy. The Institute for Information Law, Amsterdam
Kauffman Taskforce on Law, Innovation and Growth (2011) Rules for growth: promoting innovation and growth through legal reform. Kauffman Foundation, Kansas City MO
Kommerskollegium (2012) Everybody is in services: the impact of servicifcation in manufacturing on trade and trade policy. Swedish National Board of Trade, Stockholm
Kuner C (2011) Regulation of transborder data flows under data protection and privacy law: past, present and future. OECD Digital Economy Paper 187
Lanz R, Maurer A (2015) Services and global value chains—some evidence on servicification of manufacturing and services networks. WTO Working Paper ERSD 3
Leblond P (2020) Digital trade: is RCEP the WTO's future? Centre for International Governance Innovation
Manyika J et al (2011) Big data: the next frontier for innovation, competition, and productivity. McKinsey Global Institute, Washington DC
Manyika J et al (2016) Digital globalization: the new era of global flows. McKinsey Global Institute, Washington DC
Mayer-Schönberger V, Cukier K (2013) Big data: a revolution that will transform how we live, work, and think. Eamon Dolan/Houghton Mifflin Harcourt, New York
OECD (2011) The evolving privacy landscape: 30 years after the OECD privacy guidelines. OECD Digital Economy Papers
OECD (2015) Emerging policy issues: localisation barriers to trade. TAD/TC/WP(2014)17/FINAL
Peng S (2012) Renegotiate the WTO schedule of commitments? Technological development and treaty interpretation. Cornell Int Law J 45:403–430
Sacerdoti G, Yanovich A, Bohanes J (2006) The WTO at ten: the contribution of the dispute settlement system. Cambridge University Press, Cambridge
Scholz LH (2019) Big data is not big oil: the role of analogy in the law of new technologies. Tennessee Law Rev 86:863–893

Shaffer G (2021) Trade law in a data-driven economy: the need for modesty and resilience. In: Peng S, Lin C, Streinz T (eds) Artificial intelligence and international economic law: disruption, regulation, and reconfiguration. Cambridge University Press, Cambridge, pp 29–53
Shapiro C, Varian HR (1999) Information rules. Harvard Business School Press, Boston MA
The Economist (2017) The world's most valuable resource is no longer oil, but data. Print edition
UNCTAD (2021) Impacts of the Covid-19 pandemic on trade in the digital economy. UNCTAD Technical Notes on ICT for Development No. 19
United States International Trade Commission (USITC) (2013) Digital trade in the US and global economies. Part 1, Investigation No. 332–531, USITC, Washington DC
United States International Trade Commission (USITC) (2014) Digital trade in the US and global economies. Part 2, Investigation No. 332–540, USITC, Washington DC
United States Trade Representative (USTR) (2022) 2022 national trade estimate report on foreign trade. USTR, Washington DC
US Congress (2001) Bipartisan trade promotion authority act of 2001, H. R. 3005
Weber RH, Burri M (2012) Classification of services in the digital economy. Springer, Berlin
Willemyns I (2019) GATS classification of digital services—does "the Cloud" have a silver lining? J World Trade 53:59–82
Willemyns I (2020) Agreement forthcoming? A comparison of EU, US, and Chinese RTAs in times of plurilateral E-commerce negotiations. J Int Econ Law 23:221–244
World Bank (2021) World development report 2021: data for better lives. World Bank, Washington DC
WTO (2018) World trade report 2018: the future of world trade. World Trade Organization, Geneva
WTO (1998) Work programme on electronic commerce. WT/L/274
WTO (2019a) Joint statement on electronic commerce, EU proposal for WTO disciplines and commitments relating to electronic commerce, communication from the European union. INF/ECOM/22
WTO (2019b) Joint statement on electronic commerce. WT/L/1056
WTO (2020) E-commerce, trade and the Covid-19 pandemic. Information Note by the WTO Secretariat
Wunsch-Vincent S (2003) The digital trade agenda of the US. Aussenwirtschaft 1:7–46
Wunsch-Vincent S, Hold A (2012) Towards coherent rules for digital trade: building on efforts in multilateral versus preferential trade negotiations. In: Burri M, Cottier T (eds) Trade governance in the digital age. Cambridge University Press, Cambridge, pp 179–221
Yakovleva S (2020) Privacy protection(ism): the latest wave of trade constraints on regulatory autonomy. Univ Miami Law Rev 74:416–519

Mira Burri is a Professor of International Economic and Internet Law at the University of Lucerne. Her fields of interest include Internet Law, International Trade Law, Data Protection Law and Data Governance.

Safeguarding Peace and Human Wellbeing for Future Generations—Do We Need a New UN Convention?

Evelyne A. Tauchnitz

Abstract The digital transformation is affecting every aspect of our lives, from an individual to the global level. Digital technologies can be developed and used both for violent and peaceful purposes. The impact and consequences of technology for peace and human wellbeing are often difficult to predict, as even supposedly peaceful purposes are often overshadowed by ambiguity and ambivalence in their application. Both in research and policy making, the space technology inhabits and its role in social change are still being debated. In this paper, I will discuss possible governance strategies to promote the opportunities and address the risks of digital technologies. One governance option is—as the title of this paper indicates—the drafting of a new international agreement in the form of an UN-Convention for the purpose of safeguarding peace and human wellbeing in the present and for the future. Alternative governance options such as self-regulation, economic incentives, and nudging are explored regarding their advantages and shortcomings. Furthermore, the possibility of applying already existing normative frameworks, namely international human rights and humanitarian law to the digital sphere is discussed from a critical perspective. The paper concludes by assessing the potential of the presented governance strategies for safeguarding peace and human wellbeing in the digital age.

Keywords Digital technologies · Global governance · Ethics of human rights · Regulation · Peace and human wellbeing

1 Introduction

Digital change has the power to change society and has already transformed everyday life in a rapid fashion since the beginning of the millennium. The extent and way

E. A. Tauchnitz (✉)
Institute of Social Ethics ISE, University of Lucerne, Frohburgstrasse 3, 6002 Lucerne, Switzerland
e-mail: evelyne.tauchnitz@unilu.ch

K. Mathis and A. Tor (eds.), *Law and Economics of the Digital Transformation*, Economic Analysis of Law in European Legal Scholarship 15,
https://doi.org/10.1007/978-3-031-25059-0_14

people are affected varies and depends on the intention and purpose digital technologies are used for. In a peaceful context, digital technologies can help us eradicate human challenges related to poverty, exclusion, and inequalities. In a violent context, however, digital technologies are prone to create new threats and risks for humanity, most notably through the development of new cyber weapons, lethal autonomous weapon systems (LAWs), and new forms of espionage and mass surveillance. On a less dramatic front, digital technologies are shifting existing power relations between the state, citizens, and the private sector. In addition, modern communication tools are removing frictional obstacles that have long stood in the way of a swift information flow and global knowledge exchange.

On the one hand, the power of digital technologies can be of strategic importance to achieving peacebuilding objectives.[1] Early warning software, which is able to analyze big data with artificial intelligence, can produce up-to-date overviews of conflict trends. In the realm of conflict reconstruction, strategical applications are subsumed under the terms of "cyber-mediation" or digital mediation. Digital tools can be used to communicate with remote conflict parties, make peace negotiations more inclusive, improve interaction with the wider public, or evaluate the course of peace agreements. Moreover, new technologies such as cameras, drones, and satellite images can be employed to guarantee the oversight of ceasefire agreements in remote or risky areas.[2] Other scholars have discussed how new technologies supported nonviolence and peacebuilding in both Kenya and Latin America, highlighting social and political contextual factors that create a space for technology to be used for positive instead of negative outcomes.[3] Peace technologies can also contribute to programs fostering contact and collaboration between groups in conflict settings aiming to promote peaceful attitudes and supporting communities to influence pro-peace policies.[4] In addition, new technologies can increase the capacity for civilians to support nonviolence when facing a threat of insurgent violence.[5]

On the other hand, critical voices point out the considerable risks for peace that come along with the digital transformation. Even with the best of intentions, technology can produce very ambigous and ambivalent consequences that cannot always be foreseen (Kirchschlaeger 2021). Terror organizations might use artificial intelligence and drones to carry out attacks, recruit new members, and gain access to new funding sources. Repressive governments might use sophisticated surveillance for political repression of regime dissenters. Social media may promote the polarisation of political conflicts through hate speech.[6] According to the UN investigation in Myanmar, Facebook was found to be the main arena to spread hate speech and mobilisation against Rohingya Muslims.[7] Technologies are always developed for

---

[1] Cottray and Larrauri (2017).

[2] Allard and Kalrsrud (2020).

[3] Martin-Shields (2013), Muggah and Diniz (2013).

[4] Kahl and Puig Larrauri (2013).

[5] Shapiro and Siegel (2015).

[6] Singer and Brooking (2018, p. 65).

[7] Solon (2018).

a given purpose and for a given (value-) context, which can lead to ambiguity in their application when they are adapted into another context and for a different purpose. This adaption problem became apparent when the UN peace mission in Mali was under criticism for employing surveillance technologies that the United States had developed for their fight against insurgents in Afghanistan.[8] The employment of artificial intelligence (AI) bears the risk of being based on biased algorithms and data sources that can easily lead to discrimination against certain population groups.[9] The way algorithms are programmed and trained with certain pre-selected data sources reflects the values and beliefs of their programmers—who are most likely not neutral.[10] Tech criticism focussing on surveillance and power abuses by political and economic elites ranges from misgivings about censorship to social scoring techniques that undermine freedom of expression and effectively repress any potential political dissent with ruling elites. Digital manipulation and control techniques lead to the loss of individual sovereignty as we witness an increasing concentration of power, be it corporate or political, created by technological advantages and the absence of adequate regulation.[11] These patterns are heightened when the military-defence and intelligence industries develop products that progressively infiltrate our daily lives, as when the biggest arms sellers to the Middle East and North Africa also produce the surveillance technology used to monitor borders and the IT infrastructure to track population movements.[12]

As this short overview demonstrates, the impact of digital technologies on peace and human wellbeing is not yet determined, and its current uses are in flux. This ambiguity means that it is unclear whether digital technologies will graduate to be seen as tools for positive social change or whether they present new obstacles to peacebuilding processes.[13] Indeed, most scholars agree that it is not yet clear to what ends recent technological advances in the fields of Artificial Intelligence, Big Data, or Blockchain can and should be used and whether and how they should be regulated.[14] As a result of this in-betweenness and complexity of technological change, there exists a huge regulation gap in most areas when it comes to the development and use of digital technologies—including in areas that are key to safeguarding peace and human rights such as for instance the deployment of cyber weapons or intrusive surveillance techniques employed by authoritarian states to exert political control over their citizens' activities.

In order to promote and safeguard peace and human wellbeing, this paper aims to contrast the option of drafting a new UN-Convention with alternative governance strategies from a law and economics perspective. The nature of this paper

---

[8] Karlsrud (2015).

[9] Noble (2018).

[10] UN Department of Political and Peacebuilding Affairs and Centre for Humanitarian Dialogue (2019).

[11] Madrigal (2019).

[12] Akkerman (2016).

[13] Firchow and Martin-Shields (2017).

[14] Asaro (2019), Scharre (2019), Sharkey (2018), Wallach (2017).

is purely theoretical. Yet it does have practical value and may well provide guidance to academics and policy makers. The following chapter will present the concept of governance and how ethics can provide guidance to governance efforts from a philosophical perspective. The next chapter will discuss the level of governance—namely, the global versus the regional, national, or local level. The subsequent chapter will be dedicated to the question of whether self-regulation, economic incentives, and nudging are sufficient or whether we need legally binding norms. Next, the paper will discuss whether we indeed need a new international agreement (e.g. UN-Convention), or, alternatively, if it would not suffice to apply already existing legal norms, namely international human rights and humanitarian law, to the digital sphere. Finally, the paper will conclude by pointing out the main merits and shortcomings of trying to find an international and legally binding agreement—possibly in the form of a new UN Convention—on the development and use of digital technologies, which will hopefully lead to a wider public debate on the topic.

2 The Different Ramifications of Governance

Governance is important in order to promote the opportunities offered by digital technologies while at the same time addressing their risks and avoiding the development and use of digital technologies for violent purposes. There is growing recognition of the need to develop more effective policy responses to the risks associated with digital technologies.[15] Societies can respond to emerging challenges with different governance strategies, reaching from education and raising awareness to pragmatic regulation or a complete ban on certain harmful technologies.

The meaning of governance is quite broad and difficult to grasp. It has been defined as "the action, manner, or power of governing"[16] and "the act or process of governing or overseeing the control and direction of something such as a country or an organization".[17] More specifically, governance has also been described as the system by which entities are directed and controlled. It is concerned with structure and processes for decision making, accountability, control and behaviour. Governance influences how an organization's objectives are set and achieved, how risk is monitored and addressed and how performance is optimized. Governance, understood in this way, is a system and process.[18] A wide array of actors belonging to governments, international and regional organizations, the private sector, as well as an increasingly well-connected civil society engage in global processes of trying to "govern" the digital transformation. Addresses and aims of governance strategies can be to change the behaviour and decision-making process of individuals and groups,

---

[15] United Nations Human Rights Office of the High Commissioner (2019).

[16] The American Heritage Dictionary of the English Language (2022).

[17] Merriam Webster Dictionary (2022).

[18] Governance Today (2022).

regulate the conduct and business practices of private tech companies, and, last but not least, limit the power of governments and safeguard fundamental human rights.

In order to have an idea not only of what governance can do but also of what it should do, we have to turn to ethics. Ethics is a branch of philosophy that involves systematizing, defending, and recommending concepts of right and wrong behaviour. In this capacity, ethics can provide guidance with respect to how to try to "govern" the opportunities and risks associated with digital change. Within ethics, three main streams of philosophical thought can be identified: virtue ethics, deontological ethics and consequentialism. Virtue ethics, which follows the thoughts of Plato and Aristoteles, is concerned with the intentions, motivations, and purposes of actions. From this perspective, the purpose of technological developments and uses matter. Raising awareness and education about possible risks and side effects of digital technologies belong in this domain. From a deontological point of view, duty, norms, and rules matter most. According to this position, governance would need to ensure that digital technologies are developed in accordance with international law, including international human rights and humanitarian law. Consequentialism, as the name indicates, is concerned with the consequences of actions, behaviours, and events. According to this view, governance should try to maximize the benefits of technology that promote peace, while minimizing the risks and negative consequences of digital change. In addition, risks for which no responsibility can be taken due to their nature or severity must be prevented, no matter how big the potential benefits. Furthermore, and as noted by economist Uri Weiss, not only "games" that produce optimal outputs and consequences matter, but it is more relevant to avoid unjust games.[19] Technologies being used for violent purposes, such as for example lethal autonomous weapon systems (LAWs), cyber-attacks on civilian infrastructure, but also intrusive surveillance systems, can lead to or aggravate armed conflicts and wars. War, however, is undoubtedly an extremely unjust game where political and economic elites use violence to reach their goals at the cost of people's suffering and the death of innocents.

Based on the reasoning above, it could thus be argued that technologies that are developed for violent purposes (in defiance of virtue ethics), such as lethal autonomous weapon systems (LAWs), or violate international law, including human rights and humanitarian law (disregarding the principles of deontological ethics), such as for example repressive mass surveillance systems, should be banned. The same argument can be made for technologies that have an overall negative sum of expected consequences for peace and human rights (based on a consequentialist logic). This may well be the case for technologies based on biometric data collection and analysis, including facial recognition, whose effects and consequences are difficult to predict. Technologies that present a significant threat to peace should, under this logic, be banned too, including, for example, cyber-attacks on critical infrastructure and command and control systems of nuclear weapons. Technologies that are not specifically developed for violent purposes, yet are potentially ambivalent or ambigous in their use, such as for example digital identity systems or drones,

---

19 Weiss (2019, p. 2).

should be adequately regulated and brought in line with international human rights and humanitarian law. Their risks and negative consequences should be minimized through adequate regulatory measures, relying on legal norms, but also alternative means of economic incentive setting or "nudging". Where regulation is not successful in addressing existential risks, a ban or at least a moratorium should be declared until these risks can be taken care of with adequate regulation.

Not forgetting, however, that digital change harbours many benefits for humanity, governance may also try to promote the development of technology for peace (PeaceTech). Given the undefined nature of "peace", however, and remembering that many wars have been fought in the name of "peace" when interpreted in the meaning of military or national security only, PeaceTech needs to be in alignment with the promotion and respect for human rights, especially from an ethical point of view. PeaceTech that understands peace merely in military terms is not PeaceTech, but WarTech in a different rhetoric packing. Before we can, therefore, discuss the proper meaning of PeaceTech, we must first reach a common understanding of what we mean by peace in general. As a starting point, fundamental human rights norms can serve as a minimal ethical standard that any conception of peace needs to fulfil. Taking into account the universality of human rights and the global aspiration for peace as stated by the UN Charter, the aim cannot be to trade one for the other, but to aspire for global peace that promotes universal human rights for all.

One possible governance strategy is the drafting of a new international and legally binding agreement—possibly in the form of a new UN-Convention—on the purposes and values that we want technology to serve. However, also other policy options on the regional, national or local levels are possible. Self-regulatory and voluntary mechanisms such as economic incentives or "nudging" could, at least in some cases, present viable options to legally binding norms. For the cases where there is a need for legal norms, it could still be argued that there is no need to formulate new norms, but that from a pragmatic point of view, it would suffice to apply and enforce already existing norms found in international public law, including human rights and humanitarian law, to the online world. Comparing and discussing these different governance strategies from distinctive angles with the purpose of safeguarding human wellbeing and peace in the digital age will make an important contribution to the growing field of digital governance, peace technology, and tech criticism.

3 Level of Governance

An increasing number of states are already elaborating policy frameworks at the national and multi-lateral level regarding the development and use of digital technologies such as those based on Big Data, Machine Learning, and Artificial intelligence (Fjeld et al. 2020). Yet, given the global nature of the digital transformation, it is argued that we need to look for global policy strategies to guide and regulate the development and use of digital technologies. What stands in the way of a global approach, however, is the fact that the pace of technological development varies in different countries. Technologies are not emerging everywhere at the same time and do not produce the same consequences when used in different contexts. This would rather favour national or local regulatory efforts. If successful, such local governance initiatives could still be scaled up later to the national, regional, or even global level.

On a political level, the more internally diverse societies and countries are, the more difficult it becomes for national policy makers to represent and merge different interests during international negotiation processes. The larger the external differences between societies are, the more difficult it becomes to agree on how to govern the digital space between countries. Local agreements on the levels of cities or regions are potentially easier to reach, yet given the global nature of the digital transformation and the global impacts of both private technology companies and the state-military apparatus (e.g. lethal autonomous weapons (LAWs), cyber-attacks, satellite surveillance), an international agreement would undoubtedly make more sense.

Global Challenges call for global solutions, and although local initiatives can provide innovative new insights and satisfy local demands, it cannot be automatically assumed that local agreements and initiatives dealing with the digital transformation will emerge and receive the necessary political support everywhere around the globe. Authoritarian governments in particular tend to be suspicious of local initiatives. That they would be willing to give away political control when it comes to the development and use of digital technologies is unlikely. Although international agreements and the institutions behind them, namely the United Nations, face the challenge of having to convince national governments to give up some part of their sovereign control, too, when compared to local initiatives they have the advantage of possessing international legitimacy by their mere institutional setup and worldwide recognition by other countries.

Moreover, it can be argued that some technologies are so harmful to peace and human wellbeing that, from an ethical standpoint, they should be banned altogether—on a global level. Alternatively, potentially harmful technology could be put under a moratorium until there is satisfactory regulation in place that would make their use and application safe. Due to processes of normalization, however, we might not even be aware of the harmfulness of certain technological developments until it is (almost) too late. Once we have reached a tipping point, it might become close to impossible to reverse these trends. Banning or putting under a moratorium such technologies on a global level, as long as it is still possible, is therefore essential. Examples include the development of lethal autonomous weapons systems (LAWs), the use of cyberweapons to carry out cyber-attacks on civilian and military targets, biometric data collection and analysis, or intrusive brain interfaces that allow tracking and hacking of thoughts and emotions. If we want to avoid worrisome arms-technology-races between nations on an international level that could easily lead to escalation, there needs to be a global ban or moratorium on such harmful technologies. This would also protect weaker states against cyber-attacks and political interference from outside. Given the global risk and impact that emanates from certain harmful technologies, in order to be able to control this risk, the search for a global agreement is not a mere option, but the only viable solution.

Other technologies, however, are at least in principle beneficial to humanity and prohibiting them would mean denying the chance to use their potential to solve pressing global problems such as poverty, socio-economic inequalities, and climate change. A world without the internet, for instance, would be hard to imagine nowadays. And it might also not be desirable, taking into account the wide array of positive developments the internet has enabled, reaching from global information sharing and communication to the democratization of knowledge and education. The fact that some technological developments have so far been quite beneficial to humanity and already created facts that would be difficult to reverse, however, does not mean that there is no need for global regulation. Hate speech that is enabled by the internet and social media platforms is one such example where, from an ethical standpoint, the establishment and application of global norms are needed to halt the spillover from online to off-line violence in the real world on a local, national, and international level.

4 Type of Obligation

The question of whether we need legally binding norms or if voluntary and self-regulatory mechanisms are sufficient is of high political relevance for safeguarding peace and human wellbeing in the digital age. For some cases and for some actors, self-regulation, incentive setting, or nudging can be enough to guide individual and collective behaviour in the desired direction. For other cases or under other circumstances, legal norms are required in order to avoid certain risks and negative consequences, that, as a society, are not willing to take. In continuation, both the merits and shortcomings of self-regulation, economic incentives, nudging, and legally binding norms will be discussed.

4.1 Self-regulation

Self-regulation can be defined as "a regulatory process whereby an industry-level organization (such as a trade association or a professional society), as opposed to a governmental- or firm-level organization sets and enforces rules and standards relating to the conduct of firms in the industry."[20] Examples include the establishment of industry standards and best practices, the development and application of codes of professional ethics, corporate social responsibility standards, and self-policing activities of private companies and industries. With regards to digital technologies, this may include technology companies' intents to suppress hate speech and the incitement to violence on social media or develop non-discriminatory and human centric Artificial Intelligence (AI).

---

[20] Gupta and Lad (1983, p. 417).

The potential advantages of successful self-regulation, where this is possible, are numerous. When private companies, with or without social or political pressure, acknowledge the need for improvement, this can increase their competitiveness and innovation capacity. As self-regulation can make use of readily available technology and industry expertise, it is usually quite cost-efficient and relatively fast. Having fewer time gaps between the emergence of new technologies and their regulation is vital for minimizing risks. Moreover, self-regulation is a flexible mechanism that can integrate feedback more easily than long legislative processes that are bound to democratic decision-making processes. Arguably, private tech companies internalize guidelines and standards more easily if they have participated in the drafting of these norms and thus develop a feeling of ownership for their required ethical behaviour.

There are, however, also a couple of disadvantages and shortcomings associated with self-regulation. First, there is the so-called "outsider problem", which refers to companies that are not part or covered by industry agreements. This may create uneven production conditions between those who respect certain standards and those who do not. Industry-lead organizations, as compared to governments, don't have the same coercive power to oblige all companies to respect the agreed-upon rules. The resulting regulatory uncertainty may hinder investments and innovations. The fact that the enforcement of rules depends on the commitment of the industry is a main challenge of self-regulation.[21] The effectiveness of avoiding risks and safeguarding fundamental rights is thus limited. Self-regulation is not suited for "serious" problems and high-risk situations in which we often find ourselves when it comes to questions of war and peace. Furthermore, self-regulation is not suited for cases where the interests of the industry do not align with the public interest (e.g. defence industry).

4.2 *Economic Incentives*

Economic incentives can be quite efficient in promoting the desired behaviour of individuals and groups. Examples include financial rewards, subsidies, and tax benefits, versus additional taxes, fees and charges in case of non-compliance or failure to meet the agreed-upon goals. Tax benefits and subsidies can be used as a governance tool to direct financial investments and business activities towards peace. Through well-designed economic incentives, productive energies can be directed away from a destructive WarTech industry that is built on technological advances in the service of the military towards the promotion of a PeaceTech industry that searches for technological innovations in the fields of poverty reduction, education, health, and climate change, and operates in accordance with the UN Sustainable Development Goals (SDGs) and human rights in general.

The act of making impact investing financially profitable through the internalization of environmental, social, and human costs holds a huge promise that merits being explored in more depth. If arms manufacturers would have to pay for the social

---

[21] Castro (2011, pp. 3–9).

and human costs, their products create—recompensating family members of victims of armed violence and rebuilding destroyed infrastructure and property in wars—this business would undoubtedly not be profitable anymore. This is not as utopian as it may sound, but should be a mere matter of course, just as companies that pollute rivers and lakes can be held accountable for having neglected their duty of due diligence. Interesting in this regard will be the outcome of a court case that the state of Mexico filed against Smith and Wesson and other gun manufacturers in the District Court of Massachusetts, United States, in August 2021. Mexico decided to pursue civil litigation due to the extensive amount of gun violence in Mexico, for which it makes the producers of guns responsible. Mexico claims that the gun companies are negligent not only with regard to the manufacturing and design process, but also with regard to their marketing and distribution practices. This is because they do not exercise due diligence to ensure that the guns are kept from crossing the border between the United States and Mexico illegally. Inadequate legislation in the United States and a lack of meaningful enforcement of gun laws make it really easy to smuggle weapons across the border into Mexico. The weapon manufactures negligent behaviour, and lack of oversight in this regard have transborder implications for which Mexico is trying to hold these companies accountable.[22] This case is not only an important case of reference for gun control in the future but will also have financial implications for the arms industry. If successful, it could show new avenues of internalizing the human and social costs of violence that are caused by arms manufacturers not only with regard to guns, but also with regard to lethal autonomous weapons systems (LAWs) or cyber weapons. Readjusting economic incentives through the internalization of social and human costs is thus not only cost-efficient but could lead to a paradigmatic shift in making sure that new technologies do not become a tool of violence. In addition, economic incentives can promote innovation and increase competitiveness.

However, there are also some limitations to the potential of economic incentive setting. From a realistic perspective and taking into account the current state of affairs, there exist various adverse economic and financial incentives that generate huge profits for technology companies that work in collusion with national defence ministries engaged in international wars and domestic conflicts. Oftentimes, the very business model of technology companies is built on adverse economic incentives that can present a challenge to peace and human wellbeing. An example is the need of social media platforms to "engage" their users as much as possible, which can favour the formation of so-called "echo chambers", political polarization, and hate speech online. Even if and when fines are imposed on negligent tech companies, they are usually not big enough to change their behaviour as their very business models rely on such harmful practices.

[22] For more details see: Estanto (2022) and Castellanos-Jankiewicz (2021).

4.3 Nudging

Nudging has become a frequently applied method by companies and governments alike to direct individuals' and groups' behaviour towards a desired goal. A "nudge" has been defined by Thaler and Sunstein as "any aspect of the choice architecture that alters people's behaviour in a predictable way without forbidding any options or significantly changing their economic incentives."[23] A nudge makes it more likely that an individual will make a particular choice, or behave in a particular way, by altering the environment so that automatic cognitive processes are triggered to favour the desired outcome.[24] Nudge theory typically assumes that an individual's behaviour is not always in alignment with their intentions, a discrepancy known as a value-action gap.[25] If a particular unfortunate behavioural or decision making pattern is the result of cognitive boundaries, biases, or habits, this pattern may be "nudged" toward a better option by integrating insights about the very same kind of boundaries, biases, and habits into the choice architecture surrounding the behaviour, i.e. the physical, social, and psychological aspects of the contexts that influence and in which our choices take place, in ways that promote a more preferred behaviour rather than obstruct it.[26] Ideally, nudging is used to assist an individual in reaching his or her intentions with more ease or confidence. The obvious advantage of nudging is that small changes in on- or offline environments can produce relatively big effects if designed cleverly.

The risk that nudging is used for manipulating an individual's behaviour is yet already omnipresent and has become more accentuated by the means provided by data-based algorithmic nudging.[27] Ethical considerations that are concerned with the limitation of an individual's autonomy and the manipulation of behaviour need to be taken seriously as these have serious implications for our cognitive abilities and human dignity. Nonetheless, digital nudging is not without promise for peace promotion. People commonly state that they want peace, but then sometimes still end up fighting each other at the individual, group or state level. Thinking of ways how to use nudging to set peace as the default option holds huge potential for creative conflict resolution. Theoretically, it would, for instance, be possible to transcend political polarization through the breaking up of echo-chambers on social media, suggest online connections or friends from opposing religious or ethnic groups, or autoplay videos on YouTube and Netflix that promote mutual understanding and empathy for the "other".

---

[23] Thaler and Sunstein (2008, p. 6).

[24] Parkinson et al. (2014), Saghai (2013).

[25] Parkinson et al. (2014).

[26] Thaler and Sunstein (2008, p. 14).

[27] Harris, cited by Lewis (2017).

4.4 Legal Norms

Though not all ethical principles and norms need to be translated into legally binding norms, for the most fundamental norms, such as for instance international human rights, their legally binding nature is key to assuring compliance with these norms by all actors, including governments and private technology corporations. This touches directly upon the question of the gravity of the problem and how serious the risks are that are to be avoided through adequate legislation. If we are faced with a grave hazard to world peace or significant adverse impacts on the respect for fundamental human rights, we ideally do want to make sure that all actors comply under all circumstances with the norms preventing these risks. This calls for legally binding norms and a clear definition of responsibilities which can be enforced if necessary. Self-regulatory approaches, economic incentive setting, and nudging can be both very effective and efficient in promoting peaceful behaviour and practices, yet they always hold the risk of being circumvented and only adhered to as long as it is in the self-interest of the actor to do so. Trying to prohibit the proliferation of lethal autonomous weapon systems (LAWs) through economic incentives, for instance, only makes limited sense.

A look at national legislation confirms the thesis that for the protection of absolute values such as human life and individual freedom, legally binding norms are necessary to protect the individual against powerful economic and political interests. Such rights are typically enshrined in national constitutions that cannot easily be changed. The quintessential functions of constitutionalism are the protection of fundamental rights and the balancing of powers.[28] In the digital context, where both public and private actors can affect the protection of fundamental rights, digital constitutionalism involves the limitation of the power of both these categories of actors.[29] As Suzor observes, "digital constitutionalism requires us to develop new ways of limiting abuses of power in a complex system that includes many different governments, businesses, and civil society organizations."[30] The project of digital constitutionalism is to rethink how the exercise of power ought to be limited in the digital age.[31] Under the current circumstances, it is quite unlikely that voluntary and self-regulating measurements would be enough to ensure compliance of powerful technology corporations and governments with fundamental human rights and that they abstain from any actions that could endanger peace, especially if this clashes with their economic and political interests.

When presented with a serious risk to highly valued goods such as the safeguarding of peace and fundamental human rights, legally binding norms (hard law) are the most straightforward way to ensure compliance by all actors. This also provides certainty to all actors and allows private tech companies to plan and design new technologies within the agreed-upon legal framework. In order to ensure effective

---

[28] Celeste (2019), Peters (2006), Viellechner (2012), Padovani and Santaniello (2018).

[29] Celeste (2019, p. 13).

[30] Suzor (2019, p. 173).

[31] Suzor (2018).

implementation of legal norms, there must be adequate enforcement mechanisms in place, including effective access to remedy when harm occurs, which points to the important role of independent courts.

In order to have well-designed legal norms, effective institutions and expertise is needed. In particular, the latter often presents a challenge to policy makers and legislators when it comes to the regulation of digital technologies, given the fast pace of development of these technologies and their often still unknown consequences for peace and human wellbeing. Co-regulation could act as a compromise between self-regulation and conventional legislative processes. Co-regulation is defined as a process by which a private sector body authorized by public authorities adopts and implements a code of practice, and performs any function specified by the public authority pursuant to laws or sectoral legislation, in consultation with and subject to the approval of public authorities. Co-regulation refers to governance strategies in which government and non-government parties share regulatory tasks. It is a mid-point between direct government regulation ("command-and-control") and voluntary self-regulation.[32] Ideally, co-regulation could harness the advantages of tech-expertise of the industry with the legal certainty of compliance offered by legally binding norms.

5 New Agreement Versus Application of Already Existing Rules and Norms

Basically, there exist two main options when aiming to regulate or ban digital technologies through legally binding norms: (1) Formulate new norms and try to reach an international agreement on them, or (2) Improve and mainstream the interpretation and application of already existing norms to the digital sphere. Even in the case of a new international agreement, however, the formulation of new norms does not have to start from scratch but can build on an already existing treaty and customary law such as international human rights law and international humanitarian law, which is already widely accepted and universally valid. Human rights norms intend to protect human dignity and freedom at all times, while international humanitarian law applies during armed conflicts and aims to prevent unnecessary human suffering. Ideally, human rights law and international humanitarian law would be applied in a complementary manner, yet when a militarized approach is pursued, human rights are regularly dismissed or instrumentalized (Tauchnitz 2022). Whether we need a new global agreement (e.g. UN convention) or if it would be "enough" to strengthen mechanisms to effectively apply and enforce already existing normative frameworks largely depends on the effectiveness of already existent international norms to address the risks of digital technologies. So far, there does not seem to exist an agreement in this regard, at least not when it comes to controversially discussed technologies,

[32] Law Insider (2022).

such as lethal autonomous weapon systems (LAWs) or modern surveillance tools, that present a grave threat to peace and human wellbeing.

One mechanism to draft internationally binding agreements are the UN conventions. There already exist several UN conventions that aim to address a number of global challenges, such as the protection of biological diversity and children's rights, or the prohibition of certain weapons. UN-Conventions belong to the body of international treaty law. When a convention is ratified in sufficient numbers, it enters into force and becomes legally binding on the states that have ratified and signed it. The formulation of new norms is, without a doubt, a very challenging undertaking, but certainly not an impossible one. New norms are often built on already existing normative frameworks. The promotion of peace and human wellbeing can build on already existing international human rights norms, international humanitarian law, and, last but not least, the very UN Charter, which aims to maintain international peace and security. Mapping these already existent normative foundations and discussing their capacity to support a new body of international legislation around the development and use of digital technologies for the promotion of peace and human wellbeing could present a starting point for discussions. Exploring political and legal challenges to the drafting of a new UN convention on digital technologies is another key step that would merit further research into the topic. Whether the current situation would rather favour the drafting of new treaty law in the form of an international agreement, or alternatively the application of already existing normative frameworks (namely international human rights and humanitarian law) to the digital sphere remains an open question, which calls for a public debate in a multi-stakeholder approach.

A risk that needs to be discussed concerns the question whether new legislation might rather take us backwards instead of forwards. The possibility of powerful tech corporations and political elites interfering in political decision-making processes to further their particularistic interests and thus influence the very legislative processes that aim to produce laws and rules to regulate their conduct is always present. Applying, therefore, already existing international human rights norms and humanitarian law to the digital sphere more rigorously, which would potentially also include clear guidelines on its interpretation with regard to digital technologies (= a kind of minimal agreement), is thus not only easier in the sense of not having to formulate new norms and search for a new international agreement, but could also be more impactful in terms of producing the desired effect. Both international humanitarian law and international human rights law were drafted and adopted by the international community at a time of having experienced first-hand devasting wars and armed conflicts. Without such a political "window of opportunity", it is questionable if enough political consensus could be generated to facilitate the adoption of new norms that are stringent enough to actually be able to effectively protect the fundamental rights and freedoms of individuals against harm caused by the state or powerful tech corporations. There is not always a window of opportunity available to ease negotiations around a new normative framework, and when these windows are closed, it is unlikely that an agreement can be found.

No matter whether we choose to apply already existing legal norms to the digital sphere or try to formulate a new global agreement instead, at some point in time, we need to address the challenge of effective implementation and enforcement of the agreed-upon norms to the digital sphere. Even after the successful agreement and formulation of legally (and universally) binding norms and standards that could guide the development and use of digital technologies, the process of governance and constitutionalization is not yet finished. It is also key to clarify the type and intensity of responsibilities in view of these norms and standards. This concerns the question of who is responsible for what and in which way. As the global system is moving more and more away from a state-centred view only, this may also include actors such as international organizations, private corporations, and interconnected civil society. Furthermore, the question arises of how implementation and monitoring should be organized, and which (international) organization or agency should be put in charge to overview the whole process. Peter G. Kirchschlaeger (2021, p. 352) has been advocating in this context for the establishment of a new International Data Agency (IDA) to ensure the implementation of human rights and ethical standards and safeguard peace and human wellbeing for future generations.

6 Conclusions

Summarizing the discussion above, I would like to point out that there is no single, ideal approach, but that these approaches will need to be adapted to the context in which they are being applied. This context can be defined in different terms and include pragmatic aspects such as how many states would realistically vote in favour of a new legally binding agreement, to far reaching contextual factors such as the different meanings that different people and societies tend to ascribe to the meaning of peace. How we interpret the meaning of peace has implications for the significance that we ascribe to values such as freedom, human rights and security. Modern surveillance techniques, for instance, have both been praised for their contribution to peace—in the sense of security—and been vehemently criticized for violating the right to privacy and freedom of expression, which do arguably present a backbone of positive peace in a broader understanding.

Self-regulation, economic incentive setting, and nudging can provide new impetus for designing creative governance strategies that are not only cost-efficient, but can also be quite effective in altering individuals' and groups' behaviours. If we succeeded in altering the choice architecture of businesses and governments in such a way as to make peace the "default option", this would not only make the life of regulators much easier, but the world also a safer place to live in. Until then, however, legal norms or moratoriums on certain potentially harmful technologies need to fill the gap. Given the impact of powerful tech corporations, the international character of wars and armed conflicts, and the universality of human rights, a global agreement on the purposes and values that we want tech to serve would probably make the most sense. In order to avoid cherry-picking behaviour of tech companies and to make sure that all actors, governmental and private, can be held accountable in the case that harm does occur, legally binding norms would be needed to safeguard at least the most fundamental human rights and restrict any actions that could endanger peace. Effective power limitations of authoritarian regimes and tech companies present another aspect of legislation to assure sustainable and long-term positive peace that is not easy to reverse. As compared to self-regulatory and voluntary measures, legally binding norms possess the advantage of not being easily discarded. Formulating new norms and fixing them in an international agreement is one option, alternatively, efforts could be made to apply already existing norms such as international human rights and humanitarian law more effectively to the digital sphere. In both cases, the implementation of these norms is key, which raises issues of monitoring and enforcement mechanisms, including access to remedy when harm occurs. Whether an already existent international organization would be willing and able to take this role or whether a new international agency equipped with the necessary powers and competencies would be a better option is an important follow-up question that the international community needs to address, if it is serious in safeguarding peace and human wellbeing for the present and for future generations.

References

Akkerman M (2016) Border wars: the arms dealers profiting from Europe's refugee tragedy. Transnational Institute and Stop Wapenhandel. https://www.tni.org/files/publication-downloads/border-wars-report-web1207.pdf (last access 07 Sep 2022)

Allard D, Kalrsrud J (2020) Technologies of peace. In: Richmond OP, Gëzim V (eds) The Oxford handbook of peacebuilding, statebuilding and peace formation. University Press, Oxford

Asaro PM (2019) Algorithms of violence: critical perspectives on autonomous weapons. Soc Res 86(2):537–555

Castellanos-Jankiewicz L (2021) Mexico v. Smith & Wesson: U.S. court duel over extraterritorial legal issues looms with motion to dismiss. Just Security. https://www.justsecurity.org/79542/mexico-v-smith-wesson-u-s-court-duel-over-extraterritorial-legal-issues-looms-with-motion-to-dismiss/ (last access 07 Sep 2022)

Castro D (2011) Benefits and limitations of industry self-regulation for online behavioral advertising. The information technology and innovation foundation. https://itif.org/files/2011-self-regulation-online-behavioral-advertising.pdf (last access 07 Sep 2022)

Celeste E (2019) Digital constitutionalism: a new systematic theorization. Int Rev Law Comput Technol 33(1):76–99

Cottray O, Puig Larrauri H (2017) Technology at the service of peace. Stockholm International Peace Research Institute (SIPRI). April 26, 2017

Estanto D (2022) [Interview] León Castellanos-Jankiewicz: "Mexico is serious about making the US gun industry accountable for the damages caused with their products." Asser Institute. https://www.asser.nl/about-the-asser-institute/news/interview-le%C3%B3n-castellanos-jankiewicz-mexico-is-serious-about-making-the-us-gun-industry-accountable-for-the-damages-caused-with-their-products/ (last access 07 Sep 2022)

Firchow P, Martin-Shields C, Omer A, Ginty RM (2017) PeaceTech: the liminal spaces of digital technology in peacebuilding. Int Stud Perspect 18(1):4–42. https://doi.org/10.1093/isp/ekw007. https://academic.oup.com/isp/article-abstract/18/1/4/2726613

Fjeld J et al (2020) Principled artificial intelligence: mapping consensus in ethical and rights-based approaches to principles for AI. Berkman Klein Center for Internet & Society

Governance Today. What does governance mean? https://www.governancetoday.com/GT/Material/Governance__what_is_it_and_why_is_it_important_.aspx (last access 07 Sep 2022)

Gupta AK, Lad LJ (1983) Industry self-regulation: an economic, organizational, and political analysis. Acad Manag Rev 8(3):416–425

Kahl A, Puig Larrauri H (2013) Technology for peacebuilding, stability. Int J Secur Dev 2(3):1–15

Karlsrud J (2015) The UN at war: examining the consequences of peace-enforcement mandates for the UN peacekeeping operations in the CAR, the DRC and Mali. Third World Q 36(1):40–54

Kirchschlaeger PG (2021) Digital transformation and ethics: ethical considerations on the robotization and automatization of society and economy and the use of artificial intelligence. Nomos-Verlag, Baden-Baden

Law Insider (2022) Co-regulation definition. https://www.lawinsider.com/dictionary/co-regulation (last access 07 Sep 2022)

Lewis P (2017) "Our minds can be hijacked": the tech insiders who fear a smartphone dystopia. The Guardian. October 6, 2017

Madrigal A (2019) The coalition out to kill tech as we know it. The Atlantic. June 4, 2019

Martin-Shields C (2013) Inter-ethnic cooperation revisited: why mobile phones can help prevent discrete events of violence, using the Kenyan case study. Stab Int J Secur Dev 2(58):1–13

Merriam Webster Dictionary (2022) https://www.merriam-webster.com/dictionary/governance (last access 07 Sep 2022)

Muggah R, Diniz G (2013) Digitally enhanced violence prevention in the Americas. Stab Int J Secur Dev 2(57):1–23

Noble S (2018) Algorithms of oppression. New York University Press, New York

Padovani C, Santaniello M (2018) Digital constitutionalism: fundamental rights and power limitation in the Internet eco-system. Int Comm Gaz 80(4):295–301

Parkinson JA, Eccles KE, Goodman A (2014) Positive impact by design: the Wales centre for behaviour change. J Posit Psychol 9(6):517–522

Peters A (2006) Compensatory constitutionalism: the function and potential of fundamental international norms and structures. Leiden J Int Law 19:579–610

Saghai Y (2013) Salvaging the concept of nudge. J Med Ethics 39(8):487–493

Scharre P (2019) Killer apps: the real dangers of an AI arms race. Foreign Aff 98:135–144

Shapiro J, Siegel DA (2015) Coordination and security: how mobile communications affect insurgency. J Peace Res 52:312–322

Sharkey A (2018) Autonomous weapons systems, killer robots and human dignity. Ethics Inf Technol 21:75–87

Singer WP, Brooking E (2018) LikeWar: the weaponisation of social media. Houghton Mifflin Harcourt Publishing Company, New York

Solon O (2018) Facebook struggling to end hate speech in Myanmar, investigation finds. The Guardian. August 16, 2018

Suzor N (2018) Digital constitutionalism: using the rule of law to evaluate the legitimacy of governance by platforms. Soc Media Soc 4(3):1–11

Suzor N (2019) Lawless: the secret rules that govern our digital lives. Cambridge University Press

Tauchnitz E (2022) The deadly protection trap: the 'instrumentalisation'of fundamental human right norms by state actors in the Mexican Drug War. Crit Mil Stud 1–23. https://doi.org/10.1080/23337486.2021.1965819. https://www.tandfonline.com/eprint/KZDCSBACNVRJZPEAMED4/full?target=10.1080/23337486.2021.1965819

Thaler R, Sunstein C (2008) Nudge: improving decisions about health, wealth, and happiness. Penguin Books, London

The American Heritage Dictionary of the English Language (2022) 5th Edition. https://www.ahdictionary.com/word/search.html?q=governance (last access 07 Sep 2022)

United Nations Department of Political and Peacebuilding Affairs (DPPA) and Centre for Humanitarian Dialogue (2019) Report on Digital technologies and Mediation in Armed Conflict. https://peacemaker.un.org/sites/peacemaker.un.org/files/DigitalToolkitReport.pdf (last access 07 September 2022)

United Nations Human Rights Office of the High Commissioner (2019) Press release. Smart mix' of measures needed to regulate new technologies—Bachelet. April 24, 2019. https://www.ohchr.org/en/NewsEvents/Pages/DisplayNews.aspx?NewsID=24509&LangID=E (last access 07 Sep 2022)

Viellechner L (2012) Constitutionalism as a cipher: on the convergence of constitutionalist and pluralist approaches to the globalization of law. Goettingen J Int Law 4(2):599–623

Wallach W (2017) Toward a ban on lethal autonomous weapons: surmounting the obstacles. Commun ACM 60(5):28–34

Weiss U (2019) The regressive effect of legal uncertainty. J Disput Resolut 1:1–37

Evelyne A. Tauchnitz is a Senior Researcher at the Institute of Social Ethics ISE at the University of Lucerne. Her fields of interest include Peace and Conflict Studies, Ethics, Human Rights, Digital Technologies, Global Governance and Political Philosophy.

Part VII: Specific Sectors

Digitalisation of Banking and the Consumer Protection: The Regulation of Unauthorised Payments from the Perspective of Institutional Law and Economics

Mariusz Jerzy Golecki

Abstract The paper reviews the regulatory approaches taken by Polish and British regulators. Whereas Poland adopted strong consumer protection regulatory measures due to the process of implementation of the PSD2 Directive (Directive (EU) 2015/2366) into the domestic legal system, raising the level of protection on a national level, the British regulatory system attained the same result by a complex set of actions taken by English courts, the British Financial Ombudsman System and the British Payment supervisory body. In both cases, however, the final level of consumer protection defers from the one explicitly set out by the Court of Justice of the European Union, which adopted a less favourable approach in its judgment in Case C-245/18 Tecnoservice Int. Srl, in liquidation v Poste Italiane SpA. Meanwhile, the further level of protection of consumers, namely the triple authorisation rule, has not been adopted on the level of the EU law so far. This situation led to institutional alternatives in the form of either statutory actions, judicial activism, or administrative interventions. The paper thus reviews the potential response to regulatory and market failure from the perspective of institutional law and economics.

Keywords Regulation of payment services · The "incompleteness of law" theory · Unauthorised payment · PSD 2 directive

1 Introduction

One of the most important challenges to consumer protection in financial markets after the COVID pandemic seems to be related to the increase of fraud-related activities concerning electronic payments. The dynamic growth of the digitalisation of payment systems has been tested sharply during the last two years. In many countries affected by the pandemic, banking services moved to cyberspace. Branches remained

M. J. Golecki (✉)
Faculty of Law and Administration, University of Lodz, Ul. Kopcinskiego 8/12, 90-232 Łódź, Poland
e-mail: mjgolecki76@gmail.com; mgolecki@wpia.uni.lodz.pl

K. Mathis and A. Tor (eds.), *Law and Economics of the Digital Transformation*, Economic Analysis of Law in European Legal Scholarship 15,
https://doi.org/10.1007/978-3-031-25059-0_15

closed and the operations of banking systems have been based on electronic means of distant communication. Phone, mail, mobile banking functionalities, and different electronic payment systems have been specifically utilised. As a result, the number of claims concerning fraud increased in Poland from 700 to 1500 a year. The same number of frauds in the UK grew from 300 in March 2020 to almost 900 in January 2021.[1]

Meanwhile, in the EU, since 2019, the Second Payment Service Directive (PSD2) has operated, enabling both: a wider access to the market for the so-called simple payment service providers (PSP) and the cross-exchange and aces of the payment intermediaries to banking data.[2] Those changes have created a new platform for the development of financial technologies. It seems that the more sophisticated business models could operate under a single EU license with much wider access to sensitive data. Cybersecurity has also been addressed by the Directive, which has introduced the so-called double validation or authorisation system.

Any electronic payment has to be authorised by two different channels of communication; typically via the internet and an SMS code sent to a mobile phone. From the recent experience of many regulators, central banks, and the consumer protection agencies in the EU countries, including financial ombudsmen or arbitrators (Poland, Hungary, Ireland, the Czech Rep.), it seems that the recently launched double validation system no longer works. Cybercriminals effectively created schemes such as e.g. the so-called "SIM swap", which successfully circumvent any security measures based on the double authorisation system. The question of who is going to pay for the cyber fraud committed by a specialised group transferring assets to some exotic jurisdiction remains.

2 The Unauthorised Payment Case and the Reform of the Payment Services Framework

The balance between the consumer's responsibility and the PSP seems to be well defined under the framework of the PSD2. However, the experience of some states such as Germany, Ireland or Poland demonstrates that this well-weighted balance seems to be problematic. On the one hand, the directive requires the PSP to repay any unauthorised payments according to the very demanding D + 1 rule, according to which the PSP has to repay clients' assets on the next business day. On the other hand, the PSP does not have to pay in case of fraud committed by the client or in

[1] Opinion of the European Banking Authority on supervisory actions to ensure the removal of obstacles to account access under PSD2, EBA/Op/2021/02 18 February 2021, available at: https://www.eba.europa.eu/sites/default/documents/files/document_library/Publications/Opinions/2021/963372/Opinion%20on%20supervisory%20actions%20for%20removal%20of%20obstacles%20to%20account%20access%20under%20PSD2.pdf (last access 29 August 2022).

[2] Directive (EU) 2015/2366 of the European Parliament and of the Council of 25 November 2015 on payment services in the internal market, amending Directives 2002/65/EC, 2009/110/EC and 2013/36/EU and Regulation (EU) No 1093/2010, and repealing Directive 2007/64/EC.

case of gross negligence. The question remains on how to apply the concept of gross negligence to specific cases concerning different types of unauthorised payments. On the one hand, the problem of insufficient regulatory measures has been starkly demonstrated in judgments of the CJEU. In March 2019, in Case C-245/18, the court issued a judgment in an Italian leading case based on a preliminary reference procedure in *Tecnoservice Int. Srl, in liquidation v Poste Italiane SpA*. The Court stated that there was no requirement upon the payer or PSP to cross-reference the name and the IBAN.

Accordingly, it is not in PSP's interest to do so, because there is no incentive to invest in further verification and safety measures. It means that the vast number of potential invoice re-direction frauds and authorised push payment frauds (APP fraud) committed by criminals are not covered by the PSP's liability, and the loss is actually covered by the consumer, which is clearly contradictory to the PSD2 objective, namely the enhanced security of payments.

In Poland, the problem has been solved with a statutory intervention. On June 20, 2018, as a result of the legislator's actions, and as part of the implementation process of the amendment to the Directive (PSD2), the provisions of the Act of May 10, 2018, amending the Act on payment services and certain other acts entered into force in Poland. The new regulation introduces a fundamentally new standard of consumer protection in the event of making a payment that would be inconsistent with the intention of the payer-client of the payment institution within the meaning of the directive and the Polish act implementing it. The new payer's liability regime and new obligations of the payment institution concern the principles of the payer's liability and the manner of conduct of the payment institution in the event of an unauthorised payment transaction. This applies, in particular, to such phenomena as phishing or replacing the SIM card by breaking into the customer's account and making an instruction to transfer funds without his will and knowledge, and therefore especially recently spread crimes. It should be noted that the PSD 2 directive itself was intended to somehow counteract these phenomena, by introducing the principle of double authentication of payments, and one of its declared goals was to provide consumers with greater security and to increase the scope of their protection. Unfortunately, this goal has not been achieved in the European Union, and individual Member States have introduced different levels of protection through different regulatory measures. The point of reference for these measures is, of course, also the case-law of the Court of Justice of the EU, in particular the judgment in Case C-245/18, where the court issued a judgment regarding the Italian leading case based on a preliminary reference procedure in *Tecnoservice Int. Srl, in liquidation v Poste Italiane SpA*. Against this background, the Polish solution appears to be radically pro-consumer, as the Polish legislator took two steps. First, he separated two concepts: authorisation and authentication. This made it possible to increase the level of customer protection, as from now on, any operation not covered by the intention of the payer-customer cannot be considered authorised. The mere performance of authentication in accordance with the agreement with the payment service provider does not constitute authorisation yet. According to the Polish regulation, specifically Article 40 section 1 of the Act on payment services. a payment transaction should be considered as authorised only if the payer has consented to the execution of the payment transaction in the manner provided for in the contract between the payer and his provider, and at the same time, the consent of the payer in an agreed manner between the parties is the only condition for authorising the payment transaction in question. The legislator distinguished between authorisation and authentication using an agreed method. Authorisation is an expression of the actual will of the payer, and not only of the certification, which would also include the situation when it was done without the knowledge or will of the payer. Thus, if the consent for the payment transaction has not been granted by the customer of the payment institution and the provider carries out the transaction, it is in principle not entitled either to debit the payer's payment account or to demand that the payer reimburse the amount that has been transferred to the payee's payment service provider. Consequently, the authorisation must be a manifestation of the payer's informed consent, in accordance with Article 40 of the Act on payment services. This is due to the fact that the Polish legislator decided that the risk of liability for an unauthorised payment transaction rests entirely with the payment service provider, in accordance with Article 46 section 1 in conjunction joke. 45 sections 1 and 2 of the Act on payment services. An exception to this rule is when the client (payer) participates in the crime, or his behaviour is grossly negligent. Otherwise, the payer is obliged to first return the entire sum of the unauthorised transaction within one day, and then claim a recourse of this sum from the person for whom the unauthorised transaction was made.

On the other hand, in the UK, the UK Payment Systems Regulator (PSR) has recently issued a specific direction to fully implement the so-called "*Confirmation of Payee*" system in the banking sector (by 31 March 2020), adding an additional layer of protection before a payment is made. As the first step to the implementation of the further protection requirements, PSR simply issued the order addressed to Lloyds, RBS Natwest, Barclays, HSBC, Nationwide and Santander to assure implementation by 31 March 2020. In this system, the payer is able to verify that the account belongs to the person or business they intend to pay, before making the payment.[3] The bank is also able to check if the name supplied matches the name of the person holding that account.

This paper compares both regulatory regimes and evaluates them against the benchmark of law and economics. The regulatory response is thus evaluated according to the incompleteness of the law hypothesis. According to this theory, the law is incomplete, and the optimal residual lawmaker operates under the assumption of both efficiency and adequate protection of consumers' and investors' interests. The concept of incomplete law leads to the institutional comparison between judicial governance, legislative governance, and administrative measures, especially decisions, recommendations, and soft law. Against this background, this paper compares the Polish and British responses to the problem of fraud and unauthorised payments, referring to the different styles of jurisdictions (civil vs common law) and different

---

[3] Consultation paper Confirmation of Payee Requirements for further participation in CoP, Payment System Regulator May 2022, available at: https://www.psr.org.uk/media/gc1bfva1/psr-cp22-2-requirements-for-further-participation-in-cop_may-2022.pdf. (last access 29 August 2022).

regulatory settings (EU vs post-Brexit non-EU member state). Generally, it seems that the cheaper cost avoider rule clearly demonstrates that the British regulation with the triple validation seems to be superior to the much more extended PSD2 directive, which unfortunately does not cover the development of both: technology and fraud-related operations. The case of the SIM swap clearly demonstrates insufficient measures of protection, additionally involving the mobile phone operators as potential collateral perpetrators. The whole triangular regulation between the PSP, the consumer, and the operator has not been sufficiently regulated. The more systemic effect of regulatory gaps of that kind is both lack of proper incentives for PSPs to invest in cybersecurity measures and a lower level of protection. Additionally, PSPs are able to apply the concept of gross negligence and the shift of the burden of proof on the consumer in order to avoid potential liability, since the concept is notoriously vague. It seems, however, that the law and economics of tort liability offers some conducive potential solution to the problem.

3 The Incompleteness of Law Hypothesis and Different Modes of Governance

The relationship between the creation and application of the law was also of interest to Pistor and Xu. These authors attempted to answer the question of the most effective way of creating the law. They came to the belief that non-full costs could be limited by the action of residual legislature, an institution which is able to supplement the unsaid law in the context of its application process and only on a case-by-case basis. The obvious candidate who can act as residual legislator in a given system of law is, on the one hand, the courts and, on the other hand, the administrative authorities. Pistor and Xu argue that only the authority involved in the application and enforcement of the law can act as the legislature *of last resort.*[4] At the same time, Pistor and Xu formulate the theory of the optimal legislator on the basis of their proposed model of effective law-making. On the one hand, a set of factors relevant to the law-making process and its effectiveness, such as the number of potential regulated events, the potential social cost of non-regulation, and the degree of completeness of existing law, form a constituent element of the presented economic model of the optimal legislature. On the other hand, they compare the costs of law-making by the legislature, the administration, and the courts, concluding that the residual legislature is not always the optimal legislator. In this context, the challenge for the economic analysis of the law becomes, first, to empirically verify the thesis concerning which type of institution acts as a residual legislator in different, comparable in terms of data-isolated parameters, legal systems (descriptive thesis). Secondly, the purpose of the research should be to determine the conditions under which an institution, including a residual legislature, becomes the optimal legislator (normative thesis). Such research, in turn, can provide a starting point for in-depth institutional reforms. In this context,

[4] Pistor and Xu (2003, pp. 933–934).

the increase in the legal activity of the courts and of the administrative regulatory bodies can be assessed with a view to identifying the causal links underlying that process.[5]

According to some theorists of the economics of law, the thesis on the relative effectiveness of judicial law is the most important descriptive assertion of economic law. At the same time, the starting point of this theory is the interconnected verifiable relationship between the phenomenon of loopholes in the law and the precedent, which is regarded as a mechanism for filling ex-post *gaps.* In this context, it is important to analyse the so-called difficult case, that is, the anatomy of the situation of the actual conflict.

A difficult case within Dworkin's understanding is related to the concept of the *rights as trumps thesis*, which can be countered by the theory of entitlement as *prima facie claims*, which are only the starting point for determining their scope in a particular case (the concept of entitlements as claimed in a balancing operation, based on a model based on proportionality). Both concepts have their weaknesses and advantages; however, it appears that an approach that considers rights to be inviolable can be reconciled with their inclusion in the balancing category. However, this is only possible if two functions are separated as part of the application process.

On the one hand, a law-making court decision can and should take account of systemic effects, as advocates of minimalism point out. They usually advocate a more active regulatory policy of administrative bodies, relying on different regulatory technics and applying an array of flexible means of persuasion and sanctions.[6] On the other hand, however, this does not mean the automatic capitulation of *the rule of law and* the principle of non-reactivity, which, after all, take into account a form of claim of legal certainty. Therefore, the problem of difficult cases should not be regarded as a pretext for suspending the above rules where they can be taken into account at the same time. This is the case when the legal action *ex-ante* targeted by a court is assessed from the point of view of the legal rules in force at the time.

A novelty means, for one of the parties to the proceedings, a reduction in his/her powers or an increase in the scope of his duties, which constitutes a measurable economic damage of material, non-material, or mixed nature depending on the power infringed. The problem of difficult cases requires a clear solution: either pre-existing law has already granted the infringement power in question or not. In the first case, there is an infringement of the law and the granting of its protection (this situation will not be expressly referred to as a difficult case). In the second situation in question, there is significant doubt as to what a legal loophole is. This means that the legal system grants irreconcilable claims to both entities. The extension to such a power of Coase's proposal to treat impossible powers symmetrically leads, by necessity, to situations where the law is *treated as ex-ante data*, which already provides a basis at that level for establishing a distribution of rights and obligations to be called into question. At the same time, Coase says that the law is given in this situation. In *Sturges v. Bridgman,* however, there is no legal loophole in the strong or proper

[5] Pistor and Xu (2002, pp. 1–79).

[6] Cf. e.g. Ayres and Braithwaite (1992), Gunningham and Grabovsky (1998).

sense, that is, when the law is silent. The law, in this case, grants the right to use the property to both the doctor and the confectioner. At the same time, the plaintiff often asks the court to protect his right, but also to clarify it, as J. Coleman observes.[7]

In the present case, this is the situation. The fact that the action was brought in this case by a doctor and that the case was resolved on the basis of the principle that the person causing the infringement is liable for it does not mean that it has been resolved satisfactorily. The application of a clearly formulated principle combining causality and legal liability was not appropriate on the ground that it was apparent from the reasoning put forward by the court that it had carried out a balancing operation, ultimately combining not the two rights of the parties to the proceedings, but rather the reasons for protecting the optimal decision in that particular case (*the exception* in favour of the confectioner) with the systemic effect or the social consequences resulting from the adoption of a specific decision (protection of the residential area).

In that context, the question arises as to whether and under what conditions it is possible to make such a choice in favour of the systemic effect and at the expense of narrowing down the power of one of the parties, since, in fact, there is a kind of limitation of its power. In this case, according to Coase, the court appears to have directed much more towards the consequences of its own decision than the actual content of the powers. The fact that the scope of one of the entities' powers has been narrowed means that the judgment is of a legal nature. Consequently, factors relevant to the future effects and future solutions of foreseeable cases prevailed in the sense that they became the basis for such a clarification of the substantive law, which ultimately resulted in the establishment of a new legal situation, that is to say, de facto, a kind of amendment of the law by a court.[8]

But what does the interplay between statutory regulation and judicial intervention show us? It seems that courts are residual lawmakers: in case of market failure and state (legislation/administration) failure.

The comparative institutional analysis suggests three potential types of remedies being deployed in case of the so-called market failure.[9] The market structure serves as the point of departure. It should be observed that parties may insure against unpredictable events on the market. This strategy is strictly connected with the general equilibrium theorem and the concept of the complete contract (contingent contract claim) concerning all possible states of affair. Within the economic literature, this has been suggested by e.g. K. Arrow.[10] The economic theory of complete contingency contract is, however, seriously weakened by the assumption about the existence of the transaction costs. If transaction costs are high enough, then it is not profitable for a party to spend resources on filling the gaps in the contract. How the gap is to be filled ex-post is no longer the problem of market governance, given the fact that in a majority of cases, it is up to the court how to fill the gaps in incomplete contracts. Hence the market solution under the assumption of positive transaction costs is

---

[7] See Coleman (1998, pp. 33–57).

[8] Petersmann (2008, pp. 827–884), Stone Sweet (1999, pp. 147–184).

[9] Komesar (2001, pp. 19–32).

[10] Arrow (1971, Chap. 3, pp. 134–137), Ayres and Gertner (1989, pp. 96–114).

effectively being transformed into a problem of judicial governance.[11] Secondly, the government provides some regulatory measures in case of market failure. Given the fact that the existence of transaction costs leads to gaps in the contract, the state could effectively prevent the ex-post construction of contracts. The typical instrument for this purpose is a set of the default rules which operate if not bargained out by the parties. The stronger regulatory instrument is the set of mandatory rules set out in case of a typical market failure, e.g. information asymmetry. Finally, it is commonly believed that courts should supplement the market in case of high transaction costs. This part of judicial practice seems to be criticised by many.[12] Within this context, three economic models of judicial governance can be distinguished. Firstly, the Posnerian model is based on the assumption that courts should adopt the same position as the markets.[13] The reason for that is the belief according to which the market transaction is the first best choice. Courts should thus adopt the so-called "market mimicking" strategy, aligning their judgments with a potential (virtual) market solution. Thus, judicial governance becomes a perfect substitute for market allocation.[14] According to the Coasian model, judicial governance is perceived as a residual allocative framework within the high transaction costs environment (Normative Coase theorem). Additionally, judges successfully apply distributive schemes enhancing, at least in the common law, the overall efficiency of law, in accordance with the so-called efficiency of the common law hypothesis.[15] The certainty of legal position sets the limits of the efficiency-enhancing strategy. In other words: courts, under some assumptions, could be an institutional alternative to the market, but they are not ideal substitutes. Moreover, the costs of judicial governance should also be taken into account.[16] Finally, the Calabresian model is based on the assumption that different values should be preserved by the judiciary. Hence axiological pluralism becomes the background of judicial activity. Judicial governance drastically differs from the market. The decisions are left to the court exactly because of the fact that courts have to take different values into account. The market solution is not adequate in many cases, because of the fact that the market is not perfect (market failure model). Fairness, justice (distributional effects), and efficiency should be equally taken into account.[17] The question that remains is: which of those models fits the contemporary complex structure of multilevel legal systems best?

[11] Stone Sweet (2000).

[12] Komesar (1981, pp. 1356–1362), Vermeule (2006, pp. 118–153), Vermeule (2009, pp. 105–112), Golecki (2012, pp. 152–167).

[13] Posner (1993, 2003, pp. 539–551, 2008, pp. 35–40).

[14] Posner (1980, pp. 487–490, 1993, 2003, pp. 539–551, 2008, pp. 35–40).

[15] Ponzetto and Fernandez (2008, pp. 379–430).

[16] Coase (1990, pp. 8–10, 95–102).

[17] Calabresi (1982, p. 163).

4 Courts Versus Regulators: The Unauthorised Payment in the UK

In the EU, since 2019, the Second Payment Service Directive (PSD2) has been in operation: every electronic payment has to be authorised by two different channels of communication; typically, the Internet and an SMS code sent to a mobile phone. The recent experience of many regulators, central banks, and the consumer protection agencies in EU countries seems to prove the allegation that the recently launched double validation system is not effective. Although the balance between the consumer's responsibility and the PSP seems to be well defined under the framework of the PSD2, the experience of some states such as Germany, Ireland or Poland demonstrates that this balance seems to be problematic. On the one hand, the directive requires the PSP to repay any unauthorised payments according to the very demanding D + 1 rule, according to which the PSP has to repay clients' assets on the next business day. On the other hand, the PSP does not have to pay in the case of fraud committed by the client or in the case of gross negligence. The question remains on how to apply the concept of gross negligence to specific cases concerning different types of unauthorised payments. The problem of insufficient regulatory measures has been starkly demonstrated in judgments of the CJEU. In March 2019, in Case C-245/18, the Court issued a judgment in the Italian leading case based on the preliminary reference procedure in *Tecnoservice Int. Srl, in liquidation v Poste Italiane SpA*. The Court stated that there was no requirement upon the payer or PSP to cross-reference the name and the IBAN, because "when a payment order is executed in accordance with the unique identifier provided by the payment service user, which does not correspond to the payee name indicated by that user, the limitation of payment service provider liability, provided for by that article, applies to both the payer's and the payee's payment service provider." In this case, since Italian law was applicable, the court pointed out that Directive 2007/64 was transposed into Italian law (Legislative Decree No. 11 transposing Directive 2007/64/EC of 27 January 2010), hence there was no significant difference concerning the scope of the protection of the consumer under EU and Italian Law. Articles 74 and 75 of Directive 2007/64 were transposed by Articles 24 and 25 of Legislative Decree No. 11/2010, the wording of which is almost identical to that of the former provisions. This means that the vast number of potential invoice re-direction frauds and authorised push payment frauds (APP fraud) committed by criminals are not covered by the PSP's liability, and the loss is actually covered by the consumer, which is evidently contradictory with the PSD2 objective, namely the enhanced security of payments. A similar position had earlier been adopted by English courts. In *Tidal Energy Ltd v Bank of Scotland,* the Court of Appeal dismissed the appeal on the grounds that there was a clear and settled practice that the receiving bank did not need to check the beneficiary's name for correspondence with other accepted identifiers for good commercial reasons even in the case of alleged fraud and unauthorised payment.[18]

[18] [2014] EWCA Civ 1107.

The appellant was unaware that they had been a victim of fraud and that the designated receiving account did not belong to the recipient. In consequence, although the recipient's name was correct on the CHAPS transfer form, the sort code, account number, and bank name were not. The court emphasised that the customer entered into the contract on the basis of the banking practice as expressed in the case *Hare v Henty* [1861]. The judgment contained a very critical dissenting opinion of Floyd LJ, who pointed out that: "(l)urking beneath the submissions in this case is a suggestion that, if we were to decide the case against the bank, it would undermine the CHAPS system. I cannot accept that this is so for a number of reasons. The bank expressly accepted that if the instruction was an instruction to pay Design Craft rather than Barclays, then it would have no defence. In my judgment it is clear that the bank only had authority to debit Tidal's account if a payment was made which complied with the four identifiers on the transfer form. I would, for my part, have allowed the appeal and granted summary judgment to Tidal on its claim."[19] This position has not been accepted by the other judges. Thus, in fact, in the case of an unauthorised payment, the liability for the fraudulent transfer has been shifted to customers, even in the case of typical fraudulent practice. This position was, on the one hand, followed by the Court of Justice of the EU, which came to the same conclusion in Case C-245/18 *Tecnoservice Int. Srl, in liquidation v Poste Italiane SpA* in March 2019. On the other hand, some decisions of the British Financial Ombudsman were much more favourable for the victims of fraud, namely the bank's customers.[20] In a series of decisions, the Financial Ombudsman decided that in the case of fraudulent payment, the bank owes a special duty of care based on fairness and granted compensation to customers even if the case, when evaluated in accordance with the standard of duty of care as reconstructed in cases such as *Lipkin*, *Quincecare* and *Singularis,* would not give grounds for compensation from the bank.[21]

In a landmark decision DRN-8330211 against Santander PLC, the Financial Ombudsman explained the scope of banks' liability and departed from the one accepted in *Barclays Bank* v *Quincecare* [1992] 4 All ER 363. The Ombudsman relied upon the assumption that "Money can only be taken from someone's account if that person has authorised it, or the bank can prove the person was at fault. If not, the money should be refunded immediately, including any interest and charges that may have accrued as a result of the unauthorised transactions. The exceptions to this are: (i) if the bank can prove the transactions were authorised; (ii) it can prove the person was at fault because he or she acted fraudulently, or deliberately (or with gross negligence) failed to protect account details; or (iii) the person didn't tell the bank about the transactions until after 13 months has passed." This reasoning has been later applied to a vast number of decisions, including DRN-2684364, where it has been held that HSBC had to pay compensation for a delayed reaction in the case of fraud. In this decision, the Financial Ombudsmen explicitly referred to fairness and

[19] [2014] EWCA Civ 1107 [by Floyd LJ (37–38)].

[20] For an extensive analysis of FOS decisions compared to judicial rulings cf. Leow (2018).

[21] *Lipkin Gorman v Karpnale, Barclays Bank v Quincecare* and *Singularis Holdings v Daiwa Capital Markets.*

reasonableness rather than to the existing legal standards. Thus the duty of care owed by the bank to the customer in the case of fraud in practice went much further than the jurisprudence of the common law courts. On the other hand, in a recent judgment pertaining to fraud, the Court of Appeal actually adopted the approach proposed by the FSO. Lord Justice Birss proposed a more pro-customer approach in the case of the so-called authorised push payments; when giving judgment against the bank, he confirmed that "as a matter of law the duty of care identified in *Quincecare*, which is a duty on a bank to make inquiries and refrain from acting on a payment instruction in the meantime, does not depend on the fact that the bank is instructed by an agent of the customer of the bank. That is the only legal conclusion necessary to resolve this appeal. It follows from it that it is, therefore, at least possible in principle that a relevant duty of care could arise in the case of a customer instructing their bank to make a payment when that customer is the victim of APP fraud. The second part of my conclusions is that the right occasion on which to decide whether such a duty in fact arises in this case is at trial. Summary judgment in favour of the respondent bank was wrongly entered and should be set aside." This judgment coincides with the whole line of the Ombudsman's decisions which exceeded the so-called *Quincecare* standard of care owed by a bank. Certainly, the interaction of judicial decisions concerning the duty of care owed by banks to their customers and the Ombudsman's decisions pertaining to the protection of customers in the case of fraudulent bank transfer demonstrates the limited competition between the ADR and the judicial system, which at least to some extent reminds one of the historical competition between common law and equity, between royal courts and chancellors' rulings. In both cases, the competition gives more flexibility and a higher level of protection to the victim of the alleged fraud, leading to a higher level of efficiency and security in the financial market.

5 Conclusion

The fundamental assumption purported by K. Pistor and Ch. Xu is that law is, in general, inherently incomplete and that the incomplete law cannot be effectively enforced.[22] The power to interpret existing law, to adapt it to changing circumstances and to extend its application to new cases is called "residual lawmaking power". According to the "incompleteness of law" theory, residual lawmaking powers may be conferred to different but, at least to some extent, substitutive institutions: legislature, courts, or regulators. Depending on the identity of the residual lawmaker, the regulatory regime could be legislator-oriented, judiciary-oriented, or administration-oriented. While analysing the development of financial law between the XIXth and XXth centuries, the authors come to the conclusion that the legal evolution leads from the judiciary- or legislator-oriented regulatory frameworks to the more developed forms in which the administrative agencies have the last say. This hypothesis is

[22] Pistor and Xu (2002, 2003, pp. 931–1013).

illustrated by the parallel development of the English, American and German financial law, leading all jurisdictions towards the paramount influence of specialised administrative agencies, playing a crucial and double role of residual lawmakers and ultimate enforcing agencies at the same time. Both common law systems with the paramount role of judge-made law and civil law countries, where the statutory enactments responded to the problem of incomplete law, tend to develop these specialised agencies.

It has been suggested that the regulatory powers of either private or public regulatory agents developed faster in common law jurisdictions such as the US and the UK than in civil law jurisdictions such as Germany. This could be an effect of both the faster development of financial markets and the relatively greater incompleteness of law in those countries. Nevertheless, it seems that the incompleteness thesis leads to two claims. According to the positive claim, all jurisdictions, under certain assumptions such as the growth of the financial market, economic growth, and industrialisation, tend to create the specialised regulatory agencies. The normative claim suggests that such a development is the optimal path of evolution. The regulatory agencies could effectively match the alleged incompleteness of the law as the most flexible lawmakers and at the same time they could join the lawmaking function with the supervision and proactive enforcement of the relevant regulation.

The case of unauthorised payments regulation proves that this approach is generally correct. The fast action taken by some regulatory bodies, such as British Ombudsman Service and the UK Payment Systems Regulator, created a proper and efficiency-enhancing response to regulatory and market failures. On the other hand, the case of the Polish fast amendment of payment system regulation and the introduction of the distinction between authentication and authorisation provides proper protection for consumers on an even wider scale. In both cases, however, it is clear that the judicial control of administrative actions seems to be the best way of combining regulatory efficiency with the requirement of the rule of law and constitutional accountability. According to the "optimal residual enforcer" thesis, courts are optimal law enforcers when the law is more complete, or when the law is incomplete, but the costs of regulation are excessively high because the level of potential loss is relatively low and the regulated actions are heterogeneous. Regulators are better law enforcers when the law is highly incomplete, the expected level of harm is high, and the regulated actions are homogenous.[23] Thus the division of power and tasks between the regulators and the courts seems to be the constant point of reference for any feasible and realistic theory of regulation. In this context, the theory of the division of residual lawmaking and executor powers between administrative agencies and courts gives valuable insight into the key problem of the normative theory of regulation. Thus the complex network of administrative and judicial institutions seems to be the best response to both market and state failures. The second issue concerns modelling the strategy of national judges adopted within a framework of the wider multilevel judicial governance. Such a form of judicial governance creates

[23] Pistor and Xu (2002).

a feasible alternative to market transactions. Taking into account that the application of liability rules could maximise the number of transfers and the efficiency of allocation, the judicial governance plays an increasingly significant economic role.

References

Arrow KJ (1971) Insurance, risk, and resource allocation. In: Essays in the theory of risk bearing. Markham Publishing Co., Chicago, chap 3, pp 134–137

Ayres I, Braithwaite J (1992) Responsive regulation: transcending deregulatory debate. OUP, Oxford

Ayres I, Gertner R (1989) Filling gaps in incomplete contracts: an economic theory of default rules. Yale Law J 94:96–114

Calabresi G (1982) A common law for the age of statutes. Massachusetts, Cambridge

Coase RH (1990) The firm, the market and the law. University of Chicago Press, Chicago

Coleman J (1998) Markets, morals and the law. Oxford University Press, New York

Golecki MJ (2012) Evolutionary theories of derivatives regulation. Aestimatio IEB Int J Financ 4:152–167

Gunningham N, Grabovsky P (1998) Smart regulation. Clarendon Press, Oxford

Komesar N (1981) In search of a general approach to legal analysis: a comparative institutional alternative. Mich Law Rev 79:1356–1362

Komesar N (2001) Law's limits, the rule of law and the supply and demand of rights. Cambridge University Press, Cambridge

La Porta R et al (1998) Law and finance. J Polit Econ 106:113–155

Leow R (2018) Recovering mistaken payments before the financial ombudsman (September 1, 2018). [2019] Lloyds Maritime and Commercial Law Quarterly 215. https://www.i-law.com/ilaw/doc/view.htm?id=399044, available at SSRN: https://ssrn.com/abstract=3969496 (last access 29 Aug 2022)

Petersmann E-U (2008) Judging judges: from "principal-agent theory" to "constitutional justice" in multilevel "judicial governance" of economic cooperation among citizens. J Int Econ Law 11:827–884

Pistor K, Xu C (2002) Law enforcement under incomplete law: theory and evidence from financial market regulation. The Suntory and Toyota International Centres for Economics and Related Disciplines, Discussion Paper no. TE/02/442

Pistor K, Xu C (2003) Incomplete Law. N Y Univ J Int Law Polit 35:931–1013

Ponzetto GAM, Fernandez PA (2008) Case law versus statute law: an evolutionary perspective. J Legal Stud 37:379–430

Posner RA (1973) An economic approach to legal procedure and judicial administration. J Legal Stud 2:399–458

Posner RA (1980) The ethical and political basis of the efficiency norm in common law adjudication. Hofstra Law Rev 8:487–490

Posner RA (1993) What do judges maximize? (The same thing everybody else does). Supreme Court Econ Rev 3:1–41

Posner RA (2001) Frontiers of legal theory. Harvard University Press, Cambridge, Mass.

Posner RA (2008) How judges think. The University of Chicago Press, Cambridge, Mass.

Posner RA (2003) Economic analysis of law. Aspen Publishers, New York

Stone Sweet A (1999) Judicialization and the construction of governance. Comp Pol Stud 31:147–184
Stone Sweet A (2000) Governing with judges: constitutional politics in Europe. Oxford University Press, Oxford
Vermeule A (2009) Law and the limits of reason. Oxford University Press, Oxford
Vermeule A (2006) Judging under uncertainty. An Institutional theory of legal interpretation. Harvard University Press, Cambridge, Mass., London

Mariusz Jerzy Golecki is the Judge of the Polish Supreme Administrative Court and Professor at the University of Lodz, University of Lodz Faculty of Law and Administration. His fields of interest include Economic Analysis of Law, Behavioural Law and Economics, Tax Law, Legal Theory, Theory of the EU Law and Comparative Law.

Regulation of Digital Agriculture—A Law and Economics Perspective

Tilman Reinhardt

Abstract The digital transformation and the sustainability transition are the most important current challenges for European agricultural regulation. Innovation emerges as a key issue in both processes. This paper proposes an expansion of the methodological toolbox of Law and Economics to analyze how regulation can catalyze the development and diffusion of sustainable innovation.

Keywords Sustainable agriculture · Innovation systems · Digitalization

1 Digital Transformation and Sustainability Transition of Agriculture

Agriculture is becoming digital. The digital transformation concerns smart-farming technologies, i.e. software applications and corresponding hardware tools, such as variable rate technology, robotics, sensor systems, IoT, or 5G technology, but also digital business models, such as sharing-economy platforms, digital marketplaces or everything-as-a-service type applications and downstream applications in processing or logistics.

The push to digitalize all levels of the food value chain is evidenced by an accelerating pace of adoption, a growing interest in high-level policy documents, and the market entry of large outside players, such as Microsoft or IBM. More and more applications are reaching technological maturity or are integrated into new business models, such as sharing economy or e-commerce. Regulatory and administrative obligations (e.g. documentation duties, fertilizing and pesticide limits, food safety, and traceability standards) set additional incentives to digitalize processes.

T. Reinhardt (✉)
Faculty of Life Sciences: Food Nutrition and Health, University of Bayreuth,
Fritz-Hornschuch-Straße 13, 95326 Kulmbach, Germany
e-mail: Tilman.Reinhardt@uni-bayreuth.de

K. Mathis and A. Tor (eds.), *Law and Economics of the Digital Transformation*,
Economic Analysis of Law in European Legal Scholarship 15,
https://doi.org/10.1007/978-3-031-25059-0_16

The digital transformation, however, is not just an inevitable trend, it can also be considered the "best hope" for achieving sustainability in food production.[1]

There is now a broad scientific and political consensus that a sustainability transition of agriculture is needed to preserve global food security and ecological integrity. This transition needs to happen because, at the same time, a growing world population and the emerging bio-economy require a significant increase in overall agricultural production.

Digital technologies could become key solutions to bridge the gap between productivity and sustainability. Precision (livestock) farming technologies and data-driven decision-making tools based on Machine Learning or AI promise greater efficiency, but also a reduction of pesticides, fertilizers, antibiotics, and GHG-emissions, as well as better protection of soils and biodiversity. Integration of data in logistics and processing allows for completely new value opportunities and helps to reduce food waste. In addition, digital technologies also hold great potential to tailor effective policy measures.[2] Some potentially game-changing policy instruments, such as carbon sequestration, crucially depend on digital capacities to administer and control. Finally, data-driven technologies are a key enabling technology for other innovations, such as nanotechnology, new plant breeding technologies, and circular economy approaches.[3]

2 Innovation-Friendly Regulation

Many sustainability promises of digital agriculture are yet to materialize, as technologies are not ready or not being used by a large number of producers. The success of a sustainable digital transformation critically depends on the development and diffusion of innovation on all levels of the value chain. This—in turn—crucially depends on setting the right regulatory framework. The development and diffusion of sustainable innovations are not guaranteed. Also, digital technologies are no panacea for achieving sustainability. Some of their social and environmental implications are unclear and potentially dangerous.

This contribution proposes a methodological framework to analyze how regulation can catalyze the development and diffusion of sustainable digital innovations in agriculture.

Analyzing the regulations' friendliness towards sustainable innovation might seem like an unorthodox task for Law and Economics, which focuses on the efficiency and transaction costs[4] rather than the evolutionary and chaotic processes of innovation. Given the importance of innovation and sustainability in the current debate on

---

[1] Basso and Antle (2020), p. 254.

[2] Kosior (2019), p. 11.

[3] Klerkx and Rose (2020), pp. 1 et seq.

[4] Reyes y Ráfales (2014), p. 42.

agriculture, and their progressive juridification[5] and constitutionalization,[6] it seems necessary to expand the "methodological toolbox" of Law and Economics based on the substantial recent literature on innovation systems and sustainability transitions.

The central role of innovations in economic development was already described by Schumpeter more than 100 years ago. The process of "creative destruction" has remained a central theme of "heterodox" Austrian economics ever since. However, it has also been integrated into standard endogenous growth models,[7] giving rise to a wide literature on the effects of innovation on many areas of the economy.[8] Recent works, for example, show how regulation can initiate a self-sustaining push towards "clean" innovation.[9] Also, state-of-the-art firm level models of international trade consider the exit and entry of firms based on their efficiency.[10]

Whilst all these models endogenize innovation to a certain extent, they do not look at the actual innovation process and the conditions contributing to it. For this, innovation systems research has developed as a field since the 1980s, building on previous research in evolutionary economics.[11] This research emphasizes the non-linearity and complexity of innovation and the co-evolution of knowledge, organizational structures, and institutions:

The purpose of regulation and policy in this perspective is not to correct "market failure"[12] but rather to strengthen firms' capacities to internalize knowledge and become part of an "innovation system", for example, by supporting R&D networks, strengthening intermediaries,[13] as well as through resolving institutional lock-ins and path dependencies among incumbent firms and consumers.[14]

Since at least the 1990s, innovation-system-thinking has also influenced policy design, in particular the design of funding mechanisms. An example can be seen in the European Innovation Partnership (EIP)-Agri, which aims at the co-creation of innovations by multi-stakeholder groups.[15] However, as can be seen in the following analysis, innovation-system-thinking, however, has so far not affected European agricultural policy in general.

One of the most popular and accessible analytical frameworks for innovation systems is the Technological Innovation Systems (TIS)-framework.[16] It emphasizes the "functionality" of innovation systems rather than their structure. The focus is on a

[5] Mathis (2017), p. 63.

[6] Calliess (2020), pp. 129 et seq.

[7] Aghion and Howitt (1992), p. 323.

[8] Cf. the contributions in the recent Festschrift for Aghion and Howitt by Akcigit and van Reenen (2021).

[9] Acemoglu et al. (2012), p. 159.

[10] Melitz (2003), p. 1695 and subsequent literature.

[11] Greenacre, Gross and Speirs (2012), pp. 13 et seq.

[12] Dolfsma and Levdesdorff (2009), p. 932.

[13] Nilsson and Sia-Ljungström (2013), p. 171.

[14] Cecere et al. (2014), p. 1037.

[15] EU SCAR AKIS (2019), p. 316.

[16] Bergek et al. (2008a), pp. 407 et seq.

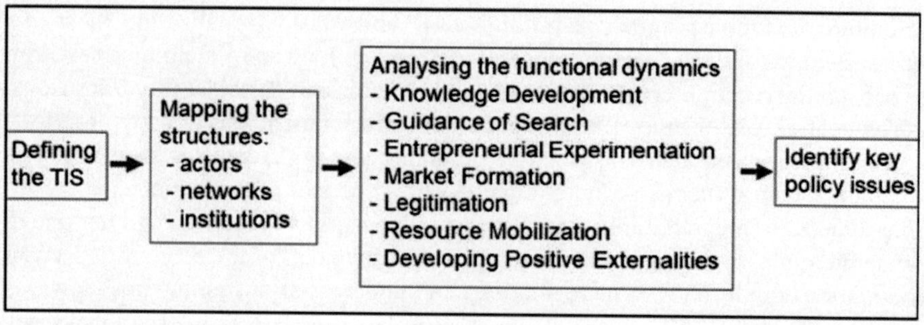

Fig. 1 Technological innovation system (TIS) Framework according to Bergek et al. (2008). *Source* Own illustration

specific technology or knowledge field, with scales ranging from "nested" to general and global Innovation Systems. Hundreds of studies have used the TIS-framework for analyzing technological development, especially in the energy sector.[17]

The TIS-framework proposes a systematic step-by-step approach for analyzing innovation systems and policies: The first step consists in defining the innovation system and mapping its main structural components, i.e. actors, networks, and institutions. In the second step, its "functional dynamics" are analyzed, i.e. seven processes seen as essential for the system's performance: Knowledge Development and Diffusion, Guidance of Search, Entrepreneurial Experimentation, Market Formation, Legitimation, Resource Mobilization, and Development of Positive Externalities. These functional dynamics are affected by technological properties but also social factors, such as beliefs or policies. For every functional dynamic, a "desired" functional pattern is contrasted with actual performance to identify inducing or blocking mechanisms. Depending on the concrete analytical interest, the framework allows for the integration of quantitative and qualitative data (Fig. 1).

3 Analyzing the Regulation of Digital Agriculture Through the Technological Innovation Systems Framework

The following chapter summarizes key results from a detailed TIS- analysis of the innovation system for digital technologies in agriculture[18]:

---

[17] Köhler et al. (2019), p. 4.

[18] Reinhardt (2022), pp. 5 et seq. with more detailed literature.

3.1 Actors, Networks and Institutions in the Innovation System

Technology providers, not farmers, are the central actors of the innovation system. This concerns "big Ag" companies, such as John Deere, but also and increasingly IT companies from outside agriculture. Start-ups play an increasing role, notably in the fields of software and field robotics.[19] Market concentration is significant, suggesting positive returns to scale and first-mover advantages.[20]

Multistakeholder Networks, which often play a central role in the development of innovation systems,[21] hardly exist so far, neither in the private sector nor at the national, European, or international level. Farmer-based organizations (FBOs), which traditionally play a huge role in shaping agricultural policy, only represent a particular interest group in the innovation system and are only starting to become active (c.f. the development of an EU Code of Conduct for Agricultural Data Sharing by the European Farmer Association COPA COGECA).[22] Compared to other sectors, public research institutions also only play a minor role, as they themselves lack relevant knowledge and do not have the necessary links to data sciences and engineering.[23]

Institutions in the TIS-framework are defined in the classical sense of institutional economics, i.e. the standards, laws, and cultural norms forming the "rules of the game".[24] They are heavily influenced by an *agricultural exceptionalism* that had prevailed for many decades with a strong orientation towards production and producer income, a dominant system of subsidies and an exception of many rules concerning competition, trade, etc.[25] For digital technologies, only few specific regulations exist. Technologies are subject to general provisions such as product safety.[26] Standard setting is mostly industry-driven, with policy makers only starting to enter the picture.[27] Digital innovation also only plays a limited role in agricultural administration.

In the terminology of the TIS-framework, it can be stated that there is a lack of "institutional alignment" in the Innovation System. This is typical for emerging innovation systems and can be seen as a central challenge for their development.

---

[19] Graff et al. (2021), p. 1.

[20] Rotz et al. (2019), p. 212.

[21] Bergek et al. (2008b), p. 419.

[22] Van der Burg et al. (2020), p. 196.

[23] Van Es and Woodard (2017), p. 101.

[24] North (1992), p. 477.

[25] Purnhagen (2019), pp. 10 et seq.

[26] Härtel (2019), pp. 580 et seq.

[27] Kosior (2019), p. 8.

3.2 *Analysis of Functional Dynamics*

3.2.1 Knowledge Development and Diffusion

Knowledge Development and Diffusion, as the first and foremost function of the innovation system, are generally strengthened by the digital transformation itself. However, significant socio-technical challenges exist in the agricultural sector: Compared to other sectors, remarkably little data is digitized. Infrastructure in rural areas is missing, digital literacy is low, and many farmers are reluctant to embrace digital technologies. Even where data is available, a lack of interoperability standards, driven by monopolistic behaviour, is complicating use by other actors.[28]

Data regulation should, in theory, pose a comparatively smaller problem, as it is generally supporting the free flow of non-personal data. Still, key questions remain unsolved, especially concerning the harmonization of data standards, access to data by independent developers, and how farmers can profit from sharing their data. The EU Code of Conduct for Agricultural Data Sharing, developed by different European Farmers' Organizations, promotes the concept of *data sovereignty*. This approach, however, seems economically inefficient and will not change distributive results between farmers and agritech companies.[29]

The new European Policy Framework under the Farm to Fork strategy clearly puts research, innovation, knowledge, and skill development at the centre of its efforts by dedicating substantial funding to research and implementation. Agricultural Knowledge and Innovation Systems are becoming a central theme that all Member States must address in their nation CAP strategic plans. The EU also promises considerable physical and digital infrastructure development such as full access to fast broadband internet in rural areas by 2025, investment in the Copernicus Earth Observation program, as well as instauration of a Farm Sustainability Data Network, and a common European Agriculture Data Space in line with the European data strategy.

3.2.2 Guidance of Search

A second key function of the TIS lies in its ability to guide actors to join the system and determine its direction. Essential factors in this respect are the visions, expectations and beliefs regarding the system's growth potential, a clear articulation of demand from lead customers, technical bottlenecks, regulatory pressure, and general trends, such as demographics.[30] So far, the adoption of digital technologies in agriculture critically depends on a quick return on investment and easy applicability.[31]

[28] Zeb et al. (2021), p. 366.

[29] Atik and Martens (2021), p. 395.

[30] Bergek et al. (2008), p. 415.

[31] Gabriel and Gandorfer (2020), p. 5.

Especially for small farmers, many technologies are not economically viable. Demographic trends do not favor technology adoption: Farmers are getting older, whilst tech developers do not seem particularly drawn to agriculture.[32]

An important role in guiding innovation can be played by increasing environmental and traceability standards. However, compared to other sectors, regulatory pressure so far is limited: new rules on fertilization and plant protection and respective documentation duties set incentives to invest in technology but only apply in certain areas. Unlike in other industrial sectors, no standard of *Best Available Techniques* exists in any area of EU agricultural regulation.[33] Also, there are no measures that directly target agritech companies, such as the fleet reduction obligations (like in Regulation (EU) 2019/1242 for heavy-duty vehicles) or phase-out obligations for certain technologies. Instruments like carbon sequestration, the bio-based circular economy, and renewable energy, that could draw new actors to the innovation system, will depend on a completely new regulatory framework.

The strong emphasis on organic agriculture in the new European Policy Framework (25% of arable land under organic farming by 2030) could, in principle, be an innovation-friendly tool. Organic farming certainly has driven some relevant technological innovations, such as mechanical weeding. However, the organic framework is inconsistent in its sustainability ambition and, in several ways, inimical to new technologies.[34] In its current status, it may even offer paradoxical incentives for farmers.

3.2.3 Entrepreneurial Experimentation

The third key function in the TIS framework relates to entrepreneurial experimentation to reduce uncertainty regarding technologies, applications, and markets.[35]

Digital technologies can generally be seen as favouring experimentation: Compared to other agrifood innovations, such as GMOs, experimentation with digital technologies also faces few regulatory restrictions. Only general regulations apply, like product safety requirements or air traffic regulations for drones.[36]

However, legal grey areas do not necessarily favour innovation. Also, the current regulatory framework only provides few niches where innovation could develop. Regulatory tools for experimentation such as the Innovation Principle from the Commission's "Better regulation toolbox", "innovation deals", or "regulatory sandboxes" are not used in agricultural regulation.

---

[32] Rotz et al. (2019), p. 208.

[33] Möckel (2015), p. 342.

[34] Purnhagen et al. (2021), pp. 602 et seq.

[35] Bergek et al. (2008), p. 415.

[36] Härtel (2019), p. 580.

3.2.4 Market Formation

Current surveys suggest that concrete markets for digital applications mostly exist for technologies that are easy to use and immediately pay off.[37] Investment costs and training needs pose significant obstacles, as financial and human capital constraints limit producers' room for manoeuvre. The market responds to these challenges, e.g. through sharing economy models or combinations of products and advisory services or financial guarantees. However, none of these approaches solves the central challenge of financially valorizing the sustainability benefits of digital technologies. As with other eco-innovations, market formation thus critically depends on regulation.

Despite the high ambition formulated in the European Farm to Fork Strategy, no fundamental reform of the subsidy mechanisms has been undertaken in the new Common Agricultural Policy (CAP) 2023–2027. New "sustainable" elements are introduced, such as the full conditionality of direct payments, enhanced standards of Good Agricultural and Ecological Conditions, new "ecoschemes" in the first pillar and a larger envelope for agri-environment-climate measures (AECMs) in the 2nd pillar. A satellite-based Area-Monitoring-System is meant to ensure full compliance.[38] However, neither conditional direct payments nor "ecoschemes" AECMs provide niche markets for innovation. They reward established procedures with cost-based subsidies and offer no perspective to get rich by pioneering new technologies. Even if pre-defined precision farming applications are subsidized through 2nd pillar funds, this central challenge remains unaddressed: Farmers cannot earn more by producing more sustainably. In fact, "ecoschemes" and AECMs, depending on their concrete conditions, might even drive farmers into investing less in innovation.

In order to initiate self-sustaining technological change, true price signals must exist. Pesticide taxation[39] or cap-and-trade schemes[40] might offer efficient options to reduce pesticide use whilst simultaneously setting incentives for innovation. Organic farming, which is rewarded by a significant premium on the market and thus delivers price signals, could also be important, but would need to be turned into an evidence-based sustainability standard (see above).

In the energy transformation, policymakers solved the issue of market formation through guaranteed feed-in tariffs. Whilst this model cannot simply be transposed to the food sector, there are certainly ways to valorize intermediate outputs, the provision of agricultural data, or introduce more competitive elements, especially for large farms.

---

[37] Gabriel and Gandorfer (2020), p. 5.

[38] NIVA (2021), p. 5.

[39] Berendse (2017), p. 315.

[40] Henning et al. (2021), p. xxiv.

3.2.5 Legitimation

Legitimation of new technologies in the eyes of all stakeholders is one of the most important functions of an innovation system in its formative phase.[41] It is a key condition for institutional alignment and usually requires the formation of new advocacy coalitions to overcome locked-in belief systems and "group thinking".

Digital technologies face few legitimation problems with consumers and policy makers.[42] The urban populace embraces their environmental benefits and increased transparency. Resistance, however, comes from potential users, namely farmers. Digitalization may bring significant changes to farmer identity, skills, and work[43]: Farmers move from being self-reliant, "hands-on" food producers to data-driven managers of complex ecosystems. Gender stereotypes are changing. In the long run, digitalization may even lead to "Farming without Farmers",[44] both in a technological and sociological sense.

Regulation and policy could play a significant role in such concerns. Unlike previous agricultural revolutions, the digital transformation does offer potential for small scale production.[45] Sustainability transitions research shows that the failure to address losers often leads to increased political resistance from advocacy groups.[46] It is typically the less innovative firms that lobby for protection. Regulation could take inspiration from behavioural economics, such as nudging and de-biasing, to overcome locked-in beliefs. It might even formulate a positive vision of future farms that could be mainstreamed throughout the legislation.

3.2.6 Resource Mobilization

The biggest challenge regarding resource mobilization mirrors the challenges of "market formation": As long as there are no clear profit opportunities for sustainable technologies, the potential to leverage external finance for transforming the agrifood sector remains limited. Again, regulatory requirements, such as the imposition of Best Available Techniques (see above), could change the playing field and help to mobilize resources for the introduction of new technologies, given the growing interest in ESG-standards in the financial sector.

---

[41] Bergek et al. (2008), p. 575.

[42] Pfeiffer et al. (2021), p. 107.

[43] Klerkx et al. (2019), p. 4.

[44] Asseng and Asche (2019), p. 1.

[45] Asseng and Asche (2019), p. 1.

[46] Köhler et al. (2019), p. 12.

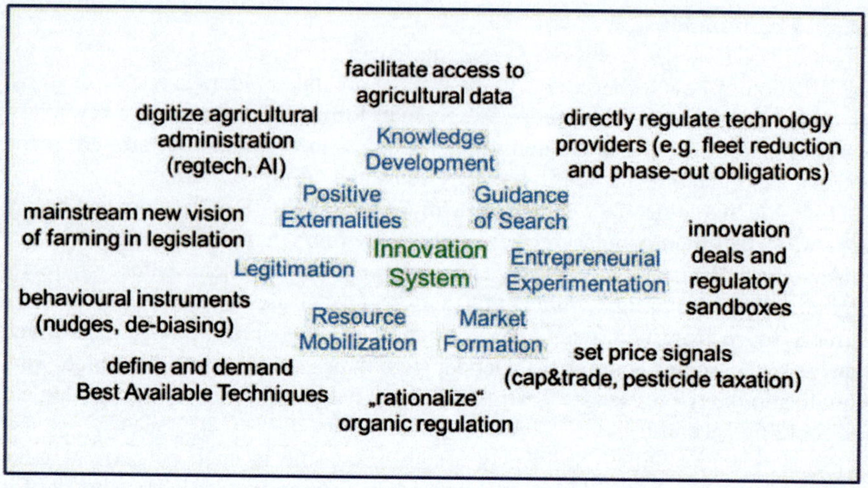

Fig. 2 Regulatory tools to support digital innovation in the agrifood sector. *Source* Own illustration

3.2.7 Development of Positive Externalities

The final function in the TIS framework consists in the development of positive externalities. To positively affect the Innovation system, externalities must not be mere side-effects of using the technology (e.g. GHG-reduction) but concrete benefits to other sectors, such as knowledge spillovers, shared intermediary goods, or a common talent pool.[47] For digital technologies in agriculture, potentials exist with neighbouring innovation systems such as the bioeconomy and renewable energy. Significant spill-overs might also concern the digitization of administration: Finding ways to creatively use the vast amount of agricultural data for the good of the sector, e.g. through AI or "regtech" (i.e. automated compliance), could set examples for many other policy areas. Finally, positive externalities may concern rural development in general. Digital infrastructures, a more sustainable image of agriculture, and some of the social changes described above (e.g. changing gender stereotypes, less manual work) could contribute to making rural life more attractive, changing current urbanization patterns, and resolving demographic challenges. Regulation could support this only indirectly by linking agricultural and regional planning. This, however, again requires a departure from many customary approaches in agricultural regulation.

Figure 2 summarizes regulatory instruments and approaches, that could address key weaknesses of the Innovation System for digital technologies in agriculture. In particular, it shows that many instruments could be adopted from other regulatory fields.

---

[47] Bergek et al. (2008), p. 418.

4 Conclusions

The above analysis has shown how the integration of the Innovation Systems approach into the "methodological toolbox" of Law and Economics can help to tackle important contemporary questions concerning agricultural regulation.

Legal scholarship on innovation often narrowly focuses on individual regulatory barriers and the role of innovation friendly instruments such as experimental clauses and innovation deals. Whilst such instruments are certainly important, it is a central insight of Innovation Systems research, that the role of regulation in the development and diffusion of innovations goes much further. As discussed above, innovation systems in their formative phase critically depend on achieving "institutional alignment". Regulation has to take an active role. It must provide a clear, coherent, and stable agenda, concrete instruments and infrastructures to support innovation and remove structural barriers to innovation, and resolve institutional lock-ins. A lack of regulation, even if it creates certain freedoms, is often not conducive to innovation, as it impedes important functions such as resource mobilization, legitimation, etc. The functional analysis can help to gain a holistic understanding of the regulatory challenges.

This seems even more true when analyzing "mission-oriented",[48] "dedicated",[49] or "eco" innovation systems.[50] These systems are characterized by strong directionality, high urgency, and an even greater role for regulatory intervention.[51] The policy must not only address blocking mechanisms but become itself a catalyst for innovation system performance.[52]

As sustainability is increasingly establishing itself as a "constitutional" meta-standard for regulation, it might eventually replace or alter the efficiency paradigm of Law and Economics. The recent judgement of the German Constitutional Court on the German climate law,[53] which establishes an intertemporal dimension of fundamental rights, can be seen as a milestone in that regard.

Concerning agricultural regulation and its historical "exceptionalism" with regard to sustainability, market mechanisms, and innovation, this analysis calls for a true paradigm shift. The EU's Farm to Fork strategy can be seen as an important step in that direction, as it specifies new values as well as concrete targets and commitments for the next decade. It looks for greater coherence between the so far disparate regulatory approaches for agriculture, environment, and food. However, significant challenges remain unsolved: Above all, the new Common Agricultural Policy of the EU (2023–2027) does not provide market conditions for innovation to thrive. It sets no incentives for pioneers and creates no risks for those who fail to keep up with

---

48 Hekkert et al. (2020), p. 76.

49 Pyka (2017), pp. 1 et seq.

50 Greenacre et al. (2012), pp. 28 et seq.

51 Cecere et al. (2014), p. 1056.

52 Nevzorova and Karakava (2020), p. 10.

53 Bundesverfassungsgericht, Beschluss des Ersten Senats vom 24. März 2021, 1 BvR 2656/18, 1 BvR 78/20, 1 BvR 96/20, 1 BvR 288/20.

technological progress. Some subsidies might even disincentivize innovation. The promise of the Farm to Fork strategy to "leave no one behind" itself seems contrary to the necessary process of "creative destruction". Experience from other sustainability transitions suggests that it might, in fact, be easier and cheaper to openly address the losers of the transition.

The strong focus of the European Union on organic farming is at least ambivalent in both regards. If the regulatory framework for organic actually concerned sustainable rather than traditional practices, it could be a powerful vector for enhancing environmental sustainability. In its current form, it risks misdirecting resources and causing leakage of environmental problems to other regions of the world.[54]

Digital technologies have huge potential to bridge the gap between agricultural productivity and sustainability. Unlike previous "revolutions", agriculture 4.0 does not necessarily favour scale or monoculture but offers perspectives for small-scale, environment-controlled food production. To reap this potential, however, regulators maybe need the central insight of Tomasi di Lampedusa's famous novel Gattopardo: "Everything needs to change, so that everything can stay the same."

Acknowledgements The article is based on: *Reinhardt, Tilman*: The farm to fork strategy and the digital transformation of the agrifood sector—an assessment from the perspective of innovation systems, Applied Economics Perspectives and Policy, 2022.

References

Acemoglu D et al (2012) The environment and directed technical change. Am Econ Rev

Aghion P, Howitt P (1992) A model of growth through creative destruction. Econometrica

Akcigit U, van Reenen J (2021) The economics of creative destruction. A Festschrift Symposium in Honor of Philippe Aghion and Peter Howitt

Asseng S and Asche F (2019) Future farms without farmers. Sci Robot

Atik C, Martens B (2021) Competition problems and governance of non-personal agricultural machine data: comparing voluntary initiatives in the US and EU. J Intellectual Property, Inform Technol E-Commerce Law

Basso B, Antle J (2020) Digital agriculture to design sustainable agricultural systems. Nat Sustain

Berendse F (2017) Add a tax to the EU agricultural policy. Nature

Bergek A, Jacobsson S, Sandén BA (2008a) "Legitimation" and "Development of Positive Externalities": two key processes in the formation phase of technological innovation systems. Technol Anal Strateg Manage

Bergek A et al (2008b) Analyzing the functional dynamics of technological innovation systems: a scheme of analysis. Res Policy

Bombardini M, Rendina OC, Trebbi F (2021) Lobbying behind the frontier. NBER Working Papers (National Bureau of Economic Research, Inc)

Calliess C (2020) Das Innovationsprinzip – Ein neues europäisches Rechtsprinzip?, Zeitschrift für Europarechtliche Studien

Cecere et al (2014) Lock-in and path dependence: an evolutionary approach to eco-innovations. J Evol Econ

[54] Henning et al. (2021), pp. 68 et seq.

Dolfsma W, Leydesdorff L (2009) Lock-in and break-out from technological trajectories: modeling and policy implications. Technological Forecasting and Social Change

EU SCAR AKIS (2019) Preparing for future AKIS in Europe: 4th report of the strategic working group on agricultural knowledge and innovation systems (AKIS)

Gabriel A, Gandorfer PDM (2020) Landwirte-Befragung 2020 Digitale Landwirtschaft Bayern

Graff G, de Figueiredo Silva FD, Zilberman D (2021) venture capital and the transformation of private R&D for agriculture. In: Moser P (ed) Economics of research and innovation in agriculture. University of Chicago Press

Greenacre P, Gross R, Speirs J (2012) Innovation theory: a review of the literature. Imperial College Centre for Energy Policy and Technology (ICEPT)

Härtel I (2019) Agrar-Digitalrecht Für Eine Nachhaltige Landwirtschaft 4.0'. Natur Und Recht

Hekkert MP et al (2020) Mission-oriented innovation systems. Environ Innov Societal Transitions

Henning C et al (2021) Ökonomische Und Ökologische Auswirkungen Des Green Deals in Der Agrarwirtschaft

Klerkx L, Rose D (2020) Dealing with the game-changing technologies of agriculture 4.0: how do we manage diversity and responsibility in food system transition pathways? Glob Food Secur

Klerkx L, Jakku E, Labarthe P (2019) A review of social science on digital agriculture, smart farming and agriculture 4.0: new contributions and a future research agenda. NJAS—Wageningen J Life Sci

Köhler J et al (2019) An agenda for sustainability transitions research: state of the art and future directions. Environ Innov Societal Transitions

Kosior K (2019) From analogue to digital agriculture. Policy and regulatory framework for agricultural data governance in the EU

Mathis K (2017) Nachhaltige Entwicklung und Generationengerechtigkeit

Melitz M (2003) The impact of trade on intra-industry reallocations and aggregate industry productivity. Econometrica

Möckel S (2015) "Best Available Techniques" as a mandatory basic standard for more sustainable agricultural land use in Europe? Land Use Policy

Nevzorova T, Karakaya E (2020) Explaining the drivers of technological innovation systems: the case of biogas technologies in mature markets. J Clean Prod

Nilsson M, Sia-Ljungström C (2013) The role of innovation intermediaries in innovation systems

NIVA (2021) Operationalising agro-climatic and agro-environmental indicators for future CAP. NIVA Policy Brief No. 2

North D (1992) Institutions, ideology, and economic performance. Cato J

Pfeiffer J, Gabriel A, Gandorfer M (2021) Understanding the public attitudinal acceptance of digital farming technologies: a nationwide survey in Germany. Agric Human Values

Purnhagen K et al (2021) Europe's farm to fork strategy and its commitment to biotechnology and organic farming: conflicting or complementary goals? Trends Plant Sci

Purnhagen K (2019) The end of agricultural exceptionalism in EU free movement law and competition law after Lisbon? Wageningen Working Papers of Law and Governance

Pyka A (2017) Dedicated innovation systems to support the transformation towards sustainability: creating income opportunities and employment in the knowledge-based digital bioeconomy. J Open Innov Technol Market Complexity

Reinhardt T (2022) The farm to fork strategy and the digital transformation of the agrifood sector—an assessment from the perspective of innovation systems. Appl Econ Perspect Policy

Reyes y Rafales FJ (2014) Überblick über die ökonomische Analyse des Rechts und ihre Applikationsmöglichkeiten auf die Europäischen Grundfreiheiten. Bonner Rechtsjournal

Rotz S et al (2019) The politics of digital agricultural technologies: a preliminary review. Sociologia Ruralis van der Burg S, Wiseman L, Krkeljas J (2020) Trust in farm data sharing: reflections on the EU code of conduct for agricultural data sharing. Ethics Inform Technol

van Es H, Woodard J (2017) Innovation in agriculture and food systems in the digital age. The global innovation index 2017: innovation feeding the world, Table 1

Zeb A, Soininen J-P, Nesli S (2021) Data harmonisation as a key to enable digitalisation of the food sector: a review. Food Bioproducts Process

Tilman Reinhardt is a Senior Researcher at the University of Bayreuth, Faculty of life sciences: Food Nutrition and Health. His fields of interest include Regulation of innovation in agriculture and food, EU and International Law, Law and Sustainability.

Index

K. Mathis and A. Tor (eds.), *Law and Economics of the Digital Transformation*, Economic Analysis of Law in European Legal Scholarship 15,
https://doi.org/10.1007/978-3-031-25059-0